THE *Good* GARDENS *Guide* 1991

Edited by

GRAHAM ROSE *and* PETER KING

BARRIE & JENKINS
LONDON

First published in Great Britain in 1991 by
Barrie & Jenkins Ltd
20 Vauxhall Bridge Road, London SW1V 2SA

A catalogue record for this book is available from the British Library

ISBN 0-7126-4604-3

Design by Clare Clements
Cartography: Malcolm Ward/Tek Art Ltd

Typeset by DP Photosetting, Aylesbury, Bucks
Printed and bound in England
by Mackays of Chatham

Contents

Introduction

This is the second annual edition of the *Guide*, containing a considerable number of gardens which were not in the 1990 edition and omitting a few that, for one reason or another, it was not appropriate to repeat. In all, over 150 'new' gardens are listed this year.

There is nothing new about visiting gardens. Henry II and Rosamund did it, John Evelyn and his diary did it, even Dr Johnson and Mrs Thrale did it, so it is not surprising that millions today say 'Let's do it'. Nor is it surprising that, despite the vagaries of the British climate, this country should be one of the most popular amongst garden-lovers from other lands. Not only have some of the greatest designers in history worked here, but the climate itself and the efforts of plant hunters have made this virtually a Botanical Garden of the World.

We decided to compile this guide because, both of us being by trade and by inclination avid garden visitors, we were constantly put off by the necessity of consulting several books at once in order to obtain the basic information needed to find the gardens of our choice. Why couldn't the facts be collected into one book? Small enough to keep in the car and with just enough information to whet our appetite, we thought it should also give some indication of the various features to be found so that choices could be made between the many wonderful offerings available to the public on a given day.

The result is a guide which we know is subjective. It is a compilation of the work of a large number of inspectors, each with different gardening interests, each with his or her favourites in the areas on which they have concentrated. This subjectivity we believe to be a benefit and we hope that our inspectors' enthusiasm will convey itself to the reader in a way which the modest descriptions written by the garden-owners themselves often fail to achieve.

Far more gardens are open to the public in the affluent south than elsewhere, and we have therefore tried to strike a balance by making a particular effort to find good gardens in other parts of the country. The same considerations apply to London and our other large cities where live huge numbers of garden lovers without gardens of their own. They find it hard to satisfy their craving for the luxury of being able to have a green thought in a green shade and our inspectors have therefore tried to help them by including parks and other public spaces which may well not be gardens in the strictest sense of the word. For this reason and others, comparison of standards between one county and another are bound to be uneven.

We have not, in general, included gardens which appeared to our inspectors to require substantial improvement, although sometimes their comments indicate that a garden might have been given a higher rating if, for instance, its maintenance could be improved. Conversely the absence of a garden from our lists does not by any means indicate that it is not praiseworthy, as exclusion might have happened for all kinds of other reasons, our ignorance being the most probable.

Graham Rose and *Peter King*, London 1991

The Garden Scene

The year 1990 could hardly have been a more difficult one for gardeners, following as it did on the gales which did so much damage in earlier years. The drought which enveloped much of the country, particularly the south where the preponderance of 'public' gardens is to be found, not only made replacement work to gale losses difficult, but also presented a grim challenge to many of those gardens whose owners had (usually months before) specified times for opening when they expected that they would be at their best.

These owners must be complimented on the great efforts they made to mitigate the effects of the drought so that visitors could enjoy their days out, almost as 'usual'. Whether the word 'usual' can continue to be applied to the British gardening scene seems somewhat open to doubt. The cause may be the so-called greenhouse effect, or some other cyclical climatic change, but the result was to bring spring forward by several weeks, delete 'flaming' June from the calendar, and make planting decisions a nightmare for the optimistic gardener. One of our inspectors told us that she had been puzzled to see in her own patch primroses and apple simultaneously in blossom, and noted that if this pattern continued it would play havoc with comments about 'best seasons' to visit.

The weather is not the only reason why some popular gardens are having to be closed to the public in 1991. Certain garden-owners have reported a considerable increase in losses due to the ravages caused by over-enthusiastic visitors snatching cuttings and seed-heads of their rarer plants. Sometimes this has become so frequent that owners are seriously considering closing their gates permanently, despite the fact that they would like to hold open days for charity. One owner in Cornwall is reported as having had to resort to 'by appointment' opening only to prevent persistent thieving. The gardens adviser to The National Trust is quoted as saying that the problem has taken on frightening proportions and at Wisley and The Savill Garden thefts by those who stayed behind, hidden, after the gates were closed, suggests that this work was executed with the cool skill of professionals. Clearly, a code of conduct is required which makes all such behaviour, whether amateur or professional, not only unpopular but unacceptable.

Another reason for the closure of fine gardens is when an owner wishes to sell his property or when one changes hands due to the death or illness of the individual who has been its inspiration. Several examples of this have resulted in exclusions from this year's *Guide*. Nothing can be done about such tragedies (for so they seem to the visitor who has come over the years to treasure his annual treat) and to an extent they are offset by the dedicated work of new owners who take over neglected gardens in order to restore them to former glory, or, better still, create a new and different experience from the remnants of the past.

That said, there are still certain private gardens which are no longer available to the public although they might be regarded as part of the national heritage. An example is Sutton Place in Surrey, a masterpiece created by that great professional Sir Geoffrey Jellicoe for Mr Stanley Seeger, and begun only in 1980. For a number of years it was open to the public by appointment, until, once the house was converted into an old people's home, this became no longer possible. Similarly Fota in Ireland has been sold to a developer and may lose its unique character as a garden. In such cases there may be cause for the local or national authority to save gardens just as houses are preserved for posterity.

Over the past ten years there has been controversy about how best to beat litter bugs. The head gardener of a famous West Country garden has told us that he is quite convinced that two factors are responsible for reducing the problem to negligible proportions in the property which he supervises. He ensures that the garden is immaculate before the public arrives. Weeds are banished from the beds, lawns are crisply edged and the gravel of the path topping is raked into a pattern of parallel striations. This, he believes, induces a sense of respect in visitors which inhibits them from blemishing the obvious order by discarding litter. He has also banished litter bins because he believes these encourage some visitors to desecrate the area round them and to continue to try to use those which become over-full.

Our inspectors continued to notice that many owners now maintain their properties without help. The days when a grand park employed a hundred men or more are gone forever, of course, but even the odd job man who would cut the lawn or weed the beds is becoming a rarity. Money for upkeep is frequently diverted away from labour to pay for electricity for power tools or bags of bark mulch to hide the weeds. Despite this, most Britons do not seem to have dropped their standards and owners slave away at the labour-intensive chores to achieve that 'well-maintained' manicured look.

We may, however, have to change our ideas, not because of shortage of labour, but because we are becoming increasingly green. Organic gardening is not synonymous with tidy gardening. Diseases have to run their course; weeds are not *verboten*. The advent or re-invention of organic gardening will mean a change in the appearance of gardens which those whose passion is for order and spruceness may have to learn to accept.

Such changes are parallelled, as we noted last year, by a continued growth in the scale of garden visiting – some individual sites alone attracting about half-a-million people in 1990. This is understandable at Sissinghurst or Wisley, but even a small town garden of our acquaintance had to cope with 800 visitors on one of the two Sundays when it was open.

On the whole our inspectors reported that the major gardens which they visited were in a fine state with a great many of them looking particularly well after considerable refurbishment or restoration. In general they thought that the substitution of mixed borders in order to reduce maintenance had done little to reduce the attraction of many gardens. They also felt that those gardens where extra dedication from the owners and their gardeners had allowed at least some area of traditional large-scale deep herbaceous beds to be maintained had an appeal and a quality unmatched elsewhere.

Almost without exception our inspectors praised the food on offer, particularly at those properties only rarely open to the public. It was the genuine 'homemade' quality of the refreshments which most impressed. As one inspector put it 'while the service was often slow and amateurish, the food was nearly always worth waiting for'.

While sipping their tea, visitors may care to spend a few moments in silent contemplation of the question 'Whither British Gardening?'. Are our garden designs and our planting to be primarily motivated by nostalgia? Should gardens be 'frozen in aspic' or returned to that state which, in the opinion of the owners, was the height of their glory? The latter question was ventilated in correspondence in *The Times* when a writer, who suggested that gardens should be left as they are and not restored, met with fierce opposition from restorers, amongst them those responsible for replanting Castle Bromwich to its appearance (or supposed appearance) in 1747.

These questions apply not only to gardens which, like Castle Bromwich, are attempting to embrace the rôle of museums, but also to those owners whose driving motivation is the past – they buy reproduction furniture, acquire 'antique' statuary, plant old roses, and no doubt serve tea made with leaves instead of bags. Of course there is nothing wrong with a healthy respect of the finest things of past times, and those owners who open their repro-gardens to the public will also acquire the merit of Government approval for their support for the British tourist industry which is to replace our lost or declining traditional businesses. It was even suggested, following publication of the Government White Paper on the Environment, that farmers might 'be invited to enter into paid contracts to conserve or restore certain types of landscape and provide public access'. In a country where landscape is so often part of the park or view around a garden, this has led to speculation that farmers who have had to give up farming may turn instead to landscape gardening their properties, presumably by returning them to past glories.

The question remains, why has Britain so few innovative gardens? Little Sparta and its like can be counted on the fingers of one hand. It is essential to produce original ideas now if we are to make a contribution to the heritage of future generations.

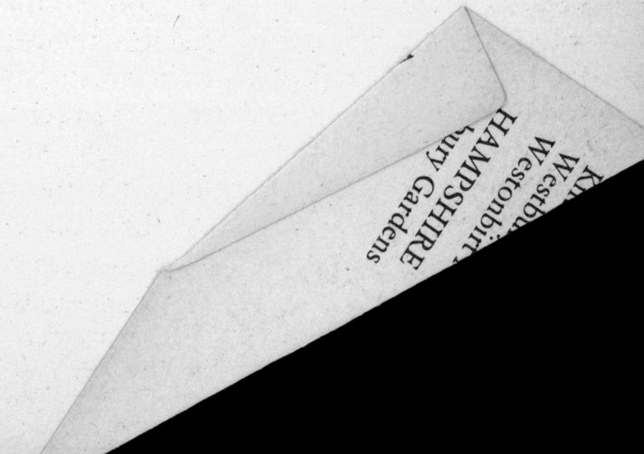

Two-starred Gardens ★★

BERKSHIRE
Folly Farm
The Old Rectory

BUCKINGHAMSHIRE
Ascott
Cliveden
The Manor House, Bledlow
Stowe Landscape Garden
Waddesdon Manor

CAMBRIDGESHIRE
Peckover House
University Botanic Garden

CHESHIRE
Tatton Park

CORNWALL
Caerhays Castle Garden
Trebah
Tresco Abbey
Trewithen

CUMBRIA
Holehird
Holker Hall
Levens Hall

DERBYSHIRE
Chatsworth

DEVON
Castle Drogo
Coleton Fishacre Garden
Knightshayes
Marwood Hill
Rosemoor Garden

DORSET
Abbotsbury Gardens
Chilcombe House
Cranborne Manor Gardens
Shute House

ESSEX
Saling Hall

GLOUCESTERSHIRE
Hidcote Manor Garden
...ftsgate Court
...ry Court Garden
...Arboretum

The Hillier Garden and Arboretum
Ventnor Botanic Garden

HEREFORD & WORCESTER
Whitfield

HERTFORDSHIRE
Hatfield House

KENT
Hever Castle
Sissinghurst Castle

LEICESTERSHIRE
Stone Cottage

LONDON (Greater)
Chiswick House
Ham House
Hampton Court Palace
Royal Botanic Gardens (Kew)
Syon Park

MERSEYSIDE
Ness Gardens

NORFOLK
Blickling Hall

NORTHAMPTONSHIRE
Cottesbrooke Hall

OXFORDSHIRE
23 Beech Croft Road
Blenheim Palace
Greys Court
Oxford Botanic Garden
Rousham House

SHROPSHIRE
Hodnet Hall

SOMERSET
Greencombe

STAFFORDSHIRE
Biddulph Grange Garden

SUFFOLK
Helmingham Hall
Shrubland Hall
Somerleyton Hall

SURREY
Painshill Park
Royal Horticultural Society's Garden
The Savill Garden
The Valley Gardens

SUSSEX (East)
Great Dixter

SUSSEX (West)
The High Beeches
Leonardslee Gardens
Nymans
Wakehurst Place Garden

WILTSHIRE
Iford Manor
Stourhead

YORKSHIRE (North)
Castle Howard
Studley Royal and Fountains Abbey

IRELAND
Anne's Grove
Birr Castle Desmesne
The Burren
Butterstream
Ilnacullin (Garinish Island)
Mount Stewart House, Garden and Temple of the Winds
National Botanic Gardens, Glasnevin
Rowallane
45 Sandford Road

SCOTLAND
Brodick Castle
Castle Kennedy and Lochinch Gardens
Crathes Castle Garden
Drummond Castle
Inverewe Garden
Little Sparta
Logan Botanic Garden
Mellerstain
Pitmedden Garden
Royal Botanic Garden (Edinburgh)
Younger Botanic Garden

WALES
Bodnant Garden
Clyne Gardens
Dyffryn Botanic Garden
Powis Castle

Using the Guide

The *Guide* is arranged by counties. Within each county the gardens are listed alphabetically by the normal name of the garden/house. The index at the end of the book can also be used to find a garden whose name only is known to the reader.

The county maps show numbers which refer to those given against each garden entry. For detailed information about how to reach gardens, use the data given in the garden entry itself. The maps also show (with un-numbered circles) where there are gardens in neighbouring counties which may be close enough to be visited by those based in the named county.

The information given is believed to be correct at the time of going to press, but changes do occur - properties sold or ownership varied and routes improved by motorway extensions etc. There may also be closures of over-visited properties, or limitations imposed on opening times. Prices of entry may be varied without notice.

Gardens in Great Britain which are open by courtesy of the owners for one of the many interested charities are included here where the gardens are of special interest even if, as on some occasions, they are open in this way on only one day in the year. However, many such gardens are also open at other specific times, such as for local charities or church restoration funds, and it is not generally possible to give dates for these locally-publicised openings. Readers should note that other nearby gardens, not listed in this guide for one reason or another, may well be open at similar times to those listed.

Readers are invited to advise the *Guide* of any gardens which in their opinion should be listed in future editions, and where possible arrangements will be made to review such suggestions.

It has not been possible for *Guide* inspectors to visit every garden which is open to the public at some time in the year, although the inspectors all have broad experience of garden visiting in their specific areas. In general, inspections have been made on an anonymous basis to ensure objectivity. Readers who would like to add information about gardens listed are warmly invited to write to the *Guide* with their comments, all of which will be acknowledged, and may be used in future editions without attribution.

Detailed use of the *Guide*

Address This is the address given by the owner or some other reputable source.

Telephone Except where specifically requested to be excluded, telephone numbers to which enquiries may be directed are given for each property. To maintain the support and cooperation of private owners it is suggested that the telephone be used with discretion. Where visits are by appointment, the telephone can of course be used except where written application, particularly for parties, is specifically requested. Code numbers are given in brackets. In all cases where visits by parties are proposed, owners should be advised in advance and arrangements preferably confirmed in writing. For the Republic of Ireland when phoning from the United Kingdom dial 353 plus area code plus number (except Dublin numbers which are 0001 plus number).

Owners Names given are those available at the time of going to press. In the case of the National Trust, some properties may be the homes of tenants of the Trust. Some other gardens are owned or managed by other trusts.

Location This information has been supplied by inspectors and is aimed to be the best available to those travelling by car. The unreliability of train and bus services makes it unrewarding to include details, particularly as many garden visits are made on Sundays. However, many properties can be reached by public transport.

Access Times of access given are the best available at the moment of going to press, but some may have been changed subsequently. In the entries, the times given are inclusive – that is, an entry such as May–Sept means that the garden is open from 1st May to 30th Sept inclusive and 2 p.m. – 5 p.m. also means that visits will be effective during that period, although some gardens may close to visitors beforehand and it is wise to arrive half an hour before closing time. Please note that many owners will open their gardens to visitors by appointment. They will often arrange to give a personally-conducted tour on these occasions.

Best season These are inspectors' suggestions though the garden concerned may well be highly attractive at other times and usually no garden will be open at a time when it does not merit a visit. The vagaries of climate prevent this information from being anything but a rough guide.

Entrance fees As far as is known, these are correct at time of going to press, but changes may be made without notice. Where there are variations, these will usually be upwards, but the amount of increase is usually small. Children are often charged at a lower rate, but are expected to be accompanied by an adult. Charges for parties are often at special rates. National Trust charges are explained in their literature with special concessions for members. Accompanied children are normally admitted by the Trust at half-price and this is why no specific charge for children is usually listed for Trust properties. Figures for the Republic of Ireland are given in punts (IR£ which is approximately equal to 85p).

Parking If there is no reference to parking this means no close convenient area available and visitors should allow time to find somewhere suitable.

Refreshments Where 'Teas' is marked, this normally implies that the owners have arranged to serve a simple tea on the property, or near at hand, at reasonable prices during opening hours. No entry means that no specific refreshment arrangements are known to the inspector.

Toilet facilities Specific facilities are marked. Where there is no entry there appear to be no specific toilets for visitors and enquiries will have to be directed to staff or owners.

Wheelchairs Inspectors have indicated where they believe a garden can reasonably be negotiated by someone in a wheelchair. No such entry means that the garden is probably unsuitable.

Dogs If dogs are allowed in a car park, or in the property on a lead, this is indicated. No entry means dogs probably not allowed.

Plants for sale No entry means plants not normally for sale. There is an increasing tendency for plants to be bought-in commercially, rather than grown on the property.

Shop This refers to special shops on the premises, such as National Trust shop selling souvenirs etc.

House open No entry means that the house is not normally open to the visiting public. Where houses are open, there is often an extra charge, usually indicated here, but again subject to change without notice.

Gardens of special distinction To help with advance information about the status of certain gardens in the view of the inspectors and editors, some 80 gardens have been marked with ★★ to indicate that in our opinion these are amongst the finest gardens in the world in terms of design and content. Many are of historic importance but some are of recent origin. Readers will appreciate that direct comparisons cannot be made between a vast estate like Chatsworth with its staff of professional gardeners and a tiny plantsman's garden in a terraced house, although that having been said both may be excellent of their kind. (★★ gardens are marked with a dark, bold ring on the maps.) Those gardens which are of very high quality, though not perhaps as unique as the ★★ ones, are given a single ★. The latter will be worth travelling a considerable distance to see, and sometimes the general ambience of the property as a whole will make the visit especially rewarding. The bulk of the gardens in the *Guide*, though not given a mark of distinction have considerable merit and will be well worth visiting when in the region. Some of them will have distinctive features of design or plant content, noted in the description, which will justify making a special journey.

County Garden of the Year Future editions of the *Guide* will recognise in each county one garden which, by popular acclaim, is the one which it appears gave the greatest pleasure to the visiting public in the previous year. The choice of this garden will be unrelated to the 'star' system, and will be chosen by nominations from readers. If you wish to nominate a garden in your county for the title of 'County Garden of the Year' please use the form which appears on page 525, after the Report Form. Inspectors in each county will make the final decision about the garden to be chosen from the various submissions. The garden should be open to the public and, except in unusual circumstances, should be featured in the 1991 *Guide*.

Calendar of Open Days The *Guide* now includes a month-by-month list of dates for those gardens which are *only open rarely*. This does *not* include gardens open regularly over several months, but some of the gardens listed here will also be open by appointment at other times. Details of these latter two categories are given under each garden in the main body of the text.

Northern Ireland The National Gardens Scheme does not extend into Northern Ireland, but the local Garden Committee of the National Trust organizes the opening of small private gardens during weekends in spring, summer and early autumn. A leaflet is printed giving times and directions, and this may be obtained from the National Trust, Rowallane House, Saintfield, County Down BT24 7LH. (Please enclose a stamped, self-addressed envelope.) On all occasions there is a charge for admission (£1.00 or 25p for children). National Trust membership is not valid for these gardens, and dogs are strictly *not* allowed in any of the gardens. The Northern Ireland Tourist Board does not provide any information about gardens in the province, but the Heritage Gardens Committee has issued a booklet describing some of the gardens and parks of outstanding historical importance (some of which are NOT open to the public). *Northern Gardens*, published by Ulster Horticultural Heritage Society, Belfast, is available for £1.50 (p&p included) by writing to Heritage Gardens Committee c/o Institute of Irish Studies, Queen's University, 8 Fitzwilliam Street, Belfast BT9 6AW.

Republic of Ireland There is no scheme operated in the Republic of Ireland similar to the National Gardens Scheme and Scottish Gardens Scheme in Britain or to the National Trust Scheme in Northern Ireland. The Irish Tourist Board does, however, issue annually a list of gardens open to the public; this may be obtained by writing to Mary Nash (Heritage), Bord Failte, Baggot Street Bridge, Dublin 2 (enclose a self-addressed envelope - and 40p (UK stamps) separately or 48p (Irish) stamps separately. This leaflet will give current admission times, entry fees, etc. for gardens in the Republic.

AVON

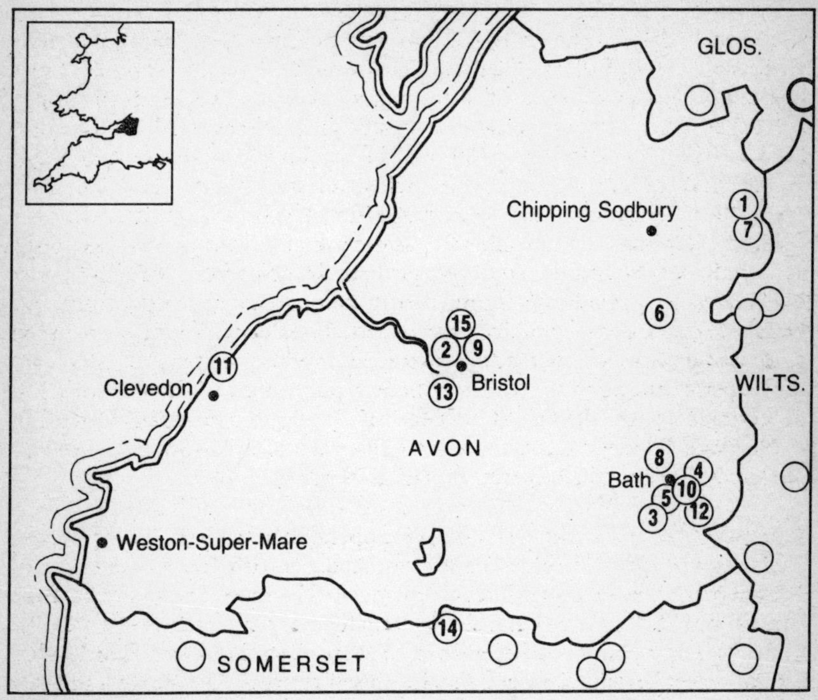

Plain circle numbers can be found by turning to neighbouring counties. Two-starred gardens are ringed in bold.

BADMINTON ★ 1

Chipping Sodbury, Avon.
The Duke and Duchess of Beaufort

5m E of Chipping Sodbury, B4040, N of M4 junction 18 • Parking • Teas • Toilet facilities • Suitable for wheelchairs • Open by appointment and 30th June, 2 - 6 p.m. Park open all year round but no cars • Entrance: £1.50, OAP £1, children under 5 free

These two private gardens have been designed in the last five years to the south and east sides of the house. Very cleverly planted, they manage to answer both the grandeur and the muddle of the house. Two conservatories on the east side are exuberant with all the best conservatory plants - large myrtle bushes in tubs and clambering cobaea. On the south side a series of enclosures or 'rooms' contain very successful mixed planting. Vistas running down and across the garden lead the eye through to an urn or doorway and glimpses of further excitement. Lilies burst out from the alchemillas and annual mallows. A cool 'room' contains only blue and white flowers. The furthest part is a heady mass of old-fashioned roses. Work is starting on the walled garden, further from the house, with huge warm, brick walls and a monumental gateway. In response to the massive scale of this garden a large allée of laburnum, wisteria and lilac has been erected. The development of this garden should be exciting.

BRISTOL BOTANIC GARDEN 2

Bracken Hill, North Road, Leigh Woods, Bristol, Avon.
Tel: (0272) 733682
University of Bristol

Cross the Suspension Bridge from Clifton, turn first right (North Road) and go ¼m up on the left • Parking • Partly suitable for wheelchairs • Become a Friend and get free plants and seeds. Otherwise plant sales are held twice a year • Open Mon – Fri except Bank Holidays, 9 a.m. – 5 p.m. • Entrance: free

The Botanic Garden moved to this site in 1959 and is very interesting for the keen plantsman. Collections of New Zealand cistus, sempervivums, campanulas. Everything is well labelled and agreeably set out. It aims to be educational, to represent most native trees and shrubs, and particularly the local flora peculiar to the Avon Gorge. Glass houses contain ferns, orchids, bromeliads, epiphytic cacti, tender bulbs. The African stone plants are fascinating, small succulents resembling pebbles in shape and colour. There are also insectivorous plants and sensitive plants which move when touched. Altogether a fascinating place which needs a lot of support in these hard pressed times – it costs only £10 to become a member of the Association of Friends.

CITY OF BATH BOTANICAL GARDENS 3

Royal Victoria Park, Bath, Avon.
City of Bath

In Royal Victoria Park • Best season: spring • Parking • Toilet facilities in Royal Victora Park • Suitable for wheelchairs • Dogs on lead • Open daily, 9 a.m. – dusk, Sun, 10 a.m. – dusk • Entrance: free

Located in the city's Royal Victoria Park the botanical gardens are a monument to Victorian taste, with splendid cedars and magnolias, a classical temple (actually 1924) and bridges over a stream and lily pond. Plants are labelled haphazardly and, as with yuccas and ornamental thistles, grow menacingly large in the humid atmosphere. The herbaceous border was replanted in 1990. Entered through a wrought iron gate the Botanic Gardens are a green refuge in the busy seven-acre park.

CLAVERTON MANOR 4

Claverton, Bath, Avon. Tel: (0225) 460503
The American Museum

2m SE of Bath of A36, signposted American Museum • Parking • Refreshments • Toilet facilities • Partly suitable for wheelchairs • Herbs for sale • Shop • House museum open • Garden open 29th March to 3rd Nov, daily except Mon (but open Bank Holiday Mons) 2 -5 p.m., Bank Holiday Sun and Mon, 11 a.m. - 5 p.m. • Entrance: £1 (house and grounds £3.50, OAP £3, children £2.50)

The house, designed by Jeffrey Wyatville, and garden are set on the side of the valley of the Avon in a stunning position with splendid views from the terrace. Despite the storms of 1989 which brought down the cedar of Lebanon on the main lawn, and many trees in the park, the grounds display good beech, ilex and cedars and have been replanted. The rather stark high walls of the house and the terrace support honeysuckle, clematis and old rose climbers, and fastigiate yews make strong buttress shapes up the south-facing wall. The Colonial Herb Garden is modest in size but the little herbarium is popular for seeds, herbs, tussie-mussies and so on. The Mount Vernon garden, a recreation of George Washington's famous garden with rampant old-fashioned roses, trained pear trees and box and beech hedges, has gone over a bit. White palings and a little raised school-house (the original was used by George Washington's grandchildren) are authentically colonial but the whole garden after thirty years as the only museum devoted to American crafts and the decorative arts might do with an imaginative overhaul.

CROWE HALL ★ 5

Widcombe Hill, Bath, Avon. Tel: (0225) 310322
Mr John Barratt

Behind Bath Spa station off the A36 to Combe Down, walking distance from station • Best seasons: late March and July • Parking on Widcombe Hill • Teas • Partly suitable for wheelchairs • Dogs • Plants sometimes for sale • Open 21st April, 9th June, 2 - 6 p.m. • Entrance: 70p, children 30p

These gardens, which extend to 30 acres on the hillside above Widcombe, are some of the most mysterious and beautiful in Bath. Through the gates there is an intriguing view of a drive, portico and terrace, and once inside the grounds few gardens in the area offer so many surprises and delights. As the owner says 'The garden is an island of classical simplicity surrounded by romantic wilderness'. Around the Regency-style house are Italianate terraces, a pond, grottos, tunnels, woods, glades, kitchen gardens and a long walk with a stone statue facing a stunning view of Prior Park, a Palladian mansion, on the horizon. Vistas and views are a feature of this steeply-banked garden where down one walk you suddenly come on the roof of the fifteenth-century church of St Thomas à Becket. The loss of 20 trees in recent storms is regarded as an improvement by the owner because new vistas have opened up. Beyond the recently restored grotto is a new meadow garden and an amusing garden dedicated to Hercules, with a theatrically ferocious hero. Magnificent trees include mulberries and nut. For its stunning setting in the meadows above and facing away from Bath and for the romantic ambiance, Crowe Hall is an experience not to be missed.

DYRHAM PARK ★ 6

Nr Chippenham, Avon. Tel: (027582) 2501
The National Trust

8m N of Bath, 12m E of Bristol on A46. Take M4 junction 18 in direction of Bath • Best season: summer • Parking • Refreshments in Orangery and picnics in park • Toilet facilities • Suitable for wheelchairs on ground floor of house and terrace only. Park suitable but many inclines • Dogs in deer park on lead only • Park open all year, 12 noon – 5.30 p.m. or dusk. House and garden open 30th March to 3rd Nov, daily except Thurs and Fri, 12 noon – 5.30 p.m. • Entrance: £4, park only £1.20

Only a tiny fragment of the London and Wise extensive 'Dutch' Garden shown in the view by Kip in 1712 survives. The terraces were all smoothed out in the early nineteenth century to form an 'English' landscape of now five mature Spanish chestnut, Lucombe oak, Red oak, Black walnut and ilex. Avenues of elms survived until the mid-1970s when they were wiped out by Dutch elm disease. They have since been replanted with limes. The cascade is still working and one can make out the form of the original garden and enjoy the terrace and the orangery which is almost certainly by Talman. It is the views towards Bristol and the elegance of the 'natural' landscape with the house tucked into the hillside that still make this an outstanding example of English landscape gardening. In all, 263 acres of ancient parkland.

ESSEX HOUSE ★ 7

Badminton, Chipping Sodbury, Avon.
Mr and Mrs James Lees-Milne

1m N of Acton Turville on B4040. M4 junction 18 • Toilet facilities nearby • Partly suitable for wheelchairs • Open by written appointment only to the seriously-interested, May to Aug

Mrs Lees-Milne is to give up having Open Days which she has done for over 20 years but says that she really enjoys showing people who are seriously interested around the garden. Those that are will be impressed. Although not large and dominated by a mammoth cedar of Lebanon which casts a swathe of dry shade across the garden one could spend longer and learn more than in any number of more showy plots. It demonstrates what intelligence in dealing with site, sureness of hand in planting, lightness of touch in design can achieve. This garden is broken up by surprises but always displays a consistency of thought. Climbers, bulbs, alliums, and annuals are woven throughout to reinforce the bones of the planting as the season progresses. The beds are full enough and the plants vigorous, everything is just in check but never too clipped or too manicured. This is a lesson to gardeners on how to achieve rampant growth and a sense of wealth (the back of the house is groaning with climbers like humulus) and yet fend off rank chaos. Clipped box and lollipop euonymus maintain order, while a garden bench is lost in a cloud of mallow or honeysuckle. There are a lot of old-fashioned roses but their short-comings are disguised by accompanying floribundas such as 'Cardinal Hume' which soldier on until November. And all this in a spot discovered by the present owner only a dozen years ago which many would have declared impossible to garden without a full-time gardener.

GEORGIAN GARDEN 8

Gravel Walk, The Circus, Bath, Avon.
Bath Museums Service

Park car in Royal Victoria Walk, enter garden by the Gravel Walk • Parking in Victoria Park • Toilet facilities in Park • Open May to Oct, Mon - Fri, 9 a.m. - 4.30 p.m. • Entrance: free

Anyone interested in seeing how a Georgian town garden looked should not miss the newly restored garden behind No 4 The Circus (but do not ring the doorbell, please). Designed to be seen from the house, the garden plan is based on excavations conducted by the Bath Archaeological Trust of the original garden, laid out in the 1770s. Surprisingly simple, there is no grass but a bed of yellow gravel edged with stone paving. Three flower beds are on a central axis. Box-rimmed borders planted starkly with scented varieties of phlox, stock, asters and a good deal of love-lies-bleeding. Honeysuckle clings to a central white pole. An eyecatcher is a curious bench copied from an eighteenth-century original. All authentic according to the Garden History Society. However, 'More George V than George III', comments one Bath garden buff.

GOLDNEY HALL 9

Lower Clifton Hill, Clifton, Bristol, Avon. Tel: (0272) 265698
University of Bristol

In centre of Bristol at top of Constitution Hill, Clifton • Teas on Open Days • Open 28th April, 12th May, 2 - 6 p.m. Grotto by special appointment for those with a serious interest • Entrance: £1.50, OAP and children 50p

Although not large or notably planted this is historically an important garden with much packed into it and a rare survival of a medium sized garden covering nine acres. The grotto is astonishingly elaborate, water really gushes through it and its walls are literally encrusted with shells and minerals. Its facade is a very striking example of early but sophisticated Gothic. The grotto is now justly famous but the entire garden (or what remains) is a thrilling discovery in the middle of this busy once bombed city. It is full of surprises not least of which is the small formal canal with orangery at its head. From the house one is lead through the shadows of an allée of Irish yews to the dank grotto entrance. Passing through the grotto and out by narrow labyrinthine passages, suddenly there is a terrace, a broad airy walk with magnificent views over the old dock. At the far end of this terrace is the Gothic gazebo and towering above the other end is the castellated water tower which holds the water for the grotto. Garden follies, parterre and herb garden.

MANOR FARM ★ 10

Church Street, Widcombe, Bath, Avon. Tel: (0255) 429273
Mr and Mrs Francis Plumbe

½m up Widcombe Hill, off A36, along Church Street, first gate on left beyond St Thomas à Becket Church • Parking in Church Street • Teas • Toilet facilities • Suitable for wheelchairs • Plants for sale • Open 16th June, 2 - 6 p.m. • Entrance: £1

Manor Farm was once part of the estate of Widcombe Manor (opposite) and in the division retained the spoils of a unique eighteenth-century dovecote with two fireplaces and chimneys to warm the birds during the breeding season, a classical pavilion (Grade I), plus a grotto, pond and towering walls of Bath stone that support 70 varieties of clematis, among other glories. The stone terrace boasts finials in the shape of acorns that came from the balustrade of the Circus in Bath. 'When we arrived 20 years ago we wanted a romantic garden', says Mrs Plumbe who cares for the clematis and the 150 varieties of roses, mostly species. Bulldozers heaved earth to build the terraces from a steep slope and a spare formal garden, resulting in a densely-planted garden with trees and shrubs creating a rolling shrub bank like a living tapestry. *Magnolia grandiflora* and catalphas, borders of tree paeonies and hydrangeas and foaming mallows, like 'Mrs Verey's Barnsley Pink' grow well in this sheltered spot. The limey soil favours scented and exotic plants, like a Chilean jasmine, mandevilla that smells of fruit and an *Abutilon megapotamicum* that flowered for a record-breading 36 months nonstop. There are rowan trees and an Irish yew and a grove of silver birches and peripatetic hostas which were lent to a film company for *The Assam Garden* - and survived. The terrace is planted in blue and white with agapanthus in pots. All this and views that include the fifteenth-century church to the west, and the eighteenth-century landscape with a Palladian villa floating above cattle in pasture with cascades to the east. *Rus in urbe* to perfection.

MANOR FARM, West Kington

(see Wiltshire)

THE MANOR HOUSE 11

Walton-in-Gordano, Clevedon, Bristol, Avon. Tel: (0272) 872067
Mr and Mrs S. Wills

2m NE of Clevedon on B3124. Entrance on N side of entry to village nearest Clevedon • Parking. Coaches by appointment only • Suitable for wheelchairs • Plants for sale • Open all year by appointment. Also 10th April to 19th Sept, Wed and Thurs, 10 a.m. – 4 p.m., and Sat and Sun, 5th, 6th, 26th, 27, May, 25th, 26th Aug, 2 – 6 p.m. • Entrance: £1, children under 14 free

A most unusual plantsman's garden of about five acres which is basically only 15 years old although the owners have taken advantage of some plantings, mostly trees, which remain from the mid-eighteenth century onwards. The Wills have aimed mainly at an informal effect and they have planted ornamental trees, shrubs, herbaceous plants and bulbs to give colour and structure throughout the year. The colour in autumn is particularly remarkable. The new plantings to the south of the house, which include the White and Silver beds, retain something of the original layout but on the other side the owners have transformed the conventional sloping lawn and rose beds by a sensitive mixture of plants including many that are unusual. There is one formal area, called the Pool Garden, with rectangular pools and fountains, and, at one end, the raised Asian bank planted with pink, blue and white colours. The yew hedges round the area are still at an early stage. Overall the Wills have achieved a remarkably attractive garden, the very opposite of what is usually meant by the description 'plantsman'. Note too their emphasis on labour saving such as the gravel mulch in the White bed.

ORCHARD HOUSE 12

Claverton, Nr Bath, Avon.
Rear-Admiral and Mrs Hugh Tracy

3½m from Bath on A36, signposted to Claverton village, or follow signs to American Museum and proceed ½m down the hill • Plants for sale. Small nursery, proceeds to charity • Open every Wed in May, 19th, 26th June, 3rd July, 2 – 6 p.m. and by appointment for groups of 15 or more • Entrance: £1, children free

On the edge of a pretty village and in the lea of an extended sixteenth-century Bath stone house this is an easy restful garden that slopes away in a series of lawns and effective rockeries. Begun as a retirement garden 25 years ago, the two and a half acres are planted with unusual species and trees for a planned and stunning foliage effect. Vistas and a secret water garden offer surprises and the vegetable garden is a treat. The garden has views into the Avon valley and Rear-Admiral Tracy has added a viewing mound which was a feature of medieval walled gardens. There are good alpines, two new tufa gardens and the glasshouses and nurseries are testimonials to Mrs Tracy's botanical expertise. The American Museum, Claverton Manor, is nearby – see entry.

THE RED LODGE 13

Park Row, Bristol, Avon. Tel: (0272) 211360
Bristol Corporation

Located in city centre • House open • Garden open June to Aug, Sat and Bank Holiday Mon, 10 a.m. - 1 p.m. and 2 - 5 p.m. • Entrance free

Good reconstruction of the seventeenth-century town garden of a merchant's house. Old varieties of fruit trees trained and espaliered. Trellis work recreated from seventeenth-century prints and similarly a knot garden. A sheet of plant names is available for 50p.

SHERBORNE GARDEN 14

Pear Tree House, Litton, Avon. Tel: (076121) 220
Mr and Mrs J. Southwell

15m S of Bristol, 7m N of Wells on B3114 ¼m beyond Litton and Ye Olde Kings Arms • Best season: June/July • Field car park and picnic area • Refreshments: tea and coffee • Suitable for wheelchairs • Dogs on lead • Gallery open with exhibition of watercolours • Open 15th June to 2nd Sept, Sat and Mon, and 15th, 16th June, 5th, 6th Oct, 11 a.m. - 6.30 p.m. Other days by appointment • Entrance: £1, children free

A rather surreal garden that displays a very personal choice of species trees, grasses and water garden features in a three and a half-acre site reclaimed from farmland. The owner gardeners are compulsive tree people who since 1963 have planted hundreds of species and exotic trees expanding the original cottage garden and pond into a mini-arboretum. Having purchased the original house because of the charm of the mature pear trees, the long narrow site now boasts a pinetum, a larch wood, nut hedges, splendid hip hedges and the latest manifestation, a prickly wood that offers 136 varieties of holly. (A list is provided for real holly lovers.) Most trees and plants are clearly labelled. This garden is an interesting example of how natural pasture land may be tamed and surface water channelled into ponds. Worth a detour to read the signpost THE HOLLYWOOD-on-Avon, and to see the evocative water-colours of winter painter, John Southwell, shown in a small gallery.

VINE HOUSE 15

Henbury, Bristol, Avon. Tel: (0272) 503573
Professor and Mrs T.F. Hewer

4m N of Bristol centre, in Henbury, next to Salutation pub • Suitable for wheelchairs • Dogs on lead • Plants for sale • Open 31st March, 1st April, 26th, 27th May, 2 - 7 p.m. and by appointment all year • Entrance: £1, OAP and children 30p

Two acres of garden developed by the present owners since 1946 which although within the city has the good fortune to back on to the woodland of the large Blaise estate landscaped by Repton. This is a particularly interesting garden because its designers started by reducing it to 'brown earth' and planning the positioning of the planting by using sticks 'surmounted by caps of white paper as though they were trees and shrubs'. The result, surprisingly, is in 'large part a wild garden' although the specimen trees are labelled and one could call this an arboretum and botanical collection. There is a glade with bulbs, cyclamen and other small plants and a pond and water garden. Collection of herbaceous and hybrid tree peonies.

GARDENS OPEN RARELY

The following gardens are open to the public on three days or less in the year, although they may also be open by appointment if this is stated in the text. For details see individual entry.

April 21 Crowe Hall; **April 28** Goldney Hall; **May 12** Goldney Hall; **June 9** Crowe Hall; **June 16** Manor Farm; **June 30** Badminton.

BEDFORDSHIRE

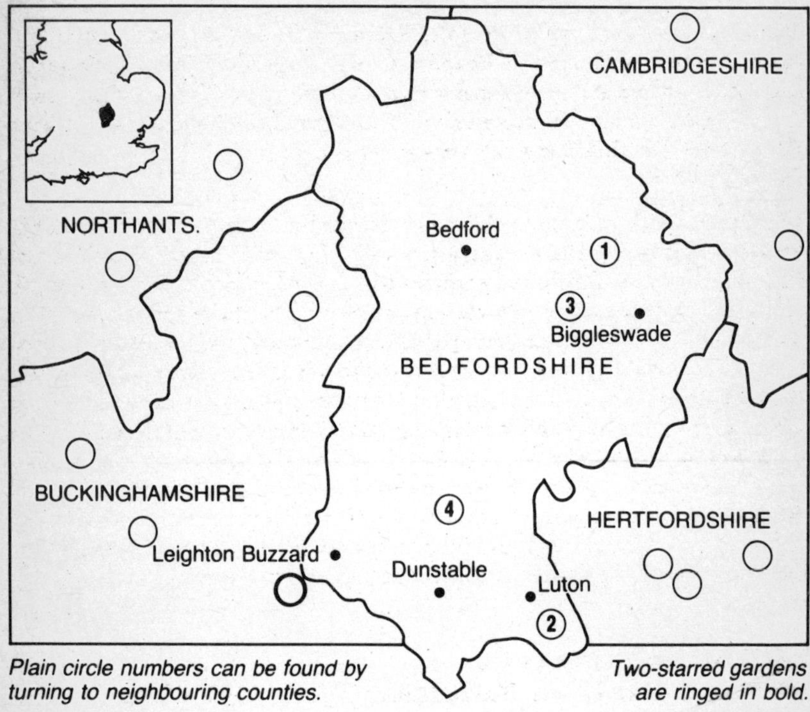

Plain circle numbers can be found by turning to neighbouring counties.

Two-starred gardens are ringed in bold.

THE LODGE 1

Sandy, Bedfordshire. Tel: (0767) 680551
Royal Society for the Protection of Birds

1m E of A1 off B1042 Sandy - Potton road • Best season: spring • Parking • Toilet facilities • Suitable for wheelchairs • Shop • Open daily, dawn to dusk • Entrance: £1.50, OAP £1, children 50p

This is one of 60 reserves established by the RSPB throughout the country. The garden has many woodland walks and nature trails with extensive bird life and the rare Natterjack toad reintroduced and breeding happily. Nature trail and Nature Discovery Room. The Lodge was bought in 1934 by Sir Malcolm Stewart, who improved the garden and made a terraced fish pond on the south side. There is a Victorian terrace and fine trees in good lawns. Other features include a large weeping birch, Wellingtonias, azalea walks to a woodland heath, colchicums, acers, sweet chestnuts. A large bignonia on the house. A huge wisteria, camellias and many big mature conifers. Two small walled gardens with *Garrya elliptica*, old wisterias and many *Clematis tangutica*. A very well planted vista of old cedar trees.

LUTON HOO ★ 2

Luton, Bedfordshire. Tel: (0582) 30909
The Wernher family

2m SE of Luton, entrance W off A6129. Enter by Park Street gates • Best season: summer • Parking • Restaurant • Toilet facilities • Suitable for wheelchairs • House open • Garden open 26th March to 13th Oct, daily except Mon, 12 noon - 6 p.m. Last admission 5 p.m. Open Bank Holidays • Entrance: £1.60, OAP £1.35, children 50p (house and garden £3.70, OAP £3.20, children £1.50)

The house stands magnificently in a landscape by 'Capability' Brown with an abundance of large cedars, oaks, ashes and other mature trees. On the south side of the house is the formal garden with a large herbacous border, recently replanted, and two vast *Magnolia* x *soulangiana*. The lower terrace forms the rose garden in eight large beds edged with box and with a sheltering yew hedge. The walls of the terrace are covered in musk roses, *Garrya elliptica* and *Wisteria sinensis*. The rock garden, built early this century as a present for Lady Wernher from her husband, has small pools running through the centre with many water lilies. Some of the maples and dwarf conifers are the original planting, including *Juniperus horizontalis* and several different forms of *Acer palmatum*. There has been much new work with scree beds of *Iris reticulata*, sedum, lewisia, thymus etc. and peat walls with erica, abies, picea and pinus. Extensive replanting in the rock gardens with shrub roses.

THE SWISS GARDEN 3

Old Warden, Biggleswade, Bedfordshire. Tel: (0234) 228330
Bedfordshire County Council

Take A1 to Biggleswade and follow signposts from A1 Biggleswade roundabout. Signposted on A600, Shefford - Bedford road • Best season: end May/June • Parking opposite Shuttleworth Collection • Refreshments at Aerodrome. Lakeside picnic area • Toilet facilities inc disabled • Suitable for wheelchairs (wheelchairs on loan) • Dogs in woodland and picnic area only • Shop • Open Easter to Oct, Wed - Sun and Bank Holiday Mondays, 1.30 - 6 p.m. Last admission 5.15 p.m. Guided tours available • Entrance: £1, OAP and children 50p. Special rates for parties

This fascinating garden is said to have been created in 1830 by Lord Ongley of the East India Company for his Swiss mistress. It was closed for 40 years from 1939, then leased by Bedfordshire County Council and restored. It has wonderful trees; cedar of Lebanon, the largest Arolla pines in England, vast pieris 300 year old underplanted with *Helleborus orientalis* and a most unusual variegated sweet chestnut. Innumerable curly iron bridges cross over miniature canals made by a Mr Hart, blacksmith of Old Warden and uncle of Lady Emma Hamilton of Nelson fame, who was a nursery maid at nearby Ickwell Bury. Little Swiss period summer houses with sheets of bulbs in the spring underplanting azaleas, rhododendrons and spring-flowering shrubs. A grotto and fernery provide dramatic contrast between the gloom of the grotto and the dazzling light of the fernery. The garden is so haunted that the gardeners will only work in twos, it is rumoured, so single visitors beware.

TODDINGTON MANOR 4

Toddington, Bedfordshire. Tel: (05255) 2576
Sir Neville and Lady Bowman-Shaw

1m NW of Toddington, 1m from M1 junction 12. First right in village, signed Milton Bryan • Parking • Teas • Suitable for wheelchairs • Plants for sale • Open 16th June, 28th July, 12 noon - 6 p.m. • Entrance: £1.50, children 50p

The Bowman-Shaws moved here in 1979 to find a wilderness, since reclaimed and planted with spring bulbs, flowering trees and other plants which lend colour on into the summer. They also inherited some wonderful old trees, especially beeches and Wellingtonias. They themselves made the pleached lime walk along a lovely old paved path, now bordered with pink and grey. A series of grey stone walled gardens are fully planted and mature with a good mixture of shrubs and plants, vines, viburnums, davidia, crinums, tree peonies, and *Hydrangea villosa*. In general planting has been of old favourites, but there are some rare and tender specimens in the greenhouse. Round the doorways between the gardens and in the borders, large daturas (both *sanguinea* and the semi-double 'Knightii') strike an unusual and interesting note. A herb garden, a nut walk and a wild garden are among newer projects. An island in a lake is planted with gunneras, amelanchier and hydrangeas.

GARDENS OPEN RARELY

The following garden is open to the public only two days in the year. For details see individual entry.

June 16 Toddington Manor; **July 28** Toddington Manor.

BERKSHIRE

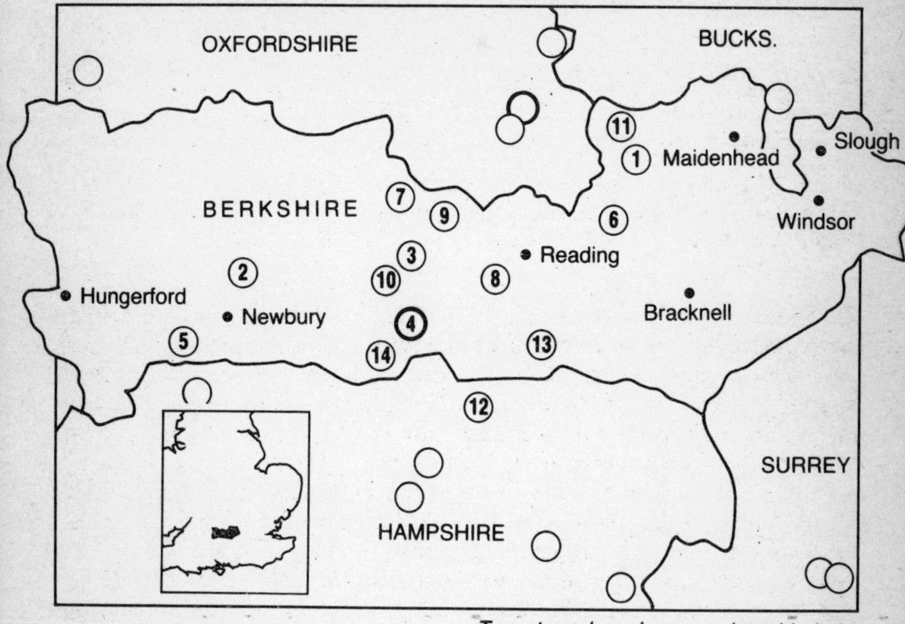

Two-starred gardens are ringed in bold.

BEAR ASH 1

Hare Hatch, Nr Reading, Berkshire. Tel: (073522) 2639
Lord and Lady Remnant

2m E of Wargrave, ½m N of A4 at Hare Hatch • Teas • Toilet facilities • Plants for sale • Open 9th June, 2 – 6 p.m. • Entrance: £1, children free

A delightful and immaculately-kept two-acre garden with a pleasant view over parkland. Silver and gold sundial border. Shrubs, old-fashioned roses, swimming pool garden, Pandora's secret garden and a small vineyard.

CHIEVELEY MANOR 2

Newbury, Berkshire. Tel: (0635248) 208
Mr and Mrs C.J. Spence

½m from M4 in Chieveley village, Mannor Lane by church • Parking in field near house • Teas • Toilet facilities • Suitable for wheelchairs • Plants for sale • Open 14th July, 2 – 6 p.m. • Entrance: £1, children free

Medium sized garden, including walled garden, swimming pool garden, herbaceous borders, shrubs and roses. Very well-maintained with new planting by owners.

ENGLEFIELD HOUSE ★ 3

Theale, Reading, Berkshire. Tel: (0734) 302221
Mr and Mrs W.R. Benyon

Entrance is on A340, near Theale • Teas in Long Gallery • Toilet facilities • Suitable for wheelchairs • Plants for sale • Open every Mon, 10 a.m. - dusk, and 21st April, 19th May, 2 - 6 p.m. • Entrance: £1, children free

A beautiful garden with a spectacular view. Deer park. Seven acres of woodland with interesting trees and shrubs. Stream and water garden. Terrace with borders, all excellently maintained. Fresh plantings this year of shrubs and herbaceous plants.

FOLLY FARM ★★ 4

Sulhamstead, Nr Reading, Berkshire.

7m SW of Reading. 2m W of junction 12 on M4. Turn left at road marked Sulhamstead at Mulligans Fish Restaurant 1m after Theale roundabout; entrance ¾m on right through a brown gate • Parking • Teas on charity open days • Toilet facilities • Partly suitable for wheelchairs • Plants for sale on open days • Open 14th April, 27th May, 30th June, 2 - 6 p.m. Individual or group applications in writing • Best season: spring/summer • Entrance: £1, children free. Individuals or parties at other times £2 per person

A sublime example of the Lutyens and Jekyll partnership in its vintage years before World War I. The intimate relationship of house and garden personifies Lutyens' genius for design and craftmanship. A complex arrangement of spaces and courts is linked by herringbone-patterned brick paths, enhancing the vernacular origins of an attractive Edwardian country house. The gardens retain much of their original character, although planting has also been chosen to suit the taste of the present owners. The formal sunken rose garden surrounded by a high yew hedge is particularly notable for its masterful design on several levels. Other features include formal entrance court, barn court, Dutch-inspired canal garden, flower parterre and tank cloister. This is one of the country's most important twentieth-century gardens.

FOXGROVE FARM 5

Enborne, Newbury, Berkshire. Tel: (0635) 40554
Miss Audrey Vockins

Enborne is 2½m SW of Newbury. From A343 turn right at The Gun Inn for 1½m, then right down Wheatlands Lane and right at T-junction • Teas on open days • Suitable for wheelchairs • Plants for sale • Open by appointment Feb and March and 24th March, 7th April, 6th May, 9th June, 2 - 6 p.m. Nursery open daily • Entrance: 60p, children free

This small garden adjoins a nursery run by the Vockins family. They specialize in bulbs especially species snowdrops, also primroses, auriculas, alpines, and small herbaceous plants. The apple tree which fell to the gales has made way for an enlarged peat bed where a flourishing *Tropaeolum speciosum* (flame flower) is doing so well that 'it is becoming a bit of a nuisance'.

HURST LODGE 6

Broadcommon Road, Hurst, Berkshire. Tel: (0734) 341088
Mr and Mrs A. Peck

On A321 Twyford – Wokingham road • Parking • Teas • Suitable for wheelchairs • Dogs on lead • Plants for sale • Open 12th May, 25th Aug, 2 – 5.30 p.m. • Entrance: £1, children 20p

This old five-acre garden was developed by Lady Ingram who died in 1989. Her placing of trees and shrubs to give sensitive colour combinations makes for attractive views. The displays of flowers, bulbs, magnolias, hydrangeas, camellias and rhododendrons give a pleasing year-round effect. The most notable features of the garden are the fine trees, old yews, copper beeches and scarlet oaks, a huge old oak and a Scots pine. A large cedar, lost in the storm, is being replaced by an extended border. Large kitchen garden. Lawns and a play area with several pieces of children's outdoor equipment make the garden inviting for young children, and overall there is an atmosphere conducive to a pleasant family day out.

LITTLE BOWDEN 7

Pangbourne, Berkshire. Tel: (0734) 842210
Mr and Mrs M. Verey

1½m W of Pangbourne on the Pangbourne – Yattendon road • Best season: mid-May, late June/earlyJuly • Parking: small groups in front of house. Open days parking in field • Refreshments on open days • Toilet fcilities • Suitable for wheelchairs • Dogs on lead • Open by appointment and May Bank Holiday Sun and 7th July • Entrance: £1

Much of this three-acre semi-formal garden and three acres of woodland garden has been developed by the Vereys since 1949. But a glade with specimen trees and borders was developed by Percy Cane early this century. In May the canopy of the cherry wood is so thick with blossom, from far off it looks like snow; underfoot there is a carpet of bluebells below flowering shrubs, especially magnolias, azaleas, camellias. In July the herbaceous border along the whole length of the house is at its best, as are two other mixed borders of roses, shrubs and herbaceous plants; disaster struck the bed of *Cardiocrinum giganteum*, burying the corms, but Mrs Verey hopes to rescue these over the next couple of years. In October the visitor should look out for the weeping lime. The terrace garden with original 1920s Italian olive jars and paved sunken garden with white flowers adjoins the house; also in the paved area is a pond with waterlilies, surrounded with plantings of roses and lilies. A silver plant border leads to a swimming pool area which is landscaped and sheltered by yew hedges and walls bearing roses, ceanothus and clematis.

THE OLD RECTORY ★★ 8

Burghfield, Reading, Berkshire. Tel: (073529) 2206
Mr and Mrs R.R. Merton

5m SW of Reading. Turn S off A4 to Burghfield village and right after Hatch Gate Inn • Parking • Suitable for wheelchairs • Plants for sale inc. unusual plants • Open last Wed in each month Feb to Oct, 11 a.m. – 4 p.m. and by appointment in writing • Entrance: 50p, children 30p

This garden has achieved wide renown and its maturity and the amazing generosity of plants skillfully planted are remarkable in a site started from scratch in 1950. Mrs Merton, described by herself as 'a green-fingered lunatic', has collected plants from all over the world notably some rare items from Japan and China. The terrace has a fine display most of the year, the herbaceous border and beds are impressive with collections of hellebores, pinks, violas, paeonies, snowdrops, old roses and many others. In the spring there are drifts of daffodils and rather rare cowslips and so many other plants to see that it is well worth making a visit month by month if you live within reasonable range. There is something here for every type of gardener most of the year. The Mertons propagate everything so sales on open days are fascinating, and there is a 'mini-market' of stalls by other plantsmen.

OLD RECTORY COTTAGE ★ 9

Tidmarsh, Pangbourne, Berkshire. Tel: (0734) 834241
Mr and Mrs A.W.A. Baker

½m S of Pangbourne towards Tidmarsh. Turn E down narrow lane • Parking • Plants for sale • Open by appointment for garden societies only and on 7th April, 5th May, 2nd June and 21st July, 2 – 6 p.m. • Entrance: 75p, children free

Although this is not a large garden it is full of rare and exciting plants, many of them collected by the owner. It has a very dry area, with early spring bulbs, a wild garden round a small lake. Lilies, roses, unusual shrubs and climbers. It is worth visiting on each of the days it is open as there is always something new to stimulate the interest of a keen gardener. The ancient apple tree was a victim of the storms but Mr Baker has interesting plans for the remaining stump. Quite rightly this garden has had much media coverage.

ST MARY'S FARM ★ 10

Beenham, Nr Reading, Berkshire.
Charles and Mary Keen

2m N of A4, halfway between Reading and Newbury • *Plants for sale* • *Open on written application only, enclosing SAE* • *Entrance: £1*

This eighteenth-century parsonage with fine trees and views has been given a wonderful uplift by the imaginative design and planting of the Keens. They have not been afraid of experimenting with bright colours, and the kitchen garden path flanked by pear trees holding hands, underplanted with brightly coloured flowers, is very striking. There is plenty to see and the herbaceous borders are particularly glorious.

THE SAVILL GARDEN

(see Surrey)

SCOTLANDS 11

Cockpole Green, Berkshire. Tel: (0628) 822648
Mr M. and the Hon. Mrs Payne

Halfway between Wargrave and Henley. At top of Remenham Hill on A423 take turning to Cockpole Green • *Parking in paddock* • *Teas* • *Suitable for wheelchairs* • *Dogs on lead* • *Open 20th, 21st April, 29th Sept, 2 - 6 p.m.* • *Entrance: £1, children free*

Well-planned and planted watergarden created by Mrs Payne from a mere trickle. Astilbes, hostas, ferns, primulas, gunneras and many more moisture-loving plants look very comfortable even after two long dry summers. There is hardly a space to be seen at the water's edge and in the surrounding shrub, fuchsia and ground cover borders even in October; a Humphrey Repton style rustic summer house marks the merging of landscaped water garden with natural woodland. Mown grass paths lead past the water garden through the woodland, around the pond and back up towards the house. On the other side of the drive and nearest the house is the formal garden, terrace awash with crevice plants, paved pool garden where a lead statue of a drummer boy holds court, among planted stone tubs, herbaceous borders and kitchen, herb and flowers-for-cutting garden.

STRATFIELD SAYE HOUSE 12

Reading, Berkshire. Tel: (0252) 882882
The Duke of Wellington

1m W of A33, halfway between Reading and Basingstoke. Turn off at Wellington Arms Hotel • *Parking* • *Refreshments* • *Toilet facilities* • *Suitable for wheelchairs* • *Shop* • *House open. Wellington Country Park, 3m from house caters for many tastes, and can be visited on combined entry ticket with house and gardens • Gardens open May to Sept, daily except Fri, 11.30 a.m. - 5 p.m. • Entrance: £3.25, children £1.60. Special rates for parties of 20 or more*

Horticulture and history are inextricably linked, from Pleasure Gardens laid out in the seventeenth century for the first owners with thousands of fine trees including many varieties of oaks, maples and walnuts to the 155 year-old *Quercus cerris* or Turkey oak under which the first duke's horse Copenhagen is buried; from *Sequoiadendron giganteum*, also known as Wellingtonia after the first duke, to the avenue of plane trees planted in 1972. In the Pleasure Gardens around 300 trees were victims of the gales and storms, among them the famous liquidambar and *Nyssa sylvatica*, but the damage has been cleared and new plantings are in hand. Fresh arrivals also in the wildfowl sanctuary which leads on from the small lake formed by a widening of the River Loddon. The walled gardens and American Garden were designed for the first duke who also placed the traditional Victorian summer house in the Pleasure Gardens. A large walled garden for vegetables and fruit is laid out in the Victorian manner, and contains a camellia house (possibly built by Paxton whose boss, the Duke of Devonshire, was a chum of the Iron Duke) from where a substantial herbaceous border leads down the centre to the Rose Garden which was replanted in 1972. Here all the roses have been chosen for their scent and new varieties are added every year. Additions also in the American Garden designed for the first duke by his head gardener. This still retains many of the original plants introduced from North America with the emphasis on azaleas, rhododendrons and kalmias but now contains plants from all over the world selected to give year round interest.

SWALLOWFIELD PARK 13

Reading, Berkshire. Tel: (0734) 883815
Country Houses Association Ltd

5m S between Reading and Wokingham on A33 under M4; 2m then left to Swallowfield village. Entrance by the village hall • Limited parking in small courtyard in front of house • Toilet facilities • Suitable for wheelchairs • Dogs on lead • Open May to Sept, Wed and Thurs, 2 - 5 p.m. • Entrance: £1, children 50p

The diarist John Evelyn called seventeenth-century Swallowfield 'a worthy house' and is said to have planted the row of yew trees (not the ancient yew hedge); Charles Dickens buried his dog Bumble in the garden, and in the hot dry summer of 1989 BBC TV transformed the existing walled garden into a formal period garden of early nineteenth-century design. Despite a second very dry summer, new plantings have survived and are doing well, although some of the rhododendrons have suffered. The gardens round the house, which is now divided into private apartments, are taken care of by the residents, and the main interest for visitors will undoubtedly be the 'new' walled garden.

WASING PLACE ★ 14

Aldermaston, Reading, Berkshire.
Sir William and Lady Mount

3m S of A4 between Reading and Newbury. Turn off at Woolhampton
• Parking • Teas • Suitable for wheelchairs • Plants for sale • Open two Suns, 2 - 6 p.m. • Entrance: £1, children free

This is a large garden on acid soil. Rhododendrons, azaleas and unusual trees and shrubs are at their best in spring. Magnificent cedars near the house. In summer the walled and kitchen garden, greenhouses and herbaceous borders all make this a beautiful place to visit.

GARDENS OPEN RARELY

The following gardens are open to the public on three days or less in the year, although they may also be open by appointment if this is stated in the text. For details see individual entry.

April 14 Folly Farm; **April 20** Scotlands; **April 21** Scotlands; **May 12** Hurst Lodge; **May 27** Folly Farm; **June 9** Bear Ash; **June 30** Folly Farm; **July 14** Chieveley Manor; **Aug 25** Hurst Lodge; **Sept 29** Scotlands.

BUCKINGHAMSHIRE

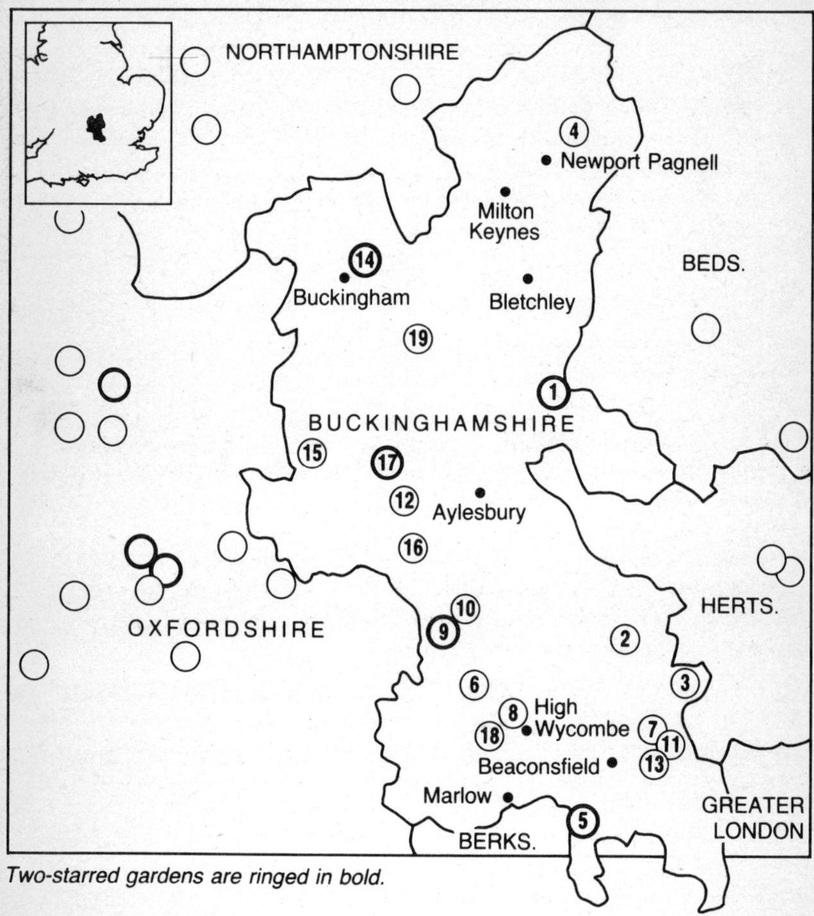

Two-starred gardens are ringed in bold.

ASCOTT ★★ 1

Wing, Buckinghamshire. Tel: (0296) 688242
The National Trust

½m E of Wing, 2m SW of Leighton Buzzard on S of A418 • Best season: spring/summer • Parking 220 yards from house • Toilet facilities • Partly suitable for wheelchairs • Dogs in car park only • House and garden open April to 19th May and 1st to 29th Sept, Tues - Sun, 2 - 6 p.m., but closed 2nd April and 7th May. Also Bank Holiday Mon. Garden only open 22nd May to 28th Aug, every Wed and the last Sun in each month and Bank Holiday Mons 27th May and 26th Aug, 2 - 6 p.m. Last admission 5.30 p.m. • Entrance: £2.20 (grounds); £3.80 (house and garden)

Thirty acres of Victorian gardening at its very best, laid out with the aid of James Veitch and Sons of Chelsea. Formidable collection of mature trees of all shapes and colours set in rolling lawns. Fascinating topiary includes evergreen sundial with yew gnomon and inscription: 'Light and shade by turn but love always' in golden yew. Wide lawns slope away to magnificent views across the Vale of Aylesbury glimpsed between towering cedars. Formal gardens include the Madeira Walk with sheltered flower borders and the bedded-out Dutch garden. Two stately fountains were created by Story – one a large group in bronze, the other a slender composition in marble. Rock garden and fernery. Interesting all year, spring gardens feature massed carpets of bulbs. A redesign of the water gardens is under way.

CAMPDEN COTTAGE 2

51 Clifton Road, Chesham Bois, Buckinghamshire.
Tel: (0494) 726818
Mr and Mrs P. Liechti

On A416 between Amersham and Chesham. Turn into Clifton Road by Catholic Church (opposite primary school). Close to traffic lights at a pedestrian crossing • Parking in road, but on open days in school car park by arrangement • Refreshments in Old Amersham • Toilet facilities in Amersham on the Hill and Old Amersham • Plants for sale • Open by appointment for parties (but no coaches) and 17th Feb, 17th March, 14th April, 5th May, 9th June, 28th July, 1st Sept, 2 – 6 p.m. • Entrance: £1, accompanied children free

A generation ago the owner described herself as 'never having given gardening a thought', and started to 'tidy' the neglected garden while builders took over the house. Straight lines have given way to a design adapted to take advantage of a magnificent weeping ash and the original network of stone paths has become a large York stone terrace surrounding the house. The owner's speciality is rare and unusual plants – when asked to point out those of interest in early September for a TV programme Mrs Liechti counted more than 400. She is also skilled in finding interesting associations of colour, shape and foliage.

CHENIES MANOR HOUSE ★ 3

Chenies, Nr Amersham, Buckinghamshire. Tel: (049476) 2888
Lt. Col. and Mrs MacLeod Matthews

Off A404 between Amersham and Rickmansworth. If approaching via M25, take junction 18 • Best season: summer • Parking • Teas • Toilet facilities • Suitable for wheelchairs • Herbs for sale • Shop • House open • Gardens open April to Oct, Wed, Thurs and Bank Holidays in May and August, 2 – 5 p.m. • Entrance: £1.40, children 70p (gardens only. House extra)

The owners have created several extremely fine linked gardens in keeping with their fifteenth/sixteenth-century brick manor house. The gardens are highly decorative and maintained to the highest standards. Planted for a long season of colour and using many old-fashioned roses and cottage plants, there is always something to enjoy here. Formal topiary in the 'white' garden, collections of medicinal and poisonous plants in a 'physic' garden, an historic turf maze and a highly productive kitchen garden. On her visits here, Queen Elizabeth I had a favourite tree and the Elizabeth Oak is named after her.

CHICHELEY HALL 4

Chicheley, Newport Pagnell, Buckinghamshire. Tel: (023065) 252
Trustees of the Hon Nicholas Beatty and Mrs John Nutting

On A422 between Bedford and Newport Pagnell, 3m from M1 junction 14 • Parking • Teas • Toilet facilities • Suitable for wheelchairs • Shop • House open • Garden open April, May, Aug and Sept, Sun and Bank Holiday Mon, 2.30 - 5.30 p.m. • Entrance: £2.75, children £1.50. Parties special rates

One of the best and least altered Georgian houses in the country is surrounded by an elegant park with fine avenues and views. Mature trees include oaks, cedars and limes. C-shaped canal lake attributed to London and Wise in 1709. Formal avenues (lime and laburnum) recently planted near the house.

CLIVEDEN ★★ 5

Maidenhead, Buckinghamshire. Tel: (06286) 5069
The National Trust

2m N of Taplow on B476 • Parking • Refreshments: light lunches, coffee, teas, in Orangery Restaurant • Toilet facilities • Partly suitable for wheelchairs • Dogs in specified woodlands only, not in gardens • Shop • House open April to Oct, Thurs and Sun, 3 - 6 p.m. Last admission 5.30 p.m. • Gardens open 29th March to Oct, daily, 11 a.m. - 6 p.m. and Nov to Dec, 11 a.m. - 4 p.m. Closed Jan and Feb • Entrance: £2.80 (House £1 extra. Timed ticket)

A famous house built in 1666 by the Duke of Buckingham in the grand manner overlooking the Thames which flows at the foot of a steep slope below. The present house and terrace designed by Sir Charles Barry incorporates a famous balustrade brought by the 1st Viscount Astor from the Villa Borghese in Rome in the 1890s. The water garden, rose garden and herbaceous borders are attractive in spring, summer and autumn respectively. The formal gardens below the house and the Long Garden, fountains, temples and statuary are pleasing throughout the year. Amongst famous designers who have worked on the grounds are John Fleming (the parterre) Leoni (The Octagon Temple) Bridgeman (walks and the amphitheatre) and Jellicoe (rose garden). Part of the house is now a luxury hotel, and there is an Open Air

Theatre Festival in the summer. Due to storms some tidying up has had to be done in the woodland areas but there was not extensive damage.

GREAT BARFIELD 6

Bradenham, Buckinghamshire.
Mr Richard Nutt

4m NW of High Wycombe. From A4010 at the Red Lion turn into village. At bottom of village green turn right and walk down no through road • Best season: spring and summer • Parking on village green • Teas • Suitable for wheelchairs • Plants for sale Feb and April only • Open 24th Feb, 28th April, 7th July, 2 - 6 p.m. • Entrance: £1, children under 16 10p

This is a plantsman's garden of one and a half acres surrounding a modern house with well-kept lawns. Designed by the owner for interest over a long season, this starts in February with snowdrops. The position and choice of plants and trees in the island beds combine with the axis of the garden in relation to the house to show to great advantage the many varieties of trees, shrubs and climbing plants. There are generous plantings of roses, lilies, bulbs and herbaceous plants.

HAREWOOD 7

Harewood Road, Chalfont St Giles, Buckinghamshire.
Tel: (0494) 763553
Mr and Mrs J. Heywood

From A404 Amersham - Richmansworth road, at miniroundabout in Little Chalfont turn S down Cokes Lane. Harewood Road is 200 yards on left • Best season: spring to autumn • Parking on street • Teas • Toilet facilities • Suitable for wheelchairs once beyond gravel driveway • Plants for sale • Open by appointment and on 5th May, 16th June, 2 - 6 p.m. • Entrance: £1, children 25p

This one-acre garden has been developed over the last decade but specimen trees planted a century ago and mature yew and box hedges give it a sense of privacy and enclosure. Many unusual roses and clematis. Interesting hardy plants have been chosen for foliage effect and climbers trained into neighbouring shrubs and trees. Other features include a pond garden. The condition throughout is very good all year round. Extensive plant list available. Woody plants are labelled.

HUGHENDEN MANOR ★ 8

High Wycombe, Buckinghamshire. Tel: (0494) 32580
The National Trust

1½m N of High Wycombe on A4128 • Best season: spring - autumn • Parking • Toilet facilities inc. disabled • Suitable for wheelchairs • Dogs • National Trust shop • House open • Garden open March, Sat and Sun only, 2 - 6 p.m., April to Oct, Wed - Sat, 2 - 6 p.m., Sun and Bank Holiday Mon, 12 noon - 6 p.m. Closed Good Fri. Last admission 5.30 p.m. • Entrance: £2.50. Party rates on application

High-Victorian garden created by Mrs Disraeli in 1860s and recently restored. Particularly pleasing is the human scale of house and gardens set in picturesque, unspoilt landscape. Woodland walks amongst ancient beeches and yews. Unusual chimaera shrub *Laburnocytisus adamii* produces yellow and mauve laburnum flowers and mauve sprays of *Cytisus purpureus* in late spring/ early summer. Last year's storms caused the loss of Hughenden's superb cedar of Lebanon.

THE MANOR HOUSE ★★ 9

Bledlow, Buckinghamshire.
The Lord and Lady Carrington

½m from B4009 in middle of Bledlow village • Best season: spring - autumn • Parking at farm next door • Teas served on June open day for charity • Partly suitable for wheelchairs • Open by written appointment, May to Sept, and 5th May, 23rd June, 2 - 6 p.m. • Entrance: £1.50, children free. Lyde Garden open free every day

With the help of landscape architect Robert Adams, Lord and Lady Carrington have created an elegant English garden of exceptionally high standard. Visit the highly productive and colourful walled vegetable garden, with York stone paths and central gazebo. Formal gardens are enclosed by tall yew and beech hedges. Mixed flower and shrub borders feature many roses and herbaceous plants around immaculately manicured lawns. To the left of the manor a new garden is taking shape with seeded lawns growing well and planting expected to be completed by summer 1991. Planned around mature existing trees on a contoured and upward sloping site with open views, the choice of shrubs is designed to display several modern sculptures to best advantage. The Lyde Garden (always open) is a water garden of great beauty and tranquillity supporting a variety of species plants.

THE MANOR HOUSE 10

Princes Risborough, Buckinghamshire.
The National Trust/Tenant Mr and Mrs R. Goode

From High Wycombe take A4010 to Princes Risborough. Turn left down High Street, left at the Market Square and then towards the church. The Manor is next to the church on right • Best season: early summer • Public car park beside church • Teas on charity day • Toilet facilities • Suitable for wheelchairs • Dogs by arrangement • House open by appointment • Gardens open 23rd June, 2 - 6 p.m. and by written appointment at weekends • Entrance: 80p, children 20p

A two-acre garden surrounds a seventeenth-century manor house restored by Lord Rothschild. Formal front garden with roses leads to walled garden with trees and mixed flower and shrub borders to which, in 1990, a new rose garden with box hedge encircling a stone pool and fountain were added. A special feature of the walled garden is the box balls and double herbaceous border. This theme is continued into the redesigned orchard where planting of a beech hedge backed by a double blue and white border and formal vegetable garden is expected to be complete by summer 1991. Mown paths will lead from the walled garden to the old orchard, past a herbaceous border, via a small woodland area to a rose garden and gazebo with blue, white and pink flowering plants at the far end of the double border, returning towards the house past the new hedge-bordered vegetable garden.

MILTON'S COTTAGE 11

Deanway, Chalfont St Giles, Buckinghamshire. Tel: (02407) 2313
Milton Cottage Trust

½ W of A413, on B4442 to Beaconsfield • Best season: early summer • Suitable for wheelchairs • Shop • Museum rooms open • Garden open Mar to Oct, weekdays except Mon (but open Bank Holiday Mons), 10 a.m. - 1 p.m., 2 - 6 p.m., Sun, 2 - 6 p.m. • Entrance: £1.50, children under 15 60p, parties of 20 or more £1.20 per person

An historic cottage where Milton completed *Paradise Lost*, it houses many of Milton's artefacts. The half an acre of attractive gardens contain a large mulberry tree which was a cutting from Milton's famous tree at Christ's College, Cambridge. Planting is informal cottage style with rose arches, vines and tapestry hedges.

NETHER WINCHENDON HOUSE 12

Nether Winchendon, Nr Aylesbury, Buckinghamshire.
Tel: (0844) 290101
Mr and Mrs R. Spencer Bernard

7m SW of Aylesbury, 5m from Thame. Near the church in Nether Winchendon village • Parking on street nearby • Suitable for wheelchairs • Open by written appointment for groups and 14th April, 4th Aug, 2.30 - 6 p.m.

These gardens surround a romantic brick and stone Tudor manor which is approached by an unusual avenue of dawn redwoods planted in 1973 continuing a centuries-old tree planting tradition by the Spencer Bernard family. Small orchards on either side of the house combine with fine specimen trees, including mature acers, catalpas, cedars, paulownias, liquidambars and, dominating the lawns at the back of the house, an eighteenth-century variegated sycamore and a late-1950s oriental plane of almost equal height. Well-kept lawns, shrub and flower borders, walled gardens including a productive kitchen garden.

SPINDRIFT 13

Jordans Village, Nr Beaconsfield, Buckinghamshire. Tel: (02407) 3172
Mr and Mrs E. Desmond

N of A40 in Jordans village, at far side of green turn right into cul de sac near school • Parking in school playground on open days • Refreshments • Toilet facilities • Partly suitable for wheelchairs • Dogs • Plants for sale • Open for groups by appointment and 1st April, 25th May, 26th Aug, 11 a.m. - 5 p.m. • Entrance: £1, children under 12, 25p

The house, built in 1933, was surrounded with trees and hedges and the present owners have extended the mature gardens on a sloping site with particularly interesting well-kept fruit and vegetable area. Productive vines under glass. Unusual trees and shrubs positioned throughout the garden. Collections of hostas and hardy geraniums.

STOWE LANDSCAPE GARDEN ★★ 14

Buckingham, Buckinghamshire. Tel: (0280) 813650
The National Trust

½m from Buckingham on A422 • Parking • Light refreshments 12 noon - 5 p.m., Dec and Jan, 12 noon - 4 p.m. • Toilet facilities in school • Partly suitable for wheelchairs • Dogs on lead • House (Stowe School) may be open in holidays for extra £1 • Garden open 23rd March to 14th April, 29th June to 1st Sept, 18th to 27th Oct, 14th to 24th and 27th to 31st Dec, 1 to 5th Jan 1992, 10 a.m. - 6 p.m. or dusk. Last admission 1 hour before closing. During summer and autumn school terms opening details on answering machine. Closed Good Fri and 25th, 26th Dec • Entrance: £2.50

The *Oxford Companion* says Stowe had an enormous influence on garden design especially after experiments there in 'natural' gardening in the 1730s. It continued to exhibit the changes of eighteenth-century taste and 'its final phase of idealized landscape still survives relatively intact'. It is a vast park with relatively few formal arrangements and the various changes made by the succession of distinguished designers who took a hand in it from the mid-seventeenth century is too long to describe here in detail. Viscount Cobham, Bridgeman, Vanburgh (who decorated the area with temples and other features) were followed by Kent who certainly designed buildings and probably the garden. 'Capability' Brown was head gardener from 1741 and his plantings were thinned out when he left 10 years later by the new owner Lord Temple. The latter also built a triumphal arch on the horizon, a focus for the main vista. Inevitably, as the work continued into the nineteenth century, the family money ran out, and the estate was sold to become a school in 1923. The governors, supported by money from the parents and ex-pupils, did well in their attempt to restore the 32 surviving buildings and the grounds as far as possible to their 1800 condition. The money that its successive owners have poured into Stowe justifies its reputation as a classic English garden. Now that the grounds are in the hands of The National Trust, which has launched an appeal for £1 million for Stowe, we may expect even greater things. If possible, the visitor should approach the gardens via the south portico of the school. The view then before him has been described as 'sudden and breathtaking' with, beyond the lawn, the Octagon Lake, the Lake Pavilions and Corinthian Arch. He may advance to walk in, and examine in detail, the Elysian fields. The Trust warns that the complete route takes 2 hours to complete. It is even possible to stay in Stowe by renting the Gothic temple owned by a private group.

THE THATCHED COTTAGE 15

Duck Lane, Ludgershall, Buckinghamshire. Tel: (0844) 237415
Mr and Mrs D. Tolman

6m from Bicester, 13m from Aylesbury, 2m S of A41 • Best season: early summer • Parking on street • Teas at owner's nursery • Toilet facilities • Dogs on lead • Plants for sale at owner's nursery • Open 12th, 19th May, 23rd, 30th June, 7th July, 25th Aug, 2 - 6 p.m. Parties by appointment on other days • Entrance: 75p, children free

A picturesque cottage garden surrounding an equally picturesque and traditional thatched hovel, both restored by the owners over the last ten years, combine to provide the visitor with examples of interesting and rare herbaceous plants in an enchanting setting. Most of these plants, together with many other varieties, are produced at the Tolman's specialist plant nursery about a mile away.

TURN END ★ 16

Townside, Haddenham, Buckinghamshire.
Tel: (0844) 291383/291817
Mr and Mrs P. Aldington

From A418 turn to Haddenham. From Thame Road turn at the Rising Sun into Townside. Turn End is 250 yards on left • Best season: spring/early summer • Parking on street • Teas on charity open days • Toilet facilities • Plants for sale • House open 29th Sept • Garden open 1st, 28th April, 9th June, 29th Sept, 2 - 6 p.m. Also groups by appointment • Entrance: £1, children 25p

Peter Aldington's RIBA award-winning development of three linked houses is surrounded by a series of garden rooms evolved over the last 25 years. A sequence of spaces, each of individual character, provides focal points at every turn. There is a fishpond courtyard, a shady court, a formal box court, an alpine garden, hot and dry raised beds and climbing roses. A wide range of plants is displayed to good effect against a framework of mature trees. This plantsman's garden is created within a one-acre town centre site.

WADDESDON MANOR ★★ 17

Waddesdon, Nr Aylesbury, Buckinghamshire.
Tel: (0296) 651211/651282
The National Trust

6m NW of Aylesbury on A41, 11m SE of Bicester. Entrance in Waddesdon village • Best season: spring - autumn • Parking • Refreshments: light lunches and teas. Picnics except on lawns at house • Toilet facilities inc. disabled • Suitable for wheelchairs • Dogs (but not allowed in aviary and children's play area) • Plants and produce for sale • National Trust shop • House closed until 1993 • Gardens open 4th April to 28th Oct. Grounds and aviary, Wed - Sat from 1 p.m. and from 11.30 a.m. on Sun. House times different. Good Fri and Bank Holiday Mon, 11 a.m. - 6 p.m. Note: closed completely on Wed following Bank Holiday • Entrance: £1.50, children 5 - 17 75p, under 5 free (grounds and aviary)

Baron Ferdinand de Rothschild's remarkable chateau (built 1874–1889), which houses a formidable art collection, is set in an appropriately grand park with fountains, vistas, terraces and walks. The gardens contain an extensive collection of Italian, French and Dutch statuary. An ornate, semi-circular aviary of sixteenth-century French style, built 1889, provides a distinguished home to many exotic birds. The park today benefits from its 100-year old plantings of native yews, limes and hornbeams with a liberal sprinkling of exotic pines, cedars, Wellingtonias and cypresses. The parterre has been replanted to restore it to its original style and appearance.

WEST WYCOMBE PARK ★ 18

West Wycombe, Buckinghamshire. Tel: (0494) 24411
The National Trust

At W end of West Wycombe, S of A40 Oxford road • Best season: spring – autumn • Parking • Suitable for wheelchairs • Dogs in car park only • House open June to Aug, Sun – Thurs, 2 – 6 p.m. Last admission 5.15 p.m. • Gardens open April to May, Sun and Wed, 2 – 6 p.m. June to Aug, Sun – Thurs, 2 – 6 p.m. Easter, May and Spring Bank Holiday Sun and Mon, 2 – 6 p.m. Last admission 5.15 p.m. Closed Good Fri • Entrance: £2.20 (grounds), £3.80 (house and grounds)

The park was largely created by the second Sir Francis Dashwood whose original designs, based on his experiences on the Grand Tour, were altered by Thomas Cook, a pupil of 'Capability' Brown, in 1779–80. Repton was called in by the next Dashwood but his plans never followed. The park survives as an important early example of the English Natural Landscape movement. Woodland and waterside walks lead to various classical temples. The music temple on an island in the lake is particularly fine. A small, pleasant park with views and vistas and a beautiful lake; this is not the place to visit if you seek flower gardens and rose beds.

WINSLOW HALL 19

Winslow, Buckinghamshire. Tel: (029671) 2323
Sir Edward and Lady Tomkins

10m N or Aylesbury, 6m S of Buckingham on A413 • Parking • Teas served in village • Partly suitable for wheelchairs • Open by appointment for groups and 6th May, 2 – 6 p.m. • Entrance: £1.50

The original gardens were created around the house completed in 1702 by Sir Christopher Wren. Apart from an English oak older than the house itself, the early London and Wise design has disappeared. Although set on a very busy main road the garden is exceptionally tranquil with a formal and high-walled terrace garden in front. Behind the house a sweep of lawn is bordered by shrubs and specimen trees mainly planted over the last 30 years by the owners and providing an unusual example of dedicated and consistent pruning to show the trees to their best advantage; among them American scarlet oak, *Prunus* 'Tai Haku' (single white cherry), willow oak, a fascinating weeping 'creeping' cedar resembling a prehistoric animal, and an 'immature' sequoia of 'only' 100 years old. Where the 300-year old oaks and elms have died, low stumps remain and provide a base for honeysuckle, roses, clematis, berberis and other climbers which are regularly clipped to make unusual flowering domes. Planted chiefly for foliage effect and autumn colour, mixed shrub and flower borders and rose beds add summer interest.

GARDENS OPEN RARELY

The following gardens are open to the public on three days or less in the year, although they may also be open by appointment if this is stated in the text. For details see individual entry.

Feb 25 Great Barfield; **April 1** Spindrift; **April 14** Nether Winchendon House; **April 28** Great Barfield; **May 5** Harewood; The Manor House, Bledlow; **May 19** Spindrift; **June 16** Harewood; **June 23** The Manor House, Bledlow; The Manor House, Princes Risborough; **July 7** Great Barfield; **Aug 4** Nether Winchendon House; **Aug 26** Spindrift.

CAMBRIDGESHIRE

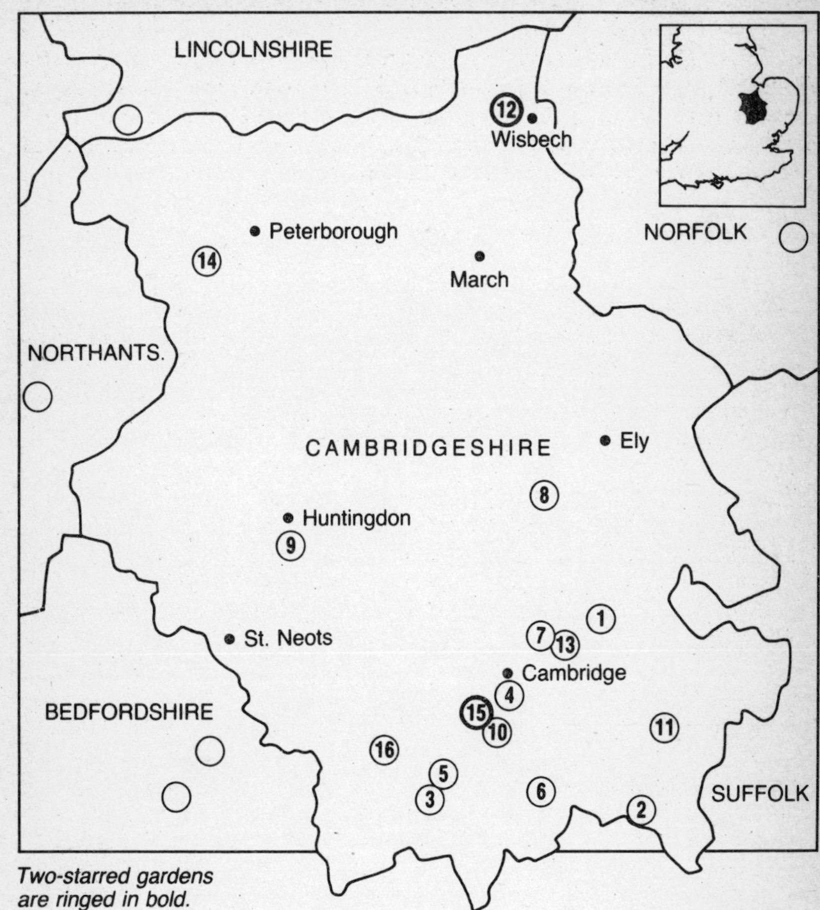

Two-starred gardens are ringed in bold.

ANGLESEY ABBEY ★ 1

Lode, Cambridgeshire. Tel: (0223) 81120
The National Trust

In village of Lode, 6m NE of Cambridge, on B1102 • Parking • Refreshments: restaurant • Toilet facilities • Suitable for wheelchairs • Plants for sale • National Trust shop • House open 30th March to 14th Oct, Wed – Sun and Bank Holiday Mon, 1.30 – 5.30 p.m. • Garden open 30th March to 14th July, Wed – Sun and Bank Holiday Mon, 11 a.m. – 5.30 p.m. Closed Good Friday. 15th July to 10th Sept, daily, 11 a.m. – 5.30 p.m. 11th Sept to 13th Oct, Wed – Sun, 11 a.m. – 5.30 p.m. • Entrance: £2 (house and gardens £4.50)

The grounds cover 100 acres and were created in the last 50 years in the park of an abbey which was later converted to an Elizabethan manor. A very visual garden with magnificent vistas down avenues of mature trees and statuary and hedges enclosing small intimate gardens. 4,500 hyacinths, spring bulbs and superb mature herbaceous borders. Silver pheasants. This is a fine garden which was let down somewhat in 1990 by a huge and exceptionally well-grown dahlia bed which displayed a mixture of garish colours.

BARTLOW PARK ★ 2

Nr Linton, Cambridgeshire. Tel: (0223) 891609
Brigadier and Mrs Alan Breitmeyer

6m NE of Saffron Walden, 1½m SE of Linton, off A604 • Parking • Suitable for wheelchairs • Open 14th April, 2 - 6 p.m. • Entrance: £1.50, children free

This garden was started 25 years ago by the Breitmeyers, helped by the renowned designer John Codrington, the former neglected garden being incorporated into the scheme. From the terraces there are splendid views of the park, through which run the headwaters of the River Granta. Other features include a formal rose garden, a tapestry beech and holly hedge, an old yew hedge and an avenue of sorbus, combined with many interesting trees and shrubs such as kolkwitzias, Judas trees and viburnums. There are good colour contrasts with *Acer platanoides*, A.p. 'Drummondii' and 'Goldsworth Purple', *Pyrus salicifolia*, *Robinia pseudoacacia* and many more. Good colour contrasts again in the border below the terrace, with *Piptanthus laburnifolius*, *Cytisus battandieri*, *Clematis tangutica* and Michaelmas daises for autumn interest.

BURY FARM ★ 3

Meldreth, Nr Royston, Cambridgeshire. Tel: (0763) 260475
Margaret Lynch

Just N of Royston on A10 to Cambridge, turn E signed to Meldreth. Opposite church • Parking in back drive, or road • Toilet facilities • Suitable for wheelchairs • Plants for sale • Open April to June, 1st Sun in the month and 16th June and by appointment • Entrance: £1, children 20p

A plantsman's garden full of interesting and architectural plants - yuccas, acanthus, box, yew, euphorbias etc. A few ancient box trees remain from what was thought to be the parterre of the twelfth-century manor house. New yew avenue terminating in a box circle. Extensive shrub/herbaceous border in soft pinks and blues. Grey/white borders. Stone wall with appropriate planting. Good use of tender plants in garden and conservatory. Moat to be developed next. Collection of irises and campanulas. Monograph on campanulas just published by the owner.

CAMBRIDGE COLLEGE GARDENS 4

Most Colleges are helpful about free access to their gardens although the Masters' or Fellows' gardens are often strictly private or rarely open. Specific viewing times are difficult to rely on because some colleges prefer not to have visitors in term time or on days when a function is taking place. The best course is to ask at the Porters' Lodge or to telephone ahead of visit. However, some college gardens will always be open to the visitor, by arrangement with porters, even if others are closed on that particular day.

It has been said that the Cambridge College gardens are superior to those of Oxford because at the former the Fellows spend money on their upkeep while at the latter it is the upkeep of the Fellows that has the priority. Be that as it may, Cambridge also has the advantage of the Backs. Although not a garden in the strictest sense of the word, this open stretch was, like many garden/parks, the subject of 'Capability' Brown's interest in the late eighteenth century. In 1779 he prepared a plan to develop this splendid stretch of land which contains the River Cam and the 'backs' of the line of colleges to the east, but the individual colleges were reluctant to collaborate. Nonetheless the Backs today are one of the country's finest pieces of green space and the outcome is probably 'hardly less beautiful than even Brown could have made it' in the words of the *Oxford Companion*.

Amongst the College gardens of particular interest are the following: *Christ's*; Note particularly Milton's mulberry; the cypress grown from seed from the tree on Shelley's grave in Rome; Charles Darwin's garden with canal with false perspective; roof garden on the new building (Open weekdays, 10.30 a.m. - 12.30 p.m. and 2 - 4 p.m. Closed Bank Holidays, Easter Week and May to mid-June and 23rd Dec to 2nd Jan). *Clare Fellows' Garden*; two-acre garden redesigned in 1946 (Open Mon - Fri, but not Bank Holidays, 2 - 4 p.m.). *Emmanuel Garden and Fellows' Garden*; large gardens with herb garden designed by John Codrington (Open daily, 9 a.m. - 5 p.m. but Fellows' Garden open only 13th July for charity). *King's Gardens and Fellows' Garden*; One of the greatest British architectural experiences is set off by fine lawns and magnificent old specimen trees. Spring bulbs (Open daily until 6 p.m. but access limited mid-April, mid-June and closed 8th, 9th Aug and 26th Dec to 3rd Jan. Fellows' Garden only 28th July). *Leckhampton* (part of Corpus Christi) at 37 Grange Road. Laid out by William Robinson, originally seven acres with two acres added (Open only one day in the summer for charity). *Magdalene Garden and Fellows' Garden* (Open daily 1 - 6 p.m. Closed May and June). *Pembroke*; Courtyard gardens with modern plantings (Daily during daylight hours). *Peterhouse*; Varied, smallish gardens and interesting octagonal court with hot and cool sides (Open Mon - Fri, 1 - 5 p.m. Limited access mid-April to mid-June). *St John's*; Huge park-like garden with eight acres of grass, fine trees and good display of bulbs in spring. Wilderness introduced by 'Capability' Brown. Rose garden and Scholars' Garden (Open daily to 5.30 p.m. but college closed to visitors May and June). *Trinity*; A garden and grounds of 45 acres with good trees. (Grounds open daily although restricted access April to Sept; opening times from Porters' Lodge. Fellows' Garden open 7th April, 2 - 6 p.m.)

CROSSING HOUSE GARDEN ★ 5

Meldreth Road, Shepreth, Cambridgeshire. Tel: (0763) 61071
Mr and Mrs Douglas Fuller

8m SW of Cambridge, ½m W of A10 • Some parking • Suitable for wheelchairs • Open every day • Entrance by collecting box

This is a tiny garden, started by the present owners 30 years ago. No matter what time of the year you visit it there is always something fascinating growing. In all there are 5,000 species to see. It is also an eye-opener as to what can be achieved in such a small space - from the use of diminutive box edges, to the yew arches that are beginning to grow, to the three tiny greenhouses packed with unusual plants. Highly recommended - a delightful garden.

DUXFORD MILL 6

Mill Lane, Duxford, Cambridgeshire. Tel: (0223) 83225
Mr R. Lea and the Hon. Mrs S. Lea

From M11 junction 10 take A505 towards Newmarket, taking the second turn to Duxford village • Best season: early July • Parking • Refreshments for parties by arrangement • Toilet facilities • Suitable for wheelchairs • Plants for sale occasionally • Open Aug Bank Holiday weekend, 12 noon - 6 p.m. and to groups of 20 or more by appointment • Entrance: 75p for charity

This nine-acre garden, started in 1948, took 20 years to complete and was planned to save upkeep with lawns which flow into each other for easy mowing and rose borders in long curves with access at front and back. Roses were bred at Duxford (there are over 2000) to give as constant a display as possible and to produce cut blooms. Vistas were planned to take advantage of the river and mill pools with statues and a Regency temple as focal points. Five hundred trees provide windbreaks, interest and winter colour, notably silver birch and other *Betula* species, such as *B. costata*, *B. jacquemontii* and *B. papyrifera*, the paper birch. Also a maple collection and specimens of the fossil tree, better known as dawn redwood (*Metasequoia glyptostroboides*), raised from cuttings from the first specimen sent to the UK in 1948. The gardens attract a variety of wildfowl.

HARDWICKE HOUSE ★ 7

High Ditch Road, Fen Ditton, Nr Cambridge, Cambridgeshire.
Tel: (02205) 2246
Mr L. and Mr J. Drake

3½m NE of Cambridge. From A45 Newmarket Road turn N by the borough cemetery • Best season: spring/summer • Parking in road opposite • Teas in Cambridge • Partly suitable for wheelchairs • Plants for sale • Open by appointment and 26th May, 9th, 16th June, 2 - 6 p.m. • Entrance: £1.50, children 50p

This medium-sized garden can be visited at any season; the spring gives a stunning display of bulbs and the colchicums give September interest. Mr Drake holds the National collection of aquilegias - 120 different varieties. There are hedges everywhere to protect the garden from its very exposed position. These have been carefully planned to create varying environments. Within the hedged enclosures there are collections of plants available in this country prior to 1660, Turkish borders and tight plantings of ground cover interspersed with plants of great rarity.

THE HERB GARDEN 8

Nigel House, High Street, Wilburton, Cambridgeshire.
Tel: (0353) 740824
Mrs Yate

5m SW of Ely on A1123 in the centre of Wilburton near the church • Best season: May to July • Parking in drive and by church • Toilet facilities • Suitable for wheelchairs • Dogs on lead • Shop • Plants for sale • Open May to Sept, most days, 10 a.m. - 6 p.m. Telephone to check • Entrance: free (collection box for charity)

For the enthusiast with a keen interest in herbs, Mrs Yate has created a small but very special garden. The narrow plot has been divided in such a way that surprise is just around each partition. The herbs are well displayed in named collections covering the aromatics, culinary, astrological, medicinal, biblical, dyers, Roman and Shakespearian herbs.

ISLAND HALL 9

Godmanchester, Nr Huntingdon, Cambridgeshire.
Tel: (0480) 459676
Mr C. and the Hon. Mrs Vane Percy

On the main street in the centre of Godmanchester • Parking in municipal car park • Teas • Toilet facilities • House open • Garden open 9th June to 8th Sept, Suns only, 2.30 - 5 p.m., and May to Sept for parties by appointment • Entrance: £2, children £1.50 (house and garden). No children under 13 in house

In a tranquil riverside setting with its own island, the garden has been reclaimed from neglect and from the Nissen huts put there when the house was requisitioned in World War II. The terrace has been removed and replaced at a lower level with gravel - to the benefit of the house. Formal shaped borders planted with different box are either side of the gravel terrace. Gaps have been left in the gravel for fastigiate yew. New shrubberies have been planted with a walk through to white and blue borders, with urns, hedges and good vistas. The island is being cleared and wild flowers encouraged. An exact replica of the original Chinese bridge over the millstream was completed in 1988. Visitors will especially enjoy the marvellous sense of history evoked by both house and garden, all of which is well documented in an excellent guide, with tales ranging from connections with William Tell and buried church plate to the restoration of the garden.

NORTH END HOUSE ★ 10

Grantchester, Nr Cambridge, Cambridgeshire. Tel: (0223) 840231
Sir Martin and Lady Nourse

2m SW of Cambridge. Approaching on the A10 from S, turn left at Trumpington (junction 11 on M11). If approaching from N on M11, take junction 12 • Parking • Teas • Suitable for wheelchairs • Open 30th June, 2 - 6 p.m. • Entrance: £2

A very well structured and maintained garden. It has the illusion of space, enhanced by a carefully-placed mirror. Created almost solely by Sir Martin and Lady Nourse, the selection of shrubs and herbaceous plants is imaginative, illustrating what beauty can be created through a knowledgeable mixing of plants. The rockery is an excellent example of a feature which does not fall into the trap of domination but adds immensely to the charm of the garden. Screening plants to the tennis court shows what can be achieved in 10 years.

PADLOCK CROFT ★ 11

West Wratting, Cambridgeshire. Tel: (0223) 290383
Mr and Mrs P.E. Lewis

On the outskirts of the village by West Wratting Park. With the Chestnut Tree public house on your right take the first right and first right again. Signed on the left • Best season: May to July • Limited parking • Teas for charity • Toilet facilities • Suitable for wheelchairs • Plants for sale • Open March to Oct, daily except Wed and Sun, 10 a.m. - 6 p.m. Wed and in winter by appointment • Entrance: 60p, children 30p on charity open days. Free at other times

A two-thirds of an acre garden created during the last 12 years solely by the owners. Mrs Lewis holds the National collection of campanula and *Campanulaceae* and is a great plant enthusiast growing plants from all over the world including the St Helena ebony (once thought to be extinct). The garden offers a number of imaginative plantings for dry, damp and alpine collections. A new rockery and a *potager* are being created.

PECKOVER HOUSE ★★ 12

North Brink, Wisbech, Cambridgeshire. Tel: (0945) 583463
The National Trust

In centre of Wisbech on N bank of the River Nene • Teas when house open • Shop • Plants for sale in house • House open (principal rooms only)

• *Garden open 30th March to 27th Oct, Mon - Wed, 2 - 5.30 p.m.* • *Entrance: £1 (house and garden £2)*

For a hundred years or so this Victorian garden has been 'the product of prudent tidiness, a period piece'. Given in 1943 to the National Trust by Alexandrina Peckover, it had been in the same family since the second half of the eighteenth century. A town house, with two and a quarter acres of garden, it contains some very interesting trees. A maidenhair tree, one of the largest in England, was planted a century ago by the donor's Peckover grandfather. Hardy palms withstand the English winter, and in the Orange House is an orange tree bearing fruit which was bought at the Hagbeach Hall sale and is at least 200 years old. In the conservatory are billbergias, daturas and monsteras. Another small house contains tender ferns. Trees and plants are rather in the Victorian taste, such as fern-leaved beech, Wellingtonias and Lawson cypresses, yuccas and spotted-leaved aucubas. The garden is divided by walls; imaginative planting of bulbs, climbers and herbaceous plants make for continuous interest throughout the year. An elegant summer-house is joined to the conservatory by matching borders edged with pinks.

THE RECTORY 13

High Street, Fen Ditton, Nr Cambridge, Cambridgeshire.
Tel: (02205) 3257
The Revd. and Mrs L. Marsh

Off A45 Cambridge - Newmarket road. Turn N by cemetery into Ditton Lane • *Best season: spring and early summer* • *Parking* • *Teas* • *Toilet facilities* • *Suitable for wheelchairs* • *Plants for sale when available* • *Open 16th June, 2 - 6 p.m. and by appointment* • *Entrance: £1.50 (fee of £1.50 for June opening covers combined admission to Hardwicke House and Old Stables in the same village)*

The garden of this late seventeenth-century house is now reduced to one acre and is in the process of being restored. Some 70 varieties of old-fashioned roses and species roses have been planted with herbaceous plants to extend the flowering season. There are many rare plants including *Arisaema candidissimum*. Also good mature trees. Many fruit trees have been planted, mulberry, walnut, medlar and apricot among others. Vegetables are grown organically and in sufficient amounts to provide vegetables and fruit for the whole year. Masses of bulbs in the spring.

THORPE HALL 14

Longthorpe, Peterborough, Cambridgeshire. Tel: (0733) 265820
The Sue Ryder Foundation

On W edge of Peterborough between A47 and A605 • *Parking* • *Refreshments* • *Toilet facilities* • *Suitable for wheelchairs* • *Plants for sale* • *Shop* • *Ground floor of house open as garden* • *Open daily except 25th, 26th*

Dec and 1st Jan, 10 a.m. – 5 p.m. • *Entrance: donations to hospice funds welcome*

The Sue Ryder Foundation Hospice at Thorpe Hall opens in spring 1991 and with it the Victorian gardens largely neglected since *c.* 1920 but now well into a five-year restoration programme started in 1989. The garden's architecture, proportions and vistas are elegant, and the restoration thus far promising, although hampered by drought in 1990. A visit in 1991, and then one later to see progress, would be most rewarding for the many Victorian garden enthusiasts. The adjacent garden centre is separately managed with a good selection of well labelled shrubs. One section of the main garden is being restored to Cromwellian style.

UNIVERSITY BOTANIC GARDEN ★★ 15

Cambridge. Tel: (0223) 336265
University of Cambridge

In S Cambridge, on E side of A10 (Trumpington Road). There is also an entrance from Hills Road on the E • *Parking in road* • *Refreshments* • *Toilet facilities* • *Suitable for wheelchairs* • *Open all year, Mon – Sat, 8 a.m. – 6 p.m. in summer (dusk in winter) and Sun, from 10 a.m.* • *Entrance: Mon – Sat, free, Sun, £1, children 50p*

This garden covers a huge area (40 acres) and is so diverse that a brief description will not do it justice. It admirably fulfils its three purposes – research, education and amenity. A visit at any time is worthwhile – even in winter when the stem garden, especially on a sunny day, is dramatic. The various cornus with red, black, green and yellow-ochre stems contrast with *Rubus thibetanus*, while the pale pink trunk of the birch *Betula albo-sinensis* var. *septentrionalis* is stunning. There is a splendid collection of native trees as well as exotic ones, including *Asimina triloba* and a good specimen of *Tetracentron sinense*. Among the collections is a fine one of salix and poplars. *Populus nigra* is now rare in England. A central area is reserved for research. There are also rockeries (both sandstone and limestone), a collection of species tulip, a scented garden, a fine range of glasshouses (hot and cool), a library and a herbarium of cultivated plants. Every specimen is clearly labelled. The new Gilmour building, named after a director who greatly expanded the garden in the 1950s and 60s, was completed in 1990.

WIMPOLE HALL 16

Arrington, Royston, Cambridgeshire. Tel: (0223) 207257
The National Trust

7m SW of Cambridge signposted off A603 at New Wimpole • *Best season: spring* • *Parking* • *Refreshments: teas and lunches* • *Toilet facilities* • *Suitable for wheelchairs* • *Minimal number of plants for sale* • *National Trust shop* • *House open 31st March to 3rd Nov, daily except Mon and Fri*

• *Gardens open 30th March to 3rd Nov, daily except Mon and Fri, 1 – 5 p.m. but open Bank Holiday Sun and Mon, 11 a.m. – 5 p.m. Closed Good Friday. Pre-booked guided tours with head gardener* • *Entrance: £4, children £2 (hall and garden)*

The gardens of this mid-seventeenth-century house followed almost every fashion in landscaping from 1690 to 1810. Today it is much changed due to Dutch elm disease. However, parterres, simplified by The National Trust, have been recently reinstated to the north of the house. Extensive and beautifully kept lawns but little else for the discerning plantsman. The surrounding landscape is of great historic and aesthetic interest and includes a two and a quarter-mile avenue, originally planted in elm in 1792, recently replanted with limes by The National Trust. Grand folly and Chinese bridge. Today, the Hall is used as a farm centre with a children's corner and agricultural museum. Also adventure playground and film loft. Flower show planned for 1991.

GARDENS OPEN RARELY

The following gardens are open to the public on three days or less in the year, although they may also be open by appointment if this is stated in the text. For details see individual entry.

April 7 Trinity College, Cambridge, Fellows' Garden; **April 14** Bartlow Park; **May 26** Hardwicke House; **June 9** Hardwicke House; The Rectory; **June 30** North End House; **July 13** Emmanuel College, Cambridge, Fellows' Garden; **July 28** King's College, Cambridge, Fellows' Garden.

CHESHIRE

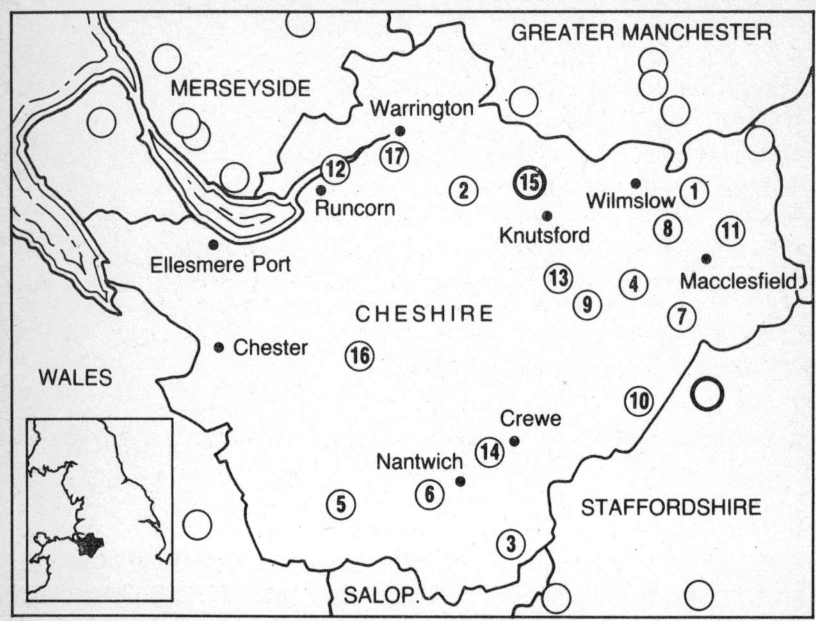

Two-starred gardens are ringed in bold.

ADLINGTON HALL 1

Macclesfield, Cheshire. Tel: (0625) 82906
Mr C.F. Legh

5m N of Macclesfield off the A523. Signposted in the village of Adlington • Best season: May/early June • Parking • Refreshments in tea rooms • Toilet facilities • Parly suitable for wheelchairs • Dogs on lead • Small shop • House open • Garden open Good Friday to Sept, Sun and Bank Holidays, 2 - 5.30 p.m., Aug, Wed, Sat, Sun and Bank Holidays, 2 - 5.30 p.m. • Entrance: £2.25, children £1, parties of 25 or more £1.75 per person

To the front of the house (fifteenth and sixteenth-century with Georgian additions) a gravel drive encircles an oval of lawn with a sundial at its centre. Beyond there is more grass, then through a pair of iron gates is a short avenue of limes dating from 1688. After these a path leads eastwards to the Shell House, a small brick building dating from 1794, with walls which were encrusted with shells in the mid-nineteenth century. To the west is a wood through which there are walks open to the visitor. The walk along the small river bank is particularly pleasant. In the centre, close to a bridge is the Temple of Diana. East from the house across a cobbled area is a formal pool. A large statue of Neptune lies at the back with water pouring into the pool from a pitcher on which he leans. There are also bright beds of annuals and a small herb garden in this area. Not much interest, then, for the plantsperson but an attractive woodland park, mostly landscaped in the eighteenth century.

ARLEY HALL AND GARDENS 2

Arley, Nr Northwich, Cheshire. Tel: (0565) 777353
The Hon M.L.W. Flower

5m W of Knutsford, 7m SE of Warrington on A50. Follow signs. Also signed from M6 junctions 19/20 and M56 junctions 9/10 • Parking • Teas. More elaborate meals by arrangement • Toilet facilities • Suitable for wheelchairs • Dogs on lead • Plants for sale • Shop • Hall open as gardens except June to Aug but not open until 2 p.m. • Gardens open Easter to early Oct, Tues – Sun, 12 noon – 6 p.m. (open at 12 noon in June to Aug and Bank Holidays) • Entrance: £2.10, children under 17, £1.05 (grounds, garden and chapel), additional £1.20, children 60p for Hall

It is thought that one of the earliest herbaceous borders in England was planted at Arley Hall. One of the few remaining landed estates in Cheshire, this is the ancestral house of the Warburtons who built their first house there in the fifteenth century, though the present Arley Hall dates only from 1840. The gardens cover 12 acres and were awarded the Christie's and Historic Houses Association Garden of the Year Award. Bounded by old brick walls and yew hedges, there is a special predilection for the tonsured, as evidenced in the splendid avenue of pleached limes which form the approach to the house and the somewhat bizarre ilex avenue which consists of 14 ilex trees clipped to the shape of giant cylinders. The walled garden, once a kitchen garden, now contains a variety of cordoned fruit trees, shrubs and herbaceous plants. There is also a collection of hybrid and species shrub roses, a rock garden planted with azaleas and rhododendrons, and a contemporary addition of a woodland garden which illustrates a continuous commitment to a family tradition.

BRIDGEMERE GARDEN WORLD 3

Bridgemere, Nr Nantwich, Cheshire. Tel: (09365) 239/381/382
Mr J. Ravenscroft

1m N of Woore on A51 between Nantwich and Stone • Parking • Refreshments: coffee shop • Toilet facilities, inc. disabled • Suitable for wheelchairs • Plants for sale • Shop • Open daily except 25th, 26th Dec, summer 9 a.m. – 8 p.m., winter 9 a.m. – 5 p.m. • Entrance: £1 for display gardens (Garden Kingdom)

Begun in 1961 with one field of roses, this 25-acre garden centre now claims to be Europe's largest. There are large areas with all types of plants for sale, garden ornaments, conservatories and greenhouses. Although some of these areas are attractively laid out, the main area of interest as a garden to view is the Garden Kingdom. This has been made mainly to show what the plants offered for sale will come to look like, and most plants are labelled. There is a rose garden, including modern and old-fashioned shrub roses, rhododendron garden, winter garden, large herbaceous border, white garden, rock and water garden, cottage garden and a vegetable and fruit garden demonstrating some unusual ways of growing your own food. Recently constructed is the 'Green and Pleasant Land', a garden that won the Chelsea gold medal in 1990 with a very notable folly built by John Bailey. Most of these areas are, as is to be expected, very well kept.

CAPESTHORNE HALL AND GARDENS ★ 4

Macclesfield, Cheshire. Tel: (0625) 861221/861439
Colonel W.A. Bromley Davenport

7m S of Wilmslow, 1m from Monks Heath on A34 • Parking • Refreshments: lunch, afternoon teas, supper by arrangement • Toilet facilities • Suitable for wheelchairs • Dogs in park only • Shop • House open as gardens but 2 - 5 p.m. only • Gardens open April, Sun; May, Aug and Sept, Wed and Sun; June and July, Tues - Thurs and Sun, 12 noon - 6 p.m. Also open Good Friday and all Bank Holidays during the summer months • Entrance: £1.50, children 5 - 16, 50p (Hall extra £1.50, OAP £1.25, children 50p)

Capesthorne is one of East Cheshire's fine historic parks showing the English style of eighteenth and nineteenth-century landscape design with belts of trees enclosing a broad sweep of park and with the house as the focal element. The gardens are best enjoyed by following the suggested woodland walks, because the outstanding features are the range of mature trees, and the views and plant-life associated with the series of man-made lakes. There is much, too, to interest those with a taste for the history of gardens - for example the site of a conservatory built by Sir Joseph Paxton. There is a pair of outstanding rococo Milanese gates, and more conventionally a formal lakeside garden planned in the 1960s by garden designer Vernon Russell-Smith.

CHOLMONDELEY CASTLE GARDENS 5

Cholmondeley Castle, Malpas, Cheshire. Tel: (0829) 720 383/203
The Marquess of Cholmondeley

On A49 between Tarporley and Whitchurch • Parking • Refreshments • Toilet facilities • Plants for sale • Shop • Open Easter Sun to Sept, Sun and Bank Holidays, 12 noon - 5.30 p.m. • Entrance: £2, OAP £1, children 50p

In spite of the ancient family name (pronounced Chumley), the Castle and more particularly the gardens are of relatively recent development, and understandably therefore they lack the maturity of other Cheshire parklands. As a site, though, it is magnificent, with the Castle straddling a hill-top and a view across parkland to a distant mere, and the classic cricket square in between. Much has been done by the present owners to develop the gardens which consisted in the 1960s of but a few (but splendid) cedars and oaks and the creation of the Temple Gardens in particular – bordered walkways around a water garden – is most satisfying with its rock garden with a fine view of the lake that leads into a stream garden planted with moisture-lovers. The grass round the tea room is filled with wild orchids and backing away from this is a good planting of rhododendrons. The rose garden contains an interesting mixture of old and new.

DORFOLD HALL 6

Nantwich, Cheshire. Tel: (0270) 625245
Mr R. Roundell

1m W of Nantwich, S of A534 • Best season: spring and early summer • Parking • Toilet facilities • Partly suitable for wheelchairs (garden only) • House open • Garden open April to Oct, Tues and Bank Holiday Mons, 2 – 5 p.m. • Entrance: £2

Dorfold Hall, impressive from the front, is approached through an avenue of limes with open parkland to each side and a large pool just to the west. The approach to the house is thought to have been laid out by William Nesfield who was chosen to design various parts of Kew. To the rear or south of the house is a large lawn at the east side of which is a statue of Shakespeare standing between two modern shrub borders. To the south is a low wall with a narrow border planted with shrub roses, beyond this is another large lawn from where there are views across a ha-ha to the flat countryside in the south. A broad grass walk leads eastwards to a dell. Here rhododendrons and other acid-loving shrubs have been planted amongst mature trees around a small stream, an area developed by the present owner. To the west is another grassed area with specimen trees, two fine gates lead to a disused walled garden.

GAWSWORTH HALL 7

Macclesfield, Cheshire. Tel: (0260) 223456
Mr and Mrs T. Richards

3m S of Macclesfield off A536. Signposted • Best season: midsummer • Parking • Refreshments: tearooms at pavilion in car park • Toilet facilities • Suitable for wheelchairs • Small shop • House open • Garden open 23rd March to 6th Oct, daily, 2 – 5.30 p.m. • Entrance: £2.70, children £1.35 (house and garden)

Gawsworth Hall is approached by a drive leading between two lakes which arrives at the north end of the hall where there is a large yew tree and lawns sloping down to one of the lakes. A formal garden on the west side of the house has beds of modern roses edged by bright annuals and many stone ornaments including a sundial and circular pool with a fountain. Stone steps lead to a sunken lawn area with borders of shrubs and perennials. To the south is another lawned garden surrounded by a high yew hedge and herbaceous borders. A grassed area containing mature trees lies to the west of these formal areas, from where there is a view of the medieval tilting ground and site of the Elizabethan pleasure gardens. A path back to the house passes a small conservatory containing classical statues.

HARE HILL GARDENS 8

Hare Hill, Over Alderley, Nr Macclesfield, Cheshire.
Tel: (0625) 828981
The National Trust

N of B5087 between Alderly Edge and Prestbury at Greyhound Road • Best season: spring/early June • Parking • Toilet facilities • Partly suitable for wheelchairs • Open 31st March to 27th Oct, Wed, Thurs, Sat, Sun and Bank Holiday Mon, 10 a.m. - 5.30 p.m. Special opening for azaleas 20th May to 7th June, daily, 10 a.m. - 5.30 p.m. 2nd Nov to March 1991, Sat and Sun, 10 a.m. - 5.30 p.m. • Entrance: £1. Car park £1 (refundable)

This garden consists of two distinct areas, a walled garden, once used for growing vegetables, and surrounding it a large woodland garden. The walled garden is rather sparsely planted. Climbing plants around the walls include vines, roses, ceanothus and wisteria, and in the centre are a few small rosebeds. A seat set into the north wall is surrounded by a white trellis pergola and nearby are two wire statues. The woodland garden is perhaps of greater interest. It contains over 50 varieties of holly, many fine rhododendrons and magnolias and there are spring-flowering bulbs and some climbing roses growing high into their host trees. In the centre is a small pond spanned by two rustic wooden bridges. Much new planting is being carried out and the garden improves each year.

JODRELL BANK ARBORETUM 9

Jodrell Bank Science Centre and Arboretum, Macclesfield, Cheshire.
Tel: (0477) 71339
Manchester University

On the A535 between Holmes Chapel and Chelford, 5m from M6 junction 18. Signposted • Parking • Refreshments: self-service cafeteria • Toilet facilities • Partly suitable for wheelchairs • Shop • Open Easter to Oct, daily, 10.30 a.m. - 5 p.m. Otherwise Sat and Sun, 12 noon - 5 p.m. • Entrance: £3, OAP £2.20, children £1.65 inc. science centre and planetarium

The garden was begun in 1972 largely at the instigation of Professor Sir Bernard Lovell and with financial support from the Granada Foundation. It is set in a flat landscape with all views to the south dominated by the massive radio telescope. Large collections of trees, heathers and old-fashioned roses are its main attractions. There are broad grass walkways and many small natural ponds in this 40-acre garden. The National collections of malus and sorbus are here, together with the Heather Society calluna collection. A visit to Jodrell Bank represents good value when all its attractions are considered and is a day out for a family.

LITTLE MORETON HALL 10

Congleton, Cheshire. Tel: (0260) 272018
The National Trust

4m SW of Congleton on the E side of the A34 between Congleton and Newcastle-under-Lyme • Parking • Refreshments: drinks and light meals • Toilet facilities • Suitable for wheelchairs • Dogs in car park and areas outside moat only • Shop • Herbs usually for sale • Open March and Oct, Sat and Sun, 1.30 - 5.30 p.m., April to Sept, daily except Tues, 1.30 - 5.30 p.m. Bank Holiday Mons, 11.30 a.m. - 5.30 p.m. Last admission 5 p.m. • Entrance: £2.30 (£2.90 at weekends and Bank Holidays), children under 18 £1.15 (£1.45 at weekends and Bank Holidays)

Little Moreton Hall is one of the best-known timber-framed buildings in the country and its gardens too are very pleasant in their own quiet way. They cover about an acre and are set within a moat. There is a cobbled courtyard in the centre of the hall and to the west a large lawn with fruit trees and an old grassed mound. To the north of the hall is a yew tunnel and the best feature of all, a knot garden, laid out under the guidance of Graham Stuart Thomas following a seventeenth-century model. It is a simple design of gravel and lawn separated by a low box hedge. There are herbaceous borders around the hall and a gravel walk that follows the inside perimeter of the moat. The garden is largely the creation of the Trust and is a fitting complement to the house.

MELLORS GARDEN 11

Hough Hole House, Sugar Lane, Rainow, Nr Macclesfield, Cheshire. Tel: (0625) 572286
Mr and Mrs G. Humphreys

Ten minutes from the centre of Macclesfield. Take the A5002 to Whaley Bridge. In the village of Rainow turn off to the north, opposite the church into Round Meadow Lane. Then turn at the first left into Sugar Lane and follow this down to the garden • Parking • Refreshments • Toilet facilities • Partly suitable for wheelchairs • Dogs on lead • Open Spring and Aug Bank Holiday Sun and Mon, 2 - 5 p.m. or by appointment for parties of more than 10 • Entrance: £1, children free

Where can you pass through the valley of the shadow of death, climb Jacob's ladder, see the mouth of hell and visit the Celestial City all within 10 minutes of Macclesfield? Here in the second half of the nineteenth century, James Mellor, much influenced by Swedenborg, designed this allegorical garden which attempts to recreate the journey of Christian in Bunyan's *Pilgrim's Progress*. Most areas are grassed with stone paths running throughout. There are many small stone houses and other ornaments to represent features of the journey. At one end a large pond is overlooked by a small octagonal summerhouse. The garden stands in a small valley in a rugged but attractive part of the Peak District. Be sure to be shown round by the owner or buy one of the excellent guide books in order to get the best from this small garden.

NORTON PRIORY MUSEUM AND GARDENS 12

Tudor Road, Runcorn, Cheshire. Tel: (0928) 569895
Norton Priory Museum Trust

From M6 at junction 11 turn for Warrington and follow Norton Priory signs. From all other directions follow Runcorn then Norton Priory signs • Parking • Refreshments: teas and snacks in Museum • Toilet facilities, inc. disabled • Suitable for wheelchairs • Dogs permitted but not in walled garden • Plants for sale • Shop • Museum open • Gardens open April to Oct, weekdays, 12 noon – 5 p.m., Sat, Sun and Bank Holidays, 12 noon – 6 p.m., Nov to March, daily, 12 noon – 4 p.m. Walled garden closed Nov to Feb • Entrance: £2, OAP and children £1. Museum and grounds £1.50, OAP, children and students 75p. Walled garden 70p, OAP, children and students 35p

Norton Priory was built as an Augustan foundation in the twelfth century and transformed into a Tudor then Georgian mansion before being abandoned in 1921. The 16 acres of gardens contain the ruins of the Priory, and also an authentic eighteenth-century walled garden. Originally built by Sir Richard Brooke in 1757 it eventually fell into disrepair, but since 1980 the owners have restored it to reflect both the Georgian and modern designs and tastes. Its range of specialities include a culinary herb and medicinal herb garden, plants for household uses, a fruit arch and cordon fruit, a new orchard, and a number of herbaceous borders.

PEOVER HALL 13

Peover Hall, Over Peover, Nr Knutsford, Cheshire.
Mr R. Brooks

3m S of Knutsford on A50 • Teas on Mons • Toilet facilities • Partly suitable for wheelchairs (many grass paths) • Dogs in park only • Plants for sale on special occasions • House open, Mon only, 2.30 – 4.30 p.m. • Gardens open May to Sept, Mon and Thurs, 2.30 – 4.30 p.m. • Entrance: £1 (hall and garden £2, children £1)

Peover Hall and its gardens are surrounded by a large expanse of flat parkland laid out in the early eighteenth century, but the gardens are mainly Edwardian. On the northern side of the hall is a forecourt, from where a broad grass walk leads through an avenue of pleached limes to a summerhouse. This overlooks a small circular lawn and both are enclosed by a high yew hedge. On the west side of the gardens is a wooded area containing many rhododendrons and a grassed dell that is particularly attractive. Clustered around the south and west of the hall are several small formal gardens, separated by brick walls and yew hedges. Some contain yew topiary. There is a rose garden, a herb garden, a white garden and a pink garden. The lily pool garden has a summerhouse with a tiled roof supported by Doric columns. A church stands in the centre of the gardens and there are fine Georgian stables.

QUEEN'S PARK, CREWE ★ 14

Victoria Avenue, Wisterton Road, Crewe, Cheshire.
Tel: (0270) 583191 ext 486
Crewe and Nantwich Borough Council

2m W of Crewe town centre, S of the A532 • Parking off Queen's Park Drive • Refreshments: cafeteria in park • Toilet facilities, inc. disabled • partly suitable for wheelchairs • Dogs on lead • Open all year, 9 a.m. - sunset • Entrance: free

Queen's Park is a very well landscaped Victorian park created in 1887–8 by the London & North Western Railway as a gift to the people of Crewe. It is oval in shape and covers 48 acres, with large grassed areas and a wide variety of mature trees. From an ornate entrance with two 'gothic' lodges and a clock tower, a drive leads through an avenue of birches to the centre of the park. Here a modern café with a terrace looks down upon the large boating lake that is surrounded by banks of trees and shrubs. From the west of the park a stream runs through a lightly wooded valley to join the lake. A path linking the entrance to this valley passes some raised beds of heathers and goes through a tunnel of laburnum. It merits a high grade for the quality of landscaping, the trees and the Victorian buildings, but in essence it is a large municipal park where a fight against vandalism and litter is fought hard.

TATTON PARK ★★ 15

Knutsford, Cheshire. Tel: (0565) 54822
The National Trust

Signposted from Knutsford and from A556 • Parking £1.20 per car • Refreshments: hot and cold lunches and snacks but from Oct to March, Suns only, 11.30 a.m. - 4.30 p.m. • Toilet facilities • Partly suitable for wheelchairs • Dogs on lead • Plants for sale • Shop • House open 29th March to Sept (closed Mons but not Bank Holiday Mons), 12 noon - 4 p.m. Oct to March 1992 (closed Mons, and 24th, 25th Dec), 11 a.m. - 4 p.m. • Gardens open 29th March to 30th Sept, daily except Mons (although open Bank Holiday Mons), 11 a.m. - 6 p.m. Oct to 28th March, daily except Mon, 24th, 25th Dec, 12 noon - 3 p.m. Park open daily except Mon, 11 a.m. - 4 p.m. Open at other times by appointment • Entrance: gardens £2, park £1.70 per car, house, park and gardens £5

The gardens here cover 50 acres and warrant an extensive exploration. On passing through the entrance visitors see to their right the Orangery. Built in 1820 by Lewis Wyatt, it contains orange trees, lemon trees, a bougainvillaea and other exotics. Next door is Paxton's fernery of 1850. This has large New Zealand tree ferns in its distinctively Victorian interior. To the east passing a large L-shaped herbaceous and shrub border, the Edwardian rose garden is reached. This is formal in design with a pool at its centre and fine stone paths and ornaments around. To the south lie large informally planted areas, an arboretum contains many conifers and rhododendrons and a lake contains water lilies and has a good variety of marginal plants growing around its banks. On the west side of the lake is a unique Japanese garden built in 1910 by workers brought especially from Japan. To the south of the house is the Italian garden possibly designed by Paxton and best viewed from the top floor of the house. The garden also contains a maze and many other features of interest. It is surrounded by a great expanse of very attractive parkland.

TIRLEY GARTH ★ 16

Utkinton, Nr Tarporley, Cheshire. Tel: (0829) 732301
Tirley Garth Trust

2½m N of Tarporley, just N of village of Utkinton on the road to Kelsall. Signposted • Parking • Teas • Toilet facilities • Partly suitable for wheelchairs and a wheelchair provided • Dogs on lead • Open 19th, 26th, 27th May, 1st, 2nd June, 2 - 6 p.m. • Entrance: £1, children 50p

Tirley Garth is a magnificent Edwardian house with gardens that complement it perfectly. They are still in much the same layout as originally designed by the architect T.H. Mawson and some of the stonework in the paths, ornaments and buildings is particularly notable. There is a circular courtyard at the western entrance and a small sunken garden to one side which leads to the large terrace on the south front which has lawns and rose beds. To the east is a lawned terrace with a view across the large semi-circular rose garden that spreads below it. In the centre of the house is a courtyard with a circular pool and fountain. Outside these formal gardens are areas of parkland and woodland; to the east is a stream running through a small valley planted with fine azaleas, rhododendrons and other acid-loving shrubs. There are good views of the surrounding countryside.

WALTON HALL GARDENS 17

Walton Lea Road, off Chester Road, Walton, Warrington, Cheshire.
Tel: (0925) 601617
Warrington Borough Council

2m SW of Warrington on S side of A56 in the village of Walton • Best season: spring and autumn • Parking. A charge is made at weekends and Bank Holidays from Easter to Oct • Refreshments • Partly suitable for wheelchairs • Toilet facilities • Dogs on lead, some restricted areas • Shop • House open Easter to Sept, Thurs - Sun, 1 - 5 p.m. (Easter, Bank Holidays) and Oct to Easter, Sun, 12.30 - 4.30 p.m. Extra charge • Gardens open daily, 8 a.m. - dusk • Entrance: free

Walton Hall, the former home of the Greenhall family, is a dark brick house with a distinctive clock tower. In front is a large lawn and to one side a modern pool and rockery, with a variety of shrubs, alpines and aquatic plants. Behind the Hall is a series of formal gardens separated by yew hedges and planted with bright annuals. Further south is a lawned area with herbaceous borders, with a path leading under some large beech trees to a rose garden. This has beds of modern roses set in an area of grass enclosed by a high conifer hedge. A walk back around the west side of the garden passes through an attractive area of shrubs and trees amongst which are many acers. Banks of mature woodland and large parkland surround the garden. The Council keeps the whole area in good condition.

CORNWALL

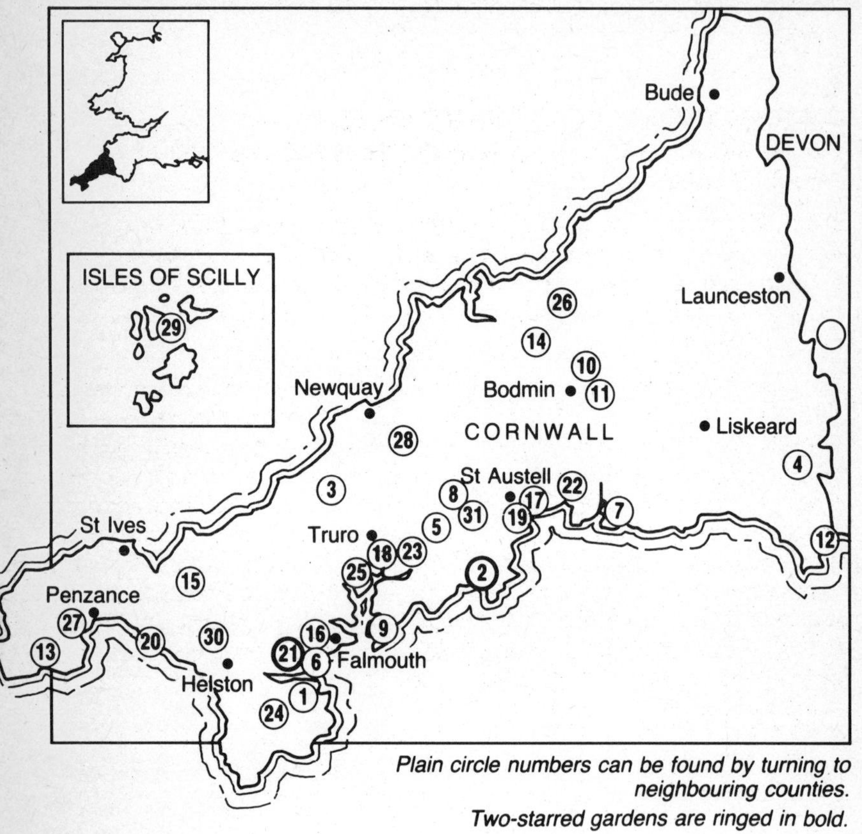

Plain circle numbers can be found by turning to neighbouring counties.
Two-starred gardens are ringed in bold.

BOSAHAN ★ 1

Manaccan, Helston, Cornwall. Tel: (0326) 23330
Captain and Mrs H.R. Graham Vivian

10m SE of Helston, 1m NE of Manaccan village • Parking in field if dry. If wet, firm area near farm • Teas • Toilet facilities • Partly suitable for wheelchairs • Dogs on lead • Plants for sale • Open 14th, 28th April, 5th, 12th May, 2.30 - 5 p.m. • Entrance: £1, children 50p

This valley garden of five acres started 100 years ago leads down to the Helford river and will give pleasure to the keen plantsman as it has both mature and newer planted trees and shrubs, including some New Zealand varieties. Its situation is said to have inspired Daphne du Maurier when creating the background for her novel *Rebecca*. In spring colour is provided by masses of camellias, rhododendrons, azaleas and magnolias along with bog plants in the water garden. There are formal beds with herbaceous plants at the top of the garden and one walks down through the valley to find the more mature specimens including pittosporums and dicksonias. There is some additional colour from ornamental pheasants. Fine views from the top of the valley.

CAERHAYS CASTLE GARDEN ★★ 2

Caerhays, Gorran, St Austell, Cornwall. Tel: (0872) 501301
Mr F.J. Williams

10m S of St Austell. On the coast by Porthluney Cove between Dodman Point and Nare Head • Parking at beach car park • Refreshments at Beach Café • Toilet facilities • Suitable for wheelchairs • Dogs on lead • Plants for sale • Open 31st March, 22nd April, 5th May, 2 - 5 p.m. • Entrance: £1.50, children under 14 free

An internationally noted garden with unrivalled collections of magnolias and shrubs raised from seed and material brought back by such plant hunters as George Forrest and E.H. Wilson, who were assisted financially in their expeditions by the Williams. The house, a vast romantic castle in the 'Gothick' style, was built by John Nash between 1805 - 1807. The garden began to take on its present form from 1896. The woodland stretches down to the sea and there are many rare specimens to be seen including tree ferns, acers, oaks, azaleas and nothofagus. J.C. Williams originlly specialized in the cultivation and hybridizing of daffodils, but turned his sheltered clearings over to a refuge for the nineteenth-century influx of new plants, and many in British gardens today originated at Caerhays. A place to be visited by the family as well as the plantsman.

CHYVERTON ★ 3

Zelah, Truro, Cornwall. Tel: (0872) 54324
Mr and Mrs N. Holman

1m W of Zelah on A30. Turn off N at Marazonvose, the entrance is ½m on right • Parking • Dogs on lead • Plants occasionally for sale • Open by appointment only March to June • Entrance: £2.50, for parties of 20 or more £2 per person. Bone fide horticultural students free. Visitors personally conducted around by owners

The outstanding feature of this garden originally landscaped in the eighteenth century is its collection of magnolias, including some bearing the name of the property and also the owner's father 'Treve Holman'. Superb trees of copper beech, cedars of Lebanon, eucryphia, and a collection of nothofagus make a beautiful backcloth to a vast collection of camellias and rhododendrons. The garden is planted to give vistas and is always being further developed. A collection of acers is being planted and there are good colour combinations with azaleas and photinias. There is an unusual hedge of *Myrtus luma* and by the stream are vast gunneras and lysichitums. Also of special interest is a

Mexican *Magnolia dealbata* believed to be the best example outside Mexico. Trees and shrubs have room to develop freely here but it is hard to realise that this beautiful and vast garden is maintained solely by the owners.

COTEHELE ★ 4

St Dominick, Nr Saltash, Cornwall. Tel: (0579) 50434
The National Trust

1m W of Calstock, 8m SW of Tavistock, 4m from Gunnislake. Turn at St Anne's Chapel • Best season: May/June • Parking • Refreshments • Toilet facilities • Partly suitable for wheelchairs • Plants for sale • Shop • House open except Fri (but open Good Fri), 11 a.m. - 6 p.m. (Oct, 11 a.m. - 5 p.m.) • Garden open daily, 11 a.m. - 6 p.m. or dusk if earlier • Entrance: £2.20 (garden and mill), £4.40 (house, garden and mill)

This ten-acre garden with terraces falling to a sheltered valley has developed gradually from Victorian times. It should give pleasure to most visitors with its combination of formal courtyards, fine terraces, walled garden, pools, herbaceous borders and valley garden. The grey granite walls of the house are a background to many climbers and from the rose terrace one walks down to the pool and dovecote. In the valley are giant conifers, hydrangeas, palms, acers and betula. There is a small acer plantation and yew hedges along with herbaceous borders.

COUNTY DEMONSTRATION GARDEN 5

Probus, Nr Truro, Cornwall. Tel: (0872) 74282
Cornwall County Council Education Committee

Just E of Probus village on A390 • Best season: summer • Parking • Refreshments: drink and biscuits • Toilet facilities • Suitable for wheelchairs • Open May to Sept, daily, 10 a.m. - 5 p.m. Oct and April, Mon - Fri, 10 a.m. - 4.30 p.m. • Entrance: £1.50, children free

This seven and a half-acre demonstration garden was started from a field in the early 1970s to serve as an advisory and education centre. A unique and fascinating display garden covering methods of growing vegetables, pruning fruit, treating lawns, weed control, compost making, design of small gardens, layouts for many aspects and situations. Fencing and walls, artificial and natural windbreaks, heath and heather planting, hanging baskets, gardening for the disabled, tree planting and staking, cloches, mulches, shrubs for shade and pruning of shrubs, herbs, rock and scree garden - in fact all aspects of gardening including various plant collections and patio and container gardening. A place to visit to get ideas and advice on problems.

GLENDURGAN GARDEN 6

Helford River, Mawnan Smith, Nr Falmouth, Cornwall.
Tel: (0208) 74281
The National Trust

4m SW of Falmouth, ½m SW of Mawnan Smith on the road to Helford Passage • Best season: spring to Sept • Parking • Toilet facilities • Open March to Oct, Tues - Sat, 10.30 a.m. - 5.30 p.m. Last admission 4.30 p.m. Closed Good Friday but open Bank Holiday Mons • Entrance: £2

This 40-acre valley garden was originally planted by Alfred Fox in the 1820s with the village of Durgan at its foot alongside the Helford river. The wooded valley contains many specimen trees including *Dicksonia antarctica*, drimys, embothrium, eucryphia, conifers and a *Davidia involucrata*. In spring there is colour from primroses, bluebells, Lenten lilies and small daffodils while in late summer there are masses of hydrangeas. An unusual feature is the laurel maze. Vast camellias and magnolias provide early colour in the garden.

HEADLAND 7

3 Battery Lane, Polruan-by-Fowey, Cornwall. Tel: (0726) 870243
Mr and Mrs J. Hill

Use public car park. Turn left (on foot) down St Saviour's Hill, left again at intersection near Coastguard Office. Gate on right • Best season: June/July • Cream teas • Beach for swimming • Open June to Sept, Thurs, 2 - 8 p.m. • Entrance: £1, children 50p

This cliff garden 100 feet above sea level, created from an old quarry on the headland, has been developed by the present owners since 1974. It is a great credit to the owners for the excellent range of plants they grow with sea on three sides of the garden where plants must withstand spray and gales. It is designed with narrow paths and archways leading round corners to discover secret areas with Australian and New Zealand plants - cordylines and olearias; sub-tropical succulents - agaves, echeverias, crassulas and lampranthus. There is a path with various eucalyptus trees. In crevices one sees sempervivum, sedum and erigeron. Monterey pines, tamarisk, Torquay pines, yuccas and fatsia all thrive and there are good plant combinations. It is surprising to find vegetables and fruit trees and bushes doing well on such a windswept slope. With the vast range of plants and clever design it is hard to believe the garden is only one and a quarter acres.

THE HOLLIES 8

Grampound, Truro, Cornwall. Tel: (0726) 882474
Mrs N.B. and Mr J.R. Croggon

6m from St Austell on A390 Truro road in the village of Grampound next to post office • Parking in side lanes - Creed Lane, Bosillian Lane, Pepo Lane

• Teas • Toilet facilities • Suitable for wheelchairs • Plants for sale • Open 14th April, 19th May, 16th, 30th June, 14th July and by appointment, 2 - 5.30 p.m. • Entrance: £1, children free

This garden has a charming 'cottage' garden effect created by the unusual design. There are island beds containing a wide range of trees and shrubs with underplanting of bulbs to provide interest and beauty throughout the year, although spring is the peak time. There are many rare plants, including alpines, to be enjoyed here.

LAMORRAN HOUSE ★ 9

Upper Castle Road, St Mawes, Cornwall. Tel: (0326) 270801
Mr and Mrs R. Dudley-Cooke

At garage above village of St Mawes turn right - signposted at Castle. In about ½m Lamorran is on left of road set behind a line of pine trees • Parking for cars in road. Coaches by prior appointment • Toilet facilities • Partly suitable for wheelchairs • Plants for sale • Open for charity on 30th March, 20th April, 25th May, 15th, 22nd June, 10 a.m. - 5 p.m. and coach parties at other times by arrangement • Entrance: £2, children free

This four-acre garden developed since 1980 contains a large and excellent collection of sub-tropical and warm temperate species which one would not expect to find on a hillside adjacent to the sea. In the main it has been designed in the Italian style with columns and other artefacts. There are 500 azaleas, many different palms and eucalyptus, yuccas, 250 rhododendrons, a wide range of conifers, a range of Australian and New Zealand plants and a fernery. There are little gardens and round every corner more unusual plants. A Japanese garden and water feature. The plantsman will enjoy this and so will other visitors as the owner has incorporated good design features and interesting colour and foliage combinations.

LANCARFFE ★ 10

Nr Bodmin, Cornwall. Tel: (0208) 72877
Mr and Mrs R. Gilbert

2m NE of Bodmin. Turn W off A30 signed Helland, then left hairpin towards Bodmin. After 400 years, turn right signposted Norton and Holton, then bear left. Adjacent to Racecourse Farm • Parking. No coaches • Refreshments • Toilet facilities • Dogs on lead • Open 12th May, 2 - 5 p.m. • Entrance: £1

Walking through this four and a half-acre garden one can enjoy its wide range of plants from *Davidia involucrata* (pocket-handkerchief tree) to beds of roses. Some beautiful trees form a backcloth to a fine collection of azaleas, camellias and rhododendrons. There is a delightful walled water garden with shrubs and climbers on the walls. Hydrangeas, eucryphias, acers, *Desfontainea spinosa*,

Campsis radicans, a *Paulownia fargesis* (foxglove tree), various cornus and embothriums are some of the specimens to be enjoyed. A magnificent splash of colour in summer is provided by a long border of dahlias. The owners are continuing to develop this very pleasant garden.

LANHYDROCK ★ 11

Bodmin, Cornwall. Tel: (0208) 73320
The National Trust

2½m SE of Bodmin off A38, or off B3268 • Best season: spring • Parking 600 yards but inc. disabled adjacent to garden • Refreshments • Toilet facilities inc. disabled • Partly suitable for wheelchairs • Dogs on lead in park • Plants for sale • Shop in house • House open (closed Mon except Bank Holiday Mon and closed Nov to March. Closes 5 p.m. in Oct). Extra charge • Garden open 29th March to Oct, daily, 11 a.m. – 6 p.m. (Oct 5 p.m.). Garden only open Nov to March 1992, daily during daylight hours • Entrance: £2.40 (garden and grounds), £4.20 (house and garden)

This superb 30-acre garden started about 1860 contains gardens within a garden and has some exceptional trees and shrubs both in the park, woodland and the more formal areas. The collection of trees started before 1634. Banks of colour are provided by magnolias, camellias and rhododendrons, and this is followed by roses which are in beds in the lawn adjacent to the house interspersed with cone-shaped Irish yews. In the terraces beds of annuals are edged with box. A circular yew hedge surrounds the herbaceous borders which contain a wide range of choice plants and provide summer colour. The woodland has walks amongst rare trees and hydrangeas and other flowering shrubs. There is a stream with bog plants.

MOUNT EDGCUMBE HOUSE AND COUNTRY PARK ★ 12

Cremyll, Torpoint, Cornwall. Tel: (0752) 822236
Plymouth City Council and Cornwall County Council

Access from Plymouth by Cremyll (pedestrian) Ferry to Park entrance. Access from Cornwall A38 to Trerulefoot roundabout then A374 and B3247 • Parking for cars and coaches, but advance booking for coaches helpful • Refreshments: lunches, teas and light refreshments 29th March to Oct daily in Orangery (0752) 822586. Picnics • Toilet facilities • Suitable for wheelchairs • Dogs on lead • Shop • House open 29th March to Oct, Wed – Sun and Bank Holidays, 11 a.m. – 5.30 p.m. • Country Park and formal gardens open daily, 8 a.m. – dusk. Earl's Garden open 29th March to Oct, Wed – Sun and Bank Holidays, 11 a.m. – 5.30 p.m. • Entrance: Country park and formal gardens free. Earl's Garden and House £2.50, concessions £1.50, children (16 and under) £1

The gardens and landscaped park were created by the Mount Edgcumbe family in the eighteenth century. They have been praised by Pepys, William Kent and Humphrey Repton. The site covers 865 acres, and stretches from Plymouth Sound to Rame Head. The Earl's Garden contains a rare, recently restored, shell grotto. This garden, which surrounds the house, was remade after having been terraced in 1941. On the east front the newly-introduced late Victorian flower beds are situated. The formal gardens at the lower end of the old tree-lined avenue encompass English, French and Italian Gardens (complete with ornamental orange trees) and two new gardens to commemorate the family's historical connection with America and New Zealand. Planted in the Amphitheatre is the National collection of Camellias. There are fine sea views to Drake's Island from the Park, where fallow deer may sometimes be seen.

PENBERTH 13

St Buryan, Nr Penzance, Cornwall. Tel: (0736) 810208
Mrs J.M.M. Banham

Leave Penzance on A30 towards Lands End. After 2m turn left on B3283 to Porthcurno and St Buryan. Keep on B3315 through the village following signs to Porthcurno. Road descends into valley. Turn left at lane signed Penberth. Approach through gatehouse • Best season: spring • Parking in field • Teas • Toilet facilities • Partly suitable for wheelchairs • Plants for sale • Open 31st March and 5th May, 2 - 5 p.m. and by appointment • Entrance: £1, children 30p

A five-acre garden in a valley leading down to the sea, created by Dr Edward Vernon Farell 70 years ago. Water garden and rock garden. Camellias, azaleas and other shrubs. Bog plants. A rushing stream. Mass of daffodils in the spring. In the grounds stands an old mill dating back to Doomsday.

PENCARROW ★ 14

Washaway, Bodmin, Cornwall. Tel: (020884) 369
The Molesworth-St Aubyn family

3m from Bodmin and Wadebridge. Signposted from the A389 Bodmin - Wadebridge road • Best season: spring • Parking • Refreshments in tearoom. Picnics • Toilet facilities • Partly suitable for wheelchairs • Dogs on lead near house • Plants for sale • Shop • Open Easter to 15th Oct daily except Fri and Sat, 1.30 - 5 p.m. Bank Holiday Mon and 1st June to 10th Sept from 11 a.m. • Entrance: £1, children 50p

The drive, one mile long, leads to the imposing Palladian mansion built in 1760. A formal garden with a circular lawn is laid out on two sides of the house. Nearby on a higher level, shrubs are placed in a rock garden made with boulders transported from Bodmin Moor when the gardens were designed by Sir William Molesworth from 1831 onwards. There are 50 acres of woodland

and parkland where over 500 different species of rhododendrons and a large collection of camellias grow. Among the many trees stands a *Picea orientalis* (Caucasian spruce) the second earliest known to have been planted in Britain. There are a large number of Monkey Puzzle trees (*Araucaria araucana*). The English name is said to have originated at Pencarrow when, in 1834, the parliamentary barrister Charles Austin who was staying at Pencarrow rashly touched one of the prickly leaves and quickly withdrew his hand, saying: 'It would puzzle a monkey'.

PENPOL HOUSE 15

Penpol Avenue, Hayle, Cornwall. Tel: (0736) 753146
Major and Mrs T.F. Ellis

4m SE of St Ives. Turn left at White Hart, Penpol Road, then 2nd left into Penpol Avenue • Best season: May to July • Parking in adjacent field • Teas • Suitable for wheelchairs • Plants for sale • Open by appointment for parties mid-May to July and on 16th and 30th June for charity, 2 – 6 p.m. • Entrance: £1, children 50p for charity

This three-acre garden surrounding the sixteenth-century house has been developed over the past 100 years. It is made up of different small gardens and there are different design features including a white painted ship's figurehead, suspended on a small building, formerly the cider house. There is a grey garden, cottage garden, an old walled garden with fruit, vegetables and a pool, a rose garden and herbaceous borders with collections of iris, delphiniums, shrubs and perennials. The old greenhouses contain a 100-year-old vine and a geranium on the wall of the same age. This garden of unique charm has an alkaline soil, unusual for Cornwall.

PENWARNE 16

Mawnan Smith, Nr Falmouth, Cornwall.
Tel: (0326) 250585/250325
Mr and Mrs H. Beister

3¼ SW of Falmouth and 1½m N of Mawnan Smith off the Falmouth to Mawnan Smith road • Best season: spring • Parking. Coaches by prior arrangement • Toilet facilities • Partly suitable for wheelchairs • Dogs on lead • Open 14th May, 2 – 5 p.m. • Entrance: £1, children 50p

There are many large trees including *Cryptomeria japonica*, beeches and oaks which form a backcloth to this woodland garden planted about 1900 in which is set a fine Georgian House. The old walled garden has roses, clematis and lilies and there are banks of azaleas, rhododendrons, camellias and magnolias, together with shrubs from New Zealand. The pool with ornamental ducks and the stream running through the garden provide areas for primulas and tree ferns. There are fruit trees and bushes along with bamboos. Many new plantings.

PINE LODGE ★ 17

Cuddra, St Austell, Cornwall. Tel: (0726) 73500
Mr and Mrs R. Clemo

Just E of St Austell off A390 between Holmbush and the turning to Tregrehan. Signs on open days • Best season: May to July • Parking • Teas • Toilet facilities • Suitable for wheelchairs • Plants for sale • Open 26th May, 16th June, 14th July, 1 - 5 p.m. or parties of 20 or more by appointment • Entrance: £1.50, children free

This four-acre garden, started 44 years ago but extended during the past 14 years, contains a wide range of plants and should be of interest to the keen gardener because there are good design features and original colour combinations. Plants labelled. Besides the usual rhododendrons and camellias so familiar in Cornish gardens there are herbaceous borders with rare and tender plants, a range of conifers, heathers, a pergola with clematis and hedera, and other climbers. A large wildlife pond, a bog garden, a vegetable garden and an arboretum with a large variety of trees are other features to enjoy.

POLGWYNNE 18

Feock, Nr Truro, Cornwall. Tel: (0872) 862612
Mr and Mrs P. Davey

5m S of Truro. Take A39, then B3289 to first crossroads. Carry straight on to ½m short of Feock • Best seasons: spring and early summer • Parking • Refreshments on open days • Toilet facilities • Partly suitable for wheelchairs • Plants for sale on open days only • Open 29th April, 12th May, 3rd June, 2 - 5 p.m. and by appointment • Entrance: £1 for charity

A three and a half-acre garden with woodlands extending to the shore of Carrick Roads. There is a *Gingko biloba* with a girth of 11ft 9ins, probably the largest specimen in Britain. Many fine trees and unusual shrubs. Beautiful setting with fine views.

PORTHPEAN 19

Porthpean House, St Austell, Cornwall. Tel: (0726) 72888
Mr and Mrs C. Petherick

Take A390 and then the road signposted Porthpean, past Mount Edgcumbe Hospice, turn left down Porthpean Beach Road. Porthpean House is the white building at the bottom of the hill just before the car park • Best season: spring • Parking in car park nearby • Refreshments: teas for parties • Toilet facilities • Suitable for wheelchairs • Dogs on lead • Plants for sale • Open Sats and Suns in April and May, and 9th, 14th April, 5th May, 2 - 5 p.m. Also by appointment • Entrance: £1.50, children free

This three-acre garden was first developed by Maurice Petherick some 40 years ago. It contains a special collection of camellias, also many azaleas and rhododendrons. The grounds have access to the beach and from the main lawn one has a magnificent view of St Austell Bay. On spring days cherry blossoms stand out sharply against the blue of the sea. There is also a nursery garden with Victorian greenhouses.

ST MICHAEL'S MOUNT 20

Marazion, Nr Penzance, Cornwall. Tel: (0736) 710507
The National Trust

½m from the shore at Marazion, ½m S of A394. Access by ferry or across causeway • Best season: spring/early summer • Parking in Marazion • Refreshments: restaurant • Toilet facilities • Plants for sale • Shop, March to Oct • Castle and Abbey open but only to guided tours Nov to March when ferry may be difficult • Garden open 29th March to Oct, Mon - Fri, 10.30 a.m. - 5.45 p.m. Last admission 4.45 p.m. Open most weekends during April to Sept for charity when NT members expected to pay for admission. Nov to March guided tours can be arranged • Entrance: £2.80, children £1.40

A unique and extraordinary 20-acre maritime garden which has been created in terraces just above the sea at the foot of a 300 ft perpendicular cliff. Here, in spite of apparent total exposure to gales and salt spray, sub-tropical species abound. The walled garden was planted in the eighteenth century by two young ladies, ancestors of the St Aubyn family who still live in the Castle. A remarkable example of micro-climate effect is in itself a fascinating study for the keen gardener. Planting has been done amongst granite boulders, some weighing hundreds of tons. There are yuccas, geraniums, euryops, hebes, phormium, fuchsias and in spring sheets of wild narcissus. Kniphofia grow wild in the bracken and provide great splashes of colour.

TREBAH ★★ 21

Mawnan Smith, Nr Falmouth, Cornwall. Tel: (0326) 250448
Major and Mrs J.A. Hibbert (The Trebah Garden Trust)

4m SW of Falmouth, 1m SW of Mawnan Smith and 500 yards W of Glendurgan Garden • Best season: March to Oct • Parking • Refreshments • Toilet facilities • Partly suitable for wheelchairs • Dogs on lead • Plants for sale • Open daily, 10.30 a.m. - 5 p.m. • Entrance: £2, disabled and children £1, children under 5 free (Nov to Feb, £1, disabled and children 50p)

A 25-acre ravine garden started by Charles Fox in the 1840s which contains many beautiful and mature trees and shrubs that provide an undulating carpet of colour. The deep ravine leads to a private beach on the Helford River. A stream runs through a water garden and a series of ponds with mature Koi carp. Extensive plantings of sub-tropical Mediterranean plants at the top of the garden blend into the rain forest of the lower reaches with glades of giant tree ferns, bananas and bamboos. Three acres of blue and white hydrangeas carry the colour through to Christmas. A paradise for the artist, the plantsman and the family.

TREGREHAN 22

Par, Nr St Austell, Cornwall. Tel: (072681) 2438
The Carlyon Estate. Mr T. Hudson

On A390 Lostwithiel to St Austell road. The entrance is opposite the Britannia Inn • Best season: spring • Parking • Toilet facilities • Partly suitable for wheelchairs • Plants for sale, esp. camellias • Open mid-March to June and Sept, Wed, Thurs and Sat, 10.30 a.m. - 5 p.m. • Entrance: £1.50, children 75p. Parties by arrangement

The 20-acre garden contains many large and interesting trees and rhododendrons in addition to the large collection of camellias raised by the late owner. There are woodland walks carpeted with bluebells in spring and a walled garden. Other plants include clivias and nerines, but the camellias, rare trees and vast rhododendrons are of particular interest to the keen plantsman. Magnificent Victorian greenhouses.

TREHANE 23

Nr Probus, Cornwall. Tel: (087252) 270
David and Simon Trehane

Turn N off A39 between the Wheel Inn and Tresillian Bridge. Signposted • Best season: spring/summer • Parking in field. Coaches by special arrangement for a different route • Teas • Toilet facilities • Partly suitable for wheelchairs • Dogs on lead • Plants for sale • Open by appointment and 24th March, 7th, 28th April, 5th, 19th May, 16th June, 1st, 21st July, 18th Aug, 2 - 5 p.m. • Entrance: £1, children 50p

This is a plantsman's garden containing a wonderful variety and many good collections - geraniums, hemerocallis, romneyas and trilliums. There are lovely camellias, many actually raised here. Interesting climbers cover the old walls and in spring the woodland area is carpeted with bluebells, claytonias and campions. A very old *Pieris japonica*, a davidia and vast rhododendrons, azaleas and magnolias provide a background to a large collection of herbaceous plants. This garden will also be enjoyed by the general visitor as it has a great sense of peace and half of its 10 acres is woodland.

TRELEAN 24

St Martin-in Meneage, Nr Helston, Cornwall. Tel: (032623) 255
Squadron Leader and Mrs G.T. Witherwick

7m SE of Helston on B3293. After 4m turn left for Mawgan 1m from the village of St Martin-in-Meneage • Best season: spring/autumn • Parking in field • Teas • Toilet facilities • Dogs on lead • Plants for sale • Open by appointment and Spring Bank Holiday Sunday and 28th Oct 12 noon - 5 p.m. • Entrance: £1, children 20p

This 20-acre garden set in a valley with superb views of the River Helford is for the keen plantsman as it contains a superb collection of beautiful and rare trees and shrubs including 14 different nothofagus, 50 different acers, various eucalyptus, cistus, enkianthus, olearias and robinias. The winding steep paths are bordered on either side by ilex, hazels, Scots pine and many varieties of rhododendrons and 70 different conifers. The owner, who started this garden from an area of woodland and bracken in 1980, is certainly creating a paradise for the botanist.

TRELISSICK ★ 25

Feock, Nr Truro, Cornwall. Tel: (0872) 862090
The National Trust

4m S of Truro on B3289 above King Harry Ferry • Best season: April/May • Parking £1 (refundable) • Refreshments: restaurant open 11 a.m. - 6 p.m., Sun, 12 noon - 6 p.m. Limited opening Nov and Dec, phone (0872) 863486 • Toilet facilities • Partly suitable for wheelchairs • Dogs on lead on woodland walk and park only • Plants for sale • Art and Craft Gallery in grounds open • Garden open March to Oct, Mon - Sat, 11 a.m. - 6 p.m. Sun, 1 - 6 p.m. (Mar and Oct closes 5 p.m.) • Entrance: £2.50

This 25-acre garden with woodland was originally planted with exotic things and became known as the fruit garden of Cornwall. Now it contains a wide variety of interest with its collection of hydrangeas, a dell, aromatic, fern and fig gardens along with some very large trees including *Quercus ilex*, *Fagus sylvatica* and a beautiful Japanese cedar *Cryptomeria japonica* in a lawn backed by herbaceous borders containing a range of perennials. Near the entrance is a lovely border of heliotrope - a tradition of Trelissick. The dell has tree ferns, hostas and hellebores and there are many beautiful shrubs. Small walled garden with aromatic plants.

TREMEER 26

St Tudy, Nr Bodmin, Cornwall. Tel: (0208) 850313
The Haslam-Hopwood family

NW of St Tudy between A39 and B3266. Take Wadebridge road from the centre of St Tudy • Best season: April to June • Parking in garden. Coaches at village hall by arrangement • Toilet facilities • Dogs on lead • Open April to Sept, daily, 2 - 6 p.m. • Entrance: free. Donations to charity at the entrance

By Cornish standards this seven-acre garden is exposed and cold and has a high rainfall, but manages to produce vivid colour and pervading scent. A large bank of heathers is backed by dwarf rhododendrons and camellias. The terrace beneath the house looks out to a backcloth of fine mature trees. After crossing the lawn, walks meander through beautiful shrubs - rhododendrons, azaleas, camellias - and at the bottom of the garden is a small lake with ducks. Primulas, hostas and other water plants. Herbaceous borders provide summer colour and the walls have good climbers and perennials beneath.

TRENGWAINTON GARDEN ★ 27

Nr Penzance, Cornwall. Tel: (0736) 63021
The National Trust

2m NW of Penzance on B3312, or ½m off A3071 • Best season: spring • Parking • Teas usually at Trengwainton Farm • Toilet facilities • Suitable for wheelchairs • Dogs on lead • Open March to Oct, Wed - Sat, Bank Holiday Mon and Good Fri, 11 a.m. - 6 p.m. (closes 5 p.m. in March and Oct) • Entrance: £1.80

Trengwainton means 'House of the Spring' and was acquired by the Bolitho family in 1867. It will appeal to both the plantsman and the ordinary gardener because it contains a magnificent collection of magnolias, rhododendrons and camellias and a series of walled gardens with many tender and exotic shrubs and plants that would not survive in less mild areas of England. The stream garden alongside the drive backed by a beech wood provides masses of colour from candelabra primulas, lilies, lysichitum and other bog plants. Many of the rhododendrons were raised from seed collected by Kingdon Ward's expedition to NE Assam and the Mishmi Hills of Burma. New Zealand tree ferns, pittosporums from China, Japanese maples, embothriums, olearia, acacia, eucryphia, and Chatham Island forget-me-not are just a few of the beautiful plants to be seen during the spring and summer. There are magnificent views of the hills leading down to the sea and a space has been cut in the woodland to reveal St Michael's Mount

TRERICE 28

Nr Newquay, Cornwall. Tel: (0637) 875404
The National Trust

3m SE of Newquay via A392 and A3058. Turn right at Kestle Mill • Best season: summer • Parking • Refreshments • Toilet facilities • Partly suitable for wheelchairs • Plants for sale • Shop in house • House open • Garden open 29th March to Oct, daily except Tues, 11 a.m. - 6 p.m. (closes 5 p.m. in Oct). Last admission ½ hour before closing • Entrance. £3.20

A small garden by Cornish standards developed around an Elizabethan manor house where one can enjoy many unusual and lovely rare plants. It has been planted with shrubs, climbers and perennials to provide very good foliage and colour combinations. In the front walled courtyard are herbaceous borders. An Elizabethan knot garden has recently been developed. The back court has a range of cottage garden plants - fuchsia, lonicera, roses and climbers on the house. An orchard has been planted with apples, pears, quince, plums in the quincunx pattern used in the seventeenth century, and there are figs elsewhere in the garden. The design features of the garden are of particular interest.

TRESCO ABBEY ★★ 29

Tresco, Isles of Scilly.
Tel: (0720) 22849 Mike Nelhams (Head Gardener)
Mr R.A. Dorrien-Smith

On the Island of Tresco. Travel: by helicopter from Penzance Heliport to Tresco Heliport - 12 months (reservations (0736) 63871 and (0720) 22646) or from St Mary's by launch • Refreshments • Toilet facilities • Suitable for wheelchairs (availble at garden gate) • Dogs on lead • Plants for sale • Shop • Open daily, 10 a.m. - 4 p.m. • Entrance: £2.50, children £1

One of the most spectacular of all Britain's 'sub-tropical' gardens on an island which lies in the warming Gulf Stream. Protected from the Atlantic gales by windbreaks, the garden is arranged on several terraces mounting a hillside which are linked by flights of steps. They serve as a home for myriad exotic plants like proteus from South Africa, the tender geranium *G. maderense* from Madeira and trees and shrubs from the North Island of New Zealand and Australia which could not thrive out-of-doors in many places on the British mainland. This 17-acre garden is both formal and informal. Many of the plants are self-seeded. The grounds also house the Valhalla collection of ship figureheads from the National Maritime Museum.

ISLES OF SCILLY

There are over one hundred islands in addition to Tresco. Only five are inhabited. Spring comes very early, bringing abundant flowering of daffodils and narcissi. In 1868 William Trevellick of St Mary's sent some flowers to Covent Garden in a hat box and since then the industry has grown steadily and now between December and April some 800 tons of flowers are transported, many in bud so as to reach market in peak condition. February is perhaps the best month for the visitor. Then there is a wide variety of wild flowers in the fields and hedgerows. The *soleil d'or* grows in the bulb fields and the pink sea thrift is everywhere on the cliffs. One mile from Hugh Town, St Mary's, a two-acre garden is being created in a quarry by volunteer gardeners. Entrance is free. Contact Mr R Letherbridge (0270) 22404.

TREVARNO 30

Helston, Cornwall. Tel: (0326) 572022
Mr and Mrs P. Bickford-Smith

3m N of Helston on B3303 and E of Crowntown • Best season: spring • Parking. Coaches by arrangement • Refreshments • Toilet facilities • Open 28th April, 12th May for charity, 1.30 - 5 p.m. Parties by arrangement • Entrance: £1, children 50p

This fine woodland garden of 15 acres includes a large ornamental lake at the foot of the garden and alongside is the bog garden. It contains a vast range of rare trees and shrubs along with a collection of oaks, species rhododendrons and *Acer palmatum* 'Dissectum Nigrum'. There is a collection of ilex, a shady garden and a grotto, and a collection of geraniums. Beside the waterfall are primulas, rheums, astilbes and aruncus. A plantsman's garden.

TREWITHEN ★★ 31

Grampound Road, Nr Truro, Cornwall.
Tel: (0726) 882418/882763/882764
Mr A.M.J. Galsworthy

On A390 between Truro and St Austell, adjacent to the County Demonstration Garden • Parking • Toilet facilities • Suitable for wheelchairs • Dogs on lead • Plants for sale • Garden shop (0726) 883794 • House open April to July, Mon, Tues, 2 - 4.30 p.m. • Garden open March to Sept, Mon - Sat, 10 a.m. - 4.30 p.m. • Entrance: £1.75 (£1.50 in Sept), children £1

This is an internationally famous garden, known for its great collection of magnolias, rhododendrons and camellias along with many other beautiful and rare trees and shrubs. It is fitting that its founder George Johnstone named a camellia after his daughter 'Elizabeth Johnston', and there are rhododendrons 'Alison Johnston' after his wife, 'Trewithen Orange' and 'Jack Skelton' after his head gardener. The lawn in front of the house is edged with banks of a wide range of shrubs including viburnums, azaleas, potentillas, euonymus, berberis. There is a sunken garden with tree ferns, azaleas and acers. There are many nothofagus, embothriums, pieris, enkianthus, eucryphias, griselinias. The walled garden has a pool and some choice climbers including *Clianthus puniceus*, and *Mutisia decurrens*, and there is a pergola with wisteria. Newly planted beds of young trees of sorbus and birch, mahonia, cornus, phygelius and roses and island beds with heathers and dwarf conifers. The beech trees that provide shelter for the garden are magnificent. A half hour video describes the creation of the garden over the years.

GARDENS OPEN RARELY

The following gardens are open to the public on three days or less in the year, although they may also be open by appointment if this is stated in the text. For details see individual entry.

March 31 Caerhays Castle Garden; Penberth; **April 22** Caerhays Castle Garden; **April 28** Trevarno; **April 29** Polgwynne; **May 5** Caerhays Castle Garden; Penberth; **May 12** Lancarffe; Polgwynne; Trevarno; **May 14** Penwarne; **May 26** Pine Lodge; **June 3** Polgwynne; **June 16** Penpol House; Pine Lodge; **June 30** Penpol House; **July 14** Pine Lodge; **Oct 28** Trelean.

CUMBRIA & THE ISLE OF MAN

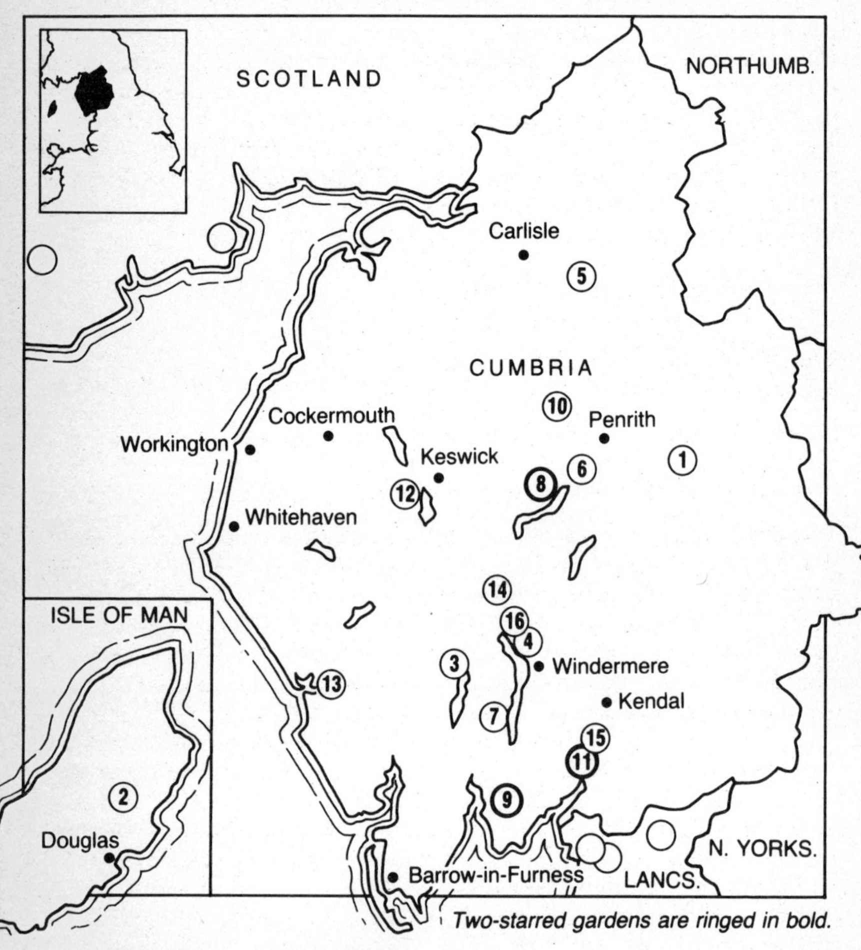

Two-starred gardens are ringed in bold.

ACORN BANK GARDEN 1

Temple Sowerby, Penrith, Cumbria. Tel: (07683) 61893
The National Trust

6m E of Penrith of A66 N of Temple Sowerby • Best season: spring and early summer • Parking • Picnic area only • Toilet facilities inc. disabled • Mostly suitable for wheelchairs • Guide dogs only in gardens, on lead in picnic area • Plants for sale • Shop • Admission to house by prior written permission Sue Ryder Society • Open 29th March to 3rd Nov, daily, 10 a.m. – 6 p.m. Last admission 5.30 p.m. • Entrance: £1.20

The 'acorn bank' is the ancient oakwood sloping down to the Crowdundle Beck behind the house. In spring it is a mass of daffodils and narcissi in many varieties planted profusely in the 1930s (e.g. some 60,000 Lenten lilies). The walled gardens are then also a mass of blossom from the old varieties of apple, medlar, pear and quince in the sheltered orchards, with their carpet of wild tulips, anemones and narcissi. The orchard's trees include apple varieties which blossom late and are therefore suitable for cooler northern areas. Along the three sheltering walls are carefully modulated herbaceous and shrub borders, with good clematis and climbers. A bed of species roses (*Rugosa* and others) flanks the steps to a picturesque sunken garden (a pond and alpine terraces). Through a gateway lies a splendid herb garden - a well tended collection of some 250 medicinal and culinary herbs, all comprehensively labelled and documented.

BALLALHEANNAGH ★ 2

Glen Roy, Lonan, Isle of Man. Tel: (0624) 861875
Mr and Mrs C. Dadd

In Glen Roy on E side of island, 2m inland from Laxey • Best season: spring • Parking • Plants for sale at nursery • Open daily, 10 a.m. - 1 p.m., 2 p.m. - 5 p.m., but closed on weekends from Nov to Feb • Entrance: £1

Take a steep-sided valley, a ladder, some seedlings of exotic rhododendrons and forget all about digging pits to accommodate the roots. Just stick them into crevices among the mosses and ferns. Wait a few years, never giving up. Outcome - paradise for plant-lovers. You expect to find a garden like Ballalheannagh in Cornwall or Kerry but this is in the middle of the Isle of Man. Every visitor with an interest in gardening, who is marooned on that island, need not fear boredom. This is a botanical garden, not in name, but surely in content. Steep winding paths cling to the valley sides. Crystal water cascades below carry the bells of pieris to the Irish Sea. The lower portion is well stocked with lofty rhododendrons while the upper parts of the valley contain newer plantings that will certainly delight in years to come. Here are pieris, eucalyptus, drimys, epacris, epigaea, megacarpea and betula (species with wonderful names like *Betula tatewakiana*), and a host of others. It's not all shrubs and trees, there are choice bulbs too, and the native mosses and ferns are a wonderful sight.

BRANTWOOD 3

Coniston, Cumbria. Tel: (05394) 41396
Brantwood Trust

E side of Coniston Water off B5285, signposted. Possibly water taxi from Coniston • Best season: spring, autumn • Parking • Tea room and restaurant • Toilet facilities inc. disabled • Dogs • Plants for sale planned • Shop • House open, £2.25, children £1.25, family £6 (2 plus 5 maximum)

• *Garden open mid-March to mid-Nov, daily, 11 a.m. - 5.30 p.m. winter, Wed - Sun, 11 a.m. - 4 p.m.* • *Entrance: 50p, children 25p (nature trail)*

This is a superb site with wonderful views, atmosphere and potential. The rocky hillside behind the house is threaded with a wandering network of paths created by Ruskin (who lived here 1872 - 1900) to delight the eye and please the mind. Rhododendrons and azaleas flourish in the acid soil to make a lovely woodland garden. Now in the capable hands of Sally Beamish, it is being restored to its former glory after long neglect and enhanced by imaginative planting. The water features will also be revived. Given time and hard work it should become a classic.

BROCKHOLE ★ 4

Lake District National Park Centre, Windermere, Cumbria.
Tel: (09662) 6601
Lake District Special Planning Board

1½m N of Windermere on A591 • *Best season: spring, early summer, autumn* • *Parking* • *Refreshments: restaurant and cafeteria* • *Toilet facilities inc. disabled* • *Partly suitable for wheelchairs* • *Dogs on lead* • *Shop* • *Open Easter to early Nov, daily, 10 a.m. - 5 p.m. (July and Aug to 10 p.m.)* • *Entrance: £1.90, children 90p, family and group rates available.*

A garden blessed with the Lakeland combination of western aspect and water to the hills beyond, in this case notably the Langdale Pikes. To frame this view Mawson worked closely (c. 1900) with his architect colleague, Gibson. The ornamental terraces drop through rose beds, herbaceous borders and shrubbery to a wild flower meadow flanked by mature woodland. The original kitchen and herb garden has been restored by Sue Tasker. Special features are rock plants, Chilean and other half-hardy shrubs and rarities and the constantly changing colour from spring rhododendrons and azaleas through to the late Chilean hollies.

CORBY CASTLE 5

Great Corby, Cumbria. Tel: (0228) 560246
Mr and Mrs John Howard

6m E of Carlisle, turn off A69 at Warwick Bridge to Great Corby village • *Best season: spring, early summer* • *Parking* • *Dogs on lead* • *Open April to Oct, daily, 1 - 5 p.m.* • *Entrance: 40p (honesty box)*

Created by Thomas Howard in the early eighteenth century the grounds run along the River Eden for about one mile, with fine trees and architectural features. The cascade was restored in 1957 and takes the water from the park down a series of steps to the river.

DALEMAIN ★ 6

Dalemain Estate, Dacre, Penrith, Cumbria. Tel: (07684) 86450
Mr and Mrs Bryce McCosh

On A592 2m N of Pooley Bridge on Penrith road • Best season: early summer • Parking • Licensed restaurant and tea room • Toilet facilities • Suitable for wheelchairs • Plants for sale • Shop • House open • Gardens open Easter Sun to 6th Oct, Sun - Thurs, 11.15 a.m. - 5 p.m. • Entrance: £2.80, children free (house and garden £3, children £2, family £8 (2 plus own children)). Special prices for prebooked parties. Guided tours of gardens £2.50 per person

Dalemain has evolved in the most natural way from a twelfth-century pele tower with its kitchen garden and herbs. The Tudor-walled knot garden is there, as is the Stuart terrace (1680s) and the walled orchard where apple trees like 'Nonsuch' and 'Keswick Codling', planted in 1728, still bear fruit. The gardens have been finely re-established by Mrs McCosh with shrubs, species roses and other rarities, together with herbaceous replanting along the terraces and around the orchard. There is a wild garden on the lower ground featuring the Himalayan blue poppy in early summer and a walk past the Tudor gazebo into woods overlooking the Dacre Beck.

GRAYTHWAITE HALL ★ 7

Ulverston, Hawkshead, Cumbria. Tel: (05395) 31248
Esthwaite Estate Company

4m up W side of Windermere from Newby Bridge, A590 • Best season: spring • Toilet facilities • Dogs on lead • Open April to July, daily, 10 a.m. - 6 p.m. • Entrance: £2, children free

Essentially a spring garden landscaped by the late Victorian Thomas Mawson in partnership with Dan Gibson in a beautiful parkland and woodland setting. Azaleas and rhododendrons lead to late cultivars of spring-flowering shrubs. Formal terraced rose garden. The finely wrought sundials and gate by Gibson, the Dutch garden and the stream and pond all add charm to this serene garden.

HOLEHIRD ★★ 8

Troutbeck, Windermere, Cumbria.
Tel: (09662) 6238
Lakeland Horticultural Society

2m N of Windermere on A592 Troutbeck road • Parking • Toilet facilities • Partly suitable for wheelchairs • Dogs on lead • Annual plant sale 1st Sat in May in local school • Open all year, daily, sunrise - sunset. Garden guides available April to Oct, 11 a.m. - 5 p.m. • Entrance: free

This is a garden run by members of a Society dedicated to promoting 'knowledge on the cultivation of plants, shrubs and trees especially those suited to Lakeland conditions'. It lies on a splendid site with a natural water course and rock banks looking over Windermere to Scafell Pike. The Society has part of the former orchard, the rock garden and now the walled kitchen garden. Much earlier planting has been preserved, including survivors from plant-hunting expeditions to China and many fine specimen trees (e.g. 60ft handkerchief tree). Highlights are the summer-autumn heathers, winter-flowering shrubs, alpines and the national astilbe and hydrangea collections. The walled garden now has herbaceous specimens, herbs and climbers. Good ferns.

HOLKER HALL ★★ 9

Cark-in-Cartmel, Grange-over-Sands, Cumbria. Tel: (05395) 58328
Lord and Lady Cavendish

4½m W of Grange-over-Sands on B5278 between Haverthwaite (A590) and Grange-over-Sands • Best season: spring, summer • Parking • Refreshments: cafeteria lunches, snacks and teas • Toilet facilities inc. disabled • Mostly suitable for wheelchairs • Dogs • Plants for sale • Shop • House open • Gardens open Easter Sun to Oct, Sun – Fri, 10.30 a.m. – 4.30 p.m. • Entrance: 1991 prices not available. 1990 prices: £2.20, children £1.20. Group rates £1.65, children £1.10 (gardens, grounds and exhibitions. Hall and motor museum extra)

Set in acres of parkland, the woodland walks and formal gardens have been constantly developed by the family ever since Lord George Cavendish established his 'contrived natural landscape' some 200 years ago. The woods now contain many rare and beautiful specimens, all tagged and chronicled in the excellent guide to the walks. Other features are the recent cascade, evocative of the Villa d'Este, and a beautifully contrived transformation of the croquet lawn into summer gardens. This combination of formal beds and inventive planting (e.g. spire lilies rising out of massed rue) makes a wonderful Italianate-cum-English garden that typifies the spirit of Holker. There is also Mawson's rose garden, now being sensitively renewed (his pergola and balustrade still survive). The early blaze of rare rhododendrons and azaleas, carpets of spring bulbs and the colour and scent of summer and autumn displays provide year-round interest and pleasure.

HUTTON-IN-THE-FOREST ★ 10

Skelton, Penrith, Cumbria. Tel: (08534) 449
Lord and Lady Inglewood

3m from M6 junction 41, along B5305 to Wigton • Best season: summer • Parking • Teas when house open. Other meals on request • Toilet facilities • Suitable for wheelchairs up to house • Dogs on lead • Shop • House open 30th May to 29th Sept, Thurs, Fri and Sun, 1 – 4 p.m. inc. Bank Holidays • Garden open daily except Sat and 25th Dec, 11 a.m. – 5 p.m. Private parties by arrangement daily from April • Entrance: £1, children free (house and grounds £2.80, children 7–16 £1)

This garden was inspired by William Gilpin, eighteenth-century pioneer of the picturesque, who was brought up in the Border Country. It has great visual appeal, with a magnificent view from the Victorian topiary terraces. There are good herbs and fruit trees and excellent beds and borders in the walled garden. Some of the mature woodland trees were imported from the Indies by Henry Fletcher, an ancestor of the owners, in the early eighteenth century. Recent planting includes rhododendrons and other spring displays in the woodland low garden and there is an extensive park with forest walks, where conducted tours take place by arrangement. Other features include a seventeenth-century dovecote and pools.

LEVENS HALL ★★ 11

Levens Hall, Kendal, Cumbria. Tel: (05395) 60321
Mr C.H. Bagot

5m S of Kendal on A6 (M6 junction 36) • Best season: summer • Parking • Teas • Toilet facilities inc. disabled • Suitable for wheelchairs • Plants for sale • Shop • House open. Combined ticket £3.25, children and students £1.65, groups of 20 or more and others £2.65 per person • Garden open Easter Sun to Sept, Sun - Thurs, 11 a.m. - 5 p.m. • Entrance: £1.90, children 95p, groups of 20 or more and others £1.70 per person

James II's gardener, Guillaume Beaumont, designed this famous topiary garden in 1692. It is one of very few to retain its original trees and design. The impeccably clipped yews and box hedges are set off by colourful spring and summer bedding and borders. Massive walls of beech hedge open to vistas over parkland. One avenue leads to the earliest designed ha-ha. There is a picturesque herb garden behind the house, and another now planted up to match the recently discovered seventeenth-century plan. The record of only 10 gardeners in 300 years, and the affectionate care by the Bagot family, account for the rare harmony of this exceptional garden.

LINGHOLM GARDENS ★ 12

Lingholm, Keswick, Cumbria. Tel: (07687) 72003
The Viscount Rochdale

W side of Derwentwater, 2m from Keswick off A66 • Best season: spring, early summer and autumn • Parking • Teas • Toilet facilities • Suitable for wheelchairs • Plants for sale • Open Easter to Oct, daily, 10 a.m. - 5 p.m. • Entrance: £1.95, accompanied children free, groups £1.60 per person

A most pleasing lakeland garden with view south to Borrowdale. Colour from early spring with bulbs and long-lasting display of azaleas and rhododendrons (note *Rhododendron auriculatum* and *Rhododendron* 'Shilsonii') right through to August. Much other blossom and a particularly good mix of trees (e.g. silver firs, cedars and maples) keep up the interest throughout the season. Careful labelling in the formal gardens and along the delightful woodland walk enhances the pleasure. Beatrix Potter stayed and wrote 'Squirrel Nutkin' here.

MUNCASTER CASTLE ★ 13

Ravenglass, Cumbria. Tel: (06577) 614/203
Mr and Mrs Gordon-Duff-Pennington

15m S of Whitehaven on A595 • Best season: May and June • Parking • Teas • Toilet facilities • Suitable for wheelchairs • Dogs on lead • Garden centre plants for sale • Shop • House open: Tues - Sun, 1 - 4.30 p.m. Combined ticket £3, children £1.50 • Garden open April to Sept, daily, 11 a.m. - 5 p.m. • Entrance: £1.50, children £1

The splendid backdrop of Scafell and the hills, the acid soil and the Gulf Stream warmth provide ideal conditions. One of the finest collections of species rhododendron in Europe has been built up, many from plant-hunting expenditions to Nepal in the 1920s (Kingdon-Ward, Ludlow and Sheriff). There are excellent azaleas, camellias, magnolias, hydrangeas and maples, plus many unusual trees (e.g. *Nothofagus* species). The garden is at its best in May and June but intensive new planting is ensuring constant pleasure for visitors in all seasons. Tony Warburton of TV fame also runs an Owl Centre here - a national centre for breeding and conservation of endangered owls, including many worldwide species.

RYDAL MOUNT 14

Ambleside, Cumbria. Tel: (05394) 33002
Mrs Henderson

1m N of Ambleside on A591 • Best season: spring • Parking • Toilet facilities • Dogs on lead • Shop • House open • Garden open Mar to Oct, daily, 9.30 a.m. - 5 p.m., Nov to Feb, daily except Tues, 10 a.m. - 4 p.m. • Entrance: £2, children 80p, groups £1.70 per person

The carefully maintained grounds of Wordsworth's house still follow the lines of his own plan and it is easy to imagine the poet wandering along the upper terrace walk (Isabella's) and down through winding, shaded paths to the lawns, or across a terrace to the ancient mound with its distant glimpse of Windermere. Apart from its poetic association the garden is also a visual delight with good herbaceous borders, shrubs and unusual trees (e.g. the fern-leaved beech). An addition to the spring display is the bank of dancing daffodils in nearby Dora's field. A word of praise for some good labelling.

SIZERGH CASTLE ★ 15

Kendal, Cumbria. Tel: (05395) 60070
The National Trust

1m S of Kendal on A591 (M6 junction 36) • Best season: spring to autumn • Parking • Teas: 1.30 - 5 p.m. • Toilet facilities • Partly suitable for wheelchairs • Shop • House open same days as garden, 1.30 - 5.30 p.m. • Garden open 31st March to 3rd Nov, Sun to Thurs, 12.30 - 5.30 p.m. Last admission 5 p.m. • Entrance: £1.25 (castle and garden £2.80). Parties of 15 or more reduced rate by arrangement

An exceptionally varied garden with colour from early spring daffodils to summer borders and climbers culminating in glorious autumn tints (the vine-clad tower all fiery red is a memorable spectacle). Other features encountered along shady paths are the Hayes' rock garden (Japanese maples, dwarf conifers, primulas, gentians, etc.) the long wall (*Clematis flammula*, *Hydrangea petiolaris*, brooms and much else) and the rose garden (specimen roses and clematis). The pond and rockery are now being refurbished.

STAGSHAW 16

Ambleside, Cumbria. Tel: (05394) 32109
The National Trust

½m S of Ambleside on A591 • Best season: spring, early summer • Limited parking, access dangerous • Open 29th March to June, daily, 10 a.m. - 6.30 p.m., July to Oct, by appointment (please send SAE) • Entrance: £1

Created by C.H.D. Acland, this is a carefully blended area of azaleas and rhododendrons among camellias, magnolias and other fine shrubs on a west-facing hillside of oaks looking over the head of Lake Windermere. Rather difficult of access but worth the effort.

DERBYSHIRE

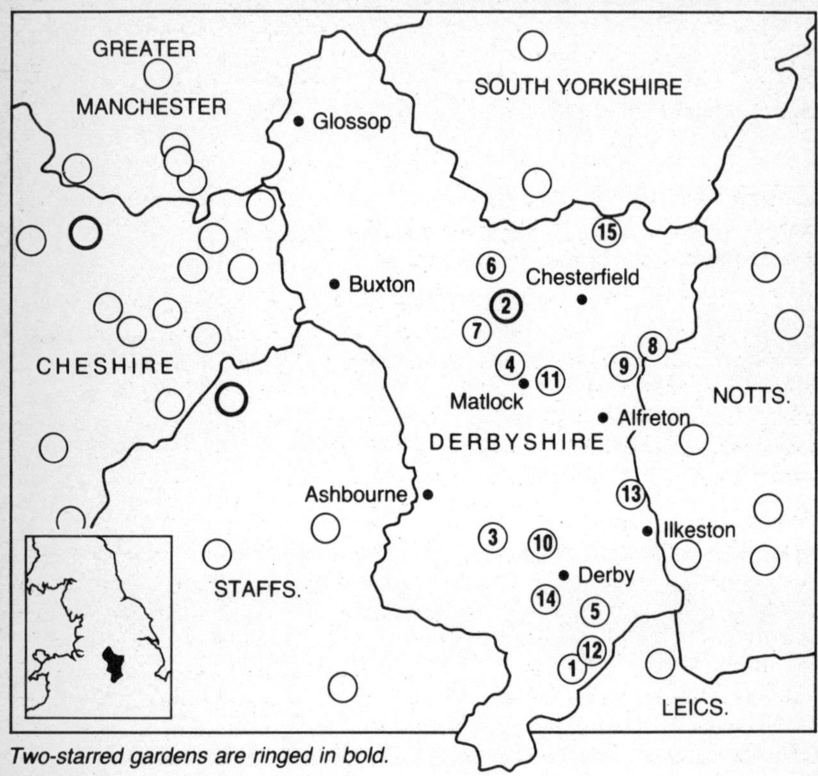

Two-starred gardens are ringed in bold.

CALKE ABBEY 1

Ticknall, Derbyshire.
Tel: (0332) 864444 (24 hr recorded information or (0332) 863822 (office)
The National Trust

9m S of Derby, off A514 at Ticknall • Parking • Refreshments: restaurant • Toilet facilities • Partly suitable for wheelchairs • National Trust shop • House open but tickets are timed and there may be some waiting • Gardens open 30th March to Oct, Sat – Wed and Bank Holiday Mons, 11 a.m. – 5 p.m. Closed Good Friday • Entrance: £3.70, children £1.80 (house and gardens). £1 vehicle charge entry to park, which is open during daylight hours all year, refundable on entry to house

Previously owned by an eccentric family and recently taken on by the Trust, Calke House and park overshadow the gardens at present. These latter have a long history and with a sympathetic approach could be another Trust jewel.

There are frames, pits, an orangery and grotto, and an auricula stand all waiting to be restored. Only two gardeners are on the staff at present but the work done in recent years is magnificent. The flower garden is delightful with a pattern of beds and basket-weave ironwork round a little fountain pond. The Trust hopes to restore the gardens to their former glory given enough funds, and for locals it will be worth making periodic visits to see its resurrection to eighteenth and nineteenth-century status.

CHATSWORTH ★★ 2

Bakewell, Derbyshire. Tel: (0246) 582204
The Duke and Duchess of Devonshire

4m E of Bakewell, 10m W of Chesterfield on B6012, off A619 and A6
• Parking: cars £1, coaches free • Refreshments: hot meals and salads in the Carriage House restaurant, snacks near Orangery Shop • Toilet facilities • Suitable for wheelchairs (but not house) • Dogs on lead • Plants for sale • Shop • House open • Garden open Easter to Oct, daily, 11 a.m. - 5 p.m. • Entrance: £2.25, OAP and students £1.75, children £1.10, (house and garden £4.25, OAP and students £3.50, children £2)

The 100 acres of garden at Chatsworth have developed over 300 years and many areas still reflect the garden fashions of each century. The seventeenth-century gardens of London and Wise remain only as the cascade and canal pond to the south. During the eighteenth century 'Capability' Brown destroyed much of the formal gardens to create a landscaped woodland park. Notable is the vista created by Brown from the Salisbury Lawn to the horizon, which remains unchanged as does the lawn itself since no liming or fertilizer has been used, allowing many varieties of wild flowers, grasses, moss and sedges to thrive. The orange borders and blue and white borders are twentieth-century additions as is the terrace, display greenhouse, rose garden and old conservatory garden which has lupin, dahlia and Michaelmas daisy beds. The Duke and Duchess continue to work on the garden improving the arboretum and pinetum by removing the suffocating rhododendron, laurels and sycamores and planting many new trees - labelling of these different trees is excellent. The serpentine hedge of beech was planted in 1953 and the double rows of pleached red-twigged limes were planted in 1952, both now rewarding features. Paxton's work still gives pleasure: there is the large rockery, some rare conifers, the magnificent 276 ft water jet from the Emperor fountain. Alas, the Great Conservatory was a casualty of the 1914–18 war and three and a half foot stone walls in the old conservatory garden are all that remain to give an idea of its size. The epitome of a cottage garden has been created near the 'Plant Sales' area. A useful booklet 'The Garden at Chatsworth' can be bought in the shop before entering the garden.

DAM FARM HOUSE 3

Yeldersley Lane, Brailsford, Derbyshire. Tel: (0335) 60291
Mrs S.D. Player

5m SE of Ashbourne on A52. Opposite the Ednaston village turn, the gate is 500 yards on right • Parking in field next to garden • Teas • Partly suitable for wheelchairs • Plants for sale • Open by appointment and 28th April, 19th May, 23rd June, 21st July, 2 - 5 p.m. • Entrance: £1, children 25p

The scree garden has a large number of choice alpines. Climbers are used abundantly for clothing walls, trees, pergolas - even spilling down over high retaining walls and all achieved in 10 years. Collection of old roses. Plenty of informative labelling. This garden promises to be a most important one as it continues to develop under the expertise of Mrs Player.

DARLEY HOUSE ★ 4

Darley Dale, Matlock, Derbyshire. Tel: (0629) 733341
Mr and Mrs G.H. Briscoe

2m N of Matlock on A6 to Bakewell, on right just past Whitworth Hospital • Best season: spring/summer • Limited parking beside entrance • Refreshments: tea and biscuits • Partly suitable for wheelchairs • Plants for sale. Extensive seed list • Open 28th April to Oct by appointment • Entrance: 60p, children 20p. Special arrangements for private parties

This serene garden was originally set out by Paxton in 1845. Plantsman's gardens can be bogged down by the sheer number of different plants but here, although there is a wealth of beautiful and unusual plants, all harmonise. There are a number of mature tender shrubs and plants which surprisingly survive the Derbyshire weather - thoughtful planting obviously paying dividends. Extensive seed list.

ELVASTON CASTLE COUNTRY PARK ★ 5

Nr Derby, Derbyshire. Tel: (0332) 571342
Derbyshire County Council

6m SE of Derby on B5010 between Borrowash A6005 and Thulston A6. Signposted from A6 and A52 • Parking: mid-week 50p, weekends and Bank Holidays £1 • Refreshments: Parlour tearoom, Easter to Oct • Toilet facilities • Suitable for wheelchairs • Dogs on lead in Old English Garden • Shop • Estate Museum open Easter to Oct, daily except Mon and Tues (but open Bank Holiday Mons) • Garden open all year, daily, 9 a.m. - dusk • Entrance: free

A fine garden to visit at any time of the year. Within the 200 acres there is a large variety of mature trees with many recent trees planted from donations as a memorial to a loved one - an excellent idea. A tree trail is planned. The Italian garden with its clipped yews has limited appeal visually. The original walled kitchen garden is now the Old English Garden containing herbaceous borders, rose garden and herb garden. The history of the garden is displayed in the Information Centre; of particular interest is that in 1851 there were 90 gardening staff. William Barron, the professional gardener who developed the garden at that time, was an expert on transplanting mature trees - the cedars here were moved by the Barron method - Kew has a 'Barron transplanter'. He had erected 11 miles of yew hedge by 1850 and in 1880, when he had left his employment here, he caused a controversy by transplanting a 1000-year-old yew tree in Buckland churchyard to save the church.

FIR CROFT 6

Froggatt Road, Calver, Derbyshire.
Dr and Mrs S.B. Furness

4m N of Bakewell. Between the Q8 filling station and the junction of B6001 and B6054 • Best season: spring/early summer • Limited parking • Partly suitable for wheelchairs • Plants for sale at adjoining nursery • Open 28th April, 12th May, 9th, 23rd June, 2 - 6 p.m. Also for groups by appointment. Nursery open March to Dec, Sat and Sun, 1 - 6 p.m., Mon, 10 a.m. - 6 p.m. • Entrance: by collection box for charity

The owner is a botanist and botanical photographer who has put his expertise into an extensive alpine garden - a 'must' to visit if interested in alpine and scree gardens, particularly as the garden was started from scratch in 1985.

HADDON HALL 7

Bakewell, Derbyshire. Tel: (062981) 2855
The Duke of Rutland

2m SE of Bakewell, 6½m N of Matlock on A6 • Parking: cars 30p, coaches free • Refreshments: lunches and teas in Stables tearoom • Toilet facilities • House open • Garden open Easter to Sept, daily except Mon in April to June, and except Sun and Mon in July and Aug, but open Bank Holiday Sun and Mon, 11 a.m. - 6 p.m. • Entrance: £3, OAP £2.40, children £1.80 (house and garden)

The castle and gardens of seventeenth-century origin - reconstructed this century - stand on a limestone bluff. The gardens are mainly on the south side and are laid out in a series of stone-walled terraces with the River Wye at their feet. The thick stone walls of the castle and terrace walls face south and west and look well as a background for the extensive collection of climbing and rambling roses. The plants, shrubs and roses all have legible labels. The upper terrace with balustraded parapet and fine stairway is particularly memorable.

HARDWICK HALL ★ 8

Doe Lea, Chesterfield, Derbyshire. Tel: (0246) 850430
The National Trust

6½m NW of Mansfield, 9½m SE of Chesterfield. Approach from M1 junction 29 then A617 • Best season: summer • Parking. Gates close at 6.30 p.m. • Refreshments in Great Kitchen of Hall on days Hall is open 12 noon - 4.45 p.m. • Toilet facilities • Suitable for wheelchairs • Dogs in park only, on lead • National Trust shop • House open 30th March to Oct on Wed, Thurs, Sat, Sun and Bank Holiday Mon, 12.30 - 5 p.m. or sunset if earlier. Last admission 4.30 p.m. • Garden open 30th March to Oct, daily, 12 noon - 5.30 p.m. Country park open, daily, dawn - dusk • Entrance: £1.80 (house and garden £4.50, children £2.20). No reduction for parties

This famous Elizabethan mansion house was built for Bess of Hardwick by Robert Smythson in the late sixteenth century. Mature yew hedges and brick walls provide necessary shelter to an otherwise exposed hilltop site. The borders of the Great Court have spring-flowering shrubs to give colour for a longer period than herbaceous plants can provide. Some herbaceous borders have strong, hot colours as an overall grouping, others have soft hues. In order to rest the soil to rid it of a build-up of pests and diseases the borders were replanted in October 1989. The herb garden is outstanding in variety of plants and display. There is some 300 acres of country park. One of the two magnificent cedars has been badly wind-damaged.

THE HERB GARDEN 9

Hall View Cottage, Hardstoft, Pilsley, Nr Chesterfield, Derbyshire.
Tel: (0246) 854268
Mrs Raynor

3m SE of Chesterfield. Turn off A619 and follow B6039 • Best season: summer • Limited parking • Suitable for wheelchairs • Plants for sale • Shop • Open April to Oct, daily, 10 a.m. - 6 p.m. • Entrance: free

A rich herb garden in a rural setting with a now established parterre. This garden is only a short distance from the other excellent herb garden in Hardwick Hall (see entry). A large range of herbs for sale.

KEDLESTON HALL ★ 10

Kedleston, Derbyshire. Tel: (0332) 842191
The National Trust

4½m MW of Derby on the Derby-Hulland road between A6 and A52. Well signposted • Best season: summer/autumn • Parking • Refreshments: tearoom, 12 noon - 5 p.m. • Toilet facilities • Not suitable for wheelchairs unless by prior written arrangemet • Shop • Hall open, April to Oct, Sat - Wed, 1 - 5.30 p.m. contains Curzon's Indian Museum • Gardens open 30th

March to Oct, Sat - Wed, inc. Bank Holidays, 11 - 6 p.m. Closed Good Friday. Nov to 23rd Dec, Sat and Sun only, 12 noon - 4 p.m. Park only April to Oct, daily, 11 - 6 p.m. and Nov to 22nd Dec, Sat and Sun only, 12 noon - 4 p.m. • *Entrance: park: £1 vehicle entry charge on Thurs and Fri. Hall and garden: £3.50, children £1.70. Coach parties must pre-book by writing to the Administrator*

The ancient home of the Curzon family, their most famous member being George Nathaniel, one time Viceroy of India. The extensive gardens do not compete with this classical Robert Adam palace, but are of mature parkland where the eye is always drawn to the house. The rhododendrons when in flower are worth visiting in their own right, otherwise visit the gardens as a pleasurable way not only to view Adam's magnificent south front but his octagonal-domed summerhouse, his orangery, a Venetian-windowed water-side house, the bridge across the lake, the aviary - now a loggia - and the main gateway. The formal gardens have a heart-shaped sunken rose garden and beds by Lutyens (1925). The Hackforth Fountain is another attraction.

LEA GARDENS 11

Lea, Nr Matlock, Derbyshire. Tel: (0629) 534380
Mr and Mrs Tye

5m SE of Matlock E off A6 • *Parking. Coaches by appointment* • *Refreshments: light lunches, teas* • *Suitable for wheelchairs* • *Plants for sale* • *Open 20th March to July, daily, 10 a.m. - 7 p.m. Oct and Nov, Wed, Thurs and Sun, 2 - 5 p.m.* • *Entrance: season ticket £1.50, children 50p*

This garden, featured in a 1990 *Gardener's World* programme, has a comprehensive collection of rhododendrons, azaleas, alpines and conifers all brought together here in a beautiful woodland setting. The excellent booklet describes the contents of the garden with a suggested route. John Marsden Smedley started his rhododendron garden in 1935, inspired by his visits to Bodnant and Exbury. Under the Tye family the collection now comprises some 550 varieties of rhododendrons and azaleas.

MELBOURNE HALL ★ 12

Melbourne, Derbyshire. Tel: (0332) 862502
Lord Ralph Kerr

8m S of Derby off B587 in village of Melbourne (between A514 and A453) • *Best season: spring/summer* • *Limited parking* • *Refreshments: hot and cold meals in tea room* • *Toilet facilities* • *Suitable for wheelchairs* • *Shop* • *House open, Aug, most days, 2 - 5 p.m. £2, OAP £1.50, children 75p* • *Garden open April to Sept, Wed, Sat, Sun and Bank Holiday Mon, 2 - 6 p.m.* • *Entrance: £2, OAP £1*

There has been very little alteration to Sir Thomas Coke's formal garden so this is a visual record of a complete late seventeenth-century/early eighteenth-century garden in the style of Le Nôtre laid out by London and Wise. It is in immaculate condition with avenues culminating in exquisite statuary and fountains including the lead urn The Four Seasons by van Nost whose other lead statuary stands in niches of yew. A series of terraces run down to a lake, the Great Basin. A grotto has an inscription thought to be that of Byron's troublesome mistress Caroline Lamb. Unique in English gardens is the Birdcage iron arbour of 1706 which can be seen from the house along a long walk hedged with yews. It is well worth buying the booklet 'Melbourne Hall Gardens' at the entrance, giving the history and a suggested guided tour.

210 NOTTINGHAM ROAD 13

Woodlinkin, Langley Mill, Derbyshire. Tel: (0773) 714903
Mr and Mrs R. Brown

12m NW of Nottingham on A610 near Codnor. It is the first house past a garage on the left • Best season: late spring/early summer • Limited parking • Suitable for wheelchairs • Dogs on lead • Open by appointment and 24th June, 2 - 5 p.m. • Entrance: 50p, children free

A plantsman's garden of half an acre with an emphasis on shrub roses - the garden is packed with many good examples. There are also some rarer shrubs and trees. Geraniums, hellebores, symphytums and similar plants provide all-year interest in the herbaceous section. The brick base of a disused greenhouse is used for a display of alpines.

57 PORTLAND CLOSE 14

Mickleover, Derbyshire. Tel: (0332) 515450
Mr and Mrs A.L. Ritchie

From A111 (Derby ring road) take A516. At first roundabout take B5020 (signposted Mickleover). In Mickleover take right turn into Cavendish Way, then second left into Portland Close • Best season: spring/summer • Limited parking • Plants for sale • Open by appointment and 28th April, 26th May, 2 - 5 p.m. • Entrance: 50p, children free

A plantsman's small garden with something unusual planted in almost every inch of it. The knowledgeable owner propagates most of the huge variety of hostas, primulas, auriculas, violas and cyclamen, with many of the plants for sale. Alpines, sink gardens.

RENISHAW HALL 15

Eckington, Derbyshire.
Sir Reresby and Lady Sitwell

6m from Sheffield and Chesterfield on A616. From M1 at junction 30, take A616 towards Sheffield for 3m, over the railway bridge S-bend, and immediately turn left. From the traffic lights in Eckington take the third turning right – up a slight rise and the entrance is ahead • Best season: summer • Parking • Teas • Toilet facilities • Partly suitable for wheelchairs • Dogs on lead • Plants for sale • Open 26th, 27th May, 30th June, 28th July, 25th, 26th Aug, 2 – 5 p.m. • Entrance: £1.50, OAP £1, children 50p

An entry in *The Guinness Book of Records* states that Renishaw has 'the most northerly vineyard in western Europe'. Also astonishing to see at this northerly latitude and on top of a hill (albeit on a south-facing wall) are enormous specimens of *Acacia dealbata*, *Cytisus battandieri* and *Fremontodendron californicum*. There are other rare, slightly tender specimen shrubs within the garden. Presumably the fact that the soil is light, the aspect southerly and shelter provided by yew hedges and parkland trees overcome the disadvantages of latitude and height. Sir George Sitwell spent much of his life in Italy and hence this is the style he recreated at Renishaw. The sound of splashing water, always in the background, adds to the Italianate atmosphere. Osbert Sitwell's memoirs give amusing anecdotes about his father's plans for the gardens which could certainly have included, had he been alive today, the attainment of a star in the Guide.

GARDENS OPEN RARELY

The following gardens are open to the public on three days or less in the year, although they may also be open by appointment if this is stated in the text. For details see individual entry.
April 28 57 Portland Close; **May 26** 57 Portland Close; **June 24** 210 Nottingham Road.

DEVON

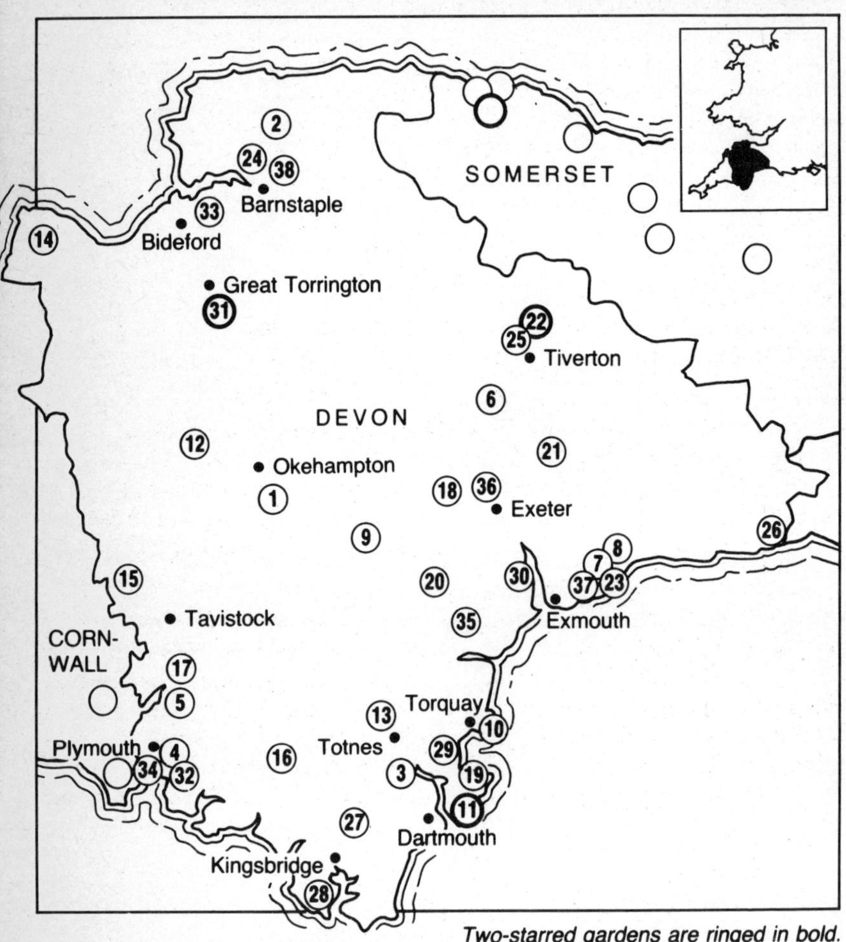

Two-starred gardens are ringed in bold.

ANDREW'S CORNER 1

Belstone, Nr Okehampton, Devon. Tel: (0837) 840332
H.J. and Mr and Mrs R.J. Hill

3m E of Okehampton, signed to Belstone • Parking • Teas on open days • Suitable for wheelchairs • Plants for sale • Open by appointment and 14th April, 5th, 26th, 27th May, 2nd, 23rd June, 21st July, 2.30 - 6 p.m. • Entrance: 50p, children 25p

Nine hundred feet above sea level, on north Dartmoor, facing to the Taw valley and across to the high moor. In its two thirds of an acre (amazing that it is not larger) grow a wide variety of plants of all sorts not normally seen at such an altitude. The sense of space is achieved by the division of the garden into different levels by rhododendrons and trees, each area being a small region with its own micro-climate, and all with glimpses through to other areas and to the wide landscape. There are herbaceous plants, many roses and lilies, conifers and heathers in island beds; in spring flowering bulbs and meconopsis; in autumn colour from maples and gentians. There are dry stone walls (a speciality of the area) a paved area and a pond with water plants and among the stone and paving are lewisias and other alpines. The owner does not like the description 'plantsman'; he says it is a hobby he loves – it is certainly an inspiration.

ARLINGTON COURT 2

Arlington, Nr Barnstaple, Devon. Tel: (027182) 296
The National Trust

6m N of Barnstaple on A39, turn E • Parking 300 yards away • Refreshments when house open. Tearooms Nov to March 1992 • Toilet facilities in house • Dogs in grounds only on leads • Shop • House open • Garden open April to Oct, daily except Sat but open Sat of Bank Holiday weekends 11 a.m. – 6 p.m., Oct, 11 a.m. – 5 p.m. Last admission ½ hour before closing. Park open all year, daily during daylight hours • Entrance: £2 (house £4)

The Georgian house is set in a magnificent park where Shetland ponies and Jacob sheep graze. There are a number of woodland walks with many remains of the old stone-built water courses or leats that were used to irrigate the park in times of drought two centuries ago. The planned 'wilderness' was a popular eighteenth-century feature, a semi-wild area between the garden and the parkland. The woodland is managed to protect wildlife including red deer. The lake is approached by an avenue of monkey puzzle (araucaria) trees.

AVENUE COTTAGE GARDENS 3

Ashprington, Totnes, Devon. Tel: (080423) 769
Mr R.C.H. Soans and Mr R.J. Pitts

Take the A381 from Totnes towards Kingsbridge. Turn left to Ashprington. Facing the Durant Arms in Ashprington turn left uphill past the Church (No through road). The gardens are 300 yards on the right • No coaches • Plants for sale • Open April to Sept, Tues – Sat, 11 a.m. – 5 p.m. Also by appointment • Entrance: by donation

These gardens were originally part of the eighteenth-century landscape gardens of Sharpham House, separated 50 years ago. They are approached along a splendid avenue of Turkey oaks planted in 1844. Many of the rhododendrons and azaleas planted in the last century are enormous and magnificent. Over the years the garden had become overgrown in some places and it is now undergoing a major transformation with overcrowded areas being cleared to give more space and light to new plantings and to open up new vistas. There are new plantings of many unusual herbaceous plants including species asters, hydrangeas and several giant grasses including pampas and miscanthus. It is probably best in spring and early summer but there is late summer colour, too, particularly in the large acers.

41 BEAUMONT ROAD 4

St Judes, Plymouth, Devon. Tel: (0752) 668640
Mr and Mrs A.J. Parsons

½m from Plymouth city centre, 100 yards from Beaumont Park. Take Ebrington Street exit from Charles Cross roundabout in city centre • Parking in nearby street • Teas • Open 9th, 16th June, 2–6 p.m. • Entrance: 50p

A prize-winning garden in a north-facing, narrow Victorian backyard, 60 feet long. Plants intensively grown in pots and containers include clematis, ceanothus, parthenocissus. Variagated ivies grow out of tubs over arches; there is a rockery and even a pool and waterfall. Pieris, viburnums, camellias, many clematis, and scented plants such as philadelphus, *Viburnum farreri* and Regal lilies, make this matchbox garden an inspiration for small town garden owners. Mr and Mrs Parsons aptly quote Horace: 'This is one of my prayers: for a parcel of land, not so very large'.

BICKHAM HOUSE 5

Bickham, Roborough, Plymouth, Devon.
Lord and Lady Roborough

8m N of Plymouth on A386. Take Maristow turn left on Roborough Down and follow poster directions • Best season: spring • Parking • Teas • Toilet facilities • Plants for sale • Open 31st March to 2nd June, Suns only and 1st April, 6th, 27th May, 16th June, 2 – 5.30 p.m. • Entrance: £1

This is a spring garden in a valley with magnificent views. There is a mass of bulbs and many camellias as well as magnolias and rhododendrons. There are two ponds with aquatic plants and a walled garden with old roses.

BICKLEIGH CASTLE 6

Nr Tiverton, Devon. Tel: (08845) 363
Mr and Mrs O.N. Boxall

4m S of Tiverton off A396. At Bickleigh Bridge take A3072 and follow signs • Best season: spring/early summer • Parking • Teas • Suitable for wheelchairs (ground floor of house only) • House open. Private tours for groups by appointment • Gardens open Easter week (Good Friday – Fri), then Suns, Weds and Bank Holiday Mons, 2 – 5 p.m. until late May Bank Holiday and then daily except Sat until early Oct, 2 - 5 p.m. • Entrance: £2.50, children 5 - 15 £1.30 (house, garden and exhibitions). Family tickets available

These gardens are situated in the valley of the Exe around the ancient buildings which are historically fascinating with much to see. The gatehouse is fourteenth-century, the thatched chapel eleventh and twelfth-century, and the Castle became the home of the Carew family, Sir George Carew being the Vice Admiral of the Mary Rose. Beyond the eighteenth-century Italian wrought iron courtyard gates is a large mound planted in the 1930s with most of the known varieties of rhododendron. There is a 300-year-old wisteria and many more mature trees including *Gingko biloba*, magnolias, a Judas tree and a tulip tree. The Castle moat is planted with iris and water lilies.

BICTON COLLEGE OF AGRICULTURE 7

East Budleigh, Devon. Tel: (0395) 68353

By Sidmouth Lodge, halfway between Budleigh Salterton and Newton Poppleford on A376 • Parking in main college car park, short walk to gardens • Toilet facilities • Suitable for wheelchairs • Plants for sale sometimes • Open all year Wed and Fri only, 2 - 5 p.m. Closed Christmas • Entrance: £1, children free. Membership of Friends of the College gives unlimited access and free gardening advice on Fri afternoons

The gardens of this Georgian house form the horticultural department of Bicton Agricultural College, and as such contain a large number of plants laid out for both study and general interest. As well as the fascinating herbaceous beds there is an arboretum with spring-flowering trees and an old walled garden with glasshouses, all approached by an avenue of araucarias (monkey puzzle trees). Amongst the plants which provide both information and effect are the NCCPG collections of agapanthus and pittosporums. Garden and arboretum guides are available.

BICTON PARK ★ 8

East Budleigh, Budleigh Salterton, Devon. Tel: (0395) 68465
Bicton Park Trust Company

2m N of Budleigh Salterton on A376. Entrance near St Mary's Church • Parking • Refreshments: self-service restaurant and licensed bar, picnic areas • Toilet facilities • Suitable for wheelchairs • Dogs on lead • Shop • Museum open, extra charge • Park open March to Oct, 10 a.m. - 6 p.m. • Entrance: £3.75, OAP £3.50 (OAP 'Golden Days' (Wed and Thurs) £2.50), children 3 - 15 £2.75. Family ticket £2.75 per person. Special rates for parties of 20 or more

There is much to see here in the 50 acres - don't be put off by the 'fun and family entertainment'. The formal and informal gardens date from 1734 and the Italian garden is attributed to Le Nôtre; there is an Oriental garden with a 150 year old mulberry, azaleas, camellias, flowering cherries and a paeony border (bush and tree); an American Garden established in the 1830s with a snowdrop tree (*Halesia carolina*), calico bushes and a handkerchief tree (*Davidia involucrata*); a Hermitage Garden with lake and water garden and a pinetum with some rare conifers including a Mexican juniper, yuccas, Korean thuya and Tasmanian cedar. The pinetum was established in 1838 and extended in 1910 to take the collection of the famous botanist and explorer 'Chinese' Wilson. Perhaps Bicton's greatest glory is the Palm House built between 1815 and 1820, one of the oldest in the country and recently refurbished; in it, Kentia palms up to 20 feet, tree ferns and bromeliads, and outside an Assam tea plant. There are also geranium and fuchsia houses and a tropical and a temperate house for bananas, coffee trees and bougainvilleas. Bicton College of Agriculture is also open (see entry).

CASTLE DROGO ★★ 9

Drewsteignton, Devon. Tel: (06473) 3306
The National Trust

4m S of A30 or 4m N of Moretonhamstead on A382, turn E to Drewsteignton • Parking. Coaches by appointment only • Refreshments: coffee and light lunches (licensed) and teas, 10.30 a.m. - 5.30 p.m. • Toilet facilities inc. disabled • Suitable for wheelchairs. Special parking and access by arrangement at shop. Scented plants for visually handicapped • Shop sells brochure • House open at extra charge. Croquet can be played with hired equipment • Open 29th March to Oct, daily except Fri, 11 a.m. - 6 p.m. Last admission ½ hour before closing • Entrance £1.60 (garden and grounds only). Reduced rates for parties by appointment

The last castle to be built in England (begun 1910) was designed by Sir Edwin Lutyens, with the great Gertrude Jekyll much involved with the garden design and planting. Apart from the evergreen oaks above the magnificent views over the Teign Gorge, and a valley planted with rhododendrons, magnolias, camellias, cherries and maples, there is a series of formal terraces and borders with walls of granite and sharp-edged yew hedges. One terrace has rose beds, with white flowers and arbours of yew and *Parrotia persica* 'the iron tree'. In the main formal gardens, with galleries round a sunken centre, paths are serpentine (an Indian touch typical of Lutyens who built New Delhi in the 1920s when he was supervising here), and herbaceous borders are full of old varieties of lupins, lychnis, campanula, hollyhocks and red hot pokers. Under the granite walls are perennials like euphorbias, hellebores, alchemilla and veronica, with spring bulbs. Steps lead to a second terrace with yucca and wisterias and herb borders; more steps to shrub borders of lilac, azaleas, magnolias and lilies, and finally a splendid circular lawn surrounded by a tall yew hedge at the top, a huge green circle and a perfect stage set for croquet.

CASTLE TOR 10

Wellswood, Torquay, Devon. Tel: (0803) 214858
Mr L. Stocks

In Torquay. From Higher Lincombe Road, turn E into Oxlea Road. Entrance is 200 yards on right with eagle-topped pillars • Parking • Open by appointment • Entrance: 50p, children 25p

Half a century ago the then owner of Castle Tor approached Sir Edwin Lutyens and asked him to design a smaller version of Castle Drogo; being too busy Sir Edwin nominated a pupil of his, Frederick Harrild, and the result is this fascinating architectural garden with magnificent views over Lyme Bay and Tor Bay. Gertrude Jekyll's ideas about garden colour - no violent juxtapositions or circular beds full of salvias were incorporated, and the whole is framed in terraces of Somerset limestone (a pleasant change from granite) and cubic green walls of yew hedges; there is topiary in both green and golden (Irish) yew. There are architectural type follies like a pillared orangery with a domed roof and a tower with portcullis and gatehouse; best of all a long ornamental water course or small canal. Over the years the owner has collected suitable statuary and bright annual flowers are seen as accents in urns and tubs against the stone background.

COLETON FISHACRE GARDEN ★★ 11

Coleton, Kingswear, Dartmouth, Devon. Tel: (080425) 466
The National Trust

2m from Kingswear, take Lower Ferry Road and turn off at toll house • Parking • Very limited for wheelchairs • Open 3rd, 10th, 17th, 24th March, 2 - 5 p.m., and 29th March to Oct, Wed - Fri and Sun, 11 a.m. - 6 p.m. or dusk if earlier • Entrance: £2. Reduced rates for parties

Oswald Milne who was a pupil of Edwin Lutyens designed the house and the architectural features of this garden for Sir Rupert and Lady D'Oyly Carte; the house was completed and the garden begun in 1926. Exceptionally mild and sheltered, it is in a Devon combe, sloping steeply to the cliff tops and the sea, and sheltered by belts of Monterey pine and holm oaks planted in 1925. There are many streams making a humid atmosphere for the moisture-loving plants like the magnificent bamboos (inch thick canes) and mimosas, and many other sub-tropical plants, rarely grown outside in this country. There is a collection of unusual trees like dawn redwood and swamp cypress and Chilean myrtle, and dominating all a tall tulip tree the same age as the house. Formal walls and terraces make a framework round the house for a large number of sun-loving tender plants; there are various water features, notably stone-edged channels and a circular pool in the lawn in the herbaceous-bordered walled garden. Scented herbs and plants.

CROSSPARK 12

Northlew, Nr Okehampton, Devon. Tel: (040922) 518
Mrs G. West

8m NW of Okehampton. From Okehampton take A30 to Launceston for 1m, turn right onto B3218, then 2nd right to Northlew, then follow Highampton road for 1m • Parking • Toilet facilities • Only a small area suitable for wheelchairs • Plants for sale • Open end March to Sept, Fri and Sun and Bank Holiday Mons, 2 - 6 p.m., and Easter to mid-Sept by appointment • Entrance: 50p

This plantswoman's garden, created from a field by the owner, would provide interest for a visit at most times of the year. A heather bed and pleasant separate colour beds and also an attractive white garden. The pool and waterfall are surrounded by a range of bog plants and there is a good selection of climbers on the house. Also dwarf conifers and a rockery.

DARTINGTON HALL ★ 13

Dartington, Nr Totnes, Devon. Tel: (0803) 862271
Dartington Hall Trust

2m NW of Totnes, E of A384 • Parking. Coaches by appointment (0803) 863614 • Refreshments by appointment • Toilet facilities • Plants for sale • Open daily, dawn - dusk • Entrance: by donation

The gardens were begun by Dorothy and Leonard Elmhirst in 1925 when the Hall was derelict and the estate and parkland overgrown. Several garden designers have been advisers - Beatrix Farrand designed the courtyard and cobbled drive round the central lawn and opened up the woodland walkways. There are three woodland walks using bay, yew, and hollies as a background for a collection of camellias, magnolias and rhododendrons. Landscape designer Percy Cane made the glade and the azalea dell. The overall design is strongly architectural with sunken lawns and terraces and formal clipped yews contrasting with the mature woodland. Fine sculpture by Henry Moore and others.

DOCTON MILL ★ 14

Spekes Valley, Nr Hartland, Devon. Tel: (237) 441369
Mr N.S. and Mrs I.D. Pugh

Off A39 from Hartland village to Stoke, turn left and follow Elmscott signs to Lymebridge in Spekes Valley • Parking • Open March to Sept, daily, 10 a.m. - 5 p.m. • Entrance: £1.50, children free

Mr and Mrs Pugh took over this then derelict water mill nine years ago and embarked upon a large scale clearance of the waterways; there are ponds, leats, footbridges over the river and many smaller streams as it is only 1500 yards from Speke's Mill Mouth coastal waterfall and the beach. A boggy area was drained to make a stream and a bog garden with ligularaes and primulas and ferns; the whole purpose has been to make everything as natural as possible, integrating the garden into the wild with indigenous plants such as brooms, cytisus and many grasses. Near the house the garden abounds in roses, mostly old shrub roses, there is a hedge of 'Felicia' and 'Pax' hybrid musk roses and a climbing 'Felicia' - a rarity. Roses are underplanted with many varieties of perennial geraniums, another favourite plant, and these are also used on the rockery which is wet clay and north facing and not suitable for alpines, together with hebes and small conifers.

ENDSLEIGH HOUSE AND GARDENS 15

Milton Abott, Nr Tavistock, Devon. Tel: (082287) 248
Endsleigh Charitable Trust

4m W of Tavistock on the A384 • Parking • Refreshments: hotel open by appointment for lunch and tea • Open April to Sept, Sat, Sun and Bank Holidays, 12 noon - 4 p.m., and by appointment, Tues and Fri, 12 noon - 4 p.m. • Entrance: by donation (suggested minimum £1)

Endsleigh was built, starting in 1811, for the 6th Duke of Bedford from designs by architect Jeffry Wyatville and landscape designer Humphrey Repton. The house is a good example of the 'Cottage Orné' and was used as a fishing and hunting lodge by the Duke. It is now a Country House Hotel popular with salmon fishermen. The park and garden have magnificent views over the Tamar Valley. There is a shell house with a terrace, an arboretum mainly planted in the first years of the last century, a rock pool with alpines and newly-planted ferns, an ornamental pool with carp, a waterfall and a yew walk. These gardens will also be of great interest to birdwatchers.

FARDEL MANOR 16

Ivybridge, Devon. Tel: (0752) 892353
Dr A.G. Stevens

1¼m NW of Ivybridge, 2m SE of Cornwood, 200 yards off railway bridge • Parking • Teas • Plants for sale • Open 29th July, 11 a.m. - 4.30 p.m. and for specialist groups by appointment • Entrance: 75p, children 30p

A five-acre garden, half of it recently planted, with secluded areas or 'rooms', including a herb garden, a formal fountain garden, herbaceous borders and shrubberies surrounding the fourteenth-century manor house. Climbing roses cover the south wall, joined by Canary creeper in late summer; there is an orangery with Black Hamburg grapes and *Citrus mitis*, vegetable and fruit gardens and an orchard, a bog area with parsley, thistles, day lilies and wild iris and the giant *Gunnera manicata*. A stream leads to a lake surrounded with iris and primulas - a habitat for waterfowl of all kinds. The cultivation is totally organic.

THE GARDEN HOUSE ★ 17

Buckland Monachorum, Yelverton, Devon. Tel: (0822) 854769
The Fortescue Garden Trust

10m N of Plymouth, W of Yelverton off A386 • Parking • Plants for sale • Open April to Sept, daily, 10.30 a.m. - 5 p.m. • Entrance: £1.50, children 50p

An eight-acre garden created after 1945 by Lionel Fortescue, a great plant collector and perfectionist, the charming two-acre walled garden was originally part of a mediaeval monastery. It contains a good collection of herbaceous plants giving the appearance of a cottage garden. Hedges planted for shelter on different levels surprise one as new areas come into view. There are some lovely old trees and some unusual specimens, mainly shrubs, herbaceous and alpines. An alpine house is of special interest. Courses in gardening are held at specified times.

THE GLEBE HOUSE 18

Whitestone, Nr Exeter, Devon. Tel: (039281) 200
Mr and Mrs S.J. West

4m W of Exeter, adjoining Whitestone church • Parking but narrow lanes unsuitable for coaches • Open May and June, Sun and 7th, 14th, 21st July and by appointment, 2 - 5 p.m. • Entrance: £1, children free

A two-acre garden round a former rectory, fifteenth-century with a Georgian façade, and a fourteenth-century tithe barn (Ancient Monument), with magnificent views to the south over the estuary of the Exe, and towards Dartmoor. On the lower level are lawns, trees and a heather garden; above, divided by coniferous hedges and windbreaks, are walks among clematis, vitis and a collection of over 200 varieties of shrub roses - old-fashioned, species and modern hybrid. The middle level of the garden, with the house and tithe barn, features many varieties of climbing roses, clematis, jasmine and honeysuckle. The most impressive and memorable plant is an enormously vigorous *Rosa filipes* 'Kiftsgate' which is trained along the tithe barn, and extends over 120 feet. Flooding the courtyard with scent when in flower in early July this must be one of the largest climbing roses in the South West.

GREENWAY HOUSE 19

Nr Greenway Ferry, Churston Ferrers, Devon. Tel: (0803) 842382
Mr and Mrs A.A. Hicks

4m W of Brixham. From B3203 Paignton - Brixham road, take road to Galmpton, then towards Greenway • Parking • Teas • Suitable for wheelchairs • Plants for sale in nursery open Tues, Wed, Fri p.m., Sat a.m. and by appointment • Garden open 25th April, 2nd May, 2 - 6 p.m. • Entrance: £1, children 50p

Another large (30-acre) and ancient Devon garden on a steep slope, on the bank of the tree-lined Dart river which has woodland walks. There are a large number of indigenous trees over 150 years old and a giant tulip tree. In the walled garden are many camellias, 30 varieties of early magnolias, ceanothus, wisterias and abutilons, and a cork oak. The banks of primroses and bluebells make it magical in spring. On the Georgian façade are *Magnolia grandiflora*, *Akebia quinata* and *Mutisia oligodon*; in the natural glades are foxgloves, white iris, herb Robert, pennywort, ivy and hart's tongue and male ferns.

HIGHER KNOWLE 20

Lustleigh, Devon. Tel: (06477) 275
Mr and Mrs D.R.A. Quicke

8m NW of Newton Abbot, 3m NW of Bovey Tracey on A382 towards Moretonhamstead. In 2½m, turn left at Kelly Cross for Lustleigh; after ¼m straight on at Brookfield for Manaton; after ½m steep drive on left • Teas in village • Open 21st April to 2nd June, Sun and Bank Holiday Mons, 2 - 6 p.m. • Entrance: £1, children 50p

A woodland garden only 30 years old situated on a steep hillside with Dartmoor views. The old beech wood is carpeted with bluebells in spring, and magnolias and rhododendrons, ornamental cherries and heather banks; there is also a tall *Embothrium coccineum* flowering in early summer. A beech hedge encloses a lawn, with the main display of deciduous and evergreen azaleas. Giant Dartmoor granite boulders and much natural sculpture to the woodland walks.

KILLERTON ★ 21

Broadclyst, Nr Exeter, Devon. Tel: (0392) 881345
The National Trust

7m NE of Exeter, on W side of B3181 • Parking • Licensed refreshments same time as house. Tearoom 29th March to 22nd Dec and Jan to March • Toilet facilities • Partly suitable for wheelchairs but motorised buggy with driver available for higher levels • Shop • House and costume museum open 29th March to Oct, daily except Tues, 11 a.m. - 6 p.m. (Oct 11 a.m. - 5 p.m.). Last admission ½ hour before closing. House £3.60 • Park and garden open all year during daylight hours • Entrance: £2.20 (park and garden). Winter Rate £1

This large garden was made on a hill with woods extending in all to 4000 acres, first by John Veitch in the 1770s and then by the famous Victorian William Robinson. The actual garden area of 15 acres will provide interest and pleasure to all, but to the tree and shrub enthusiast it is a haven of delight. Beside the avenues of beeches there are Wellingtonias and Lawson cypresses which provide colour and form and many broad-leaved trees including oaks and maples, as well as the usual conifers. Terraced beds provide summer colour and there are dwarf shrubs and herbaceous specimens to follow the fine display of rhododendrons. A garden to give pleasure at most times of the year. There is a bear house.

KNIGHTSHAYES ★★ 22

Bolham, Tiverton, Devon. Tel: (0884) 254665
The National Trust

2m N of Tiverton, turn right off A396 at Bolham • Parking inc. disabled • Refreshments: restaurant for coffee, lunches and teas. Licensed • Toilet facilities • Suitable for wheelchairs • Dogs on lead in park only • Plants for sale • Shop • House open, daily except Fri but open Good Friday, 1.30 - 6 p.m. (Oct 1.30 - 5 p.m.). Last admission ½ hour before closing • Open 29th March to Oct, daily, 11 a.m. - 6 p.m. (5 p.m. in Oct) • Entrance: £1.80 (garden and grounds only)

This 40-acre garden should give pleasure to everyone with its extensive parkland and large range of trees including Douglas firs, willows, cedar of Lebanon, and nothofagus. The formal Victorian gardens were completely transformed by the formers owners, Sir John and Lady Heathcote Amory, and continued by the Trust. An unusual piece of topiary - the Fox Hunt - leads one on to masses of camellias, azaleas, magnolias, acers and rhododendrons. A formal paved garden contains silver, lilac and pink plants and there is a circular pool surrounded by a yew hedge. The borders have many tender and rare specimens and in the peat-block beds are cyclament, hellebores and primulas. Something of interest at all seasons.

LEE FORD 23

Budleigh Salterton, Devon. Tel: (03954) 5894
Mr and Mrs N. Lindsay-Fynn

3½m from Exmouth • Parking • Teas on open days, 3 - 5.30 p.m. • Suitable for wheelchairs • Plants for sale • Open by prior appointment for parties only and 27th May, 1.30 - 5.30 p.m. • Entrance: £1, OAP 80p, children 50p. Parties of 20 or more 80p per person

Inspired by the Savill Gardens at Windsor, the present owner's father developed this wild woodland garden in the 1950s and 60s and it is one of the longest established open-to-the-public gardens in Devon, best seen perhaps in early summer when the magnolias are in flower. The mown glades are surrounded with masses of species and ponticum rhododendrons, and there is a large collection of camellias, many from the Channel Islands, including white camellias which are often in flower on Christmas Day. There is also a treat of an old-fashioned walled vegetable garden with an Adam pavilion.

MARWOOD HILL ★★ 24

Marwood, Nr Barnstaple, Devon. Tel: (0271) 42528
Dr J.A. Smart

4m NW of Barnstaple. Turn off B3230 to Marwood • Best season: April to Aug • Parking in roadway • Teas on Sun and Bank Holidays or for parties by prior arrangement • Partly suitable for wheelchairs • Dogs on lead • Plants for sale • Open daily except 25th Dec, dawn - dusk • Entrance: £1, children 10p

With the wonderful collection of plants this 20-acre garden is of special interest to the connoisseur but could not fail to give pleasure to any visitor. Over 3000 different varieties of plants covering collections of willows, ferns, magnolias, embothriums, rhododendrons and hebes, and a fine collection of camellias in a glasshouse. Tender plants from Tasmania, Australia and New Zealand are in another greenhouse and the walled gardens are clothed with a beautiful range of clematis and other climbers. A rock garden has been created from an old quarry and contains many alpines, and round the pools are primulas and bog plants.

MIDDLE HILL 25

Washfield, Nr Tiverton, Devon. Tel: (03985) 380
Mr and Mrs E. Boundy

4½m NW of Tiverton, via B3221. Through the village of Washfield and the garden is 1½m on left • Best season: May • Parking • Partly suitable for wheelchairs • Plants for sale • Open 14th April to 22nd Sept, Sun only (except 28th April, 9th June, 25th Aug) and by appointment 7th April to 29th Sept, 2 - 5 p.m. • Entrance: 50p, children 25p

This small garden has been created over 20 odd years to include some specialist plants. There are raised beds, a rockery, island beds growing gentians, ferns, hostas, clematis, crocosmias, penstemons, and pittosporums and, being so exposed, shelter has been provided. Interesting colour and foliage combinations offer some good tips.

THE MOORINGS 26

Rocombe, Uplyme, Lyme Regis, Dorset. Tel: (02974) 3295
Mr and Mrs A. Marriage

2m NW of Lyme Regis. Take A3070 out of Lyme Regis, turn right 150 yards beyond Black Dog pub, over cross roads, fork right into Springhead Road. Top gate to garden is 500 yards on right • Parking • Open by appointment and 31st March, 1st, 21st April, 5th, 6th, 26th, 27th May, 3rd Nov, 11 a.m. - 5 p.m. • Entrance: 50p, children free

Especially rewarding to visit in spring and autumn, this garden has been made by Mr Marriage since 1965 out of three fields on a sheltered, steep, west-facing slope. Impressively, most of the newly-planted arboretum trees have been grown from seed; there is a collection of eucalyptus, many unusual pines including umbrella and maritime pines (grown from seed gathered in the south of France) and nothofagus, including *N. obliqua* and *N. procera*, and the woodland is underplanted with snowdrops. *Hibiscus mutabilis*, a hardy shrub with very large flowers in August, is very rare in this country; there are camellias and a 35 foot high magnolia, and a buddleia flowering rose-red in June. A great point of interest is the collection of over 50 different species of fern, all grown from spores.

THE OLD RECTORY 27

Woodleigh, Nr Loddiswell, Devon. Tel: (0548) 550387
Mr and Mrs H.E. Morton

3½m N of Kingsbridge, E off Kingsbridge - Wrangaton road at Rake Cross (1m S of Loddiswell), 1½m to Woodleigh itself • Parking • Suitable for wheelchairs • Open by appointment only • Entrance: 50p, children 10p

A three-acre woodland garden, and walled garden, rescued from neglect 27 years ago. In the woodland are several individual glades of mature trees, underplanted with magnolias, azaleas, camellias and rhododendrons. There is great attention to form in the planting; evergreens and shrubs are planted for scent and winter effect, and the wild garden is most colourful in spring with crocus and daffodils, while the walled garden is designed with summer in mind. The garden is a haven for wildlife, and chemicals have never been used.

OVERBECKS MUSEUM AND GARDEN ★ 28

Sharpitor, Salcombe, Devon. Tel: (054884) 2893
The National Trust

1½m S of Salcombe, SW to South Sands • Best season: spring - early summer • Parking. Coaches by appointment • Picnic area • Toilet facilities • Dogs on lead • Shop • Museum open, 29th March to Oct, 12 noon - 5 p.m. £2.60 • Garden open daily 10 a.m. - 8 p.m. or sunset if earlier • Entrance: £1.80 (garden only). Parking charge refundable

Palms stand among the bluebells in this exotic garden high above the Salcombe estuary, giving a strongly Mediterranean atmosphere. The mild, maritime climate enables it to be filled with exotics such as myrtles, daturas, agaves and an example of the large camphor tree, *Cinnamomum camphora*, a great rarity. The Himalayan *Magnolia campbellii* is nearly 90 years old and 40 feet high and wide and a sight to see in March. The steep terraces were built in 1901 and lead down through fuchsia trees, fruiting banana palms and myrtle trees to a wonderful *Cornus kousa*. In formal beds near the house is the Chatham Island forget-me-not - *Myosotidium hortensia* (hydrangea-like) with flowers as clear as blue china, phormiums, and tender roses among the rocks.

PAIGNTON ZOO AND BOTANICAL GARDEN ★ 29

Totnes Road, Paignton, Devon. Tel: (03954) 57479

Parking • Refreshments: restaurants • Toilet facilities • Suitable for wheelchairs • Shop • Open daily except 25th Dec, 10 a.m. - sunset

Those not keen on zoos may be won over by Paignton; it is in the forefront of animal and plant conservation and one of the zoos worldwide involved in the breeding of endangered species. As well as the very healthy and happy animals there are the plants. Paignton (over 100 acres in size) was the first zoo in the country to combine animals and a botanic garden, laid out 60 years ago and added to over the years. Choice of plants has been dictated by their harmlessness to teeth and beaks and their ability to provide shade, perches and swinging and basking places; there are geographical collections of plants in the paddocks, and plants also make the fences safer. Hardy Chinese plants surround the baboon rocks. Paignton has the R.H.S. National Collection of sorbaria and buddleia. There are two large plant houses, one sub-tropical with tender plants and trees and magical birds flying, and a tropical house with a jungle pool and areas of tropical plants (indoor plants par excellence) and small areas of different plant families - orchids, African violets and lilies; everything is extensively and informatively labelled - both flora and fauna.

POWDERHAM CASTLE 30

Kenton, Exeter, Devon.
Lord and Lady Courtenay

From Exeter take the A379. Signposted • Parking • Teas, ices and soft drinks • Toilet facilities • Shop • House open • Garden open 26th May to 12th September, daily except Fri and Sat, 2 - 5.30 p.m. • Entrance: £3.20 (house and garden), children £1

The house is believed to date back in parts to 1390, with major additions and a terraced garden in 1840. Broad steps lead down from the terrace to a formal rose garden (formerly another terrace) with gravelled paths and rose beds in a raised lawn; the roses include modern (flowering in September) and a good selection of old-fashioned shrub roses. The garden has urns, a sundial and topiary and one wing of the house is covered in a giant wisteria where lives a grand tortoise aged 150. More climbing roses and honeysuckles grow from the gravel along the castellated wall which gives a magnificent view over the park with its splendid trees and large herd of fallow deer to the sailing boats on the Exe estuary.

ROSEMOOR GARDEN ★★ 31

Great Torrington, Devon. Tel: (0805) 24067
The Royal Horticultural Society

1m SE of Great Torrington on B3220 • Best season: May to Sept • Parking • Refreshments: in restaurant (licensed) • Toilet facilities • Suitable for wheelchairs • Plants for sale in plant centre • Shop in Visitors' Centre open March to 15th Dec, 10 a.m. - 6 p.m. (summer) • Garden open all year • Entrance: £1.75, children 50p

First opened to the public 35 years ago, the original eight-acre garden was made by Lady Anne Palmer: it contains a collection of 3500 plants from all over Europe, North and South America, New Zealand and Japan. There is a large collection of rhododendrons, heathers, waterside plants and old roses; it is also the home of specialist collections of ilex (hollies) and cornus (dogwoods) - over 100 varieties. There are scree gardens, an arboretum, alpines and bulbs. Recently Rosemoor was given to the Royal Horticultural Society as its first regional centre, second only to Wisley. An extra 32 acres have been given, and after much earth moving and drainage work the extensions have begun, including a new rose garden and a visitors' centre, and there is a developing plan to include cottage and herb gardens, a *jardin potager*, alpine lawns, fruit and vegetables and a trial garden to illustrate how specific groups of plants will perform in different conditions. This is truly a great National Garden in the making.

SALTRAM HOUSE ★ 32

Plympton, Plymouth, Devon. Tel: (0752) 336546
The National Trust

3m E of Plymouth. On A379 turn N to Billacombe. After 1m turn left to Saltram • Best season: April to June • Parking • Licensed refreshments • Toilet facilities • Suitable for wheelchairs • Dogs • Shop April to Oct • House open 29th March to Oct, 12.30 - 6 p.m. (Oct 12.30 - 5 p.m.). £4.40 • Gardens open 29th March to Oct, daily except Fri and Sat, but open Sat of Bank Holiday weekends, 11 a.m. - 6 p.m. (Oct 11 a.m. - 5 p.m.). Last admission ½ hour before closing • Entrance: £1.20 garden only

The original garden dates from 1770, slightly altered in the last century; there are three eighteenth-century buildings - a castle or belvedere, an orangery (due to the mild climate the orange and lemon trees are moved outside in the summer) and a classical garden house named Fanny's Bower after Fanny Burney who came here in 1789 in the entourage of George III. There is a long lime avenue underplanted with narcissi in spring, *Cyclamen linearifolium* in autumn and a central glade with specimen trees like the stone pine and Himalayan spruce. There is a beech grove, a Melancholy Walk, and walks with magnolias, camellias, rhododendrons and Japanese maples which, with other trees, make for dramatic autumn colour.

TAPELEY PARK ★ 33

Instow, Devon. Tel: (0271) 860528
Mr H.T.C. Christie

2m N of Bideford S off A39 Barnstaple - Bideford road • Parking • Teas in Queen Anne dairy. Picnic places • Toilet facilities • Suitable for wheelchairs • Dogs • Plants for sale • House open. Tours for parties of 6 or more • Garden open Easter to Oct, daily except Sat, 10 a.m. - 6 p.m. • Entrance: by collecting box

The house is basically William and Mary, set on a splendid site above the River Torridge and Bideford, with much to see and a family with a fascinating history - The Christies of Glynbourne. There are three formal terraces, an Italian garden with ornamental water, yew hedges, an ilex tunnel, a shell house, ice house, and a variety of roses, fuchsias, lavender, dahlias as well as more exotic plants like *Abelia floribunda*, sophora and feijoa from Brazil. On the south of the house are yuccas, *Magnolia grandiflora*, agapanthus and mimosas; on the east, wisteria and *Drimys winteri*, a rare honeysuckle. A woodland walk is lined with camellias, hydrangeas and rhododendrons with primroses and primulas in spring under the giant beeches and oaks; this leads to a water-lily-covered pond in late summer, in the background fall firs and *Thuya plicata*. Walled kitchen garden.

TUDOR GARDEN 34

New Street, The Barbican, Plymouth, Devon.
Plymouth Corporation

In the centre of the old town • Parking difficult • Dogs • Open daily • Entrance: free

An integral part of an area of Plymouth that is being refurbished, this is an interesting reconstruction of the type of Tudor garden that would have existed behind the house in this ancient street. As far as possible only plants which grew in Elizabethan England have been established. Elsewhere in Plymouth the Corporation commemorates great Victorian seaside gardening with colourful carpet bedding by traditional methods.

UGBROOKE PARK 35

Chudleigh, Devon. Tel: (0626) 852179
The Lady Clifford

Follow signs on A380 Exeter - Torby road, and on A38 Exeter - Plymouth road • Parking • Refreshments 1.30 - 5 p.m. • Toilet facilities • Suitable for wheelchairs • Dogs • House open. Private tours for groups by appointment • Park open Sat, Sun and Bank Holiday Monday from late May Bank Holiday to Aug Bank Holiday • Entrance: £1.50, children 75p

The magnificent park around this house (originally twelfth-century and redesigned by Robert Adam) was laid out by 'Capability' Brown. There are extensive lakeside walks. Much new planting is going on, including an interesting Japanese water garden at the entrance gates. There is an eighteenth-century orangery and the conservatory houses tropical plants. Much of the outside planting is semi-tropical.

UNIVERSITY OF EXETER ★ 36

Northcote House, The Queen's Drive, Exeter, Devon.
Tel: (0392) 263263
University of Exeter

On N outskirts of Exeter on A396, turn E on to B3183 • Best season: April to June • Parking • Dogs on lead • Shop open weekdays sells guide books • Open daily • Entrancee: free. Coaches by appointment only

There is much to see on a one mile tour of these extensive gardens based on those made in the 1860s by an East India Merchant millionaire who inherited a fortune made by blockade-running in the Napoleonic wars. The landscaping and tree planting was carried out by Veitch whose plant collectors went all over the world (among them E.H. 'Chinese' Wilson) and at that time many of the trees were unique in Europe. There is a series of lakes with wildfowl, dogwoods, birches, hazel and alder, callistemon shrubs (bottle brushes) wingnut trees (*Pterocarya stenoptera*) brought from China in 1860 and a maidenhair tree (*Gingko*) sacred in Buddhist China. Rockeries have collections of alpines; there is a banana tree (*Musa basjoo*), a large *Gunnera chilensis* and palm trees introduced by Robert Fortune in 1849. Formal gardens and bedding plants lead to a sunken, scented garden. Exeter will house the National collection of Azara, evergreens from Chile, with scented yellow flowers. There are, of course, rhododendrons, magnolias, camellias in a woodland walk; roses, eucalyptus and *Opuntia humifusa*, the prickly pear cactus flowering in summer.

VICARS MEAD 37

Hayes Lane, East Budleigh, Devon. Tel: (03954) 2641
Mr and Mrs H.F.J. Read

From A376 Newton Poppleford - Budleigh Salterton road, turn off left for East Budleigh • Car park 50 yards from entrance • Toilet facilities • Partly suitable for wheelchairs • Plants for sale • Open 31st March, 1st April, 5th, 6th, 26th, 27th May, 9th, 16th, 23rd, 30th June, 7th, 14th July, 25th, 26th Aug, 8th Sept, 2 - 6 p.m. • Entrance: £1, children free

On and around a red sandstone escarpment this three and a half-acre garden has been created since 1977. It is most interesting to keen plantsmen in that it contains many rare and unusual shrubs and houses four National collections - dianellas, libertias, liriopes and ophiopogons.

WOODSIDE

38

Higher Raleigh Road, Barnstaple, Devon. Tel: (0271) 43095
Mr and Mrs M. Feesey

Off A39 Barnstaple to Lynton road, turn right 300 yards above fire station • Limited parking in road outside • Open 12th May, 23rd June, 21st July, 2 - 5.30 p.m. • Entrance: 60p, children 20p

A sloping two-acre garden in a suburban area with an unusual collection of plants including ornamental grasses, bamboos and sedges. Many parts of the garden are shaded but rare dwarf shrubs, trees and conifers survive. There are raised beds and troughs with alpines and peat-loving specimens. A collection of New Zealand plants along with peat-loving shrubs make this a garden with a difference.

GARDENS OPEN RARELY

The following gardens are open to the public on three days or less in the year, although they may also be open by appointment if this is stated in the text. For details see individual entry.

April 25 Greenway House; **May 2** Greenway House; **May 12** Woodside; **May 27** Lee Ford; **June 9** 41 Beaumont Road; **June 16** 41 Beaumont Road; **June 23** Woodside; **July 21** Woodside; **July 29** Fardel Manor.

DORSET

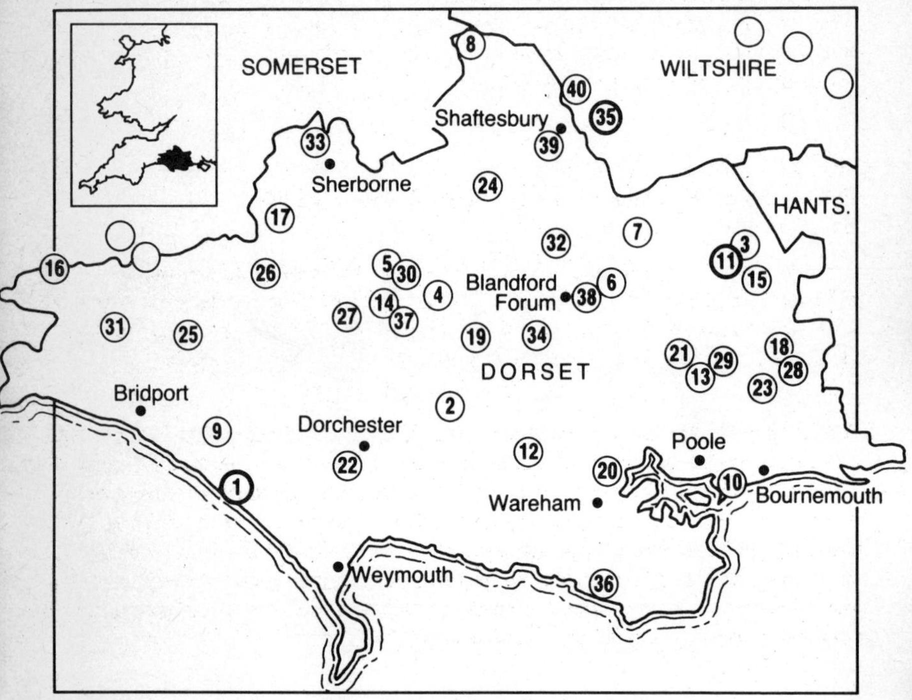

Plain circle numbers can be found by turning to neighbouring counties. Two-starred gardens are ringed in bold.

ABBOTSBURY GARDENS ★★ 1

Abbotsbury, Dorset. Tel: (0305) 871387
Ilchester Estates

9m NW of Weymouth, 9m SW of Dorchester off B3157 • Parking • Refreshments • Toilet facilities • Partly suitable for wheelchairs • Dogs on lead • Plants for sale • Shop • Open March to Oct, daily, 10 a.m. - 5 p.m., Nov to Feb, daily except Mon, and 25th, 26th Dec, 10 a.m. - 4 p.m. • Entrance: £2.50, OAP £2, children 60p. Joint tickets with Swannery and group booking discounts available

Proximity to the sea helps to provide the 'micro-climate' which makes Abbotsbury so special. Within its 20 acres there is much of great interest to the plantsperson in the many rare species on display, while amateur gardeners can get pleasure from the banks of colour and the shaded walks - particularly in the spring. People travel a long way to visit these gardens - often called 'sub-tropical', but probably technically better described as 'wet Mediterranean'. The new visitor centre, shop and refreshment area are an excellent additional bonus for the many coach parties who come for both gardens and nearby Swannery (not to be missed when open!). Pure garden enthusiasts will be more interested in the redesigned plant sales area which, while not extensive, has a good range of healthy stock on tempting display. It is good to see that the recent severe damage from wind and flood has not diminished the tranquillity of this fascinating garden.

ATHELHAMPTON ★ 2

Puddletown, Dorchester, Dorset. Tel: (0305) 848363
Lady Du Cann

On A35 1m E of Puddletown, near Dorchester • Best season: May/June • Parking • Refreshments • Toilet facilities • Partly suitable for wheelchairs • Shop • House open • Garden open Easter to Oct, Wed, Thurs, Sun and Bank Holidays (Also July, Tues; Aug, Mon and Tues; Sept, Tues), 2 - 6 p.m. • Entrance: £1.50, children free (£3 house and gardens)

Athelhampton garden was rescued and re-designed by Alfred La Fontaine in 1891, a process continued by subsequent owners, latterly the late Robert Cooke. Courts and walls follow the original plan with beautiful stonework in walls and arches. Apart from some of the most impressive topiary in England there are pools, fountains, a rectangular canal with water lilies and a pleached lime walk. It is not a great flower garden but rambling roses, clematis and jasmine (in their seasons) make it memorable. With one and a half gardeners instead of the original 12 you can't have everything!

BOVERIDGE FARM 3

Cranborne, Dorset. Tel: (07254) 241
Mr D.J. Dampney

Nr Cranborne on Martin Road (unclassified). Take 2nd turn on right • Best season: April to June • Parking • Teas at Ashley Park in next village of Damerham • Toilet facilities • Plants for sale in Ashley Park • Open 21st April, 12th May, 16th June, 2 - 5.30 p.m. • Entrance: 75p, children free

The house lies on a steep north-facing slope, and the garden has been laid out below it, to the west of it and above. The plants and shrubs on the lower side are on chalk, whilst the fern bank and shrubbery above is on neutral clay. There is a fine view across the rooftops and along the valley, which is largely arable with wooded hilltops. As a busy farmer, Mr Dampney has had to fit his enthusiasm for uncommon plants around his working life. It has taken over 35 years to create the garden as it is today, a colourful and interesting collection much of which he has himself grown from seed or cuttings. He has recently developed a farm and woodland walk at Damerham (3 miles away). The walk leads through ancient woods which now include 40 different varieties of oak tree, with underplanting of spring shrubs.

BROADLANDS ★ 4

Hazelbury Bryan, Nr Sturminster Newton, Dorset. Tel: (0258) 817374
Mr and Mrs M.J. Smith

4m S of Sturminster Newton off A357 Blandford – Sherborne road at signpost. ½m beyond Antelope pub • Parking • Toilet facilities • Suitable for wheelchairs • Plants for sale • Open by appointment and 7th, 21s April, 5th, 19th May, 2nd, 16th June, 14th July, 4th Aug, 8th Sept and every Wed in July and Aug, 2 – 5.30 p.m. • Entrance: £1, accompanied children free

This is a two-acre garden in which the design and planting have the curious effect of obscuring the full size of the area while at the same time extending the apparent distance the visitor covers in walking round it. This is achieved by the clever siting of island beds, with grass walkways leading to features such as ponds, rockeries and paved seating areas. There are screening hedges to enhance the surprise of discovering the greenhouse, the vegetables, the ornamental woodland. Round every corner the visitor comes upon some new feature of interest and delight, and everywhere there are uncommon plants to give pleasure in all seasons. Begun in 1975, this is a most successful layout, excellently labelled and refreshingly imaginative, which should inspire gardeners of all levels of competence. New features include an area devoted to shrub and climbing roses, and further development and underplanting in the woodland area.

CANNINGS COURT 5

Pulham, Nr Sherborne, Dorset. Tel: (0258) 817210
Mr and Mrs J.D. Dennison

13m N of Dorchester, 8m SE of Sherborne. Turn E at crossroads in Pulham • Parking • Refreshments • Toilet facilities • Suitable for wheelchairs • Plants for sale • Open 19th May, 30th June, 21st July, 2–6 p.m. • Entrance: 75p, children free

Over twenty years of loving labour have gone into this farmhouse garden, developed virtually from scratch at the same time as the owners were busy with the rescue of the farm itself. The bare walls of the Georgian façade have been clothed with thriving creepers, the open land behind is sheltered by tree screens and contains colourful borders and shrubberies, a pond and an arboretum. The *potager* which was in preparation last year has now been developed into a thriving plot of unusual and colourful vegetables. Based on those at Villandry, it is being edged with box and cotton lavender. Not content, they have plans for a woodland walk, more tree screens and arbours – probably enough to occupy the next 20 years. Do not leave without looking in the tool store-cum-workshop which is entered through a huge Elizabethan fireplace rising 20 feet up a blackened chimney. The farm name is a corruption of 'Canon's Court' and it has probably been in continuous occupation for over 1000 years, as the surrounding buildings could testify.

CHARLTON COTTAGE 6

Tarrant Rushton, Blandford, Dorset. Tel: (0258) 452072
The Hon. Penelope Piercy

3m SE of Blandford on B3082. Fork left at top of hill, right at T-junction, first left to village • Parking in adjacent field • Suitable for wheelchairs • Open 26th May, 9th June, 2 - 5.30 p.m. • Entrance: £1, children 25p

Charlton Cottage lies at the end of the village where the garden surrounds what used to be two terraced cottages, now all one property. In place of the long narrow cottage strips, the back garden has two lawn areas separated by colourful borders and leading up a gentle slope among shrubs and trees to a vegetable area. In front of the house the road from the village peters out into a narrow track, so the owner has acquired land on the other side where there are further borders through which the visitor descends to a shady water garden and wild area.

CHETTLE HOUSE 7

Blandford Forum, Dorset. Tel: (0258) 89209
Mr and Mrs P. Bourke

6m NE of Blandford on A354, turn left to Chettle • Parking • Refreshments at weekend • Toilet facilities • Suitable for wheelchairs • Plants for sale • Art gallery • House open • Garden open April to Oct, daily except Tues, 11 a.m. - 5 p.m. • Entrance: £1.50, children free

The wide lawns frame the attractive Queen Anne house with many chalk-loving varieties of shrubs and herbaceous plants (some quite rare) in the borders. Visitors can experience a very peaceful and relaxing atmosphere in this garden, and if interested can purchase plants raised from garden stock in the good small nursery not far from the house.

CHIFFCHAFFS 8

Chaffeymoor, Bourton, Gillingham, Dorset.
Mr and Mrs K.R. Potts

3m E of Wincanton off A303 at W end of Bourton village • Best season: spring • Parking in road • Teas on first and last Suns • Toilet facilities • Plants for sale • Open 24th March to 29th Sept, Wed, Sun (except second Wed and Sun in the month), 2 - 5.30 p.m. • Entrance: £1, children 25p

An impressive avenue of flowering cherries leads to the house and gardens, the nursery and the woodland walk surrounding fields, which extend to a total of 12 acres. The terraces and viewpoints afford fascinating glimpses of open country around and the varied and colourful beds and borders are delightful. Special interest is provided by the new underplanting in the woodland area and by the collection of dwarf rhododendrons and old-fashioned roses. The nursery is well-stocked with a wide variety of healthy-looking plants.

CHILCOMBE HOUSE ★★ 9

Chilcombe, Nr Bridport, Dorset. Tel: (03083) 234
Mr and Mrs J. Hubbard

5m E of Bridport off A35 • Parking • Teas • Plants for sale • Open 16th, 30th June, 2 - 6.30 p.m. • Entrance: £1.20, children 50p

There are wild areas, courtyards and a walled garden divided into smaller sections. Mixed plantings of shrubs, flowers and herbs cover every inch of ground to great advantage, and there is also a bank of mixed heather, angelica plants, fruit trees and vegetables with good clematis and many old roses. This garden is a marvellous creation in a beautiful setting.

COMPTON ACRES ★ 10

Canford Cliffs, Poole, Dorset. Tel: (0202) 700778
Mr and Mrs L. Green

From Poole/Bournemouth road onto Canford Cliffs road (near Sandbanks) • Parking • Refreshments • Toilet facilities • Suitable for wheelchairs (can be supplied) • Guide dogs only • Plants for sale • Shop • Open 24th March to Oct, daily, 10.30 a.m. - 6.30 p.m. • Entrance: £2.70, OAP £1.70, children 85p

Keen gardeners might be put off by the huge coach park, the frankly commercial and rather down-market approach. They should persevere, because the gardens themselves are well-designed, immaculately kept and stocked with many interesting and well-labelled plants, trees and shrubs. Water abounds in streams, waterfalls, ponds and formal lakes, the home of fat, multi-coloured carp. An enterprise aimed obviously (and very accurately) at the tourist, Compton Acres has the feel of a very opulent public park, a sort of pop-concert of the gardening world - but none the worse for that.

CRANBORNE MANOR GARDENS ★★ 11

Cranborne, Dorset. Tel: (07254) 248
The Viscount and Viscountess Cranborne

10m N of Wimborne on B3078 • Parking • Refreshments • Toilet facilities • Partly suitable for wheelchairs • Plants for sale • Shop • Open April to Sept, Weds 9 a.m. - 5 p.m. Also 8th June • Entrance: £2.50, OAP £2

Tradescant established the basic framework in the early seventeenth century, but little is left of the original plan. Neglected for a long period, the garden has been revived in the last three generations and now includes several smaller areas surrounded by tall clipped yew hedges, a walled white garden at its best in midsummer, wide lawns (again yew-lined) and extensive woodland and wild areas. Best of all is the high-walled entrance courtyard to the south which is approached through an arch between the two Jacobean gate houses. Here the plant selection along the lengthy borders is delightfully imaginative, providing the perfect introduction to what has been called 'the most magical house in Dorset' (not least for the garden which surrounds it). The excellent nursery garden specializes in traditional rose varieties, but also carries a wide selection of other plants. Italian statuay and stone ornaments are also featured, together with very high quality garden furniture.

CULEAZE 12

Bere Regis, Dorset. Tel: (0929) 471209
Col. and Mrs A.M. Barne

1½m S of Bere Regis on the road to Wool. Take 2nd left (signposted) then right • Parking • Refreshments in Bere Regis • Toilet facilities • Suitable for wheelchairs • Dogs on lead • Plants for sale • Farm shop • Open 5th, 6th May, 2 - 6 p.m. • Entrance: 75p

Most of the trees and plants in this well-established garden have been grown from seeds or cuttings raised by the owners. They include some rare and unusual specimens successfully reared despite the warning advice of experts – always ready to say it couldn't be done. There is a rhododendron-lined drive, a large lawn bordered by interesting trees, and a good-sized walled area with many more special and often sought-after plants, not to mention an extensive cut flower and Christmas tree plantation. This is a very large enterprise to be attempted with only part-time staff, and the visitor will readily appreciate the effort required to maintain it.

DEAN'S COURT 13

Wimborne Minster, Dorset.
Sir Michael and Lady Hanham

In the centre of Wimborne off B3073 • Parking nearby • Refreshments • Toilet facilities • Suitable for wheelchairs • Organically-grown herb plants for sale • Open Easter to Sept, Bank Holidays and certain Thurs and Suns. Also additional opening during Arts Festival. Contact Wimborne Tourist Information Office for details. Tel: (0202) 886116 • Entrance: £1, children 50p

A mellow brick house set in 13 acres of parkland containing a number of interesting and very large trees. A swamp cypress towers near the house, and a 92 foot tulip tree covers one wall. The many fine specimens include Lucombe oak, Wellingtonias, Caucasian wing nut, Chilean fire bush, Japanese pagoda tree, blue cedars and horse chestnuts. There are few formal beds, but a courtyard contains an unusually comprehensive herb garden with almost 100 different plants. The walled kitchen garden, in which many of the old varieties of vegetables are grown by organic production methods, is extensive and obviously successful. A peaceful haven from the busy town just a few yards away, and well worth a visit.

DOMINEY'S YARD 14

Buckland Newton, Dorset. Tel: (03005) 295
Captain and Mrs W. Gueterbock

11m from both Dorchester and Sherborne, 2m E of A352 or take B3143 from Sturminster Newton. Take 'no through road' between church and pub next to phone box. Opposite new houses • Parking in lane • Refreshments • Toilet facilities • Partly suitable for wheelchairs • Open 5th May, 2 - 6 p.m., 14th July, 2 - 6.30 p.m., 11th Aug, 2 - 6 p.m., and by appointment • Entrance: £1.20, children 30p

An inviting swimming pool and an immaculate lawn tennis court are features of this attractive family garden; they are so placed that they neither dominate nor detract from the borders and shrubberies which will interest and delight amateurs and plantsmen alike. Blessed with three different soil types within two acres, the owners have been able to grow a wide variety of unusual plants during the 25 years they have lived here. Camellias and magnolias grow on greensand. Shrubs and trees provide year round colour to enhance the lovely seventeenth-century cottage.

EDMONDSHAM HOUSE 15

Edmondsham, Nr Cranborne, Dorset. Tel: (07254) 207
Mrs J. Smith

2m S of Cranborne. From the A354 turn at Sixpenny Handley crossroads to Ringwood and Cranborne • Best season: spring • Parking • Refreshments on open days • Toilet facilities • Suitable for wheelchairs • Plants and vegetables for sale • House open 15th April, all Bank Holiday Mons, Weds in April and Oct, 2 - 5 p.m. • Garden open April to June and Oct, Wed - Sat, 10 a.m. - 12 noon. Also by appointment • Entrance: 75p, children 30p (£1.50, children 60p house and garden)

A vast, walled kitchen garden in which only organic methods are used provides the major interest here. This is very much a Victorian kitchen garden in origin, having been intensively cultivated since the mid-nineteenth century, but several modern and interesting vegetable variants are grown for sale. Herbaceous borders line the walls. Wide lawns surround the house, bordered by many fine and rare trees growing to a good height. An unusual circular grass hollow is said to be a cockpit, one of only a few 'naturalised' areas of the sort in the country. The massed spring bulbs together with the many spring-flowering shrubs make this the best season to visit, but the peaceful, mellow atmosphere pervades the garden at all seasons. The house is of Tudor origin and the church nearby is also of historic interest.

FORDE ABBEY ★

Chard, Somerset.
Tel: (0460) 21366 (in Dorset but postal address Somerset)
Mr M. Roper

7m W of Crewkerne, 4m SE of Chard off A30 • Parking • Refreshments • Toilet facilities • Suitable for wheelchairs • Dogs • Plants for sale • House open • Garden open all year, daily, 10 a.m. - 4.30 p.m. • Entrance: £2.30, OAP £2, children free

This unique and fascinating former Cistercian abbey, inhabited as a private house since 1649, is set in a varied and pleasing garden. Old walls and colourful borders, wide sloping lawns, lush ponds and cascades, graceful statuary and huge mature trees combine to create an atmosphere of timeless elegance. There is something here for every gardener to appreciate; the bog garden displays a large collection of primulas and other Asiatic plants; the shrubbery contains a variety of magnolias, rhododendrons and other delightful specimens. There is a rock garden and a very fine arboretum built up since 1947; at the back of the abbey is an extensive kitchen garden and a nursery selling rare and unusual plants which look in fine health.

FRANKHAM FARM 17

Ryme Intrinseca, Nr Sherborne, Dorset. Tel: (0935) 872304
Mr and Mrs R.G. Earle

3m S of Yeovil, turning off A37 at crossroads with garage. Drive ¼m on left • Best season: spring/summer • Parking • Suitable for wheelchairs • Open 31st March, 5th May, 23rd June • Entrance: 80p, children free

Approached by an impressive tree-lined drive the entrance yard has colourful climbing plants clinging to its grey walls. There is more colour and greenery in the beds and screening hedges that help to distance the farm house itself from the working buildings behind. To the south of the house, a lawn has curving borders on each side framing a low wall and leading the eye on to the fields beyond. The variety and success of the planting in the borders is evidence of the owners' flair for colour and form as well as their knowledge of unusual and interesting plants. From the end wall the visitor can begin to see the extent of the tree-screening which protects the garden on either side. This is a very exposed site around which shelter belts of quick-growing species have gradually been extended to allow replacement by a variety of plantings that should interest keen tree-lovers. On the west side, beyond the drive, a small orchard has been enlarged by the same means into a delightful arboretum, underplanted with spring bulbs, camellias and other shrubs. There is much to learn and admire here for all gardeners facing the problems of an exposed position.

HIGHBURY 18

West Moors, Dorset. Tel: (0202) 874372
Mr and Mrs S. Cherry

8m N of Bournemouth off B3072. Woodside Road is the last road at the N end of West Moors village • Parking in road • Refreshments • Toilet facilities • Suitable for wheelchairs • Plants for sale • Open by appointment for parties and on Suns and Bank Holidays, from last Sun in March to first Sun in Sept, 2 - 6 p.m. • Entrance: 65p, OAP and parties 45p, children 25p

Mr and Mrs Cherry have amassed in their small botanical garden a fascinating collection of unusual specimens which will interest plantsmen and keen amateurs alike. With excellent labelling and much other general information available, this is a garden which delivers more to the enthusiast than is conveyed by the initial impression. It must be admitted that the average gardener might find the closely surrounding trees and the emphasis on rarity as against form and colour rather less than exciting.

IVY COTTAGE ★ 19

Aller Lane, Ansty, Dorset. Tel: (0258) 880053
Mr and Mrs A. Stevens

8m W of Blandford, 12m N of Dorchester. Take A354 Puddletown/Blandford road, turn first left after Blue Vinney, through Cheselbourne • Parking in road • Teas on Suns only • Partly suitable for wheelchairs • Plants for sale • Open April to Oct, Thurs, 10 a.m. - 5 p.m. and on 14th April, 26th May, 25th August, 22nd September, 2 - 5.30 p.m. Parties by appointment only • Entrance on Thurs, April to Oct, £1, on Sun, £1.50 (combined with Aller Green)

Mrs Stevens trained and worked as a professional gardener before coming to her cottage 27 years ago. Although chalk underlies the surrounding land, this garden is actually well watered and is therefore an ideal home for plants such as primulas, irises, gunneras, and in particular trollius and moisture-loving lobelias, for both of which this is the NCCPG National collection. A thriving and ordered vegetable garden (which never needs a hose), large herbaceous borders giving colour all year round, drifts of bulbs and other spring plants surrounding specimen trees and shrubs and two most interesting raised beds for alpines. This garden has been justifiably featured in print and on television, and merits a wide detour. Just up the road is Aller Green, a typical peaceful Dorset cottage garden of approximately one acre in an old orchard setting. The two share some charity opening days with a combined admission charge.

KESWORTH 20

Kesworth Farm House, Sandford, Wareham, Dorset.
Tel: (09295) 51577
Mr H.J.S. Clarke

1½m N of Wareham off A351 opposite Sandford School (Keysworth Drive) • Parking • Toilet facilities • Suitable for wheelchairs • Dogs • Open 12th, 19th May, 12.30 – 7 p.m. • Entrance: £1, children free

Kesworth is a twentieth-century park and garden scheme conceived on the scale of 'Capability' Brown, but carried out under unfavourable conditions. Bordered on the south side by the marshy edge of Poole Harbour, to the north by a busy road and railway line, and with industrial estates, both active and derelict formerly in full view, it is hardly surprising that Mr Clark's friends feared for his sanity when he acquired Kesworth. His intention of revitalising the farmland and building his own residence there was to prove even more difficult than he imagined. Poor soil, voracious wildlife, wind and fire took constant toll of his plantings. Twenty-five years of effort and 40,000 trees have gone into the project, with the result that Kesworth farmhouse (a modern evocation of the mid-eighteenth century) now stands fronted by a wide yew-lined lawn, with flagged courts and borders to the rear linking it with the original farm outbuildings. On all sides are graduated screens of trees set in broad grassland. The eyesores have been successfully obliterated, the land revived. Kesworth may not stand among the foremost as a gardener's treasure trove, but with its avenue, groves and marshland scenery and wildlife it provides a wonderful example of conservation started 20 years before the concept became generally fashionable.

KINGSTON LACY ★ 21

Wimborne, Dorset. Tel: (0202) 883402
The National Trust

1½m W of Wimborne on B3082 • Best season: spring • Parking 100 yards • Licensed refreshments and teas, 11.30 a.m. – 5.30 p.m. Picnics in north park only • Toilet facilities • Suitable for wheelchairs • Dogs on lead and in car park and north park only • Shop • House open 12 noon – 5.30 p.m. Last admission 5 p.m. (£4.50) • Garden open 25th March to 3rd Nov, daily except Thurs and Fri, 12 noon – 5.30 p.m. Last admission 5 p.m. Park 11.30 a.m. – 6 p.m. • Entrance: £1.40 (park and garden)

The terrace, modelled by Barry on the Queen's house at Greenwich, displays urns, vases and lions in bronze and marble. There are six interesting marble wellheads or tubs for bay trees, also an Egyptian obelisk and sarcophagus. The small informal 'Dutch Garden' was laid out in 1899 for Mrs Bankes in memory of her husband and is still planted in the seasonal schemes designed for her. The restored Victorian fernery leads to the once fine Cedar Walk where one of the trees was planted by the Duke of Wellington in 1827, others by visiting royalty and family members. Sadly many of these trees were among the 1000 or so lost in the storms of January 1990, the devastation from which will take another 18 months to clear. However, there is still the laurel walk, the ancient lime avenue, and many areas of spring bulbs in the 400-acre park to enjoy.

KINGSTON MAURWARD ★ 22

Dorset College of Agriculture, Dorchester, Dorset. Tel: (0305) 264738
Dorset County Council

E of Dorchester off A35. Turn off at roundabout at end of bypass • Best season: spring/summer • Parking • Toilet facilities • Partly suitable for wheelchairs • Open Easter to Sept, 11 a.m. - 5 p.m. Guided tours by appointment • Entrance: £2, children £1 (inc. Farm Animal Park)

As might be expected, the requirements of a busy agricultural and horticultural teaching centre have inevitably altered the character of what was for many generations an impressive private mansion. The garden, with its splendid stone terraces, balustrades and steps, was laid out to the west of the house during and soon after World War I and the hedges and topiary of box and yew which form such a feature also date from this period. From 1939 to 1947 the property suffered misuse and total neglect, and it has taken many years of dedicated work by staff and students to restore it to something of its former glory. Sadly, features such as statuary and a Grecian temple have gone for good, with the result that recesses in the hedges stand empty, carefully planned vistas lead to nothing. Nevertheless, the planting is colourful and interesting (the National Collection of penstemons and salvias is held here); drifts of bulbs in spring, mainly crocus and anemone species and later cyclamen and autumn crocus surround some fine specimen trees. The large lake below the wide, sloping lawn dates back to the late eighteenth century. The nature trail provides shady walks around its margin, is full of wildlife and gives superb views over the lake and water meadows. Also surviving are the remains of what was once a Japanese garden, and a graceful folly and pond. The former walled kitchen garden provides a demonstration and practical working area for students. Much good restoration work is still being done, but to return it to its former status this garden needs the sort of lavish resources which are not available to a local authority in these times. Linked to the garden is the Farm Animal Park which contains unusual breeds.

KNOLL GARDENS 23

Stapehill Road, Wimborne, Dorset. Tel: (0202) 873931
Mr K. Martin

Between Wimborne and Ferndown, near village of Hampreston • Parking • Refreshments • Toilet facilities • Suitable for wheelchairs • Plants for sale • Shop • Open March to Nov, 10 a.m. - 6 p.m. or dusk if earlier • Entrance: £2.60, OAP £2.15, children £1.30

Some six acres of gardens contain over 3000 different named plants. A new box-hedged formal garden has been added, while the borders and terraces round the waterfall and ponds are maturing well. Interesting trees and shrubs (particularly the Australian Section) are grouped on pleasant lawns. There is much to be learned here about what can be done in a short space of time to redesign and rebuild a garden. The well-stocked nursery offers a good choice of healthy plants.

THE MANOR HOUSE 24

Hinton St Mary, Sturminster Newton, Dorset. Tel: (0258) 72519
Mr and Mrs A. Pitt-Rivers

1m NW of Sturminster Newton on B3092 • Parking • Refreshments • Toilet facilities • Suitable for wheelchairs • Open 29th, 30th June, 2 – 6 p.m. • Entrance: £1.50, children 20p

The Manor House lies in the Blackmore Vale and has splendid views. There is a pleasant sunken pond with fountains, an interesting arboretum to the side of the house, a further sunken rose garden, again with statuary and fountains screened by yew trees, a lime tree walk and an unusual stone gazebo as part of a walled garden by the barn. Individually each part of this garden has interest and attraction for the visitor, but taken together the result is somehow rather disappointing. Perhaps the loss of some fine elm trees which used to surround the garden has something to do with it; perhaps it may need the application of an overall design to link the various sections. Plans are in hand to replant in some areas, and hopefully the opportunity can be taken to provide the coherence and 'heart' which currently this garden seems to lack. Events are held from time to time in the large restored barn.

MAPPERTON ★ 25

Beaminster, Dorset. Tel: (0308) 862645
The Montagu family

5m NE of Bridport, 2m SE of Beaminster • Parking • Toilet facilities • House open to parties of 15 or more by appointment • Garden open March to Oct, daily except Sat, 2 – 6 p.m. • Entrance: £1.20, children 60p, children under 5 free

A garden with a difference, Mapperton runs down a gradually steepening valley dominated by the delightful sixteenth/seventeenth-century manor house. Terraces in brick and concrete descend through formal Italian-style borders towards the summer house, which itself stands high above two huge fish tanks (how have they resisted turning them into an Olympic-length swimming pool?) On all sides there is topiary in yew and box. Beyond the tanks, the valley becomes a shrubbery and arboretum, much of it recently planted by the present owners. Many of the concrete features depicting animals and birds, both natural and stylistic, are in need of attention, but in general the numerous ornaments provide interest and surprise.

MELBURY HOUSE 26

Evershot, Dorset. Tel: (0935) 83222 (Estate Office)
The Hon. Mrs C. Morrison

13m N of Dorchester on A37 Yeovil – Dorchester road. Signposted • Best season: spring • Parking • Teas • Toilet facilities • Suitable for wheelchairs • Plants for sale • Open 23rd, 30th May, 13th, 20th June, 4th, 11th July, 2 – 6 p.m. • Entrance: £1.80, OAP and children 85p

This historic house (not open to the public) is approached from the north by a long drive through open parkland. Visitors are directed round the east side, passing the ancient family church (open) set above a wooded valley. Lawns sweep down to a small lake beyond which rise more wooded hills. A shrub-enclosed lawn leads to a flower garden on the west side, with colourful herbaceous borders beneath mellow brick walls. Beyond this are two other vast walled areas largely used as paddock or open lawn, but with a small part still maintained as a productive kitchen garden. To the south-west of the house an interesting arboretum with shrubs and massed spring bulbs. This is a pleasant country-house garden which, lacking any outstanding features, seems to be waiting, like an unfinished canvas, for creative inspiration to make it a a worthy foil to the fascinating and historic building it enfolds.

MINTERNE 27

Minterne Magna, Dorchester, Dorset. Tel: (0300) 341370
Lord and Lady Digby

9m N of Dorchester on A352 • Parking • Toilet facilities • Dogs on lead • Open April to Oct, daily, 10 a.m. – 7 p.m. • Entrance: £2, children (accompanied only) free, in honesty box

An interesting collection of Himalayan rhododendrons and azaleas, spring bulbs, cherries and maples. Many rare trees. One and a half miles of walks with palm trees, cedar, beech, etc. Alas no labelling to help the amateur. The first half of the walk is disappointing in midsummer although evidence remains of some spectacular spring colour. At the lower end of the valley the stream with its lakes and waterfalls is surrounded by splendid tall trees among which the paths wind back towards the house. A very restful and attractive atmosphere, but both lakes and undergrowth could do with attention. Tree colour in autumn should be special.

THE MOORINGS

(see Devon)

MOULIN HUET 28

15 Heatherdown Road, West Moors, Dorset. Tel: (0202) 875760
Mr H. Judd

8m N of Bournemouth. Look for cul-de-sac off the road • Parking in road • Open by appointment for parties and on 12th, 19th May, 2 - 5 p.m. • Entrance: 50p, children free

Mr Judd (now in his eighties) and his late wife built their garden from open heath over 20 years. Although only a third of an acre and triangular in shape, it seems to stretch and enlarge as the visitor is conducted from area to area through archways and along winding paths. All the plants, some of them quite rare, have been grown from seed or cuttings. There is also a fine collection of bonsai, grown by Mr Judd's own unique method which apparently defies all the rules.

NORTH LEIGH HOUSE 29

Colehill, Wimborne, Dorset. Tel: (0202) 882592
Mr and Mrs S. Walker

1m NE of Wimborne. Turn off B3073 by Sir Winston Churchill pub into North Leigh Lane (¾m) • Parking • Refreshments • Toilet facilities • Partly suitable for wheelchairs • Dogs on lead • House open by appointment • Garden open 7th April, 5th May, 4th Aug, 2 - 6 p.m. • Entrance: 70p, children 20p

The restoration of this delightful house and its once impenetrable grounds has taken over 22 years to achieve, and the work continues. There are five acres of informal parkland, with mature trees, a small lake and grassy banks covered in drifts of wild orchids and naturalised spring bulbs. The Victorian features include a balustraded terrace, a fountain, a small walled garden and a magnificent conservatory in which a heavy-fruiting vine flourishes alongside other interesting specimens. There is a strong sense of the past being recaptured here; it is not difficult to imagine in such surroundings the tennis or croquet parties of 100 years ago, and the urbane butler bringing forth cooling drinks on a long-distant summer afternoon. Today, figs from the tree may be taken with afternoon tea.

THE OLD RECTORY 30

Pulham, Dorchester, Dorset. Tel: (0258) 817595
Sir John and Lady Garnier

13m N of Dorchester, 8m SE of Sherborne on B3143. Turn E at crossroads in Pulham • Parking • Refreshments • Toilet facilities • Suitable for wheelchairs • Dogs on lead • Plants for sale • Open 19th, 22nd May, 9th, 12th, 30th June, 3rd July, 2 - 6 p.m. • Entrance: £1, children free

A wide lawn runs away southward from this delightful Georgian building, leading to a ha-ha and a really spectacular view over open countryside to distant hills. The main part of the three-acre garden is set to the west and includes some fine mature trees as well as interesting younger ones, a fenced pond, a rose arbour containing many varieties of bush, shrub and climbing plants, and a pleasant vista down a yew-lined lawn, back towards the west front. This is a lovely, peaceful, mature garden which fully compensates for the somewhat startling impression some visitors may experience when greeted by the castellated Gothic façade of the north front.

PARNHAM HOUSE ★ 31

Beaminster, Dorset. Tel: (0308) 862204
Mr and Mrs J. Makepeace

½m S of Beaminster on A3066 • Parking • Refreshments: licensed buttery • Toilet facilities • Partly suitable for wheelchairs • Dogs on lead • Shop • House and workshop open • Garden open April to Oct, Wed, Sun and Bank Holidays, 10 a.m. - 5 p.m. • Entrance: £3, children 10 - 15 £1.50, under 10 free (house, workshop and garden)

The imposing stone terracing to the west of the house frames the many large clipped yews through which descend spring-fed water channels. A wide lawn leads to the balustrade and a small lake. There are large woodland and wild areas to the north and east, and sheltered borders along the brick wall of the old kitchen garden - the earliest part. Here Mrs Makepeace has used her gift for colour and form to create some splendid displays, notable as much for their shape and texture as for the well-chosen colour schemes. There are also delightful small and large courtyards to the south of the house with interesting plantings. Because the house is regularly open to the public in connection with John Makepeace's furniture design and workshops, there are asphalted drives and parking areas near the house, as well as a large grassed car park. This together with the proximity of the southern fencing to the house itself creates a somewhat disturbed and truncated effect which tends to take away from the overall excellence. Mr Makepeace, as well as being a designer with an international reputation, has recently taken an interest in the design of timber buildings.

RUSSETS 32

Rectory Lane, Child Okeford, Nr Blandford, Dorset.
Tel: (0258) 860703
Mr and Mrs G.D. Harthan

6m NW of Blandford off A357. Turn N after Shillingstone • Parking in Rectory Lane • Teas • Suitable for wheelchairs • Dogs on lead • Plants for sale • Open by appointment and on 27th May, 30th June, 21st, 28th July, 2.30 - 5.30 p.m. • Entrance: £1, children free

This property, which used to be part of an old orchard, was acquired as a building plot in the early seventies. The garden has been more than 16 years in the making and under the care of compulsive plant lovers now surrounds the house in a delightful variety of colour and shape. Although described as a 'plantsman's garden' this is much more than just a collector's display, and should give pleasure to any gardener who, like the owners, cannot resist acquiring plants simply for the love of their infinite variety.

SANDFORD ORCAS MANOR 33

Nr Sherborne, Dorset. Tel: (096322) 206
Sir Mervyn Medlycott, Bart.

2½m N of Sherborne, turning off B3148, next to village church • Parking • Toilet facilities • Dogs on lead • House open • Garden open Easter Mon, 10 a.m. - 6 p.m., then May to Sept, Sun, 2 - 6 p.m. and Mon, 10 a.m. - 6 p.m. • Entrance: £1.50, children 70p (house and garden). Pre-booked parties of 10 or more at reduced rates on other days if preferred

Looked at purely as a garden, Sandford Orcas is not exceptional. An old, flagged path slopes up between bordered lawns towards an open field. The stone walls at either side are attractive enough, but they stop suddenly at the wire fence and the view lacks a frame and a focal point. There is a herb garden with small box-bordered beds and a pleasant view across a lower lawn along the south side of the house. At the end of this lawn another viewpoint back towards the south front allows the attractive planting below the herb garden to show at its best. Roses and other climbing plants clinging to the honey-grey walls harmonize well with this gracious setting. It is the house, ancient and redolent of its long history, which permeates the scene and transforms the garden. On its own the visitor might enjoy but remain unmoved by the garden; but to see house and garden in perfect harmony on a warm summer's day is a pleasure not to be lightly foregone.

SHEPHERD'S COTTAGE 34

Whatcombe, Nr Blandford, Dorset. Tel: (0258) 880190
Rev. and Mrs R. East

5m SW of Blandford. Take A354 to Winterborne Whitchurch, at the bottom of the hill take the road to Winterborne Stickland. After 1m, take sharp left on bend, then immediately right along Forestry Commission road • Parking • Toilet facilities • Suitable for wheelchairs • Dogs • Open by appointment only

This is a tiny jewel of a garden decorating a 300 year-old thatched cottage which nestles into a green parkland valley. Seen on a sunny autumn afternoon, this colourful plot is radiant with the care and interest that have been lavished upon it. Informal beds of shrubs, herbaceous plants, winter heathers and foliage plants.

SHUTE HOUSE ★★ 35

Donhead St Mary, Shaftesbury, Dorset.
Lady Anne Tree

4m E of Shaftesbury, N off A30 on far side of village • Parking on road • Partly suitable for wheelchairs • Open 25th May, 2.30 – 5.30 p.m. • Entrance: £2, OAP £1, children 50p

Designed by Sir Geofffrey Jellicoe in the 1960s the beauty of Shute House garden depends entirely upon the water supplied by a bountiful spring. It is used throughout, in streams, in formal and informal pools, and above all in the 'Kashmiri' garden – the centrepiece of the design – where it falls from level to level over cascades arranged to vary the sound it makes; it runs through channels between octagonal pools, each with its own source so that the surface is never still; framed by grass and trees, reflecting and refracting the sunlight and culminating in a statue, beyond which are the fields and hills of open countryside. Vistas abound in this garden. There are statues to draw and satisfy the eye, varied and interesting trees to frame the view. Although there is colour particularly in spring, form is the key, in timberwork, in stone, in plant-entwined arches, in box-bordered flower beds, shaped pools and twisting paths. This theme is still being developed in a new area, where tall metal frames are to support ivy and other climbing plants in geometrical patterns. Even in the bog garden, perhaps the least ordered area, a primitive African figure enigmatically presides, and near to the house is an amusing 'bedroom' of clipped box, furnished with a dressing table and a four poster bed framed with climbing vines. Conceived with skill and wit, this is a garden not to be missed.

SMEDMORE HOUSE 36

Kimmeridge, Nr Wareham, Dorset.
Dr Philip Mansel

7m S of Wareham. Right off A351 at sign to Kimmeridge • Best season: June to July • Parking • Refreshments at post office in Kimmeridge • Toilet facilities • Suitable for wheelchairs • Dogs on lead • Plants for sale • House open • Garden open May to Sept, Wed, and 25th Aug for charity, 2.15 – 5.30 p.m. Also by appointment with the Administrator Major Peter James, Tel: (0929) 480719 • Entrance: 90p, children free (house and gardens £1.80, children 90p)

The gardens at Smedmore are of necessity either surrounded by walls or protected by screens of trees in order to mitigate the damage from sea winds. The mellow walls are admirably used to display many attractive and interesting climbing plants, including fine double mauve and white wisterias and the tender *Clianthus puniceus*, while among the trees are some splendid mature and unusual specimens. The large kitchen garden is now being prepared for use as a nursery. There are three very pretty small walled gardens as well, but the main pleasure at Smedmore is derived from the colourful principal garden with its air of age and tranquillity.

STICKY WICKET 37

Buckland Newton, Dorset. Tel: (03005) 476
Peter and Pam Lewis

11m from Dorchester and Sherborne, 2m E of A352 or take B3143 from Sturminster Newton. At T-junction midway between church and school • Parking in road • Refreshments • Toilet facilities • Partly suitable for wheelchairs • Plants for sale • Open 26th May to 8th Sept, Thurs, and 14th July, 14th, 15th Sept, 10.30 a.m. - 6 p.m. • Entrance: £1, children 50p

A design of concentric circles and radiating paths has enabled the creation of many separate beds showing different planting styles. A very fragrant and colourful display is enhanced by many unusual and/or variegated plants and bordered by species roses. The garden is designed to attract birds, butterflies and bees and to provide spectacular flowerheads for drying. There is a small pond and a wet area which is also attractive to wildlife. This is very much the garden of conservationist-minded plantlovers; plans are afoot to develop a white woodland area to carry the idea further. If the progress of recent years is maintained this garden is destined to become outstanding.

STOUR HOUSE 38

East Street, Blandford, Dorset. Tel: (0258) 452914
Mr T.S.B. Card

In Blandford, 100 yards from Market Place on the one-way system • Parking in town • Toilet facilities • Suitable for wheelchairs • Open 7th April, 14th July, 18th Aug, 2 - 6 p.m. • Entrance: 50p, children 20p

A wooden bridge of unusual design leads onto a long island set in the River Stour at the end of this garden. Mature trees and shrubs flourish on a lush green sward underplanted with massed spring bulbs. Walk westwards to the end of the island to enjoy a perfect view of the weir below a distant, graceful bridge. It is easy to imagine the romantic picnic parties that must have been held here in the past. The main garden has wide-bordered lawns with some interesting plants and shrubs, and an orchard and vegetable area. It might perhaps benefit by offering more interesting focal points, and needs some further screening from the presence of a supermarket and car park alongside, but the surprise and pleasure afforded by discovering such a pleasing, tranquil area in the heart of a busy market town makes this hidden garden well worth a visit.

14 UMBERS HILL 39

Shaftesbury, Dorset. Tel: (0747) 53312
Mrs K. Bellars

From Shaftesbury take B3091. Turn right into Breach Lane at small crossroads, then right into Umbers Hill • Best season: April to Sept • Parking • Toilet facilities • Open by appointment only • Entrance: 75p inc. tea and coffee

Mrs Bellars and her husband have created a garden worthy of the splendid position in which their bungalow was built more than 20 years ago. Although only a small plot it has shrubberies, beds and borders filled with thriving and well-chosen plants. There are over 50 varieties of clematis and also numerous stone sinks containing alpines and rockplants. (Mrs Bellars lectures frequently on these and other plants about which she is a recognised authority.) From the sunny terrace visitors can view 25 miles down the lovely Blackmore Vale.

WINCOMBE PARK 40

Shaftesbury, Dorset. Tel: (0747) 52161
The Hon Martin and Mrs Fortescue

2m from Shaftesbury signed to Wincombe off A350 to Warminster • Best season: summer • Parking • Teas • Toilet facilities • Dogs on lead • Unusual plants occasionally for sale • Open 9th June, 2 - 6 p.m., and to groups by appointment • Entrance: £1, children 25p

This is essentially a beautifully landscaped park. The house is set upon the side of a valley, screened behind tall trees and approached by a winding drive. There is a high bank beside the drive containing an interesting and well-judged selection of shrubs and small trees. Below and to the side of the house are small lawns and a walled kitchen-garden, itself worth a look. The borders are full of specimens to interest the plantsperson. But the real pleasure for the visitor lies in the wide, sloping lawn below the lake, and then up the steep wooded valley side beyond. In addition to the newly planted walled garden, the owners are heavily involved in removing and replacing the 1500 trees destroyed in winter storms around the valley. The garden alone would not justify a long detour but the whole ensemble is memorable.

GARDENS OPEN RARELY

The following gardens are open to the public on three days or less in the year, although they may also be open by appointment if this is stated in the text. For details see individual entry.

May 31 Frankham Farm; **April 7** North Leigh House; Stour House; **April 21** Boveridge Farm; **May 5** Culeaze; Dominey's Yard; Frankham Farm; North Leigh House; **May 6** Culeaze; **May 12** Boveridge Farm; Kesworth; Moulin Huet; **May 19** Cannings Court; Kesworth; Moulin Huet; **May 25** Shute House; **May 26** Charlton Cottage; **June 9** Charlton Cottage; Wincombe

Park; **June 16** Boveridge Farm; **June 23** Frankham Farm; **June 29** The Manor House; **June 30** Cannings Court; The Manor House; **July 14** Dominey's Yard; Stour House; **July 21** Cannings Court; **Aug 4** North Leigh House; **Aug 11** Dominey's Yard; **Aug 18** Stour House.

DURHAM

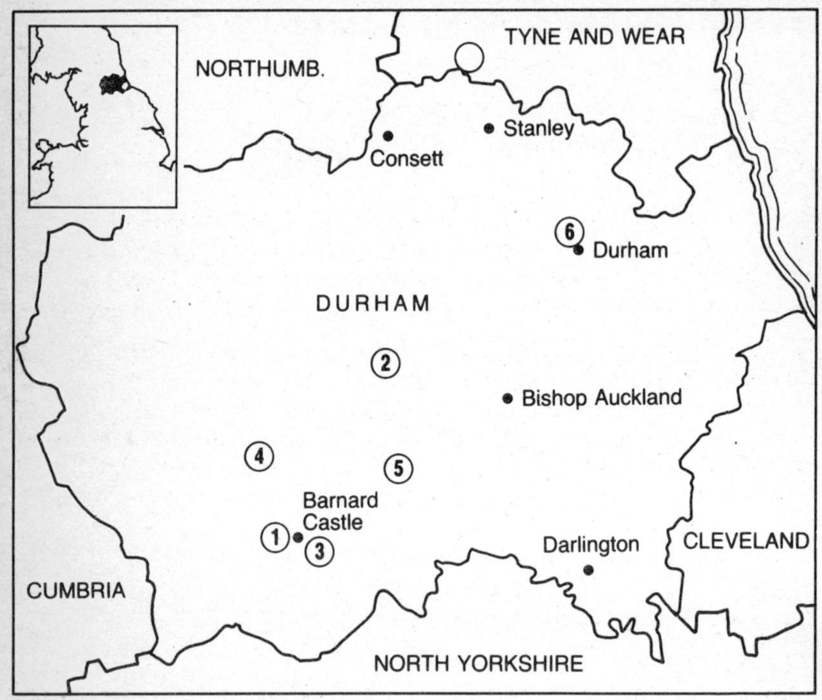

BARNINGHAM PARK 1

Barningham, Barnard Castle, Co. Durham. Tel: (0833) 21202
Sir Anthony Milbank

10m NW of Scotch Corner off A66 at A66 Motel crossroads • Parking • Teas • Partly suitable for wheelchairs • Plants for sale • Open 2nd June, 26th July, 15th, 22nd Sept, 2 - 6 p.m. • Entrance: £1, children 50p

Predominantly a woodland garden, continuing to be developed by the present owner, this has interesting walks and good stands of specimen trees. A garden for recreation rather than serious horticultural study.

BEDBURN HALL GARDENS 2

Hamsterley, Bishop Auckland, Co. Durham. Tel: (038888) 231
Mr I. Bonas

9m NW of Bishop Auckland. W off A68 at Witton-le-Wear. 3m SE of Wolsingham off B6293 • Parking • Teas • Partly suitable for wheelchairs • Plants for sale • Open by appointment and as advertised on certain days in summer, 2 - 6 p.m. • Entrance: £1, children 25p

A medium-sized terraced garden, largely developed by the present owner, it is beautifully situated by Hamsterley Forest. The garden is dominated by a lake with associated rhododendrons and bamboos. A new conservatory contains figs, bougainvilleas, passion flowers and other exotics. Woodland.

BOWES MUSEUM GARDENS ★ 3

Barnard Castle, Co. Durham. Tel: (0833) 690606
Durham County Council

From Barnard Castle E on the road towards Westwick • Best season: spring/summer • Parking • Refreshments: coffee, lunch, teas in museum restaurant and picnic areas all during summer • Toilet facilities • Suitable for wheelchairs • Shop in museum • Open daily, dawn – dusk • Entrance: free

The formal gardens reflect the grandeur of the museum buildings (built in the 1870s) which are like a large French chateau. The parterre has been recut in the style of the seventeenth century using elaborate shapes formed by box hedges and coloured gravels. The nineteenth-century tradition is continued by planting a succession of flowers during the spring and summer months and the whole impression is of a period-piece. Bowls and tennis facilities available.

EGGLESTON HALL GARDENS 4

Eggleston, Barnard Castle, Co. Durham. Tel: (0833) 50378
Mrs W.T. Gray

5m NW of Barnard Castle on B6278 • Parking • Catering for parties can be arranged • Partly suitable for wheelchairs • Plants for sale • Shop at house on weekdays only by prior arrangement • Open daily, 10 a.m. – 5 p.m. • Entrance: £1, children 50p

The current garden was developed by the present owner within the framework of an older garden that, apart from mature trees and an original walled garden, retains little of its early identity. It is largely informal with an excellent collection of unusual plants and flowers suitable for floral art. Extensive lawns and a kitchen garden run on organic lines to produce ingredients for the cookery courses run at the Hall. Interesting cool greenhouse.

RABY CASTLE GARDENS 5

Staindrop, Co. Durham. Tel: (0833) 60202
The Rt Hon. The Lord Barnard

1m N of Staindrop on A688 Barnard Castle – Bishop Auckland road • Parking • Teas • Toilet facilities • Partly suitable for wheelchairs • House open (extra charge) • Gardens open 30th April to June, Sat – Wed. July to Sept, daily except Sat. Bank Holiday weekends, 11 a.m. – 5.30 p.m. • Entrance: 80p, OAP and children 60p

This formal garden dating from the mid-eighteenth century was designed by Thomas White, 2nd Earl of Darlington, and has a wide array of trees, shrubs and herbaceous plants. The garden walls from locally hand-made bricks have flues which used to enable sub-tropical fruits to be grown on the south terrace. The famous white Ischia fig tree brought to Raby in 1768 still survives. Rose garden, shrub borders, original yew hedges and ornamental pond.

UNIVERSITY OF DURHAM BOTANIC GARDEN ★ 6

Hollingside Lane, Durham, Co. Durham. Tel: (091) 3742670
Durham University

1m from centre of Durham City. Turn off A167 at Cock O' The North roundabout towards the city for 1m, garden off Hollingside Lane • Parking • Toilet facilities • Partly suitable for wheelchairs • Open April to Oct, Mon - Fri, 10 a.m. - 12 noon, 2 - 4 p.m., Sat, Sun and Bank Holidays, 2 - 4 p.m., Nov - March, Mon - Fri, 10 a.m. - 12 noon, Sat and Sun except Christmas week, 2 - 4 p.m. • Entrance: free

Established in 1970 as a centre for botanical study, this is now one of the few botanical gardens in the north of England. It contains fine labelled collections, especially of trees and shrubs, and conducts basic research into many aspects of the plant kingdom. There are demonstrations of major forest systems and cactus and tropical greenhouses. A garden for the keen plant lover rather than the landscape designer. On economic grounds, some of its previous collections and features have been rationalized.

ESSEX

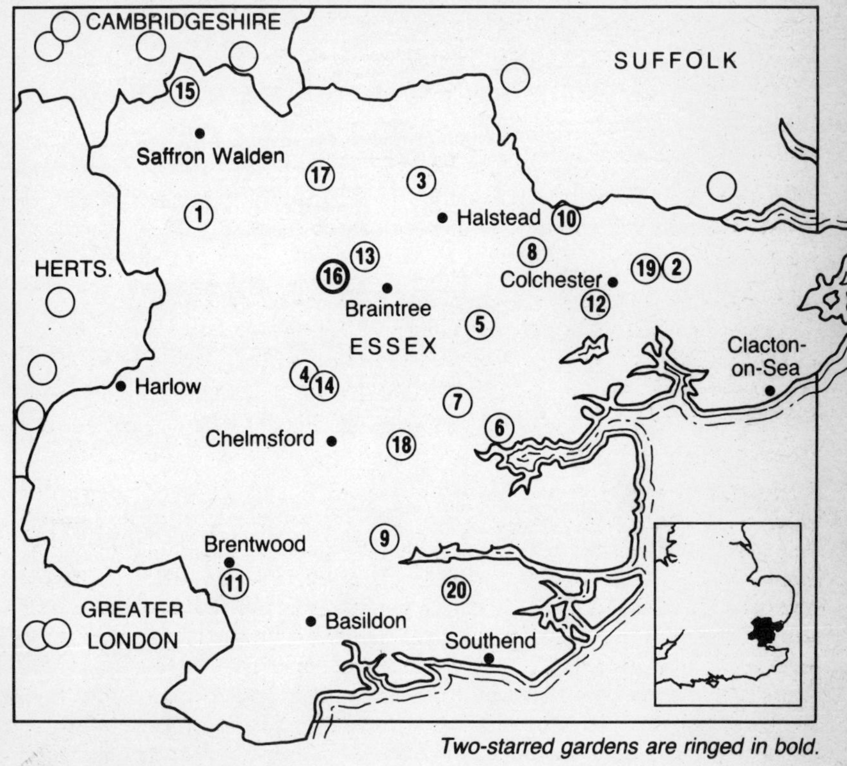

Two-starred gardens are ringed in bold.

AMBERDEN HALL 1

Widdington, Nr Saffron Walden, Essex. Tel: (0799) 40402
Mr and Mrs D. Lloyd

6m from Saffron Walden. E off B1383 near Newport, follow signs to Mole Hall Wildlife Park, ½m past park on right • Parking • Teas • Toilet facilities • Suitable for wheelchairs • Open 14th July, 2 - 6 p.m. • Entrance: £1, children free

Some lovely old walls enclose this medium-sized garden set at one side of a fine house. A pair of life-sized lead giraffes greet you as you step through the gate. The borders are well designed, so that not all the garden is visible at once. All are planted in specific colours - the red border being the newest with roses, dahlias, hemerocallis, etc. The walls are covered in a variety of climbers, many rare, like *Trachelospermum jasminoides*. To hide a barn roof, a Leylandii hedge has been clipped with a crenellated top. Good vegetable garden. Mrs Lloyd has plans to extend the garden beyond the walls with an avenue of different ivies grown up stakes.

THE BETH CHATTO GARDENS ★ (2)

Elmstead Market, Colchester, Essex. Tel: (0206) 822007
Mrs Beth Chatto

¼m E of Elmstead Market on A133 • Parking • Toilet facilities • Plants for sale in nursery adjoining gardens. • Open March to Oct, Mon - Sat, 9 a.m. - 5 p.m., Nov to Feb, Mon - Fri, 9 a.m. - 4 p.m. Closed Bank Holidays. Groups by arrangement. • Entrance: £1, children free

Beth Chatto, the Gertrude Jekyll of today, designed this garden in the 1960s from a neglected hollow which was either boggy and soggy or exceedingly dry. She, more than anyone else, has influenced gardeners by her choice of plants for any situation - dry, wet or shady - and her ability to show them off to perfection. The planting of her garden is a lesson to every gardener on how to use both leaf and flower to best advantage.

CRACKNELLS ★ 3

Great Yeldham, Essex. Tel: (0787) 237370
Mr and Mrs T. Chamberlain

Off A604 between Halstead and Haverhill • Parking • Suitable for wheelchairs • Open by appointment • Entrance by charity box donation

Mr Chamberlain started contouring this large garden even before he started building his house. The garden rolls away from the house down to the lake, also excavated at the start. This is not a garden in the accepted sense but 'a garden picture painted with trees', to use Mr Chamberlain's own words. He has collected trees from all over the country and has an impressive collection. Here is the rare cut-leaved beech, *Fagus sylvatica* var. *heterophylla* and its purple and pink-leaved forms, '*Rohanii*' and '*Roseomarginata*' as well as the variegated tulip tree *Liriodendron tulipifera* 'Aureomarginatum'. There are also collections of birches, acers, sorbus and oaks. If you are a lover of trees, make your pilgrimage.

FANNERS GREEN 4

Great Waltham, Nr Chelmsford, Essex. Tel: (0245) 360035
Dr and Mrs T.M. Pickard

4m N of Chelmsford. Take A130 from Chelmsford to Great Waltham, turn left into South Street, opposite Six Bells pub. Drive 1¼m • Limited parking • Plants for sale • Open 12th, 13th May, 9th, 10th June, 7th, 8th July (Suns and Mons), 2 - 6 p.m. • Entrance: 60p, children 30p

Mrs Pickard is a garden designer and it certainly shows in this small country garden. Here are compartments in miniature with hedges of thuya and beech, each compartment having a different theme. The vegetable garden is divided by paths into tiny squares with vegetables grown for their decorative qualities as well as their culinary uses. There is a large range of plants and shrubs, including a half-standard purple-leaved sambucus, a herb garden and a well-kept conservatory.

FEERINGBURY MAJOR ★ 5

Coggeshall Road, Feering, Essex. Tel: (0376) 561946
Mr and Mrs Giles Coode-Adams

On B1024 between Coggeshall and Feering • Parking • Suitable for wheelchairs • Open May and June, weekdays, 9 a.m. - 1 p.m. and by appointment • Entrance: £1.50

For all its size (seven acres) and variety this is a peaceful garden. The large natural ponds are well planted with rare and unusual bog plants - gunneras and primulas, blue and yellow meconopsis, and kirengeshomas. There are fine trees, shrub borders and a long 'old rose' border backed up by a wall with clematis and honeysuckles growing up it. Clematis are Mr Coode-Adams' speciality. Here are many exciting plants tucked into corners, by walls or on the terrace.

FOLLY FAUNTS HOUSE 6

Goldhanger, Maldon, Essex. Tel: (0621) 88213
Mr and Mrs J.C. Jenkinson

On B1026 between Maldon and Colchester • Parking • Teas • Toilet facilities • Suitable for wheelchairs • Dogs on lead • Plants for sale • Open 9th, 13th, 23rd, 27th June, 2 - 5 p.m. and by appointment for coach parties • Entrance £1, children 50p

A large five-acre garden, created by the owner in the last 27 years, divided into compartments each with a different theme. A hedge of *Hypericum* 'Hidcote' makes a splash of colour next to the large pond. Mr Jenkinson is fond of the Japanese wineberry which is planted or has seeded in different parts of the garden. Its red prickly stems and edible fruit make an unusual feature. The latest venture has been the planting of five avenues of trees radiating from the drive - here, in contrast, is a purple-leaved acer and *Betula albo-sinensis*.

GLEN CHANTRY 7

Wickham Bishops, Nr Witham, Essex. Tel: (0621) 891342
Mr and Mrs W.G. Staines

SE of Witham. Turn left off B1018 towards Wickham Bishops. Cross River Blackwater bridge and turn left up track by Blue Mills • Parking • Teas • Toilet facilities • Suitable for wheelchairs • Large range of unusual plants for sale • Open 21st April, 5th, 19th May, 2nd, 16th, 30th June, 14th, 28th July, 25th Aug, 8th, 29th Sept, 2 - 5 p.m. • Entrance: 75p, children 35p

This large undulating garden has been created by the owners since 1977. The huge informally-shaped borders are filled with a variety of plants and colours. Kniphofia 'Little Maid' was looking pretty, mixed with monardas, eryngiums, roses and hemerocallis. The unusual *Stokesia laevis* 'Blue Star' was particularly noticeable. Large rock gardens and a stream with waterfalls running through them to a pond make a dominant feature amongst the very wide selection of herbaceous plants and heather and conifer beds.

HILL HOUSE 8

Chappel, Nr Colchester, Essex. Tel: (0787) 222428
Mr and Mrs R. Mason

On A604 between Colchester and Earl's Colne • Limited parking • Plants for sale • Open by appointment • Entrance: by donation to charity box

This is a large garden at the beginning of its life. It has been designed by the owners on formal lines using yew hedging and walls to create vistas. A mixed planting of tough native trees, sorbus and hawthorn, etc. has been established as a windbreak. A new lime avenue is the latest addition – sited to lead the eye out into the country. The pond area will be planted next. The bones of the garden are now in place including urns, statues and seats. All the colour and secondary planting will come next. In a small courtyard, reminiscent of a London garden, is a raised pool planted only with green-leaved plants and white flowers.

HYDE HALL GARDEN ★ 9

Rettendon, Nr Chelmsford, Essex. Tel: (0245) 400256
Hyde Hall Garden Trust

7m SE of Chelmsford, signposted from A130 and A132 • Parking • Light refreshments • Toilet facilities • Suitable for wheelchairs • Dogs on lead • Plants for sale • Open Good Fri to Oct, Sun, Wed and Bank Holidays, 11 a.m. – 6 p.m. Open at other times by appointment • Entrance: £1.50, OAP £1, children free

This is a huge garden containing many different collections of plants. There is a comprehensive rose garden showing both bedding roses and climbers. There are large borders filled with a variety of shrubs including magnolias and the NCCPG collections of viburnums and malus. The greenhouses are well kept and colourful. Near them are containers, urns, pots and troughs planted with pelargoniums and helichrysum, also great mounds of *Chrysanthemum frutescens* now called *Argyranthemum frutescens*, phormiums and felicias. There is a newly-planted area, in hedge 'bays', in specific colour schemes. Good ponds and trees.

LOWER DAIRY HOUSE 10

Little Horkesley, Colchester, Essex. Tel: (0206262) 220
Mr and Mrs D.J. Burnett

7m N of Colchester off A134. Left at bottom of hill before Nayland Village, into Water Lane. Garden ½m on left after farm buildings • Parking • Teas • Toilet facilities • Plants for sale • Open by appointment and 30th, 31st March, 1st, 13th, 14th April, 4th to 6th, 25 to 27th May inc., 1st, 2nd, 22nd, 23rd, 29th, 30th June, 2 - 6 p.m. • Entrance: £1, children 50p

This immaculately-kept garden of one and a half acres is a riot of colour. Mrs Burnett fills any spaces in between the perennials with annuals - marigolds and larkspur and geraniums - all old-fashioned plants. Many unusual plants intermix with cottage garden varieties, including a good selection of cistus, diascias and other sun lovers. There is a newly-created pond where the thick planting consists of primulas, hostas and mimulus. A bridge crosses to a path which runs along the bank, much loved by the children who visit the garden.

THE MAGNOLIAS 11

18 St Johns Avenue, Brentwood, Essex. Tel: (0277) 220019
Mr and Mrs R.A. Hammond

From A1023 turn S to A128. After 300 yards turn right at traffic lights, over railway bridge. St Johns Avenue is third on right • Restricted parking • Teas • Plants for sale • Open 31st March, 14th, 28th April, 5th, 12th, 26th May, 9th June, 14th July, 11th, 25th Aug, 8th Sept, 13th Oct, 2 - 5 p.m. Certain other days and parties by appointment • Entrance: 70p, children 30p

This fascinating half-acre plantsman's garden illustrates what can be achieved in a small space. Lawns are minimal. Paths wind through jungle-like borders filled with acers, camellias and magnolias underplanted with smaller shrubs and ground-cover plants. There is a large collection of hostas and unusual and rare bamboos. Mr Hammond also keeps the National collection of Arisaemas. Some huge koi live in raised pools and turtles swim happily in their greenhouse. Something of interest here at any time of the year.

OLIVERS ★ 12

Olivers Lane, Colchester, Essex. Tel: (0206) 330575
Mr and Mrs David Edwards

3m SW of Colchester between B1022 and B1026 (signposted). From Colchester via B1022 Maldon Road turn left at Leather Bottle pub miniroundabout into Gosbeck's Road, right into Olivers Lane • Parking • Teas • Toilet facilities • Suitable for wheelchairs • Plants for sale • Open May to July, Wed, 2 - 5 p.m., also 11th, 12th May and 30th June, 2 - 6 p.m. Other times and parties by appointment • Entrance: £1, children free

The moment you drive down to the attractive Georgian-fronted house and step on to the large York paved terrace, beautifully planted in soft sympathetic colours, you are entranced. Around you are 20 acres of garden and woodland in fine condition. From the terrace you look down over lawn, pools and woods to a natural meadow (cut only to encourage wild flowers and grasses) and to trees bordering the river. A 'willow pattern' bridge crosses the first of a succession of pools which drop down to an ancient fish pond. *Taxodium distichum*, metasequoia and ginkgo flourish by the pools. There are yew hedges and the delightful woodland walk. Here mature native trees shelter rhododendrons, azaleas and shrub roses in the rides.

PANFIELD HALL 13

Nr Braintree, Essex. Tel: (0376) 24512
Mr and Mrs R. Newman

2m from Braintree. N off A120 through Great Saline, right to Panfield, through village and right into Hall Road • Parking • Cream teas • Toilet facilities • Suitable for wheelchairs • Dogs on lead • Plants for sale occasionally • Open 14th July, 2 - 6 p.m. • Entrance: £1, OAP and children 50p

This four-acre garden surrounding an old house (1520) has been restored in the last six years. There are plans for further development. The rose garden is completed. Leading from there is a pergola with laburnum, wisterias and clematis already looking established. Crossing the bridge over the ponds is a sunken garden near the house, box-edged, with rose 'Little White Pet' and soft-coloured ground-cover. There is a box and topiary maze here too. The long formal canal-like pool and statue are in memory of Mr Newman's parents. The clipped box crowns add to the formality. Herbaceous borders due to be replanted for 1991.

PARK FARM 14

Chatham Hall Lane, Great Waltham, Chelmsford, Essex.
Tel: (0245) 360871
Mr D. Bracey and Mrs J.E.M. Cowley

5m N of Chelmsford. Take A130 towards Braintree, on Little Waltham bypass left into Chatham Hall Lane • Parking • Teas • Toilet facilities • Plants for sale • Open May to July, Sun, and 13th, 20th, 27th May, 10th, 17th, 24th June, 8th, 15th July, 2 - 6 p.m. • Entrance: 75p, children 30p

Mrs Cowley immediately infects the visitor with her enthusiasm and energy. She is still creating her two-acre garden on the site of an old farmyard. Each part of her garden is different. A small copse by the drive leads to raised borders for plants that like hot dry conditions, which in turn lead back to the house. The garden surrounds the house and is divided up by hedges. Climbing roses cover the trees. The difficult *Romneya coulteri* mingles happily with other herbaceous plants. Shrub roses abound as they are special favourites. There are vistas and cross vistas all cleverly combined to lead you on. After visiting China and getting some cuttings (legally) Mrs Cowley has made her own Chinese garden. Giant hogweed and *Crambe cordifolia* fight over the pool.

REED HOUSE 15

Manor Lane, Great Chesterford, Saffron Walden, Essex.
Tel: (0799) 30312
Mrs Felicity Mason

11m S of Cambridge, 4m N of Saffron Walden, 1m S of Stump Cross M11 junction. On B184 turn into Chesterford High Street. Turn left at Crown and Thistle public house in Manor Lane • Open by appointment and combined opening with Manor Farm nearby 7th July, 2 – 6 p.m. The owners of Manor Farm are Mr and Mrs W. Hamilton. Tel: (0799) 30279 • Entrance (to both) £1.75, children 50p

Mrs Mason moved to her present house only a few years ago, leaving a large garden crammed with treasures that used to be open to the public four times a year. Her new garden is a revelation as to what can be achieved in a short time. She designed the garden and planted everything herself. Features include sink gardens, koi carp in the pool, bulbs everywhere, clematis, a greenhouse bursting at its panes, and a new conservatory rapidly filling up with rare plants.

SALING HALL ★★ 16

Great Saling, Nr Braintree, Essex.
Mr and Mrs Hugh Johnson

6m NW of Braintree, halfway between Braintree and Dumnow on A120 turn N at the Saling Oak • Parking • Suitable for wheelchairs • Open for charity Weds in May, June and July, 2 – 5 p.m. and 30th June, 2 – 6 p.m. Parties by appointment • Entrance: £1, children free

The extensive planting of trees will interest any gardener. It includes oaks, pines, prunus, willows, birches, junipers, maples and other species suited to the chalky boulder clays and gravels. A row of tall Lombardy poplars leads up to the seventeenth-century manor house. But there is much to admire besides the trees. The old walled garden facing the new conservatory is exuberantly planted with shrubs, bulbs and herbaceous plants bordered by clipped juniper, cypress and box. There is a vegetable garden, a Japanese garden, a water garden (recently planted with gunnera, primulas, irises, etc.), a valley garden and a rose glade. This last is mainly dedicated to pink shrub roses, including *Rosa* 'Complicata', R. *soulieana* and R. *glauca* (*rubrifolia*).

SPAINS HALL 17

Finchingfield, Essex. Tel: (0371) 810266
Colonel Sir John Ruggles-Brise, Bart.

1m NW of Finchingfield. Signposted • Parking • Toilet facilities • Suitable for wheelchairs • Dogs on leads • House open by appointment • Garden open May to July, Sun, 2 - 5 p.m. • Entrance: 50p, children 25p

The flower garden by the charming Elizabethan house includes a large cedar of Lebanon, planted in 1670, with a spread of 186 feet. At each side of the sundial (made in 1799 by Adams, who also made those in the gardens of Buckingham Palace) are perpetually-flowering pink China roses 'Hermosa' from Sir Walter Gilbey's vineyard in France. The park (private) and kitchen garden were landscaped by Humphrey Repton in 1807, and walled in 1828. The greenhouse contains bougainvilleas brought from Sir John's sister's previous home in Kenya. The Chinese *Paulownia* occasionally produces its blue foxglove-shaped flowers.

STONE PINE ★ 18

Hyde Lane, Danbury, Chelmsford, Essex. Tel: (024 541) 3232
Mr and Mrs David Barker

E of Chelmsford 1m off A414 • Limited parking • Plants for sale occasionally • Open by appointment • Entrance by charity box

This small plantsman's garden is owned by the Chairman of the Hardy Plant Society. Mr Barker has filled it with choice and unusual plants. The area of grass is minimal and paths wind around borders crammed with trees, acers being particularly popular, and shrubs. Surprising plants appear around each corner like the rarely-seen *Paris quadrifolia*. Mr Barker is also knowledgeable on lilies, hemerocallis, hostas and grasses of all kinds. National reference collections of Epimedium and Japanese anemonies.

TYE FARM 19

Elmstead Market, Colchester, Essex. Tel: (0206) 222400
Mr and Mrs C. Gooch

2m from Colchester on A133, ½m before Elmstead Market • Parking • Teas • Open 29th, 30th June, 2 - 6 p.m. • Entrance: £1, children 50p

This one-acre garden is cleverly planted with hedges to make compartments to break the prevailing wind. There is a neat vegetable garden with espaliered peach trees, a white garden and over 60 varieties of old roses planted with spring-flowering or autumn-flowering shrubs. Outside the conservatory is a formally-planted area for herbs, box-edged. The conservatory has many unusual plants in it, including a lemon tree, a mature *Rhododendron fragrantissima*, a frangipani and a *Grevillea banksii*.

VOLPAIA ★ 20

54 Woodlands Road, Hockley, Essex. Tel: (0702) 203761
Mr and Mrs D. Fox

2¾m NE of Rayleigh. On B1013 Rayleigh - Rochford road, turn S from Spa Hotel into Woodlands Road • Limited parking • Teas • Open April to June, Thurs and Sun, 2.30 - 5.30 p.m. • Entrance: 70p, children 30p

Here is a garden for plant lovers - not a garden for lovers of massed colour. From the lawn at the rear of the house, paths lead into natural woodland of mature oak, hornbeam and birch where all kinds of rhododendron, camellia and magnolia have been planted and now flourish. *Davidia involucrata*, cornus and eucryphia flower in turn. Woodland plants seldom seen elsewhere are at home here: trilliums, uvularias, disporums, erythroniums and Solomon's seal. Corners have been cut back to allow lilies to flower in summer and the willow gentian in autumn. There is a bog garden where primulas, gunnera, ferns, and hostas and the skunk cabbage find the moisture they love.

GARDENS OPEN RARELY

The following gardens are open to the public on three days or less in the year, although they may also be open by appointment if this is stated in the text. For details see individual entry.

June 29 Tye Farm; **June 30** Tye Farm; **July 7** Reed House; **July 14** Amberden Hall; Panfield Hall.

GLOUCESTERSHIRE

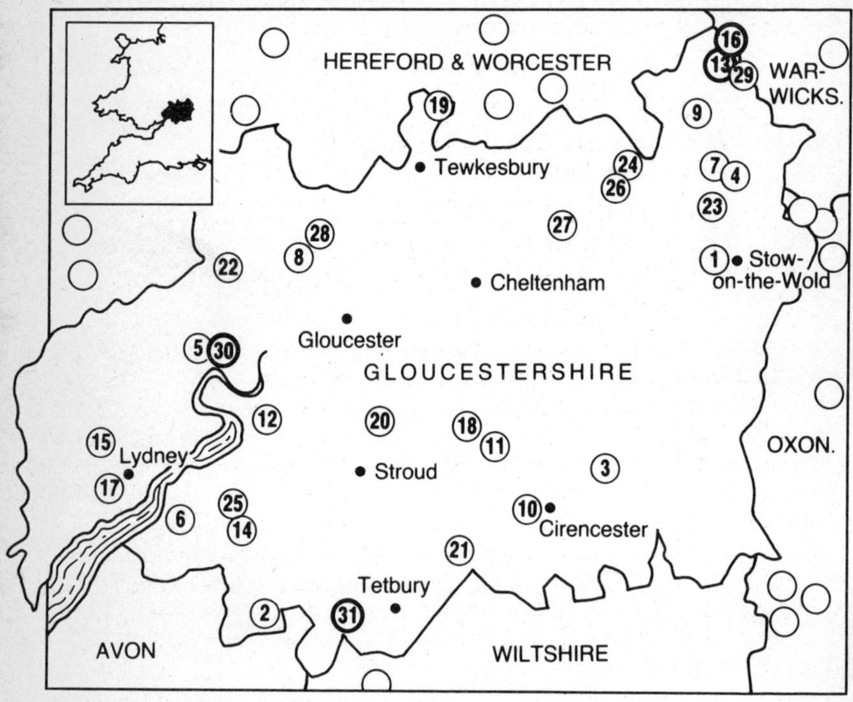

Plain circle numbers can be found by turning to neighbouring counties. Two-starred gardens are ringed in bold.

ABBOTSWOOD ★ 1

Stow-on-the-Wold, Gloucestershire. Tel: (0451) 30366
Dikler Farming Co

1m W of Stow-on-the-Wold on B4077 • Best season: spring • Parking free in grounds but no coaches. Coaches can drop passengers at top gate and park in Stow • Teas • Toilet facilities • Partly suitable for wheelchairs • Open 31st March, 14th, 28th April, 12th May, 1.30 - 6 p.m. • Entrance: £1.50, children free

The house is in one of the most beautiful of Cotswold settings. From the car park it is approached up a descending stream and pools, the woodland carpeted with spring flowers and bulbs, including one of the world's largest displays of fritillarias. The woods continue above and beyond the house and have been planted with rhododendrons, flowering shrubs and specimen trees. Near the house are formal gardens and terraces including a box-edged rose garden and a water garden. Extensive heather plantings. The house (not open) was formerly owned by Harry Ferguson, inventor of the modern tractor, who spent part of his considerable fortune developing the estate which has a somewhat park-like character. Nearby are the Swells, Cotswold villages renowned for their cottagey planting.

ALDERLEY GRANGE ★ 2

Alderley, Gloucestershire. Tel: (0453) 842161
Mr Guy and the Hon. Mrs Acloque

2m S of Wotton-under-Edge. Turn NW off A46 Bath - Stroud road at Dunkirk • Best season: April to July • Parking • Suitable for wheelchairs • Open 9th June, 2 - 6 p.m. and by appointment for parties during June • Entrance: £1, children free

Garden of exceptional beauty and character in tranquil walled setting, renowned for its collection of aromatic plants and scented flowers. Designed by Alvide Lees-Milne and believed to be the last garden in which Vita Sackville-West had a hand, Alderley Grange was acquired by the present owners in 1974 and has been immaculately maintained and developed with discretion and style. The fine house and a mulberry tree date from the seventeenth century; a pleached and arched lime walk leads to a series of enclosed gardens. There is a notable hexagonal herb garden with many delightful perspectives of clipped, trained or potted shrubs and trees. There are abundant plantings of old roses. Many tender and unusual subjects flourish in this cherished and exquisite space, which has been much photographed and drawn.

BARNSLEY HOUSE ★ 3

Barnsley, Gloucestershire. Tel: (028574) 281
Mrs Rosemary Verey

4m N of Cirencester on A433 in village of Barnsley • Parking, inc. coaches • Toilet facilities • Suitable for wheelchairs • Plants for sale • Open Mon, Wed, Thurs and Sat, 10 a.m. - 6 p.m. • Entrance: £2, OAP £1, children free. Dec to Feb no charge. Parties by appointment

A splendid small garden under three acres, but comprising many garden styles from the past, carefully blended by the Vereys since they acquired the house and garden in the early 1960s. The Queen Anne stone house is set in an array of small gardens and vistas that blend perfectly to give a harmonious overall effect. The standard of horticulture and maintenance is very high. Great attention has been given to colour and texture. The kitchen garden is a particular delight with numerous small beds, ornate paths, box hedges, trained fruit trees etc. This garden was the recipient of the Christie's Award for the Best Garden in 1988.

BATSFORD ARBORETUM ★ 4

Moreton-in-Marsh, Gloucestershire. Tel: (0386) 700409/(0608) 50722
The Batsford Foundation

1½m NW of Moreton-in-Marsh on A44 to Evesham. Opposite the entrance to Sezincote (see entry) • Best season: spring and autumn • Parking • Refreshments: coffees, light lunches and teas except Mons. Picnic area at garden centre • Toilet facilities • Dogs on lead in arboretum • Plants for sale at garden centre open all year 10 a.m. - 5 p.m. • Open April to Oct, daily, 10 a.m. - 5 p.m. • Entrance: £2, OAP and children £1

Over 1000 species of different trees in 50 acres of typical Cotswold countryside plus an unusual collection of exotic shrubs and bronze statues from the Far East, originally collected for the garden by Lord Redesdale. It was expanded into an arboretum by Lord Dulverton in the 1960s. For students, a guidebook gives the details, but everyone will enjoy the effects, particularly the autumn colours. Fine views of the house (not open). There is also a water garden, and, nearby, a falconry centre.

BELL HOUSE 5

Westbury-on-Severn, Gloucestershire. Tel: (0452) 76388
Mr and Mrs G.J. Linklater

9m S of Gloucester off A48, beside church close to Westbury Court Gardens • Refreshments • Toilet facilities • Suitable for wheelchairs • Plants for sale • Open 31st March, 1st, 14th April, 5th, 6th, 26th, 27th May, 16th June, 25th, 26th Aug, 8th Sept, 11 a.m. - 5 p.m. and by appointment • Entrance: £1, children 50p

Attractively laid-out two-acre mature garden in process of restoration and extension by present owners with help from their young family. The Bell House is near the village church and the garden contains mature trees, a stream, an interesting water garden and ponds. Established colonies of cyclamen, daffodils and fritillarias flourish among specimen shrubs and trees whose strong outlines and contrasting textures are now fulfilling the promise of a design laid out 50 years ago. The relaxed and welcoming atmosphere here is a pleasant complement to the prevailing sense of formality at nearby Westbury Court.

BERKELEY CASTLE 6

Berkeley, Gloucestershire. Tel: (0453) 810332
Mr R.J.G. Berkeley

W of M5 between junctions 13 and 14 just off A38 • Parking • Refreshments and picnic area • Toilet facilities • Shop • House open • Butterfly house • Open April, daily except Mon, 2 - 5 p.m., May to Sept, Tues - Sat, 11 a.m. - 5 p.m., Sun, 2 - 5 p.m., Oct, Sun, 2 - 4.30 p.m., Bank Holiday Mon, 11 a.m. -

5 p.m. • Entrance: £1, children 50p (castle and gardens £2.90, OAP £2.60, children £1.45). Special prices for parties

Apart from Windsor, Berkeley is the oldest inhabited castle in Britain. Its history, full of incident, includes the brutal murder of Edward II after his failure to succumb to the stench of putrefying carcasses in the dungeon below his prison room. The castle grounds remain the home of the Berkeley Hunt, distinguished by their yellow jackets since the eighteenth century when Berkeleys hunted their hounds to Charing Cross and back on their own land. An entertaining guided tour of the immaculately-maintained castle may be followed by a walk in the extensive parkland, with lovely views over gentle, unspoilt Gloucestershire landscape. There is an Elizabethan bowling lawn, a lily pond and terraced beds simply planted with many unusual shrubs and ramblers which tumble and climb against the imposing castle walls, their colours in the sun reminiscent of rose and lavender pot pourri.

BOURTON HOUSE 7

Bourton-on-the-Hill, Nr Moreton-in-Marsh, Gloucestershire.
Tel: (0386) 700121
Mr and Mrs R. Paice

2m W of Moreton-in-Marsh on A44 • Parking across road • Refreshments: DIY tea and coffee in historic barn • Toilet facilities • Suitable for wheelchairs • Open 23rd May to 26th Sept, Thurs, 12 noon – 5 p.m. • Entrance: £1.50, children free

This exceptionally handsome eighteenth-century Cotswold village house with fine views is enhanced by a medium-sized garden largely created under the present ownership. The diminutive geometrical *potager* is a particular delight. Well-kept lawns, quiet fountains, a knot garden in the making and Cotswold stone walls set off a number of herbaceous borders in which the choice and arrangement of plants and shrubs skilfully use current fashions in garden design. Nearby Sezincote and Batsford, and Hidcote as well as Kiftsgate less than half an hour away, make Bourton House a sensible location to include in garden touring in this part of Gloucestershire.

CAMP COTTAGE 8

Highleadon, Gloucestershire. Tel: (0452) 79352
Mr L.R. Holmes and Mr S. O'Neill

6m W of Gloucester. From Gloucester take A40 Ross road, turn right onto B4215 Newent road. 2½m along, turn right at sign for Upleadon (Highleadon garage on left side at turn). Cottage is 100 yards up lane on left hand side • Best season: May to July • Parking on main road outside • Refreshments: tea and soft drinks • Suitable for wheelchairs • Plants for sale • Open all year, Sun, and 31st March to Oct, Tues, Thurs and Bank Holidays, 2 – 6 p.m. or dusk • Entrance: 75p, children 25p

Picturesque seventeenth-century timbered cottage in a sheltered setting surrounded by richly-planted cottage garden. An extensive network of pergolas and arches bears a splendid collection of old roses, honeysuckles, unusual climbers and ramblers. Old-fashioned herbaceous plants and self-sown annuals pack every niche in the garden, whose rich river silt base supports prodigious colonies of opium and Welsh poppies. It is hard to believe that the present owners have built up this lavish, multi-tiered display only since 1988.

CHIPPING CAMPDEN GARDENS 9

Chipping Campden, Gloucestershire.

N of A44 between Evesham and Stow-on-the-Wold and S of Stratford-upon-Avon off A46 E of Broadway • Parking • Refreshments: ample facilities in town for all needs • Toilet facilities

Because of its position near Hidcote, Kiftsgate and Stratford the town is a popular holiday stopping-off point for garden visitors, so it is fortuitous that it has two small gardens frequently open. Mr and Mrs Lusty's is entered through their house The Martins in the main street which is itself next door to Mrs Lusty's interior decorating shop The Green Dragon and behind the butter market. It is a long, narrow town garden, with houses and a drive on one side, which has triumphed over its location by being cleverly designed to give surprises, informality, shelter and a wide variety of plants. Two levels are used, forming divisions with grass paths around small borders and beds. There is a splendid mulberry tree. Visitors are invited to contribute to an autistic charity, and the garden is open in the summer 'when it looks good' and is closed when it rains so check with the shop (0396) 840379.

Another town garden normally open during the year is the Ernest Wilson Memorial Garden, also in the High Street. It was opened in 1984 in memory of 'Chinese' Wilson, who was born in Chipping Campden in 1876. The famous collector is estimated to have introduced 1200 species of trees and shrubs during his career and the garden includes several of his finds including *Acer griseum*, the paperbark maple, *Davidia involucrata*, the handkerchief tree, and the plant for which he wished to be remembered, the *Lilium regale*. It is a peaceful oasis, with seats and shade, backed by the beautiful church tower. Admission is free with a box for contributions to its upkeep set in the stone wall beside the entrance arch.

Other gardens in Campden and neighbouring Broad Campden are open for charity and for the past three years a charity has arranged for 30 gardens to open over a June weekend. This will probably become an annual event. The choice of gardens appears to have been dictated by a desire for quantity rather than quality, and in general their appeal will be to those who like what is now called the traditional Cotswold style.

One of the pleasantest hotel gardens is to be found in the centre of the town, behind the King's Arms, where food and drink is served in the summer.

CIRENCESTER GARDENS 10

Cecily Hill, Cirencester, Gloucestershire. Tel: see below

On W side of Cirencester, leading up to entrance to Cirencester Park • Parking • Teas • Toilet facilities • Partly suitable for wheelchairs • Plants for sale on 14th July • Open: 38 Cecily Hill: 9th, 16th, 23rd, 30th June, 7th, 14th, 21st, 28th July, 4th, 11th, 18th Aug, 2 - 5.30 p.m. (except 14th July when 2 - 6 p.m.). Also by appointment May to Sept. 42 Cecily Hill: 9th, 16th, 23rd June, 14th, 21st July, 11th, 18th Aug, 2 - 5.30 p.m. (except 14th July when 2 - 6 p.m.). Cecily Hill House: 14th July only, 2 - 6 p.m.

The grandest garden in the town, Cirencester Park, is usually only open once a year in aid of charity but the park is open all the year round, courtesy of Earl Bathurst. Three gardens in Cecily Hill are open occasionally for charity and one of them, the most publicised in the media, is at No 38. For those who like to see a garden full of flowers and colour this could be their Mecca, although another name would be more appropriate as it is owned by Mr and Mrs John Beck. Entered through the house is a small walled garden of great interest, but beyond this and concealed from view is a long low flower garden with some 500 perennials including many varieties of geranium. Mrs Beck is pleased to open the garden by appointment, (0285) 653778. One of the other gardens open, Cecily Hill House, has a small ornamental kitchen garden of original design and unusual vegetables. Five to ten minutes walk from Cecily Hill at 20 St Peter's Road is a tiny 70 foot garden entirely without grass, with a small rockery, cascade and pond and 18 varieties of clematis which would be of considerable interest to anyone having to design for such a small space. Meg and Jeff Blumson open by appointment as well as their charity Sun openings twice in the summer. Telephone (0285) 657696.

COTSWOLD FARM 11

Duntisbourne Abbots, Gloucestershire. Tel: (0285) 653856
Major and Mrs P.D. Birchall

5m N of Cirencester on A417; signed immediately W of Five Mile House Inn • Best season: May to July • Parking at house • Refreshments by appointment • Toilet facility • Open by appointment • Entrance: £1.50

Mature garden planted in grand style and sustained with sensitive artistry surrounding fine old house in superb Cotswold setting. Formal walled gardens with pools and planted with shrub roses, lavender and a collection of scented flowers. Established plantings of shrubs, herbaceous plants and many small treasures overlooking an unspoilt wooded valley. A charmed garden redolent of another age in a remote and lovely situation.

FRAMPTON COURT 12

Frampton-on-Severn, Gloucestershire. Tel: (0452) 740219
Mrs Peter Clifford

SW of Gloucester near Stonehouse, 2m from M5 junction 13. Signposted. Left hand side of village green, entrance through imposing gates in long wall between two large chestnut trees • Best season: May to Sept • Parking • Refreshments in village hall on selected days • Suitable for wheelchairs • House open by appointment. £2.50 • Garden open all year by appointment • Entrance: 50p

Home of the lady artists who painted *The Frampton Flora*, Frampton Court remains an elegant family establishment on land owned by the Clifford family since the twelfth century. The house, dating from the 1730s, is of the Vanburgh School, with exquisite interior woodwork and furnishings which may be shown by appointment to visitors, preferably in parties, by the present owner Mrs Peter Clifford. The five-acre grounds are maintained with a minimum of labour and contain a lake, fine trees and a formal water garden of Dutch design, believed to have been built by the architects of the larger Westbury Court Garden on the other side of the Severn. A Strawberry Hill Gothic Orangery (not open but available for letting) where the ladies are believed to have executed their work, stands reflected in the still water, planted with lilies and flanked by a mixed border. This garden is open in association with that of Frampton Manor, also occupied by Cliffords, where a strongly-planted walled garden with many old roses is splendidly set off by a fine fifteenth-century timbered house.

HIDCOTE MANOR GARDEN ★★ 13

Hidcote Bartrim, Chipping Campden, Gloucestershire.
Tel: (0386) 438333
The National Trust

Follow signposts from Chipping Campden or Mickleton near Stratford-upon-Avon • Parking but coaches by prior arrangement • Refreshments: café for morning coffee, licensed light lunches, teas 11 a.m. - 5 p.m. Party bookings. No picnics. • Toilet facilities • Partly suitable for wheelchairs • Plants for sale • Shop • Open 30th March to Oct, daily except Tues and Fri, 11 a.m. - 8 p.m. Last admission 7 p.m. or 1 hour before sunset if earlier • Entrance: £3.80, family (2 adults and up to 4 children) £10.45

It is unnecessary to describe this garden in detail, one of the most famous in Britain and an essential visit for garden lovers of every persuasion. Created by Lawrence Johnston in the early years of the twentieth century, the original condition of the site may be judged from the early photographs in the entrance area. Johnston had a strong sense of design and great skill in planting, using mainly nineteenth-century specimens. Many varieties now bear the name Hidcote. Given to the National Trust in 1948, its splendid architectural effects and bold plantings have been retained, although these days some visitors are offended by the use of annuals. Johnston's achievement is all the more remarkable because of the isolation of the hill-top site whose scale can be appreciated by the view from the entrance to Kiftsgate garden which is within walking distance (see entry). See also Vale House.

HUNTS COURT 14

North Nibley, Dursley, Gloucestershire. Tel: (0453) 547440
Mr and Mrs T.K. Marshall

2m NW of Wotton-under-Edge nr North Nibley. Turn E off B4060 in Nibley at the Black Horse Inn and fork left after ¼m • Best season: June • Parking • Teas on Suns only • Toilet facilities • Suitable for wheelchairs • Plants for sale • Open all year except Aug, Tues - Sat, 2 - 6 p.m. Also for charities on last four Suns in June and first one in July and by appointment • Entrance: £1

An informal garden next to a nursery and working farm, designed to show off a fine collection of more than 400 varieties of old roses, climbers, species and shrubs. In June, there is a stunning display of fully grown climbers cascading from old apple trees.

JASMINE HOUSE 15

Bream, Nr Lydney, Gloucestershire. Tel: (0594) 563688
Mr V.M. Bond

W of the Severn estuary, 3m N of Lydney. At Bream Maypole Garage turn right to Park End. Immediately after crossroads, turn right by insurance office. House is 200 yards on left • Best season: summer • Parking in village only • Plants for sale • Open all year by appointment. Easter to Sept, Thurs, 2 - 5 p.m. • Entrance: 50p, children free

A plantsman's garden developed over the last few years, virtually from scratch, on a three quarters of an acre cottage garden. Naturally there are cottage plants but the main interest is the alpines, heathers and fuchsias. There are many species of herbaceous plants. Among the fruit trees in the orchard are 'beds' - small wild gardens of differing types. Not far away is Lydney Park, a rather grand garden at its most spectacular in spring (see entry).

KIFTSGATE COURT ★★ 16

Chipping Campden, Gloucestershire. Tel: (0386) 438777
Mr and Mrs A.H. Chambers

3m NE of Chipping Campden and near Mickleton. Kiftsgate is next to Hidcote Manor which is signposted • Parking • Plants for sale • Open 30th March to Sept, Wed, Thurs, Sun, 2 - 6 p.m. Also Bank Holiday Mons (NB not identical opening times with Hidcote) • Entrance: £2.20, children 80p

The house was built mid-nineteenth century on this magnificent site surrounded by three steep banks. The garden was largely created by the present owner's grandmother who with her husband moved there after World War I. Her work was continued by her daughter, Diana Binny, who made a few alterations but continued the colour schemes of the borders. In spring, the white sunken garden is covered with bulbs and there is a fine show of daffodils along the drive. June and July are the peak months for colour and scent but the magnificent old and species roses are the glory of this garden, home of *Rosa* 'Kiftsgate'. Other features are perennial geraniums, a large wisteria and many species of hydrangea, some very large. In autumn, Japanese maples glow in the bluebell wood. This garden should not be missed, not only because of its proximity to Hidcote, but because of its profusion of colour and apparent informality. Unusual plants are sometimes amongst those available for sale. See also Vale House.

LYDNEY PARK GARDENS 17

Lydney, Gloucestershire. Tel: (0594) 42844
Lord Bledisloe

20m SW of Gloucester. N of A48 between Lydney and Aylburton • Parking • Refreshments: teas. Picnics in deer park • Toilet facilities • Partly suitable for wheelchairs • Dogs on lead • Shrubs for sale • Shop • Roman site and museum open • Gardens open Easter Sun and Mon. Every Sun, Bank Holiday and Wed from 31st March to 9th June and daily, 26th May to 2nd June, 11 a.m. - 6 p.m. Parties by appointment in season • Entrance: £1.50 except Wed when £1. Car and accompanied children free

The park dates back to the seventeenth century and although it has been in the hands of one family since 1723, a new house was built in 1875 and the old one demolished. A new start was made on the garden in 1950 when the terrace was paved and a line of *Chamae cyparis Lawsoniana* 'Kilmacurragh' planted to frame the view. An area near the house has an interesting collection of magnolias but the most picturesque sight is the bank of daffodils and cherries, splendid in season. From 1957, a determined attempt has been made to plant rhododendrons and azaleas in the wooded valley, behind and below the house, with the aim of achieving bold colour at different times between March and June. Near the entrance to the main part of the gardens there is a small pool surrounded by azaleas and a collection of acers. From here the route passes through carefully-planted groups of rhododendron and by a folly, brought from Venice as recently as 1961. This overlooks a valley and bog garden. Criss-crossing the hillside, there are rare and fine rhododendrons and azaleas, including an area planted with un-named seedlings. Enormous effort has gone into the plant design, colour combination and general landscaping, and those who are enthusiastic about rhododendrons, azaleas and camellias will find enough to enjoy for a whole day. Another interest for visitors is the Roman camp, excavated by Sir Mortimer Wheeler, and the museum which contains the famous bronze Lydney Dog, one of the finest pieces of Romano-British sculpture. Guide book with map available.

MISARDEN PARK GARDENS ★ 18

Miserden, Stroud, Gloucestershire. Tel: (028582) 309
Major T.N.H. Willis

7m SW from Gloucester, 3m from A417. Signposted • Parking • Toilet facilities • Suitable for wheelchairs • Nursery adjacent to garden • Gardens open 3rd April to 27th Sept, Wed and Thurs, 9.30 a.m. - 4. 30 p.m. and 31st March, 7th April, 9th June, 7th July, 2 - 6 p.m. • Entrance: £1.50 (inc. printed guide), children free. Reduction for booked parties

This lovely, timeless English garden has most of the features that one expects from a garden of the early twentieth century. There are extensive yew hedges, a York stone terrace, a loggia overhung with wisteria, a fine specimen of *Magnolia* x *soulangiana*. The south lawn sports very fine grass stairs. The west of the house descends to the nursery in a series of fine grassed terraces. There are two very good herbaceous borders leading to a traditional rose garden beyond. The grounds are planted with many fine specimen trees. The spring show of blossom and bulbs is particularly good. The gardens command excellent views over the famous Golden Valley.

THE OLD MANOR 19

Twyning, Nr Tewkesbury, Gloucestershire. Tel: (0684) 293516
Mrs Joan Wilder

3m N of Tewkesbury via A38; follow signs to Twyning. The garden is at the T-junction at west end of the village • Best season: April to June • Parking • Tea and biscuits on Bank Holiday Mons • Toilet facilities • Suitable for wheelchairs • Plants for sale • Open all year, Mon, 2 - 6 p.m. or dusk if earlier • Entrance: £1.20, accompanied children free

Plantswoman's garden packed with treasures developed over 35 years partly on the site of a Queen Anne Manor. Ancient abbey masonry, churchyard headstones and old brick walls with pineapples give atmosphere to a series of separated contained spaces featuring a pool garden, fern, peat and scree beds, troughs and a renowned 'snake bed'. A connoisseur's collection of plants including many species; unusual plants are available from the small nursery.

PAINSWICK ROCOCO GARDEN 20

The Stables, Painswick House, Painswick, Gloucestershire.
Lord and Lady Dickinson

½m from Painswick on B4073. Signposted • Best season: spring • Parking • Refreshments: teas and lunches • Toilet facilities • Suitable for wheelchairs • Plants for sale • Shop • Open Feb to mid-Dec, Wed - Sun and on Bank Holiday Mons, 11 a.m. - 5 p.m. • Entrance: £2.20, OAP £1.90, children £1.10. Coaches by appointment

A great deal of time, money and effort is going into the restoration (almost complete redevelopment) of this rare rococo survival. Most of the work is new, plantings are incomplete and very young. Whole sections are yet to be restored. But, given time, it will be splendid. At present, the best features are the eighteenth-century garden buildings, the views into especially beautiful surrounding countryside, and the marvellous snowdrop wood spanning a stream that flows from a pond at the lower end. This must be one of the best displays of naturalized snowdrops in England. There are some splendid beech woods and older specimen trees. Wildflowers are allowed complete freedom. Rococo gardening was an eighteenth-century combination of formal geometric features with winding woodland paths, revealing sudden incidents and vistas – in essence, a softening of the formal French styles, apparent from about 1715 onwards in all forms of art. A painting by Thomas Robins (1716–1778) is the basis for Painswick's restoration.

RODMARTON MANOR ★ 21

Rodmarton, Gloucestershire. Tel: (028584) 219
Mrs Anthony Biddulph

6m SW of Cirencester, 4m NE of Tetbury off A433 • Best season: May/June • Refreshments: teas on charity Suns and by prior arrangement • Suitable for wheelchairs • Plants for sale • Open March to Aug, Thurs, 2 – 5 p.m. and on two Suns in summer for charity. Also by appointment • Entrance: £1.50, children free

This much praised garden has been featured in numerous books and magazines over the years. It is a good example of an 'English' garden in the classical sense, but firmly of this century. The garden is famous for its fine hedges of yew, hornbeam, beech and holly. The drive to the manor house, designed by Ernest Barnsley, lies between two immaculately clipped tall beech hedges. There are many good topiaries, a lovely hornbeam avenue and many fine vistas. The herbaceous borders, terrace and leisure gardens are of particular interest. The overall maintenance may have seen better days but as in so many large gardens, great emphasis has had to be placed on labour-saving schemes. This garden will appeal to those who like their design strong and undiluted.

RYELANDS HOUSE 22

Taynton, Gloucestershire. Tel: (045279) 251
Captain and Mrs E. Wilson

8m W of Gloucester, midway between Huntley (A40) and Newent (B4215) • Best season: spring • Parking • Refreshments • Toilet facilities • Suitable for wheelchairs in dry weather • Dogs welcome on country and woodland walk • Plants for sale • Open by appointment for parties and on 31st March, 1st, 7th, 14th, 21st, 28th April, 5th, 6th May, 2nd, 9th June, 25th, 26th Aug, 2 – 6 p.m. • Entrance: £1.50, children free

Carefully cultivated garden designed, developed and maintained by owners since 1964 surrounding a fine creeper-clad early-nineteenth-century house in a peaceful country setting. Yew and box hedges subdivide a sunken garden, pergolas and arches frame well-placed statuary and lead the eye to inviting seats, a water garden and specimen shrubs. Mature trees shade immaculately-maintained beds planted with an experienced eye, in sophisticated tonal harmonies. A mile walk across the owners' land to a tranquil two-acre secluded lake, rich with wildlife, should not be missed especially in spring when the wild daffodils carpet the surrounding woodland. A garden of character with a warm welcome from the owners.

SEZINCOTE ★ 23

Bourton-on-the-Hill, Nr Moreton-in-Marsh, Gloucestershire.
Mr and Mrs D. Peake

1½m from Moreton-in-Marsh on A44 just before reaching Bourton-on-the-Hill • Parking • Teas on charity open day • Toilet facilities • Dogs on lead • House open May to July and Sept, Thurs, Fri, 2.30 - 6 p.m. • Garden open Jan to Nov, Thurs, Fri and Bank Holiday Mon, 2 - 6 p.m. Also 30th June for charity. Closed Dec • Entrance: £2, children £1, children under 5 free (house and garden £3)

The estate, acquired in the early nineteenth century, was developed in the Indian style by the architect, Thomas Daniell, who combined this with Palladian motifs. In the twentieth century a canal pool, a curving conservatory and a little pavilion also in Indian style have been added. The garden reflects what the *Oxford Companion* calls its architectural dichotomy, and, despite some work by Repton, the mixture of traditional landscape with eastern ornamentation, such as the Indian bridge, is not one which every visitor finds satisfactory. However it is certainly unique, although there are echoes of Brighton Pavilion, for which Repton drew designs of an oriental nature.

SNOWSHILL MANOR ★ 24

Nr Broadway, Gloucestershire. Tel: (038685) 2410
The National Trust

3m S of Broadway off A44 and off A424 between Broadway and Stow-on-the-Wold. 4m W of junction of A44/A424 • Parking • No refreshments but nearby pub serves morning coffee and lunches • Partly suitable for wheelchairs, but liable to overcrowding on Suns and Bank Holiday Mons • Open Easter Sat, Sun and Mon, 11 a.m. - 1 p.m. and 2 - 6 p.m., April and Oct, Sat, Sun, 11 a .m. - 1 p.m. and 2 - 5 p.m. May to Sept, Wed - Sun and Bank Holiday Mon, 11 a.m. - 1 p.m. and 2 - 6 p.m. Last admission ½ hour before closing • Entrance: £3.50. Parties by written appointment only and no concessions

From a design by M.H. Baillie-Scott, the owner Charles Wade transformed a 'wilderness of chaos' on a Cotswold hillside into an interconnecting series of outdoor 'rooms' in Hidcote style from the 1920s onwards. Wade was, according to the *Oxford Companion*, a believer in the arts and crafts rustic ideal and the garden, like the house, expresses his eccentricities. Seats and woodwork are painted 'Wade' blue, a powdery dark blue with touches of turquoise which goes well with the Cotswold stone walls. The simple cottage style conceals careful planting with blue, mauve and purple as the motif. Organic gardening is employed here. The visitor may care to contrast Wade's success with some of the less happy attempts at the Cotswold garden style by others in this picture-postcard village no longer inhabited by traditional villagers.

STANCOMBE PARK 25

Stinchcombe, Gloucestershire. Tel: (0453) 542815
Mr and Mrs Barlow

Between Wotton-under-Edge and Dursley on B4060 • Best season: June • Parking in field by park • Teas and home-made cakes • Toilet facilities • Partly suitable for wheelchairs • Plants for sale • Open 23rd June, 2 - 6 p.m. and by appointment for parties • Entrance: £1.50 for both gardens

When Stancombe Park - built in the 1840s - was opened for charity last June, 1400 people rushed to view the most curious park and garden south of Biddulph Grange. Set on the Cotswold escarpment, Stancombe Park boasts the ingredients of a Gothic best-seller. A narrow path drops into a dark glen, roots from enormous oaks, copper beeches and chestnuts trip your feet, ferns brush your face, walls drip water, and amonites and fossils loom in the gloom. A dark lake reflects an eerie Doric temple. Rocks erupt with moss. Egyptian tombs trap the unwary. Tunnels turn into gloomy grottos. Even plants live in wire cages. Metal arches flake with rust. Family parties become confused, divided and lost. Folly freaks are in their element. Everyone has a good time in this Victorian theme park turned horror movie. Escape can be found in the pretty rose garden, tea and further twentieth-century follies around the charming house.

STANWAY HOUSE 26

Cheltenham, Gloucestershire. Tel: (038673) 469
Lord Neidpath

1m E of B4632 Cheltenham - Broadway road, 4m from Winchcombe • Parking • Refreshments: coffee and tea. Bakehouse tea rooms in village. Picnics permitted in park • Toilet facilities • Partly suitable for wheelchairs • Dogs • House open • Garden open June to Aug, Tues and Thurs, also 28th April, 9th June, 2 - 5 p.m. Other times by appointment • Entrance: £1.75, OAP £1.50, children 75p (house and garden)

Stanway is a honey-coloured Cotswold village with its Jacobean 'great house' which has been in the hands of only two families since. It was much frequented by Arthur Balfour and 'The Souls' in the latter years of the last century. More recently, the garden was used to film part of *The Draughtsman's Contract* so one need to say no more to those who favour grand design and effects. Contrariwise it offers nothing to the plantsperson as there is hardly a flower in sight. Behind the house, the garden rises in a series of dramatic lawns and a (rare) formal terraced mound to the pyramid folly which, in the eighteenth century was the pivot of the vast cascade descending to a lake by the house. The present owner plans to restore this with its 170m-long waterfall, its canal 35m wide, and to extend the lime avenue and vista. Alas the estimated cost is £¼ million. Other features include the fourteenth-century tithe barn, church and a dog cemetery whose inmates go back to 1700.

SUDELEY CASTLE ★ 27

Winchcombe, Gloucestershire. Tel: (0242) 604357/8
Lord and Lady Ashcombe

6m N of Cheltenham Spa on A46. Entry through the town of Winchcombe • Parking • Meals and refreshments. Picnic facilities in play area only • Toilet facilities • Suitable for wheelchairs • A good selection of plants for sale. Plant centre open 16th Feb to 24th Dec, 10 a.m. - 5.30 p.m. Information (0242) 602308 • Shop • Castle open 12 noon - 5 p.m. • Garden open 28th March to Oct, 11 a.m. - 5.30 p.m. • Entrance: £2.75, children £1.20 (castle and grounds £4.20, children £2.20)

There has been a house on this magnificent site for over 1000 years but today the emphasis is on tourism with pleasant facilities, craft and other exhibitions such as falconry. The main attraction of the extensive grounds are the clipped yews by the park balustrade and the sculptural yew hedges with openings and tunnel walks round the so-called Queen's garden. This imitation of a medieval knot garden, made in the nineteenth century by an ancestor of the owners, has well-clipped rosemary, lavender and other herbs. Otherwise, the planting is rather patchy. The owners are renovating the Queen's garden under the guidance of Jane Fernley Whittingstall to 'become one of the major rose gardens of England'.

TREVI GARDENS 28

Hartpury, Gloucestershire. Tel: (0452) 70370
Mr and Mrs G.D. Gough

5m NW of Gloucester via A417. In village turn sharp back right over Old Road before war memorial • Parking in road outside • Teas • Toilet facilities • Suitable for wheelchairs • Plants for sale • Open 21st March to 6th June, Thurs only and 5th May, 20th June, 4th, 18th July, 1st, 4th, 15th Aug, 5th, 19th Sept, 2 - 6 p.m. Coaches and groups at other times by appointment • Entrance: £1, accompanied children free

This carefully-planned and maintained garden gives the impression of more space than its one acre and aims to be full of interest and variety at all times of the year. Meandering paths lead through arches, around well-planted beds, under a laburnum and clematis walk, through a stream garden and alongside a decorative vegetable garden flanked with espaliered fruit trees. The owners have invested much hard work in achieving a garden displaying colour and good-looking plants at every season and have created a sense of enclosed and charmed oasis within an area of recently-built housing. There are unusual species and cultivars to catch the plantsman's eye as well as colourful annuals and old favourites, and there is a welcoming informality here to make any visitor feel at home.

VALE HOUSE 29

Hidcote Boyce, Chipping Campden, Gloucestershire.
Tel: (0386) 438 228
Miss Bettine Muir

On the road from Chipping Campden to Hidcote Manor and Kiftsgate Gardens (see entries). On the edge of Hidcote Boyce • Parking in mown paddock • Partly suitable for wheelchairs • Open May to July, Wed, 2 - 5 p.m. • Entrance: £1, children 50p

Miss Bettine Muir is the second daughter of Heather Muir, the creator of Kiftsgate and remembers the planting of the famous rose. She is a born gardener and her skill is reflected in the most unusual and exciting planting in her own garden. She moved to Vale House in the early 1970s, beginning work on the 'flat field' which surrounded it in 1972. Within dense windbreaks which do not impede the lovely view west across the Cotswolds to Bredon are a series of small gardens linked by grass paths. Around the house are climbers and borders of unusual plants, to the east more hedges and new shrub plantings.

WESTBURY COURT GARDEN ★★ 30

Westbury-on-Severn, Gloucestershire. Tel: (045276) 461
The National Trust

9m SW of Gloucester on A48, close to the church • Parking • Picnic area • Toilet facilities • Suitable for wheelchairs • Open 30th March to Oct, Wed - Sun and Bank Holiday Mon, 11 a.m. - 6 p.m. Other months by appointment only • Entrance: £1.60. Groups of 15 or more by prior arrangement

Seventeenth-century Dutch water garden restored and maintained in pristine condition by The National Trust. Formally-clipped yew hedges sporting stalked pyramids and globes flank rectangular canals planted with water lilies and containing huge carp. A contemporary tall pavilion gives an overview of the parallel canals, one widening to a T-shaped lake with Neptune rising from the deep. The Forest of Dean makes a spectacular backdrop but the great house has gone, alas, and has been replaced by a purpose-built residential home for elderly people. Carefully selected contemporary plants and fan-trained fruit trees flourish against the old walls, and a collection of herbs and medicinal plants, old tulips, dianthus and roses has been assembled and planted in a parterre in an enclosed garden which gives the feel of an outdoor room.

WESTONBIRT ARBORETUM ★★ 31

Westonbirt, Gloucestershire. Tel: (066688) 220
The Forestry Commission

3m SW of Tetbury on A433, 5m NE of junction with A6 • Best seasons: spring and autumn • Parking • Light refreshments at café (closed late Nov to Easter). Picnic area • Toilet facilities • Suitable for wheelchairs • Dogs allowed in most areas • Visitor Centre with exhibition and shop (closed late Nov to Easter) • Open all year, 10 a.m. - 8 p.m. or dusk • Entrance: £2, OAP and children 5 - 16, £1

This is perhaps the finest arboretum in Britain. Started in 1829 by R. Staynor-Holford, Westonbirt was expanded and improved by successive generations of the same family until it was taken over by the Forestry Commission in 1956. Numerous grass rides divide the trees into roughly rectangular blocks, within which are various open spaces and glades used for special plantings such as the famous Japanese maple collection. Westonbirt is noted for its vast range of notable mature specimen trees. Colour is best in spring (rhododendron, magnolias etc) and autumn (Japanese maples, fothergilla). The Forestry Commission is continuing with new planting, for example the Hillier Glade with ornamental cherries. Across the valley from the original arboretum is Silk Valley with collections of native and American species that in spring are carpeted with primroses, wood anemones and bluebells. 17,000 numbered trees and 17 miles of paths.

GARDENS OPEN RARELY

The following gardens are open to the public on three days or less in the year, although they may also be open by appointment if this is stated in the text. For details see individual entry.
June 9 Alderley Grange; **June 23** Stancombe Park.

HAMPSHIRE & ISLE OF WIGHT

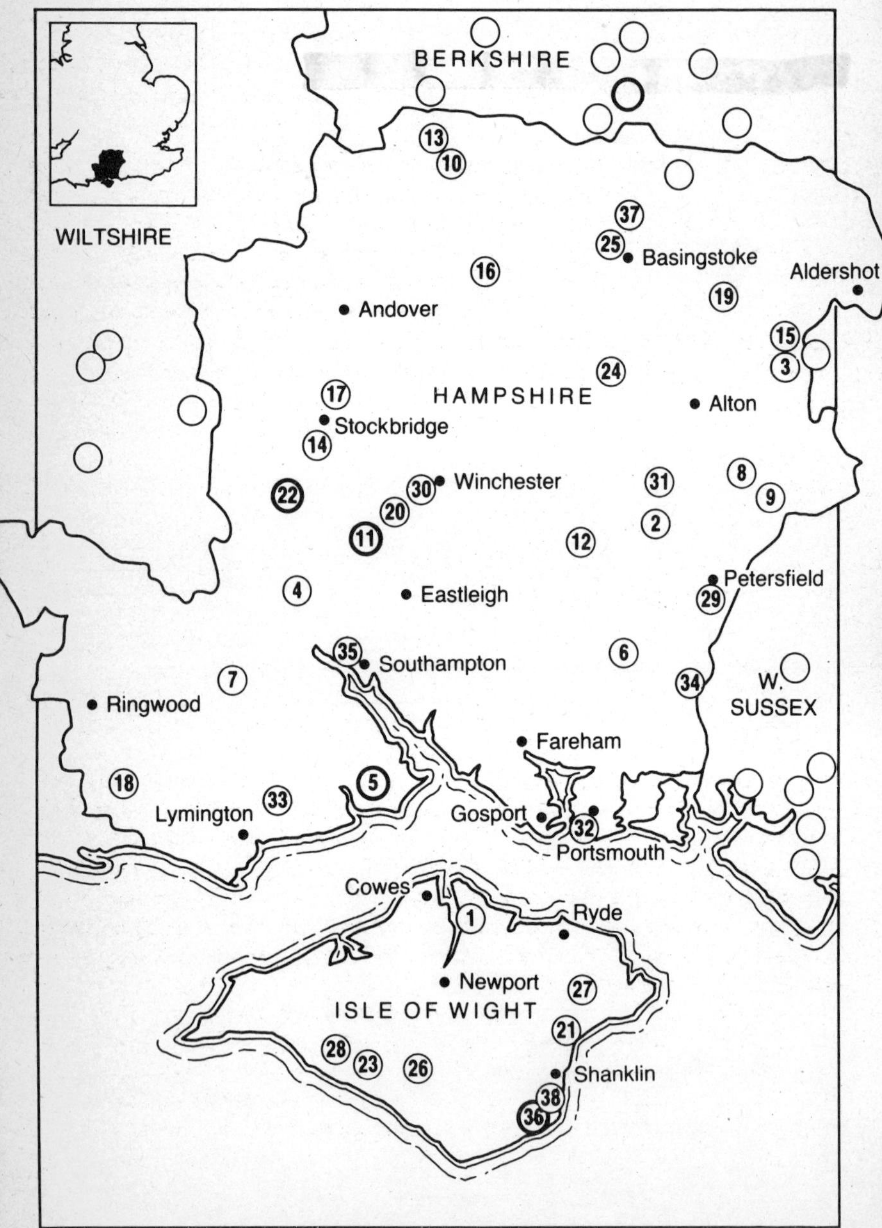

Plain circle numbers can be found by turning to neighbouring counties.
Two-starred gardens are ringed in bold.

BARTON MANOR ★ 1

Whippingham, East Cowes, Isle of Wight. Tel: (0983) 292835
Mr and Mrs A. Goddard

From E. Cowes A3021, 500 yards beyond Osborne House on left • Best season: mid-May/Aug • Parking • Refreshments: cafeteria and wine bar – all day licence • Toilet facilities • Suitable for wheelchairs • Plants for sale • Shop • Open Easter; 6th to 30th April, Sat and Sun; May to 13th Oct, daily • Entrance: £3.50 (inc. souvenir tasting glass, wine tasting and guide leaflet), children (one per adult) free

Prince Albert's original design included fine trees and the cork grove. The grand terraces were added by Edward VII, sloping down towards Osborne Bay. In 1924 no less than 225,000 daffodils were planted around the lake, which give a fine display in spring. There is also a secret garden planted with azaleas and roses, impressive herbaceous borders and a productive vineyard, wine from which is on sale. In 1968 Hilliers laid out an intriguing water garden on the far side of the lake, on what was originally Queen Victoria's skating rink. The present owners, running the garden and vineyard as a commercial operation, have spared no effort in restoring and maintaining the estate to an immaculate standard. The NCCPG's National collection of red hot pokers (kniphofia) is here.

BRAMDEAN HOUSE ★ 2

Bramdean, Nr Alresford, Hampshire. Tel: (0962) 771214
Mr and Mrs H. Wakefield

10m E of Winchester on A272 at W end of Bramdean • Best season: summer • Parking • Refreshments • Toilet facilities • Plants for sale • Open by appointment and 17th, 31st March, 1st, 21st April, 19th May, 16th June, 21st July, 18th Aug, 2 – 5 p.m. • Entrance: £1, children free

A bumbling hedge of yew and box swelling out between a pair of armorial gates lends a slightly eccentric air to the south front of the eighteenth-century house and effectively conceals the fine country house garden to the north. A grass path rises steadily from the centre of the garden front forming a vista through the three main sections. The first is dominated by the famous double herbaceous border, lawns and mature trees; a walled kitchen garden defines the second and an orchard watched over by a cupoláed gazebo the last. The careful composition of colours, foliage and views is a continuous and successful feature of these 'gardens', from *Crambe cordifolia* and onopordums, the spreading *Prunus subhirtella*, yew topiary and huge beeches to the classical and meticulously maintained kitchen garden. The view from the orchard through the wrought iron gates of the walled garden with sundial to the herbaceous borders and lily pond in midsummer is much admired.

BROADHATCH HOUSE 3

Bentley, Nr Alton, Hampshire. Tel: (0420) 23185
Bruce and Elizabeth Powell

4m NE of Alton on A31. Turn right at pond ½m up School Lane, bear right at fork • Parking • Suitable for wheelchairs • Dogs on lead • Plants for sale • Open 23rd June, 2 - 6 p.m., 24th June, 10 a.m. - 6 p.m., 14th July, 2 - 6 p.m., 15th July, 11 a.m. - 6 p.m. • Entrance: £1, children free

Spreading from the east, south and west of the house the three and a half acres are divided into a series of garden rooms which, although extremely well laid out, are sometimes let down by the absence of a strong feature. However the view through the sunken rose garden with its 'Peace' and hybrid musks to the double herbaceous borders will be sufficient reward for any visitor. The kitchen garden is well-maintained.

BROADLANDS ★ 4

Romsey, Hampshire. Tel: (0794) 516878
Lord Romsey

S of Romsey on A31. Signposted • Parking • Refreshments and picnic site • Toilet facilities • Suitable for wheelchairs • Shop • Open 28th March to 29th Sept, daily except Fri, 10 a.m. - 4 p.m. Closed Fri except Aug, Sept and Good Friday • Entrance: £4.50, OAP £3.60, children £3

This former home of Lord Louis Mountbatten has a smooth lawn running from the steps of the porticoed west front to the River Test and spreading parkland trees of beech and cedar come together in a composition that epitomises the eighteenth-century English Landscape School. The elegant Palladianism of Broadlands could only be the work of 'Capability' Brown. To the south of the house a large circular pool and fountain hold centre stage within an enclosure of topiary yew hedges and, to the north and east a series of disappointing walled gardens. In addition to the house, arguably the finest in Hampshire, a classical orangery, ice house and a small garden are perfectly sited in the immaculate lawns amongst noteworthy specimens of magnolias, taxodiums, limes and huge plane trees. It is for these overall impressions rather than details that Broadlands has gained its popularity.

EXBURY GARDENS ★★ 5

Exbury, Nr Southampton, Hampshire. Tel: (0703) 891203
Mr E.L. de Rothschild

2½m SE of Beaulieu, 15m SW of Southampton, via B3054 SE of Beaulieu after 1m turn right for Exbury • Best season: spring/autumn • Parking • Refreshments • Toilet facilities • Suitable for wheelchairs • Dogs on lead • Plants for sale • Shop • Open mid-March to mid-July/Sept to late Oct, 10 a.m. - 5.30 p.m. • *Entrance: spring £3, OAP/children/parties per person £2.50 (children under 12 free), autumn £2, OAPs £1.50*

Established in the 1920s and 1930s these outstanding gardens are synonymous with the name of Rothschild and with the development of new hybrid rhododendrons and azaleas over the last 70 years or so. Work on this most beautifully tended woodland garden is continuing and the 200 acres provide aspects of planting from early nineteenth-century cedars and *Sequoiadendron gigantium* (Wellingtonias) to huge swathes of colour such as the apricot or the spectacular 'Lady Chamberlain's Walk' beneath the high canopy of oak and pine. In compositional terms it would be hard to better the layout of the area around the high and low ponds where Japanese maples, cercidiphyllum, *Salix fargesii* and primulas are the pick of the plants and the glimpsed views across the Beaulieu river refreshing. Three separate walks amongst conifers, camellias, wisteria, rock gardens, winter gardens and pools demand that nothing less than a day is spent here.

FAIRFIELD HOUSE ★ 6

Hambledon, Portsmouth, Hampshire.
Tel: (070132) 431
Mr and Mrs P. Wake

10m SW of Petersfield on B2150 • *Best season: June to July* • *Parking* • *Refreshments* • *Toilet facilities* • *Suitable for wheelchairs* • *Dogs on lead* • *Plants for sale* • *Open by appointment and 16th June, 2 - 6 p.m.* • *Entrance: £1, children 50p (suitable for groups)*

There can be little doubt that Lanning Roper, who assisted in the establishment of this excellent garden, would approve of the continuing development of the planting at Fairfield, particularly the climbing, shrub and bush roses around and on the elegant white Regency 'colonial' house. Set on a south-facing slope beneath chalk down and sheltered by hedges, walls and a legacy of fine trees, cedars of Lebanon and a stooled lime tree worthy of note, this largely informal garden has been skilfully shaped by the Wakes. The four acres not only host an impressive range of roses, of which there are over 160 in number, but mixed borders of choice specimens, clematis and solanum are very successful, and in spring drifts of bulbs.

FURZEY GARDENS ★ 7

Minstead, Nr Lyndhurst, Hampshire. Tel: (0703) 812464
Mrs M.A. Selwood (Manager)

8m SW of Southampton, 1m S of A31, 2m W of Cadnam and the end of M27, 3½m NW of Lyndhurst • *Best season: spring* • *Parking* • *Refreshments at Honey Pot café ½m away* • *Toilet facilities* • *Plants for sale* • *Sixteenth-century cottage open daily in summer, weekends in winter* • *Gardens open daily except 25th and 26th Dec, 10 a.m. – 5 p.m. Dusk in winter • Entrance: £1.95, children 95p, winter £1, children 50p. Reductions for parties by arrangement*

This eight-acre garden was laid out by Hew Dalrymple in the early 1920s using plants from the nursery at nearby Bartley. The range of plants, particularly those of Australasian descent, make this garden a must for horticulturalists and plant historians. Situated on a south-facing slope, winding paths lead to many noteworthy and surprisingly large specimens. There is relatively little herbaceous planting but this is more than compensated for by the boldness and density of some of the most colourful planting schemes with the vermilion of Chilean Fire trees in May/June outstanding. Recent replanting has left some gaps in the borders but there does not seem to be anything from lawns to the shaded plants of the water garden that will not flourish here.

THE GILBERT WHITE MUSEUM 8

'The Wakes', Selborne, Alton, Hampshire. Tel: (042050) 275
Oates Memorial Trust

4½m S of Alton, 8m N of Petersfield on B3006 • Best season: spring • Parking: public car park behind Selborne Arms • Toilet facilities • Suitable for wheelchairs • Shop • House open • Garden open Easter to Oct, Wed – Sun and Bank Holidays, 11 a.m. – 5.30 p.m. Last admission 5 p.m. Also open Tues in July and Aug • Entrance: £1.50, OAP/student £1, children 50p

'The Wakes' through the great naturalist Gilbert White's 'Garden Kalender' is probably one of the best documented gardens of the eighteenth century. Since their purchase in 1954 the gardens have been steadily restored to period form and now show many of the flowers described in White's journals. Of the many interesting and period features, the yew topiary, laburnum arbour, herb garden and rose garden should be noted. An original brick path may be followed past an ancient yew and out into the 'Great Mead' where from the shelter of an arbour Selborne Hanger, the parkland trees and the early ha-ha can be enjoyed. Visitors may ponder on the fact that it was at 'The Wakes' that White made the first observations of the value of the earthworm to gardens and farms.

GREATHAM MILL ★ 9

Greatham, Nr Liss, Hampshire. Tel: (04207) 219
Mrs E.N. Pumphrey

7m SE of Alton on B3006 turn off at Hawkley, 5m N of Petersfield, from A325 at Greatham turn onto B3006 towards Alton. After 600 yards left into No Through yard • Parking • Refreshments: picnic area • Toilet facilities • Plants for sale • Open mid-April to Sept, Sun and Bank Holiday, 2 – 6 p.m. Also by appointment • Entrance: £1, children free

Seemingly protected by the moat-like River Rother and a mill race the 'cottage-style' garden of Greatham Mill harbours a wide-ranging collection of many unusual varieties as well as attractive planting associations of the more usual kind. The seventeenth-century mill half hidden by wisteria provides a romantic backdrop to a water garden at the front where large leaves and luxuriance of hostas, royal ferns, rodgersias and gunnera dominate more sensitive planting. Passing beside and behind the house the full extent of the Pumphreys' achievements since their arrival here in 1949 can be appreciated. Alpines, in spreading middle age, grasses and herbaceous plants provide constant ground cover interest amongst carefully laid out grass paths, enticed by groupings of choice foliage shrubs, including a curious pencil-thin hedge, and trees.

HIGHCLERE CASTLE 10

Highclere, Nr Newbury, Hampshire. Tel: (0635) 253210
Lord and Lady Carnarvon

4½m S of Newbury on W side of A34 • Parking • Refreshments and picnic area • Toilet facilities • Suitable for wheelchairs • Plants for sale at plant centre • Shop • House open • Garden open 30th June to 29th Sept, Wed – Sun and Bank Holiday Mons, 2 – 6 p.m. Last admission 5 p.m. • Entrance: £3.50, OAP £3, disabled and children under 16, £2. Special group rates

Though much altered by 'Capability' Brown in the 1770s, Highclere Park will still reward students of the earlier rococo style with a rare and fine collection of early eighteenth-century follies. Around Charles Barry's huge battlemented house an equally fine collection of cedars – North Indian Deodar, Mount Atlas and Lebanon – may be identified, the near horizontal branches of the latter framing views to first of the house and then seemingly of all the district. Relegated to the slopes away from the house, the walled and secret garden is planted in an uncharacteristically cautious manner for Highclere and saved only by James Russell's eye for good spring and summer colour. It was on Lord Carnarvon's estate here that in 1909 the young Geoffrey de Havilland made some of the early powered tests in his wood and fabric flying machine. The savage winter storms of 1990 damaged many lime and beech avenues and tragically destroyed more than 50 cedars of Lebanon depriving the house and estate of many of its memorable and stately vistas. See also entry for Hollington Herb Garden.

THE HILLIER GARDENS AND ARBORETUM ★★ 11

Jermyns Lane, Ampfield, Nr Romsey, Hampshire. Tel: (0794) 68787
Hampshire County Council

3m NE of Romsey, 9m SW of Winchester, ¾m W of A31 along Jermyns Lane. Signposted from A31 and A3057 • Parking • Light refreshments at weekends and Bank Holidays April to Oct, 12 noon – 5 p.m. • Toilet facilities • Suitable for wheelchairs • Plants for sale at Hilliers Nursery/Garden Centre • Open all year Monday – Fri, 10.30 a.m. – 5 p.m. Weekends and Bank Holidays from March to 2nd Sun in Nov, 10.30 a.m. – 6 p.m. For summer evening and winter weekend opening telephone for further details. Brentry Woodland open late spring only • Entrance: £1.80, OAP £1.40, children under 15, 50p at weekends and Bank Holidays, free on weekdays. Season tickets £7.50. For parties exceeding 30 adults, £1.40 per head

Administered by Hampshire County Council since 1977 this enormous collection of trees and shrubs was begun in 1953 by the late Sir Harold Hillier using his house and garden as a starting point. Extends to 160 acres and includes approximately 14,000 different species and cultivars, with many rarities. With a total of 36,000 plants it is impossible not to be impressed or to learn something about how, what and where to plant. Seasonal interest maps and labelling will lead the visitor to herbaceous, scree, heather and bog gardens. Amongst the trees and shrubs, *Eucalyptus nitens* and *niphophila*, *Magnolia cylindrica* and the acers are worthy of note. Much more than an arboretum this attractively laid-out garden can be enjoyed at many levels and can only increase in interest as the immense collection of young trees gains in maturity. Keen gardeners should partake little and often and always be armed with a notebook.

HINTON AMPNER ★ 12

Hinton Ampner, Bramdean, Nr Winchester, Hampshire.
Tel: (096279) 361
The National Trust

1m W of Bramdean village, 8m E of Winchester on A272 • Parking. Special entrance for coaches through village • Homemade teas in tearoom 2 – 5 p.m. • Toilet facilities • Partly suitable for wheelchairs • House open Tues and Wed only and Sat and Sun in Aug, 1.30 – 5.30 p.m. Last admission 5 p.m. £1.20 extra • Garden open 29th March to Sept, Sat, Sun, Tues, Wed and Bank Holiday Mons, 1.30 – 5.30 p.m. Last admission 5 p.m. • Entrance: £1.70. Pre-booked parties to house and garden £2.50 per person. Bookings and enquiries to: NT Regional Office, Polesden Lacey, Dorking, Surrey RH5 6BD. Tel: (0372) 53401

Located on the shoulder of a ridge, the ascent to the house through almost routine parkland in no way prepares the visitor for the view to the south of classic English downland scenery over a series of descending terraces laid out in the Hidcote style. From his inheritance of the estate in 1935 onwards Ralph Dutton, later Lord Sherborne, set about transforming the remnants of a Victorian/Edwardian park into a series of gardens on different levels linked by the 'Long Walk' and the 'main terrace'. The skill with which features such as the temple, obelisk and statue of Diana are sited and with which many surprise vistas were created is testimony to Lord Sherborne's knowledge of garden history. Although areas of the garden are in the process of restoration and some large shrubs need to be rescued, both from rampant climbers, Russian vine and Kiftsgate roses and undisciplined pruning, the masterly design of this garden and the elegance of its topiary, yew and box hedges deserve wide recognition.

HOLLINGTON HERB GARDEN 13

Woolton Hill, Nr Newbury, Hampshire. Tel: (0635) 263908
Mr and Mrs S.G. Hopkinson

4m S of Newbury off A343. Follow signs to Herb Garden • Best season: summer • Parking • Refreshments • Toilet facilities • Suitable for wheelchairs • Plants for sale • Shop • Open March to Sept, daily, 10 a.m. - 5.30 p.m., Oct to Mar, Mon - Fri, 10 a.m. - 5 p.m., Sun and Bank Holidays, 11 a.m. - 5 p.m. • Entrance: free. Collecting box for charity

Interestingly laid out, this small garden modestly but successfully combines the function of a sales pitch for its specimen plants with the art of garden design. Set within an old walled garden, a small fountain, knot garden and rampant hop climbing over gnarled espalier provide the visual treats, but is the pot-pourri of aromas that distinguishes this garden and nursery. It could be combined with a visit to Highclere Castle nearby (see entry).

HOUGHTON LODGE ★ 14

Stockbridge, Hampshire. Tel: (0264) 810177/071 352 7478
Captain and Mrs M. Busk

6m S of Andover, 1½m S of Stockbridge on minor road signposted Houghton • Best season: spring • Parking • Refreshments on Easter Sun, Bank Holidays and charity days. Picnic area • Suitable for wheelchairs • Plants for sale • House open by appointment only • Open March to Sept, Mon, Tues, Easter Sun and Bank Holidays, 10 a.m. - 1 p.m., 2 - 4 p.m. Hydroponicum open Fri - Tues and Bank Holidays by appointment • Entrance: £1.50, children 50p. Extra charge for hydroponicum

Built shortly before 1801 Houghton Lodge is probably among the most 'picturesque' of Gothic cottage ornés both in its architectural fantasy and its perfect garden setting alongside the River Test. Marie Antoinette would certainly have approved of this idyll. A succession of snowdrops and massed daffodils beneath fine parkland specimens of plane, oaks and horse chestnuts clothe the ridge beyond the lawns from where a unique rustic flint grotto can be reached; in autumn the colours of Indian gums and maples can be observed reflected in the river. A well-maintained walled garden with espalier fruit trees and glasshouses stocked with vines seems to be able to pass without comment in a garden such as this but needless to say it is quite as excellent as the rest. The Hampshire Hydroponicum, believed to be the first set up for public display of plant culture without soil in England, was opened in early 1990 within the chalk cob walls of the kitchen garden. Replanting of the gardens is being undertaken with the advice of the landscape historian David Jacques.

JENKYN PLACE ★ 15

Bentley, Nr Alton, Hampshire. Tel: (0420) 23118
Mrs Patricia Coke

4m SW of Farnham on A31, signposted 400 yards N of Bentley crossroads • Parking • Toilet facilities • Suitable for wheelchairs • Plants usually for sale • Open 11th April to 8th Sept, Thurs - Sun and Bank Holiday Mons, 2 - 6 p.m. • Entrance: £1.50, children 75p

Since their arrival just after World War II Mr and Mrs Coke have created a remarkable garden that is somewhat reminiscent of Hidcote, both in spirit and structure. Falling steadily to the south-east the high ground of this garden is dominated by a series of formal rooms arranged on terraces of which the sundial garden, an elegant rose garden (note the *Caesalpinia japonica* and loquat shrub), and a scented Dutch garden are the pick. A classically-perfect double herbaceous border backed by high hedges ends the sequence of walled and hedged enclosures and leads by way of cross axis to a succession of less intensively and informally planted areas which do tend to be less successful in design. A long sloping lawn returns to the house revealing the handsome seventeenth-century façade and a superb Cedar of Lebanon planted in 1828. This is a garden to be visited more than once.

LAVERSTOKE HOUSE 16

Laverstoke, Nr Whitchurch, Hampshire. Tel: (0256) 770245
Mr and Mrs Julian Sheffield

2m E of Whitchurch, 10m W of Basingstoke on B3400 • Parking • Suitable for wheelchairs • Dogs on lead • Open by appointment • Entrance: 80p, children 20p

Rebuilt by Joseph Bonomi in 1796-98, Laverstoke was home to the Portal family, founders of the nearby paper mills where Bank of England notes were made for over 200 years. Beneath the imposing yellow brick façades and giant portico, the owners had laid out a terrace and garden of great style and poise; a collection of old-fashioned shrub roses underplanted with *Alchemilla mollis* is particularly effective. If it is the great imagination of the Sheffields that is shaping the gardens immediately around the house, it is their good fortune that many good hands planted the impressive parkland trees that accompany the descent from Laverstoke to the River Test.

LONGSTOCK PARK GARDENS ★ 17

Longstock, Nr Stockbridge, Hampshire. Tel: (0264) 810894
John Lewis Partnership (Leckford Estates Ltd)

2m N of Stockbridge. From A30 turn N on A3057. Signposted • Parking • Refreshments at Leckford • Toilet facilities • Suitable for wheelchairs • Plants for sale • Open occasionally for charities: April to Sept on 3rd Sun in each month, 2 - 5 p.m. • Entrance: £1.50, children 50p

The huge leaves of gunnera, the stilts (pneumatophores) of *Taxodium distichum*, varied nymphaeas and a giant white lily *Cardiocrinum giganteum* are just a few of the many interesting features and unusual plants to be found in this most immaculate and loveliest of water gardens. Developed between 1946 and 1953 the garden is fed by the River Test and is located some way from the house. Approached with an air of increasing expectation between a high hedge and old oak trees the garden reveals itself all at once as a veritable archipelago connected by narrow bridges and causeways beneath which clear waters and golden carp slowly move. The background is formed by woodland trees into which a variety of acid-loving trees and shrubs and wild flowers have been introduced as a contrast to the sometimes over-disciplined planting of this successful garden.

MACPENNYS NURSERIES 18

Burley Road, Bransgore, Nr Christchurch, Hampshire.
Mr and Mrs T.M. Lowndes

Midway between Christchurch and Burley. Turn N off A35 Lyndhurst - Bournemouth road at Hinton Admiral (Cod and Fiddle), right at Bransgore crossroads (Crown) on ¼m on right • Best season: spring • Parking • Teas at Holmsley Old Station Tearooms or Burley Forest Tearooms • Suitable for wheelchairs • Dogs on lead • Plants for sale • Open daily except 25th, 26th Dec and 1st Jan, Mon - Sat, 9 a.m. - 5 p.m., Sun, 2 - 5 p.m. • Entrance: by collecting box

There is something about the very name Macpennys that promises the well-stocked nursery that one finds at Bransgore. The gravel pit alongside provides a highly successful way of extending the plant collection into a most unusual woodland garden. Magnolias, camellias, pieris and rhododendrons all flourish beneath a canopy of pine somewhat savaged by the recent severe winter storms. A labyrinthine series of paths (from which one is invited to scramble to reach labels) eventually return to the nursery where many of the plants seen can be purchased.

THE MANOR HOUSE 19

Upton Grey, Nr Basingstoke, Hampshire. Tel: (0256) 862827
Mr and Mrs J. Wallinger

6m SE of Basingstoke in Upton Grey village on hill immediately behind church • Best season: May to July • Parking. Coaches by appointment only • Plants for sale • Open by appointment and 7th, 15th June, 2 - 5 p.m. • Entrance: £2.50

Here are formal gardens and terraces with excellent herbaceous borders and dry-stone walling. They have been meticulously restored by the present owners over the past five years to the original plans prepared by Gertrude Jekyll in 1908–1910 and this garden illustrates many of the designer's favourite herbaceous planting combinations. The yew hedging in the formal garden is far from maturity and consequently deprives the scene of much needed structure but the colour and shape are clearly evident. To the south-west is an informal wild garden and pool. The house was designed by Ernest Newton for Charles Holmes, editor of *The Studio* magazine.

MERDON MANOR 20

Hursley, Nr Winchester, Hampshire. Tel: (0962) 75215
Mr and Mrs J.C. Smith

4m SW of Winchester. From the A3090 Winchester - Romsey road at Standon turn onto the Slackstead road and continue for 1½m • Parking • Teas • Plants for sale • Open by appointment, 2 - 6 p.m. • Entrance: 80p, children 20p

It is difficult to imagine a more surprising feature for this or any other garden than the enclosed pool garden that is revealed only by opening a heavy door in a barn wall. The sheltered microclimate protects many tender plants grown in raised troughs and a myriad of pots and urns surround two formal pools. The whole effect is quite extravagant and a marvellous foil to the sophistication of the rest of the garden. There is a large area of parkland.

MORTON MANOR 21

Brading, Sandown, Isle of Wight. Tel: (0983) 406168
J.B., J. and J.A. Trzebski

3m from Ryde on A3055, turn right at Brading traffic lights, signposted 100 yards up hill • Best season: April to June • Parking • Refreshments: morning coffee, lunch, cream teas. Fully licensed • Toilet facilities • Suitable for wheelchairs • Dogs on lead • Home-grown plants and vines for sale • Shop • House open • Garden open 1st Sun in April to Oct, daily except Sat, 10 a.m. - 5.30 p.m. • Entrance: £2.25, OAP £2, children £1 (inc. house, garden, winery and video on wine production)

The history of Morton dates back to the thirteenth century. The Elizabethan sunken garden is surrounded by a 400 year old box hedge and old-fashioned roses and shaded by a magnificent *Magnolia grandiflora*. The terraces are nineteenth-century with extensive herbaceous borders and a huge London plane. Masses of spring bulbs are followed by rhododendrons and traditional herbaceous displays. Among the wide range of fine trees is an Indian Bean (*Catalpa bignonioides*). Little remains of the old walled garden but in the corner behind the herbs are the restored bee boles; also a turf maze has been made for children, and there is a vineyard.

MOTTISFONT ABBEY ★★ 22

Mottisfont, Nr Romsey, Hampshire. Tel: (0794) 40757
The National Trust

4½m NW of Romsey, ¾m W of A3057 • Best season: midsummer • Parking • Refreshments at local post office • Toilet facilities • Suitable for wheelchairs • Dogs in car park only • Shop • Part of house open Wed afternoons only but numbers restricted. 50p extra • Open April to Sept, daily except Fri and Sat, 2 – 6 p.m., last admission 5 p.m. Evening opening of rose garden Tues, Wed, Thurs and Sun, 7 – 9 p.m. during rose season only (check first). Last admission 8.30 p.m. • Entrance: £1.50 • Bookings and enquiries to The Head Gardener, The White House, Hatt Lane, Mottisfont, Nr Romsey SO51 0LJ. Tel: (0794) 41220 during opening hours

Established in only 1972, the walled rose garden designed by Graham Stuart Thomas is already famous and deservedly so. Between the gravel paths, meeting at a small pool and fountain, are assembled one of the most comprehensive collections of old French roses of the nineteenth century, seen and smelt at its best in midsummer when the scent is trapped within its walls. Broad herbaceous borders containing pinks, aubretias, saponarias and much else ensure that from very early in the season there is always something to enjoy. It is to be hoped that the visitor will not miss, if it is possible to miss, the enormous London plane trees, *Platanus* x *hybrida (acerfolia)* (the largest in the country) that occupy parkland sweeping down to the River Test. Pockets of formal gardens can be found around the house created by such accomplished designers as Geoffrey Jellicoe (the pleached lime walk underplanted with *Chionodoxa luciliae*) and Norah Lindsay. The Abbey (tenanted) contains a drawing room decorated by muralist Rex Whistler but access is limited.

MOTTISTONE MANOR 23

Mottistone, Newport, Isle of Wight. Tel: (0983) 740946
The National Trust

SW of Newport on B3399 between Brighstone and Brook • Best season: May/June • Parking on village green when garden open • House open 26th Aug only. £1 extra • Garden open April to 25th Sept, Wed only and Bank Holiday Mon, 2 - 5.30 p.m. Last admission 5 p.m. • Entrance: £1.20, children 60p

A terraced garden, best seen in spring for a glorious display of irises, laid out to gain maximum effect from the views over the Needles, Channel and south-west coast of the island. Not so much a plantsman's garden as an impressive frame for the Manor.

MOUNDSMERE MANOR 24

Preston Candover, Nr Basingstoke, Hampshire. Tel: (025687) 207
Mr and Mrs Andreae

6m S of Basingstoke on B3046. Drive gates on left just after Preston Candover sign • Parking. Coaches by appointment • Suitable for wheelchairs • Dogs on lead • Open 30th June, 2 - 6 p.m. • Entrance: £1, children 50p

Inspired by Hampton Court and designed in 1908, the pleasing relationship of house to garden to landscape marks Moundsmere Manor as one of Sir Reginald Blomfield's (1856-1942) best surviving gardens. To the south of the 'Wrenaissance' house the principal formal garden descends in terraces framed by clipped yews with deep herbaceous borders. This is Edwardian gardening on a grand scale, characteristically architectural, and will not disappoint students of Blomfield's *The Formal Garden in England* in which he attacked the informal style of gardening supported by William Robinson. For Blomfield, gardens were primarily works of art. Other examples of his work are found at Godington Park (Kent) and Athelhampton (Dorset) (see entries). There is a pinetum to the north.

MOUNTBATTEN HOUSE

(formerly Gateway House) 25
Basing View, PO Box 117, Basingstoke, Hampshire.
Tel: (0256) 56144
IBM plc

In central Basingstoke, just off A339, adjacent to AA HQ • Parking by prior arrangement • Closed at present for security reasons but excellent views can be gained from the nearby park

Designed by Arup Associates and James Russell in 1976 for Wiggins Teape, this is one of the foremost roof gardens in Britain and illustrates what can be achieved when landscape design is given proper consideration at the design stage of a modern building. Essentially a ziggurat-building, access to six levels can be gained directly from the offices to terraces which by their luxuriance of planting, cascading foliage and climbing wisteria belie the fact that you are all the time standing on the roof of an office or car park. Romantic combination of building and planting will delight plantspersons and designers alike.

NORTHCOURT ★ 26

Shorwell, Newport, Isle of Wight. Tel: (0983) 740415
Mr and Mrs J. Harrison

4m S of Newport on B3323. Entrance on right after rustic bridge, opposite thatched cottage • Best season: May/June • Parking • Refreshments • Partly suitable for wheelchairs • Dogs on lead (under sufferance) • Plants for sale • Open 19th May, 22nd June (The period 18th to 25th May is Heritage Week for the Isle of Wight Gardens Trust and John Harrison has arranged for several beautiful Isle of Wight gardens to be open at that time which are not normally open to the public) • Entrance: approx. £1 (varies according to charity)

Twelve acres of wooded grounds surround a Jacobean manor house. There are three varied gardens (divided between members of the Harrison family) consisting of landscaped terraces leading down to the stream and water gardens; herbaceous borders, woodland walks, walled rose garden and walled kitchen garden containing over 50 varieties of apples. The more interesting plants include *Echium pininana* (biennial from the Canaries) on the top terrace by the pond; eucryphias; and the dainty little daisy *Erigeron mucronatus* in the rose garden that may have been inspired by Gertrude Jekyll. Northcourt offers bed and breakfast accommodation and could be the ideal spot for a gardener's tour of the Isle of Wight.

NUNWELL HOUSE 27

Coach Lane, Brading, Ryde, Isle of Wight. Tel: (0983) 407240
Col. and Mrs. J.A. Aylmer

3m S of Ryde, signed off the A3055 in Brading into Coach Lane • Best season: July and September • Parking • Toilet facilities • Shop • House open • Gardens open 30th June to 20th Sept, daily except Fri and Sat, 10 a.m. - 5 p.m. • Entrance: £2.30, OAP £1.80, children 60p (house and garden)

Nunwell House stands in six acres of gardens with wonderful views across the park to Spithead. The rose garden (originally a bowling green in the seventeenth century) is set at the top of a slope, in front of the walled garden (not open), which leads down the Long Walk past the side of the house, where stand two very handsome paulownias, to the front. The fountain came from the Crystal Palace and below the balustrade is a lily pond, formerly a swimming pool. Among the varied plants in the borders there is a pretty mallow 'Barnsley' and on the front of the house are two large myrtles. A steep flight of steps bordered by lavender leads up to the woods. To the rear of the house is an arboretum laid out by Russel Vernon Smith in 1963. The Aylmers are gradually restoring the gardens to their former glory.

OWL COTTAGE ★ 28

Hoxall Lane, Mottistone, Newport, Isle of Wight.
Tel: (0983) 740433
Mrs A.L. Hutchinson, Miss S.L. Leaning

From B3399 turn down Hoxall Lane by Mottistone green. Owl Cottage is 200 yards on right • Best season: late June/early July • Refreshments: homemade teas by appointment • Toilet facilities • Suitable for wheelchairs • Dogs • Open May to Aug, 2 - 6 p.m., by appointment for parties of 10 or more (max 24) • Entrance: £1

A brilliant cottage garden with sea views (the thatched cottage is sixteenth-century), planted to give year round colour. There are 23 flowering cherries and over 50 varieties of clematis, including the *balearica* flowering in sequence from January to October and the *armandii.* In addition to a large herbaceous section there are colourful bulbs and flowering shrubs, euphorbias, amaryllis lilies, agapanthus and delphiniums. The garden is the creation of the present owners.

PETERSFIELD PHYSIC GARDEN 29

16 High Street, Petersfield, Hampshire. Tel: (0730) 64709
Hampshire Gardens Trust

Located to the rear of No 16 High Street, Mackarness and Lunt solicitors office. Access at side • Best season: spring and summer • Public car park • Suitable for wheelchairs • Plants for sale • Open all year except 25th Dec, 9 a.m. - 5 p.m. • Entrance: free, donations welcome

Held within the arms of a walled garden that reach out to the rear of Petersfield High Street is the latest of a series of remarkable historic garden recreations undertaken by the Hampshire Gardens Trust. A small physic garden attended by beds holding the John Goodyer collection, named after the seventeenth-century Petersfield botanist, is rapidly establishing itself as a retreat for research or pleasure, for local residents, horticulturalists and a circle of latterday students of medicine and botany. The care and attention to detail is worthy of note and promises much for the knot garden and topiary walk to follow. Such ambition should be encouraged by contributing to the collection box and returning often.

QUEEN ELEANOR'S GARDEN 30

Great Hall, Castle Avenue, High Street, Winchester, Hampshire.
Tel: (0962) 84647
Hampshire County Council (sponsored by Hampshire Gardens Trust)

Through the Great Hall, central Winchester • Public car park nearby in Sussex Street • Suitable for wheelchairs • Shop • Open daily, 10 a.m. - 5 p.m., except winter weekends, 10 a.m. - 4 p.m. • Entrance: free

Faced with a wedge of land 90 × 30 feet and bounded by buildings, the designer, Dr Sylvia Landsberg, has achieved the only authentic recreation of its type in Britain of a thirteenth- century medieval pleasure garden. When viewed against the neighbouring wall of the Great Hall the maturing Queen's herber, tunnel arbour and the detailed research behind the rill and fountain make it just possible to forget that this is a garden of so recent creation.

ROTHERFIELD PARK 31

East Tisted, Alton, Hampshire. Tel: (042058) 204
Sir James and Lady Scott

4m S of Alton on A32 • Parking • Teas on charity open day. Picnickers welcome • Dogs on lead • Plants for sale • House open on charity open day • Garden open April to Sept, Sun, Tues and Thurs, 2 - 4 p.m. Also for charity 23rd June, 2 - 5 p.m. and by appointment • Entrance: £1, children free (house and gardens £2.50, children 50p)

Living at Chawton, less than 10m north, Jane Austen would have counted herself a neighbour, and an approving one, to Rotherfield estate which underwent picturesque improvement in the hands of J.T. Parkinson from 1815-1821. The elevated and exposed position of the house is superb and ideally suited to the lofty gothic architecture if not the sweet chestnuts and oaks which just survived the hurricanes of 1987 and 1990. The garden sensibly leaves the slopes to parkland and finds shelter in the walled area away from the watchful castellations, collonades and turrets of the house. Approached between yew hedges, buttressed with the golden variety, wrought-iron gates open to herbaceous borders, fan-trained apricots and apples and espalier fruit trees. Mindful of the disapproval of Miss Austen, remnants of the earlier eighteenth-century gardens are hidden in the park's woodlands.

SOUTHSEA COMMON and ESPLANADE SEAFRONT GARDENS 32

Clarence and Southsea Esplanade, Portsmouth, Hampshire.
Inquiries to Tourist Information Centre. Tel: (0705) 826722

Follow directions for Old Portsmouth but from Anglesey Road one way system turn left into Hampshire Terrace, continue to Pier Road and turn left down Clarence Esplanade • Best season: June to Sept • Southsea Castle car park and public parking nearby • Toilet facilities • Suitable for wheelchairs • Dogs • Open all year • Entrance: free

The heathland origins of Southsea Common and Esplanade could not be further from the minds of the many thousands of tourists as they admire year after year the extensive bedding out and manicured gardens. Quintessentially English, a tour of approximately four and a half miles will brazenly confirm the highest, or worst expectations of what the pleasure grounds of a seaside resort should be.

SPINNERS ★ 33

School Lane, Boldre, Nr Lymington, Hampshire. Tel: (0590) 673347
Mr and Mrs P.G.G. Chappell

1½m N of Lymington. From A337 Brockenhurst - Lymington road, turn E for Boldre. Signposted • Parking • Wide selection of plants for sale in nursery • Open April to Aug, daily, 10 a.m. - 6 p.m. Other times by appointment. Nursery open all year • Entrance: £1

Created and developed by the Chappells on a wooded slope falling westwards towards the Lymington river it is not difficult to understand why Roy Lancaster and many other plantsmen have so highly praised this garden. The spirit of the nearby New Forest has been carefully maintained and shade and acid-loving plants flourish beneath a canopy of indigenous and specimen shrubs and trees. *Cornus kousa chinensiss*, a grove of eucalyptus and unusual magnolias catch the eye amongst many other specimens that are improved by good plant associations. Cyclamen, erythroniums, trillium and hellebores in spring; lush hostas, primulas, ferns and rodgersias in the bog garden; magnolias in summer and the autumn colours of *Nyssa sinensis* and many maples ensure that wherever the meandering paths lead in this excellent informal garden there is always something of interest and apparently something of everything.

STANSTED PARK 34

Rowlands Castle, Hampshire. Tel: (0705) 412265
The Earl and Countess of Bessborough

1m N of Emsworth, just off the B2149 • Best season: early summer • Parking • Refreshments • Toilet facilities • Plants for sale • Shop • House open • Garden open Easter Sun and Mon, May to Sept, Sun - Tues inc. Bank Holidays, 2 - 6 p.m. Last admission 5.30 p.m. • Entrance: £1.50, OAP £1, children under 12 60p (house and grounds £2.50, OAP £2, children under 12 £1. Parties of 20 or more £2, children 80p per person)

A woodland walk with fine spring bulbs encloses walled gardens with good greenhouses with muscat vines and other organically-grown produce. There is an elegant Dutch-style rose garden, which is set off beautifully by the mellow red brick eighteenth-century house, and a fine arboretum which is quickly recovering from the gale damage of 1987. There is also a prettily set cricket ground with cricket every Sunday, taking place in view of the tea room.

THE TUDOR HOUSE MUSEUM 35

Tudor House, Bugle Street, Southampton, Hampshire.
Tel: (0703) 332513
Southampton City Council

A36 to West Quay Road or Western Esplanade or A33, follow signs to Docks and Town Quay • Parking by public swimming pool • Toilet facilities • Suitable for wheelchairs • Shop • Museum open • Garden open Tues - Fri, 10 a.m. - 12 noon, 1 - 5 p.m., Sat, 10 a.m. - 12 noon, 1 - 4 p.m., Sun, 2 - 5 p.m. • Entrance: free

This must be many people's favourite museum, not particularly for its collection although it is good, but for its timber-framed building and garden setting. Designed by Dr Sylvia Landsberg and completed in 1982 the garden is a convincing distillation of ornamental gardens of the Tudor period. Packed with authentic details, heraldic beasts, camomile lawn, knot garden and many old English flowers and sixteenth-century roses this is a surprisingly peaceful place.

VENTNOR BOTANIC GARDEN ★★ 36

The Undercliffe Drive, Ventnor, Isle of Wight. Tel: (0983) 855397
South Wight Borough Council

Follow signs from A3055 • Paying car park • Refreshments: restaurant/café, licensed bar • Toilet facilities • Suitable for wheelchairs • Dogs • Limited plants for sale • Shop • Garden open all year. Temperate House, Easter to Oct, daily, 10 a.m. - 5 p.m., Oct to Easter, Tues - Thurs, 11 a.m. - 3 p.m., Sun, 1 - 4 p.m. • Entrance: free (50p, children 20p for Temperate House)

Twenty-two acres, sheltered from north and east and planted with *Quercus ilex*, *Pinus nigra* and cypresses interspersed with escallonia, griselinia and viburnums to give shelter from sea winds to the south. Many tender plants (including olives; *Berberis asiatica* and *Acer sikkimensis* from the Himalayas; *Cestrum elegans* from Mexico; *Pittosporum daphniphylloides* from China all of which flourish in the mild climate). The rose garden has over 700 hybrid teas and floribundas also modern shrub, Banksian, climbing, rambler, rugosa, etc. The pinetum has many exotic species from the Canary Islands, New Zealand and China and in the palm garden banana plants from Japan and *Citrus ichangensis* are but a few of the rare plants displayed to maximum effect in surroundings designed by Geoffrey Hillier. There is also a magnificent temperate house with a worldwide collection of plants from the warmest zones of the world, together with impressive written and pictorial displays. There is an Australian section, a central bed of flowers from southern Africa, an island section with palms from Crete and a unique collection from St Helena. Damage by gales in 1987 and 1990 has caused the management to begin replanting with windproof varieties.

THE VYNE 37

Sherborne St John, Nr Basingstoke, Hampshire. Tel: (0256) 881337
The National Trust

4m N of Basingstoke between Sherborne St John and Bramley on A340, turn E at NT signs • Parking • Refreshments: light lunches, homemade teas, 12.30 - 2 p.m., 3 - 5.30 p.m. • Toilet facilities • Suitable for wheelchairs • Dogs in car park only • Shop • House open 1.30 - 5.30 p.m., Mon, 11 a.m. - 5.30 p.m. Last admission 5 p.m. • Garden open 29th March to Oct, daily except Mon and Fri, 12.30 - 5.30 p.m. Open Good Fri and Bank Holiday Mon (but closed Tues following), 11 a.m. - 5.30 p.m. • Entrance: £1.70 (house £3.40). Parties £2.20 per person Tues - Thurs only

This example of the English School was landscaped by John Chute between 1755 and 1776 to complement the early classical portico and garden houses designed by John Webb, disciple of Inigo Jones. Though not as grand or extensive as many country houses in the ownership of The National Trust this early sixteenth-century house provides to the west of its modest entrance one of the best though small, herbaceous borders of such properties and to the north broad lawns and fine trees that perfectly match the famous Corinthian portico. The framed views to the house from across the lake will amply reward those who venture the woodland walk. Other features include stone seats in architectural yews, great oaks, the Garden House lake and *Phillyrea latifolia* specimens.

YAFFLES 38

Bonchurch, Ventnor, Isle of Wight. Tel: (0983) 852193
Mrs Wolfenden

Immediately above St Boniface Church in Bonchurch • Best season: April/May • Parking in road • Refreshments: home-made teas • Dogs on lead • Plants for sale • Shop • Open 26th May, 16th June, 2.30 - 5 p.m. • Entrance: probably £1, children free

A quarter of an acre of sheltered cliff garden with spectacular sea views, sculpted by Mrs Wolfenden from a precipice overgrown with weeds and scrub. Years of very hard work have made this garden of ledges and glades, with a variety of flowering shrubs, spring bulbs and plants of botanical interest. Taking advantage of the mild climate of the island's undercliff the owner has succeeded in creating a sheet of colour all the year round.

GARDENS OPEN RARELY

The following gardens are open to the public on three days or less in the year, although they may also be open by appointment if this is stated in the text. For details see individual entry.

May 19 Northcourt; **May 26** Yaffles; **June 7** The Manor House; **June 15** The Manor House; **June 16** Yaffles; **June 22** Northcourt; **June 30** Moundsmere Manor.

HEREFORD & WORCESTER

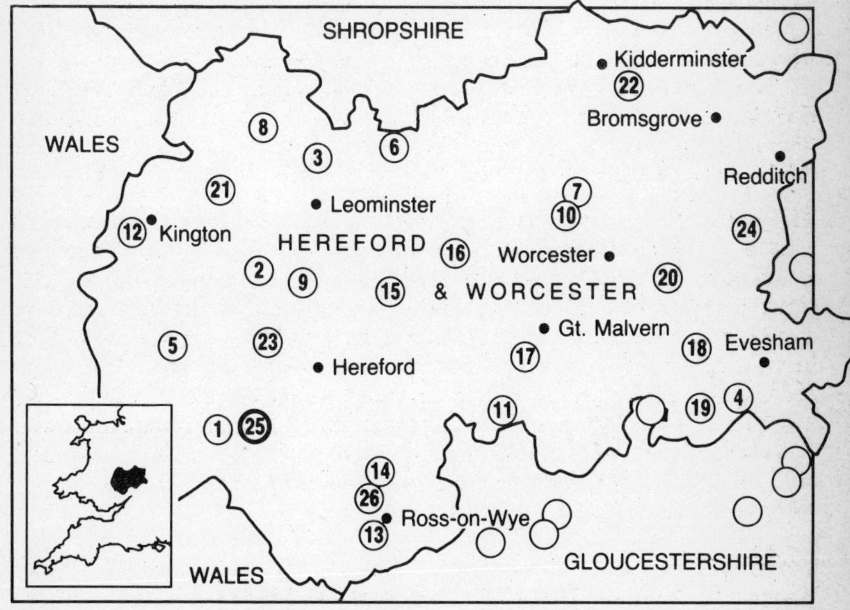

Plain circle numbers can be found by turning to neighbouring counties. Two-starred gardens are ringed in bold.

ABBEY DORE COURT 1

Abbey Dore, Hereford, Hereford and Worcester. Tel: (0981) 240419
Mrs C.L. Ward

11m SW of Hereford • Parking • Refreshments: from 11.30 a.m. • Toilet facilities • Partly suitable for wheelchairs • Plants for sale • Gift gallery • Open 3rd Sat in March to 3rd Sun in Oct, daily except Wed, 11 a.m. - 6 p.m. • Entrance: £1.25, children 50p

Mrs Ward is a noted plantswoman and the large garden has much of interest. Two old sequoias dominate the garden once edged by the river but now extended into a meadow with a pool and well-planted rockery. Another recent area of expansion contains a more formal arrangement in which greys and whites are much in evidence and in large beds near the walled fruit garden there is the NCCPG collection of sedums.

ARROW COTTAGE GARDEN 2

Ledgemoor, Weobley, Hereford and Worcester. Tel: (00544) 318468
Mr and Mrs L. Hattatt

10m NW of Hereford • Best season: May/June • Parking on roadside • Open March to July, Sept, Wed – Fri and Sun, 2 – 5 p.m. Closed Aug. At other times by appointment • Entrance: £1, children free

Designed as a series of small gardens by the present owner and his family since 1972. The older part of the garden, planted long before the expansion over the little stream that winds through the property is, perhaps, rather reminiscent of the surroundings of an ideal Wendy House and there is a marked contrast on crossing the tiny bridge to later and more formal areas, much of them still in the preliminary stages of planting. However, the one and a half acres contain some interesting flowers, trees and shrubs and everything is very well maintained.

BERRINGTON HALL 3

Leominster, Hereford and Worcester. Tel: (0568) 5721
The National Trust

3m S of Leominster on W side of A49 • Parking • Refreshments: lunches and teas (opening 12.30 p.m.). Picnic tables in car park • Toilet facilities • Suitable for wheelchairs • National Trust shop • House open 30th March to April, Sat, Sun and Bank Holiday Mon, 1.30 – 5.30 p.m. May to Sept, Wed – Sun and Bank Holiday Mon, 1.30 – 5.30 p.m. Oct, Sat and Sun, 1.30 – 4.30 p.m. Last admission ½ hour before closing. Grounds open from 12.30 p.m. • Entrance: £1 (house and grounds £2.70)

This late eighteenth-century house designed by Henry Holland is set in mature grounds landscaped by 'Capability' Brown. The gardens have seen better times but are well-maintained. The new woodland area needs time to mature and a new orchard planting scheme has been undertaken in the walled garden. There is a joint entry ticket with Croft Castle nearby (see entry) and the best value for intending visitors is the joint ticket giving entry to both houses and gardens, although those not interested in the houses may feel that the afternoon becomes a little expensive.

BREDON SPRINGS 4

Ashton-under-Hill, Evesham, Hereford and Worcester.
Tel: (0386) 881328
Mr R. Sidwell

6m SW of Evesham • Best season: early summer • Small free car park 300 yards from garden • Dogs • Open April to Oct, Sat, Sun, Wed, Thurs, also Bank Holiday Mons and following Tues, 10 a.m. – dusk • Entrance: 75p, children free

A plantsman's garden created by the owner over the last 40 years with a diverse collection of material, carefully arranged and planted in an old cottage garden. Areas of woodland have been added to increase the range of growing conditions. There are signs of a decline and some of the plantings are becoming overgrown. In several parts of the garden the aggressive weed *Hippuris vulgaris*, marestail and horsetail, is becoming well established. Nevertheless, a garden which still retains some unusual and interesting plants.

BROBURY GARDENS AND GALLERY 5

Brobury, Hereford and Worcester. Tel: (09817) 229
Mr E. Okarma

11m W of Hereford • Parking • Toilet facilities • Art Gallery open • Garden open May to Sept, Mon - Sat, 9 a.m. - 4.30 p.m. • Entrance: £1.50, OAP £1, children 50p

This is what might be expected to have been enjoyed by a well-to-do Victorian gentleman. Conifers, some formal terracing, good trees, herbaceous borders as well as modern planting including a nice young stand of *Betula jacquemontii* and clever use of conifers to conceal electricity poles. More interesting plants can be found in antique prints in the Gallery which has a very wide selection, both horticultural and general. Brobury, facing, as it does, both Moccas and Bredwardine where the diarist Kilvert was vicar for the last few months of his life and where he is buried, is a convenient stop on the Kilvert Trail. A walk through the famous avenue of Scots Firs to Monnington will take the literary pilgrim to where he baptised, in 1879, Francis Theodora, the daughter of his brother-in-law, the Rector. More than half-a-century later she destroyed the major part of his voluminous diary before publication.

BURFORD HOUSE GARDENS ★ 6

Tenbury Wells, Hereford and Worcester. Tel: (0584) 810777
Mr J. Treasure

1m W of Tenbury Wells on A456 • Best season: summer • Parking close to garden • Refreshments: tea room • Toilet facilities • Suitable for wheelchairs • Plants for sale in nursery open Mon - Sat, 9 a.m. - 5 p.m., Sun, 2 - 5 p.m. • Bookshop in tea room • Open 16th March to 20th Oct, Mon - Sat, 11 a.m. - 5 p.m., Sun, 2 - 5 p.m. • Entrance: £1.95, children 80p. Parties 25 and over £1.60 per person

The Georgian house dates from 1728 but the gardens today from only 1954 when the present owners took over. The garden and adjoining nursery is best known for its collection of clematis. However, it is very diverse in its plants and plantings. Formal water gardens at the rear of the house give way to a variety of informal shrub and herbaceous borders. Good autumn colour is provided by the woodland planting. A garden that cannot fail to please throughout the growing season.

CLACKS FARM 7

Boreley, Ombersley, Hereford and Worcester. Tel: (0905) 620250
Mr and Mrs A. Billitt

1m N of Ombersley on A449. Turn left into Woodfield Lane and follow signs for about 2m • Refreshments: tea, coffee, soft drinks • Toilet facilities • Suitable for wheelchairs • Dogs on lead • Plants for sale • Open 11th, 12th May, 8th, 9th June, 13th, 14th July, 10th, 11th Aug, 7th, 8th Sept and 27th, 28th July for 'Gardening Time' show. Coaches by appointment at any time • Entrance: £1, children 50p

This garden was created by the Billitts with T.V. demonstrations in mind. There are eight glasshouses, a large fruit and vegetable garden. Ornamental and water gardens. It is very much a learning garden and planted to teach the amateur, particularly the lover of annuals. Mr Billett has a lifetime's experience of fruit growing and, with his wife, thinks nothing of planting out 15,000 bedding plants a year. Several of the beds are trial grounds for major seedsmen and, in season, offer as much colour and more information than a major city's Parks Department. It has been featured many times on *Gardener's World*.

CROFT CASTLE 8

Leominster, Hereford and Worcester. Tel: (056885) 246
The National Trust

5m NW of Leominster off B4362 • Parking • Refreshments: light lunches and teas. Picnics in parkland • Toilet facilities • Partly suitable for wheelchairs • Dogs in park only on lead • Plants for sale • House open • Garden open Easter Sat, Sun, Mon, 2 - 6 p.m., May to Sept, Wed - Sun and Bank Holiday Mon, 2 - 6 p.m. Last admission ½ hour before closing • Entrance: £2.40. Parkland and Croft Ambrey open all year

This is a traditional estate garden with formal beds around the house which dates from the fourteenth century. It is well-kept and pleasant to walk through but lacks specific interest for the specialist except perhaps for the walled garden which is in good condition and the fine avenue of Spanish chestnuts. There are charming walks in the Fishpool valley. Berrington Hall is nearby (see entry).

DINMORE MANOR 9

Dinmore, Leominster, Hereford and Worcester. Tel: (043271) 240
Mr R.G. Murray

6m N of Hereford on A49. 1m driveway signposted • Best season: summer • Parking • Teas occasionally during summer • Toilet facilities • Suitable for wheelchairs • Open daily, 9.30 - 5.30 p.m. • Entrance: £2, OAP £1, accompanied children under 14 free

The site includes the twelfth – fourteenth-century church of the Knights Hospitaller. An unusual garden centred around the small church, its outstanding feature is the rock garden with some excellent specimens of *Acer palmatum*. This part of the garden is bordered on two sides by modern cloisters linking the house to a small tower which help to evoke a medieval atmosphere. The house and garden are built on high ground with surrounding stone wall giving way to lower ground and some fine views.

EASTGROVE COTTAGE GARDEN NURSERY 10

Sankyns Green, Nr Shrawley, Little Witley, Hereford and Worcester. Tel: (0299) 896389
Mr and Mrs J. Malcolm Skinner

8m NW of Worcester between Shrawley (B4196) and Great Witley (A443) • Best season: June/July • Parking. Coaches by appointment • Toilet facilities • Suitable for wheelchairs • Plants for sale • Open April to July, Sept to Nov, daily except Tues and Wed, 2 – 5 p.m. Closed Aug • Entrance: £1, children 20p

This delightful cottage garden with a superb range of hardy plants has been created and maintained by the present owners since 1970. The garden is full of colour, spring to autumn. It has the benefit of being connected with a commercial nursery developed by the owners and is highly recommended to plantspersons and others.

EASTNOR CASTLE 11

Eastnor, Ledbury, Hereford and Worcester. Tel: (0531) 2304/5
Eastnor Estates

2m E of Ledbury on A438 • Best seasons: spring and early autumn • Parking • Refreshments on Castle open days • Toilet facilities • Dogs on lead • Shop • Castle open selected days for collection of armour and tapestries. Parties by appointment any day • Open Easter Sun and Bank Holiday Mons, end May to Sept, Sun, July and Aug, Wed and Thurs, 2.15 – 5.30 p.m. Parties by appointment at other times • Entrance: £1.50 (house and garden £2.50)

Essentially an arboretum, Eastnor has one of the best nineteenth-century plantings in the country with many mature specimens. It is worth visiting early in the year for the display of spring bulbs. The house is an early nineteenth-century castle in medieval style surrounded by a deer park now, alas, much overgrown. Maintenance is largely confined to the vicinity of the Castle and the trees rise, and, in some cases, lie fallen amid a jungle of saplings and weeds. The view of the Castle from the far end of the large lake is still striking although a considerable area of the latter is covered in summer with a thick growth of 'Pattypans', *Nuphar lutea*, the common yellow waterlily, and around the edges are clumps of khaki shelters which, by day, partially conceal the coke cans of the common white fisherman. To judge by the number of tractors, the estate is not without staff, and it is sad to see such a noble and extensive park degenerating. Despite the great variety of both conifers and broad-leaved trees there are no labels. However, some replanting has been undertaken in parts of the estate and paths have been kept clear, and the keen tree enthusiast will enjoy the long walks in the woodland.

HERGEST CROFT GARDEN ★ 12

Kington, Hereford and Worcester. Tel: (0544) 230160
W.L. Banks and R.A. Banks

½m W of Kington off A44 • Parking • Teas • Toilet facilities • Partly suitable for wheelchairs • Dogs on lead • Plants for sale • Shop • Open April to Oct, daily • Entrance: £1.60, children 80p, season ticket £6

This has been the family home of the Banks family since 1896, and the garden design was much influenced by the writings of William Robinson and Gertrude Jekyll. There is an interesting collection of plants including huge rhododendrons in delightful woodland setting which extends to 50 acres and has general appeal as well as to the plantsperson. Formal garden. Half a mile through the park is a wood containing, in season, vast sheets of rhododendrons quite 30 feet high. By following the path at the top of the dingle you can look down on a scene not far removed from those in their native habitat. In late May, wellington boots are usually necessary not least in crossing the park in which many sheep graze.

THE HILL COURT 13

Hom Green, Ross-on-Wye, Hereford and Worcester. Tel: (0989) 64144
Mr C. Rowley

2¼m SW of Ross-on-Wye. Take B4228 towards Walford, after ½m bear right and follow garden signs for 1½m to lodge gates on right • Best season: summer • Parking • Refreshments: tearoom open daily • Toilet facilities • Suitable for wheelchairs • Dogs on lead • Plants for sale at garden centre open daily • Walled garden, Yew walk and water garden open daily without charge. Private gardens open for charity on certain Sundays, 2 – 5.30 p.m. • Entrance: £1.50, OAP and children 75p

An eighteenth-century Grade I listed house (not open). The Hill Court is set in a park, the house itself being approached by a splendid avenue. A large walled garden has been set out with symmetrical beds, clipped low hedges and garden furniture, the borders being arranged to highlight in turn those plants at their best in each of the twelve months. Old pear trees, carefully trained, a large glasshouse and well-kept paths preserve the image of what was, presumably, the kitchen garden while at the same time offering an elegant and educational place in which to walk. Another smaller walled garden of great charm is used for teas with accommodation under cover if it is wet. Large outbuildings and an area surrounded by hedges house a small garden centre with well-grown, if slightly pricey, general stock. The private gardens include a bronze and silver fountain garden.

HOW CAPLE COURT 14

How Caple, Hereford, Hereford and Worcester. Tel: (0989) 86626
Mr and Mrs Peter Lee

10m SE of Hereford on B4224, turn right at How Caple crossroads • Best season: summer • Parking • Refreshments on Sun and Bank Holidays. Parties by appointment • Toilet facilities • Partly suitable for wheelchairs • Dogs on leads • Plants for sale • Shop • Open Easter to Oct, Mon - Sat, 9.30 a.m. - 5 p.m., also May to Sept, Sun, 10 a.m. - 5 p.m. • Entrance: £2, children £1

A large house and medieval church set in 11 acres of grounds with fine trees lining a valley which flows down to a bend in the River Wye. Much of the Edwardian planting is being re-established, there are good formal terraces, and a big pool surrounded by a curious pergola. A large ruined Florentine garden is in the process of restoration and if the original water supply can be replaced the whole should be spectacular. There is a fabric shop on one side of the stable yard and a small area selling some unusual shrubs and old roses. Recent plantings in the valley are maturing well, but there is still a good deal of work to be done if the gardens' former glory is to be recaptured.

LOWER HOPE 15

Ullingswick, Hereford and Worcester.
Mr and Mrs Clive Richards

At the roundabout on the A465 nr Burley Gate take the A417 towards Leominster. After 2m turn right. Lower Hope is about ½m on left. Signposted • Parking • Refreshments • Toilet facilities • Suitable for wheelchairs • Open 14th April, 7th July, 2 - 6 p.m. • Entrance: £1, children free

On entering this five-acre garden through a gate in the hedge which largely conceals it from the road, the effect is of finding the south banks of the Chelsea Flower Show transported bodily to Herefordshire. Artfully contrived streams meander, crossed by Japanese-style bridges under which swim Koi carp; beds backed with shrubs and filled with perennials and annuals in profusion; serried masses of roses; herbaceous borders; a laburnum tunnel; fruit and vegetable gardens; two conservatories full of giant begonias, ferns and the grander kind of indoor pot display, a swimming pool surrounded by fashionable garden furniture, a paved yard with a weather-vaned stable block. There are many interesting shrubs and everything is a great tribute to the Richards' gardeners.

MARLEY BANK 16

Bottom Lane, Whitbourne, Hereford and Worcester. Tel: (0886) 21576
Mr and Mrs R. Norman

10m W of Worcester on A44. Turn right to Whitbourne. At T junction by church after 1m turn left for 600 yards • Restricted parking • Plants for sale • Open 6th April to 12th Oct, Sat, 10 a.m. - 5.30 p.m. and by appointment. Closed 13th to 20th July • Entrance: 80p

Sue and Roger Norman are experts and the garden not only contains a great variety of plants in terraced beds but has been created with a designer's eye for form and texture. Very few of these plants are at all common, unusual cultivars are the norm, and rare treasures, particularly alpines, abound. The many paths are carefully constructed of different materials to complement the plantings and the whole looks out over a very fine view. All plants for sale are propagated at Marley Bank and purchasers need have no qualms about nomenclature and provenance - factors not always found in sales from private gardens.

OLD COURT NURSERIES 17

Colwall, Malvern, Hereford and Worcester. Tel: (0684) 40416
Mr and Mrs P. Picton

3m W of Malvern on B4218 • Best season: Sept/Oct • Limited parking • Suitable for wheelchairs • Plants for sale • Open April to Oct, daily except Tues, 10 a.m. - 1 p.m., 2.15 - 5.30 p.m. • Entrance: £1

This small garden has been created on the site of the Old Court Nurseries. It retains a nursery atmosphere (old frames now contain alpine beds) and plants for sale in neat rows. Herbaceous borders and shrubs create diversity. Holds the NCCPG Michaelmas daisy collection, a genus on which the owner, Paul Picton, the son of the late Percy Picton, is an acknowledged expert.

PERSHORE COLLEGE OF HORTICULTURE 18

Avonbank, Pershore, Hereford and Worcester. Tel: (0386) 552443
Hereford and Worcester County Council

1m S of Pershore on A44. 7m from M5 junction 7 • Best season: summer • Parking • Toilet facilities • Suitable for wheelchairs • Dogs on lead • Plants for sale • Open 1st June, 10.30 a.m. - 5 p.m. (College open day), 23rd June, 2 - 5.30 p.m. for charity. Also weekdays for RHS members, and every Thurs and Fri for retail plant sales, 2 - 4.30 p.m. • Entrance: free for RHS members

The gardens are designed with a definite bias towards education so although not picturesque they are worth visiting. Extensive ornamental grounds include an arboretum, orchard, vegetables, automated glasshouses and a large commercial nursery. The RHS Centre at Pershore and Alpine Garden Society Headquarters are situated on the College estate.

THE PRIORY 19

Kemerton, Tewkesbury, Hereford and Worcester. Tel: (038689) 258
Mr and the Hon. Mrs Peter Healing

5m NE of Tewkesbury off B4080 • Parking • Suitable for wheelchairs • Dogs on lead • Plants for sale at small nursery • Open 26th May, 23rd June, 14th July, 4th, 25th Aug, 15th Sept and June to Sept, Thurs, 2 – 7 p.m. • Entrance: £1, children free

A garden of herbaceous borders, planted in colour groups with many unusual trees and shrubs. A stream garden, sunken garden and fern garden add diversity and the careful use of colours and textures using a wide range of plants, many of them unusual, make the borders outstanding. Mr Healing is a most accomplished plantsman and, when he is present in the small plant sales area, is always happy to answer questions.

SPETCHLEY PARK 20

Spetchley, Nr Worcester, Hereford and Worcester.
Tel: (090565) 224/213
Mr J. Berkeley

3m E of Worcester on A422 • Parking • Refreshments on Sun and Bank Holidays • Toilet facilities • Suitable for wheelchairs • Plant centre • Open 29th March to Sept, daily except Sat, weekdays 11 a.m. – 5 p.m., Suns and Bank Holidays, 2 – 5 p.m. • Entrance: £1.70, children 90p

Rose Berkeley was sister of the great Ellen Willmott and in her day the garden was one of the wonders of England. Now, this formal garden provides many vistas along borders and walls, through clipped yew hedges and open arches. Combined with the successive planning and planting it has a rich and abundant feel. The old kitchen garden is now surrounded by splendid borders although the beds within the walls would be improved by thinning out. There are large drifts of naturalised Turk's Cap lilies, in early July, and the new rock beds near the entrance are maturing well. As one would expect, fine specimen trees abound and the wooden rusticated arbour must be one of the best examples of Victorian taste in garden furniture still standing.

STAUNTON PARK 21

Staunton-on-Arrow, Leominster, Hereford and Worcester.
Tel: (05447) 474
Mr E.J.L. and Miss A. Savage

3m from Pembridge, 6m from Kington on the Titley road. Signposted • Best season: spring/summer • Parking inside garden • Teas • Toilet facilities • Suitable for wheelchairs • Dogs on lead • Plants for sale • Shop • Norman church adjoining open • Garden open April to mid-Oct, Tues, Wed and Sun, 2 – 6 p.m. • Entrance: £1, children 50p

Suffering somewhat after two years of drought this 14-acre garden, now in its fourth year of opening, offers a spacious setting for some fine trees, mixed borders, a lake and a herb garden laid out on traditional lines. If the heavy Victorian planting of *Rhododendron ponticum* and the rampant bracken could be eliminated from the far side of the lake the effect would be much enhanced.

STONE HOUSE COTTAGE GARDENS 22

Stone, Kidderminster, Hereford and Worcester. Tel: (0562) 69902
Major and the Hon. Mrs Arbuthnott

2m SE of Kidderminster via A448 • Parking • Toilet facilities • Suitable for wheelchairs • Plants for sale • Open March to Oct, Wed - Sat, and May and June, Suns, 10 a.m. - 6 p.m. • Entrance: £1, children free

This sheltered walled garden is an absolute delight for plantsman and amateur alike. Not only for the rare herbaceous plants, shrubs and climbers but for the overall picture they create. There is also a nursery adjacent to the garden with a large selection of plants for sale, emphasis being on the less hardy. Major Arbuthnot is as handy with a bricklayer's as with a gardener's trowel and the skyline is ornamented with several handsome towers from which, during the local Music Festival, suitable music is played by professional wind ensembles and you are invited to picnic in the garden for a modest fee. The effect is akin to a non-pretentious Glyndebourne or a transplanted San Gimingnano. At other times you may ascend the towers to view the garden as a whole for the price of a donation to the Mother Theresa charity.

THE WEIR GARDEN 23

Swainshill, Hereford and Worcester.
The National Trust

5m W of Hereford on A438 • Best season: spring • Parking • No coaches • Open 14th Feb to Oct, Wed - Sun and Bank Holiday Mon, 11 a.m. - 6 p.m. Closed on Good Friday • Entrance: £1

This garden offers a pleasant walk along the banks of the Wye. The main interest is to visit in the spring since the chief charm resides in the drifts of bulbs. It is terraced in an informal way on a cliffside and would be improved by extensive replanting. Features include a small Japanese-style garden.

WHITE COTTAGE (Cranesbill Nursery) 24

Earls Common Road, Stock Green, Hereford and Worcester.
Tel: (0386) 792414
Mr and Mrs S.M. Bates

7m E of Worcester off A422 • Best season: May/June • Limited parking • Teas at Jinny Ring Craft Centre, Hanbury (approx 5m) • Toilet facilities

• Suitable for wheelchairs • Plants for sale • Open Easter to Oct. Daily in early months except Thurs, 10 a.m. - 5 p.m. but by appointment only in Aug and Oct • Entrance: 75p for charity, children free

A two-acre garden with large lawns bordered by interesting shrub and herbaceous borders created by the owner over the last 8 years. Artificial stream bordered by peat blocks creates good conditions for primula collection. Extensive collection of hardy geraniums. Part of the garden has been set aside for a small nursery selling many of the plants featured in the garden.

WHITFIELD ★★ 25

Wormbridge, Hereford and Worcester.
Mr G.M. Clive

8m SW of Hereford on A465 to Abergavenny • Picnic parties welcome • Suitable for wheelchairs • Open 9th June, 2 - 6 p.m. and occasionally for local charities - see local press for details • Entrance: £1, children 50p

Within this large park, the owner has created one of the largest private gardens made in Britain in the last half-century. The park itself has some fine old trees which may be seen on the one-and-a-half-mile woodland walk, including an 1851 redwood grove and what is said to be the tallest oak in Britain. Near the house, a new terrace with fine planting and statuary was the first step towards developing the grand garden which expands across the lawn to the south of the house. To the east a large cedar dominates an area now managed as a wildflower meadow, cut only twice a year. To the north, Mr Clive has created superb water features, including a lake and, rare in this century, a folly ruin. Attractive planting too, for the plantsperson.

WOODLANDS 26

Bridstow, Hoarwithy Road, Nr Ross-on-Wye, Hereford and Worcester.
Tel: (0989) 62972
Mr and Mrs Shadforth

1m from Ross. At junction of A40 and A49, turn for Hereford and then turn right towards Hoarwithy. Woodlands is ½m on left • Parking • Suitable for wheelchairs • Open April to Sept by appointment • Entrance: £1, children 50p

Truly a labour of love, the garden makes clever use of the lie of the land and the many winding beds are generously filled with a wide variety of shrubs and herbaceous plants. Clematis twines through trees and shrubs, there are many different penstemons, ivies, roses, bulbs and climbers. From every part of the garden the eye is led gently to another. A small formal pond contains water lilies. Paths and lawns wind immaculately through the whole. A walled and trellised *potager* seems almost too pretty to allow for harvesting. Woodlands provides bed and breakfast and so is a useful centre for a garden tour of the area.

GARDENS OPEN RARELY

The following gardens are open to the public on three days or less in the year, although they may also be open by appointment if this is stated in the text. For details see individual entry.

April 14 Lower Hope; **June 1** Pershore College; **June 9** Whitfield; **June 23** Pershore College; **July 7** Lower Hope.

HERTFORDSHIRE

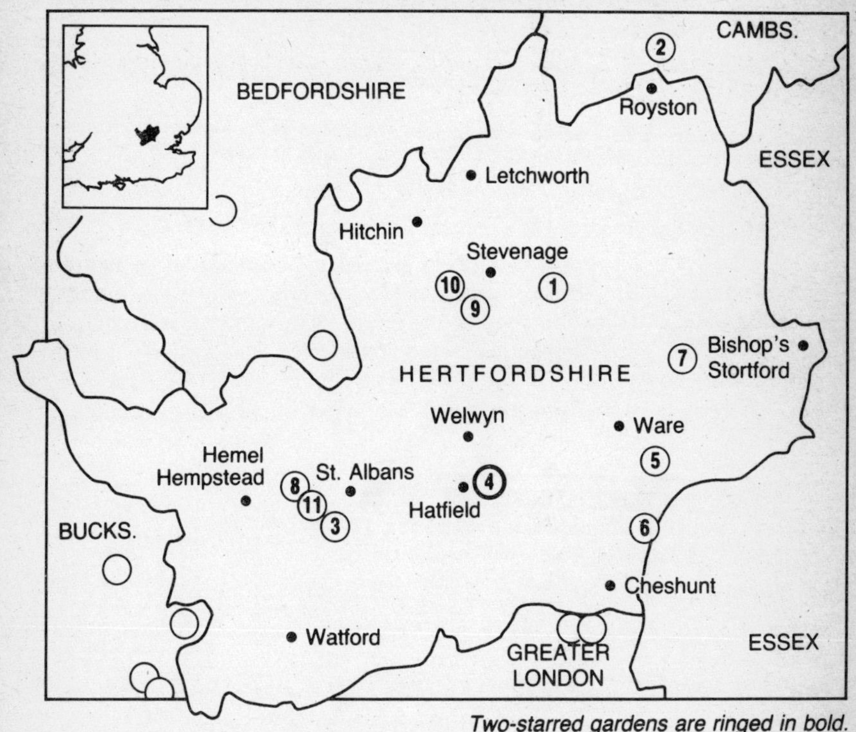

Two-starred gardens are ringed in bold.

BENINGTON LORDSHIP ★ 1

Benington, Nr Stevenage, Hertfordshire. Tel: (043885) 668
Mr and Mrs C.H.A. Bott

5m E of Stevenage • Parking • Refreshments • Toilet facilities • Plants and pots for sale • Open Easter and Summer Bank Holiday, 12 noon – 5 p.m., April to Sept, Wed, 12 noon – 5 p.m., April to Aug, Sun, 2 – 5 p.m. • Entrance £2, OAP £2, children free

Here is a garden that has almost everything: wonderful views, lakes to wander round, a Victorian folly and a Norman keep and moat, as well as a colourful rockery and big double herbaceous borders. Borders in the kitchen garden are in the process of being made – one in shades of gold and silver, another full of penstemons.

CAPEL MANOR

(see London)

DOCWRA'S MANOR 2

Shepreth, Royston, Hertfordshire.
Tel: (0763) 261473, 261537, 260235
Mrs John Raven

8m SW of Cambridge, ½m W of A10. Opposite war memorial • Best season: May - July • Parking in street • Toilet facilities • Suitable for wheelchairs • Small nursery with hardy plants for sale • Open all year, Mon, Wed, Fri, 10 a.m. - 5 p.m. and 7th April, 5th May, 2nd June, 7th July, 4th Aug, 1st Sept, 2 - 6 p.m. Also by appointment. Parties welcome • Entrance: £1, accompanied children under 16 free

This two and a half-acre garden round a Queen Anne house has been created by the owner since 1954. It is divided into different areas by using buildings, hedges and walls, thus enabling choice and tender plants to be protected from winds. Collections of euphorbias and clematis species. The garden has been encouraged to grow jungle-like and seedlings are left to grow where they will unless they are near something too small. Many bulbs and unusual plants.

GARDENS OF THE ROSE ★ 3

Chigwell Green, St Albans, Hertfordshire. Tel: (0727) 50461
Royal National Rose Society

2m S of St Albans on B4630 (signposted) • Parking • Refreshments: licensed cafeteria • Toilet facilities • Suitable for wheelchairs with good facilities for disabled • Dogs on lead • Miniature rose plants for sale, growers' catalogues available • Open 15th June to 20th Oct, Mon - Sat, 9 a.m. - 5 p.m., Suns and Bank Holidays, 10 a.m. - 6 p.m. • Entrance: £2.20, OAP and disabled £1.50, groups £1.70 per person. Members and children free

The Royal National Rose Gardens provide a wonderful display of one of the best and most important collections of roses in the world. There are some 30,000 rose trees and at least 1700 varieties including hybrid teas, floribundas and climbing roses of every kind, miniature roses and ground-cover roses. Some of the roses are thought to differ little from the roses admired in the classical world. Part of the gardens is the trial grounds for roses from all over the world. The Society is now trying to introduce other plants which harmonize with roses and enhance the planting schemes to give a more natural effect. Already there is a touch of blue from a bank of geraniums and an edging of golden *Alchemilla mollis*. H.M. The Queen Mother is particularly fond of old roses and the garden named for her contains a fascinating collection of Gallicas, Albas, Damasks, Centifolias, Portlands and Moss roses. Here can be seen what is thought to be the original red rose of Lancaster and white rose of York. Among the Gallicas is the 'Rosa Mundi' said to have been named for Fair Rosamond, the mistress of Henry II. This is an historic wonderland which could be explored indefinitely by rose lovers and will have interest for all gardeners. (Note: for those who wish to be up-to-date, hybrid teas and floribundas are now known as large-flowered and cluster-flowered roses respectively.) The garden is being enlarged over the next ten years from its current 12 to some 60 acres.

HATFIELD HOUSE ★★ 4

Hatfield, Hertfordshire. Tel: (0707) 262823
The Marquess and Marchioness of Salisbury

Opposite Hatfield railway station on A1000. 2m from A1(M) junction 4 • Parking • Refreshments: light meals and teas, 11 a.m. - 5 p.m. • Toilet facilities • Suitable for wheelchairs • Plants for sale • Shops • House open • Garden open 25th March to 13th Oct. West Gardens, daily except Good Friday, 11 a.m. - 6 p.m. East Garden (Lord and Lady Salisbury's private garden) Mon except Bank Holidays, 2 - 5 p.m. • Entrance: £2.15, OAP £2, children £1.60 (house supplement £1.75, children £1.10). Enquire for party rates

Originally laid out in the early seventeenth century by Robert Cecil and planted by John Tradescant the Elder. Nothing new can be written about this fascinating garden with its presiding genius the Marchioness of Salisbury except to say do visit it. Try to choose a time when the private gardens in front of the house are open for it is here that some of the most beautiful plants are to be seen. See the mop-headed *Quercus ilex* imported especially for the garden and the great double anemone said to have been given to Tradescant, now re-introduced and growing. Amongst the many features are the varied knot gardens, the wilderness and the scented gardens. There is an annual midsummer festival at Hatfield, part country fair, part garden party and part flower show, which gives an opportunity to visit the gardens, including the splendid East Garden, normally only open on Monday afternoons in season.

HILL HOUSE ★ 5

Stanstead Abbots, Ware, Hertfordshire. Tel: (0920) 870013
Mr and Mrs R. Pilkington

Halfway between Hertford and Harlow. From A10 turn E on to A414, and at roundabout take B181 for Stanstead Abbots, left at end of High Street and first right past church • Parking • Teas • Toilet facilities • Suitable for wheelchairs • Dogs on lead • Plants for sale • Picture gallery • Open 5th May, 2nd, 9th June, 7th July, 2 - 5.30 p.m. • Entrance: £1.50, OAP £1, children 50p

Six acres of very varied garden including woodland, a bog garden, a fine herbaceous border and a highly recommended conservatory. The owners tend the immaculate borders themselves and employ help to mow the extensive lawns. A delightful cottage garden. A magnificent conservatory. The position is an interesting one, on a south-facing slope overlooking Stanstead Abbotts and as a bonus, ospreys have been seen in the valley.

HIPKINS 6

Broxbourne, Hertfordshire.
Mr Stuart Douglas Hamilton and Mr Michael Goulding

1m from Broxbourne. From A10 to Broxbourne turn up Bell or Park Lane to Baas Lane • Parking • Teas • Toilet facilities • Suitable for wheelchairs • Dogs on lead • Plants for sale • Open 19th May, 2.30 - 6.00 p.m. for charity • Entrance £1, children 20p

Mr Goulding is a famous flower arranger and lecturer and grows much of his material in this charming oasis in Hoddesden. The three-acre garden is in a delightful setting with azaleas and rhododendrons and a bog garden with *Lysichiton americanus.* Good and unusual herbaceous borders. Well-kept kitchen garden. Slightly disappointing for the plantsman, but the garden claims highest attendance in any one day in Hertfordshire.

HOPLEYS ★ 7

Much Hadham, Ware, Hertfordshire. Tel: (027984) 2509
Dr and Mrs David Barker, Mr A. Barker

50 yards N of Bull public house in centre of Much Hadham • Parking • Teas • Toilet facilities • Suitable for wheelchairs • Plants for sale • Open by appointment, and all year except Jan and Aug; Sun, 2 - 5 p.m., Mon, Wed - Sat, 9 a.m. - 5 p.m. Also on special days for charities • Entrance: between 80p and £1.50, children 40p

The owners have been working on this garden for many years and it has been expanding yearly. The relatively new pool and bog area look well established. There are numerous borders filled with shrubs and hardy plants, most of which are for sale in the nursery. The long-established conifer bed illustrates the different sizes and shapes of mature conifers. There is also a border for tender plants which have come through the last two winters well. Shrub seed seems to germinate well in the fertile soil and Dr and Mrs Barker have found self-seeded gems.

KING CHARLES II COTTAGE 8

Leverstock Green, Hemel Hempstead, Hertfordshire. Tel: (0442) 64233
Mr and Mrs F.S. Cadman

Via A4147, midway between Hemel Hempstead and St Albans • Parking • Teas at Westwick Cottage nearby • Suitable for wheelchairs • Plants for sale elsewhere in village on charity days • Open 30th June, 11 a.m. - 5 p.m. • Entrance: £2 (combined entrance to four gardens)

This one-acre garden has evolved over 30 years from an overgrown orchard. A huge gnarled apple tree and a yew hedge are survivors from a former garden. The roses are a special feature, planted in long beds and following the curve of the drive, with some splendid shrub roses in island beds. One remembers especially a rock pool beneath the willows planted with foliage plants; the terrace with cushions of pinks and small bedding plants between the York paving stones; climbers on the black and white cottage walls, mainly roses and clematis; and a vista across the lawn through the beech hedge of a mixed border beyond planted with a successful mixture of unusual shrubs, herbaceous plants, azaleas in late spring, providing a succession of good colour and foliage. Other gardens in this village and Gorhambury also open, including Westwick Cottage (see entry).

KNEBWORTH HOUSE 9

Knebworth, Nr Stevenage, Hertfordshire. Tel: (0438) 812661
The Lord Cobbold

28m N of London, 3m from Stevenage. Direct access from A1 junction 7 • Parking • Refreshments: In sixteenth-century tithe barn • Toilet facilities • Suitable for wheelchairs • Open 22nd March to 19th May, 9th to 29th Sept, weekends and Bank Holidays, 25th May to 8th Sept, daily except Mon (but open Bank Holiday Mons), 12 noon – 5 p.m. Closed 28th June to 1July • Entrance: £3.50, OAP and children £3 (house and garden)

As the historic home of the Lytton family, the garden evolved from a simple Tudor green and orchard to Sir Edward Bulwer Lytton's elaborate Victorian design. After his marriage into the family, Edwin Lutyens made alterations and simplified the main central area. In 1980 a programme of restoration was started with the aim of reinstating as much as possible of the original Lutyens designs. The twin pleached lime avenues planted by Lutyens lead to an upper lawn of rose beds and herbaceous borders with tall yew hedges behind. These are mixed borders of blue, pink, silver, mauve and white. Clematis 'Perle d'Azur' and rose 'New Dawn' are grown on iron frames. The 'Wilderness' is a mass of daffodils in spring. Other features are a vast 300-year-old oak tree, a small pinetum of exotic pines and a large leaning Wellingtonia. *Clematis montana* and the 'Garland' rose are draped over Lutyens' garden bothy.

ST PAUL'S WALDEN BURY ★ 10

Whitwell, Nr Hitchin, Hertfordshire. Tel: (0438) 871218
Mr and Mrs Simon Bowes Lyon

5m S of Hitchin, ½m N of Whitwell on B651 • Best season: spring • Parking • Teas • Suitable for wheelchairs • Dogs on lead • Open 21st April, 12th May, 2nd June, 2 – 7 p.m., 30th June, 2 – 6 p.m., followed by lakeside concert. Other times by appointment • Entrance: £1.50, children 75p

This is a formal landscape garden, laid out about 1730, and influenced by French tastes. Long rides and avenues span about 40 acres, leading to temples, statues, lake and ponds. There are also more recent flower gardens and a woodland garden planted with rhododendrons, azaleas and magnolias.

WESTWICK COTTAGE 11

Leverstock Green, Hemel Hempstead, Hertfordshire.
Tel: (0442) 521291
Mrs Sheila MacQueen

On A4147, midway between Hemel Hempstead and St Albans • *Parking* • *Teas, coffees and light refreshments* • *Suitable for wheelchairs* • *Plants for sale* • *Open 30th June, 11 a.m. - 5 p.m.* • *Entrance: £2 (combined entrance to four gardens), children free*

Created by the owner 40 years ago, and planted with the idea of picking for flower arranging. A large border designed to be viewed end on from the house is full of colour and interest, with mixed perennials and annuals, white delphiniums, *Alchemilla mollis*, phlox and interesting shrubs to give it body and texture. Staddle stones under a big flowering cherry, *Prunus* 'Kanzan', catch the eye, as does a stone trough in front of the house. A stone urn filled with nicotiana, pelargoniums, etc. shows Mrs MacQueen's skills as a flower arranger. Other Leverstock Green gardens are open on the same day.

GARDENS OPEN RARELY

The following gardens are open to the public on one day only in the year. For details see individual entry.
May 19 Hipkins; **June 30** King Charles II Cottage.

HUMBERSIDE

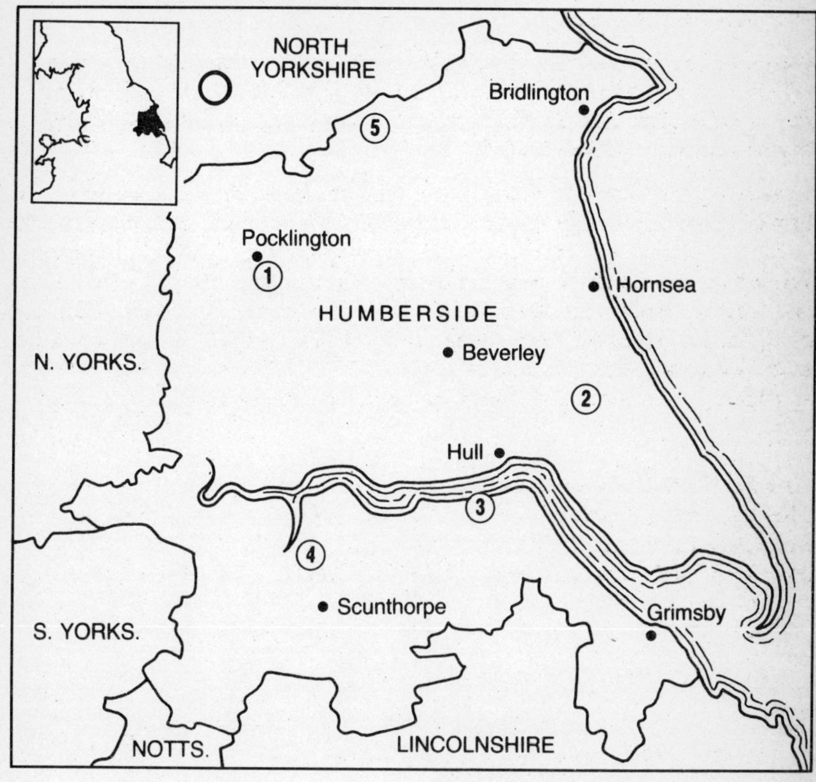

Two-starred gardens are ringed in bold.

BURNBY HALL ★ 1

Pocklington, Humberside. Tel: (0759) 302068
Stewart's Burnby Hall Gardens and Museum Trust

13m E of York on B 1247 on the outskirts of Pocklington • Best season: June to Sept • Parking, inc. coaches • Refreshments: cafeteria for teas in garden • Toilet facilities • Suitable for wheelchairs • Shop • Open Easter to mid-Oct, daily, 10 a.m. - 6 p.m. • Entrance: £1.50, OAP £1, children 5 - 16 50p, under 5 free. Parties £1 per person

The gardens were established in 1904 by Major Stewart, the original ponds being constructed for fishing and swimming, but in 1975 they were converted to water lily cultivation. They are now one of the finest water gardens in Europe covering two acres. A large collection of hardy water lilies forms a subsidiary of the National collection. Lilies may be seen from May to mid-September in a normal year and in July there are some 5000 blooms of 60 different varieties.

BURTON CONSTABLE HALL 2

Nr Hull, Humberside. Tel: (0964) 562400
Mr J. Chichester Constable

7½m NE of Hull. Take A165 between Hull and Skirlaugh and follow signs • Parking • Cafeteria • Toilet facilities • Suitable for wheelchairs • Shop • House open as garden, 1 - 4.30 p.m. • Garden open Easter, May and Spring Bank Holiday Suns and Mons. Also Suns in June and July and 21st July to 1st Sept, Sun - Thurs, 12 noon - 5 p.m. Parties at any time by arrangement with administrator • Entrance: £2 (house and grounds)

A fine Elizabethan house surrounded by parkland which 'Capability' Brown, whose plans can still be seen, laid out in the 1770s. His 20 acres of lakes are spanned by a good stone bridge, and while his trees have not all survived they are being replaced by new plantings, still in their infancy. Around the house is a four-acre garden with handsome eighteenth-century orangery, statuary and borders.

THE COTTAGES 3

Ferry Road, Barrow-Haven, Nr Barton-on-Humber, South Humberside. Tel: (0469) 31614
Mr and Mrs E.C. Walsh

4m E of Barton-on-Humber off A1077 adjacent to Barrow-Haven railway station • Parking • Teas • Partly suitable for wheelchairs • Plants for sale • Open 26th, 27th May, 25th, 26th Aug, 11 a.m. - 5 p.m. and by appointment • Entrance: £1, OAP and children 50p

Situated on a disused tile works near the River Humber this one and a quarter-acre garden is on a direct flight path for many migratory birds. By careful management the owners have maximised the number of food sources, nest sites and habitats for visiting and resident species. There are bird-watching hides for the enthusiast. The result is a pastoral haven of old thorn trees intermingled with more recently-planted trees, shrubs and herbaceous plants. Grassy paths meander to a dyke planted with bog plants, a pond and reed bed and an organic vegetable plot. In contrast, the well-manicured area around the house has beds, borders and trellises brimming with plants providing year-round colour.

NORMANBY HALL 4

Normanby Hall Country Park, Nr Scunthorpe, South Humberside. Tel: (0742) 720588
Run by Scunthorpe Borough Council

4m N of Scunthorpe on B1430 • Best season: June/July • Parking • Refreshments • Toilet facilities • Suitable for wheelchairs • Dogs on lead • Shop • House open April to Nov, Mon - Fri, 11 a.m. - 5 p.m., Sat and Sun,

1 – 5 p.m., Bank Holiday Mon, 11 a.m. – 5 p.m. • Farm Museum open April to Nov, daily, 1 – 5 p.m. • Park open all year, dawn – dusk • Entrance: small fee to car park

Although the parkland and woodland at Normanby is extensive, with superb nature trails, rhododendron walks, lakes and accessible deer park, the actual pleasure gardens are rather limited. They are, however, well-maintained and as an addition to the many attractions here are worth seeing. Next to the Regency house are formal rose beds and a lavender-edged sunken garden with a fish pond. Further away, and easily missed, is a lovely, walled 'secret garden'. Enclosed by mellow brick walls, holly and conifer hedges are double-sided herbaceous borders, grass paths and good wall shrubs and climbers, a peaceful retreat from the often busy park. Within the grounds is a small farm museum which, like the house, has no entry charge and allows all the family to find something of interest at a minimal cost.

SLEDMERE HOUSE 5

Sledmere, Great Driffield, Humberside. Tel: (0377) 36208
Sir Tatton Sykes, Bart.

9m NW of Great Driffield, signposted off A166 • Parking • Teas • Toilet facilities • Suitable for wheelchairs • Plants for sale • Shop • House open as garden • Open May Bank Holiday to Sept, daily except Mon and Fri, 1.30 – 5 p.m. Open Bank Holidays • Entrance: £1, children 60p (house and garden)

A listed garden, Sledmere is among the most well-preserved of 'Capability' Brown's landscape schemes. Dating from the 1770s it clearly reveals his characteristic belting and clumping of trees and carefully controlled diagonal vistas to distant 'eye-catchers'. His use of a ha-ha allows the park to flow up to the windows of the house (whence it is best seen) across extensive tree-planted lawns. To the rear of the house are a well-stocked herbaceous border, a newly planted knot garden and an interesting Italian paved sculpture court (1911) which is undergoing restoration. The eighteenth-century walled gardens are now grassed over and planted with mainly spring-flowering shrubs and are entered through a small but attractive rose garden set off by garden urns.

KENT

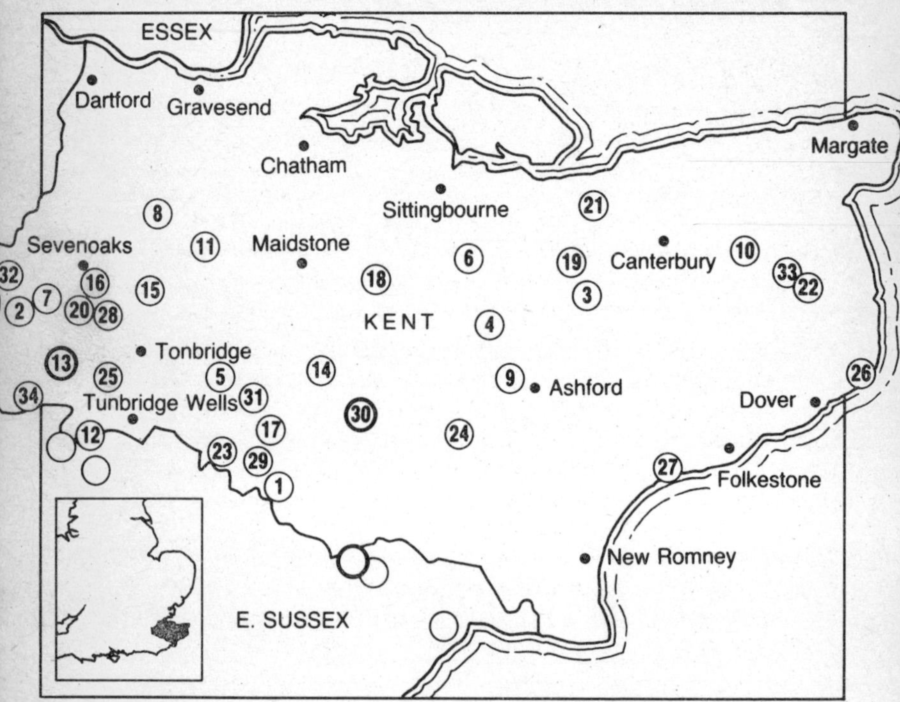

Two-starred gardens are ringed in bold.

BEDGEBURY NATIONAL PINETUM ★ (1)

Nr Goudhurst, Cranbrook, Kent. Tel: (0580) 211044 (Curator)
Forestry Commission

On B2079 Goudhurst - Flimwell road off the A21 • Parking. Disabled persons may be brought to and collected from lake • Refreshments: ice creams available in car park. Light refreshments available at shop in garden at weekends only • Toilet facilities • Suitable for wheelchairs • Dogs on lead • Shop open Easter to Sept, 11 a.m. - 5 p.m. • Garden open April to Sept, daily, 10 a.m. - 8 p.m. or dusk if earlier, Oct, Mon - Fri, 12 noon - 4 p.m. • Entrance: £1, children 50p. Exact money required at certain times

The Pinetum lies on sandy soil too infertile for sustained agriculture, being silty, very acid and deficient in phosphates. Specimen trees were initially cultivated with the addition of essential nutrients. However, although the size of some of the conifers is inevitably limited, the variety of species is not, and the Pinetum offers a comprehensive collection of the conifers that can be grown in Britain. It has been planted so that the form, colour and texture of the mature trees can readily be seen. As well as being a valuable educational resource for schools and students of forestry and related subjects, it is also a place for quiet enjoyment.

CHARTWELL 2

Westerham, Kent. Tel: (0732) 866368
The National Trust

2m S of Westerham off B2026 • Parking • Refreshments: licensed self-service restaurant • Toilet facilities • Partly suitable for wheelchairs • Dogs on lead • Shop • House open but entry by timed ticket • Open 30th March to Oct, Tues, Wed and Thurs, 12 noon - 5.30 p.m., Sat, Sun and Bank Holiday Mon, 11 a.m. - 5.30 p.m. Closed Good Fri and Tues following Bank Holiday Mon • Entrance: £1.50 (house and garden £3.70)

The effect of the 1989 drought on the lawns and shrubs is evident as is that of the 1987 gales which devastated the wooded combe surrounding the grounds - now extensively replanted. The lawns to the front of the house slope down to two large lakes and a swimming pool (constructed by Sir Winston Churchill). A walled rose garden at the side of the house leads to a loggia, with grapevine, adjoining the Marlborough Pavilion which contains bas reliefs of the Battle of Marlborough. Another main feature, adjoining an orchard, is the Golden Rose Garden and Walk - extending to the kitchen garden, where Sir Winston built the summer house and part of the brick wall. Lady Churchill had a good deal to do with the original design of the garden. This is a garden worth exploring and for enjoying the sense of space and history, but it is not of particular interest to the plantsperson.

CHILHAM CASTLE 3

Chilham, Nr Canterbury, Kent. Tel: (0227) 730319
The Viscount Massereene and Ferrard

S side of A252, just W Chilham village • Best seasons: spring, summer • Parking • Occasional refreshments • Toilet facilities • Dogs on lead • Shop • Garden open week before Easter to mid-Oct, Sun - Sat, 11 a.m. - 5 p.m. • Entrance: Mon and Fri, £2.20, other days with birds of prey display £2.50

Considerable work over the last year has brought about many improvements. Signs of the '87 hurricane are receding. The lake has been restored as a central feature. A new rose bed has been started and herbaceous beds show signs of renewed vigour. Above all one visits Chilham to see the outstanding view down to the Stour Valley and the terracing supposedly designed by John Tradescant. This was later destroyed by 'Capability' Brown in the interests of naturalism, then restored in the 1920s. All the elements of garden history are here - Jacobean terracing, mid-eighteenth-century deer park, viewing mound, formal Victorian garden, lake garden. Old trees that survived the hurricane include a fine *Quercus ilex* planted to mark the completion of the house, and a splendid cedar of Lebanon. Use your imagination and think of Old England while others in your party enjoy the tourist attractions at the side.

CHURCH HILL COTTAGE GARDENS 

Charing Heath, Ashford, Kent. Tel: (023371) 2522
Mr and Mrs M. Metianu

Follow sign S from dual-carriageway section of A20, ½m W of Charing, to Charing Heath and Egerton. Fork right at Red Lion pub after 1 mile, take next right and 250 yards on right • Best season: May to July • Parking • Toilet facilities • Suitable for wheelchairs • Plants for sale • Garden and nursery open March to May, daily, June to Nov and Feb, daily except Mon and Tues. Closed Dec and Jan • Entrance: £1, children free

In spite of current works for the M20 in the vicinity, Church Hill Cottage Gardens have an air of peace and tranquillity rarely equalled in much larger gardens. There is a strong sense of design in the curves of borders and island beds but these are so well matched by the fine and well-developed planting that the whole seems natural and much more established than one normally expects after only eight years. Established birches form a central point. Beds are varied, some with colour themes, others with shrubs heavily underplanted with a wide range of unusual hardy plants, bulbs in season, foliage plants, etc. One point of plantsman's interest is the large collection of dianthus, which includes between 30 and 40 types of old forms dating from the sixteenth to eighteenth centuries. This garden is always evolving and will soon feature a new woodland area.

CRITTENDEN HOUSE ★ 5

Crittenden Road, Matfield, Nr Tonbridge, Kent. Tel: (089283) 2554
Mr B.P. Tompsett

6m SE of Tonbridge on B2160. Turn left in village along Chestnut Lane, house on right after 1m • Best seasons: spring and early summer • Parking • Refreshments: at Cherrytrees on Matfield Green • Toilet facilities • Partly suitable for wheelchairs • Open 31st March, 1st, 14th April, 6th, 19th, 26th, 27th May, 2nd, 16th June, 2 - 6 p.m. • Entrance: £1, children 50p. Parties by appointment

An extraordinary range of soil types has led to a wide variety of species blending within the labour-saving concept of the owner's design; with spring bulbs, rhododendrons, roses, lilies, waterside plantings and autumn colours, this garden teems with interest throughout the year. Curved lawns sweep to island beds and interestingly-planted water fringes within a framework of trees. The local native flora, such as *Primula vulgaris* and *Dactylorhiza fuchsii*, mingle strikingly with more rarified species such as *Paeonia lutea ludlowii* ('Sherriff's Variety'), a gift from George Sherriff, and *Malus* 'Crittenden' (awarded First Class Certificate in 1971). *Crataegus* varieties, such as *monogyna* 'Pink May', x *lavallei* and *laciniata*, contrast with *Davidia involucrata* var. *involucrata* (with its outstanding autumn colours) and *Rhododendron* 'Elizabeth', *R.* 'Unique', *R. yakushimanum* 'Exbury' and *R. auriculatum* 'Lady Chamberlain'. Several trees have been raised from seeds collected by the owner – *Pinus ayacahuite* from Popacatapetl, Mexico, and *Hippophae salicifolia* from Nepal, for example. The local stone used in the garden has many fossil sand-ripples and even a fossil footprint of a dinosaur – possibly Iguanodon.

DODDINGTON PLACE 6

Doddington, Nr Sittingbourne, Kent. Tel: (079586) 385
Mr R. and the Hon. Mrs Oldfield

6m S of Sittingbourne. From A20 turn N at Lenham. From A2 turn S at Teynham. Signposted • Best season: May/June • Parking • Refreshments: morning coffee, light lunch, afternoon tea • Toilet facilities • Suitable for wheelchairs • Dogs on lead • Plants for sale when available • Shop • Open Easter Mon, May to Sept, Wed and Bank Holidays, 11 a.m. – 6 p.m. Also Sun in May • Entrance: £1.50, children 25p

Created in the nineteenth century by Nessfield and developed in the 1910s with woodland garden added in the 1960s by Mr and Mrs Oldfield, the gardens are set in open countryside in 10 acres of landscaped grounds surrounding a Victorian country house. They include lawns with established oaks, a Wellingtonia walk, a sunken garden, rock garden and much fine yew hedging. The main feature for the plantsman is the well-designed woodland garden set, in the 1960s, on acid soil to the side of the main garden. Here are rhododendrons and azaleas, numerous acers and a variety of other trees and shrubs, some rare. The ideal time for this is spring and early summer, but there is year round interest – the rest of the garden has a sense of space and fine views. Plans for redevelopment in the rockery and sunken garden should bear fruit in a few years. This garden continues to develop, with new planting throughout.

EMMETTS GARDEN ★ 7

Ide Hill, Sevenoaks, Kent. Tel: (073275) 429
The National Trust

1½m S of A25 on Sundridge to Ide Hill road. 1½m N of Ide Hill off B2042 • Best season: spring to midsummer • Parking. Buggy available from car park to entrance • Teas 2 – 5 p.m. • Partly suitable for wheelchairs • Dogs on lead • Open 29th March to Oct, Wed – Sun and Bank Holiday Mon, 2 – 6 p.m. Last admission 5 p.m. There is a country fair 17th, 18th Aug • Entrance: £2, children £1. Pre-booked parties £1.50, children 80p

Set on the top of Ide Hill, Emmetts Garden gives a superb view over the Weald of Kent and provides an impressive setting for this plantsman's collection of trees and shrubs. This is a garden to visit at any time although it is particularly fine in spring, with its bluebell woods and flowering shrubs. First planted by Frederick Lubbock, the owner, from about 1890 until his death in 1926, it is specially noted for its rhododendrons and azaleas. It follows the late nineteenth-century style of combining exotics with conifers to provide a 'wild' garden, all well listed in the Trust guide. Recent additions to extend the interest throughout the season include a rose garden, a rock garden and extensive planting of acers for autumn colour. The enforced clearance of some trees and shrubs after the gales of 1987 has enabled new planting to keep the traditions of the garden but also to expand it. Planting is developing well.

FAIRSEAT RECTORY 8

The Rectory, Vigo Lane, Fairseat, Sevenoaks, Kent. Tel: (0732) 822494
The Reverend and Mrs David Clark

½m W A227 at the Vigo pub, 1½m N of Wrotham • Parking in village • Refreshments • Toilet facilities • Suitable for wheelchairss • Plants for sale • Open 16th June, 27th July, 2 - 5.30 p.m. • Entrance: £1, children 25p

This is a delightful garden in the grounds of the only weather-boarded rectory in Kent. Though still on the North Downs, there is a good layer of soil (Bagshot clay) over the chalk, permitting pieris and magnolia to flourish. The present incumbent and his wife have created the garden over the last 20 years. With 14 island beds set in and around a large lawn, the plant succession is excellent, giving colour in all seasons. Individual beds have different colour themes, combining shrubs and herbaceous plants. It is worth visiting to see how to bring a sense of garden design into a relatively small space. The garden is only open two days a year, in its best seasons, thus enabling the owners to have ready a plant description written for each occasion in minute and lively detail.

GODINTON PARK ★ 9

Ashford, Kent. Tel: (0233) 620773
Mr Alan Wyndham Green

1½m W of Ashford on A20 at Potter's Corner • Best season: summer • Parking • Toilet facilities • Partly suitable for wheelchairs • Dogs on lead • Plants for sale sometimes • House open • Garden open Easter weekend Sat - Mon, other Bank Holiday Mons, and June to Sept, Sun 2 - 5 p.m. and parties by appointment • Entrance: 70p (house and garden £1.50, children 70p. Parties of 20 or more £1.20 per person)

The key features of the formal areas are the water garden, well stocked with lilies and surrounded by shrubs and beds; and the small enclosed Italian garden; two statues, draped in wisteria, guard the entrance to this peaceful spot with its cruciform pool, statuary, loggia and summerhouse. There are also several shrubbed areas, a rose garden with triangular beds of annuals, and much statuary, reflecting the architectural interest of the designer. The layout was developed by Sir Reginald Blomfield when remodelling the house between 1902-6, and he used yew hedges to separate the gardens from the park, marking the different areas with lesser hedges and level changes, evolving a happy mix of balance and order. Much of the topiary reflects the outlines of the Jacobean house, although some of the symmetry has been lost with time. The garden is important evidence of Blomfield's formal style which was so much at variance with Robinson's. Round the house and gardens is an ancient park, of some 240 acres, containing some of the oldest trees in England. Unfortunately all the grey poplars (*Populus canescens*) which lined the avenue in the park were lost in the winds of Jan 1990.

GOODNESTONE PARK ★ 10

Nr Wingham, Canterbury, Kent. Tel: (0304) 840218
The Lord and Lady FitzWalter

5m E of Canterbury on A257 turn S onto B2045, after 1m turn E • Parking • Refreshments: Teas on Sun and Wed 19th May to 28th Aug • Toilet facilities • Suitable for wheelchairs • Plants for sale • Shop • Open April to 25th Oct, Mon - Fri and Bank Holidays, 11 a.m. - 5 p.m., 31st March to 7th July, 28th July to 29th Sept, Sun, 2 - 6 p.m. • Entrance: £1.50, OAP £1.30, Disabled in wheelchairs £1, children under 12 20p, parties over 25 or more £1.30 per person (£1.50 per person for guided tour)

Goodnestone (pronounced Gunston) Park is a 14-acre garden in rural setting round the eighteenth-century house. First built in 1700, by Brook Bridges, this Palladian-style house was rebuilt and enlarged by his great-grandson, Sir Brook Bridges, 3rd Bart. whose daughter Elizabeth married Jane Austen's brother, Edward. Jane Austen refers frequently to Goodnestone and her Bridges cousins in her letters. There are pleasant vistas within the garden and good views out to open countryside. The garden ranges in planting from the mid-eighteenth-century parkland with fine trees and cedars to the walled area behing the house designed since the early 1970s by the present Lady FitzWalter. The garden tour leads along a broad terrace in front of the house, planted with an abundance of roses and mixed shrubs. Behind the house a small woodland garden, laid out in the 1920s, gives pleasant walks and welcome shade. Here are rhododendrons, camellias, magnolias and hydrangeas among many others. A cedar walk leads between spring borders on the left and more roses on the right, to a new walled garden overlooked by the church tower. Old roses mingle with mixed underplanting. Walls bear clematis, jasmine, climbing roses. New planting in the woodland area shows continued development of this fine garden.

GREAT COMP ★

Borough Green, Sevenoaks, Kent. Tel: (0732) 882669
Great Comp Charitable Trust

2m E of Borough Green. Take B2016 S from A20 at Wrotham Heath, right at first crossroads, then ½m ahead on left • Best season: July and Aug • Parking • Teas by arrangement for parties • Toilet facilities, but not adapted for wheelchairs • Suitable for wheelchairs • Plants for sale • Open April to Oct, 11 a.m. - 6 p.m. • Entrance: £2, children £1

Great Comp consists of seven acres of mature gardens round a seventeenth-century house and an original Edwardian-style garden created by Mr and Mrs Roderick Cameron since 1957. This is a delightful garden with semi-woodland walks, changing vistas and plantsman's interest. Extended from an original four and a half acres of garden, rough woodland and paddock, Great Comp now contains 3,000 named plants. Each area or walk makes a separate entity yet is designed to lead on to another part. Some stonework gives added interest at focal points, and there have been some cement additions to mock ruins during the winter of 1989/90. Carefully mixed deciduous and evergreen planting provides all-year round variety, including magnolias, rhododendrons, azaleas, maples, underplanted with heathers, hostas and geraniums. Good herbaceous planting. A guide book is available at the gate.

GROOMBRIDGE PLACE 12

Groombridge, Kent. Tel: (0892) 864226
Mrs R. Newton

5m SW of Tunbridge Wells on B2110 • Parking • Refreshments • Toilet facilities • Partly suitable for wheelchairs • Open 21st July, 2 - 6.30 p.m. • Entrance: £1, children 50p

Peacocks roam amongst the yews and along the terraces. Swans and mallards enjoy the lake by the drive. The herbaceous borders are well kept, neat and tidy. Wild mimulus can be seen in the damper areas, with hostas and primulas. The greenhouses, vegetable and flower areas for the house are orderly and altogether the gardens enhance this mid-seventeenth-century listed moated manor house set in a typical and attractive Kent village.

HEVER CASTLE ★★

Hever, Edenbridge, Kent. Tel: (0732) 865224
Broadlands Properties Ltd

3m SE of Edenbridge, midway between Sevenoaks and East Grinstead between B2026 and B2027 • Refreshments • Toilet facilities • Suitable for wheelchairs • Plants for sale • Shop • Castle open 19th March to 10th Nov, 12 noon - 6 p.m. Last admission 5 p.m. • Gardens open 19th March to 10th Nov, 11 a.m. - 6 p.m. Last admission 5 p.m. • Entrance: £3, OAP £2.60, children 5 - 16 £1.80, family ticket £7.80. Groups per person: £2.60, students £2.30, children £1.60 (castle and gardens, £3.70, OAP £3.40, children £1.90)

The gardens were laid out between 1904–8 to William Waldorf Astor's designs. One thousand men were employed, 800 of whom dug out the 35-acre lake; steam engines moved rock and soil to create apparently natural new features and teams of horses moved mature trees from the Ashdown forest. Today the gardens have reached their maturity and are teeming with colour and interest throughout the year. Amongst the many superb features is an outstanding four-acre Italian garden, the setting for a large collection of classical statuary. Opposite, there is a magnificent pergola, supporting camellias, wisteria, crab apple, Virginia creeper and roses. It fuses into the hillside beyond which has shaded grottos of cool damp-loving species such as hostas, astilbes and polygonum. Less formal areas include the rhododendron walks, Anne Boleyn's orchard and her walk, which extends along the full length of the grounds and is particularly attractive in autumn.

IDEN CROFT HERBS 14

Frittenden Road, Staplehurst, Kent. Tel: (0580) 891432
Rosemary and David Titterington

Sign from A229 S of Staplehurst. Turn down Frittenden Road at Amoco garage and follow signposts • Parking • Light refreshments • Toilet facilities • Suitable for wheelchairs • Plants for sale • Shop • Open all year, Mon - Sat, 9 a.m. - 5 .m., additional opening from April to Sept, Sun and Bank Holidays, 11 a.m. - 5 p.m. • Entrance: by donation box

Gardens situated in quiet backwater near Staplehurst. There are acres of herbs bordered by grass paths and a large walled garden. A variety of demonstration gardens help the garden planner and over 600 varieties of herbs are available in pots for planting according to seasonal variations. The origanums here were designated as The National collection in 1983. The latest garden is specially designed for the enjoyment of blind and disabled visitors.

IGHTHAM MOTE ★

Ivy Hatch, Nr Borough Green, Kent. Tel: (0732) 810378
The National Trust

6m E of Sevenoaks, off A25 and 2½m S of Ightham off A227 • Parking • Tea bar open from 11.30 a.m. weekdays, 10.30 a.m. Sun and Bank Holidays. Closes 5 p.m. • Toilet facilities inc. disabled • Suitable for wheelchairs with special parking available • Shop • House open • Garden open 29th March to Oct, Mon, Wed - Fri, 12 noon - 5.30 p.m., Sun and Bank Holiday Mon, 11 a.m. - 5.30 p.m. Last admission 5 p.m. 'Midsummer magic' concert 5th, 6th July • Entrance: weekdays £3. Sun and Bank Holidays £3.50 (no ticket for garden only)

Situated in a wooded cleft of the Kentish Weald, this medieval and Tudor manor house lies in the valley of Dinas Dene, where a stream has been dammed to form small lakes and the moat which surrounds the house. The medieval design of the gardens has evolved over several centuries. The present lawn replaces the stew pond, which was used for breeding fish for the table. Further household needs were satisfied with vegetables and herbs for culinary and medicinal purposes, and flowers for decorating and scenting the house were also prevalent. During the nineteenth century the garden emerged as an excellent example of the ideal 'old English' garden, and The National Trust is gradually restoring this with extensive replanting. Six acres of woodland walks with fine rhododendrons are re-established and the long border has returned to its former glory.

KNOLE 16

Sevenoaks, Kent. Tel: (0732) 450608
The National Trust

At S end of Sevenoaks town centre, just E of A225 • Parking £5.50 inc. one admission to house • Refreshments in Sevenoaks but few teashops • Wheelchairs in Great Hall, park and garden only • Dogs in park on leads • House open 29th March to Oct, Wed - Sat and Bank Holiday Mons, 11 a.m. - 5 p.m., Sun, 2 - 5 p.m. £3 • Garden open May to Sept, first Wed in each month only (garden only) but park open daily to pedestrians by courtesy of Lord Sackville • Entrance: park free, garden 50p

The garden here, which contains a herb and wilderness garden, is not of great consequence, but it will be much visited by those who watched the TV programme about the Nicolsons. However the prurient should be advised that according to a National Trust spokesperson 'Nothing of that sort happens on Trust property.'

LADHAM HOUSE ★ 17

Goudhurst, Kent. Tel: (0580) 211203
Betty Lady Jessel

NE of village off A262 • Best season: May and July • Parking • Toilet facilities • Dogs on lead • Open 5th, 12th May, and 7th July (charity celebration with teas and Silver Band), 11 a.m. - 6 p.m. • Entrance: £1.50, children 50p

This Georgian farmhouse with additional French features has been in the family for over 100 years and the garden developed over that period. Interesting features are the newly-planted bog garden, replacing a leaking pond, and the arboretum, in an early stage of development, with the outlines of the old kitchen garden still much in evidence. The mixed shrub borders are attractive; notable are the magnolias - two *watsonii* over 30ft and a deep red flowering 'Betty Jessel'. Amongst the other rarer trees and shrubs are

American oaks, *Aesculus parviflora* and *Carpenteria californica*. The newly-planted arboretum replaces over 250 trees and shrubs lost in the 1987 storm and the Fountain Garden has been completely reconstructed since the storm.

LEEDS CASTLE AND CULPEPER GARDENS

Maidstone, Kent. Tel: (0622) 765400
Leeds Castle Foundation

On B2163 off junction 8 of M20 • Best season: Culpeper Gardens in spring, rose season and high summer, Castle grounds, spring and autumn • Refreshments • Toilet facilities • Suitable for wheelchairs with transport from car park to castle • Dogs in car park only • Shop • House open • Garden open 18th March to Oct, daily, 11 a.m. - 5 p.m. and winter weekends • Entrance: £4.10 (park and gardens), OAP and students £3.10, children £2.40, family ticket £11.40

Visit Leeds Castle and grounds for its romantic, wooded setting, designed by 'Capability' Brown. The woodland walk with old and new plantings of shrubs is especially beautiful in daffodil time. The atmosphere is also much enhanced by wildfowl. The Culpeper Garden alone, in a secluded area beyond the Castle, provides the main interest for the keen gardener. This is not the herb garden as often thought, though a small area does include some herbs, but is named after a seventeenth-century owner of Leeds Castle, distantly related to the herbalist. Started in 1980 by Russell Page on a slope overlooking the River Len, and surrounded by high brick walls of stabling and old cottages, the garden already gives an established feel of old world charm. A simple pattern of paths lined with box contains areas full of old roses (40 varieties), riotously underplanted with herbaceous perennials. The National collection of bergamots (nepetas and monardas) is situated in one corner. The new grotto has been much publicised. There is also a maze, duckery and aviary.

LONGACRE

Perry Wood, Selling, Kent. Tel: (0227) 752254
Dr and Mrs G. Thomas

5m SE of Faversham. From A2 (M2) take A251 S then follow signs for Selling. Pass White Lion on left, 2nd right, then left, continue for ¼m. From A252 at Chilham, take road to Selling at Badgers Hill Fruit Farm, turn left at 2nd crossroads, first right, next left, then right • Best season: spring and summer • Parking • Teas • Suitable for wheelchairs • Plants for sale from own nursery • Open by appointment and 21st April, 5th, 6th, 19th, 27th May, 2nd, 16th, 30th June, 14th, 28th July, 25th, 26th Aug, 8th Sept, 2 - 5 p.m. • Entrance: 75p

Longacre remains a first-class small garden. Whatever the weather, it continues to delight. Created entirely by the present owners, it provides year-round plantsman's interest with a wide variety of unusual hardy plants.

d section, alpine section and pleasantly designed beds stand out for their colour themes with attractive foliage base. Numerous spring bulbs and flowers give way to summer herbaceous plants. Nearby Perry Woods give good opportunity for walking dogs and children.

LONG BARN 20

Long Barn Road, Weald, Nr Sevenoaks, Kent.
Brandon and Sarah Gough

3m S of Sevenoaks. Follow signs to Weald from junction of A21 and B245. Continue through village • Parking • Refreshments • Toilet facilities • Open 23rd June, 14th July, 2 – 5 p.m. • Entrance: £1, children 30p

Three acres of sloping garden round a fourteenth-century Wealden hall house are being restored by the owners following the basic design by Harold Nicolson and Vita Sackville-West when they lived here before buying Sissinghurst. The main feature is a Dutch knot garden, said to have been designed by Lutyens. This contains in season a fine display of mixed herbaceous planting. New features include a small rhododendron glade, rose walk, pergola and herb gardens. Well situated with fine views over the Weald, this is a garden to watch as it develops further. See also Knole.

MOUNT EPHRAIM 21

Hernhill, Nr Faversham, Kent. Tel: (0227) 751496
Mrs M.N. Dawes and Mr and Mrs E.S. Dawes

Take A299 N from A2/M2, then right to Hernhill at Duke of York pub, through village on left • Parking • Refreshments: homemade lunches and teas on Sun and Bank Holidays except in July. Licensed to sell wine from own vineyard • Toilet facilities • Partly suitable for wheelchairs • Dogs on lead • Shop • Open daily, 11 a.m. – 6 p.m. • Entrance: £1.50, children 25p

Mount Ephraim is remarkable for its variety on seven sloping acres with distant views of the Thames Estuary, surrounding fruit orchards and new vineyards. With a backdrop of trees of outstanding shapes and contrasts, it includes rose gardens, rock garden, a small Japanese garden and a lake. Restored, from 1950 onwards after years of neglect, it retains much of the original design of the 1800s, laid out again in 1912 by William Dawes, including topiary effects and the original rock garden. It has continuously evolved and a new water garden will soon extend the range and diversity even further. Spring bulbs, prunus in blossom, and rhododendrons make spring to early June an ideal time to visit but herbaceous borders and shrubs extend the interest through the season. A three quarters of a mile orchard walk on Sundays gives extra interest, explaining growth, development and types of fruit farming. Kent Countryside Productions produce Shakespeare in grounds at the end of June.

NORTHBOURNE COURT 22

Northbourne, Deal, Kent. Tel: (0304) 360813
The Hon. Charles James

1½m W of Deal. From A258 at W of Deal take turning W towards Great Mongeham and Northbourne • Best season: June and July • Parking • Refreshments sometimes • Toilet facilities: unisex • Partly suitable for wheelchairs • Dogs on lead • Plants for sale when available • Open 5th, 25th May, 9th, 30th June, 7th, 21st July, 4th, 25th Aug, 15th Sept, 2 - 6 p.m., and June to Aug, Wed, 2 - 5 p.m. • Entrance: £2, children £1. Coach parties by arrangement. Enquiries to the Hon. Charles James, Betteshanger Home Farm Office, Northbourne, Deal, Kent.

Originally created in Tudor times, with Jacobean structure providing the basis, the garden in its present form was the creation of the father of the present Lord Northbourne. The main feature of this delightful garden, set within high walls to protect it from easterly winds, is the series of small and enclosed gardens with profuse and colourful, cottage-style planting. The old tiered terraces give further character and a distinctive setting for chalk-loving plants. Specially noticeable are grey-foliage plants, including lavender and dianthus. Also distinctive fuchsias and geraniums. Numerous pots and urns.

OWL HOUSE 23

Mount Pleasant, Lamberhurst, Kent. Tel: (0892) 890230
Marchioness of Dufferin and Ava

Off A21 in Lamberhurst • Best season: spring and early summer • Parking • Toilet facilities • Dogs on lead • Plants for sale • Shop • Open daily except 25th Dec and 1st Jan, 11 a.m. - 6 p.m. • Entrance: £2, children £1

During the sixteenth century the house (with the crookedest chimney in Kent) was the hiding place for wool smugglers known as owlers (they hooted by way of warning). The present owner planted prunus, malus and particularly roses along the many walks with their ample seats and sculptured owls. One water garden is attractively surrounded with azaleas and lilies; the other is wilder and danker. This is not a visit for the avid plantsman but a pleasant place for a family walk along the woodlined paths. It suffered badly from the hurricane, followed by high winds and the drought. The first impression is of neglect, but away from the cottage, especially around the water gardens, there is a feeling of great peace.

PEDDAR'S WOOD 24

14 Orchard Road, St Michael's, Tenterden, Kent. Tel: (05806) 3994
Mr and Mrs B.J. Honeysett

From A28 1m N of Tenterden turn W to Grant Road at Crown Hotel, 2nd right Orchard Road • Refreshments • Open 11th May, 8th, 29th June, 17th July, 10th Aug, 2 - 6 p.m. and by appointment • Entrance: £1, children 20p

This plantsman's garden of exceptional opulence and interest is approximately a quarter of an acre behind a typical small semi-detached town house. Great imagination and expertise have been used to develop it over the last six years into a garden of many delights. Other than potash only the usual organic composts are used but a two inch mulch of peat has been laid over the loamy soil. Amongst the clematis which trail rampantly are 'Victoria' and 'Margo Kosta'. Pink abutilon, solanum, vines, wisterias and roses vie for space while specimens such as cannas, the almost black viola 'Molly Sanderson' and impatiens 'Congo Cockatoo' are evident. There are in fact over 100 varieties of clematis including some of the owner's own seedlings as well as 40 varieties of lilies, 50 varieties of climbing roses and ferns in abundance.

PENSHURST PLACE ★ 25

Penshurst, Tonbridge, Kent. Tel: (0892) 870307
Lord De L'Isle

S of Tonbridge on B2176, N of Tunbridge Wells on A26 • Parking • Refreshments: 12.30 - 5 p.m. • Toilet facilities • Suitable for wheelchairs in grounds • Guide dogs only • Shop • House open • Garden open 28th March to 29th Sept, daily except Mon, 12.30 - 6 p.m. Open Bank Holidays • Entrance: £3.50, OAP £3, children under 16 £1.75, inc. entrance to house, toy museum and venture playground.

The 600-year-old gardens, contemporary with the house, reflect their development under their Tudor owner Sir Henry Sidney and the restoration by the present owner and his grandfather Lord De L'Isle. The many separate enclosures, surrounded by trim tall yew hedges, offer a wide variety of interesting planting, with continuous displays from spring to early autumn. The Italian garden with its oval fountain and century-old gingko dominates the front of the magnificent house. The herbaceous border is teeming with colour from irises, phlox, anemones, anchusa, coreopsis and yuccas amongst others. Contrast is made by the nut trees and over a dozen different crab apples underplanted with daffodils, myosotis, tulips, bluebells, Lenten lilies and a magnificent bed of peonies which borders the orchard. Even in late summer the rose garden is colourful with 'King Arthur' and 'Elizabeth Glamis' and their perfumes mingle with that from mature lavender bushes. A new lake and nature trail are being developed so that the style of design so much enjoyed here by Gertrude Jekyll and Beatrix Farrand is fully recaptured. Numerous seats make it easy to enjoy the garden and the views. Two medieval fish ponds have been reclaimed and are to be stocked with fish. The nature trail which was damaged by the January 1990 gales is being replaced.

THE PINES GARDEN 26

Beach Road, St Margaret's Bay, Kent. Tel: (0304) 852764
St Margaret's Bay Trust

3m NE of Dover off B2058, S of the village of St Margaret's at Cliffe • Best seasons: spring and summer • Parking nearby in road • Toilet facilities • Suitable for wheelchairs • Plants for sale when available • Open daily except 25th Dec, from 10 a.m. • Entrance: small admission charge

It is hard to believe that this well-stocked and perfectly maintained garden was a rubbish dump until 1970. Fred Cleary, founder of St Margaret's Bay Trust, and his wife transformed the original three acres, with a second three-acre site known as the Barrack Field, once home and training ground for soldiers during the Napoleonic Wars. Now the garden is established, with a good variety of trees, including conifers, flowering shrubs, bulbs and bog plants. An avenue of elms is an encouraging sight. A lake, well-stocked with fish, and a rockery provides further interest. A huge bronze statue of Sir Winston Churchill seems intrusive but is understandable in this cliff-top situation near to Dover cliffs.

PORT LYMPNE 27

Lympne, Nr Hythe, Kent. Tel: (0303) 264646
Mr J. Aspinall

3m W of Hythe • Parking • Mansion open. A Lutyens-style house with Rex Whistler and Spencer Roberts murals • Open daily except 25th Dec, 10 a.m. - 5 p.m. (summer) and to 1 hour before dusk (winter) • Entrance: £5, OAP and children £3

This is one of those gardens which some people enjoy very much and leaves others pretty cold. It stands in a 300-acre zoo park with views across the Channel. Before World War I Sir Philip Sassoon began building a new house and garden with the help of Sir Herbert Baker and Ernest Willmote and, after the war, with much assistance from the architect Philip Tilden. After a period of distinction in the 1920s and 30s it fell into decay until it was rescued in the 1970s by John Aspinall who wanted the surrounding land for his private zoo. He has reconstructed the 15-acre garden to something like its original design with advice from experts like the late Russell Page. Visitors enter down a great stone stairway of 125 steps, flanked by clipped Leyland cypress, to the paved West Court with lily pool. Beyond is the Magnolia Walk and a series of terraces planted with standard fig trees and vines. Everywhere there is fine stone paving and walls with appropriately-placed urns, caryatids etc. There is extensive bedding and use of bedding-out. Arthur Hellyer admits that 'for years it has been fashionable to denigrate Port Lympne' but he admires it.

Others, however, feel that it lacks 'soul' - that vital element that every great garden must have, however extensive the resources that have been poured into it. Arthur Hellyer waxes lyrical about the beautiful wrought ironwork by Bainbridge Reynolds.

RIVERHILL GARDENS 28

Sevenoaks, Kent. Tel: (0732) 452557
Mr John Rogers (correspondence to Mrs David Rogers)

On A225 left-hand side of road, 2m S of Sevenoaks • Best season: spring and early summer • Parking. Coaches by appointment • Home-made teas • Toilet facilities • Plants for sale • Shop • House open only to bona fide booked parties • Open Easter to June, Sun and Bank Holidays, 12 noon - 6 p.m. • Entrance: £1.50, children 50p (house and garden £2 per person for parties of 20 or more, but no children inside house)

This was originally one of the great smaller country-house gardens, housing a plantsman's collection of trees and species shrubs as introduced by John Rogers, a keen horticulturist, in the mid-1800s. The twin stresses of the 1987 hurricane, when Riverhill received the full force of the winds, and the recent drought have taken their toll. However, massive rhododendrons, many of them species, topped by cedar of Lebanon planted in 1815, also azaleas, and outstanding underplanting of bulbs still make Riverhill a fine sight in early summer. Other features include wood garden, rose walk and old orchard with Wellingtonia (planted in 1815), magnolias etc. Work continues to restore and develop the gardens and undoubtedly the immense care lavished on it will enable it in time to be restored to its rightful distinction.

SCOTNEY CASTLE ★ 29

Lamberhurst, Tunbridge Wells, Kent. Tel: (0892) 890651
The National Trust

1½m of Lamberhurst on E side of A21, 8m SE of Tunbridge Wells • Best seasons: spring and autumn • Parking • Refreshments in Goudhurst village • Toilet facilities • Partly suitable for wheelchairs but hilly approach • Plants for sale • Shop • Castle open May to Aug Bank Holiday Mon same times as garden: 30th March to 10th Nov, Wed - Fri, 11 a.m. - 6 p.m., Sat, Sun and Bank Holidays, 2 - 6 p.m. or sunset if earlier. Last admission ½ hour before closing • Entrance: Wed - Sat, £2. Sun and Bank Holidays, £2.80. Pre-booked parties, £1.60, children £1

This is an unusual garden designed in the romantic manner by the Hussey family following the tradition established by William Kent. The sloping grounds include many smaller garden layouts in the overall area. A formal garden overlooks a quarry garden. The grounds of the old castle enclose a rose garden. Herb garden. Lakeside planting adds an air of informality. Evergreens and deciduous trees provide the mature planting. They link shrubs and plants to give something in flower at every season. Daffodils, magnolias, rhododendrons and azaleas are the most spectacular. Also notable are the kalmias and hydrangeas. In a good autumn, the colours are spectacular. In some ways the planting seems occasional and haphazard, but visit this garden for its setting on a slope that gives fine views of open countryside, and for the romantic eighteenth to nineteenth-century theme uniting it. The old castle beside the lake gives added interest. At the end of August a Shakespeare play will be performed in the grounds.

SISSINGHURST CASTLE ★★

Sissinghurst, Nr Cranbrook, Kent. Tel: (0580) 712850
The National Trust

2m NE of Cranbrook, 1m E of Sissinghurst on A262, 13m S of Maidstone • Parking but parties by appointment only and no coaches at weekends • Refreshments: Tues - Fri, 12 noon - 6 p.m., Sat and Sun, 10 a.m. - 6 p.m. Picnics in car park and grass field in front of castle only • Toilet facilities • Wheelchairs restricted to two chairs at one time because of narrow uneven parths • Limited choice of plants for sale • Shop • Tower and library open • Garden open 29th March to 14th Oct, Tues - Fri, 1 - 6.30 p.m., Sat, Sun and Good Fri, 10 a.m. - 6.30 p.m. Closed every Mon inc. Bank Holidays. Last admission 6 p.m. • Entrance: Tues - Sat, £4, Sun, £4.50

'Profusion, even extravagance and exuberance within the confines of the utmost linear severity' is Vita Sackville-West's description of her design when creating Sissinghurst with her husband Harold Nicolson. It is a romantic garden with seasonal features throughout the year. Certain colour schemes have been followed, as in the purple border, the orange and yellow cottage garden, and the white garden, which is probably the most beautiful garden at Sissinghurst, itself one of the outstanding gardens in the world. The Nicolsons added little to, but saved much of the Elizabethan mansion. The site was first occupied in the twelfth century, when a moated manor was built where the orchard now stands. The library and tower are open and the latter is well worth climbing in order to see the perspective of the whole garden and surrounding area. The garden is in immaculate condition, well-labelled, well-restored after the gales of 1987, with changing vistas at every turn of the winding paths or more formal walks. The rose garden contains many old-fashioned roses as well as flowering shrubs such as *Ceanothus impressus*, *Hydrangea villosa* which together with yuccas, clematis and pansies fill the area. There is a thyme lawn leading to the herb garden filled with fragrance and charm. It is a truly magnificent example of Englishness and has had immense influence on garden design because of its structure of separate 'gardens' within the garden - but be warned that it is liable to be very crowded at weekends and afternoons. See also Long Barn and Knole.

SPRIVERS GARDEN 31

Sprivers Estate, Lamberhurst Road, Horsmonden, Kent.
Tel: (089272) 3266
The National Trust (Tenant: Chilstone Garden Ornaments)

From A21 nr Lamberhurst turn onto B2167 and Sprivers is signposted on the left opposite the turning to Horsmonden church • Parking • Suitable for wheelchairs • Shop with Chilstone garden ornaments on sale • Open Mon – Fri, 9 a.m. – 5 p.m., Sun, 10 a.m. – 4 p.m. Also May to 25th Sept, Wed, 2 – 5 p.m. for Trust members • Entrance: by purchase of brochure. £1.10 on Wed open days

A decorative garden, consisting of small gardens divided by old brick walls and yew hedges surrounding an early seventeenth-century house. There is a water garden which, like the rest of the area, is laid out to display to their best advantage garden statuary and ornaments made by the Trust's tenants.

SQUERRYES COURT 32

Westerham, Kent. Tel: (0959) 62345/63118
Mr and Mrs John Warde

½m W of Westerham on A25, 10 minutes from M25 junctions 5 or 6 • Parking • Teas • Toilet facilities • Partly suitable for wheelchairs • Dogs on lead • House open. £2.40, children £1.20 • Open March, Suns only, April to Sept, Wed, Sat, Sun and Bank Holiday Mons, 2 – 6 p.m. • Entrance: £1.40, children 70p. Parties of 20 or more by appointment

The gardens are divided into about 20 acres of formal areas and 200 of parkland. Lime groves, which are the oldest in the country, lead to a gazebo, built around 1740, from where a former member of the family used to watch his racehorses in training; nearby is a fine old dovecote. The main feature is the newly restored formal area to the rear of the house; a 1719 print has been used as an outline on which to base the ongoing developments, which reflect the mellowed brickwork of this handsome house. Beds, edged with box, contain lavender, rue, purple sage and *Nicotiana affinis*, with contrasting magenta and pink of penstemon and verbena; all are framed by well-kept yew hedges. There are several rose gardens, heather beds and azalea and rhododendron shrubberies and fine examples of topiary, which, together with a broad variety of spring bulbs, make this a garden for all seasons. Many fine magnolias around the house, a cenotaph in memory of General Wolfe (a close family friend), and a large lake complete this most attractive garden, which even when viewed towards the end of its opening period at the end of a difficult summer, was colourful and well-kept.

UPDOWN FARM 33

Betteshangar, Deal, Kent. Tel: (0304) 611895
Mr and the Hon. Mrs Willis-Fleming

3m S of Sandwich. From A256 Sandwich - Dover road, turn first left S of Eastry, signed Northbourne, Mongeham. Turn first left and into the first house on the right • Parking • Refreshments • Toilet facilities • Suitable for wheelchairs • Open 26th May, 30th June, 2 - 6 p.m. • Entrance: £1, OAP 70p, children 30p

Standing on chalk downland in open country, this is a delightful garden with many facets. A mixture of formal, enclosed areas lead to open and informal gardens with a good variety of shrubs and with quiet woodland area. The present owners have created it over the last fifteen years and it is continually developing. Shrub and climber roses are a special feature. Well worth visiting in conjunction with nearby Northbourne Court.

WAYSTRODE MANOR 34

Cowden, Kent. Tel: (0342) 850695
Mr and Mrs Peter Wright

4½m S of Edenbridge, off B2026 Edenbridge - Hartfield road • Parking • Teas • Toilet facilities • Partly suitable for wheelchairs • Plants for sale • Open by appointment and 26th May, 2 - 6 p.m., 29th May, 1.30 - 5.30 p.m., 12th June, 1.30 - 5.30 p.m. and 30th June, 2 - 6 p.m. Last admission ½ hour before closing • Entrance: £1.50, children 50p

The half-timbered sixteenth-century house and its surrounding gardens, developed by the present owners over the past 25 years, are set deep in the wooded Kentish countryside on Wealden clay. Plants tumble over the paving stones around the house and borders of shrubs and perennials, the wisteria walk and the laburnum tunnel all make more formal contrasts. Clipped yew hedges surround the island beds which are arranged in varying colour schemes; for example the oranges and reds of dahlias and roses in one and grey-foliate plants in another. The plants are well-labelled and there is also an ineresting small collection of garden statuary.

GARDENS OPEN RARELY

The following gardens are open to the public on three days or less in the year, although they may also be open by appointment if this is stated in the text. For details see individual entry.

May 5 Ladham House; **May 12** Ladham House; **May 26** Updown Farm; **June 16** Fairseat Rectory; **June 23** Long Barn; **June 30** Updown Farm; **July 7** Ladham House; **July 14** Long Barn; **July 21** Groombridge Place; **July 27** Fairseat Rectory.

LANCASHIRE

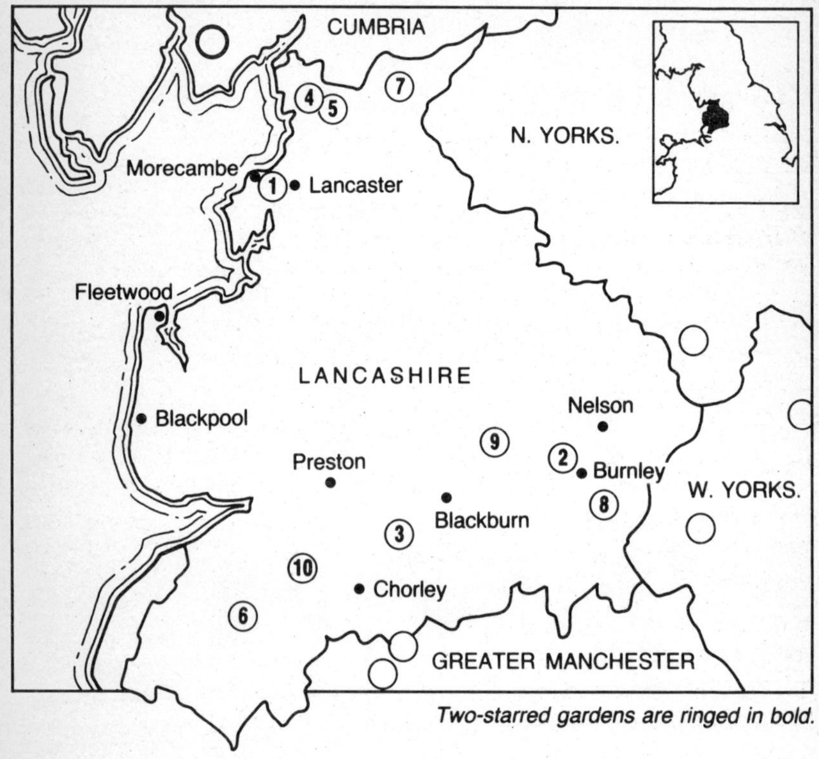

Two-starred gardens are ringed in bold.

ASHTON MEMORIAL 1

Williamson Park, Lancaster, Lancashire. Tel: (0524) 33318
Lancashire County Council

E of Lancaster town centre. Signposted • Best season: spring • Parking • Refreshments: tea shop • Toilet facilities inc. disabled • Suitable for wheelchairs • Dogs • Shop • Memorial open. Entrance to viewing gallery 40p, ground floor with exhibition free. Butterfly house £1.75 • Open daily except 25th, 26th Dec and 1st Jan, Easter Sat to Sept, 10 a.m. – 5 p.m., Oct to Good Fri, 10 a.m. – 4 p.m. • Entrance: free to gardens

Ashton Memorial was described by Pevsner as 'the grandest monument in England'. It stands at the highest point of Williamson Park looking down on the town of Lancaster. There are many views of the surrounding country from various points in the superbly landscaped park. Broad paths run through the grounds much of which is woodland with an underplanting of rhododendrons and other shrubs. There is a small lake spanned by a stone bridge, and from near here is a large stairway that leads to the huge domed monument.

Behind the monument across a cobbled area and mosaic is the palm house which now houses a collection of tropical butterflies. To the rear is a small garden containing plants attractive to local butterflies. Both monument and palm house were designed in 1906 in the style of the Baroque revival.

GAWTHORPE HALL 2

Padiham, Nr Burnley, Lancashire. Tel: (0282) 78511
The National Trust

N of A671 just E of Padiham town centre • Best season: spring • Parking • Refreshments: Tues - Fri, 11 a.m. - 5 p.m., Sat and Sun 1 - 5 p.m. • Toilet facilities inc. disabled • Partly suitable for wheelchairs • Dogs on lead • Craft gallery and shop • House open 29th March to Oct, daily except Mon and Fri but open Good Friday and Bank Holiday Mon, 1 - 5 p.m. Last admission 4.15 p.m. • Gardens open all year 10 a.m. - 6 p.m. • No charge for gardens (house and gardens £2)

This garden, though not particularly special in botanical terms, does set off the Elizabethan Hall. To the front is a formal layout of lawns and gravel paths, to the rear a parterre by Barry in the form of a sunburst overlooks the River Calder. The woodlands that surround the formal garden are planted with rhododendrons and azaleas. Through them are many walks with views back to the house and across the valley.

HOGHTON TOWER 3

Hoghton, Nr Preston, Lancashire. Tel: (025485) 2986
Sir Bernard de Hoghton

5m SE of Preston N of A675 midway between Preston and Blackburn • Best season: summer • Parking • Refreshments: tearooms • Toilet facilities • Partly suitable for wheelchairs • Dogs on lead in grounds but not garden • Shop • House and gardens open Easter Sat to Oct, Sun, also July and Aug, Sat and all Bank Holidays, 2 - 5 p.m. • Entrance: £2.50, children £1 (house and gardens)

Hoghton Tower, a sixteenth-century house built of stone, occupies a hilltop position with good views to all sides. The house and outbuildings are built around two courtyards which although not qualifying as gardens are fine areas. Surrounding the house are three walled gardens; the first contains a large lawn and herbaceous borders. The second has a smaller rectangular lawn at the centre of which is a raised square pond with an elaborate stone fountain; to one end is a statue and at the other a sundial on a stone pedestal; clipped yews flank two sides of the lawn. The third is mainly lawn with access to the tops of two small crenellated towers. Around the walled gardens runs 'the long walk' which passes under some large beech trees and is newly planted with shrubs, mainly rhododendrons and azaleas. Excellent views of the surrounding countryside.

LEIGHTON HALL 4

Carnforth, Lancashire. Tel: (0524) 734474
Mr R.G. Reynolds

2m W of Yealand Conyers, signposted from M6 junction 35 • Parking • Teas • Toilet facilities • Suitable for wheelchairs • Dogs on lead in park only • Shop • House open • Garden open May to Sept, daily except Sat and Mon, 2 - 5 p.m. • Entrance: £2.50, OAP £2, children £1.50, parties of 25 or more £2 per person (house and grounds).

Very striking when first seen from the entrance gates, the white stone façade (*c.* 1800) shines out in its parkland setting with the hills of the Lake District visible beyond. The most interesting area of the gardens, which lie to the west of the house, is the walled garden with its unusual labyrinth in the form of a gravel path that runs under an old cherry orchard. Opposite is a vegetable garden made in a geometric design with grass paths. There are also herbaceous borders and a very aromatic herb garden containing a wide variety of perennials with climbing roses on the wall behind.

LINDEN HALL 5

Borwick, Carnforth, Lancashire.
Mr and Mrs E.P. Sharpe

Off A6070, 300 yards along the road to Priest Hutton from Borwick village green • Best season: summer • Parking in road • Partly suitable for wheelchairs • Plants for sale • Open Easter Monday to 1st Aug, Mon - Fri and 5th May, 2nd June, 7th, 20th, 21st July, 2 - 5 p.m. • Entrance: honesty box

An informal garden of five acres, surrounded by a high stone wall to three sides and a ha-ha to the south. There are extensive lawned areas with irregularly-shaped beds containing a wide collection of mature shrubs and trees including many magnolias and cherries. From close by the attractive Victorian house at the east end of the garden a stream runs through the centre to a pool on the west side. Along the stream are borders of moisture-loving plants and in the pool a Chinese pagoda stands on a wooden platform. A variety of herbaceous plants, many climbers, a knot garden and a small greenhouse. Although most areas are well-tended a gentle relaxed feel pervades the whole garden.

RUFFORD OLD HALL 6

Rufford, Nr Ormskirk, Lancashire. Tel: (0704) 821254
The National Trust

7m N of Ormskirk, N of Rufford village on E of A59 • Best season: spring • Parking • Refreshments: lunches and teas, teas only on Sun • Toilet facilities • Suitable for wheelchairs • Dogs on lead • Shop • House open as garden. Last admission 4.30 p.m. • Open 30th March to 3rd Nov, daily except Fri, 1 - 5 p.m., Sun, 2 - 5 p.m. • Entrance: £1.20 (house and garden £2.30)

Rufford Old Hall is an exceptional fifteenth-century timber-framed house whose gardens complement it perfectly, having been laid out by the Trust in the style of the 1820 period. On the south are lawns and gravel paths laid out in a formal manner. The many island beds are formal in layout, too, but the shrubs, small trees and herbaceous plants they contain are planted in a more relaxed way. In the centre a path leads from two large topiary squirrels to a beech avenue that goes beyond the garden towards Rufford. There are many mature trees and rhododendrons in this area. To the east of the house by the stables is an attractive cobbled area with climbing plants on the surrounding walls. When visiting, look for the gardener's own garden to the north side of the house, in which grow many old-fashioned plants enclosed by a rustic wooden fence.

SELLET HALL GARDENS 7

Kirkby Lonsdale, via Carnforth, Lancashire. Tel: (05242) 71865
Mrs J. Gray

1m SW of Kirkby Lonsdale, signposted from B6254 • Best seasons: spring and summer • Parking • Toilet facilities • Partly suitable for wheelchairs • Plants for sale • Shop • Open daily except 25th Dec, 1st Jan, 10 a.m. - 5 p.m. • Entrance: 50p, children free

Created over the last 20 years, this garden is set around an old and attractive grey stone house in a beautiful part of North Lancashire. A fairly large herb garden is its best feature, formal in layout and surrounded by a high yew hedge. The symmetrical beds contain a great number of herbs and other perennials; there are good collections of lavenders, thymes and artemisias. Behind the herb garden is a wild-flower garden and to one side a bee garden. Also a small Japanese garden and other areas of shrubs, perennials, dwarf conifers and heathers. The small courtyard has been attractively planted. Some areas are still being developed, and the results are impressive for this exposed part of the country.

TOWNELEY PARK 8

Todmorden Road, Burnley, Lancashire. Tel: (0282) 24213
Burnley Corporation

1½m SE of Burnley town centre on A671 • Best season: spring • Refreshments: cafeteria • Toilet facilities • Suitable for wheelchairs • Dogs on lead • Gift shop in Hall • Hall open daily except Sat, weekdays 10 a.m. - 5 p.m., Sun, 12 noon - 5 p.m. Closed Christmas week • Garden open all year during daylight hours • Entrance: free

The Hall dates from 1500 but its exterior is largely the work of 1816–20. The gardens are not its main attraction but are pleasantly grassed and contain many mature trees. Parkland laid out in the late eighteenth century forms the basis of today's gardens. The front of the house looks out over a pond and beyond a ha-ha to open parkland. There are some formal beds to the east of the house planted with bright arrangements of annuals. Further to the east as well as to the south and west are extensive woodlands containing many large rhododendrons and long walks. There is also a craft museum and a nature centre.

WHALLEY ABBEY 9

Whalley, Blackburn, Lancashire. Tel: (025482) 2268
Diocese of Blackburn

8m NNW of Burnley, Whalley is S of A59 between Clitheroe and Blackburn • Best season: summer • Refreshments: in coffee shop • Toilet facilities • Partly suitable for wheelchairs • Dogs on lead • Shop • Open all year, dawn – dusk • Entrance: 75p, OAP 40p

Whalley Abbey is visited mainly by those wishing to see the ruins of the fourteenth-century abbey, and the gardens run round their periphery. These gardens are of recent creation and consist mainly of herbaceous borders and shrubs; in one area there are conifers and heathers. The stone terraces that have been made against the north outer wall of the garden are perhaps its most attractive feature. To the south of the ruins is an avenue of mixed trees flanking the River Calder that runs behind them. Development of the gardens is continuing.

WORDEN PARK 10

Arts and Crafts Centre, Leyland, Lancashire. Tel: (0772) 455908/ 421109
Borough of South Ribble

Take B5248 S from Leyland and at Leyland Cross follow signs to Worden Park • Parking • Refreshments: coffee shop and snacks at Craft Centre • Toilet facilities • Partly suitable for wheelchairs • Dogs • Craft centre • Open daily, 8 a.m. – sunset • Entrance: free, except first Sat in June when a charge is made

These gardens are set around part of an old house and a stable block that now contains a craft workshop (the rest of the house was burnt down in the 1950s). There are formal gardens with brightly planted beds amongst cobbled paths and a garden for the blind with scented plants grown in raised beds. The maze is quite unusual being made of hornbeam hedges in a circular pattern. A little distance away is a large conservatory with a rockery to one side and a herbaceous border to the other. They face a formal lawned area that is enclosed by a low balustrade and some fine ironwork gates. On occasions a walled garden can be entered; this has a mulberry tree and a greenhouse with a vine. Large areas of open parkland surround the gardens.

LEICESTERSHIRE

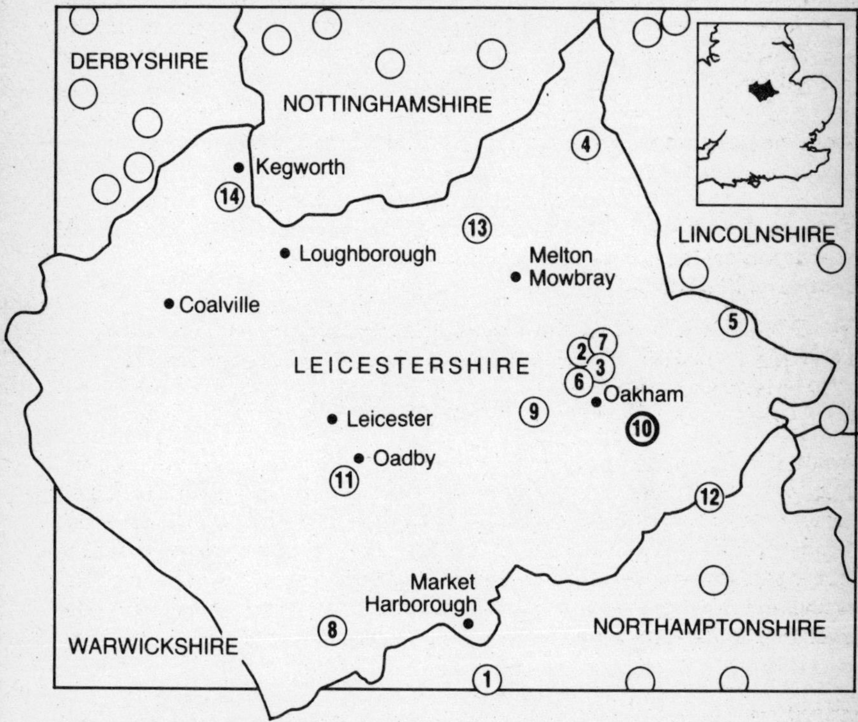

Plain circle numbers can be found by turning to neighbouring counties.
Two-starred gardens are ringed in bold.

ARTHINGWORTH MANOR 1

Arthingworth, Nr Market Harborough, Leicestershire.
Mr and Mrs W. Guinness

5m S of Market Harborough. Turn left off A508 to Arthingworth, fork right past the church, left by the white cottage over a cattle grid • Best season: June/July • Parking in field • Teas • Toilet facilities • Plants for sale • Open 23rd June, 2 - 5.30 p.m., 6th July, 2 - 5 p.m. • Entrance: £1.20, children 50p

A six and a half-acre garden designed by John Codrington 20 years ago. Shrub borders contain interesting colour combinations. Walls of roses, clematis and wisteria. Beside the ruined manor house is the white garden. The rose garden is a major feature and there are also fruit and vegetable gardens and herbaceous borders. The most recent addition is a three-acre arboretum.

ASHWELL HOUSE 2

Ashwell, Leicestershire. Tel: (0572) 722833
Mr and Mrs S.D. Pettifer

3m N of Oakham via B668 towards Cottesmore, turn left to Ashwell • Parking • Toilet facilities • Suitable for wheelchairs • Plants sometimes for sale • Open for parties by appointment • Entrance: £1 per person

An old garden, well-planned with colour combinations to provide all year colour, and golden plants to light up the various borders. There are peaches, plums, pears and blackberries on the old walls and soft fruits in the garden along with a range of vegetables, and some nut trees. A wide range of shrubs and perennials in the borders, and a large variety of flowers grown for drying.

ASHWELL LODGE 3

Ashwell, Nr Oakham, Leicestershire. Tel: (0572) 722825
Mrs B.V. Eve

3m N of Oakham between A606 to Melton Mowbray and B668 Oakham - Cottesmore road • Parking in street • Teas • Toilet facilities • Suitable for wheelchairs • Plants for sale • Open 28th April, 2.30 - 6 p.m. • Entrance: £1

A one and a half-acre garden redesigned by Percy Cane about 1973 and divided up into little gardens by hedges of beech and yew. A paved rose garden with shrub and pillar roses and a crown-shaped trellis with roses, as well as clematis with roses on arches provide masses of colour. A border of peony. A good range of cottage-garden plants in the herbaceous borders and also shrubs and acers. Water and a greenhouse are other features in this very pleasant garden which in spring is colourful with bulbs. There are fruit trees, and smaller plants on the patio.

BELVOIR CASTLE 4

Belvoir, Grantham, Leicestershire. Tel: (0476) 870262
The Duke of Rutland

6m from Grantham, S of A52 Nottingham - Grantham road and N of Melton Mowbray road. By Belvoir village. Signposted • Parking • Refreshments: lunches and teas. Picnics in car park • Toilet facilities • Partly suitable for wheelchairs • Shop • Castle open • Gardens open 29th March to 1st Oct, Tues - Thurs and Sat, 12 noon - 5.30 p.m., Sun and Bank Holiday Mon, 11 a.m. - 6 p.m. • Entrance: £3, concessions £2 (house and gardens)

From a distance this castle (pronounced Beaver) has all the appearance of a medieval fortress, although on arrival it is clearly a more solid eighteenth-century erection. The house is famous for its rooms by James Wyatt. The mid-nineteenth century garden descends from the castle in a series of terraces and slopes with some small gardens created by hedging. Bulbs, early-flowering shrubs, roses and arbours. Some seating. Good views of Belvoir Vale. Friendly peacocks.

CLIPSHAM HOUSE 5

Clipsam, Leicestershire. Tel: (0780) 410238
Mr and Mrs R. Wheatley

10m NE of Oakham, E of A1 on B668 • Parking in grounds or nearby lane • Teas • Toilet facilities • Suitable for wheelchairs • Dogs on lead • Open by appointment • Entrance: by donation when open for charity

This garden is set in parkland with some good trees and various conifers and acers. There is a lovely walled garden with island beds and grass paths and a pool and fountain. Herbaceous borders contain a wide range of shrubs, ground-cover plants and roses, and on the walls are climbers and fruit trees. A conservatory houses more tender plants and there is a vegetable garden and orchard. Designed to give pleasure and colour throughout the summer.

LANGHAM LODGE 6

Langham, Nr Oakham, Leicestershire. Tel: (0572) 722912
Mr and Mrs H.N. Hemsley

½m out of Langham on Burley Road. Go up farm road beside pair of cottages • Best season: June/July • Parking • Suitable for wheelchairs • Dogs on lead • Plants for sale • Open by appointment • Entrance: £1, children free

This one-acre garden, with rich soil, should be of interest to plantspersons for its imaginative foliage combinations and good sense of shape and colour contrasts. Old-fashioned roses, a peony border, iris, azaleas, hebes, sedums, berberis, dogwoods, eucalyptus, elaeagnus and hostas. There is a hot-coloured bed, an evergreen border, and bulbs in spring. A delightful walled garden with water and a wide range of cottage-garden plans together with a greenhouse and vegetable garden are other features to enjoy.

OLD HALL 7

Ashwell, Leicestershire. Tel: (0572) 722823
Mrs N.L. McRoberts

3m N of Oakham via B668 towards Cottesmore, turn left to Ashwell • Best season: mid-June to late July • Parking • Toilet facilities • Open for parties by arrangement • Entrance: £1 per person

Fine old garden with some good colour combinations both with shrubs and in the herbaceous borders, and a range of variegated foliage specimens. A large yew hedge forms a screen and the church provides a backcloth to the raised border of shrubs and trees. In the walled garden is a good range of cottage garden plants and perennials and climbers on the wall add further colour. A pleasant garden with a peaceful atmosphere.

ORCHARDS 8

Hall Lane, Walton, Nr Lutterworth, Leicestershire. Tel: (0455) 556958
Mr and Mrs G. Cousins

8m S of Leicester. Take A50, turn right for Bruntingthorpe then follow signs for Walton • Best season: summer • Parking in nearby roads • Toilet facilities • Suitable for wheelchairs • Dogs on lead • Plants for sale • Open by appointment • Entrance: £1, children free

A fine example of how to create variety in a small area round a village bungalow. The courtyard has many unusual plants on the walls. There are raised beds around a pool, old brick paths, troughs with alpines, island beds, a cottage garden with shrub roses, lavender, verbascum and geraniums. Full of ideas and original plant combinations in foliage and colour.

ROCKINGHAM CASTLE

(see Northamptonshire)

ROSE COTTAGE 9

Owston, Nr Oakham, Leicestershire. Tel: (066477) 545
Mr J.D. Buchanan

6m W of Oakham via Knossington, 3m S of Somerby • Parking outside village hall • Home-made teas • Toilet facilities • Suitable for wheelchairs • Plants for sale • Open 21st April, 16th June, 2 - 6 p.m. Also by appointment • Entrance: £1, children free

This one and three quarter-acre garden made from an old sand quarry over the past 12 years on clay and lime conditions has a wide range of plants and the design features are very good. There is a beautiful hedge of *Rosa rugosa*, island beds, a raised bed with conifers and heathers, ground-cover plants, collections of hollies, roses, hardy geraniums, hebes, ferns, alpines and potentillas. In addition a peat bed, scree border and a good vegetable garden. Pool. A garden full of interesting ideas.

STONE COTTAGE ★★ 10

Hambleton, Oakham, Rutland, Leicestershire. Tel: (0572) 722156
Mr J. Codrington

3m E of Oakham, turn S off A606 for Hambleton • Plants for sale on application • Open by appointment April to Oct. Also 5th May, 16th June, 2.30 - 6 p.m. • Entrance: £1, children 50p for charity

John Codrington has been one of the most influential of designers over the post-war years and his small garden is essential viewing for all who are interested in the subtleties of planting. The garden is also notable for the clever way in which the designer has divided his plot - linking the separate areas by cross walks which make the garden seem much longer than it is. There is particular interest for the specialist because of the range of plants from all over the world. There is a tropical house and tropical garden, gardens of individual colours, a woodland area, water, tree peonies, a collection of grasses and ferns, a herb garden and many roses.

UNIVERSITY OF LEICESTER BOTANIC GARDEN ★ 11

Stoughton Drive South, Oadby, Leicestershire. Tel: (0533) 717725
Leicester University

3m SE of city centre, just off the A6 opposite Oadby race course • Parking in nearby roads • Toilet facilities • Suitable for wheelchairs • Plants for sale when available • Open all year, Mon - Fri, 10 a.m. - 4.30 p.m. (3.30 p.m. on Fri) or dusk if earlier • Entrance: free

A 16-acre garden founded in the early 1900s incorporating the gardens of four large houses with many interesting features ranging from the large trees of *Pinus nigra*, *Sequoiadendron giganteum*, *Fraxinus excelsior* and *Juglans regia* to the alpine houses' lewisias and drabas. A cactus house, shrub borders with a wide range of acers and conifers, a fern house, fuchsias and herbaceous borders. Borders of ericas, climbers on the wall and on a stone pergola, a formal pool and a raised-bed garden. National collections of aubretias, hardy fuchsias and skimmias. A typical Leicestershre meadow has been recreated. Visitors can learn much botanically.

WAKERLEY MANOR 12

Wakerley, Nr Uppingham, Leicestershire. Tel: (057287) 511
Mr and Mrs A.D.A.W. Forbes

6m from Uppingham. Turn right off A47 through Barrowden to Wakerley • Best season: July • Parking • Refreshments • Suitable for wheelchairs • Dogs on lead • Plants for sale when available • Open by appointment and 30th June, 2 - 6 p.m. For weekdays March to Nov, telephone Stuart Baines on the above number evenings only • Entrance: £1, OAP 50p, children 10p

A four and a half-acre garden landscaped 15 years ago and being developed by the present owners with large areas of lawn and mature trees - weeping ash, *Cedrus atlantica* and sequoiadendron. Autumn colour is provided by several acers, sorbus and fagus and new trees and shrubs are being planted to provide shelter. Herbaceous borders with perennials, shrubs and shrub roses provide summer colour. Climbers adorn the house walls and there is a pool with fish and plants. A hedge of lavatera gives a splash of colour and in the greenhouses are a range of good pot plants. Vegetable garden.

WARTNABY GARDENS 13

Wartnaby, Nr Melton Mowbray, Leicestershire.
Lord and Lady King

4m NW of Melton Mowbray. From A606 turn W in Ab Kettleby for Wartnaby • Best season: end May to mid-Aug • Parking • Refreshments • Dogs on lead • Plants for sale • Open 19th May, 23rd June, 21st July and by written appointment on weekdays. • Entrance: £1, children 20p

This garden has delightful little gardens within it, including a grey garden, a sunken garden and a purple border of shrubs and roses, and there are good herbaceous borders, climbers and old-fashioned roses. A large pool has an adjacent bog garden with primulas, ferns and astilbe and several varieties of willow. There is an arboretum with a good collection of trees and shrub roses, and alongside the drive is a beech hedge in a Grecian pattern. Greenhouses contain peaches, orchids and a vine and there is a new fruit garden with fruit arches and cordon trees. Fine views.

WHATTON HOUSE ★ 14

Nr Kegworth, Leicestershire. Tel: (0509) 842268
Lord Crawshaw

4m NE of Loughborough on A6 between Kegworth and Hathern. 1m from M1 junction 24 • Best season: spring • Parking in grounds • Refreshments in tea room • Toilet facilities • Partly suitable for wheelchairs • Dogs on lead • Plants for sale • Open 31st March to 29th Sept, Sun and Bank Holiday Mons, 2 -6 p.m. Weekdays by appointment • Entrance: £1, OAP 50p, children 40p

This 15-acre garden created by Lord Crawshaw and developed over the years contains wide interest with the lovely herbaceous border, the unusual Chinese garden and the many large trees and more recently-planned arboretum. Note the Art Nouveau gate. There is an ice-house, a dog cemetery, rose garden, woodland garden and the Canyon garden. Water adds to the beauty with pools and there are brick channels that can be filled with water. There is a large walled kitchen garden and in the early part of the year masses of wild flowers. Some areas are somewhat overgrown but an air of peace surrounds the whole.

GARDENS OPEN RARELY

The following gardens are open to the public on three days or less in the year, although they may also be open by appointment if this is stated in the text. For details see individual entry.

April 21 Rose Cottage; **April 28** Ashwell Lodge; **May 5** Stone Cottage; **May 19** Wartnaby Gardens; **June 16** Rose Cottage; Stone Cottage; **June 23** Arthingworth Manor; Wartnaby Gardens; **July 6** Arthingworth Manor; **July 21** Wartnaby Gardens.

LINCOLNSHIRE

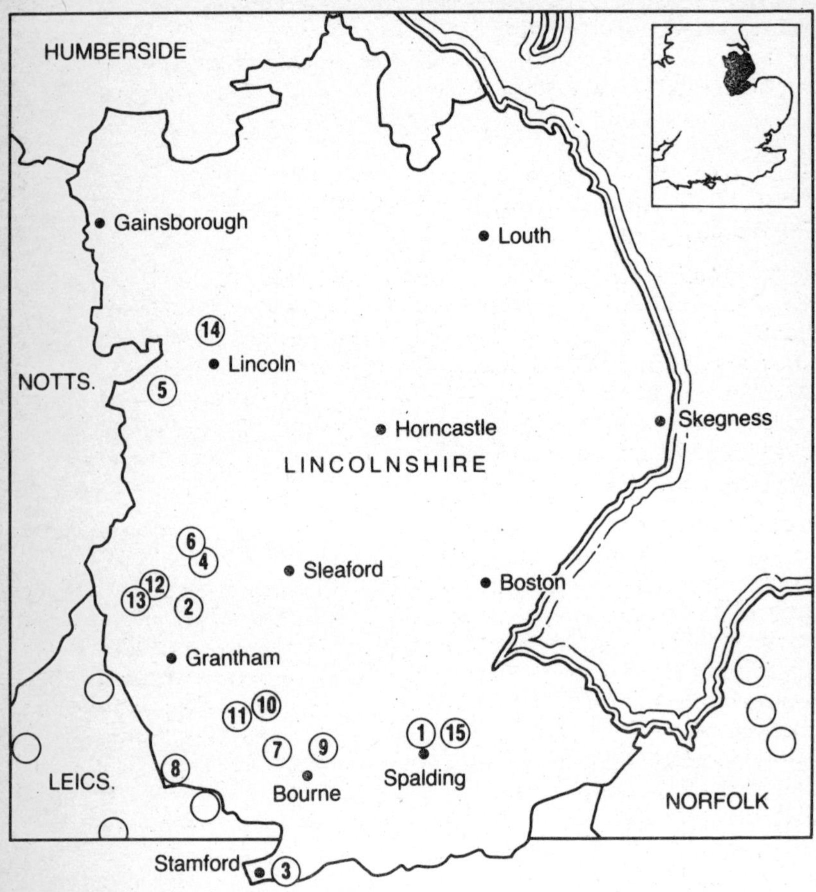

Plain circle numbers can be found by turning to neighbouring counties.

AYSCOUGHFEE HALL AND GARDENS 1

Churchgate, Spalding, Lincolnshire. Tel: (0775) 725468
South Holland District Council

Centre of Spalding • Parking on Churchgate • Refreshments: café open seasonally • Toilet facilities inc. disabled • Suitable for wheelchairs • Dogs on lead • House open: Mon - Thurs, 10 a.m. - 5 p.m., Fri, 10 a.m. - 4.30 p.m., Mar to Oct, Sat, 10 a.m. - 5 p.m., Sun, 11 a.m. - 5 p.m. • Gardens open daily, Mon - Sat, 8 a.m. - 5 p.m. or ½ hour after sunset, Sun, 10 a.m. - 5 p.m. or ½ hour after sunset. Closed 25th Dec • Entrance: free

Next to the River Welland the gardens of this public park are in a beautiful setting. Entirely enclosed by lovely old walls, they are worth visiting for the bizarrely-shaped, clipped yew walks, its old rectangular fish pond with fountains and the fascinating medieval red-brick hall now housing the museum of South Holland. In addition there are good bedding display, lawns, formal rose garden, pergola, and wall shrubs including a fruiting vine.

BELTON HOUSE ★ 2

Belton, Nr Grantham, Lincolnshire. Tel: (0476) 66116
The National Trust

4m N of Grantham off A607 • Parking • Refreshments: light lunches, teas, etc., 12 noon – 5.30 p.m. • Toilet facilities inc. disabled • Suitable for wheelchairs • Dogs on lead • Gift shop • House open, 30th March to Oct, Wed – Sun and Bank Holiday Mons, 1 – 5.30 p.m. Closed Good Friday • Gardens open 30 March to Oct, Wed – Sun and Bank Holiday Mons, 11 a.m. – 5.30 p.m. Last admission 5 p.m. Free access to park on foot from Lion Lodge gates all year but this does not give admittance to house, garden or adventure playground • Entrance: £3.50 (house and gardens)

The gardens at Belton are large and impressive. The extensive woodland area has two lakes, a small canal and good cedars; a children's adventure playground makes it ideal for families. However, it is the formal area to the north of the house, completed with the superbly restored and replanted Jeffrey Wyatville orangery, that makes the garden memorable. The 'Dutch garden' has clipped yew hedging, formal beds with lavender edging, standard 'Iceberg' roses and well-planted stone urns. The earlier Italian garden has a large central pond with fountain, a lion-headed exhedra, lawns and clipped yews. The gradual but extensive restoration of the garden, including the reforming of herbaceous borders and the old statue walk, ensures a garden of great merit and authenticity. 200 trees were blown down during recent gales in the park, 29 of which were in the garden, including six cedars of Lebanon and two large beeches.

BURGHLEY HOUSE 3

Stamford, Lincolnshire. Tel: (0780) 52451
Burghley House Preservation Trust
Custodian: Lady Victoria Leatham (née Cecil)

½m E of Stamford on Barnack Road, close to A1. Well signposted • Parking • Refreshments • Toilet facilities • Limited access for wheelchairs • Dogs on lead in park only • Shop • House open except 14th Sept • Garden open 29th March to 6th Oct, daily, 11 a.m. – 5 p.m. Avoid Burghley Horse Trials, 12th to 15th Sept 1991 • Entrance: £3.80, OAP £3.50, children £2.30, family £10 inc. guided tour of house and entrance to special exhibition

The main attraction at Burghley is the magnificent Elizabethan house with its immense collection of art treasures, built by Richard Cecil, created Lord Burghley by his Queen. Both the house and its custodian, Lady Victoria Leatham, have appeared on many television antiques programmes. The parkland, landscaped by 'Capability' Brown, is delightful and extensive. There is only a small area of formal rose garden with oval pond, lavender, fountain and urns so Burghley is of limited interest to visitors with more botanical leanings. In addition to creating a large serpentine lake, Brown built a new stable block, an orangery, a gamekeeper's lodge, a dairy and an ice-house. The finest surviving small building is a lakeside summer house.

CAYTHORPE COURT 4

Lincolnshire College of Agriculture and Horticulture, Caythorpe Court, Caythorpe, Grantham, Lincolnshire. Tel: (0400) 72521

10m N of Grantham off A607 • Parking • Refreshments on open day • Toilet facilities • Partly suitable for wheelchairs • Plants and produce for sale • Open 1st June, 1.30 – 5 p.m. for College Open Day and 9th, 16th, 21st May in the evening by appointment • Entrance: £2 per car on open day

One of three centres for the Lincolnshire College of Agriculture and Horticulture, this is reflected in its glasshouses and display beds of roses, shrubs, bedding and herbaceous plants. However, it is the original garden around the 1899 hunting lodge that makes a visit worthwhile. Three large terraces built on a west-facing slope are wonderfully romantic with Ancaster stone walls, balustrades and stairways. For ease of maintenance all are quite simply planted. The upper terrace has a good shrub border and lawn with a specimen monkey-puzzle tree. The middle terrace, a delight in spring, has walls covered in aubretia, and a row of flowering cherries. The third has Virginia creeper and wisteria swathing the balustraded stairs, and a wide rose border underplanted with flag irises and backed by clematis-covered walls from the upper terrace; walks lead through the surrounding woodland. To the east of the house, from the central lavender-edged bed, shrub-lined drives lead to other parts of the college.

DODDINGTON HALL 5

Doddington, Nr Lincoln, Lincolnshire. Tel: (0522) 694308
Mr and Mrs A.G. Jarvis

5m W of Lincoln on B1190 • Parking • Refreshment: restaurant • Toilet facilities inc. disabled • Suitable for wheelchairs • Dogs on lead • Shop • House open • Open Easter Mon and May to Sept, Wed and Sun inc. Bank Holiday Mons, 2 – 6 p.m. Parties at other times by arrangement • Entrance: £1.50, children 75p (house and garden £3, children £1.50), special rates for parties of 20 or more

The romantic gardens of the Elizabethan house successfully combine many different styles and moods. The simplicity of the gravel, box and lawned courtyard, the formal croquet lawn and the gravel walk along the kitchen garden wall contrasts with the walled west garden with its elaborate parterres of roses, iris and clipped box edging with borders of herbaceous plants and old roses. (The parterres were restored in Elizabethan style in 1900.) Fine eighteenth-century Italian gates open from here on to a formal yew alley, more old roses and a good wild garden. Here the meandering walks take in a turf maze, stream, ancient specimens of sweet chestnut, cedar, yew and holly, and the Temple of the Winds built by the present owner. The more recently-planted herb garden, pleached hornbeams and dwarf box-edging continue to harmonize the different areas and create more interest in this peaceful garden.

FULBECK HALL 6

Fulbeck, Nr Grantham, Lincolnshire. Tel: (0400) 72205
Mr and Mrs Fry

On A607 Lincoln – Grantham road • Parking • Picnic area • Toilet facilities • Suitable for wheelchairs • Dogs on lead • Plants for sale • House open Easter, May and Aug Bank Holiday Suns and Mons and 7th to 28th July, daily, 2 – 5 p.m. Extra charge • Gardens open Easter to Oct, Tues and Wed, and Easter May and Aug Bank Holiday Suns and Mons, and 7th to 28th July, daily, 2 – 5 p.m. • Entrance: £1.50, OAP and children £1, season ticket £4 (house and garden £2.50, OAP £2, children £1)

The 11-acre garden at Fulbeck is varied and interesting with newly-planted informal areas together with a formal Victorian terrace. Many of the trees here are as old as the house (1733). The top terrace with a gravel walk is backed by a superbly-shaped clipped yew hedge. The bottom lawn has shrubs, roses, unusual clematis and ramblers climbing into the surrounding trees. Against a lime-stone wall at the south of the house is a herbaceous border with many choice plants. Beyond the immediate garden is a pleasant wild garden and nature trail. In 1990, 500 native trees and shrubs around the north and western edge of the garden were planted, and a pond was constructed near the northern boundary by the nature trail. Planting plans available for the whole formal area of the garden which visitors may buy or borrow.

GRIMSTHORPE CASTLE 7

Grimsthorpe, Nr Bourne, Lincolnshire. Tel: (0778) 32205
Grimsthorpe and Drummond Castle Trust Ltd

4m NW of Bourne on A151 Colsterworth – Bourne road • Parking • Teas • Toilet facilities inc. disabled • Suitable for wheelchairs • House open Sun, 2 – 6 p.m. • Garden open Sat, Sun and Bank Holiday Mons, 4th May to 15th Sept, 10 a.m. – 6 p.m. Also on other dates to be advertised locally or on application to Estate Office • Entrance: £1, OAP and children 50p (house and garden £3, OAP and children £1.50)

The impressive house, part-medieval, part-Tudor and part-eighteenth-century, of Vanbrugh design, is surrounded on three sides by good pleasure gardens in which 'Capability' Brown had a hand. The Victorian knot garden to the east of the house has beds of lavender, roses and catmint with edges of clipped box. To the south are two yew-hedged rose gardens with topiary, a yew 'broad walk' and a retreat. Leading to the west terrace is a double yew walk with classic herbaceous borders and beyond a shrub rose border and row of 70-year-old cedars. The yew hedging throughout the garden is superbly maintained and differs in design from one area to another. Beyond the pleasure gardens are the arboretum, wild garden, an unusual geometrically-designed kitchen garden with clipped box and bean pergola, and extensive parkland. Views of the old oak and chestnut avenues and the parkland with its lake and Vanbrugh summer house are provided by cleverly positioned vistas and terraces.

GUNBY HALL ★ 8

Gunby, Nr Spilsby, Lincolnshire.
The National Trust

2½m of Burgh-le-Marsh on S of A158 • Parking • Toilet facilities • Suitable for wheelchairs • Dogs on lead • Plants for sale • House and garden open April to Sept, Wed, 2 - 6 p.m. Other weekdays by written appointment. Last admission 5.30 p.m. Garden also open Thurs, 2 - 6 p.m. Also open Tues, Thurs and Fri by written appointment to Mr and Mrs J.D. Wrisdale • Entrance: £1 garden (house and garden £2)

The early eighteenth-century house, with its walls smothered in fine plants, is set in parkland with avenues of lime and horse chestnut. The shrub borders, wild garden, lawns with old cedars and the restrained formal front garden of catmint and lavender beds backed by clipped yew provide a startling contrast to the main attraction of Gunby - its walled gardens. The dazzling pergola garden with its apple-tree walkway has a maze of paths leading to beds of old roses, herb garden and brimming herbaceous and annual borders. The second walled area houses an impressive kitchen garden reached after passing more borders of perfectly-arranged herbaceous plants and hybrid musk roses. Backing on to its wall is another wonderfully classic herbaceous border and beyond an early nineteenth-century long fish pond and orchard completing an altogether enchanting garden. It is fitting that it was the subject of Tennyson's 'Haunt of Ancient Peace'.

32 MAIN STREET 9

Dyke, Nr Bourne, Lincolnshire. Tel: (0778) 422241
Mr and Mrs D. Sellars

1m N of Bourne, off A15 • Parking • Teas • Toilet facilities at nearby village hall • Dogs on lead • Plants for sale • Open May Bank Holiday and some Suns in April and Aug. Also by appointment • Entrance: 80p, children 20p

This small area of 100 × 50 feet is subdivided into tiny compartments allowing an astonishing number of planting schemes. Every available space is crammed with a choice plant, ornament, trough or architectural feature and by careful planning and underplanting overflows with a continuous display of colour. Such is the enthusiasm of the owner that the garden is constantly changing and may well vary significantly from year to year; it is daunting to recall that it has been developed over a period of only six years.

MANOR FARM 10

Keisby, Nr Lenton, Bourne, Lincolnshire.
Mr and Mrs C.A. Richardson

9m NW of Bourne, N of A151 • Parking • Teas • Toilet facilities on ground floor • Suitable for wheelchairs • Dogs on lead • Plants for sale • Open 5th May, 30th June, 2 – 6 p.m. • Entrance: £1, children free

This pretty, informal garden is a delight with its artistic planning and colour harmonization. The tiny paths to the vegetable plot, pergola and stream meander through the beds and so allow close inspection of the many choice plants, including shrub roses, ramblers and clematis. The garden was featured on *Gardeners' World*.

MANOR HOUSE 11

Bitchfield, Grantham, Lincolnshire. Tel: (047685) 261
Mr John Richardson

Centre of Bitchfield village on B1176 SE of Grantham • Best season: June/July • Parking • Toilet facilities • Suitable for wheelchairs • Open for parties of 15 or more by appointment only. No children • Entrance: donations to charity

The restrained courtyard entrance has walls of soft apricot-pink, perfectly matching the gravel, and is decorated merely with clipped box in French-style planters. Just south of the house is a formal box-edged garden with a central armillary sphere, planted with the grey-foliated, white-flowering *Cerastium tomentosum* var. *columnae* that gives a welcome winter colour and interest for this is a summer garden, magnificent in June and July. There are 94 rose varieties mixed with herbaceous plants in formal and informal borders. Roses also provide colour round the pond and ramble happily through old apple trees in the lawn and over the house walls. By careful design, views over a ha-ha to the paddock are never lost, even with the owner's generous planting schemes. Much recommended for lovers of shrub roses and summer-flowering herbaceous plants. Robin Lane-Fox helped with the design.

MARSTON HALL 12

Marston, Nr Grantham, Lincolnshire. Tel: (0400) 50225
Reverend Henry Thorold

6m NW of Grantham, 1½m off A1 • Teas • Toilet facilities • Suitable for wheelchairs • Dogs on lead • Plants for sale when available • House and garden open 19th May, 16th, 23rd June, 21st July, 2 - 6 p.m. Other times by appointment • Entrance: £1.50, children 75p

The gardens reflect the intimate nature of the beautiful and ancient Ancaster stone house. A series of small, walled and high-hedged gardens, courtyards and walks house formal rose beds, cottage garden, knot garden planted with herbs, and vegetables screened by herbaceous borders and trellising. To the south of the house are lawns, clipped yews and walks through the newly-planted laburnum avenue and ancient trees including an enormous laburnum and a 400-year-old wych elm. The Lancing avenue of Lombardy poplars stretches from the orchard to the nearby River Witham and perfectly unites the garden with the parkland beyond.

ORCHARD NURSERIES 13

Tow Lane, Foston, Grantham, Lincolnshire.
Janet and Richard Blenkinship

7m NW of Grantham off A1 • Parking • Refreshments when open for charity • Toilet facilities • Suitable for wheelchairs • Plants for sale • Open March to Sept, daily, 10 a.m. - 5 p.m. • Entrance: on certain days 50p, otherwise voluntary donation to charity

Set around the owners' nursery and propagating areas, the one-acre garden offers an ideal opportunity for viewing the many herbaceous plants in which they specialise. The small areas of lawns and grassy paths, separated by hedges and plant-laden arches, provide a foil for the many borders. Varying from shady shrub-backed borders to bright and cottagy beds, they are filled with labelled, choice plants. A small meadow, bog garden and a pond are additional features of especial interest to the plantsperson.

RISEHOLME HALL 14

Lincolnshire College of Agriculture and Horticulture, Riseholme Hall, Riseholme, Lincoln. Tel: (0522) 522252
Lincolnshire County Council

5m N of Lincoln off A15 • Parking • Refreshments on Open Day and in evenings if booked • Toilet facilities • Suitable for wheelchairs • Plants for sale • Farm shop • Open 15th June, 1.30 - 5 p.m. for College Open Day and 12th, 25th, 26th June, 9th July, guided tours by appointment at 7, 7.15, 7.30 and 7.45 p.m. • Entrance: £2 on Open Day

Typically eighteenth-century landscaped parkland, with a picturesque lake, surrounds the house and gardens. Reflecting its educational as well as decorative function the garden provides a rare opportunity to view a vast selection of labelled plants. The horticultural department's demonstration plots show rock, water, low maintenance and heather gardens as well as demonstration hedges, genus beds, bedding, vegetables and glasshouses. The long Bishop's Walk has a yew hedge to the north and a warm brick wall to the south allowing the cultivation of many tender wall shrubs and climbers normally only found in more southerly districts. Along the walk is a herbaceous border and island beds of flowering shrubs. Also a newly restored, walled organic vegetable garden, an arboretum planted in 1971, mixed borders, rose beds and conservation areas.

SPRINGFIELDS GARDENS 15

Springfield, Spalding, Lincolnshire. Tel: (0775) 724843
Springfields Horticultural Society

1½m from Spalding on A151 • Best season: April and Sept • Parking • Refreshments: café, tea shop and licensed restaurant • Toilet facilities • Suitable for wheelchairs • Plants for sale • Shop • Open 29th March to 29th Sept, daily, 10 a.m. - 6 p.m. • Entrance: £2, children free (£3, OAP £2, children 5 - 16, £1 special events)

The 25 acres of gardens have been designed to maximize areas of show bedding - whether of the colourful spring displays of thousands of bulb varieties or of the later roses and annuals. Subdivided into smaller areas by shrub borders and small copses, the garden boasts many different features all easily accessible for wheelchairs. However, with the exception of an excellent herbaceous border, with its bold plantings, the gardens and glasshouses can be monotonous. The colour schemes are dazzling but wearing and the gardens themselves - the lake, the pergolas and the architecture - are all somewhat dated.

GARDENS OPEN RARELY

The following gardens are open to the public on three days or less in the year, although Caythorpe Court may also be open by appointment. For details see individual entry.
May 5 Manor Farm; **June 1** Caythorpe Court; **June 30** Manor Farm.

LONDON (Greater)

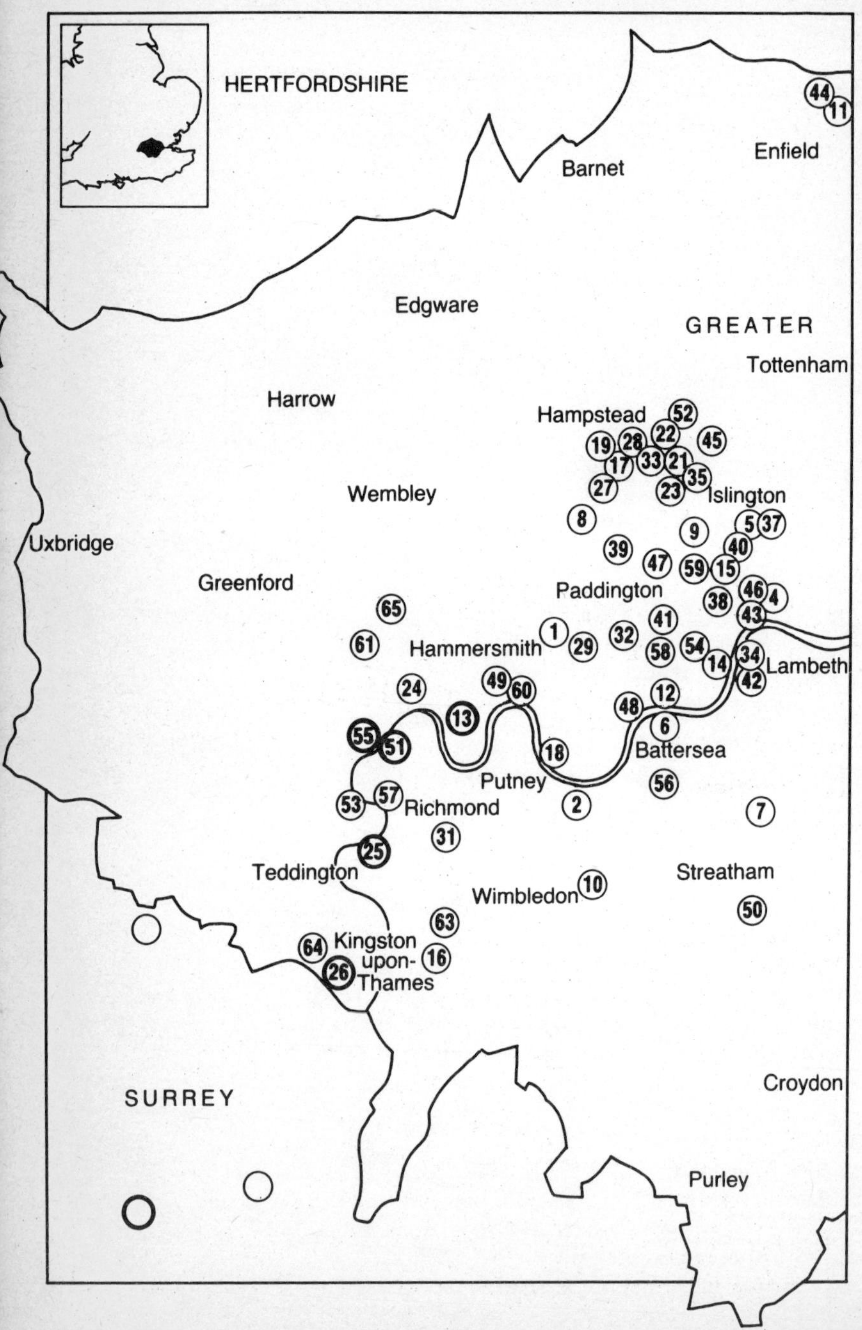

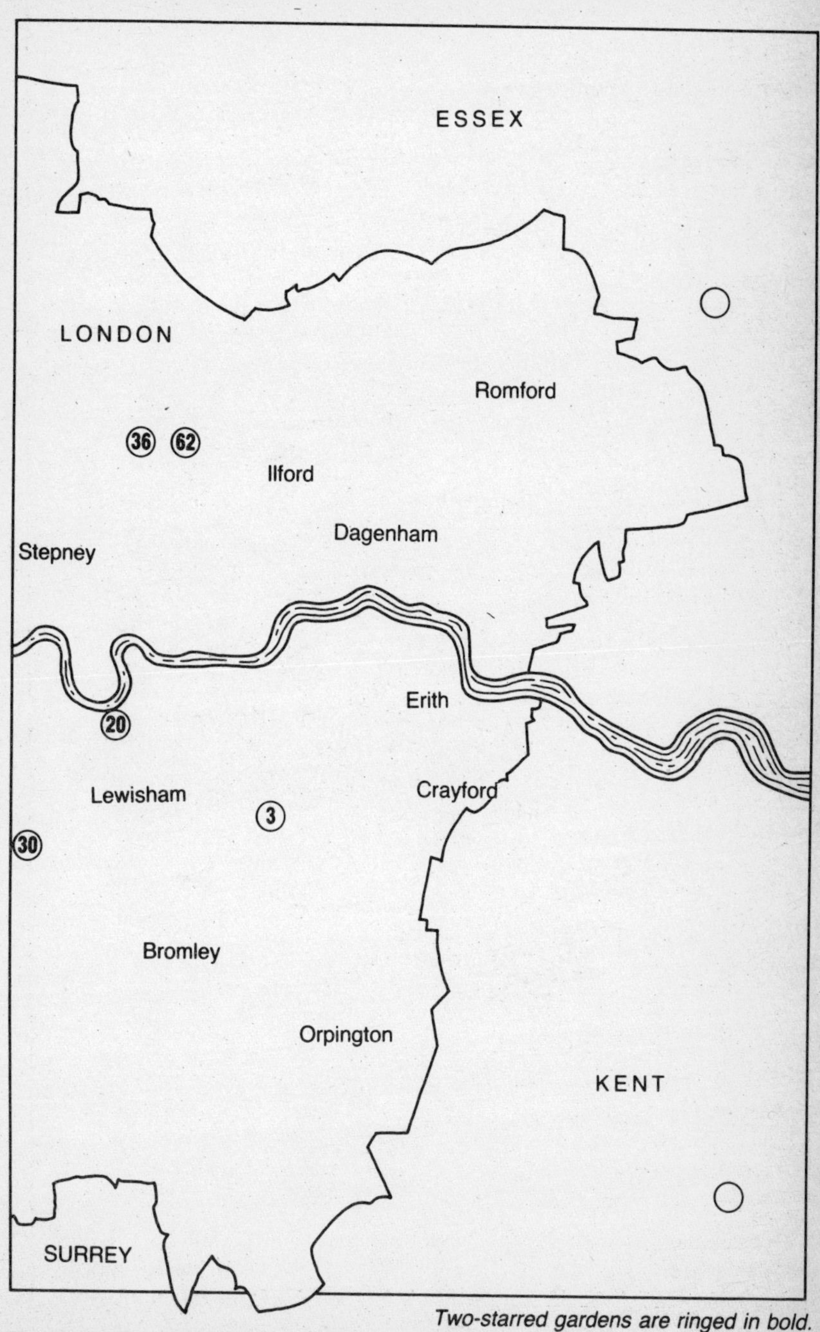

Two-starred gardens are ringed in bold.

29 ADDISON AVENUE 1

London W11. Tel: (0603) 2450
Mr and Mrs D.B. Nicholson

Off Holland Park Avenue, W of tube station. Cars must enter via Norland Square and Queensdale Road • Best season: summer • Parking • Open 21st July, 2 - 6 p.m. • Entrance: 80p

Meticulously kept and well-designed small town walled garden (about 30 × 40 feet) with a profusion of plants on every surface. It makes the best use of every inch of space. A tiny lawn is dominated by two venerable pear trees. Beyond them are perennial borders, slightly raised, and formally laid out but informally planted with an emphasis on phlox and hardy geraniums. To one side of the studio workshop at the end of the garden is a small shade garden, complete with statue. In late summer *Solanum jasminoides* blossoms profusely on one of the walls. The colour themes of the borders (pink, blue and white) and the variegated foliage help to unify the garden, which is an excellent balance between design and planting. Interestingly 'everything is used to being moved and hardly ever sulks'.

32 ATNEY ROAD 2

Putney, London SW15. Tel: (0785) 9355
Mrs Sally Tamplin

Off Putney Bridge Road • Parking in street • Teas • Partly suitable for wheelchairs • Open by appointment and 2nd June, 7th July, 15th Sept, 2 - 6 p.m. • Entrance: 80p

A spacious London garden with attractively planted terrace and wide lawn beyond, which has been described as 'brilliant'. Wide borders along the boundaries are packed with herbaceous plants, roses, hydrangeas and other shrubs to ensure a long season of interest. A central rose arch leads to the rear of the garden where young hedges are establishing, and a scree garden has been recently created. A tiny 'woodland dell'.

AVERY HILL PARK 3

Eltham, London SE9. Tel: (081) 850 3217
London Borough of Greenwich

Off Bexley Road and Avery Hill Road • Parking • Refreshments: small café • Toilet facilities • Suitable for wheelchairs • Some restrictions on dogs • Open 7.30 a.m. - dusk. The winter garden open Mon - Thurs, 1 - 4 p.m., Fri, 1 - 3 p.m., Sat and Sun, 10 a.m. - 4 p.m. Closed 24th, 25th December and 1st Jan • Entrance: free

More remains of the garden at Avery Hill Park than the 50-room mansion, which was badly damaged in the Blitz. The house, built by Colonel John North, otherwise known as The Nitrate King because he made a fortune from

Chilean nitrates which were much in demand as fertiliser, was the perfect example of the excesses of the Victorian nouveaux-riches. Since 1906 it has been used as a teachers' training college, while the gardens are enjoyed by the local inhabitants. There are rose gardens and three giant conservatories which look like icebergs which have come to a halt on the southern slope of Shooter's Hill. Storms have damaged some of the glass but the domed temperate house is bursting with bougainvilleas and staghorn ferns. The tropical house attracts school parties to see bananas, coffee and ginger while the camellias draw the crowds to the cold house in the spring. There is also an aviary.

BARBICAN CONSERVATORY ★ 4

The Barbican, London EC2. Tel: (071) 638 4141
City of London

In the Barbican Centre, on the 8th floor • Parking • Refreshments at Waterside Café in Barbican Centre • Toilet facilities • Partly suitable for wheelchairs • Shop in Barbican Centre • Open weekends and Bank Holidays only, 12 noon – 5 p.m. Ring to confirm opening times as the conservatory is sometimes used for conferences • Entrance: 75p, OAP and children 50p, family ticket (2 adults and up to 4 children) £2

The lift to the eighth floor of the Barbican transports you from a concrete jungle to a lush jungle of temperate and semi-tropical plants. Planted in the autumn of 1980–81, using 1,600 cubic metres of soil, the conservatory was opened in 1984. Twin *Cupressus cashmeriana* grace the main entrance while a vast banyan tree (*Ficus bengalensis*) in the eastern section is in need of pruning before it goes through the roof. Many familiar houseplants, like *Ficus benjamina* have reached giant proportions and a colossal Swiss Cheese plant (*Monstera deliciosa*) produces edible fruits after flowering. The Arid House on the second level, added in 1986, contains epiphyllum and cacti, including the largest *Carnegiea gigantea* in Europe. Fred, as it is affectionately known, was a gift from the Mayor of Salt Lake City. There are finches in the aviary and the ponds are alive with fish and terrapins. There is a fresh stock of chameleons which live in tanks rather than the trees. Natural predators and pathogens are used to keep down pests, and the hard Thames water is softened to stop nutrients becoming locked in the soil. Floodlighting has recently been installed, but the limited winter opening hours don't allow visitors to take full advantage of it.

28 BARNSBURY SQUARE 5

London N1.
Mr F.T. Gardner

Off Thornhill Road • Parking in road • Refreshments • Open 16th June, 2 – 6 p.m. • Entrance: £1 (£1.50 for combined admission with 338 Liverpool Road, N7 – see entry)

A real period piece! For the most part, an un-reconstructed Victorian garden, cared for by the third and fourth generation of owners. There is a re-discovered grotto dating from the nineteenth century, linked with a pool (exceptionally full of frogs), waterfall and fountain, all previously run with rationed mains water but now pumped in the conventional manner. There is a traditional 1930s wooden greenhouse and a Victorian gazebo of real distinction, though slightly askew. Magnificent trees lent by surrounding gardens create a London oasis effect. Interesting planting reflects changing fashions and styles and gives year round interest.

BATTERSEA PARK 6

Battersea, London SW11. Tel: (081) 871 7530/1
Wandsworth Borough Council

S side of Thames, from Chelsea Bridge to Albert Bridge • Parking free in car park • Refreshments • Toilet facilities • Suitable for wheelchairs • Dogs • Open daily, 7 a.m. - dusk • Entrance: free

Laid out in 1852–8 on Battersea Fields, an old duelling rendezvous. It has been much improved by the late-lamented GLC and contains many interesting features such as the Buddhist temple, zoo, aviary, sculptures, large boating lake and also frequent entertainments in tented accommodation. The plantsperson should make a point of visiting the glasshouses near Albert Bridge. Interesting sub-tropical garden, water garden and modern wooden arbourwork. It is to be hoped that the improvements will continue under the new regime.

BROCKWELL PARK 7

Tulse Hill, London SE24. Tel: (081) 6141
Lambeth Council

Take A205 then A215, entrances at Herne Hill Gate, Norwood Road, Brockwell Gardens Road etc. • Best season: summer (July) • Parking: Herne Hill Gate, Norwood Road, Brockwell Gardens Road • Refreshments • Toilet facilities inc. disabled • Partly suitable for wheelchairs • Dogs, except in walled garden • Open daily, 9 a.m. - dusk • Entrance: free

A peaceful and attractive refuge from nearby Brixton shopping centre, within a surprisingly large park, Brockwell has both a pretty and secluded old English walled garden, with rose beds, and a delightful mixture of herbaceous bedding, providing almost year-round interest. (Radios, cassettes, and dogs are banned from the walled garden - and children under 14 have to be accompanied by an adult.) On the hilltop surrounding the clock-tower are a variety of shrubs and trees and formal bedding. Both park and gardens are very well-maintained. The parkland is well provided with benches. Ground staff are helpful and informative. There are three ponds. Good views to the north over a London of many towers and a few spires which looks surprisingly attractive and even romantic.

15A BUCKLAND CRESCENT ★ 8

London NW3.
Lady Barbirolli

Near Fitzjohn's Avenue at Swiss Cottage end. 5 mins from Swiss Cottage tube station and various buses • Parking in neighbouring streets • Suitable for wheelchairs • Plants for sale • Open 23rd June, 2.30 - 6.30 p.m. • Entrance: £1

The strong sense of space and line that musicians often possess is expressed in this dignified third-of-an-acre town garden. The ground plan combines flowing unfussy lines and ingenious geometry. Planting ranges from a functional but decorative vegetable patch to some remarkable mature tree specimens, such as *Cornus alternifolia* 'Variegata' and *Metasequoia glyptostroboides*; it is everywhere discriminating. A generous terrace is enhanced by boldly planted urns. Recent gales have culled the southern boundary of vast mature trees to good effect.

CAMLEY STREET NATURE PARK 9

Camley Street, London NW1. Tel: (071) 833 2311
London Borough of Camden; managed by the London Wildlife Trust

Behind King's Cross gasometers, turn off Goods Way or Pancras Way • Parking in nearby streets • Toilet facilities • Partly suitable for wheelchairs • Small shop • Open daily, Mon - Fri, 9.30 a.m. - 5 p.m., Sat and Sun, 11 a.m. - 5 p.m. • Entrance: free. Donations welcome

Now threatened by the King's Cross Development scheme, this is an example of an extremely successful urban wild garden created against all the odds. Plants, wildlife and people thrive in it. In two and a fifth acres set between the Regent's Canal, imposing black and red gasometers and a noisy skipyard, it has been landscaped with a large pond at its centre. This tranquil space has a fine record of sighted birds and other wildlife. A simple pergola next to a small area of flower beds frames a view of the canal and passing long boats; the whole is somewhat romantically framed by relics of Victorian industry.

CANNIZARO PARK 10

Westside, Wimbledon, London SW19. Tel: (081) 946 7349
Merton Council

Westside, Wimbledon • Best season: May • Parking: Westside and surrounding side roads • Teas Sun only, 2 - 5 p.m., provided by Wimbledon Guides and Brownies • Toilet facilities • Wheelchairs have reasonable access to top gardens • Dogs on lead • Open daily, Mon - Fri, 8 a.m. - sunset, Sat, Sun and Bank Holidays, 9 a.m. - sunset • Entrance: free

Formerly the grounds of Cannizaro House, the approach is through imposing gates and a formal drive, lined with beautifully-kept seasonal bedding. Cannizaro's trees are its principal attraction: cork oaks, mulberry and sassafras (until a few years ago it had the oldest sassafras in England). Some enormous and beautiful beeches have been slightly damaged. In the midst of the trees a secluded picnic area, set with tables, contains - somewhat unexpectedly - a bust of the Emperor Haile Selassie of Ethiopia, who sought refuge in Wimbledon. There is a small aviary, a pretty walled rose garden, an azalea and rhododendron collection and a heather garden. The old garden, the rather disappointing formal Italian garden and the pool are found down a steep slope directly in front of Cannizaro House. A wild garden is being created in the same location. Sculpture exhibitions are sometimes held in the park.

CAPEL MANOR 11

Horticultural and Environmental Centre
Bullsmoor Lane, Enfield, Middlesex. Tel: (0992) 763849
London Borough of Enfield

From the M25 junction with the A10, it is AA signposted via Turkey Street/ Bullsmoor Lane • Parking • Teas • Toilet facilities • Suitable for wheelchairs • Dogs on lead • Plants for sale sometimes at weekends • Open April to Oct, daily, 10 a.m. - 4.30 p.m., Nov to March, weekdays, 10 a.m. - 4.30 p.m. • Entrance: £1.25, OAP and children 60p

These gardens are intended to show the history of gardening from the sixteenth century to the present. They also function as a design centre for the garden industry. The contrast with Myddelton House, along the road, could not be stronger: at Capel, maintenance is excellent but a unifying sensibility completely lacking. The gardens here are from first to last a curate's egg; good areas, such as the garden for the disabled, jostle with aberrations and queasy inventions, such as 'A Lover's Garden'. Detailing is mixed; jagged rocks are sunk in the middle of smooth, rounded pebbles. But there is lots of interest for the family outing, enhanced by an adjoining 'educational farm'. In 1990 the *Sunday Times* Beginner's Garden, featured at Chelsea, was moved here for display, and funds are being collected for further development.

CHELSEA PHYSIC GARDEN ★ 12

66 Royal Hospital Road, Chelsea, London SW3. Tel: (071) 352 5646
Trustees of Chelsea Physic Garden

One entrance in Swan Walk, off Chelsea Embankment, and another in Royal Hospital Road • Parking: meters in side street • Teas on Sun • Toilet facilities • Partly suitable for wheelchairs • Plants for sale • Open 3rd April to 23rd Oct, Wed, Sun, 2 - 5 p.m., also during Chelsea Flower Show, 12 noon - 5 p.m. Entrance: £2, students, children and unemployed £1

Founded to train London's apothecaries in herbal medicine in the seventeenth century, the Chelsea Physic Garden is still actively involved in research into herbal medicine, as well as playing an important botanical role. Its three and a half acres, tucked between Cheyne Walk and Swan Walk, are well worth visiting, not only for the fascinating range of medicinal plants grown there, but also for their rare and interesting ones, including beautiful trees like the magnificent golden rain tree (*Koelreuteria paniculata*). The gardens also house what is believed to be the earliest rock garden in Europe, created in basaltic lava brought back by the botanist Joseph Banks from Iceland in 1772. The main part of the garden is devoted to systematic-order beds of plants, but there are also displays associated with the plant hunters and botanists who have played their part in the development of the garden, including Banks, Philip Miller, William Hudson and Robert Fortune, as well as an attractive woodland garden. The National collection of cistus is housed here. You can become a Friend of the Chelsea Physic Garden for a smallish sum, entitling you and a guest to free entry on all public open days, and to entry at other times in office hours.

CHISWICK HOUSE ★★ 13

Burlington Lane, Chiswick, London W4. Tel: (081) 742 1225
London Borough of Hounslow

5m W of central London, just off A4 • Parking. Entrance on A4 • Refreshments • Toilet facilities • Suitable for wheelchairs • Dogs on lead, not admitted in Italian garden • House open • Garden open daily, dawn – dusk • Entrance: free

Handsome, semi-classical gardens, stretching over many acres, with lakes, statues, monuments and magnificent trees. Created by William Kent to complement the Palladian villa built by Lord Burlington in 1729, the gardens are full of splendid vistas, avenues and changes of contour. There is a formal Italian garden with parterres filled with technicolour bedding plants in front of the handsome conservatory (both introduced after Kent's day) and a large canal-shaped lake, with informal woodland planting around it. The gardens are well worth visiting at any time of the year, but particularly in autumn and winter when many other gardens have lost their charm. Mature cedars and gingkos were felled as part of the restoration programme to recreate the original gardens, causing much local outrage. Public access to sections of the park is restricted while the work continues.

COLLEGE GARDEN AND LITTLE CLOISTER 14

Westminster Abbey, London SW1. Tel: (071) 222 5152
Dean and Chapter of Westminster

Off Dean's Yard, next to Abbey shop • Best season: spring • Suitable for wheelchairs • Abbey shop • Abbey open • Garden open April to Sept, Thurs, 10 a.m. – 6 p.m., Oct to March, Thurs, 10 a.m. – 4 p.m. Closed Maundy Thurs • Entrance: free

The eleventh-century college garden has been under cultivation for more than 900 years making it possibly the oldest garden in England. Whereas it was once tended by monks who would have produced herbs for the kitchen and infirmary it is now a communal garden for members of the Abbey staff whose houses overlook it. The garden has a utilitarian atmosphere and uninspired planting. Large plane trees, a large fig, propped up and underplanted with laurel, rose beds and beds of canna lilies. There are brass band concerts during August and September. The tiny Little Cloister garden has far more atmosphere with a gentle fountain just catching the sun at its centre. More figs are trained against the walls and the beds beneath a curtain of Virginia creeper are filled with acanthus, rosemary and hostas. Overlooking the Thames, across Millbank, is the Victoria Tower Garden, with a replica of Rodin's *Burghers of Calais*. Lovers of sculpture should also look at Henry Moore's bronze *Knife Edge*.

COLVILLE PLACE 15

London W1.
London Borough of Camden

Between Charlotte Street and Whitfield Street, near Tottenham Court Road • Parking very difficult • Suitable for wheelchairs • Open 7.30 a.m. - dusk • Entrance: free

Fortunate houses in Colville Place look across a paved path on to what is a cross between a *hortus conclusus* and a small piazza. This imaginative tiny public garden was created a few years ago on a bomb site. There is a lawn, a pleasing pergola, fruit trees and, slightly tucked away, a children's play area. Planting is bold, simple and pleasing, with lots of lavender. This seems to be London's nearest equivalent to modern garden design in the public arena, and the result has enormous charm. A haven from Oxford Street.

THE ELMS 16

13 Wolverton Avenue, Kingston-on-Thames, Surrey.
Tel: (081) 546 7624
Dr and Mrs R. Rawlings

1m E of Kingston on A308, 100 yards from Norbiton station. Entry opposite Manorgate flats in Manorgate Road • Parking in street • Teas by Home Farm Trust • Seeds and plants for sale • Open 22nd, 24th March, 20th, 21st April, 11th, 12th May, 15th, 16th June, 2 - 5 p.m. and groups by appointment • Entrance: 80p

Recently re-designed by the owners (Mrs Rawlings is a professional landscape gardener), this is a true collector's garden with some rare and unusual plants, featuring rhododendrons, magnolias, camellias, dwarf conifers and a wide range of evergreen and deciduous shrubs. Small trees, ground cover (herbaceous), a two-level pool with geyser and well planted margins, also interesting alpine trays featured. This very small garden (only 55 × 25 feet) even has fruit, plum, pears and soft fruit.

FENTON HOUSE 17

Hampstead Grove, London NW3. Tel: (071) 435 3471
The National Trust

Centre of Hampstead in area known as Holly Hill behind Heath Street • Parking difficult • Toilet facilities only if house is also visited • Partly suitable for wheelchairs • House open • Garden open March, Sat and Sun, 2 - 6 p.m., April to Oct, Sat - Wed, 11 a.m. - 6 p.m. Last admission 5 p.m. Parties on weekdays by appointment • Entrance: free (house £2.80)

Handsome seventeenth-century house and walled garden (about half an acre). The formal south garden is seen through an impressive iron gate (not open) and can be approached from the house. The entrance to the house is via the side door. Directly behind the house the walled garden is formal with standard *Prunus lusitanica* in tubs, gravel walks and herbaceous borders edged with neatly-clipped box. Standard lavenders are an unusual feature, and here as in the rest of the garden the walls are particularly well-planted. There is an interesting collection of varieties of *Clematis viticella*. The garden is terraced on several levels with yew hedges (eight years old) dividing the areas, which become less formal further from the house. There is a sunken rose garden with secluded seating, good vistas and many scented plants. The far wall hosts a beautifully-trained *Magnolia grandiflora*. Adjacent to the main garden below another wall is an old orchard, carefully cut at three mower heights, and a small kitchen/cottage garden. The garden is surprisingly peaceful and has the delightful, unhurried atmosphere of the traditional old-world garden. Particularly good views of it are to be had from the attic floor of the house.

FULHAM PALACE 18

Fulham Palace Road, London SW6. Tel: (071) 736 5821
London Borough of Hammersmith and Fulham

Fulham Palace Road and Bishop's Avenue to the N • Parking • Suitable for wheelchairs • Dogs • Plants for sale. Nursery nearby • Open daily except 25th Dec, 1st Jan, 8 a.m. - dusk • Entrance: free

The palace, surrounded by a moat in its prime, was the former home of the Bishops of London where in the sixteenth century Bishop Compton used his missionaries to help him establish here a collection of shrubs and trees sent back from America. Today it is rather sad in a faded way, like an overgrown country house garden, but it is a charming place for a peaceful walk, far superior to many other open spaces in London, and the two gardeners are doing their best in the impossible position in which they are placed by the Borough Council's financial problems. The 37-acre area to wander round is seldom crowded. The south front of the house looks over lawns with enormous cedars and other trees. The remains of the old walled garden contains a very long ruined glasshouse built along a curved wall and a box-edged garden. Another part has order beds. A large rough area with beech hedges. The small courtyard at the front of the house (part Henry VII, part Victorian) has euphorbias, some climbers and other plants and a fountain. It must be said that some visitors find the overall atmosphere depressing but that is not the general view. Do not mistake this for Bishop's Park which extends to the south as far as the river. There are rumours that this garden, which is of great historical importance, will shortly be refurbished, and it has also been proposed as a potential site for a national museum of garden history.

GOLDERS HILL PARK 19

North End Way, Hampstead, London NW3. Tel: (081) 455 5183
Corporation of London

From Hampstead, past Jack Straw's Castle on road to Golders Green, opposite Bull and Bush pub. The flower garden is on right of park, past café • Best season: spring, summer, autumn • Refreshments: North End Way entrance, March to Oct • Toilet facilities • Partly suitable for wheelchairs • Dogs on lead • Greenhouses open weekends, 2 - 4 p.m. • Garden open daily, 7.30 a.m. - dusk • Entrance: free

The manicured 39-acre park was created in 1899 in the grounds of a manor house (bombed in World War II). The two-acre dazzling flower garden on the north side is designed in a series of garden rooms, with a mixture of perennial and bedding plants. It has an almost Victorian feel with its neat, brilliantly coloured displays of flowers, although the colour schemes can appear on the vulgar side. On a less strident note is the canal feature planted with water-loving and woodland plants, leading down to the ornamental pool with its ducks and flamboyant flamingoes. Plenty of seats at strategic points ensure that the garden is much used by elderly local residents. (The park itself has a large menagerie with deer, goats, wallabies, oryx and many birds.)

GREENWICH PARK 20

Greenwich, London SE10. Tel: (081) 858 2608
Department of the Environment

Entrances in Greenwich (Romney Road) and in Blackheath (Charlton Way). Good service to Greenwich by river, tel: (071) 376 3676 or (081) 305 0300 for winter timetables • Parking easier at Blackheath entrance • Refreshments • Toilet facilities • Suitable for wheelchairs but quite steep in places • Dogs • Observatory and Maritime Museum, Greenwich Theatre and Ranger's House. Ships at Greenwich pier. Thames Barrier Visitors' Centre • Open dawn - dusk • Entrance: free

Greenwich appears to have been a royal residence as early as 1300. Henry VIII was born here and in the seventeenth century Charles II commissioned Le

Nôtre to lay out Greenwich Park which covers some 190 acres. Pepys noted in his diary of April 11th 1662 'the king hath planted trees and made steps in the hill up to the castle which is very magnificent.' Le Nôtre's wonderful avenue of sweet chestnuts and elms still forms the backbone of this magnificent park, but the gales have taken their toll. The panoramic view from The Observatory, overlooking the Naval College and curving river, is the most spectacular in London. Massive new building developments, including Canary Wharf, have made the visitor's map of the City skyscape hopelessly out of date and not everyone approves of what the developers have done to the view. The Victorian garden, in earshot of the bandstand, is a classic example of municipal planting – island beds dotted among specimen trees. Visitors take bread to feed the ducks and geese in a nearby lake and there is a paddock with deer. The Royal Observatory and the Maritime Museum justifiably draw the crowds. Music recitals take place in the eighteenth-century Ranger's House, facing Blackheath.

4 THE GROVE ★ 21

Highgate, London N6.
Mr Cob Stenham

In Highgate village, off Hampstead Lane • Parking in street • Open 23rd June, 2 – 5 p.m. • Entrance: 50p

The seventeenth-century house sits behind a dignified front courtyard, beautifully paved with brick (as is the rear terrace) with restrained planting of skimmias and other evergreens. A side passage brings the visitor through to an outstanding vista; the terrace, with a formal pool surrounded by dramatic planting, is the foreground to an immaculate lawn with well-planted, mixed borders. Beyond this is an extensive backdrop to the wooded slopes of Hampstead Heath. An arbour of silver pears overlooks this stunning view and a ceanothus arch leads one down, through a tunnel of *Vitis coignetiae*, to the lower garden. This comprises an orchard with an old mulberry tree and some good statuary. One yew hedge conceals the well-ordered compost/bonfire area, and another balances this to enclose a tiny secret garden dominated by a *Cladrastis lutea*. *Rosa laevigata* 'Cooperi' flourishes on the south wall of the house, and the whole garden, which is beautifully designed and maintained, has exceptional charm.

7 THE GROVE ★ 22

Highgate, London N6. Tel: (081) 340 7205
The Hon. Mrs Judith Lyttelton

In Highgate village • Best season: summer • Parking in street • Suitable for wheelchairs • Open 5th May, 2 – 5 p.m. • Entrance: £1

A huge half-acre London walled town garden behind a very handsome Georgian house *c.*1815, splendidly designed by the owner for low-maintenance, but with lots of interest. Tunnels, arbours, screens abound. A series of brick built arches across the width of the garden separate it into two compartments. The area near the house is formal with a lawn, the area beyond the screen much less so, with many fine compartments and features. Full of secret paths and unexpected views. A magic garden for children. Much use is made of evergreens and there are some exquisite shrubs, including a row of camellias down one wall and a massive *Hydrangea petiolaris* with a trunk as thick as a boxer's biceps! There are many species and varieties of a particular genus - five varieties of box and even more of ivies for example. The owner describes it as a gold, green and red garden. The canal feature, planted with yellow irises, has become very overgrown, as have some of the allées and tunnels, but the layout and choice of planting is still sufficiently retained to provide inspiration for busy garden-owners who would still like to have an interesting garden. Several other gardens in The Grove are open on charity days.

24 GROVE TERRACE 23

London NW5.
Lucy Gent

Off Highgate Road • Parking in street • Open 20th May, 28th July, 2 - 6 p.m. and by written appointment • Entrance: £1, children 50p

An extra long, narrow garden crammed with plants arranged in such a way as to create an illusion of greater space and to forget that one is in a crowded London terrace. Different areas of interest and many unusual plants including a Cercis 'Forrest Pansey' and Gleditsia 'Ruby Lace'. Imaginative use is made of pots, the most interesting and handsome of them made by Jeni Jones, to establish points of focus and differing heights. One large pot contains a robust Lonicera 'Reflexa' trained into a standard. The small garden at the front of the house contains an unusual rosemary 'Benenden Blue', lavenders and wild roses. Very much the plantsman's garden, with expert guidance for visitors from the owner.

GUNNERSBURY PARK 24

London W3. Tel: (081) 992 1612
London Borough of Ealing and Hounslow

½m N of Chiswick roundabout turn left off A406 • Parking: entrance from Popes Lane, no coaches • Refreshments • Toilet facilities • Suitable for wheelchairs • Dogs • Museum open Mon - Fri, 1 - 5 p.m., winter, 1 - 4 p.m., Bank Holidays, March and Sept, 2 - 6 p.m., winter, 2 - 6 p.m. Closed Christmas • Park open daily, 7.30 a.m. - dusk • Entrance: free

Little remains of the grandiose gardens of the Rothschild days except the rose gardens in the traditional 'Clock' pattern. Formal flower beds near the museum are well kept and colourfully planted, with a background of parkland.

Beyond the trees the sports grounds, golf course and tennis courts are hidden from view from the terrace where it is difficult to realize one is only a few miles from Marble Arch. Amongst the gardeners who have toiled here are William Kent and J.C. Loudon. For children, there is a boating pool.

HAM HOUSE ★★ 25

Ham Street, Richmond, Surrey. Tel: (081) 940 1950
The National Trust

On S bank of Thames, W of A307 at Petersham • Parking 400 yards by river, disabled in courtyard • Refreshments: teas, light lunches by arrangement with manager • Toilet facilities inc. disabled • Partly suitable for wheelchairs • National Trust Shop • House open April to Sept, daily except Mon and Fri. £2. Pre-booked parties £1 per person • Gardens open daily except Mon, 11 a.m. – 5.30 p.m. • Entrance: free (house £2)

Relatively recently restored by the National Trust, the gardens at Ham House now retain their seventeenth-century appearance in which formality predominates. In the south garden, below a wide gravel terrace, are eight square lawns divided by paths. The strong architectural nature of the hornbeam avenues, gravel terraces and parterres of box and cotton lavender mean that the garden looks good in any season, and the authenticity of the restoration, down to replicas of the seventeenth-century garden furniture, adds to its charm. Even the tea room, in part of the old orangery, with tables and chairs on the lawns in summer, has a stately elegance.

HAMPTON COURT PALACE ★★ 26

East Molesey, Surrey. Tel: (081) 977 8441
Historic Royal Palaces Agency

On A308 at junction of A309 on N side of Kingston bridge over Thames • Limited parking • Toilet facilities • Mostly suitable for wheelchairs • Dogs on lead • Shop • Palace open (admission charge) • Gardens open daily, dawn – dusk • Entrance: free

Hampton Court Palace is worth a visit to study the activities of British monarchs from Henry VIII onwards, and the gardens are an exciting and eclectic mixture of styles and taste, with many different areas of interest. Most famous for its Great Vine, planted in 1796, which still produces hundreds of 'Black Hamburg' grapes each year (on sale to the public when harvested in September or October) and its maze, replanted in 1690, with half-a-mile of densely hedged paths. The pond gardens offer a magnificent display of bedding plants (best seen in summer), and there is a Tudor knot garden with interlocking bands of dwarf box, thyme, lavender and cotton lavender, infilled with bedding plants. On a truly grand scale, the great fountain gardens, an immense semi-circle of grass and flower beds with a central fountain, is probably the most impressive element, but the wilderness garden in spring, with its mass of daffodils and spring-flowering trees - principally cherry and crab - has the most charm. The laburnum walk off the wilderness garden - a tunnel of trained trees with butter-coloured rivulets of flowers in May - is another great attraction. The former kitchen garden now houses a rose garden, mainly comprising old-fashioned roses. The 40p guide book gives an excellent potted history of the gardens and a much-needed map. Too much to see in one day - plan at least two trips; one in spring and one in summer. Last summer saw the launch of a major flower show which is intended to become an annual event. Although very thin in its first year considering the price of the tickets, some interesting nurseries exhibited, and the organisers anticipate a better show in 1991.

37 HEATH DRIVE 27

London NW3. Tel: (071) 435 2419
Mr and Mrs C. Caplin

Off Finchley Road • Best seasons: late spring and summer • Parking • Refreshments • Suitable for wheelchairs • Plants for sale • Open 12th May, 2.30 - 6 p.m. • Entrance: 60p, children 30p

Largish, square garden (about one fifth of an acre) with a vast number of plants packed into it. There is an attractive pergola walk and unusual and interesting plants, including a wisteria grown as a standard (now 30 years old and about 20 feet tall) which makes an attractive small tree. Lots of lavatera - several species and varieties, tree paeonies, rhododendrons (including a climbing form), palms (trachycarpus), a fig and a mulberry tree. The large pool was well stocked with fish until a heron had them. Now there are only black ones (the heron can't see these apparently!). Other features of the garden include a fruit tree tunnel (apple and pears), raised beds and a greenhouse and conservatory for exotics. The garden boasts a very well-hidden compost heap behind a hedge of attractive cut-leaved alder. In the front garden there is a particularly good semi-evergreen *Buddleia colvillei* with magenta hanging flower heads in June and July. The Caplins have won the Frankland Moore Trophy (for gardens with help) six times.

THE HILL 28

Inverforth Close, North End Way, London NW3. Tel: (081) 455 5183
Corporation of London

From Hampstead past Jack Straw's Castle on road to Golders Green, on left hand side • Partly suitable for wheelchairs • Open daily, 9 a.m. - dusk • Entrance: free

Created by Lord Leverhulme in the 1920s, the garden was designed by Thomas Mawson, an architect. Overgrown in parts, its chief charm lies in its secluded setting and the romantic pergola walk, festooned in unchecked climbers, although part of this is now closed. Wonderful views across the heath from many points in the garden. There is a large formal lily pond (slightly unkempt) as well as herbaceous borders, undulating lawns, and many shrubs and trees.

HOLLAND PARK 29

Kensington, London W8. Tel: (071) 602 9483
Royal Borough of Kensington and Chelsea

Between Kensington High Street A31 and Holland Park Avenue, with several entrances • Parking from Abbotsbury Road entrance • Refreshments: light lunches etc. Restaurant (rather expensive) • Toilet facilities • Dogs on lead • Open daily, 8 a.m. - sunset • Entrance: free

Most of the famous Holland House was destroyed by bombs in World War II. The formal gardens, created in 1812 by Lord Holland, have been maintained. The small park contains some rare (unlabelled) trees such as Pyrenean oak, Chinese sweet gum, Himalayan birch, violet willow and the snowdrop tree which flowers in May. The rose walk has now been replanted with a variety of hybrid teas. There is a small iris garden round a fountain. Peacocks strut the lawns and drape the walls with their tail feathers and in the woodland section birds and squirrels find sanctuary from London's noise and traffic. There is a children's play area. One of the nicest small London parks. Next to the entrance in Kensington Road/High Street, opposite the cinema, is the Commonwealth Institute, whose gardens have seen better days.

HORNIMAN GARDENS 30

Forest Hill, London SE23.

Refreshments: at tearoom in Museum. Picnics allowed • Toilet facilities • Horticultural demonstrations March to Sept, first Wed in the month at 2.30 p.m. • Open all year except 25th Dec, Mon - Sat, 7.15 a.m. - dusk, Sun, 8 a.m. - dusk • Entrance: free

Charming, rather old-fashioned park in fine situation with extensive views over, alas, rather hideous south London, on three sides. Formal bedding, rose pergola, bandstand (with band on summer Sunday afternoons), steep hill garden with rocks, stream, conifers, etc. Large and impressive Victorian conservatory rebuilt recently behind the Horniman Museum which does not contain any plants but is used for functions from time to time.

ISABELLA PLANTATION ★ 31

Richmond Park, Richmond, Surrey. Tel: (081) 3209
Department of the Environment, Royal Parks

Richmond Park, Broomfield Hill • Best season: late spring • Parking: Broomfield Hill car park, Pembroke Lodge (Roehampton Gate), disabled at north entrance by way of Ham Gate • Refreshments (Pembroke Lodge) • Toilet facilities • Suitable for wheelchairs • Dogs on lead • Open daily, dawn - dusk • Entrance: free

A wooded enclosure, this features many fine indigenous forest trees - oaks, beeches and birch - as well as more exotic specimens like the pocket handkerchief tree (*Davidia involucrata*) and many species of magnolia. The principal glory, however, is the collection of rhododendrons and azaleas, the earliest rhododendron 'Christmas Cheer' blossoming in the New Year, but the garden is at its best from April until June, when the dwarf azaleas and the waterside primulas around the pond are also in flower. The garden is a notable bird sanctuary - nuthatches, treecreepers, kingfishers, woodpeckers and owls have all been spotted here, and badgers have their own entrance to the gardens. The Waterhouse Plantations in neighbouring Bushy Park are also very fine (see entry).

KENSINGTON GARDENS 32

London SW7. Tel: (071) 262 5484
Royal Parks

Entrances off Kensington High Street, Exhibition Road and Bayswater Road • Best seasons: spring and summer • Refreshments (new management at café in Hyde Park) • Toilet facilities • Suitable for wheelchairs • Dogs • Palace Museum open Mon - Sat, 9 a.m. - 5 p.m., Sun, 1 - 5 p.m. • Open daily, 5 a.m. - dusk • Entrance: free

These 274 acres of the finest park, adjoining Hyde Park, have their own pleasures, including sculpture by Henry Moore and G.F. Watts and, for children and older enthusiasts, the Peter Pan statue. The orangery probably by Hawksmoor, with decoration by Grinling Gibbons, is well worth a visit. So, too, is the sunken water garden surrounded by beds of bright seasonal flowers which can be viewed from 'windows' in a beech walk. From the Broad Walk south to the Albert Memorial, semi-circular flower beds are kept planted against a background of flowering shrubs. Many different species of nannies and prams are in evidence along the Flower Walk at the South side near the Albert Memorial.

KENWOOD 33

Hampstead Lane, London NW3. Tel: (081) 348 1286
English Heritage

N side of Hampstead Heath, on Highgate to Hampstead Road • Parking at West Lodge car park, Hampstead Lane • Refreshments • Toilet facilities • Suitable for wheelchairs • Dogs on lead • House open April (or Maundy Thurs if earlier) to 1st Oct, 10 a.m. - 6 p.m., Oct to April (or Maundy Thurs), 10 a.m. - 4 p.m. • Park open daily, dawn - dusk • Entrance: free

Vistas, sweeping lawns from the terrace of Kenwood House and views over Hampstead Heath (and London) predominate. Magnificent mature trees, mainly oak and beech. Large-scale shrubberies, dominated by rhododendrons – among which nestles Dr Johnson's summer house (used by the great man on visits to his friends, the Thrales, in Streatham). There is also some magnificent modern sculpture including a Henry Moore. The garden slopes down towards two large lakes known as the Lily pond (the largest) and the Concert pond (where open air concerts are held in summer). Woods fringe the heath side of the gardens, with several gates onto the heath itself. A good place to walk at any season, but particularly when the trees are turning in autumn.

LAMBETH PALACE GARDENS 34

Lambeth Palace Road, London SE1. Tel: (071) 928 8282
Church of England

S side of the Thames, next to Lambeth Bridge • Best seasons: spring and summer • Suitable for wheelchairs • Open 13th April, 2 - 5.30 p.m. • Entrance: £2, OAP and children 10 - 16 £1, children under 10 free

Only Buckingham Palace, apparently, has bigger grounds in central London. Lambeth Palace stands in 10½ acres, roughly nine of them devoted to the gardens. There is a magnificent fig tree in the entrance garden to the palace. Behind the palace, and facing it, is a restored rose terrace, fronted by a perennial border designed by Beth Chatto. Beyond, more or less around the walled perimeter of the garden, is what will eventually be a woodland walkway that will encompass at various points a scented garden, a wild garden (with lily pond) and a Chinese garden. Close to the house is a relatively newly commissioned herb garden (by Faith and Geoff Whitten) and design of which, though attractive, seems at odds with the nearby rose terrace. Mrs Runcie undertook a great deal of restoration work in the garden over the last few years and over 2000 trees and shrubs were planted. Despite the attractive setting, the gardens have a curiously bitty and disconnected feel to them, although some of that may be due to the newness of a lot of the planting which needs a good five or six years before its impact begins to be felt. Not far from Lambeth Palace, towards Waterloo is St Thomas's Hospital. Inside one of the large courtyards is a pleasant garden, abutting the foot of Westminster Bridge, which contains one of the most spectacular modern sculpture water fountains in the world. This is the stainless steel *Revolving Torsion* by Naum Gabo.

15 LANGBOURNE AVENUE 35

Holly Lodge Estate, London N6. Tel: (081) 340 5806
Mr Peter Partridge

Off Swain's Lane, which is off Highgate Road • Parking in neighbouring roads • Open 15th June to 15th July strictly by appointment • Entrance: free

A front garden with a large hamamelis and other striking shrubs tell that this is no ordinary town garden. Behind the semi-detached house the ground rises steeply. Starting with a tree fern *Dicksonia antarctica* and *Bergenia ciliata*, there are many interesting plants in excellent associations: *Brunnera* 'Langtrees', *Melianthus major*, *Rosa glauca*, *Acer negundo* 'Flamingo' and, behind, *Phormium tenax*. At the top of the garden sits a wide terrace with pond. Foliage, dramatic throughout, is especially good here: gunneras, lysichitums, rodgersias and *Peltiphyllum peltatum*. Trees include a tulip tree and a corkscrew willow so large as to be positively statuesque in its central position.

1 LISTER ROAD ★ 36

London E11. Tel: (081) 556 8962
Mr Myles Challis

Off High Road, Leytonstone about 10 minutes walk from the tube station • Parking on Lister Road • Toilet facilities • Plant exchanges • Open June to Aug by appointment

This is one of London's greatest surprises; a 40 ft × 20 ft garden of subtropical and bold foliage hidden away in Leytonstone. An Abyssinian palm, canna lilies, daturas, gingers and tree ferns, all wintered under cover, flourish in a matrix of hardy plants, such as bamboos, gunneras, phormiums and euphorbias. A narrow path leads past a screen of bamboos to a pond. This garden strikes a note of rich fantasy, not least in the wind's sound in the giant leaves. It is also a unique store of ideas easily adapted to more conventional gardens, and as Myles Challis is a garden designer, this is in effect his showroom.

338 LIVERPOOL ROAD 37

London N7.
Mr and Mrs Simon Relph

The house is on the corner of Furlong Road. 5 minutes' walk from Highbury and Islington tube station • Parking in side streets • Teas • Open 16th June, 2 - 6 p.m. • Entrance: £1 (£1.50 for combined admission with 28 Barnsbury Square, N1 - see entry)

A densely-planted front garden of mainly grey and silver plants, with a basement area of ivy and ferns is entered from Liverpool Road, while the entrance to the back garden is round the corner in Furlong Road. Although small, this is beautifully designed to show many interesting plants. An unusual and very successful water feature comprises a narrow canal right across the garden.

LONDON SQUARES

Many other cities have squares but probably none has more than London. They were mostly built in the eighteenth and nineteenth centuries to provide an outlook for the fashionable houses which surrounded them and in not so fashionable areas like Pimlico so that the lesser classes could imitate the behaviour of their betters. A few squares still remain the joint property of the owners of houses (and today, flats) round them, the grandest being Belgrave Square built by Basevi in 1825, Eaton Square and Cadogan Square. Other private squares, hardly less grand, include Montpelier, Brompton, Carlyle, Lowndes, Onslow and others to the west of Hyde Park Corner. Since they so rarely appear to be occupied by the residents, particularly at weekends when they have gone to their houses in the country, it is surprising that there has been no movement to agitate for their occasional unlocking to admit the public at large. However, some squares (and 'gardens' as other areas are called) have over the years become places where the public may be admitted and these include the following:

Central area: ***Berkeley Square***, ***Cavendish Square***, ***Grosvenor Square***, and ***St James's Square*** (this is the earliest, begun 1665, and the quietest). Eastern area: ***Gray's Inn*** (where Field Court is open to the public during weekday lunchtimes in the summer), ***Inner and Middle Temple Gardens***, with entrance in Fleet Street, ***Lincoln's Inn***, with one of its 'squares', New Hall, open to the public Mon - Fri, 12 noon - 1.30 p.m. only. Northern area: ***Fitzroy Square***, the work of Geoffrey Jellicoe, not open but viewable; ***Gordon Square***, closed weekends; ***Russell Square***, and ***Soho Square***. Southern area: ***Dolphin Square***, part of the large block of flats.

At least one private Square has begun limited opening to the public, ***Eccleston Square*** in Pimlico. This four and a half acre square, run by a committee of residents and normally reserved for the use of the residents, has something for everyone - a tennis court well screened at one end, grassy areas for children to play in and 'secret' paths through the shrubbery in which to hide, pleasant curving paths for strollers and a paved area where the fortunate residents can have a barbecue. Some large, well-planted pots, many clematis and other climbing plants on the surrounding railings and even some productive fruit trees. Even if one can't get in, there's a lot to be seen from the street. (Open for charity 21st April, 9th June.)

22 LOUDOUN ROAD 39

London NW8.
Mrs Ruth Barclay

Less than 5 minutes' walk from St John's Wood tube station, between Abbey Road and Finchley Road. Also near bus stop • Parking in street • Teas • Open 26th May, 2 - 6.30 p.m. • Entrance: £1, children 50p

In this small front garden maximum use of the space is achieved by good design and interesting plant associations. There is a charming sheltered courtyard at the back where peaches and grapes ripen annually and passion flowers romp. Some statuary is well-positioned and one's eye is raised by a glowing canopy of golden acacia cascading at the boundary.

1–8 AND 10 MALVERN TERRACE 40

London N1.

Off Thornhill Road • Best season: April to Aug • Parking in neighbouring streets • Refreshmens and music on open day • Suitable for wheelchairs • Open for charity 5th May, but visible to the public any day • Entrance: 80p

This is a touch of Edinburgh's Anne Street: fair-sized – and south-facing – front gardens come right down to the cobbled cul-de-sac. Across it in Thornhill Gardens mature trees complete the illusion of remoteness from London. Generous planting plays against well-tended grass and paths. All is in scale with the pleasing 1830s housing; the occasional vast pot or shrub adds a bit of piquancy. There is a nice flow through these front patches; a detour to see them if you're in the neighbourhood is well worthwhile.

MOUNT STREET GARDENS 41

Mount Street, London W1. Tel: (071) 828 8070
Westminster Borough Council

Access from Mount Street, South Audley Street near the Public Library and South Street, Mayfair • Dogs on lead • Open spring and summer, weekdays, 8 a.m. – up to 9.30 p.m.; autumn and winter, 8 a.m. – 4.30 p.m. Sun and Public Holidays, open from 9 a.m. • Entrance: free

This well-hidden leafy retreat is much loved by locals while the throng of the city seems to pass it by. Tasteful planting and lofty trees make it the perfect spot to take your ease after shopping. Versailles tubs planted with palms, beds of sugar pink and white geraniums can be enjoyed from dozens of wooden benches donated by those who have enjoyed this garden's charm.

MUSEUM OF GARDEN HISTORY 42

St Mary-at-Lambeth, Lambeth Palace Road, London SE1.
Tel: (071) 261 1891 (11 a.m. – 3 p.m.)
The Tradescant Trust

Lambeth Palace Road, parallel to River Thames on S bank, hard by Lambeth Bridge • Best seasons: spring and summer • Refreshments in church • Toilet facilities • Suitable for wheelchairs • Limited selection of plants for sale • Shop • The displays in The Museum of Garden History include garden tools and artefacts and Gertrude Jekyll's desk • Open Mon – Fri, 11 a.m. – 3 p.m., Sun, 10.30 a.m. – 5 p.m. Closed Sat • Entrance: free, donations welcomed

A small formal knot garden in the churchyard of St Mary-at-Lambeth features the plants originally collected by the John Tradescants (Elder and Younger) on their plant-hunting trips to America and Asia in the sixteenth and seventeenth centuries, many of them now so familiar we think of them as indigenous to this country. The knot garden designed by Lady Salisbury has 32 compartments of dwarf box, densely infilled with herbs and perennials. The centrepiece of the knot is a handsome clipped holly, *Ilex* 'Silver King'. Plants are all labelled. Although small the garden has a few well-placed benches. Part of its charm are the old brick and stone paths and the tombs and tombstones. A detailed planting plan of the knot is available (price 25p) in the museum shop, and some of the plants featured in the knot are on sale as well. Lambeth Palace (see entry) is next door.

MUSEUM OF LONDON GARDEN COURT 43

The Museum of London, London Wall, London EC2.
Tel: (071) 600 3699
Museum of London

Park in the Barbican Centre and follow signs to the Museum • Best season: summer • Refreshments: licensed restaurant • Toilet facilities • Suitable for wheelchairs but steps make assistance necessary • Museum shop • Open April to Oct, Tues - Sat, 10 a.m. - 6 p.m., Sun, 2 - 6 p.m. Last admission 5.30 p.m. Closed Mon • Entrance: free

Last year the Museum of London put on a much welcomed exhibition called 'London's Pride' which traced the history of the capital's gardens. The exhibition was an excuse to bring in garden designers Colson and Stone and totally revamp the internal courtyard. The team transformed an almost lifeless area into a living history of plantsmanship in the City from medieval times to the present day. Legendary names like Henry Russell, who sold striped roses in Westminster, to James Veitch, who sold exotica like the monkey puzzle tree from his nursery in Chelsea, are represented. This tiny roof garden is flanked on four sides by high buildings yet the designers have still managed to incorporate a tumbling rill and a rock garden. A visit here should be combined with the Barbican Conservatory.

MYDDELTON HOUSE ★ 44

Bulls Cross, Enfield, Middlesex. Tel: (0992) 717711
Lea Valley Regional Park Authority

From M25/A10 junction 25, turn W from A10 on Bulls Moor Lane, bear left into Bulls Cross and Myddelton House is on right at junction with Turley Street • Parking • Toilet facilities • Suitable for wheelchairs • Plants for sale occasionally • Open weekdays, 10 a.m. - 3.30 p.m. Closed weekends and Bank Holidays • Entrance: £1, children 50p

A magnificent diverse plant collection set in four acres built up by the famous E.A. Bowles and now restored. Splendid spring bulbs, followed by iris, followed by autumn crocus and impressive varieties of autumn-remontant iris make this garden a joy all year round. Zephyranthus, nerines, belladonna lilies, acidantheras are a few of the autumn bulbs and there is a fine *Crinum moorei* near the conservatory. This is by no means a municipal garden and the impressive plant collection is displayed attractively, in a well-designed garden surrounding the impressive Regency house of mellow golden brick. Serious understaffing has resulted in some untidiness but the garden is still unified by Bowles's plants and vision.

NOEL-BAKER PEACE GARDEN 45

Elthorne Park, Hazelville Road, London N19.
London Borough of Islington

There are several entrances to Elthorne Park, including those in Beaumont Road and Sunnyside Road • Best season: summer • Parking in adjacent roads • Toilet facilities in adjacent playground • Suitable for wheelchairs • Open daily, Mon - Fri, 8 a.m. - dusk, Sat, 9 a.m. - dusk, Sun, 10 a.m. - dusk • Entrance: free

This is a small well-designed formal garden within a London park, created in 1984 in memory of Philip Noel-Baker, winner of the Nobel Peace Prize in 1959. It is a lovely example of late twentieth-century garden design and planting, centering on an interesting water feature and a striking bronze figure (with horizontal bronze reflection). Much use is made of brick and York stone paving, and raised beds together with lawns; the overall effect is softened and enlivened by the excellent planting, with many unusual species (e.g. *Feijoa sellowiana*, *Clerodendrum bungei* and *C. trichotomum*). The emphasis is on green, grey and white, lifted here and there by splashes of colour and linked by the strong lines of the asymmetric design which creates several secluded sitting areas. It receives extensive use and support from the local community and although the results of limited maintenance are sometimes apparent, the overall impression is of well-loved amenity. There is a good children's playground and a fitness trail in adjacent Elthorne Park.

POSTMAN'S PARK 46

St Martins Le Grand, London EC1.
City of London Corporation

Close to St Paul's Cathedral • Parking difficult. Some meters near Smithfield Market after 2 p.m. • Suitable for wheelchairs but access limited to one entrance • Open Mon - Fri, 7 a.m. - dusk. Closed weekends and Bank Holidays • Entrance: free

Normally an oasis of calm in the midst of City chaos, the attractions of this small garden are temporarily diminished by the dirt and noise from surrounding building work. An area of formal bedding in the centre with mature trees, bushes and shrubs and a fine sculpture by Michael Ayrton. There is also a small fountain with goldfish and tombs and headstones from the time it was a churchyard. An arcade protects a tiled wall commemorating the noble deeds of those who died in their efforts to save others. Heartrending stuff in high Victorian style.

QUEEN MARY'S ROSE GARDEN 47

Inner Circle, Regent's Park, London NW1. Tel: (071) 486 7905
Department of the Environment

Off Marylebone Road. Many other entrances to the park • Best season: June, July and Aug • Parking: Inner Circle, weekdays, from 11 a.m., Sat and Sun, all day • Refreshments • Toilet facilities • Suitable for wheelchairs • Open daily, dawn - dusk • Entrance: free

These sedate, well-laid out and beautifully manicured gardens are justly famous. Playing host to more than 60,000 roses - dominated by Hybrid Teas and floribundas, although also including old-fashioned, shrub and species roses - the sight and scent of the gardens in high summer is a magnet for thousands of visitors. It must be said, however, that this style of rose garden is not to everyone's taste. The roses are grown with almost military precision and are in perfect condition. Swagged and garlanded climbers surround the circular rose garden, but the herbaceous borders are also worth visiting, particularly in late July and August, as is the large ornamental lake with its central island. It attracts many varieties of waterfowl, including herons which nest on the island. The Broad Walk (five minutes from the Rose Gardens) between the Inner and Outer circle towards Cambridge Gate is another exquisitely-maintained Victorian-style area of planting. St John's Lodge, on the north side of the Inner Circle and now part of what was Bedford College, has a secluded garden including a rose garden. The park as a whole is one of the most pleasant in London.

RANELAGH GARDENS ★ 48

Royal Hospital Road, London SW3. Tel: (071) 730 0161
Royal Hospital Chelsea

Chelsea Bridge Road. Through Chelsea Hospital main gate in Royal Hospital Road, then small gate on left. Also gates in Lower Sloane Street, Chelsea Embankment • Parking difficult in street • Suitable for wheelchairs • Open daily except 25th Dec and during Chelsea Flower Show, 10 a.m. - 1 p.m., 2 - 6 p.m. • Entrance: free

Elegant and attractive gardens with over a mile of wide walkways through undulating park-like grass and handsome tree and shrub planting, with a few perennial and shrub borders. Formerly the pleasure grounds of Ranelagh, complete with a large rotunda (now demolished) and laid out in formal style, they were redesigned by Gibson in the nineteenth century, but turned into allotments for pensioners between the World Wars. They were later reconstructed according to Gibson's plan. A summerhouse by Sir John Soane, near the entrance to the garden, houses several seats plus glass cases with a history and a map of the gardens with the major trees marked on it. These include many species of poplar, birch, beech, holly, cherry, chestnut, lime, oak and so on, with a couple of more exotic ones - the tree of heaven and the maidenhair tree. The serenity of the gardens is slightly marred by traffic in Chelsea Bridge Road. To one side of the park is the area used to house the Chelsea Flower Show. A long avenue of plane trees marks the western edge of the garden.

RAVENSCOURT PARK 49

King Street, London W6.
Hammersmith and Fulham Borough Council

Near junction of King Street and Chiswick High Street • Best season: June/July • Parking outside • Refreshments: summer, 10 a.m. - 7 p.m., winter, 10 a.m. - 5 p.m. • Toilet facilities • Suitable for wheelchairs • Dogs in dog zones • Plants for sale Wed - Sat, 10.30 a.m. - 4.45 p.m., Sun 10.30 a.m. - 5.45 p.m. • Open 7.30 a.m. - 6 p.m. • Entrance: free

A delightful park, with dog zones and dog-free zones, and a variety of trees and shrubs relatively unscathed by recent gale damage. A scented garden, a pond with Canada geese and other waterfowl, a bowling green, an impressive cactus house and extensive playing facilities for children. One of the best park cafeterias in London in a former coach house.

THE ROOKERY 50

Streatham Common South, London SE25. Tel: (081) 764 5478
Lambeth Council

Streatham High Road, then Streatham Common South • Best season: July • Parking top of Streatham High Road • Light refreshments • Toilet facilities • Partly suitable for wheelchairs • Dogs on lead on top terrace only • Open daily, 10 a.m. - dusk. Closed 25th Dec

This secluded and once beautifully-kept mixed garden is beginning to decline because the two ladies who looked after it for many years have retired. The rock garden has been let go badly, many plants have died in the drought and the bindweed is thick and eight feet into the trees and shrubs. Help please! Formerly the walled garden of a private house and the surrounding hillside - with sloping lawns and terraces. Views over Streatham Vale. Walled garden, the beautiful white garden best seen in July, extensive rock garden with a small stream and goldfish pond. Orchard. Delightful old English garden, beautifully scented, with large variety of annual and perennial plants. An orchard picnic area with tables. Abundance of benches donated by grateful Streatham residents for this peaceful and pretty garden a quarter of a mile (uphill) off the busy High Road. Plenty of litter bins. Children enjoy the orchard area (no ball games), the dense shrubbery and hidden, winding paths leading up through the rock garden area and stream.

ROYAL BOTANIC GARDENS ★★ 51

Kew, Richmond, Surrey. Tel: (081) 940 1171
Trustees

Kew Green, S of Kew Bridge • Parking Kew Green/Queen Elizabeth's Lawn car park (Brentford Gate) • Refreshments: Orangery restaurant, pavilion and tea bar • Toilet facilities inc. disabled • Suitable for wheelchairs which may be reserved in advance free of charge • Shop • Kew Palace open sumer, Queen Charlotte's cottage open summer weekends and public holidays (April to Sept) • Open daily, 9.30 a.m. - 4/6 p.m. depending on season, glasshouses, 10 a.m. - 4 p.m. • Entrance: £3, OAP and students £1.50, children £1, season ticket (for Kew and Wakehurst Place) £12, family season (2 adults and 3 children) £23

Internationally renowned, and primarily a botanic institution, collecting, conserving and exchanging plants from all over the world, Kew's delighful and varied gardens and grounds of more than 300 acres have something for everyone. In spring, the flowering cherries, crocuses, daffodils, and tulips and the lovely rock garden, in May and June, the bluebell wood, its lilacs (made famous by the song) and the water-lily house, in summer the herbaceous garden, the rose and cottage gardens, in the autumn bulbs and trees, and in the winter, the heath garden, the winter flowering cherries and (indoors) the alpine house, as well as the year-round pleasure of Decimus Burton's Palm house, the temperate and arid houses, and the Princess of Wales Conservatory with its computer-controlled micro-climates. The recently-opened Sir Joseph Banks building houses seasonal exhibitions on economic botany.

Kew's grounds also contain four temples, the famous Pagoda, Japanese Gateway, a campanile, the wood museum, the Marianne North gallery, (filled with 832 oil paintings of plants) besides Kew Palace itself, and the charming Queen Charlotte's cottage. The grass garden has over 600 grasses - besides those of the bamboo garden. About fifty per cent of the herbaceous garden's 2000 species are of wild origin. There is a somewhat formal rose garden, a delightful rock garden - originally of limestone, but completely replaced by sandstone. The Cambridge cottage gardens, the Queen's garden (in the style of a seventeenth-century garden) and the heather garden should not be missed.

The huge glasshouses, some of which are kept at tropical temperatures, are well worth visiting in winter, with their unique collections of exotic and unusual plants, ranging from banana trees to giant water lilies. In the Princess of Wales Conservatory are imaginative mangrove swamps and deserts, carnivorous plants and orchids.

The trees range from ash and birch collections, through conifers, eucalyptus and mulberry to walnut. The wood museum contains not only specimens of different woods but also inlay work, a history of the manufacture of paper, etc. The lake, once a disused gravel pit, has an abundance of wildfowl. The orangery does not contain oranges – which are to be found in the Citrus Walk (the orangery now has a bookshop, exhibition area and waiter-service restaurant).

It is well worth buying the souvenir guide (price £1.35) and planning a route for the elderly or unenergetic. The disabled will find most parts of Kew very accessible. Children will particularly enjoy the Princess of Wales Conservatory, with its Namib deserts and carnivorous plants, as well as the Palm House to see 'real' bananas. Tree-climbing, ball-games, and other sports are not allowed. Neither are radios, cassettes, etc.

SOUTHWOOD LODGE 52

33 Kingsley Place, Highgate, London N6.
Mr and Mrs Christopher Whittington

Off Southgate Lane, Highgate village • Parking in street • Plants for sale • Open 12th May, 16th June, 2 – 6 p.m. • Entrance: 80p

An imaginatively-designed garden created in 1963 from a much larger, older garden, set at the highest part of London with a magnificent view to the east 'as far as the Urals'. In approximately a third of an acre of a fairly steep site, there is much variety of mood and planting. By the house, which is clad in many fine clematis, a densely-planted paved area is enclosed on two sides by a high beech hedge through which steps lead down to a grassy walk planted with bushes, shrubs, more clematis and herbaceous plants. A wooded area in the lowest part of the garden, with many shade-loving plants leads one up past two pools with the soothing sound of trickling water and suitable bog plants. Alpines growing in troughs on a low wall.

7 ST GEORGE'S ROAD ★ 53

St Margaret's, Twickenham, Middlesex. Tel: (081) 982 3713
Mr and Mrs R. Raworth

Off A316 between Twickenham Bridge and St Margaret's roundabout • Best season: May to July • Parking in road • Teas on open day and by arrangement • Plants for sale • Open by appointment and 16th, 30th June, 2 – 6 p.m. • Entrance: £1, children free

A most successful result of garden design inspired by Hidcote and Tintinhull, on a miniature scale, nearly a generation ago. Mature garden of grace and peacefulness only yards from one of London's main routes to the west. The various rooms, Italianate patio, herb garden and knot garden lead through to an emerald carpet of grass and flower borders backing onto old trees in a private park. There are honeysuckles, old roses and many rare shrubs to interest the plantsperson and also the contents of a large elegant greenhouse on the north-facing wall of the wisteria-covered house.

ST JAMES'S PARK ★ 54

The Mall, London SW1. Tel: (071) 930 1793
Department of the Environment

From Buckingham Palace on the W to Horse Guards Parade on the E, the Mall on the N and on the S by Birdcage Walk • Parking difficult • Refreshments in park • Toilet facilities • Suitable for wheelchairs • Dogs • Open daily • Entrance: free

One of the smaller royal parks but one of the prettiest. It was Henry VIII who turned this swampy field into a pleasure ground and nursery for deer. After the Restoration, in 1660, Charles II employed the French garden designer Le Nôtre, who planned the gardens at Versailles, to refashion the park into a garden. Le Nôtre drew up plans for the lake and islands and included an aviary along Birdcage Walk. He also incorporated a 600-yard pitch for King Charles to play the old French game of Paille Maille (a crude form of croquet). The game gave its name to Pall Mall. Nash remodelled the lake in 1827–29 but the islands are still home to a wide variety of birds from ducks to pelicans. The park is also a sanctuary for politicians and civil servants as well as weary sightseers who can doze on deckchairs.

SYON PARK ★★ 55

Brentford, Middlesex. Tel: (081) 560 0881
His Grace the Duke of Northumberland

2m W of Kew Bridge, road marked from A315/310 at Bush Corner • Parking • Refreshments • Toilet facilities • Suitable for wheelchairs • Plants for sale • Shop • House open, Easter to Sept, 12 noon – 5 p.m. • Park open daily, 10 a.m. – 6 p.m. • Entrance: £1.75, OAP and children £1.25 (house and gardens £3.30, OAP and children £2.25)

The house built by Robert Adam *c.*1760 was the London seat of the Percy family which also employed 'Capability' Brown. From woodland garden to Charles Fowler's Great Conservatory (1830), Syon Park shows British gardening on a grand scale. The lakeside walk is of great interest; specimen trees planted in the eighteenth century by Brown still survive, supplemented by irises, day lilies and clumps of Chilian rhubarb. The six-acre rose garden, separated from the park (entrance 10p coin) created on the raised terrace that was constructed by the Protector Duke of Somerset in the sixteenth century, is well worth the extra effort of visiting, especially in June.

TRINITY HOSPICE ★ 56

30 Clapham Common North Side, London SW4. Tel: (071) 622 9481
Trustees of the Hospice

Off N side of the Common • Best season: spring, mid-summer • Parking on Common • Refreshments • Toilet facilities • Suitable for wheelchairs

• Plants for sale • Open several times a year in April, June, July and Sept for charity. Other times by appointment • Entrance: 50p, children free

The gardens at Trinity Hospice were designed primarily for the benefit of patients, their families and the staff. Stretching over nearly two acres, the gardens are set out on slightly rolling park-like terrain and designed by John Medhurst and David Foreman of London Landscape Consortium on the principles adhered to by Lanning Roper. The latter had originally been asked by the Sainsbury Family Charity Trust to design these gardens on a dilapidated site but his illness caught up with him before he could do much. The gardens were finished because of donations made by his friends and called the Lanning Roper Memorial Garden. Perennials and shrubs predominate but there is also a wild garden at one end and a large pool with a modern nubile sculpture and a duck house as slightly incongruous company.

TRUMPETER'S HOUSE AND LODGE GARDEN ★ 57

Old Palace Yard, Richmond, Surrey.
Mrs Pamela and Miss Sarah Franklyn

On Richmond Green • Best season: summer • Parking • Refreshments • Toilet facilities • Suitable for wheelchairs • Plants for sale • Open 23rd June, 14th July, 10.30 a.m. - 5.30 p.m. • Entrance: £1.50

Three acres of garden stand on the site of the former Richmond Palace. The garden feature ponds, many varieties of roses, Judas and mulberry trees and extensive lawns. Behind ironwork gates lies a 'secret garden' where Queen Elizabeth I walked and where a raised Georgian gazebo overlooks one of the loveliest stretches of the river. Here the garden has been laid out with plants of the Elizabethan period and the eye is drawn to a fine white aviary housing white doves. Very well maintained, this is one of the most interesting middle-sized gardens in the London region.

VICTORIA AND ALBERT MUSEUM 58

Cromwell Road, London SW7. Tel: (071) 938 8500
Trustees and Department of the Environment

Cromwell Road, close to South Kensington tube station and in walking distance of Harrods • Parking difficult • Toilet facilities • Suitable for wheelchairs • Open daily, weekdays, 10 a.m. - 5.50 p.m., Sun, 2.30 p.m. - 5.50 p.m. • Entrance: £3 (50p OAP, students and Friends of the V & A) suggested voluntary donation for museum and garden

Only rarely does the owner of a run-down garden find himself in the position of being offered vast sums by a sponsor who will foot the bill for a complete redesign. This was the case with Sir Roy Strong, former director of the V & A, and his benefactor Pirelli. It is strange that Sir Roy, who is a distinguished writer on gardening and has developed a beautiful garden of his own, should have approved a scheme which is so desiccated, although perhaps he was influenced by the desire to acknowledge his debt to the Italians by making this large open space at the heart of the museum a classic geometry which would shine under a blue Roman sky of the kind rarely prevailing in South Kensington. Whatever the reason, what was done was done with elegance and is maintained to a high standard.

WALLACE COLLECTION 59

Manchester Square, London W1. Tel: (071) 935 0687
Trustees of the Wallace Collection

N of Wigmore Street, behind Selfridges • Parking difficult • Toilet facilities (most elegantly tiled in London) • Suitable for wheelchairs • Shop • Gallery open • Open daily, weekdays, 10 a.m. - 5 p.m., Sun, 2 - 5 p.m. Closed Good Friday, May Day Bank Holiday and 24th to 26th Dec • Entrance: free

A secluded paved courtyard in the centre of Hertford House, a mansion built in 1776–88 for the then Duke of Manchester. When this storehouse of paintings, china and other treasures, collected by the Marquis of Hertford, was bequeathed to the nation, the government bought this mansion to display them. This stylish courtyard is like a stage set, dramatised by four magnificent bronze urns, two of which once stood in the Chateau de Bagatelle, the home of the Marquis and his son, Sir Richard Wallace. The centrepiece is an elegant fountain with a golden snake recoiling from the fish in the pool. The planting is kept simple with beds edged with clipped box and filled with santolina.

WALPOLE HOUSE ★ 60

Chiswick Mall, London W4.
Mr and Mrs Jeremy Benson

S of Great West Road (M4) between Hammersmith flyover and Hogarth roundabout • Parking in adjacent roads • Refreshments • Toilet facilities • Seeds for sale from excellent lists, packed with information and from 10p a packet • Open for parties 21st April, 2 - 6 p.m., 19th May, 2 - 7 p.m. • Entrance: £1, children 20p

This is one of the beautiful old houses on the Mall with two thirds of an acre of formally-designed and informally-planted garden whose sheer size (for London) takes your breath away as you come out into it from the house. A large paved area leading up steps to wide lawns with mature and handsome trees including two poplars, a tulip tree, several large ornamental cherries, acers, a magnolia and a strawberry grape from which cuttings are sometimes for sale. Beyond a yew hedge is a woodland area, heavily shaded, and intersected with old brick paths. A formal lily pond (larger than many town gardens) is surrounded by borders and a fence covered with climbers. Many varieties of peonies, irises, climbing roses, clematis, etc. Other borders and further small pool. Much self-seeding in the borders which accounts for the informality within the mostly formal lay-out. Note the 'front' gardens across the road (other owners) which are regularly flooded by the river. The nearby Strawberry House, splendidly developed by Lady Rothes, is up for sale and closed to the public.

WALPOLE PARK 61

Ealing, London W5. Tel: (081) 579 2424
London Borough of Ealing

Centre of Ealing, access from Uxbridge Road and High Street • Parking in surrounding residential roads • Toilet facilities • Suitable for wheelchairs • Dogs on lead • Open daily, 8 a.m. - dusk • Entrance: free

The gardens were acquired by the Borough Council and opened to the public in 1901. Large walled rose garden with a pergola. Formal beds set in lawn framed by old cedar trees. Centrepiece of topiary in the shape of a peacock but its tail is a bed of suitably-coloured flowering plants. There is also a water garden in Oriental style.

WANSTEAD PARK 62

Wanstead, London E11. Tel: (081) 530 4594
Corporation of London

Its western boundary is close to Leytonstone High Road, and its southern boundary to Manor Park. There are several entrances from Overton Drive and Warren Road • Parking at any of the several entrances • Suitable for wheelchairs • Dogs • Open at all times • Entrance: free

A skeleton of an eighteenth-century garden, obscured by a golfcourse. Popular with dog walkers and the occasional fisherman who can compete with the herons in the perch pond on payment of a toll to the bailiff. The old house, frequented by Elizabeth I, was rebuilt in 1715. The new mansion was considered one of the noblest houses in Europe. In 1755 Walpole was rather dismissive or jealous of the garden which he was told cost as much as the house - £100,000. Nothing remains of the house which was pulled down in 1822 to meet family debts. The garden boasts little more than a delapidated grotto and a hint of the elaborate water features. Look out for the map at the gates which details the Serpentine, reservoir and basin. The clogged up canals and lakes might be a haven for wildlife but they are a depressing sight for garden-lovers. The London Corporation is talking about the possibility of trying to rescue what it can of the garden. It should certainly do something - in the middle of the week, when the park is at its quietest, it would be the perfect location to film a murder.

THE WATER GARDENS ★ 63

Warren Road, Kingston Hill, Kingston, Surrey.
Octagon Developments Ltd

From Kingston take the A308 (Kingston Hill) towards London. About ½m on right, turn right into Warren Road • Parking on street • Partly suitable for wheelchairs • Open 12th May, 6th Oct, 2 - 5 p.m. • Entrance: £1, children 50p

A new development of luxury apartments has been built on part of the site, overlooking what is thought to be the oldest Japanese-style garden in Britain. An idyllic woodland setting of azaleas, acers, rhododendrons and magnolias among mature broadleaf trees and conifers. Gravel paths and stepping stones wind through these magnificent gardens, and you are never far from the sound of water, which runs in streams and cascades into tranquil ponds.

WATERHOUSE PLANTATION ★ 64

(also known as Woodland Garden)
Bushy Park, Hampton, London. Tel: (081) 979 1586
Department of the Environment

On A308 Hampton Court road, ¼m W of Hampton Court roundabout. Short walk from car park, gate on main road alongside • Best season: spring • Parking • Suitable for wheelchairs • Open daily, 9 a.m. - dusk • Entrance: free

There are two Plantations, both in Bushy Park, adjoining Hampton Court. Planting similar to the Isabella Plantation in Richmond Park (see entry) concentrating on masses of shrubs - rhododendrons, azaleas and camellias. The artificial river, the Longford, is a dramatic feature with many small bridges. Waterhouse suffered in the 1987 gales but has recovered well and there is something to see at all times of the year, such as a heather garden and wild flowers in season.

42 WOODVILLE GARDENS 65

London W5. Tel: (081) 998 4134
J. Welfare

Off Hanger Lane (off A40) • Best season: early summer • Parking in street • Open by appointment only • Entrance: by donation to charity

Larger than average town garden laid out predominantly to accommodate the owner's love of plants. The beds surrounding the lawn have grown in size as the need for more plant space demanded. There are a number of interesting and unusual ones, including a *Cestrum parqui* on the house wall, a small bed under an apple tree with four different pulmonarias and a large number of silver-leaved and variegated perennials and shrubs. The small raised terrace by the house is interplanted with low-growing silver-foliage plants and geraniums. Below it is a densely planted bed of dwarf alpines. At the bottom is a small bog garden.

GARDENS OPEN RARELY

The following gardens are open to the public on three days or less in the year, although they may also be open by appointment if this is stated in the text. For details see individual entry.

April 21 Walpole House; **May 5** 7 The Grove; 1-8 & 10 Malvern Terrace; **May 19** Walpole House; **May 20** 24 Grove Terrace; **May 26** 22 Loudoun Road; **June 2** 32 Atney Road; **June 16** 28 Barnsbury Square; 338 Liverpool Road; 7 St George's Road; **June 23** 15A Buckland Crescent; 4 The Grove; Trumpeter's House; **June 30** 7 St George's Road; **July 7** 32 Atney Road; **July 14** Trumpeter's House; **July 21** 29 Addison Avenue; **July 28** 24 The Grove; **Sept 15** 32 Atney Road.

MANCHESTER (Greater)

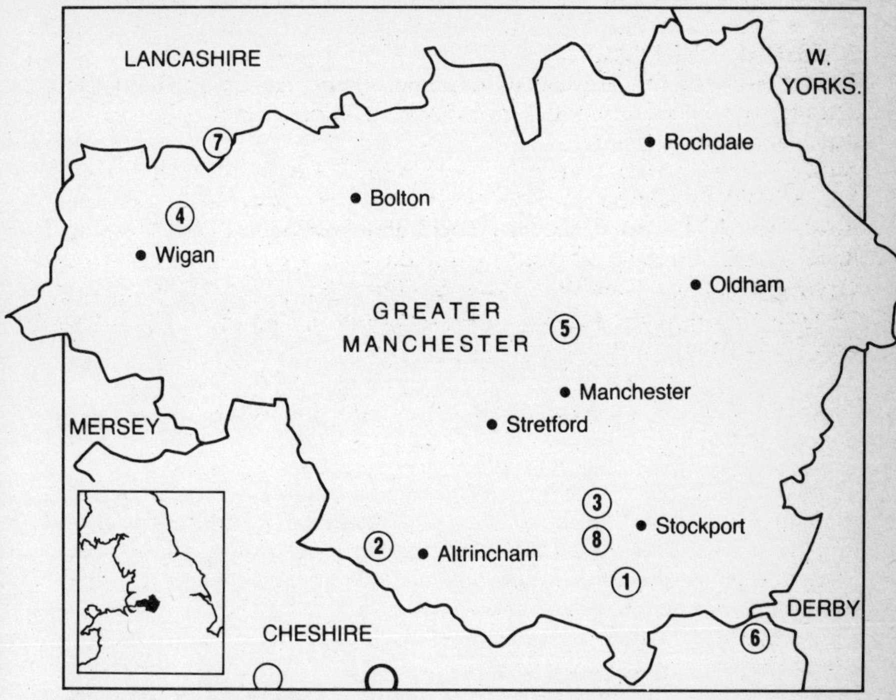

Plain circle numbers can be found by turning to neighbouring counties. Two-starred gardens are ringed in bold.

BRAMALL HALL 1

Bramhall Park, Bramhall, Stockport, Greater Manchester.
Tel: (061) 485 3708
Stockport Metropolitan Borough Council

2m S of Stockport on A5102 between Bramhall and Stockport, follow signposts • Best seasons: late spring/early summer • Parking • Refreshments in tea shop in converted stables • Toilet facilities • Partly suitable for wheelchairs • Dogs on leads in some areas • Shop in Hall • House open April to Sept, daily, 1 – 5 p.m., Oct to Dec, Feb to March, daily except Mon, 1 – 4 p.m. Closed January, 25th, 26th Dec. Entrance: £1.60, OAP and children, 80p • Gardens open all day • Entrance: free (to gardens only)

The gardens of Bramall Hall are a missed opportunity. At the front of this magnificent black and white timber-framed house is a courtyard covered in tarmac. To the back a slope down from the house has been terraced using brick retaining walls. These are in bad repair and of an unfortunate choice of brick.

The best parts of the gardens are a little distance to the front of the house where, in a narrow strip of land, are some formal beds containing bright annuals and a herbaceous border enclosed by a hedge. The parkland is another matter. In the valley of a small river are broad areas of grassland and a number of small lakes. Woods, which contain some very large beech trees, surround the park and hide all sign of the suburbs of Stockport. Along the river there is a walk, the banks of which are covered in wild flowers.

DUNHAM MASSEY ★ 2

Nr Altrincham, Greater Manchester. Tel: (061) 941 1025
The National Trust

3m SW of Altrincham off A56 • Parking • Refreshments: licensed self-service restaurant • Toilet facilities • Suitable for wheelchairs • Dogs on lead in park only • Shop • House open 31st March to Oct, daily except Fri, 1 - 5 p.m., Sun and Bank Holiday Mons, 12 noon - 5 p.m. • Gardens open 31st March to Oct, daily, 12 noon - 5.30 p.m., Sun and Bank Holiday Mons, 11 a.m. - 5.30 p.m. • Entrance: £1 garden only

Dunham Massey has extensive parkland with much of its layout dating from the eighteenth century and earlier. The gardens close to the house have many historic elements, too. The lake that borders the north and west sides of the house was formerly part of a moat and overlooking it is a mount that dates from the Tudor period, now grassed over and planted with false acacias. On the north side of the house, in front of the lake, is an Edwardian parterre planted in purple and gold; to the east is a large lawn bordered by shrubs and trees where there is an eighteenth-century orangery and an old well house. The Trust has carried out much replanting with the aim of restoring it 'in the character of the late-Victorian Pleasure Ground'. The result appears extremely successful. In the centre of the house is an attractive courtyard with four beds of shrubs and herbaceous plants. One of the rooms of the house contains paintings of the gardens made at various periods in history.

FLETCHER MOSS BOTANICAL GARDENS and PARSONAGE GARDENS ★ 3

Mill Gate Lane, Didsbury, Greater Manchester. Tel: (061) 434 1877
Manchester City Council (Recreational Services)

5m S of Manchester city centre on Mill Gate Lane which runs S of the A5145 close to the centre of the village of Didsbury • Limited parking • Refreshments: in small café (the building where the first meeting of the RSPB took place) but opening times uncertain • Toilet facilities inc. disabled • Partly suitable for wheelchairs • Dogs allowed in certain areas only • House open • Garden open all year, 9 a.m. - dusk • Entrance: free

Much of this garden is set on a steep south-facing bank that is planted with a great variety of shrubs, heathers, bulbs, alpines, azaleas and small trees.

Amongst them are rocky streams running down to a water garden and lawned area where there are moisture-loving plants including a large clump of gunneras. Across some tennis courts is a large grassed area containing specimen trees. Within a short walking distance are the Parsonage Gardens which are the grounds of the Fletcher Moss Museum. They were laid out in Victorian times and are more formal, containing lawns, good herbaceous borders, camellias and rhododendrons. There is also an Orchid House and some fine trees, notably a swamp cypress and a mulberry. Excellent well-maintained gardens.

HAIGH HALL GARDENS 4

Haigh Country Park, Haigh, Nr Wigan, Greater Manchester.
Tel: (0942) 832895
Metropolitan Borough of Wigan (Department of Leisure)

2m NE of Wigan on N side of B5238. Signposted • Parking (50p during peak summer season) • Refreshments: café • Toilet facilities • Suitable for wheelchairs which are available from the information centre • Dogs on lead • Shop • Parkland open all year, daily during daylight hours. Zoo open, daily except 25th, 26th Dec and 1st Jan • Entrance: mainly free, but some areas of the gardens are entered through the zoo for which there is a charge

Haigh Hall is surrounded by mature parkland, and a short distance to the east of the hall are some formal gardens probably of Victorian and Edwardian origin. In an open area of lawn there is an oval pool around which are rose beds and specimen shrubs. Close by are three adjoining walled gardens, the middle one containing a good herbaceous border and a well-stocked shrub border. The second, to the south, has shrubs around the walls and young specimen trees planted in a lawn in the centre; the wall to the south is low and gives a view across a wild garden with a pond. The third walled garden at the northern end can only be entered from the zoo, and here against the south facing wall is a cactus house and a butterfly house. On the west side is a landscaped area with heathers and conifers. The rest is a formal layout with roses, yew hedges and lawns and, against the east wall, a border of shrub roses.

HEATON HALL 5

Heaton Park, Prestwich, Greater Manchester.
Tel: (061) 773 1085 (Park)
Manchester City Council

4m N of the city centre on A576 just S of junction with M66 • Best season: spring • Parking • Refreshments: café • Toilet facilities • Some areas suitable for wheelchairs, but ring for advice before visiting • Dogs • Shop • House open summer months only • Gardens open all year during daylight hours • Entrance: free

Heaton Hall, built in 1772 by Wyatt, was described by Pevsner as 'the finest house of its period in Lancashire'. To the front of the lovely Hall is an area of formal, brightly planted gardens that would perhaps go better in front of a Victorian house. To the rear are some stables, with a small heather garden at their front and behind a large formal rose garden. A path leads through a tunnel to an attractive dell planted with a variety of mature trees and many rhododendrons. From here a path follows a stream through a series of pools and waterfalls with many new plantings on its surrounding banks leading to a large boating lake. On the Prestwich side of the park is an old walled garden where small demonstration gardens have been created, including a low-maintenance garden, a cottage garden and an alpine garden. A large greenhouse is also open to view.

LYME PARK ★ 6

Disley, Stockport, Greater Manchester. Tel: (0663) 62023
The National Trust

6m SE of Stockport just W of Disley on A6 • Parking • Refreshments: teas sometimes available in hall, kiosk in car park • Toilet facilities • Special help is available with wheelchairs. Phone in advance • Dogs on leads • Shop • House open at different times and at extra charge • Park open all year, daily except 25th and 26th Dec. Summer 11 a.m. - 6 p.m. Winter 11 a.m. - 4 p.m. Guided tours at special times • Entrance: pedestrians free, car £3 to include occupants. This charge applies to National Trust members

Lyme Park has immense character and the gardens contrast well with the rugged hills (and usually clouds) that surround it. A lawn at the front of the house leads down to a lake beyond which is a woodland garden underplanted with rhododendrons and other shade-loving plants. To the east is a fine orangery and below the terrace to the west is a well-kept geometric Dutch garden. An extensive programme to restore the gardens to their original design is nearly complete.

RIVINGTON TERRACED GARDENS 7

Rivington, Greater Manchester. Tel: (0204) 691549
(Rivington Information Centre)
North West Water

2m NW of Horwich. Follow the signposts to Rivington from the A673 in Horwich or in Grimeford village. The gardens are reached by a 10-minute walk from Rivington Hall and Hall Barn • Best season: June • Parking, refreshments, toilet facilities and shop at Hall Barn • Dogs • Open at all times • Entrance: free

These are not gardens as such but the remains of gardens that were built by Lord Leverhulme in the early part of this century. They are set mainly in woodland on a steep west-facing hillside and have fine views across Rivington reservoirs. It is worth buying the guide which leads the visitor round and explains the various features. Particularly impressive is a rocky ravine, the remains of a Japanese garden and the restored pigeon tower. There are a variety of mature trees and many rhododendrons and once this must have been a very grand estate. When visiting be prepared for a stiff walk and beware of the paths which can be slippery in some areas.

WYTHENSHAWE HORTICULTURAL CENTRE 8

Wythenshawe Park, Wythenshawe Road, Baguley, Greater Manchester. Tel: (061) 945 1768
Manchester City Council

7m S of Manchester city centre, ¼m from M63 junction 9, ½m from M56 junction 3, S of B5167 • Parking • Refreshments: cafeteria at hall, weekends only, 10 a.m. - 5 p.m. • Toilet facilities inc. disabled • Partly suitable for wheelchairs • Plants for sale Wed, 1 - 4 p.m., also Sat and Sun, 10 a.m. - 4 p.m. • Open daily, 10 a.m. - 4 p.m. • Entrance: free

Set on the site of an old vegetable garden, this centre is now the nursery that provides most of the bedding stock for the city's parks. It also houses many surprisingly large collections of plants. Outside are herbaceous beds, vegetable plots, heather beds and an area of small trees and conifers. Among the many greenhouses is a cactus house containing many large specimens, a temperate house, a fern and orchid house, an alpine house and a chrysanthemum house. There is also a Visitors' Centre where the staff are always willing to help with advice. To the east of the Centre is the Hall, with some formal garden, including a large bed devoted to spiraeas.

MERSEYSIDE

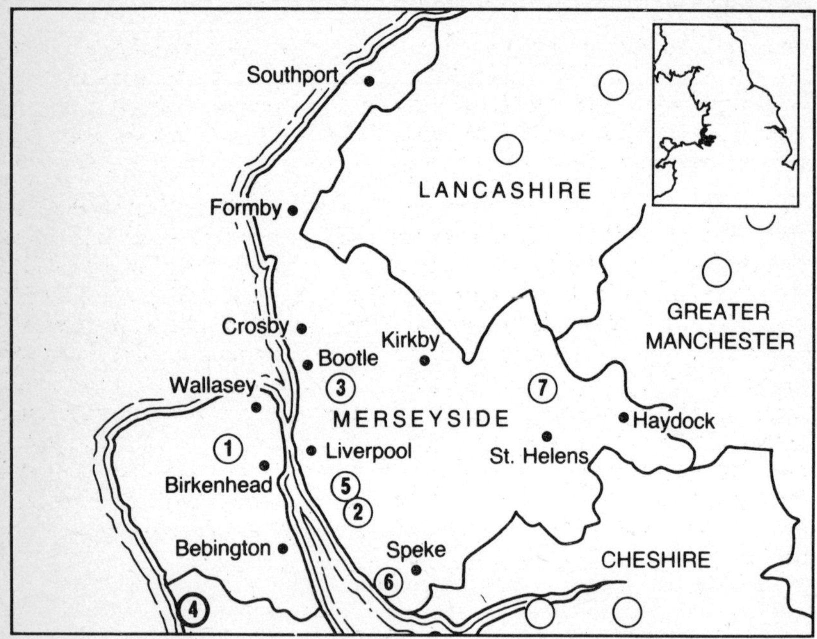

Plain circle numbers can be found by turning to neighbouring counties.
Two-starred gardens are ringed in bold.

BIRKENHEAD PARK ★ 1

Birkenhead, Wirral, Merseyside. Tel: (051) 647 2366
Metropolitan Borough of Wirral

1m from the centre of Birkenhead on S of A553 • *Best season: autumn* • *Parking around park* • *Refreshments: tea kiosk sometimes open* • *Partly suitable for wheelchairs* • *Dogs in some areas only* • *Open during daylight hours* • *Entrance: free*

Birkenhead Park is rich in history. Opened in 1847, it was the world's first park to be built at public expense. Joseph Paxton produced its design which was highly influential in the creation of New York's Central Park. It is split into two by a road; on the eastern side is a lake with well-landscaped banks planted with trees and shrubs. A Swiss-style bridge links two islands and to one end is a fine stone boathouse, that has been recently restored. In the west part is another lake with weeping willows and rhododendrons planted round its edge. There is also an enclosed area of more ornamental plants. This park is so well landscaped and planted that it is possible to overlook the litter and vandalism from which it suffers.

CALDERSTONE PARK ★ 2

Liverpool, Merseyside. Tel: (051) 225 4835
Liverpool City Council, Environmental Services

4m SE of Liverpool city centre, S of A562 • Parking • Refreshments in teashop • Toilet facilities • Suitable for wheelchairs • Dogs in park only • Park open at all times. Old English Garden and Japanese Garden open April to Sept, 8 a.m. - 7.30 p.m., Oct to March, 8 a.m. - 4 p.m. Closed 25th Dec • Entrance: free

This is a large landscaped park with mature trees, shrubs, a lake and rhododendron walk. In its centre are three gardens set around an old walled garden which are a credit to the city council gardener here. The first is the Flower garden which has semiformal beds of perennials and grasses, formal beds of annuals and a long greenhouse. Next is the Old English garden, where amongst a formal layout of paths are beds containing a huge range of perennials, bulbs and shrubs. There is a circular pond at the centre and pergolas carrying clematis, vines and other climbers cross the paths at various points. Finally the Japanese garden has a chain of rocky streams and pools around which are pines, acers and clumps of bamboo. A greenhouse contains the National Collection of the genus *Aechmea*. Altogether this must be one of the best 'free' gardens in the country. Alas, the park itself is badly affected by litter.

CROXTETH HALL AND COUNTRY PARK 3

Liverpool, Merseyside. Tel: (051) 228 5311
Liverpool City Council, Environmental Services

Turn N off A5058 Liverpool ring road into Muirhead Avenue on NE side of city. Croxteth Park is well signposted • Best season: summer • Parking • Restaurant • Toilet facilities • Partly suitable for wheelchairs • Dogs in outer park only • Shop in house • House open • Gardens open Good Fri to Sept, daily, 11 a.m. - 5 p.m., winter times on request • Entrance: 50p for walled garden (all facilities £2). Reductions for OAP and children

Croxteth Hall stands in 500 acres of parkland in which there are large areas of woodland and many rhododendrons. The centre of interest to gardeners is the large walled garden to the north of the house. Divided up by gravel paths, this garden contains areas growing a great variety of fruit, vegetables and decorative plants; fruit espaliers are grown against the walls and trained on wire fences and the south-facing wall has a broad herbaceous border containing a good variety of perennials and ornamental grasses. In the north east corner several greenhouses and a mushroom house are all open to the visitor. To the south end is a small weather station surrounded by herb beds, and, close by, some working beehives.

THE ISLE OF MAN
(see Cumbria)

NESS GARDENS ★★ 4

University of Liverpool Botanic Gardens, Ness, South Wirral, Merseyside. Tel: (051) 336 2135
University of Liverpool

2m off A540 on Neston Road between Ness and Burton • Parking • Refreshments • Toilet facilities • Partly suitable for wheelchairs • Plants for sale • Shop • Open daily except 25th Dec, March to Oct, 9.30 a.m. - dusk, Nov to Feb, 9.30 a.m. - 4 p.m. • Entrance: £2.50, OAP and children 10 - 18 years £1.50, family ticket £6

A Mr Bulley began gardening on this site in 1898 using plants collected for him by George Forrest, the noted plant hunter. His daughter gave the gardens to the University in 1948. They extend over 60 acres. Those who have experience of the north west winds blowing off the Irish Sea will marvel at the variety and exotic nature of the plant life. The secret is in the Lombardy poplars, holm oaks and Scots pines which have been planted as shelter belts shielding the specialist areas. The aim has been to provide all-year round interest from the spring, through the herbaceous and rose gardens of the summer to the heather and sorbus collections of the autumn. There are in addition areas of specialist interest such as the Nature Plant Garden which houses plants raised from seed or cuttings from wild plants and used for propagation or the re-stocking of natural habitats. For all its specialist and academic background the labelling of plants is somewhat inadequate and though there are a number of signed 'walks' of varying distances (including one suitable for wheelchairs) here again the signs could be clearer without being obtrusive. The coloured illustrated guide (at £1) is therefore a must.

SEFTON PARK 5

Liverpool, Merseyside. Tel: (051) 724 2371
Liverpool City Council (controlled by Environmental Services, Calderstone Park)

3m SE of Liverpool city centre, N of A561 • Best season: spring • Parking at various points around park • Refreshments at café in centre of park • Suitable for wheelchairs • Dogs • Open at all times • Entrance: free

Although this large park suffers badly from litter and vandalism it remains an extremely fine Victorian park, with many of its monuments, gateways and shelters as well as the large houses surrounding it built in the Gothic style of the late 1800s. A large serpentine boating lake has two small streams entering at its northern end. One stream flows from the east through a lightly wooded valley that has been landscaped with large rocks and planted with rhododendrons. The other flows from the north through a series of small lakes passing a replica of Piccadilly's Eros, a statue of Peter Pan and an ornate bandstand. In the centre of the park is a magnificent palm house now in bad repair but a restoration scheme is soon to be undertaken.

SPEKE HALL 6

The Walk, Liverpool, Merseyside. Tel: (051) 427 7231
The National Trust

8m SE of Liverpool city centre, S of A561. Signposted • Best season: spring • Entrance: 50p • Parking 50p • Refreshments in teashop from 12 noon. Picnics in orchard • Toilet facilities inc. disabled • Partly suitable for wheelchairs • Shop • Hall open April to Oct, daily except Mon. £2, children 50p. Reductions for parties • Gardens open 30th March to 1st Nov, daily except Mon, 1 - 5.30 p.m., Nov to March 1992, daily except Mon, 12 - noon - 4p.m. Closed 24th to 26th, 31st Dec and 1st Jan • Entrance: 50p (house £2.50)

The gardens at Speke are neither as old nor as impressive as the Elizabethan Hall. They are remarkable, however, for although they are situated amidst the industrial areas of south Liverpool they seem to be set in the heart of the countryside, despite their proximity to Liverpool airport. In front of the house is a large lawn with shrub borders to the sides containing mainly rhododendrons and hollies. On the side opposite the house is a ha-ha allowing views to the fields and woodland. A stone bridge leads over a drained moat to the ornate stone entrance of the hall. The moat continues to the west where there is a herbaceous border with a variety of perennials; a large holm oak stands opposite. To the south is a formal rose garden containing fragrant varieties of old-fashioned roses. In the centre of the house is a large cobbled courtyard in which grow two enormous yews. The Trust is continuing to develop many areas of the gardens.

MIDLANDS (West)

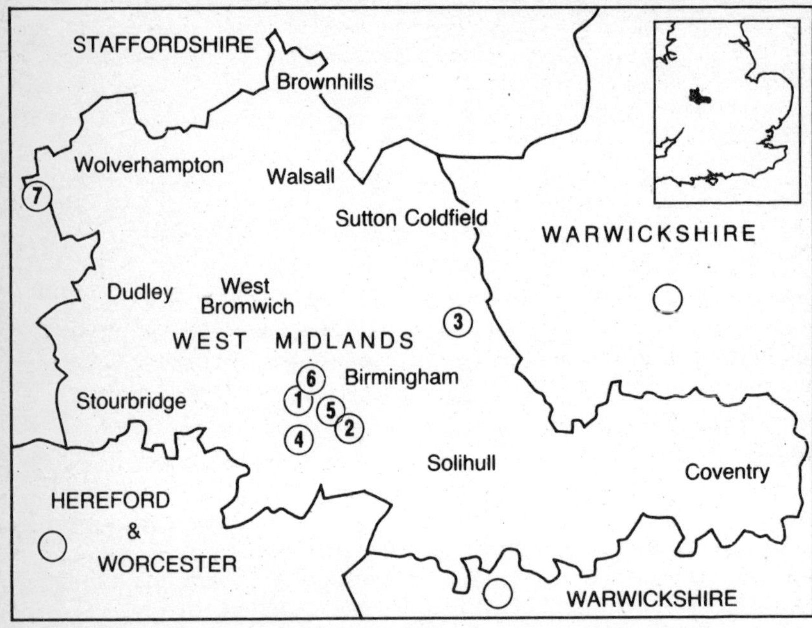

Plain circle numbers can be found by turning to neighbouring counties.

BIRMINGHAM BOTANICAL GARDENS AND GLASSHOUSES ★ 1

Westbourne Road, Edgbaston, Birmingham, West Midlands. Tel: (021) 454 1860

2m from city centre. Approach from Hagley Road or Calthorpe Road • Parking • Refreshments: restaurant. Picnics allowed • Toilet facilities • Suitable for wheelchairs. Two chairs available for use free of charge • Plants for sale • Shop • Open summer, Mon - Sat, 9 a.m. - 7.30 p.m., Sun, 10 a.m. - 7.30 p.m., winter closes at 6 p.m. or dusk • Entrance: £2.40 (£2.70 on summer Suns), OAP, disabled, students and children £1.20. Parties £2.10 per person (£1 for concessions)

This garden will appeal to the keen plantsperson and also to the everyday gardener. In addition to the unusual plants in the Tropical house and the orangery, there is a cactus and succulent house, and cages with parrots and also guinea fowl, ducks, peacocks, geese and other birds. Some beautiful old trees, a border for E.H. Wilson plants, a raised alpine bed and a raised garden area to give ideas and enjoyment to disabled visitors. Good colour foliage contrasts and a small area laid out with model domestic gardens. The rock garden contains rhododendrons, primulas, astilbes and azaleas and there are also herbaceous borders and a rose garden. There is a small display of carnivorous plants. A children's playground and adventure trail makes the garden a pleasant place for a family outing. The model domestic gardens perhaps should be called theme gardens. They cover low maintenance, children, colour and a plantsman's garden.

CANNON HILL PARK 2

Moseley, Birmingham, West Midlands. Tel: (021) 449 0238
Birmingham City Council

2m from Birmingham city centre opposite Edgbaston Cricket Ground • Best season: spring/summer • Parking • Refreshments: lunches and snacks in park restaurant. Picnic area • Toilet facilities in Midlands Art Centre open 9 a.m. – 9 p.m. • Suitable for wheelchairs • Dogs • Art Centre in park, bookshop, gallery and restaurant • Open daily, 8 a.m. – dusk • Entrance: free

Eighty acres of park with formal beds, wide range of herbaceous plants, shrubs and trees. Glasshouse with collection of Tropical and sub-tropical plants open 10 a.m. – 4 p.m. Nature trails. Children's area. Also boating, miniature golf, bowls and tennis available. A model of the Elan Valley is set in the garden area.

CASTLE BROMWICH HALL ★ 3

Old Chester Road, Castle Bromwich, Birmingham, West Midlands. Tel: (021) 749 4100
Castle Bromwich Garden Trust

4m E of Birmingham city centre. 1m from junction 5 of M6 northbound • Parking • Refreshments • Toilet facilities • Suitable for wheelchairs • Seeds for sale • Shop • Open 31st March to Sept, Mon – Thurs, 1.30 – 4.30 p.m., Sat, Sun and Bank Holidays, 2 – 6 p.m. Guided tours on Wed, Thurs and Sat • Entrance: £1.50, OAP £1, children 6 – 15 50p. Special rates for parties

The hall, built at the end of the sixteenth century, was sold to Sir John Bridgman in 1657 and his wife created the garden with expert help. It fell into decay, and now a series of formal connecting gardens is being restored to give them the appearance and content of a garden of 1680/1740. The perimeter wall and orangery have been rebuilt and all planting completed. There are fan- and espalier-trained fruit trees and orchard, a kitchen garden, holly walk, ponds, cold bath, archery ground, maze, wilderness, parterres and herbaceous borders. A new orchard of period varieties was planted winter 1990/91. Visitors have the rare opportunity to see a period garden being restored year-by-year.

MARTINEAU ENVIRONMENTAL STUDIES CENTRE 4

Priory Road, Edgbaston, Birmingham, West Midlands.
Tel: (021) 440 4883
City of Birmingham Education Department

Turn off A38 road into Priory Road and entrance is 100 yards on right opposite Priory Hospital • Parking • Tea on open day • Toilet facilities • Suitable for wheelchairs • Plants for sale • Open 14th July and weekdays by arrangement, 10.30 a.m. - 6 p.m. • Entrance: £1, children 50p

This is a two-acre educational garden designed for teachers and children but the wide range of features make it interesting for all, and a good place for the family with children interested in gardening. There are annuals, herbaceous and shrub borders, roses, raised beds, herbs, alpines, bulbs, miscanthus and the greenhouse with a collection of cactus, tomatoes and peppers along with tropical things such as a banana, fig and coffee plant. In the woodland area there are native plants and a pool with plenty of wildlife. The vegetable plots contain brassicas, root crops and legumes and the fruit trees and soft fruit include a medlar, greengage, apricot, blueberry and tayberry. The children work on some of the plots - so with school holidays everything cannot always be weed free. There are now some sheep, ducks and hens.

UNIVERSITY OF BIRMINGHAM BOTANIC GARDEN ★ 5

Winterbourne, 58 Edgbaston Park Road, Edgbaston, Birmingham, West Midlands. Tel: (021) 414 5613
University of Birmingham School of Continuing Studies

Off A38 Bristol Road leading out of the city, adjacent to the University campus • Parking • Toilet facilities • Suitable for wheelchairs • Plants sometimes for sale on open days • Open for parties by arrangement

About seven acres of garden originally belonging to a large house owing much to the landscape style developed by Edward Lutyens and Gertrude Jekyll. Because of its wide range of plants and different features it should be of interest to the botanist as well as the ordinary gardener. There are geographical beds showing typical trees and shrubs from Europe, Australasia, the Americas, China and Japan. The pergola is covered with clematis and roses and there are herbaceous borders backed by brick walls covered with climbers. A miniature arboretum contains interesting specimens including giant oaks, acers, conifers and a *Gingko biloba* along with hedges of yew, *Taxus baccata* and copper beech. In a fairly new Commemorative Garden is a Black Mulberry planted to mark the 100th anniversary of the City of Birmingham. The range of plants continues with the sandstone rock garden, troughs, rhododendrons, heathers and alpines. There is an unusual nut walk containing several varieties of *Corylus avellana* trained over an iron framework. A special feature is the walled garden laid out with beds of roses showing the History of the Rose, and elsewhere are more recent plantings of roses.

8 VICARAGE ROAD 6

Edgbaston, Birmingham, West Midlands. Tel: (021) 455 0902
Charles and Tessa King-Farlow

1½m W of city centre off A456 Hagley Road. Going out of the city, turn left into Vicarage Road • Best season: May/June and early July • Parking in local roads • Teas • Suitable for wheelchairs • Plants for sale at certain times • Open 23rd June, 7th July, 2 - 6 p.m. and by appointment • Entrance: £1, OAP and children 50p

A visit to this garden should give pleasure to most gardeners as there is a sense of mystery as one moves from one area to the next. Plenty of good planting ideas can be seen with the clever use of colour and foliage combinations - a range of grey and variegated foliage. Roses and clematis scramble through old fruit trees and other shrubs. There is a bank of shrub roses, and the herbaceous border consists of three tiers and contains a wide range and some rare plants. There is a conservatory, pool and 1920s rock garden providing year-round colour. The walled kitchen garden has fruit and vegetables, and improvements are planned for this area. It is hard to believe that one is walking through a garden so near the centre of a large city.

WIGHTWICK MANOR 7

Wightwick Bank, Wolverhampton, West Midlands.
Tel: (0902) 761108
The National Trust

3m W of Wolverhampton off A454. Turn by the Mermaid Inn up Wightwick Bank • Parking • Minimal refreshments • Toilet facilities • Suitable for wheelchairs • Dogs on lead • Shop • House open same days as garden, 2.30 - 5.30 p.m. Timed tickets • Open March to Dec, Thurs and Sat, Bank Holiday Sun and Mon, 2 - 6 p.m. Closed 25th, 26th Dec. Pre-booked parties accepted Wed and Thurs • Entrance: £1 (house £3)

This 10-acre garden, designed by Alfred Parsons, surrounds an 1887 house strongly influenced in its design by William Morris and his movement; it contains a collection of pre-Raphaelite paintings. Large trees form a delightful framework to the garden with a central octagonal arbour with climbing roses and clematis. Moving through an old orchard one reaches a less formal area with pools surrounded by shrubs and rhododendrons. There are herbaceous borders, two rows of barrel-shaped yews and beds containing plants from gardens of famous men. As a surprise round a corner one comes across a line of boulders from Scotland and the Lake District which were left when the great glaciers melted in the last Ice Age.

GARDENS OPEN RARELY

The following garden is open to the public on two days in the year, although it may also be open by appointment. For details see individual entry.
June 23 8 Vicarage Road; **July 7** 8 Vicarage Road.

NORFOLK

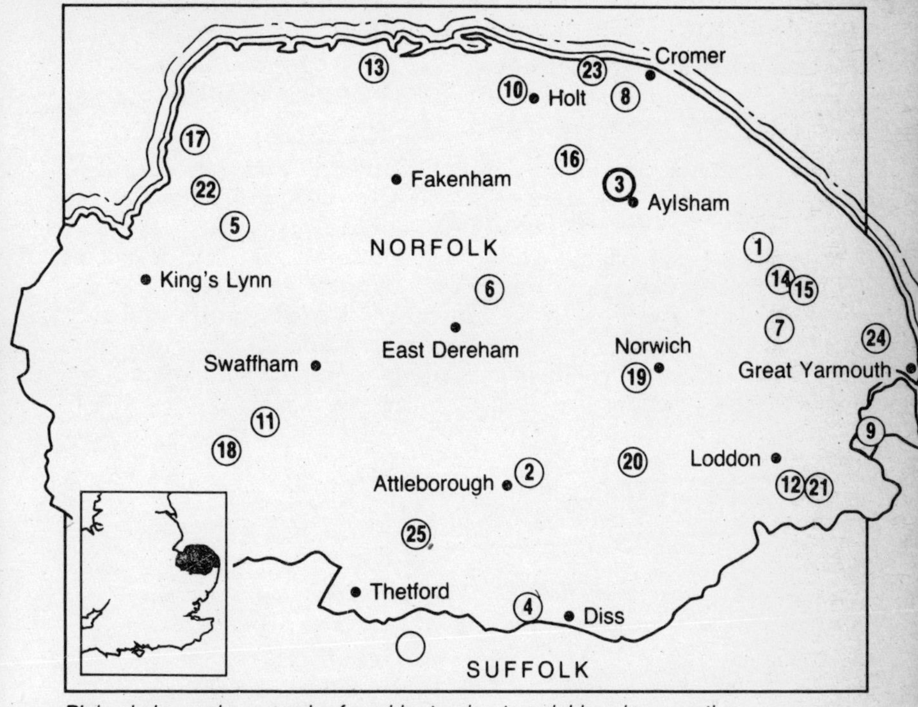

Plain circle numbers can be found by turning to neighbouring counties. Two-starred gardens are ringed in bold.

BEESTON HALL 1

Beeston St Lawrence, Wroxham, Norfolk. Tel: (0692) 630771
Sir Ronald and Lady Preston

2¼m NE of Wroxham on road to Stalham off A1151 • Best season: early summer • Parking • Refreshments: tearoom • Toilet facilities • Suitable for wheelchairs • Shop • House open • Garden open April to mid-Sept, Fri, Sun, Bank Holiday Mon, also Wed in Aug, 2 – 5.30 p.m. • Entrance: £2, children £1, grounds only 60p

The Gothic house of 1786 stands on rising grounds overlooking a long serpentine lake. The gardens to the south of the house are pretty although not extensive. There is a brick orangery, herbaceous and shrub borders, and some mature trees of early nineteenth-century planting. The park originally laid out by Richmond (a contemporary of 'Capability' Brown) is now largely given over to farming and a broad path winds down through corn fields to woodland where there is an ice-house and a lakeside walk.

BESTHORPE HALL ★ 2

Besthorpe, Attleborough, Norfolk. Tel: (0953) 452138
Mr J.A. Alston

1m E of Attleborough on Bunwell Road. Entrance on right, past church • Best season: June • Parking • Refreshments • Toilet facilities • Suitable for wheelchairs • Plants for sale • Open by appointment and 16th June, 2 - 5.30 p.m., 14th July, 2 - 5 p.m. • Entrance: £1

A pool and fountain occupy the centre of the entrance forecourt. Beyond the house, more pools and fountains are set among lawns skirted by high clematis-hung walls of Tudor brick which form a backdrop to long herbaceous borders. The largest lawn, believed to have once been a tilt yard, has developing topiary, while on another is an enormous and shapely Wellingtonia. There are many other fine trees among which are paulownia, and a variety of birches, acers and magnolias including the sumptuous *M. delavayi*. There are walled kitchen gardens, a nuttery, a herb garden, and a small lake with wildfowl. On another lushly planted pool live a pair of black swans.

BLICKLING HALL ★★ 3

Aylsham, Norfolk. Tel: (0263) 733084
The National Trust

1½m NW of Aylsham on N side of B1354 • Best seasons: spring and summer • Parking • Refreshments 12 noon - 5 p.m. Picnic area in walled garden • Toilet facilities • Suitable for wheelchairs • Dogs in park on leads • Plants for sale • Shop • House open 1 - 5 p.m. • Cycle hire on house open days • Open 30th March to 27th Oct, daily except Mon and Thurs, 12 noon - 5 p.m. and daily in July and Aug. Open Bank Holiday Mons. Closed Good Fri • Entrance: £2 (house and gardens £4.50)

Although the gardens of Blickling Hall seem so suited to the style and beauty of the Jacobean house, they consist of a blend of features from the seventeenth to the twentieth centuries. From the earliest period come the massive yew hedges flanking the south approach. To the east is the parterre planned by Nesfield and Wyatt in 1870 with its topiary pillars and blocks of yew shaped like grand pianos. Complicated flower beds were replaced in 1938 with Norah Lindsay's four large square beds of herbaceous plants in selected colours with surrounding borders of roses edged with catmint. The central pool has a seventeenth-century fountain bought from nearby Oxnead Hall. A high retaining wall bounds the southern side while in the centre of the eastern side flights of steps mount up to the highest terrace with a central vista through blocks of woodland to the Doric temple of 1730 raised above parkland beyond. The two blocks are intersected by allées in seventeenth-century style although planted in 1861–64. Recent gales have done much damage but replanting has been undertaken using Turkey oak, lime and beech. On the southern side is the Orangery of 1782 by Samuel Wyatt which houses half-hardy plants and a statue of Hercules by Nicholas Stone made for Oxnead in the 1640s. In the corner of the northern block is the secret garden, a remnant of a larger eighteenth-century garden for which Repton made recommendations. It now consists of a lawn with a central sundial surrounded by high beech hedges. The shrub border through which it is approached is by Norah Lindsay who was also responsible for the planting of the dry moat around the house. North of the parterre is a raised grassy area, possibly a remnant of the Jacobean mount; here grow enormous, sprawling Oriental planes. To the north-west is landscaped parkland where woods descend to the curving lake formed before 1729 and later extended. West of the house are cedars of Lebanon and a collection of magnolias around a nineteenth-century fountain. Elsewhere in the park are the Gothic Tower of 1773 and the Mausoleum of 1796, a pyramid 45 ft square by Joseph Bonomi.

BRESSINGHAM HALL GARDENS ★ 4

Bressingham, Diss, Norfolk. Tel: (037988) 386/382
Mr Alan Bloom and Mr Adrian Bloom

3m W of Diss on A1066 • Parking • Refreshments • Toilet facilities • Suitable for wheelchairs • Plants for sale • Shop • Open May to Sept, daily, 10 a.m. – 5.30 p.m. Adrian Bloom's garden open 14th July, 7th, 8th Sept, 6th Oct • Entrance: £2.50, children £1.50 (joint entrance to both gardens £3)

The six acres of this garden are chiefly occupied by island beds, a scheme which allows for the display of over 5000 kinds of hardy perennials, and the beds are full of colour and interest throughout the spring, summer and autumn. Although a miniature railways runs through to one side of the garden, the owners believe that it and the associated steam museum are not a distraction, particularly as they run only on Sun, Wed and Thurs, leaving four days for those who prefer to come solely for the garden. This is of a very high standard and comparisons have been made with Wisley. The large plant centre offers a wide range of trees, shrubs and herbaceous plants. The adjoining garden of Adrian Bloom contains over 300 varieties of conifers, some 50 different heathers and at least 1000 shrubs and perennials.

CONGHAM HALL HOTEL 5

Lynn Road, Grimston, Nr King's Lynn, Norfolk. Tel: (0485) 600250
Mr and Mrs T. Forecast

NE of King's Lynn. Go to A149/A148 interchange, then follow A148 signed Sandringham/Fakenham/Cromer for 100 yards. Turn right for Grimston. Hotel is 2½m on left hand side of road • Parking • Suitable for wheelchairs • Open April to Sept, daily except Sat, 2 – 4 p.m. Small parties by arrangement at other times. No coaches • Entrance: free

Herb garden. Over 300 varieties grown in about two acres of hedged *jardinière* set near the Georgian manor house, now a hotel, which is itself surrounded by 40 acres of parkland. Mrs Forecast began the herb garden a few years ago as part of a vegetable and soft fruit supply for the kitchen. Now it has become an obsession, and includes medicinal herbs which, it goes without saying, are rarely if ever required by diners. Anyone interested in herbs should certainly visit. *Bon viveurs* will find the hotel in the *Good Food Guide*.

ELSING HALL ★ 6

Elsing, Nr East Dereham, Norfolk. Tel: (0362) 637224
Mr and Mrs D.H. Cargill

5m NE of East Dereham. Elsing signposted off A47 and B1067 • Parking • Refreshments • Dogs on lead • Open 30th June, 7th July, 2 - 6 p.m. and by appointment • Entrance: £1, children free

The romantic appearance of this garden is in complete harmony with the moated flint and half-timbered house which it surrounds. The garden, although mostly of recent planting, is rich, lush and unrestrained and in mid-summer is filled with the scene of the old garden roses which cover the walls and fill the borders. The lawn between the house and the moat has been abandoned to wild orchids: wildfowl nest in the reedy lake. Both the lake and a nearby stewpond are encircled by moist borders supporting luxuriant growth. On the walls of the kitchen garden grow old roses many of which seem unique to this place. A large variety of new trees has been planted, a knot garden is being developed, and an avenue of gingkos has been established.

FAIRHAVEN GARDEN TRUST ★ 7

South Walsham, Norwich, Norfolk. Tel: (060549) 449
Fairhaven Garden Trust

9m NE of Norwich off B1140 • Best season: May/June • Parking • Refreshments • Toilet facilities • Suitable for wheelchairs • Dogs on lead • Plants for sale • Open Easter to 5th May, Sun and Bank Holidays. 8th May to 8th Sept, Wed - Sun and Bank Holiday Mons, 15th, 22nd, 29th Sept, all 11 a.m. - 6 p.m., except Sat 2 - 6 p.m. 27th Oct, 10 a.m. - dusk • Entrance: £1.50, OAP £1, children 70p

A garden created in natural woods of oak and alder extending to about 230 acres surrounding the unspoiled South Walsham Broad. Paths wind among banks of azaleas and large-leaved rhododendrons and lead to the edge of the broad itself. Much of the area is wet and supports a rich variety of primulas, with lysichitons, astilbes, ligularias and gunneras of exceptional size, merging into the natural vegetation among which are many Royal ferns and some majestic oaks. Although particularly colourful during the flowering of the azaleas in the spring, this garden gives pleasure at all times of the year when natural beauty is preferred to man-made sophistication.

FELBRIGG HALL ★ 8

Felbrigg, Cromer, Norfolk. Tel: (026375) 444
The National Trust

3m SW of Cromer off A148. Main entrance on B1436 • Best season: summer • Parking • Refreshments: April to 27th Oct, 11 a.m. - 5 p.m. 28th Oct to 22nd Dec, 11 a.m. - 3.30 p.m., 4th Jan to March; Sat and Sun only, 11 a.m. to 3.30 p.m. • Toilet facilities • Suitable for wheelchairs • Dogs in park only on leads • Plants for sale • Shop • House open • Gardens open 30th March to 27th Oct, daily except Tues and Fri, 11 a.m. - 5.30 p.m. Woodland walks all year except 25th Dec, daily, dawn - dusk • Entrance: £1.50 (house and gardens £4)

The house faces south across the park which is notable for its fine woods and lakeside walk. A ha-ha separates the park from the lawns of the house where there is an orangery planted with camellias. To the north the ground rises and there are specimen trees and shrubs. At some distance to the east there is a large walled kitchen garden now richly planted with a combination of fruit, vegetables and flowers in a formal design behind clipped hedges. There is also a vine house and great brick dovecote. In early autumn there is a display of many varieties of colchicums: the National collection is kept here. The gardens are kept in immaculate order. Sheringham Park is nearby (see entry).

FRITTON LAKE 9

Fritton, Great Yarmouth, Norfolk. Tel: (0493) 488208
Lord and Lady Somerleyton

5m SW of Great Yarmouth off the A143 • Best season: summer • Parking • Refreshments • Toilet facilities • Suitable for wheelchairs • Shop • Open Good Friday to 1st Oct, daily 10 a.m. - 6 p.m. • Entrance: £3, OAP and children £2

Visitors should not be put off at the entrance by the paraphernalia associated with the development of Fritton Lake as a country park. The large lake remains almost unspoilt and separate from the tea rooms and other commercial attractions. An unusual feature is a Victorian garden of about half an acre in the gardenesque style with irregular beds surrounded by clipped box hedges and filled with shrubs and herbaceous perennials that give a colourful display in the summer.

GLAVENSIDE 10

Letheringsett, Nr Holt, Norfolk. Tel: (0263) 713181
Mr and Mrs John Cozens-Hardy

1m W of Holt on A148 • Best seasons: spring and summer • Parking • Refreshments • Toilet facilities • Suitable for wheelchairs • Mill shop

• Working water mill overlooking the garden is open • Open daily, 10 a.m. - 6 p.m. • Entrance: £1, children 20p

A three-acre garden on the banks of the River Glaven which is crossed by a high arched bridge. Sloping lawns flank the river and there are further streams and pools, a small rock garden, rose garden and kitchen garden. In spite of the number of recently established trees and shrubs, this could not be described as a plantsman's garden but the flower beds are colourful and well-maintained. Five other gardens are open in Letheringsett usually for one day in April.

GOODERSTONE WATER GARDENS 11

Crow Hall, Gooderstone, King's Lynn, Norfolk. Tel: (0366) 21208
Mr and Mrs W.H. Knights

4m SW of Swaffham. E of Gooderstone village. Signposted. Gardens on opposite side of road to car park • Best season: summer • Parking • Tea and biscuits • Toilet facilities • Suitable for wheelchairs • Open weekdays, 10.30 a.m. - 6 p.m., Sun, 1.30 - 6 p.m. • Entrance: £1, children 30p

Somewhat difficult to find, the entrance to these gardens is along a concreted path between modern industrial buildings. A series of broad streams, with many recently-added trees and shrubs, and a small lake have been excavated in open woodland. These are bordered by a variety of aquatic plants and crossed by numerous wooden bridges connecting wide grassy paths. There is no great variety of design and one part of this extensive garden is very much like another but the effect is pleasing.

HALES HALL 12

Hales, Loddon, Norfolk. Tel: (050846) 395
Mr and Mrs T.E. Read

14m SE of Norwich, signposted off A146 • Parking • Plants for sale • Fifteenth-century Great Barn open as nursery • Open July and Aug, Wed, 2 - 5 p.m. Party visits at other times by arrangement. The nursery, Reads, is open Tues - Sat, 10 a.m. - 5 p.m. (closed 1 - 2 p.m.) and at other times by appointment. The owners plan to extend the garden open times • Entrance: collection box

A moat surrounds the remaining wing of a vast house of the early sixteenth century and a central lawn with well-planted borders backed by high brick walls. Work is continuing on the restoration of the garden after centuries of neglect. The owners specialise in growing rare and unusual perennial plants, and look after the National collection of citrus, figs and greenhouse grapes. The associated nurseries offer an extensive range of conservatory plants, vines, figs and mulberries.

HOLKHAM HALL ★ 13

Holkham, Wells-next-the-Sea, Norfolk. Tel: (0328) 710374
The Viscount Coke

2m W of Wells on A149 • Parking • Refreshments • Toilet facilities • Suitable for wheelchairs • Plants for sale in garden centre • Pottery and gift shop • House open • Terrace gardens open 27th May to 30th Sept, daily except Fri and Sat, 1.30 - 5 p.m. and Easter, May, Spring and Summer Bank Holiday Suns and Mons, 11.30 a.m. - 5 p.m. Garden centre gardens open throughout the year, Mon - Sat, 10 a.m. - 5 p.m., Sun 2 - 5 p.m. • Entrance: £2, OAP £1.75, children 75p (State rooms and terrace gardens). Discounts for pre-paid parties of 20 or more. Parking 50p. Garden centre gardens free

The vast park at Holkham was laid out originally by William Kent and later worked on by both Brown and Repton. The park is famous for its holm oaks and contains an arboretum with many rare trees and shrubs. On the west side of the house, lawns sweep down to the great lake. The terrace which fronts the south façade was added in 1854 but the scale of the house and park is so large that, from a distance at least, this does not seriously disrupt the vision of the two, in spite of the garish and inappropriate beds of polyantha roses. These formal beds flank a great fountain representing Perseus and Andromeda. The garden centre walled gardens in the grounds extend to over six acres, subdivided into six areas with perennial borders and the original greenhouses. Alpines, shrubs, perennials, herbs, roses, bedding and house plants for sale.

HOW HILL FARM ★ 14

Ludham, Norfolk. Tel: (069262) 558
Mr P.D.S. Boardman

2m W of Ludham. Follow signs to How Hill, Farm Garden S of How Hill • Parking • Refreshments • Toilet facilities • Partly suitable for wheelchairs • Open 12th May, 2 - 5 p.m. Parties at other times by arrangement • Entrance: £1.50, children free

This garden adjoins that of the How Hill Trust and is not open at the same time for fear of being overwhelmed. The garden around the farm is comparatively conventional except for a large Chusan palm planted in a dog cage from which it threatens to escape. Here, too, is a collection of over 50 varieties of *Ilex aquifolium* as well as many rare species of the holly genus. Over the road in the river valley is a rich combination of exotics mingled with native vegetation. Around a series of pools, banks of azaleas merge into reed beds, rhododendron species rise over thickets of fern and bramble, wild grasses skirt groves of the giant *Arundo donax*, with birches and conifers against a background of a recently-created three-acre broad, thick with water lilies. The soil in places is exceptionally acid, as low as ph 2.8, other parts vary up to ph 7.5 supporting a wide variety of trees and shrubs.

HOW HILL GARDEN ★ 15

Ludham, Norwich, Norfolk. Tel: (069262) 555
How Hill Trust

2m W of Ludham, signposted from village • Parking • Refreshments • Toilet facilities • Suitable for wheelchairs • Shop • House open • Garden open 28th April, 5th, 12th May, 2 - 6 p.m. • Entrance: £1.50, children 50p

There are two gardens here, a formal Edwardian garden terraced into rising ground overlooking the valley of the River Ant, and a separate water and woodland garden. The formal garden has herbaceous borders surrounded by high yew hedges forming a series of linked enclosures and backed by a great brick wall above which rises the dramatically-positioned house. Unfortunately the borders have lost much of their Edwardian character and a white border has gone entirely. Some informal planting leads towards the woodland in which the water garden is set, where quiet waterways, crossed by wooden bridges, are lined with native and exotic aquatic plants. This area is thickly planted with azaleas, highly colourful at the time of the spring open days.

MANNINGTON HALL ★ 16

Nr Saxthorpe, Norfolk. Tel: (026387) 4175
Lord and Lady Walpole

18m NW of Norwich, signposted at Saxthorpe off B1149 • Best season: June/July • Parking • Refreshments • Toilet facilities • Suitable for wheelchairs • Plants for sale • Shop • Open Easter Sun to Oct, Sun, 12 noon - 5 p.m., also May to Aug, Wed - Fri, 11 a.m. - 5 p.m. • Entrance: £2, OAP and students £1.50, children free

The romantic appearance of this garden of 20 acres is only matched in Norfolk by Elsing Hall where the house is also of the fifteenth century. Lawns run down to the moat which is crossed by a drawbridge to herbaceous borders backed by high walls of brick and flint. The moat also encloses a secret, scented garden in a design derived from one of the ceilings of the house. Outside the moat are borders of flowering shrubs flanking a Doric temple, and beyond are woodlands containing the ruins of a Saxon church. Within the walls of the former kitchen garden, a series of rose gardens has been planted following the design of gardens from medieval to modern times and featuring roses popular at each period. A lake, woods and meadowland with extensive walls are other features.

NORFOLK LAVENDER LTD 17

Caley Mill, Heacham, King's Lynn, Norfolk. Tel: (0485) 70384
Norfolk Lavender Ltd

13m N of King's Lynn on A149 • Best season: June to Sept • Parking • Refreshments • Toilet facilities • Suitable for wheelchairs • Plants for sale • Shop • Open all year except 25th Dec, 10 a.m. - 5 p.m. • Entrance: free

Here is the National collection of lavenders, displaying all the species and varieties which can be grown in this country, set in two acres around a Gothic watermill on the banks of the Heacham river. The fields of lavender are a fine sight in July and August, and there is also a rose garden and a herb garden.

OXBURGH HALL 18

Oxborough, Swaffham, Norfolk. Tel: (036621) 258
The National Trust

7m SW of Swaffham off A134 • Parking • Refreshments • Toilet facilities • Suitable for wheelchairs • Plants for sale • Shop • House open 30th March to Sept, daily except Thurs and Fri, 1.30 - 5.30 p.m., Bank Holiday Mons, 11 a.m. - 5.30 p.m. Oct, Sat and Sun, 1.30 - 5.30 p.m. • Entrance: £3.30

The neat gardens of this fine moated house, carefully tended by the National Trust, lack the romantic appeal of Elsing or Rainthorpe. There are some good trees, pleasant lawns, and well-stocked herbaceous borders. On the north side of the house is a parterre with bedding plants in colour masses, said to be of French design but somewhat modest by French standards and, while worth inspecting, somehow seeming inappropriate here.

THE PLANTATION GARDEN 19

Earlham Road, Norwich, Norfolk.
Tel: (0603) 713174 (Mr John Watson)
Plantation Garden Preservation Trust

Entrance off Earlham Road, shared with hotel immediately to W of R.C. cathedral • Best season: summer • Suitable for wheelchairs • Open by appointment • Entrance: donations welcome

Designed by the architect Edward Boardman in the 1850s this garden shows the possible influence of Sir Charles Barry's 'Shrublands' near Ipswich. It was formed in a narrow steep-sided chalk quarry not far from the centre of Norwich. Now crowded around with mature trees, lawns cover the quarry floor reached by an extraordinary series of terraces constructed of a jumble of architectural fragments and slag, and other industrial waste. The centre piece is a tall, multi-tiered fountain. Flower beds with typical Victorian bedding have been reinstated although more, now covered by grass, have yet to be recovered. Dedicated volunteers have made themselves responsible for restoration and although there is still much to do, this has been revealed as a most remarkable garden which will merit a higher rating in due course.

RAINTHORPE HALL GARDENS ★ 20

Tasburgh, Norwich, Norfolk. Tel: (0508) 470618
Mr G.F. Hastings

8m S of Norwich off A140. At Newton Flotman fork right on Flordon Road by garage, on 1m to red brick gates on left • Best season: May to Sept • Parking • Refreshments • Toilet facilities • Suitable for wheelchairs • Plants for sale • House open by appointment only • Gardens open Easter to Oct, Wed, Sat, Sun and Bank Holiday Mon, 10 a.m. - 5 p.m. • Entrance: £1.50, OAP and children 75p

The gardens here at one of the most beautiful houses in Norfolk extend to five acres. Of the sixteenth-century garden there are some remains in the knot garden, the nuttery, and an ancient yew tree. The lawn runs down to the River Tas and there is a recently developed conservation lake. There are many fine and rare trees and a collection of bamboos. What this garden lacks in overall cohesion of design, it makes up for in the peace and beauty of its setting.

RAVENINGHAM HALL ★ 21

Raveningham, Norwich, Norfolk. Tel: (050846) 206/222
Sir Nicholas Bacon

14m SE of Norwich off A140, left at Hales on B1136, then 1st right • Parking • Refreshments • Toilet facilities • Suitable for wheelchairs • Plants for sale • Open April to Sept, Suns and Bank Holidays, 2 - 5 p.m. Nursery open daily, 9 a.m. - 4 p.m. • Entrance: £1.50, children free

This garden, in a fine landscaped park, has a rich variety of trees, shrubs and herbaceous plants dating from the eighteenth century to the present day. There is a large collection of galanthus species and varieties. The walled kitchen garden and greenhouses are still in use, and the associated nurseries offer an exceptional range of shrubs, climbers and herbaceous plants, many rarely available elsewhere. A new arboretum is currently being developed.

SANDRINGHAM HOUSE ★ 22

Sandringham, King's Lynn, Norfolk. Tel: (0553) 772675
H.M. The Queen

9m NE of King's Lynn on B1440 near Sandringham Church • Best seasons: spring and autumn • Parking • Refreshments in restaurant and cafeteria • Toilet facilities • Suitable for wheelchairs • Plants for sale • Shop • House open as garden but closed 22nd July to 10th Aug • Ranger's Interpretation Centre and country park • Garden open 21st April to Sept (except 22nd July to 10th Aug), Sun - Thurs, 11 a.m. (12 noon on Sun) - 4.45 p.m. • Entrance: £1.70, OAP £1.30, children £1 (house and grounds £2.20, OAP £1.70, children £1.40)

The house stands among broad lawns with an outer belt of woodland through which a path runs past plantings of camellias, hydrangeas, cornus, magnolias and rhododendrons with some fine specimen trees including *Davidia involucrata* and *Cercidiphyllum japonicum*. The path passes the magnificent cast and wrought iron 'Norwich Gates' of 1862. In the open lawn are specimen oaks planted by Queen Victoria and other members of the royal family. To the south-west of the house is the upper lake whose eastern side is built up into a massive rock garden using blocks of the local carstone, and now largely planted with dwarf conifers. Below the rock garden, opening onto the lake, is a cavernous grotto, intended as a boathouse, while above is a small summerhouse built for Queen Alexandra. There are thick plantings of hostas, agapanthus and various moisture-loving plants around the margin of the lake. The path passes between the upper and largest lower lake set in wooded surroundings. To the north of the house is a garden designed by Sir Geoffrey Jellicoe for King Georve VI. A long series of beds is surrounded by box hedges and divided by gravel and grass paths and flanked by avenues of pleached lime, one of which is centred on a gold-plated statue of a Buddhist divinity.

SHERINGHAM PARK ★ 23

Upper Sheringham, Norfolk. Tel: (0263) 823778
The National Trust

4m NE of Holt off A148 • Best season: May/June • Parking: £2 per car to include all occupants • Refreshments at Felbrigg Hall (also NT) during their opening hours (see entry) • Partly suitable for wheelchairs • Dogs on lead in park • House occupied, but limited access to some rooms by appointment in writing, April to Sept only • Park open daily, dawn – dusk • Entrance: £2 per car inc. parking

Sheringham Park stands in a secluded valley at the edge of the Cromer/Holt ridge, close to the sea but protected from its winds by steep wooded hills. Both house and park are now the property of the National Trust although the house remains in private occupation. The park is remarkable not only for its great beauty and spectacular views but also for an extensive collection of rhododendrons which thrive in the acid soil. Crowning an eminence is a classical temple based on a design by Repton and erected to mark the 60th birthday of Mr Thomas Upcher, the last descendant of the original owner to live at Sheringham. Since coming into its ownership the Trust has begun to remove some inappropriate twentieth-century planting and to restore the original form of the garden, the favourite and best-preserved work of Repton.

THRIGBY WILDLIFE GARDENS 24

Thrigby Hall, Filby, Great Yarmouth, Norfolk. Tel: (0493) 369477
Mr K.J. Sims

6m NW of Great Yarmouth, signposted at Filby on A1064 • Best season: summer • Parking • Refreshments • Toilet facilities • Suitable for wheelchairs • Shop • Open daily, 10 a.m. - 5 p.m. or dusk • Entrance: £3, OAP, £2, children £1.50

The chief attraction of these gardens is a collection of Chinese plants arranged to form the landscape of the Willow Pattern plate, complete with pagodas and bridges across a small lake. Complementing a collection of Asiatic animals, the plants are those particularly associated with temple gardens and include *Gingko biloba*, *Pinus parviflora*, *Paeonia suffruticosa*, *Nandina domestica* and *Chimonobambusa quadrangularis*, set against a background of willows of many species. Planted 1989 but interesting even in an immature state.

WRETHAM LODGE ★ 25

East Wretham, Thetford, Norfolk. Tel: (095382) 366
Mrs A. Hoellering

6m NE of Thetford. Left by village sign, right at crossroads then bear left • Best season: May to July • Parking • Refreshments • Toilet facilities • Suitable for wheelchairs • Plants for sale • Open 5th, 12th May, 30th June, 7th July, 2.30 - 5.30 p.m. and by appointment • Entrance: £1, children 50p

Extensive lawns surround the handsome flint-faced former rectory set in its own walled park. There are herbaceous borders and hundreds of old, species and climbing roses massed in informal beds or covering high flint walls. Walls surround the kitchen garden supporting espalier and fan-trained fruit trees - pears, cherries and apricots. There is a vine house and a variety of figs. Roses and herbaceous plants are mixed with the vegetables and in the spring there is a display of many species of tulip. A wide grassy walk runs round the park through a range of mature and recently established trees where spring-flowering bulbs are naturalised, with a mass display of bluebells in May.

GARDENS OPEN RARELY

The following gardens are open to the public on three days or less in the year, although they may also be open by appointment if this is stated in the text. For details see individual entry.

April 28 How Hill Garden; **May 5** How Hill Garden; **May 12** How Hill Farm; How Hill Garden; **June 16** Besthorpe Hall; **June 30** Elsing Hall; **July 7** Elsing Hall; **July 14** Besthorpe Hall.

NORTHAMPTONSHIRE

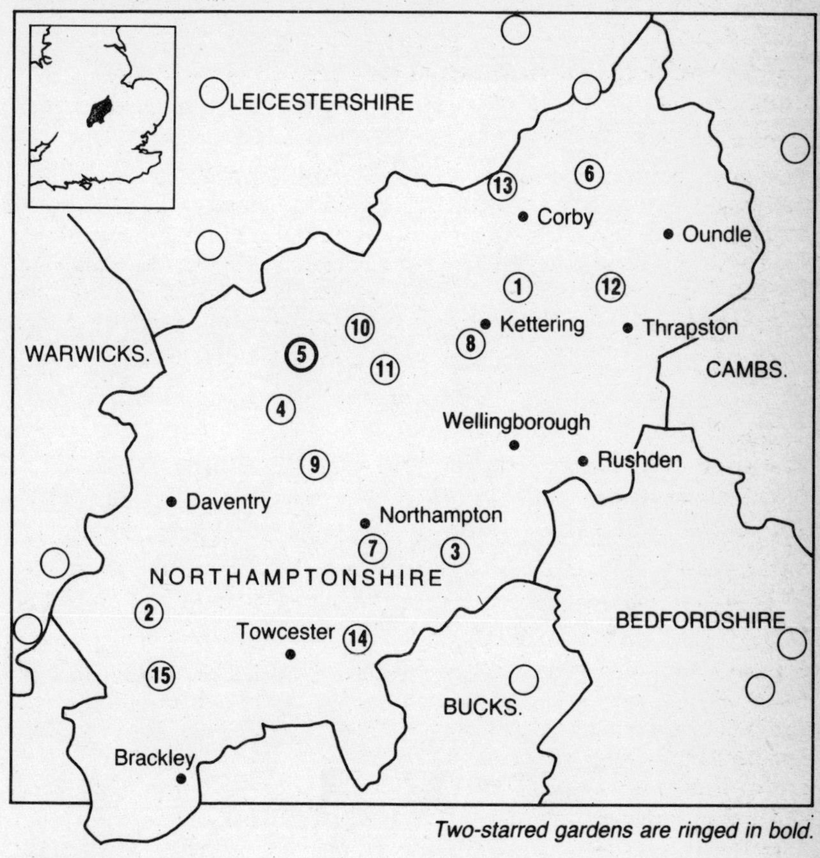

Two-starred gardens are ringed in bold.

BOUGHTON HOUSE GARDEN 1

Kettering, Northamptonshire. Tel: (0536) 515731
The Duke and Duchess of Buccleuch and Queensberry

On A43, N of Kettering, between Weekley and Geddington • Parking • Refreshments weekends and Aug • Toilet facilities • Partly suitable for wheelchairs • Dogs on lead • Plants for sale • Shop • House open (times differ from garden) • Garden open 27th April to Sept, daily except Fri, 2 - 5 p.m. • Entrance: £1, children 50p

Magnificent and extensive sixteenth/seventeenth-century manor house with collections of paintings, tapestries, furniture, porcelain, etc., and with grounds laid out by Bridgeman rather than gardens surrounding. An outstanding rectangular lily pond, nature walks and woodland adventure play area in a working estate. An unusual relic is a portable summerhouse or tea house made of oil-cloth over a wooden framework whose roof interior still retains original decoration. Excellent selection of pot, herbaceous and shrub plants at nursery garden. Good choice for a family visit with historic house, walks, play area and plants for sale. No formal gardens.

CANONS ASHBY HOUSE ★ 2

Woodford Halse, Nr Daventry, Northamptonshire.
Tel: (0327) 860044
The National Trust

6m S of Daventry on the B4525 Northampton - Banbury road • Parking 200 yards from house. Disabled ring in advance and park near house • Refreshments • Toilet facilities • Suitable for wheelchairs, two wheelchairs available. Taped guide for blind visitors • Dogs on lead in Home Paddock only • House open • Garden open April to Oct, Wed - Sun and Bank Holiday Mon, 1 - 5.30 p.m. or dusk if earlier. Last admission 5 p.m. • Entrance: free (garden only), £2.50, children £1.20 (house and gardens)

This well-maintained garden is being extensively restored by the National Trust. Formal with axial arrangements of paths and terraces, high stone walls, lawns and gateways, it dates almost entirely from the beginning of the eighteenth century. Borders with majestic plants such as acanthus and giant thistles. Yew court with fine topiary. Old varieties of pear, apple, plum trees and soft fruit. Cedar planted in 1715. Espaliers grown from original stock planted by Edward Dryden whose family has owned the house since the sixteenth century.

CASTLE ASHBY GARDENS ★ 3

Castle Ashby, Northamptonshire. Tel: (060129) 234
The Marquess of Northampton

5m E of Northampton, between A45 Northampton - Wellingborough road and A428 Northampton - Bedford road • Best season: March to May • Parking • Refreshments at farm shop in village, 400 yards • Suitable for wheelchairs, paths not very smooth • Dogs on lead • Plants rarely for sale • Farm shop in village • House open and tours for parties by appointment during 'Country Fair', 1st week July, check by phone • Gardens open daily, 10 a.m. - 6 p.m., with occasional closures for events • Entrance: £1, OAP and children 50p. (Tickets from machine when car park unattended)

Originally Elizabethan, then a park landscaped by 'Capability' Brown, and later a Matthew Digby Wyatt Terrace, Italian garden and arboretum, Castle Ashby is now primarily an 'all function centre' for company and private events. There is public access to most of the gardens (except East terrace although good views from near the church) which present a glorious combination of views. A nature walk past mature trees leads over a terracotta bridge and to the 'knucklebone arbour', a summerhouse with what are probably sheep and deer knuckles set in the floor. Among the wild and naturalised plants are carpets of aconites and snowdrops, winter heliotrope, butterbur, daffodils, bluebells, wood anemones, celandines, bush vetch, wood buttercups and a wide selection of lake and pondside plants. Features include an orangery and archway greenhouses, topiary and well-planted large vases. Restoration of the garden and its architectural features is continuing.

COTON MANOR GARDENS 4

Ravensthorpe, Northamptonshire. Tel: (0604) 740219
Cdr H. Pasley-Tyler

10m N of Northampton, signs A428 and A50 • Parking • Home-made teas • Toilet facilities • Partly suitable for wheelchairs • Dogs on lead • Unusual plants and shrubs for sale • Shop • Open Easter to Sept, Sun and Bank Holidays, June to Aug, Wed, 2 – 6 p.m. • Entrance: £2.50, OAP £2, children 50p

A carefully planned and tended garden on several sloped acres which provide colour and interest throughout the year. There is an excellent variety of foliage plants, herbaceous borders, lawns and hedges plus lakes with ornamental waterfowl. It is a garden which will appeal most to those seeking inspiration for their own medium-sized gardens, and those who enjoy waterfowl.

COTTESBROOKE HALL ★★ 5

Cottesbrooke, Northampton, Northamptonshire. Tel: (060124) 808
Captain and Mrs J. Macdonald-Buchanan

10m N of Northampton between A50 and A508 • Parking • Toilet facilities • Suitable for wheelchairs • Plants for sale • House open • Garden open 6th June to 26th Sept, Thurs only, also Bank Holiday 26th Aug, 2 – 5.30 p.m. Last admission 5 p.m. • Entrance: £1.50, children 75p (£3.50 house and gardens). Parties by appointment when possible

An excellently-maintained formal garden surrounding a fine Queen Anne house, set in a large park (also open) with lakes and a stream, vistas and avenues. Design and planting work by Edward Schultz, Geoffrey Jellicoe, Sylvia Crowe and the late Macdonald-Buchanan is being continued by the present owners and their head gardener, Mrs Daw. The result is a series of delightful enclosed courtyards and gardens around the house with superb borders, urns and statues. The spinney garden is at its best in spring with bulbs and azaleas. New trees, borders, yew hedges, walls, gates and vistas are still being added. Beyond the thatched Wendy house the wild garden surrounds a series of small lakes and cascades, with azaleas, rhododendrons, acers, cherries, spring bulbs and wild flowers. The magnolia, cherry and acer collections and the ancient cedars are notable. The house (possibly the model for Jane Austen's *Mansfield Park*) is open to the public for the first time in 1991.

DEENE PARK 6

Corby, Northamptonshire. Tel: (078085) 278/223
Mr Edmund Brudenell

6m N of Corby off A43 Kettering to Stamford road • Parking • Teas • Toilet facilities • Partly suitable for wheelchairs • Dogs in car park only • Shop • House open • Garden open June to Aug, Sun, 2 - 5 p.m. and Bank Holiday Suns and Mons, Easter to Aug. Groups by appointment • Entrance: £3, children £1, inc. house

The glory of Deene, which was created by generations of the Brudenell family, is its trees. Fine mature specimens and groups fringe the formal areas and frame tranquil and enchanting views of the parkland and countryside. Main features of its garden are the long borders, old-fashioned roses and the lake. The gardens, parkland, church and house together provide a delightful, interesting and relaxing afternoon for visitors in what was the home of the Earl of Cardigan who led the Charge of the Light Brigade in 1854.

DELAPRE ABBEY 7

London Road, Northampton, Northamptonshire. Tel: (0604) 762129
Northampton Borough Council Leisure Department

1m S of Northampton on A508 • Best season: summer • Parking • Toilet facilities • Suitable for wheelchairs • Dogs on lead • House open. Parts of building shown on Thurs throughout year after 2 p.m. (phone in advance to confirm) • Garden open daily, early March to Sept, 10 a.m. - sunset. Rest of park continuously • Entrance: free

Largely rebuilt in the seventeenth century, the house on the site of the former nunnery of St Mary of the Meadow, together with 500 acres of land, passed into public ownership in 1946. With improving standards of maintenance (although some associated buildings are in need of repair) it is still possible to glimpse the hey-day of a lovely garden. Beyond the walled former kitchen garden, and well-tended lawns, perennial, annual and rose beds and an eighteenth-century thatched game larder, are walks through the wilderness garden with fine trees, shrubberies and lily ponds. There are lakes and a golf course in the park, and at the roadside close to the entrance one of the country's Queen Eleanor Crosses commemorates the funeral procession in 1290 of Edward I's queen.

31 DERWENT CRESCENT 8

Kettering, Northamptonshire. Tel: (0536) 520070
Mr and Mrs B.J. Mitchell

W side of Kettering, off A43 to Northampton. Travelling away from Kettering town centre, turn right along Bowhill after going under railway bridge, then 1st right, 1st right, 1st left or phone for instructions • Parking on street • Teas, proceeds to charity • *Toilet facilities* • *Plants for sale occasionally, proceeds to charity* • *Open by appointment* • *Entrance: 50p, children 20p*

Strictly for the plantsperson, but an absolute jewel for herbaceous, bulb, alpine and fern enthusiasts. Owners' knowledge of their plants and propagation methods (over 33 years experience here) is enormous and enthusiastically passed on to satisfy the curiosity of visitors.

HOLDENBY HOUSE GARDENS 9

Holdenby, Northampton, Northamptonshire. Tel: (0604) 770241
Mr and Mrs James Lowther

7m W of Northampton, signposted A40 and A428 • *Parking* • *Refreshments: teas. Meals by appointment* • *Toilet facilities* • *Partly suitable for wheelchairs* • *Dogs on lead* • *Plants and herbs for sale* • *Shop inc. croquet mallet hire* • *House open Bank Holiday Mons* • *Gardens open July to Aug, Thurs, 2 - 6 p.m., Sun, Bank Holidays, Easter to Sept, 2 - 6 p.m. Groups by appointment* • *Entrance: £2, children £1*

Only grassed terraces and a fish pond remain of the extensive Elizabethan garden which surrounded the vast mansion built by Elizabeth I's chancellor, Sir Christopher Hatton, in the late sixteenth century. The recent gardens still link the surviving remnant of the house (only one eighth of its former size) to its past, especially the delightful Elizabethan garden, planted in 1980 by Rosemary Verey as a miniature replica of Hatton's original centrepiece, using only plants available in the 1580s. Other features include the fragrant border, part of the nineteenth-century garden also replanted by Mrs Verey. The rare breeds and falcons displayed in the old kitchen garden, and occasional events in the gardens, attract school and family visits.

KELMARSH HALL 10

Kelmarsh, Northampton, Northamptonshire. Tel: (060128) 276
Miss C.V. Lancaster

On A508 5m S of Market Harborough, 11m N of Northampton • *Best season: spring* • *Parking* • *Refreshments* • *Toilet facilities* • *Dogs on lead* • *Plants and produce for sale occasionally* • *James Gibb's Palladian house open with escorted visits* • *Garden open Easter to Aug, Sun and Bank Holidays, 2.15 - 5 p.m., April and Sept, by appointment (minimum 12 persons)* • *Entrance £1.50, OAP and children over 12 £1, children under 12 free (house and gardens)*

The drive is an avenue of lime trees bordering the park of 20 acres where a herd of rare British white cattle graze. Maze-like close-clipped box and yew hedges and colonnades lead to secret and quiet gardens with views of a lake. There are herbaceous borders and a rose garden. Seats are provided at vantage points and spring flowers and rhododendrons are special features. Keen gardeners will probably wish to visit only if they are combining it with a tour of the house.

LAMPORT HALL GARDEN 11

Lamport Hall, Northampton, Northamptonshire. Tel: (060128) 272
Lamport Hall Trust

8m N of Northampton on A508 • Parking • Refreshments • Toilet facilities • Suitable for wheelchairs • Dogs on lead • Shop • House open • Garden open Easter to Sept, Sun and Bank Holidays, July and Aug also Thurs, 2.15 - 5.15 p.m. Coach parties/groups at any time by arrangement • Entrance: £2.50, OAP £2, children £1 (house and gardens)

The main attraction here is Lamport Hall itself, now essentially an event (dog shows, antique fairs) and school study centre. Grounds initially laid out by Gilbert Clarke in 1655 are in the process of restoration and provide a pleasant setting, but at this stage will mainly interest those who want to follow the progress of restoration. Ultimately the local ironstone rock garden and the refurbished nineteenth-century Italian garden with its fine urns should be most attractive. Also public access to the attractive park.

THE OLD RECTORY ★ 12

Sudborough, Northamptonshire. Tel: (08012) 3247
Mr and Mrs Anthony Huntington

Off A6116 Corby - Thrapton road • Best season: June/July • Teas by prior request • Toilet facilities • Suitable for wheelchairs • Plants for sale occasionally • Open by appointment and 30th June, 2 - 6 p.m. for charity • Entrance: £1

Delightful three-acre rectory garden in beautiful stone and thatch village. Much has been accomplished in last six years to develop a garden of interest to all. Copious planting in the mixed borders, around the pond and with climbers. Vegetable garden fascinating, small beds with brick paths leading to a central wrought-iron arbour. Standard roses and gooseberries and tents of runner beans provide vertical features. A wilder garden along the stream completes the picture, while excellent labelling throughout will help visitors keen to improve their knowledge of plants.

ROCKINGHAM CASTLE GARDENS 13

Corby, Northamptonshire. Tel: (0536) 770240
Commander Michael Saunders Watson and family

2m N of Corby on A6003. Signposted • Best season: June • Parking. Disabled may park near entrance • Teas • Toilet facilities • Partly suitable for wheelchairs • Dogs on lead • Shop • House open • Garden open Easter Sun to Sept, Sun and Thurs, Bank Holiday Mons and the Tues following, also Tues in Aug, 1.30 - 5.30 p.m. Groups by appointment at other times • Entrance: £2.70, children £1.40 (castle and grounds)

Rockingham sits on a hilltop fortress site with stunning views of three counties. It has remnants of all periods of its 800-year history. The garden's major features range from formal seventeenth-century terraces and yew hedges to the romantic wild garden of the nineteenth century. There is a circular rose garden surrounded by a yew hedge and also good herbaceous borders. The wild garden was replanted with advice from Kew Gardens in the late 1960s and it includes over 200 species of trees and shrubs. The result is a delightful blend of form, colour, light and shade. Recommended for group/family outings and for those who combine interest in horticulture with history.

STOKE PARK 14

Stoke Bruerne, Towcester, Northampton, Northamptonshire.
Tel: (0604) 862172
Mr R.E. Chancellor

Clearly signposted from A5, N of Milton Keynes. ¼m W of village, opposite junction to Blisworth • Best season: summer • Parking • Suitable for wheelchairs • Dogs on lead • Pavilion open • Garden open June to Aug, weekends and Aug Bank Holiday, 2 - 6 p.m., rest of year by appointment • Entrance: £1

Stoke Park was the first house to display the Palladian plan in Britain and now (due to a fire) only the splendid pavilions with colonnaded walls remain. The outline of the original Italianate garden by Inigo Jones can be seen below the lawn so the site is of particular interest to students of historical gardens. However, the svelte lawns, herbaceous borders and a large fountain basin with water lilies are the features at Stoke Park which will be enjoyed by all who visit.

SULGRAVE MANOR 15

Sulgrave, Northamptonshire. Tel: (029576) 205
Trustees, endowed by Colonial Dames of America

7m NE of Banbury, 1m off B4525 • Parking • Refreshments sometimes available, otherwise at Thatched House Hotel opposite • Toilet facilities • House open • Garden open Feb only to pre-booked parties of 12 or more, March, daily except Wed, 10.30 a.m. - 1 p.m., 2 - 4 p.m., April to Sept, daily except Wed, 10.30 a.m. - 1 p.m., 2 - 5.30 p.m., Oct to Dec, daily except Wed, 10.30 a.m. - 1 p.m., 2 - 4 p.m. Closed 25th and 26th Dec • Entrance: £2.50, children £1.25 (house and garden). Discounts for parties of 12 or more

American visitors are in the majority here, as the house was built in 1560 by a distant ancestor of George Washington. It was acquired in 1914 and restored after World War I, with the benefit of U.S. generosity. The gardens, like the house, bear little relation to their sixteenth-century condition, but the rose garden, herb garden, herbaceous borders and kitchen garden are attractive examples of their kind.

GARDENS OPEN RARELY

The following garden is open to the public on three days or less in the year, although it may also be open by appointment. For details see individual entry.
June 30 The Old Rectory.

NORTHUMBERLAND

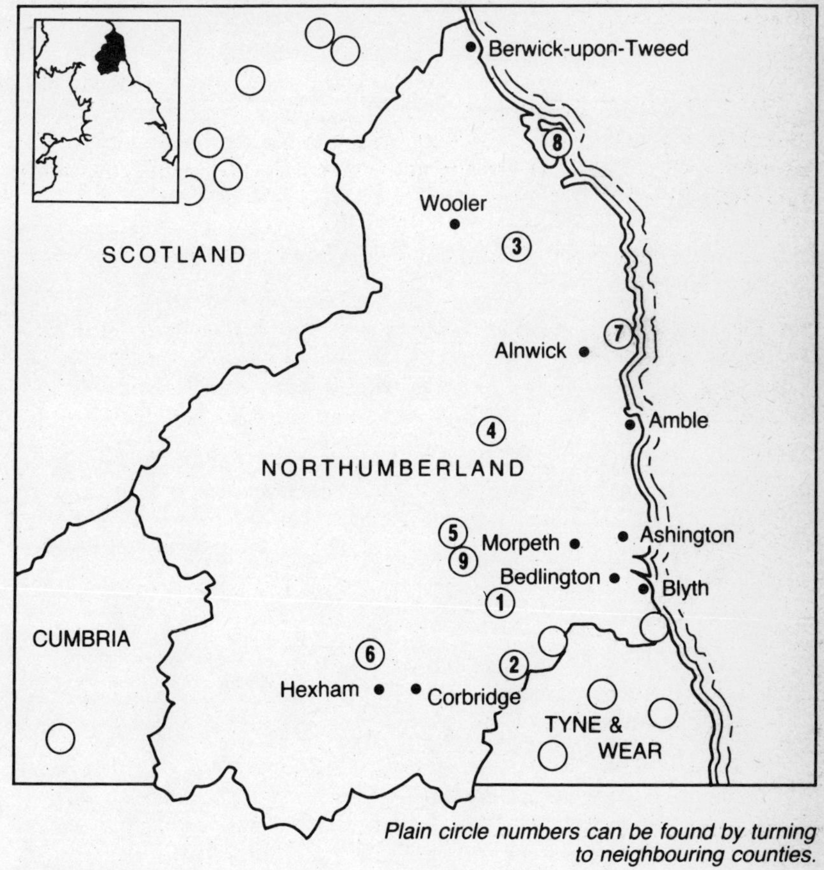

Plain circle numbers can be found by turning to neighbouring counties.

BELSAY HALL ★ 1

Belsay, Nr Newcastle-upon-Tyne, Northumberland. Tel: (0661) 881636
Sir Stephen Middleton

14m NW of Newcastle on A696 • Parking. Coaches please notify in advance • Refreshments: drinks machine, picnic area • Toilet facilities inc. disabled • Suitable for wheelchairs (available on loan) • Dogs on lead • Shop • House open • Garden open Good Friday to Sept, daily, 10 a.m. – 6 p.m., Oct to Easter, daily except Mon, 10 a.m. – 4 p.m. • Entrance: £1.50, concessions £1.10, children 75p

The gardens are the creation of two men who between them owned the Hall in succession from 1795 to 1933. Sir Charles Monck built a severe neo-classical mansion with formal terraces leading through woods to a 'garden' inside the quarry from which the house was built. His grandson took over in 1867, adding Victorian features. Both were discerning plantsmen. The result is a collection of rare, mature and exotic specimens in a fascinating sequence. The terrace looks across to massed early rhododendrons. Other areas (rose garden, magnolia terrace, winter-flowering heathers) lead to woods, a wild meadow and the quarry garden itself. Reminiscent of the ancient Greek quarries in Syracuse, it was carefully contrived and stocked to achieve a wild romantic effect and give shelter to some remarkable specimens.

BRADLEY GARDENS NURSERY 2

Sled Lane, Wylam, Northumberland. Tel: (0661) 852176
Bradley Gardens Nursery

10m W of Newcastle off A695 between Crawcrook and Wylam (well signposted) • Parking • Refreshments planned for 1991 • Toilet facilities • Suitable for wheelchairs • Dogs on lead • Plants for sale • Open mid-March to mid-Oct, Mon - Fri, 10 a.m. - 4 p.m., Sat and Sun, 9 a.m. - 5 p.m. • Entrance: free

This walled garden has particular appeal for the plantsperson. It is stocked at present with a variety of Victorian apple trees, lavenders and an extensive collection of some 200 herbs. Fresh cut herbs are sold to both public and catering trades. There are also some Victorian cottage-garden plants such as aquilegias.

CHILLINGHAM CASTLE 3

Chillingham, Northumberland. Tel: (06685) 359/390
Sir Humphry Wakefield

12m NNW of Alnwick between A1 (signed), A697, B6346 and B6348 • Best seasons: spring, midsummer • Parking • Teas • Toilet facilities • Shop • House open • Gardens open 29th March to 1st April and May to Sept, daily except Tues, 1.30 - 5 p.m. • Entrance: £2.20, OAP £1.75, children over 5 £1.50, parties of 20 or more £1.50 per person (increased rates during Flower Festival 12th to 14th July)

Not easy to find but well worth an effort, this one-time home of the Grey family is being vigorously restored along with the grounds landscaped by Wyatville (of Hampton Court fame). The Elizabethan-style walled garden has been virtually excavated by Isobel Murray to expose its intricate pattern of clipped yew and box (enlivened by scarlet tropaeolum), a central avenue and flourishing borders around the walls. Outside are lawns and a rock garden, delightful woodland and lakeside walks through drifts of snowdrops and spring displays of daffodils, bluebells and, later, rhododendrons.

CRAGSIDE HOUSE AND COUNTRY PARK 4

Rothbury, Morpeth, Northumberland. Tel: (0669) 20333
The National Trust

14m SW of Alnwick off A697 between B6341 and B6344 • Best season: early summer • Parking • Refreshments in Visitor's Centre. Picnics by Nelly's Moss Lakes • Toilet facilities inc. disabled • Partly suitable for wheelchairs • Dogs on lead in grounds only • House open 29th March to Oct, daily except Mon but open Bank Holiday Mons, 1 - 5.30 p.m. Last admission 5 p.m. • Park open 29th March to Oct, daily except Mon (but open Bank Holiday Mon), 10.30 a.m. - 7 p.m., Nov to March 1992, Sat and Sun, 10.30 a.m. - 4 p.m. • Entrance: £2 (house and park £3.50)

Lord Armstrong, the greatest of Victorian engineers, clothed this hillside above the Coquet Valley with millions of trees and shrubs as the setting for a house designed by Shaw and Norman (the first ever lit by hydro-electricity) that was then the wonder of the world. Now properly managed, the 900-acre park with its 40 miles of driveways and rambling paths is a mass of rhododendrons in June. Higher up there are enclaves of bare rock and heather, a reminder of the original state of the land, with lovely views over wooded valleys under broad Northumbrian skies. The man-made lakes, hydro-electric and hydraulic systems (also on view) add another dimension and a tribute to Victorian vigour and ingenuity at its peak.

HERTERTON HOUSE 5

Hartington, Cambo, Morpeth, Northumberland. Tel: (067074) 278
Frank and Marjorie Lawley

2m N of Cambo on B6342 • Best season: summer • Parking • Toilet facilities • Plants for sale • Open April to Oct, daily except Tues and Thurs, 1.30 - 5.30 p.m. • Entrance: 75p

The Lawleys took over this land and near-derelict Elizabethan building, with commanding views over picturesque upper Northumberland, in 1976. With vision and skill they have created three distinct areas. In front, a winter garden with tranquil vistas; alongside, a cloistered 'monastic' knot garden of mainly medicinal, occult and dye-producing herbs; and to the rear, their most impressive achievement, a flower garden. This is a carefully designed Persian carpet, with perceptively mingled hardly flowers chosen with an artist's eye. Many are unusual traditional plants (including many species from the wild) that flourish within the newly-built sheltering walls. A gem of a place, of great interest to the plantsperson.

HEXHAM HERBS ★ 6

The Chesters Walled Garden, Humshaugh, Nr Hexham, Northumberland. Tel: (0434) 681483
Kevin and Susie White

5m N of Hexham, ½m W of Chollerford on B6318 • Best season: March to Sept • Parking • Refreshments: planned • Toilet facilities: planned • Suitable for wheelchairs • Plants for sale • Shop • Open March to Nov, daily, 10 a.m. – 5 p.m., reduced hours in winter. Also by appointment • Entrance: 50p

The tall brick walls of the old kitchen garden slope gently south from the very line of Hadrian's Wall, echoing the Roman forts that lie to east and west. Within these ramparts, still with vestiges of the Victorian glasshouses and heating system, the Whites have fashioned a superb herb collection, including most fittingly a unique Roman garden with plants (myrtle, etc.) identified by archaeologists through pollen analysis. A major feature is the national NCCPG thyme bank. A rose garden (over 60 species), extensive herbaceous sections (some 800 varieties) and terraced lawns against an architectural backdrop (Norman Shaw's Chesters mansion) fill out this splendid intriguing 'fort'. A labelled wildflower meadow and woodland walk with pond are now open.

HOWICK HALL ★ 7

Howick, Northumberland. Tel: (066577) 285
Sir Charles Baring (Howick Hall Trust)

5m NE of Alnwick off B1339 • Best season: spring/summer • Parking • Toilet facilities • Partly suitable for wheelchairs • Dogs on lead • Open Easter to Oct, 2 – 7 p.m. • Entrance: £1, children and concessions 50p

The accident of woodland which sheltered this site from the blasts of the North Sea enabled Lord and Lady Grey to come here during World War 1 and start building an amazing collection of tender plants which would do credit to a Scottish west coast garden. The central terrace has a pool and excellent borders and the lawns run down through feature shrubs to a stream. Winding paths lead through shrubbery or parkland to the 'silver wood', under whose magnificent trees one passes among numerous fine shrubs and woodland flowers given to Earl and Lady Grey for their silver wedding in the 1930s. There are good varieties of rhododenron and azalea, and outstanding species hydrangea (*H. villosa*) apart from unusual flower varieties. A large pond-side garden is developing and an arboretum. Labelling is scarce but a catalogue is in preparation. This is a plantsperson's garden but there are many delights for the aesthete such as the agapanthus of varying blues on the terrace.

KIRKLEY HALL COLLEGE

(see Tyne and Wear)

LINDISFARNE CASTLE 8

Holy Island, Berwick-upon-Tweed, Northumberland.
Tel: (0289) 89244
The National Trust

On Holy Island, 6m E of the A1 across a causeway at low tide only. Tide tables printed in local papers and displayed at causeway. Access to garden on foot only, ½m from parking area • Parking by castle ½m from garden • Refreshments in village • Dogs on lead as far as Lower Battery only • National Trust shop in village • Castle open. Visitors must leave bulky objects inc. back-packs in entrance • Open April to Sept, daily except Fri, 1 - 5.30 p.m. Last admission 5 p.m. Oct, Wed, Sat and Sun, 1 - 5.30 p.m. Last admission 5 p.m. Admission to the garden is only permitted when a gardener is in attendance. • Entrance: £2.80 (inc. castle)

This garden must be unique both in design and setting. Its existence on Holy Island off the coast of Northumberland came about like this: in 1901 Edward Hudson, owner and founder of *Country Life*, on holiday saw the ruins of the castle, rapidly purchased them from their owner, the Crown, and invited the young architect Lutyens to rebuild. Lutyens had been introduced to Hudson by his friend Gertrude Jekyll. The latter advised Hudson to have a low walled garden built to the north of the castle approached by a walk across the fields. This was done in 1911. In the patterned paving, a selection of Jekyll's favourite plants were planted in gradations of colour. The original plans were recently discovered in a Californian collection and recreated by the Trust and the University of Durham. The result is not entirely entrancing. The garden is at its best in summer, as was Hudson's intention, since he asked Jekyll to design a holiday garden for August.

WALLINGTON ★ 9

Cambo, Morpeth, Northumberland. Tel: (067074) 283
The National Trust

20m W of Newcastle off A696 (signed on B6342) • Best season: spring - autumn • Parking • Refreshments: coffee, lunch and teas in Clock Tower Restaurant (067074) 274. Picnics in car park • Toilet facilities inc. disabled • Suitable for wheelchairs • Dogs on lead in garden, free in grounds • Shop • House and children's museum open 29th March to Oct, daily, except Tues, 1 - 5.30 p.m. Last admission 5 p.m. • Walled garden open 29th March to Sept, daily, 10.30 a.m. - 7 p.m., Oct to March 1992, daily, 10.30 a.m. - 4 p.m. Grounds open all year round during daylight hours • Entrance: £1.50 (house and grounds £3)

The superb house in a 100-acre landscape of lawns, terraces and flower beds has an excellent walled garden, with a great variety of climbers and an impressive summer house designed in Tuscan style by 'Capability' Brown who was a local man. The conservatory plants include a great tree fuchsia. Outside, the walks step down from a classical fountain past beds re-designed by Lady

Trevelyan in the 1930s, including notable heathers and many herbaceous varieties, through to the water meadow. Trees include two larches by the China Pond planted by the Duke of Argyll in 1738. The Hall is steeped in the history of the Trevelyan family and is associated with Ruskin and the pre-Raphaelite painters who decorated it. New circular walk.

NOTTINGHAMSHIRE

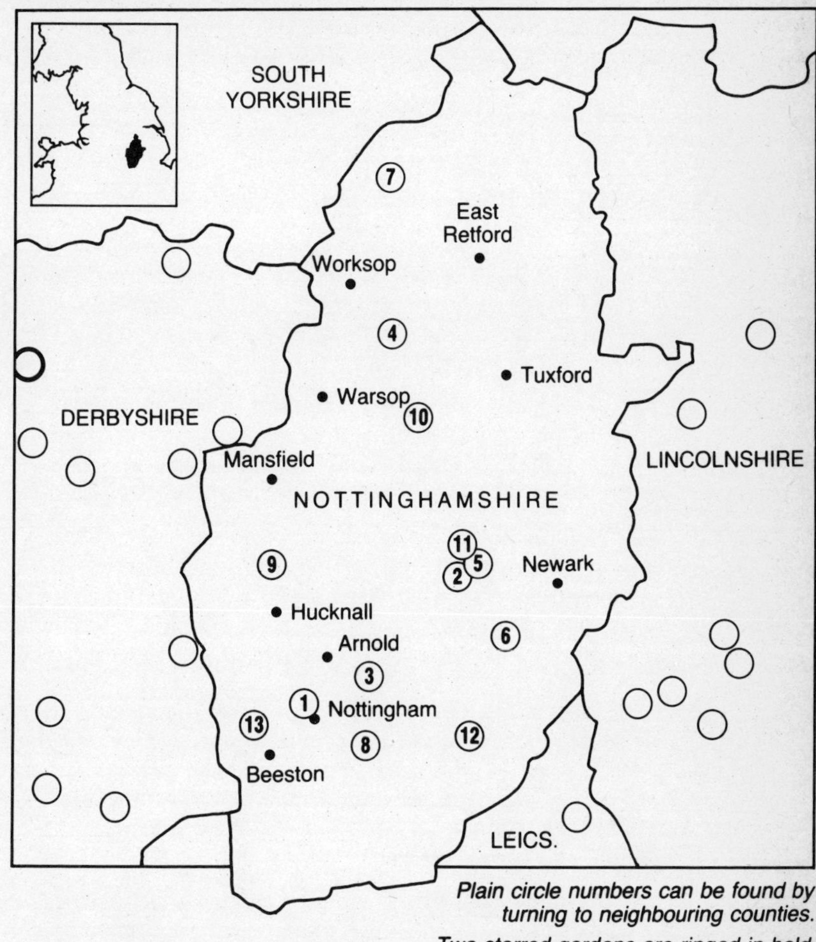

Plain circle numbers can be found by turning to neighbouring counties.

Two-starred gardens are ringed in bold.

THE ARBORETUM 1

Waverley Street, Nottingham.
Nottingham City Council

Located a short walk from the Victoria shopping centre along Shakespeare Street to Waverley Street entrance • Light refreshments at kiosk near entrance, 10 a.m. – 5 p.m. • Toilet facilities • Suitable for wheelchairs (note arboretum is on hillside) • Dogs (fouling not allowed) • Open daily, 8 a.m., Sat and Sun, 9 a.m. – 9.30 p.m. (or dusk if earlier) • Entrance: free

This is an arboretum within a city park, unusually sited on a hillside. The Royal National Rose Society's display garden within the Arboretum is at its best late June/early July – almost a total lack of labels unfortunately. This quiet, mature park, close to the city centre with aviaries and large lake and lawns is particularly suitable for children. Another spectacular feature is a 170-yard dahlia border.

BISHOP'S MANOR 2

Bishop's Drive, Southwell, Nottinghamshire.
The Rt Rev. the Lord Bishop of Southwell and Mrs Harris

12m NE of Nottingham on A612. Situated at the end of Bishops Drive on the S side of the Minster • Parking in village car parks • Refreshments: tea and biscuits • Suitable for wheelchairs • Open for charity twice a year only on Sun afternoons. Check local newspaper for dates

The charm of this garden is its unusual setting. Part of it is enclosed in the ruins of the medieval palace providing a sheltered area for the plants to flourish. The present gardener has been there five years and has created a well-maintained garden of over three acres, with rose beds and borders as well as informal areas.

17 BRIDLE ROAD 3

Burton Joyce, Nottingham. Tel: (0602) 313725
Mr and Mrs Bates

Turn N off A612 Nottingham to Southwell Road up Lambley Lane. After ½m fork right down impassable-looking Bridle Road, and the property is on the left • Best season: spring/summer • Parking very restricted in lane by the gates to the house • Partly suitable for wheelchairs • Open for charity on 21st July, 2 – 6 p.m. and most Sats by appointment • Entrance: 75p, children 25p

The one-acre garden is situated on a slope, mainly facing south and west. The mixed border is of the highest standard combining extremely well a variety of plants including dahlias and grasses. Worth looking at is the way the very steep slope on the garden's southern border has been utilized with zigzagging gravel paths. Common and unusual bulbous plants abound – those such as acidanthera and nerines are in the hot, sunny spots near the house, others in the grass, woodland and mixed border. There is a stream with naturalized ferns, primulas and the like.

CLUMBER PARK 4

Clumber Estate Office, Clumber Park, Worksop, Nottinghamshire.
Tel: (0909) 476592
The National Trust

4½m SE of Worksop off A1 and A57, 11m from junction 30 off M1 • Parking • Refreshments: cafeteria and restaurant, daily, 10.30 a.m. - 5 p.m. and in summer to 6 p.m. • Toilet facilities • Partly suitable for wheelchairs (wheelchairs inc. those for children available) • Dogs • National Trust shop • Chapel open except 25th Dec, 10 - 5 p.m. • Park always open during daylight hours. Walled kitchen garden April to Sept, Sat, Sun, Bank Holiday Mons and some weekdays during summer school holidays, 10 a.m. - 5 p.m. Last admission 4.30 p.m. • Entrance: pedestrians free, cars £2. Bicycle hire.

In 1707 the Park was enclosed from Sherwood Forest and the Dukes of Newcastle had their seat here. Only the stable block, chapel and entrance gates remain as the great house was demolished in 1938. The National Trust purchased the park in 1946. The Lincoln terrace and pleasure gardens were laid out by William Sawrey Gilpin in the early nineteenth century. Twenty-five acres out of the 3,800 acres of parkland are managed by just two gardeners. The vinery and palm house survive (being restocked) and the extensive glass houses (450 feet) are the best and longest in the National Trust's properties. The kitchen garden exhibition of late nineteenth-century and early twentieth-century tools is fascinating and reminds us that modern powered-garden tools have taken much of the heavy work out of gardening. The walled kitchen garden has some fruit bushes, a herb garden in the making and a few young fruit trees in the grassy centre but is otherwise a disappointment. The Lincoln terrace reached its height of excellence in the 1920s and after years of neglect is being restored. The cedar avenue has cedars and sweet chestnut trees of breath-taking size.

CLYDE HOUSE 5

Westgate, Southwell, Nottinghamshire.
Mr and Mrs G. Edwards

In Southwell on A612 a few hundred yards before the Minster on the right • Restricted roadside parking • Toilet facilities • Suitable for wheelchairs • Plants for sale • Open 16th June, 2 - 6 p.m. • Entrance: 75p

Totally organically-managed private gardens are regrettably rare but this example will convince visitors that it is possible to 'go organic' and still have a beautifully healthy garden. The immaculate green lawn on closer inspection was full of clover - but so what if it looked and felt luxurious underfoot? The composting area (the secret of success?) is an education in itself and Mr Edwards will explain its workings.

FLINTHAM HALL ★ 6

Flintham, Nottinghamshire.
Mr Miles Thoroton Hildyard

6m SW of Newark on A46 • Best season: summer • Parking in adjacent field • Toilet facilities • Suitable for wheelchairs • Dogs on lead • Open for charity by written appointment • Entrance: £1.50, OAP £1, children 50p

Do set aside plenty of time to visit this garden; it will not be wasted. The hall and extensive gardens are obviously loved and lavish amounts of time and effort are spent on them. It is therefore remarkable to learn that Michael Blagg is the sole gardener, though Mr Hildyard regularly attends to the gardens and lawns himself. The unique Victorian conservatory is a heady experience; the exotic plants and ornate architecture vying with each other for your attention. In the *Shell Guide to Nottinghamshire* it is described as the most spectacular in the country. It is only one of many surprises; the Regency pheasantry, recently imaginatively restored, has been frescoed by Ricardo Cinalli. The gardens were featured in *Country Life* in Sept 1989.

HODSOCK PRIORY ★ 7

Blyth, Worksop, Nottinghamshire. Tel: (0909) 591204
Sir Andrew and Lady Buchanan

1m from A1 at Blyth off B6045 Blyth – Worksop road • Parking. Coaches must book • Teas in the conservatory • Toilet facilities inc. disabled • Dogs in car park only • Plants for sale • Open 31st March, 1st, 21st April, 5th, 6th, 26th, 27th May, 23rd June, 28th July, 25th, 26th Aug, 22nd Sept, 27th Oct, 2 – 6 p.m. and Snowdrop Sunday 16th Feb 1992, 12 noon – dusk. Also 30th June to 14th July (Bassetlaw Festival), daily, 2 – 5 p.m. Other times by appointment • Entrance: £1.50, disabled persons in wheelchairs free, children 25p. Discounts for pre-booked groups of 50 or more

Historic site including a Grade I listed gatehouse *c* 1500 and a moat. There are fine trees including a huge cornus, a very old catalpa (Indian bean), tulip tree and swamp cypress, and much replanting is going on. In the spring there are the bulbs, and later, mixed borders with perennials and old roses, the latter much admired. Interesting holly hedges. Good walks, mainly grass, beyond the small lake and bog garden and into the old moat, which is accessible to the disabled.

HOLME PIERREPONT HALL 8

Radcliffe-on-Trent, Nottinghamshire. Tel: (0602) 332371
Mr and Mrs R. Brackenbury

5m SE of Nottingham off A52. Approach past the National Water Sports Centre and continue for 1½m • Parking • Teas. Other refreshments by prior arrangement • Toilet facilities • Suitable for wheelchairs • Dogs on lead

• Shop • House open • Garden open Easter Sun - Tues, May Day Bank Holiday Mon, Spring Bank Holiday Sun - Tues. Also June to Aug, Sun, Tues, Thurs, Fri, 2 - 6 p.m. and 5th May for charity • Entrance: courtyard garden £1 (house and garden £2.50, children £1), for charity £1

The Hall is a medieval brick manor house but the garden and parterre have been restored by the present owners. The box parterre is the outstanding feature of the gardens and the newly created herbaceous borders next to the York stone path (replacing old rose beds) once matured will enhance the courtyard garden further. (The Jacob sheep are very friendly lawnmowers.) Mr and Mrs Brackenbury work hard with improvements to this peaceful house and garden and willingly provide ample information. Their improvements include a winter garden.

NEWSTEAD ABBEY ★ 9

Linby, Nottinghamshire. Tel: (0623) 793557
Nottingham City Council

11m N of Nottingham on A60 • Parking • Refreshments: tea room in grounds open Good Friday to Sept • Toilet facilities • Partly suitable for wheelchairs • Dogs on lead • Shop • House open at extra charge, Good Friday to Sept, 11.30 a.m. - 6 p.m. Last admission 5 p.m. Contains Byron memorabilia • Open daily, 10 a.m. - dusk • Entrance: £1, children 50p

Water predominates in this estate that the poet Byron inherited but could rarely afford to live in. In most of the extensive and immaculate gardens there is much of interest. The Japanese gardens are justly famous and the rock and fern gardens worth visiting. Indeed the waterfalls, wildfowl, passageways, grottos and bridges provide plenty of fun for children, but in addition there is an excellent, imaginatively-equipped play area with bark mulch for safety. The tropical garden and the monks' stew pond are visually uninteresting but they are of laudable age. It is a pity that the large walled kitchen garden is now a rose garden - rose gardens however pretty are commonplace, but large kitchen gardens to the great houses are rare now and of more interest. The old rose garden is now the iris garden - an insipid area with gladioli planted in the regular plots in an effort to liven up the place.

RUFFORD COUNTRY PARK 10

Nottinghamshire. Tel: (0623) 824152
Nottinghamshire County Council

2m S of Ollerton on A614 • Parking • Refreshments: main meals - the Buttery, Mon - Sat, 12 noon - 2.30 p.m., Sun, 12 noon - 3.30 p.m. snacks at the Coach House daily, 10 a.m. - 5 p.m. • Partly suitable for wheelchairs, four available which can be booked in advance • Dogs (guide dogs only in shops and restaurants) • Shops • Rufford Abbey Cistercian area open • Park open daily, dawn - dusk • Entrance: free

Rufford Country Park contains almost everything that might be expected of an important country park e.g. lakes, lime avenues, mature cedars, etc. Recently the gardeners have created eight theme gardens including herb and scented plants, all within a larger sculpture garden. These promise to be worth another visit when established. Large areas are managed with wildlife in mind hence plenty of birdlife. Ball games are allowed on the lawns beneath cut-leaved beeches and cedars. Ample picnic areas. Conducted walks arranged during the week and weekends. Telephone for dates and times. The Reg Hookway Arboretum, established in 1983, shows promise with a good collection of oaks and birches – all well-labelled. There is a new rose garden in front of the abbey ruins which are now open to the public.

ST HELEN'S CROFT 11

Halam, Nr Southwell, Nottinghamshire. Tel: (0636) 813219
Mrs E. Ninnis

Take A614 Nottingham – Doncaster road and turn off at White Post roundabout to Southwell and Halam • Parking in adjacent field • Suitable for wheelchairs • Plants for sale • Open for charity 12th May and then first Tues in each month until 6 Oct, then 13th, 20th Oct, 2 – 5.30 p.m. and by appointment • Entrance: 75p, children 25p

A lovely three quarter-acre garden which is an inspiration for all elderly gardeners as it is still cared for by its creator despite her being in her seventies. Undaunted by the heavy clay soil she constantly introduces changes and has grand plans for future plantings. Featured in *Gardener's World* programme. An informative leaflet is provided at the entrance.

THE WILLOWS 12

5 Rockley Avenue, Radcliffe-on-Trent, Nottinghamshire.
Tel: (0602) 333621
Mr and Mrs R.A. Grout

6m E of Nottingham N of A52. From Radcliffe-on-Trent High Street P.O. turn into Shelford Road, over railway bridge, 300 yards opposite bus shelter turn left into Cliff Way, then 2nd right • Limited parking on street • Tea and biscuits on charity open days • Open for charity 3rd April, 1st May, 5th June, 3rd July, 7th Aug, 4th Sept, 2 – 5.30 p.m. Coaches strictly by appointment • Entrance: 75p, OAP, children 50p

This small private garden, designed by the owners in 1982, is of greatest appeal to those interested in rare hardy herbaceous plants. Because of its size, trees and shrubs are limited but are unusual or handled in such a way as to fit the area e.g. pollarding. Excellent labelling. Collections of hostas, hellebores, pulmonarias and snowdrops.

WOLLATON HALL 13

Nottingham. Tel: (0602) 281333
Nottingham City Council

2½m from the city centre on A609. From M1 junction 25 take A52, turn left onto A614 and left onto A609 • Parking • Refreshments: snacks near Wollaton Road car park • Toilet facilities • Partly suitable for wheelchairs • Dogs on lead because of deer • Shop • Natural History Museum in hall open April to Sept, Mon - Sat, 10 a.m. - 7 p.m., Sun, 2 - 5 p.m. Oct to March, Mon - Sat, 10 a.m. - dusk, Sun, 1.30 - 4.30 p.m. Closed 25th Dec. Free except small charge on Sun and Bank Holidays • Garden open daily all year • Entrance: free

This large park and garden is surrounded by the city but because of its size the visitor feels deep in the country - unfortunately near the park periphery the roar of traffic dispels that illusion. The polyanthus in spring are spectacular as is the summer bedding where castor-oil plants and ornamental cabbages have their place in the schemes. The formal gardens at the top of the hill give onto views of huge cedars and holm oaks and thence on to the lime avenues and the deer in the park.

GARDENS OPEN RARELY

The following gardens are open to the public on three days or less in the year, although Bridle Road may also be open by appointment. For details see individual entry.

June 16 Clyde House; **July 21** 17 Bridle Road.

OXFORDSHIRE

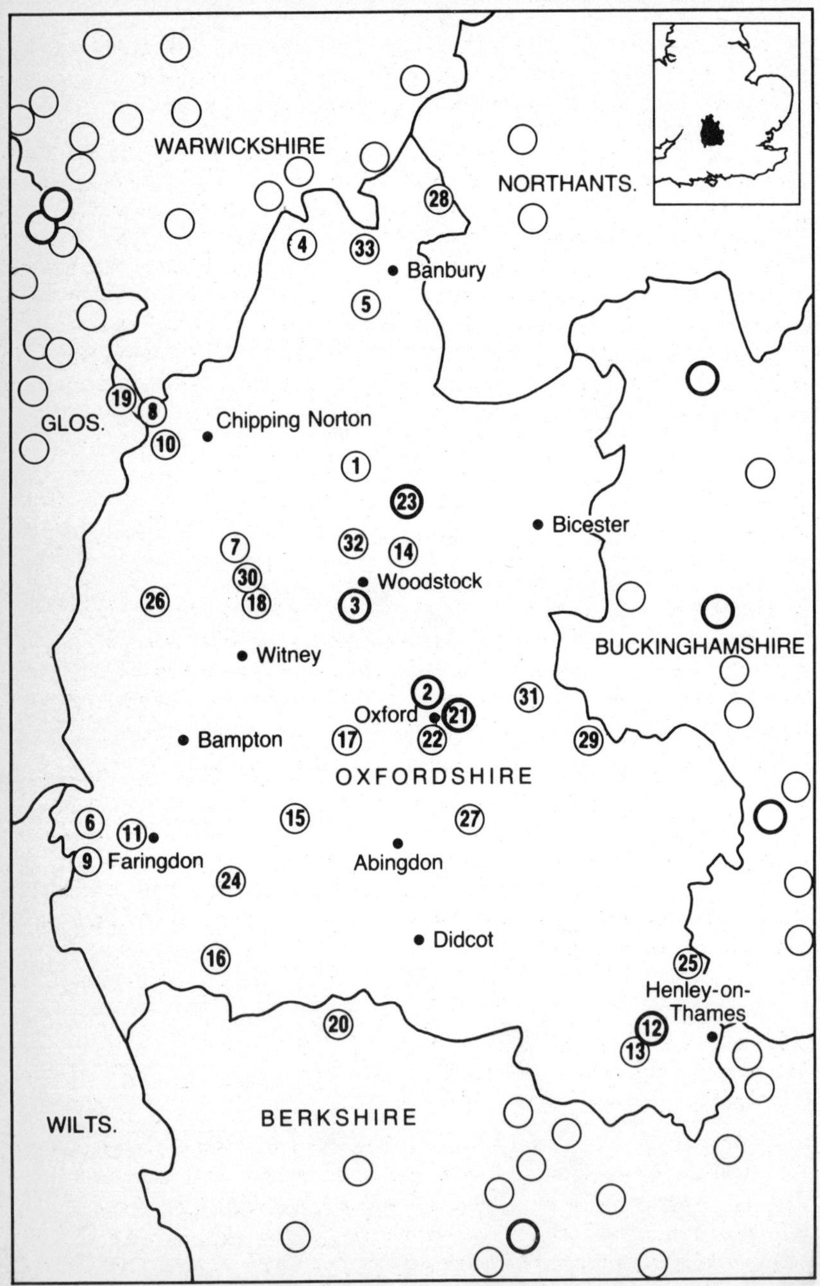

Plain circle numbers can be found by turning to neighbouring counties. Two-starred gardens are ringed in bold.

BARTON ABBEY 1

Middle Barton, Oxfordshire. Tel: (0869) 40227
Mr and Mrs J.C. Fleming

10m S of Banbury, turn W off A423 on the B4030 for 1m • Parking • Teas • Toilet facilities • Suitable for wheelchairs • Dogs on lead • Open 12th May, 11th Aug, 2 - 5.30 p.m. • Entrance: £1, children free

This is an object lesson in what to do if a place designed to be staffed by ten gardeners is reduced to having to make do with two. The Flemings have eliminated the vast beds, let the rock garden grow over and concentrated on the grandeur of the setting of the Abbey in its hollow in the hills with fine lawns running down to the lake. Two trees have been bent into a 'whalebone' arch leading to the wild garden. One economy the Flemings have not made is to reduce work on the vast Victorian walled kitchen garden. This is a model of its kind, with a large rose arch at the centre. In the unheated greenhouses beyond, nectarines and vines flourish. Note also the thatched early version of a Wendy house and the lavender walk.

23 BEECH CROFT ROAD ★★ 2

Summertown, Oxford. Tel: (0865) 56020
Mrs A. Dexter

Summertown, 2m from centre of Oxford. Beech Croft Road runs between the Banbury and Woodstock roads which connect Oxford centre to ring road • Parking limited in Beechcroft Road. Advisable to use public parking in Summertown • Open by appointment only from June to Sept • Entrance: £1.50 for charity

Clever use of perspective creates the effect of a much larger garden than would seem possible in an area of 23 × 7 yards. Foliage of different colours, textures, sizes and shapes is planted and pruned to form a backdrop to a variety of well-chosen plants. Ramondas and ferns are given room in the lower, damper end of the garden, alpines in stone troughs are placed in a sunnier position near the house. This is a tapestry garden, every inch contains unusual and interesting plants displayed with great skill.

BLENHEIM PALACE ★★ 3

Woodstock, Oxfordshire. Tel: (0993) 811325
The Duke of Marlborough

8m NW of Oxford on A34 at Woodstock. Entrances off A34 and through town • Parking • Refreshments: cafeteria, Indian Room Restaurant on Water Terraces • Toilet facilities inc. disabled • Partly suitable for wheelchairs • Dogs on lead in park only • Good garden centre open daily, 9.30 a.m. - 5.30 p.m., with refund on entrance charge for purchases • House open, mid-March to Oct, 10.30 a.m. - 5.30 p.m. (last admission 4.45 p.m.) £5.50, OAP £4.50, children £2.80 • Park open daily except 25th Dec, 9 a.m. - 5 p.m. • Entrance: park only, pedestrians 70p, children 40p, cars £3.10, gardens and park £3.10 (inc. Butterfly House and use of the train, adventure play area and nature trail but extra charges for the Marlborough Maze and rowing boat hire)

The visitor who walks through Hawksmoor's Triumphal Arch into Blenheim Park sees one of the greatest contrived landscapes in Britain. The architect Vanburgh employed Bridgeman and Henry Wise, Queen Anne's master gardener and the last of the British formalists, to contrast a bastion-walled 'military' garden and kitchen gardens. Wise also planted immense elm avenues and linked Vanburgh's bridge to the sides of the valley. However, the garden was far from ready when the first Duke of Marlborough moved into the palace in 1719. Major alterations were made by the 4th, 5th and 9th Dukes, one of the earliest of which was the grassing over of Wise's formal gardens by 'Capability' Brown after 1764. Brown also developed the two huge lakes. It is possible to spend several hours walking through the grounds, for which no charge is made. The gardens (entrance only with £2.50 garden ticket) include formal areas restored by Achille Duchene in the 1920s from those grassed by Brown in the North forecourt. He made formal gardens on the east and west, the latter two water terraces in the Versailles style. To the east of the elaborate Italian garden is a sunken garden of patterned box and golden yew, interspersed with various seasonal plantings. To the west from the terraces are the rose garden and arboretum (1984). From the vast south lawn 'one passes through a magnificent grove of cedars and on towards Wise's walled garden, part shrubberies of laurel and an Exedra of box and yew, the whole exemplifying the Victorian pleasure grounds' in the words of the *Oxford Companion*. Some visitors may doubt whether the extra money charged to see the garden is worthwhile. The rose garden is an anachronism and the pool in its centre dirty and the fountain untended. The water garden is fine but it is not Versailles. As for the Italian garden, this may only be viewed over the hedge, not entered. The grounds and the trees are another scene altogether - one of the great things in life.

BROOK COTTAGE ★ 4

Alkerton, Nr Banbury, Oxfordshire. Tel: (029587) 303/590
Mr and Mrs D. Hodges

6m W of Banbury. From A422 Banbury - Stratford road, turn W at sign for Alkerton. Soon after entering village, small war memorial on right. Turn left into Well Lane and right at fork • Partly suitable for wheelchairs • Plants for sale • Open April to Oct, Mon - Fri, 9 a.m. - 6 p.m., 6th, 7th July, 21st, 22nd Sept, 2 - 7 p.m. Other weekends, evenings and all group visits by appointment • Entrance: £1.50, OAP £1, children free

This garden, designed and planted since 1964, is on a steeply-sloping, west-facing site of four acres. The owners have used the natural features in an interesting way. For example by planting large species, old-fashioned and modern shrub roses in the grass on a steep slope. Good use is made of water and there is a large unusual-shaped pond. Indeed shape is a feature of the overall effect, such as in a sweeping crimson copper beech hedge. Note the interesting grouping of hollies and conifers. There is something here for everyone in all seasons, from the alpine scree to the small 'cottage' and vegetable gardens above the house. Most plants are labelled. On charity open days, the owner next door at Alkerton House unlocks the connecting gate to show off his two and a half acres of trees, shrubs and conifers. Upton House (see Warwickshire entry) nearby shows an earlier and more formal use of slopes.

BROUGHTON CASTLE ★ 5

Broughton, Nr Banbury, Oxfordshire. Tel: (0295) 62624
The Lord Saye and Sele

2½m SW of Banbury on B4035 • Parking • Teas on open days, refreshments for parties by arrangement • Toilet facilities • Suitable for wheelchairs • House open • Garden open 18th May to 14th September, Wed and Sun, also Thurs in July and Aug and Bank Holiday Sun and Mon, inc. Easter, 2 – 5 p.m. Also by appointment for groups throughout year • Entrance: £2.60, children £1.30

More of a house than a castle, the gardens are unexpectedly domestic within the confines of the moat. In 1900 there were 14 gardeners but the present owner and his inspired gardener have reduced the workload somewhat while retaining the overall splendour. The most important changes were made after 1969 following a visit from Lanning Roper who suggested opening up the views across the park. There are now two magnificent borders. The west-facing one, backed by the battlement wall, has a colour scheme of blues and yellows, greys and whites. The other long border is based on reds, mauves and blues. Great planting skill is evident in the serpentine flows of colour. On the south side is the walled 'ladies garden' with box-edged fleur-de-lys-shaped beds holding floribunda roses. Another wonderful border rises up to the house wall. Everywhere is a profusion of old-fashioned roses and original planting.

BUSCOT PARK ★ 6

Faringdon, Oxfordshire. Tel: (0367) 20786 (not weekends)
The National Trust

On A417 between Lechlade and Faringdon • Parking • Teas and light refreshments. Lunches for parties by prior arrangement • Toilet facilities • Plants for sale • House open • Garden open 29th to 31st March then 3rd April to Sept, Wed – Fri and every 2nd and 4th Sat and Sun immediately following, 2 – 6 p.m. Last admission 5.30 p.m. Closed Bank Holiday Mon • Entrance: £2.20, (house and garden £3.20)

Although the house was built in 1780, this garden has been developed during the twentieth century. The water garden was created by Harold Peto in 1912, although the avenues linking lake to house were added later using a goose-foot plan from the house, with fastigiate and weeping varieties of oak, beech and lime. The Egyptian avenue created by Lord Faringdon in 1969 is guarded by sphinxes and embellished with Goade stone statues copied from an original from Hadrian's Villa. The large walled kitchen garden was redesigned by Tim Rees using pleached hedges of Judas trees (which should grow into a tunnel) and hornbeam underplanted with hemerocallis. Deep borders under walls with unusual, and skilful, mixture of old roses and vegetables (gourds, marrows, red chard, parsley, etc.) Walkway outside kitchen garden between two wide borders using exterior wall and trellis as screens. Exceptionally effective planting by the late Peter Coats three years ago and, over the years, imaginative development by Lord Faringdon. The planting of the kitchen garden and the double borders is so skilful that even in the drought conditions of 1990 none of the effect was lost.

CHARLBURY GARDENS 7

Gothic House and The Priory, Charlbury, Oxfordshire.
Mr and Mrs Andrew Lawson and Dr D. El Kabir

In centre of Charlbury village on B4022 Witney - Enstone road • Parking in street • Teas • Toilet facilities • Suitable for wheelchairs • Plants for sale • Gothic House open 28th April, 22nd Sept, 2 - 6 p.m. The Priory open 26th April, 8th Sept, 2 - 6 p.m. • Entrance: £1 combined entrance

A most interesting duo. One is a third of an acre walled town garden, the other four and a half acres with open aspect, both in the centre of this large Cotswold village. Gothic House is the recent work of one of the country's leading garden photographers and his sculptress wife. Artistic flair is evident everywhere, from the entrance through a fine Gothic glass structure to the tour round the many gems picked out in miniature. The planting is highly imaginative. So is the clever use of green wood structures in treillage style including a romantic seat, and the railway sleepers which define the pond. Note the *trompe l'oeil* painting on wood by Briony Lawson. Her sculptures are everywhere, numbered and for sale. *Objets trouvée* amid the foliage and the whole effect delightful. The Priory is different as well as bigger. Visitors are given a map and description which explains that the owners took over the barish bones of a formal garden, though there was handsome topiary, including one large, surreal structure. They have added further architectural features, statues, pleached limes, etc and are growing more topiary to emphasise the 'room' format. All the beds were re-instated in late 1988 and the descriptive material lists the planting plans and makes reference to influences - Folly Farm, Hidcote, etc. The whole area is 'in the making' including a new knot garden and what will one day be an extensive arboretum.

CHASTLETON HOUSE AND VILLAGE 8

Chastleton, Oxfordshire. Tel: (060874) 355
Mrs Clutton-Brock

3m SE of Moreton-in-Marsh, 5m N of Chipping Norton off A44 • Parking • Toilet facilities in house • Suitable for wheelchairs • House open • Garden open Good Friday to last Sun in Sept, weekdays, 10.30 a.m. - 1 p.m., 2 - 5.30, Sun, 2 - 5 p.m. Will open at other times for parties of 20 or more by appointment • Entrance: £2.50, children £1.25 inc. house. Garden only free

This small and rather unkempt garden is well worth a visit because it can be combined with a tour of the 'unaltered' early seventeenth Jacobean mansion, charming especially because of its lack of sophisticated restoration. It is a simple grass affair leading to a surreal box garden dating from 1700.

CLOCK HOUSE ★ 9

Coleshill, Faringdon, Oxfordshire. Tel: (079376) 2476
Michael and Denny Wickham

3½m SW of Faringdon on B4019 • Best season: June/July • Parking • Teas in courtyard in fine weather • Toilet facilities • Suitable for wheelchairs • Dogs on lead • Plants for sale • Open by appointment and 16th June, 13th Oct, 2 - 6 p.m. • Entrance: 70p, children free

Situated on a hillside with inspiring views over the Vale of the White Horse, this exuberant, delightful garden was created by the present owners in the last thirty years in the grounds of Coleshill House, burned then demolished in the 1950s. The groundplan of the original house is being planted out in box, to show layout of walls and windows. Courtyard with collection of plants in pots, and a sunny walled garden in the old laundry-yard with roses and mixed planting. Lime avenue at the front of the house sweeps you down to the views, and a pond and terrace are sheltered by tall shrubs. Mixed herbaceous borders with interesting and unusual plants. This is an original garden, designed by an artist with a large collection of plants in imaginative settings, the atmosphere being prolific rather than tidy.

CORNWELL MANOR ★ 10

Cornwell, Nr Kingham, Oxfordshire. Tel: (0608) 658 555
The Hon Mrs Peter Ward

2m from Chipping Norton, S off A44 • Parking • Teas on charity days • Toilet facilities • Not very suitable for wheelchairs • Plants for sale • Open for parties by appointment in June and July at £1 per person. Tel: (0608) 658671 and 6th May, 2 - 6 p.m. 24th June, 11 a.m. - 5 p.m. • Entrance: £1.50

Looking at this house and garden through the wrought-iron gates on the road frontage, it seems all-year-round the quintessence of seventeenth-century gracious living. Inside, the garden has been modernised without losing any of its charm. Begin by standing on the south-facing terrace in front of the house and looking down over the croquet lawn and up to the roadside gates and the view beyond; it is as good as anything in Italy. To the east is the spring garden and a formal garden on three levels with interesting plantings such as box-edged beds of peonies. Everywhere there are trained trees and clever plantings to emphasise leaf colouring. On the other side of the house is the original one and a quarter-acre walled kitchen garden, organically cultivated and, in the owner's words 'maintained in the traditional manner, now rarely seen.' Note also the children's garden, with an early form of Wendy house, and peek in the indoor games-room window to see the mass of amazing trophies of the chase. The swimming pool area is attractively arranged. Returning to the main house, the visitor descends the south terraces to the water pools below and turns east along the woodland walk, passing on the way the rock and bog gardens. The wild garden surrounds vast and unspoilt lakes. Everywhere there is evidence of sensitive new planting. The plant sales are amongst the best. The small village nearby was refurbished by the architect of Portmeirion, Sir Clough Williams Ellis (see entry under Wales).

FARINGDON HOUSE 11

Faringdon, Oxfordshire. Tel: (0367) 240240
Miss S. Zinovieff

Entered from centre of town which is off the A420 between Oxford and Swindon • Parking • Teas on charity days • Partly suitable for wheelchairs • Open by appointment and 30th, 31st March, 26th May, 8th Sept, 2 - 5 p.m. • Entrance: £1, accompanied children free

Medium-sized apparently conventional park with fine terrace, views and trees. Its main charm lies in its eccentric features such as the coloured doves introduced by a previous owner, the dilettanti musician Lord Berners. In the orangery pool, half-submerged and looking as though he might have lunched rather too well, is a bust of General Havelock, of the Indian Mutiny. The swimming pool has a medieval influence, with lovely views over the top of old apple and pear trees, and a rare fruit walk, between two high sheltering walls. Good autumn border, lined in box, and massed bulbs down the drive in spring.

GREYS COURT ★★ 12

Rotherfield Greys, Henley-on-Thames, Oxfordshire. Tel: (04917) 529
The National Trust

3m W of Henley-on-Thames on A423 Peppard road • Best season: April to June • Parking • Teas Wed and Sat only in April and May, and Mon, Wed, Fri and Sat from June to Sept • Toilet faciliites • Suitable for wheelchairs • House open 30th March to Sept, Mon, Wed, Fri, 2 - 6 p.m. • Garden open

30th March to Sept, daily except Thurs and Sun, 2 – 6 p.m. Last admission 5.30 p.m. • *Entrance: £2.20 (house and garden £3.20)*

The statue of St Fiacre, the protector of gardeners, stands modestly in this beautiful garden, or several gardens, set against the ruins of a fourteenth-century fortified house. The largest area, an orchard, is divided by lines of morello cherries and parallel hedges of 'Rosa mundi'. An ancient wisteria forms a canopy over a walled area, approached on one side through a tunnel of younger wisterias in pinks and blues. Impeccably kept peony bed and rose garden glow against the ancient walls. Beyond the kitchen garden, across the nut avenue, is the maze, designed by Randoll Coate and inspired by one seen in a dream by the then Archbishop of Canterbury.

GREYSTONE COTTAGE ★ 13

Colmore Lane, Kingwood Common, Henley-on-Thames, Oxfordshire. Tel: (04917) 559
Mr and Mrs W. Roxburgh

5m N of Reading between B481 Nettlebed – Reading road, and Sonning Common – Stoke Row road. 1m down Colmore Lane, next to Unicorn pub • *Best season: spring/early summer* • *Parking in lane and field* • *Refreshments on special opening days* • *Suitable for wheelchairs* • *Plants for sale* • *Open by appointment April to Sept and 12th May, 2 – 6 p.m.* • *Entrance: 70p, children free*

The owners have created this garden over the past 17 years. Sunny courtyard in front of house with planting between stones: dry, Mediterranean area and small beds of mixed blue, white and yellow (nicotiana, feverfew, etc). Pear-tree alleyway (80 years old) leading away from house, with vegetable garden to right, hedges of beech beyond; lawns and woodland with long border to the west, full of unusual plants, especially a large number of hostas. Woodland with primroses, primulas and fritillaries, hellebores, azeleas, bilberries and blueberries. Golden garden behind house with wildlife pond. Lilies in border and pots in Mediterranean area.

HILL COURT 14

Tackley, Oxfordshire.
Dame Felicity Peake and Mr and Mrs Andrew C. Peake

9m N of Oxford, just E of A423. Coming from Oxford turn opposite Sturdy's Castle; if driving south turn off at earlier sign marked Tackley • *Parking* • *Teas* • *Suitable for wheelchairs* • *Plants for sale* • *Open 22nd, 23rd June, 2 – 6 p.m.* • *Entrance: £1, children free*

A two-acre, sixteenth-century walled garden, no longer physically attached to the house which was demolished *c.* 1960. Remains of the manor house, also demolished, can be seen across the park which dates from 1787. The garden, whose design was influenced by Russell Page, is unusual because it is terraced uphill from the entrance. The rose beds had to be removed about five years ago and the sensitive and original new planting is the work of Rupert Golby. Designers will find it pleasurable.

KINGSTON HOUSE 15

Kingston Bagpuize, Oxfordshire. Tel: (0865) 820259
Lord and Lady Tweedsmuir

5½m W of Abingdon at entry to Kingston Bagpuize where the A415 meets the A420 • Parking • Teas • Toilet facilities • Suitable for wheelchairs • Plants for sale • Shop • House open • Garden open April to Sept, Sun and Bank Holiday Mons, 2.30 - 5.30 p.m. • Entrance: 50p, children under 5 free (house and garden £2.25, OAP £1.75, children £1.10. Children under 5 not admitted to the house.) Groups by written appointment only - special rates

This Charles II manor house was owned in the pre-war years by Miss Marlie Raphael, a friend of Sir Harold Hillier, the great tree and shrub plantsman; accordingly she planted a woodland garden crossed by narrow curving earth paths and featuring plants from all over the world. This can be reached by an original green walk, which is to the left of the entrance. Miss Raphael's niece, Lady Tweedsmuir, continued the good work by planting the so-called Leap Wood begun on 29 February 1984. It has many rare and interesting plants although their arrangement is in some cases incongruous. A useful notated map can be purchased at the gate. In August 1990 the garden was very dessicated, and the trees and shrubs - the main features - looked in sore need of water. Perhaps the garden should be visited in the late spring to see the best effect.

KINGSTON LISLE PARK ★ 16

Wantage, Oxfordshire. Tel: (036782) 223
Mrs Leopold Lonsdale

4m W of Wantage on B4507 • Best season: June/July • Parking • Teas • Toilet facilities • Suitable for wheelchairs • Dogs on lead • Plants for sale • House open • Garden open Easter to Aug, Thurs, Bank Holiday weekends, Sat, Sun, Mon, 2 - 5 p.m. Parties at other times • Entrance: £2.50

The house, built in 1677 and extended early in the nineteenth century, is in a park setting of great tranquillity. The gardens have been restored by the present owners. Clipped yew trees surround the terrace next to the house; lawns lead to wrought-iron gates and an avenue of limes. Rose garden to the right of the lawn; a replica of Queen Mary's garden in Regent's Park, has climbing roses growing up poles and along encircling chains. Large trees at edge of lawns, mainly beech, with standard trees and shrubs. Greenhouse and vegetable gardens in walled garden with herbaceous border.

MANOR HOUSE ★ 17

Stanton Harcourt, Oxfordshire. Tel: (0865) 881928
Mr and The Hon Mrs Gascoigne

9m W of Oxford, 5m SE of Witney on B4449 • Best season: late spring/early summer • Parking • Teas • Toilet faciliites • Suitable for wheelchairs • Dogs on lead • Plants for sale • House open • Garden open 31st March, 1st, 11th, 14th, 25th, 28th April; 2nd, 5th, 6th, 16th, 19th, 23rd, 26th, 27th May; 6th, 9th, 20th, 23rd June; 4th, 7th, 18th, 21st July; 1st, 4th, 15th, 18th, 22nd, 25th, 26th Aug; 5th, 8th, 19th, 22nd Sept, 2 - 6 p.m. • Entrance: £1.50, OAP and children £1 (£3 house and garden)

Twelve acres of gardens incorporated in and around ruins of a fourteenth and fifteenth-century manor house. Entrance through courtyard into large, walled garden with yew-bush avenue leading from house to chapel. Herbaceous borders and crimson plants to right, and mixed colours on left. Old roses, viburnum, clematis and hydrangeas on walls of chapel and medieval kitchen. Alpines in troughs, geraniums in urns. Paths lead through nut-tree vistas, past shrubs round ancient stew ponds (sadly low in water after gravel-work drainage nearby). Hedges of lavender in walled garden. Rotunda in hedge gives views from garden to fields beyond. The old walled kitchen garden is being redesigned, with a collection of David Austin's New English roses, a fountain and pond in the middle, and old espaliered apple trees.

MOUNT SKIPPET 18

Ramsden, Oxfordshire. Tel: (099386) 868253
Dr and Mrs M.A.T. Rogers

4m N of Witney off B4022 to Charlbury. At crossroads marked to Finstock turn E and almost immediately turn right. Then after 400 yards turn left up No Through Way Lane • Parking • Refreshments by arrangement. Picnic area available • Suitable for wheelchairs • Plants usually for sale • Open April to Sept by appointment • Entrance: £1 to charity

Dr Rogers, now retired after a career as a research chemist, is a dedicated plantsman, preferring to grow everything from seeds or cuttings. He took over this family house of two acres and has developed a very attractive garden in a beautiful Cotswold setting. Plants are his love and there are many rare ones, including several that Wisley cannot identify. He has two rock gardens, an alpine house, interesting shrubs and trees and a bog garden adjoining the village pond. Everywhere there are collections of pots with his well-beloved plants (almost everything in the garden is labelled), some of which are sometimes for sale. Dr Rogers' enthusiasm is infectious. He is an innovator, too. In 1990 he grew tomatoes in bales of straw. Sadly, the garden has suffered badly in last summer's drought, but it is full of interesting and unusual plants. Long may this continue.

THE OLD POST OFFICE 19

Chastleton, Oxfordshire. Tel: (060874) 242
Penelope Mortimer

3m SE of Moreton-in-Marsh off A44 • Plants for sale • Parking in village street • Open 30th June, 24th Aug, 2 – 6 p.m. Also open most weekend afternoons April to Oct • Entrance: 75p for charity, children free. Note: House for sale, check opening times

The former gardener's cottage for Chastleton House (see entry), now called The Old Post Office, is described by the owner as 'a garden of ideas – some more successful than others' and amongst many worth looking at are the swing overlooking the view, the long arch of mixed climbers, the standard-gooseberry fruit bed and the various statues. The garden is also notable for two other outstanding features. It contains a very fine collection of the older rose varieties mingled with some of the best of the new hybrids. And the vast 'purple border', created in 1990, has become wonderfully established despite the very dry summer. By this summer (1991) the perennials should have developed into impressive clumps and be offering an incomparable display. For plantspersons, there are interesting things to see and a list of roses is provided; a varied selection of plants is available for sale. Another garden, Chastleton Glebe, is also open one Sunday for charity.

THE OLD RECTORY ★ 20

Farnborough, Wantage, Oxfordshire. Tel: (04882) 298
Mrs Michael Todhunter

4m SE of Wantage off B4494 • Best season: June/July • Parking • Teas sometimes • Suitable for wheelchairs • Plants for sale • Open for charity 12th May, 30th June, 7th July, 2 – 6 p.m. and by written appointment • Entrance: £1, children free

Outstanding four-acre garden created over 25 years on good original structure of large trees and hedges with magnificent views over the Downs. Deep, parallel herbaceous borders, backed by yew hedges. Subtle and effective planting next to front of house; smaller areas laid out for sun or shade-loving plants; woodland and shrubs, lawns; swimming pool surrounded by large *Hydrangea sargentiana*, potted lilies, agapanthus, with mixed roses around outside walls. Collection of old roses and small-flowered clematis. Wild flowers at edge of front lawn by ha-ha. Incidentally, those who like John Betjeman's poetry will be interested to know that he lived here 1945–50 and can look for the ghost of Miss Joan Hunter Dunn in the shrubberies. One of Oxfordshire's highest gardens, 600 feet, prey to winds from the Downs.

OXFORD BOTANIC GARDEN ★★ 21

Oxford. Tel: (0865) 276920
University of Oxford

In centre of Oxford opposite Magdalen College near bridge • Parking difficult • Picnics, while not specifically authorised, could be taken overlooking river • Suitable for wheelchairs • Professional photography and music prohibited • Open daily, 9 a.m. - 5 p.m. (4.15 p.m. during GMT), except Sun when 2 - 6 p.m. Last admission 4.45 p.m. Greenhouses 2 - 4 p.m. Closed 25th Dec and Good Fri • Entrance: free except during July and August £1 (half to charity)

This is the oldest botanic garden in Britain and one of the most attractive to the general visitor. Founded in 1621, it is surrounded by a high wall and entered through a splendid gateway by Inigo Jones's master mason. Two yews survive from the early plantings and there are a series of beds containing herbaceous plants in systematic and labelled groups. The old walls back beds with tender plants, including roses and clematis. To the left is the greenhouse area, modern ones replacing those built in 1670. There is also a rock garden. Outside the front entrance is a large rose garden donated by Americans in memory of those university staff who developed penicillin.

Several miles away at Nuneham Courtenay (south of the A 423) is the University Arboretum opened in 1968 (see entry).

OXFORD COLLEGE GARDENS 22

Most colleges are helpful about free access to their gardens although the more private ones, such as the Master's or Fellows', are rarely open. Specific viewing times are difficult to rely on because some colleges prefer not to have visitors in term time or on days when a function is taking place. The best course is to ask at the Porter's Lodge or to telephone ahead of visit. However, it is fair to say that some Oxford college gardens will always be open to the visitor, by arrangement with porters, even if others are closed on that particular day.

Amongst the college gardens of particular interest are the following: *Christ Church*; famous for Lewis Carroll's reference to the Cheshire Cat's chestnut tree in the Deanery garden. Also an Oriental plane planted 1636. Visitors in May should see the Meadow with its fritillaries. Memorial garden on St Aldates, (Memorial garden open winter 9.30 a.m. - 4.30 p.m., summer 9.30 a.m. - 5.30 p.m. Deanery and Master's garden only open once or twice a year for charity. Meadow open daily). *Corpus Christi*; the smallest college (open term time 1.30 - 4 p.m., vacations 10 a.m. - 4 p.m.). *Green College* near the Radcliffe Observatory's Tower of the Seven Winds which visitors may ascend for an aerial view, and the small gardens, part labelled, may be seen by appointment only. *Holywell Manor*; part of Balliol, a restful, well-maintained garden of one acre (open 10.30 a.m. - 6.30 p.m.). *Lady Margaret Hall*; eight acres of formal and informal, mainly designed by the Victorian architect Blomfield, also responsible for the building (open 9 a.m. - 6 p.m. or dusk if earlier). *New College*; admirers of the writings of Robin Lane Fox will be able to see examples of his plantings. The Warden's garden is a small enclosed area across the street from the main college buildings. (open term time 2 - 5 p.m., vacation 11 a.m. - 5 p.m.). *Nuffield College*; small formal garden with water features (open 9 a.m. - 7 p.m.). *Queen's College*; a garden with a fourteenth-century history, today pleasantly modernised. Good herbaceous borders in Fellows' garden and statues in Provost's garden (open 2 - 5 p.m.). *Rewley House*, Wellington Square, has an interesting roof garden, opened in 1986, which can be seen by appointment only. *Rhodes House*, not a college and not a pretty building but an unexpectedly pleasant garden behind (9 a.m. - 5 p.m. weekdays only). *St Hugh's College*; an interesting 10-acre garden largely created by Annie Rogers, a fellow, and open only by appointment. *St John's College*; landscaped in the eighteenth century and immaculately kept still. Striking in spring when bulbs in flower (open 1 - 5 p.m.). *Wadham College*; fine old trees (open 1 - 4.30 p.m.). *Wolfson College*; nine acres designed around modern college buildings by Powell and Moya, open only by appointment. *Worcester College*; the only true landscaped garden in Oxford, including a lake, made from a swampy area in 1817. Brightly-coloured beds in front quad (open term time 9 a.m. - 12 noon, vacation 9 a.m. - 12 noon and 2 - 6 p.m.).

The *University Parks*, laid out in 1864, are the perfect place for walking in all weathers and across the bridge and into Mesopotamia next to the nature reserve and woodland. The gardens near South Lodge Gate, one Edwardian with brilliant and startling colours and the other with Jekyllian subtleties of grey and silver, are well worth seeking out. (Open daily, except St Giles Fair, dawn - dusk).

ROUSHAM HOUSE ★★ 23

Steeple Aston, Oxfordshire. Tel: (0869) 47110
Family Cottrell-Dormer

Not in Steeple Aston but 2m S off A423 Oxford - Banbury road and B4030 • Parking • Toilet facilities • Suitable for wheelchairs • House open April to Sept, Wed, Sun and Bank Holidays, 2 - 4.30 p.m. • Garden open all year, daily, 10 a.m. - 4.30 p.m. • Entrance: £2, no children under 15

This is much admired because William Kent's design of 1738 is effectively frozen in time. Historical enlightenment can be combined with the enchantment of the setting and the use he made of it. In fact, before Kent it was already a famous garden described by the poet Pope as 'the prettiest place for water-falls, jetts, ponds, included with beautiful scenes of green and hanging wood, that ever I saw.' Kent's design, influenced perhaps by stage scenery, created a series of effects, and the best way to view the garden is to follow these one by one, rather than to attempt to grasp the design as a whole, although it is important to follow the various effects in the order Kent intended, and for this a guidebook is necessary. By taking the effects one-by-one, a feeling for the whole will then gradually emerge. In fact this was one of the first places where the garden took in the whole estate, also 'calling-in' the surrounding countryside, to use Pope's words. There are splendid small buildings and follies, fine sculpture, water and many seats and vantage points. The walled gardens next to the house are earlier than Kent. Allow plenty of time for a visit and plan to return another year, unless you are one of those who think a garden must be a mass of multi-coloured flowers, in which case Rousham will not be your cup of tea, except in the spring when it is mass of bulbs, including noteworthy daffodils.

STANSFIELD ★ 24

49 High Street, Stanford-in-the-Vale, Oxfordshire. Tel: (0367) 710340
Mr and Mrs D. Keeble

3½m SE of Faringdon, turn off A417 opposite Vale Garage • Best season: June to Aug • Parking in street • Suitable for wheelchairs by consultation with owners • Plants for sale • Open 16th April to 10th Sept, Tues, 10 a.m. – 4 p.m., and 9th June, 11th Aug, 2 – 6 p.m. Also by appointment • Entrance: £1

A one-acre plus plantsman's garden, not yet finished, with many island beds and borders. Large collection of plants, both for damp and dry conditions. All-year round interest in wide use of foliage and seasonal flowers, starting with species spring bulbs. Many shrubs interplanted and a new woodland area is planned. Alpines in sinks and troughs. A new scree garden has been made. Attention is focused on number and variety of plants rather than layout and design.

STONOR PARK 25

Henley-on-Thames, Oxfordshire. Tel: (049163) 587
Lord Camoys

5m N of Henley-on-Thames on B480 • Best season: June/July • Parking • Teas. Party lunches by arrangement • Toilet facilities • Suitable for wheelchairs by special arrangement • Dogs on leads • Shop • House open • Garden open April: Sun and Bank Holiday Mon only. May, June and Sept: Wed and Sun and Bank Holiday Mons. July and Aug: Wed, Thurs, Sat (Aug only), Sun and Bank Holiday Mon, 2 – 5.30 p.m. Parties by arrangement, Tues, Wed or Thurs (a.m. and p.m.) and Sun p.m. • Entrance: £3, OAP £2.40, children under 14 in family parties free. Party rates on application

The house, a red-brick Tudor E-shaped building in a bowl of hills, is the main attraction at Stonor Park. It is set on the side of a hill with open parkland and large trees in front, and with flower and vegetable garden behind and to the side sheltered against the hill. Lawns behind the house lead up to a hill terrace, pools, stone urns and planting along the steps. Orchard with cypresses and espaliered fruit trees, lavender hedges.

SWINBROOK HOUSE 26

Swinbrook, Nr Burford, Oxfordshire.
Mr J.D. Mackinnon

2m NE off Burford on road between Swinbrook and Shipton-under-Wychwood • Parking • Suitable for wheelchairs • Open 14th July • Entrance: £1

Here on the edge of the Wychwood Forest is a beautifully-preserved example of how the other half lived in the years between the wars. Old-fashioned shrub roses in immaculate beds, greenhouses full of peaches and vast beds of asparagus presumably reigned over by 'Uncle Matthew' with his entrenching tools. It was to Swinbrook House that the Mitfords moved after leaving Batsford. A substantial area is put over to breeding pheasants for the shoot. There is a fine walled garden and pleached fruit trees alongside the croquet lawn and everywhere ancient trees, presumably from the forest, as the house was not built until the late 1920s. A mile or two nearer Burford is Fulbrook, probably opening its smaller 'village' gardens on the same day and providing tea.

UNIVERSITY ARBORETUM 27

Nuneham Courtenay, Nr Oxford, Oxfordshire.
Oxford University

S of Oxford on A423 • Best season: May to Oct • Parking • Open May to Oct, Mon - Sat, 9 a.m. - 5 p.m., Sun, 2 - 6 p.m. • Entrance: free

The village and church of Nuneham were demolished in the 1670s in order to construct a classical landscape to be seen from the house; Oliver Goldsmith's poem 'The Deserted Village', written in 1770, may be based on that upheaval. Horace Walpole, in 1780, described the gardens, designed by 'Capability' Brown and William Mason (the poet gardener) as the most beautiful in the world. Most of those gardens were destroyed in the 1830s, and subsequently, with the house, became part of Nuneham Park Conference Centre. The remaining 55 acres of garden, now with the Botanic Garden under the University's care, include rhododendron walks, camellia, bamboo and heather collections under magnificent conifers.

WARDINGTON MANOR 28

Wardington, Nr Banbury, Oxfordshire. Tel: (0295) 750202/758481
The Lord Wardington

5m NE of Banbury off A361 • Parking • Teas • Toilet facilities • Suitable for wheelchairs • Plants for sale • Open 28th April, 2nd June, 11th Aug • Entrance: £1, children free

One of the great lawns of England spreads itself in front of this Jacobean manor house with its wisteria-covered walls. The topiary is impeccable too, and there are attractive borders. Away from the house, the owners have created a flowering shrub walk leading down to a pond.

WATERPERRY GARDENS ★ 29

Nr Wheatley, Oxfordshire. Tel: (08447) 226/254
School of Economic Science

8m E of Oxford, 2m N of Wheatley. Turn off M40/A40 and follow signs • Parking • Refreshments: Tea shop open 10 a.m. to ½ hour before closing. Light lunches, wine licence • Toilet facilities • Suitable for wheelchairs • Plants for sale in large nursery • In July during a 3-day event called 'Art in Action' which has a strong craft bias, increased entrance fees are charged and normal garden entry arrangements are suspended. Church open (Saxon origins) all year round • Gardens open daily, April to Sept, 10 a.m. - 5.30 p.m. or 6 p.m. at weekends; Oct to March, 10 a.m. - 4.30 p.m. Closed Christmas and New Year holidays • Entrance: Nov to Feb, no charge. March to Oct, £1.20, OAP 90p, children 60p, coach parties by appointment only

Waterperry has to be included in this guide although its 20 acres are difficult to categorize. There is a strong institutionalised/education atmosphere going back to the 1930s when a Miss Havergal opened up a small horticultural school. There is also a commercial garden centre which occupies large areas of the so-called garden, with row upon row of flowers and shrubs being grown from seeds or cuttings. Intermixed with all this are major features of the old garden, lawns and a substantial herbaceous border; also new beds containing collections of alpines, dwarf conifers and other shrubs. The South Field is a growing area for soft fruit. The Clay Bank is planted with shade lovers. Almost all the plants are labelled and the owners describe the place as one where 'the ornamental and the utilitarian live side by side'. The greenhouses in the nursery are interesting too: containing a good stock of houseplants for sale, usually including orchids and tall ficus; another, in the old walled garden, has an enormous citrus tree (it's worth the detour just to catch the scent of blossom) and other Mediterranean specimens, which are not for sale. Several hours need to be spent here to do it justice and if the visitor is overpowered by the 'utilitarian' aspect, he or she can stroll down the shady path by the little River Thame. A guide is sold at the shop. Several Wheatley gardens are also open in May for charity, together with Shotover House.

WILCOTE HOUSE ★ 30

Wilcote, Finstock, Oxfordshire. Tel: (099386) 606
The Hon. C.E. Cecil

3m S of Charlbury E off B4022 • Best season: early summer • Parking • Teas • Poor toilet facilities • Suitable for wheelchairs • Plants for sale • Open by appointment and 1st April, 27th May, 30th June, 13th Oct, 2 - 6 p.m. • Entrance: £1, children free

It is worth visiting this garden in May/June in order to walk down the laburnum tunnel planted as recently as 1984. The house is a splendid seventeenth/nineteenth-century copy in Cotswold stone of earlier periods and the large garden is also a period piece with extensive beds of old-fashioned roses and mixed borders. An unusual feature is the vast wild garden planted with an interesting selection of trees and intersected by grass paths. Very fine setting in this beautiful part of England. Arrive early for best plant sales. Mount Skippet (see entry) is nearby.

WOODPERRY HOUSE 31

Nr Stanton St John, Oxfordshire.
Mr and Mrs Robert Lush

4m E of Oxford. From Headington roundabout on ring road, take turning to Horton-cum-Studley. After 1½m cross over B4027. Road is signed to Horton-cum-Studley. Woodperry House is ½m down this road on right • Parking • Refreshments in aid of charity • Toilet facilities • Plants for sale • Open 19th May, 2nd June, 2 - 6 p.m. • Entrance: £1, children free

There is something here for most visitors, particularly those who want to see a five-acre garden built more or less from scratch (started *c.* 1987) in a style suited to the early eighteenth-century country house (not open), which Pevsner rightly described as 'strikingly beautiful'. A large formal lawned area at the back of the house looks out over Otmoor. Lime tree avenue. Elaborate beds. Stone summer houses. Beyond is a well-planted herbaceous border on one side, presumably eventually to be matched by the one opposite. Below is a very large walled vegetable garden.

WOOTTON PLACE 32

Wooton, Nr Woodstock, Oxfordshire. Tel: (0993) 811485
Mr and Mrs H. Dyer

3m N of Woodstock, turn E off the A34 • Parking • Teas • Suitable for wheelchairs • Plants for sale on spring open day • Open 21st April, 23rd June, 2 - 6 p.m. • Entrance: £1, children free

A venerable mulberry tree leans to welcome you by the front door, and huge cedars and beeches dominate the lawns to the east of the house. Over 150 varieties of daffodils and spring bulbs are the great attraction here. The old walled kitchen garden has quiet charm and nostalgic atmosphere, with ancient fruit trees, roses, herbs, peonies and romneyas, mixed with vegetables, bulbs and picking borders of annuals. A warm terrace shelters a fine plumbago, passion flower, scented geraniums and agapanthus. The park to the north of the house has more fine trees. These gardens were thought to have been laid out by 'Capability' Brown.

WROXTON ABBEY 33

Wroxton, Nr Banbury, Oxfordshire. Tel: (0295) 730551
Wroxton College of Fairleigh Dickinson University of New Jersey USA

3m W of Banbury off A422 • Parking in village • Suitable for wheelchairs • Dogs on lead • House (now used for academic purposes) open by appointment • Grounds open all year • Entrance: free

The historical interest of this garden and park is that in 1727 Tilleman Bobart (a pupil of Wise) was commissioned to construct a Renaissance-style garden with canals by the owners of the large Jacobean manor house, the 2nd Baron of Guildford. But by the late 1730s his son had this grassed over to convert it to the then fashionable landscape-style. Sanderson Miller designed some of the garden buildings *c.* 1740. The present American owners have restored much of this early landscape garden since 1978. On entering the long drive up to the house, it appears to be a conventional park, but beyond are interesting features including a serpentine river, lake, cascade which can be seen from a viewing mount, Chinese bridge, Doric temple, Gothic dovecote, obelisk, ruined arch and ice-house all restored from their derelict state. There is a rose garden and a newly-created knot garden which still needs further development. In all, the grounds cover 56 acres and offer many hours of pleasant walks. Unfortunately there is no map readily available and sign-posting is minimal.

GARDENS OPEN RARELY

The following gardens are open to the public on three days or less in the year, although they may also be open by appointment if this is stated in the text. For details see individual entry.

April 21 Wootton Place; **April 28** Gothic House; The Priory; **May 6** Cornwell Manor; **May 12** Barton Abbey; Greystone Cottage; The Old Rectory; **May 19** Woodperry House; **June 2** Woodperry House; **June 16** Clock House; **June 22** Hill Court; **June 23** Hill Court; Wootton Place; **June 24** Cornwell Manor; **June 30** The Old Rectory; **July 14** Swinbrook Manor; **Aug 11** Barton Abbey; **Sept 15** Gothic House; The Priory; **Oct 13** Clock House.

SHROPSHIRE

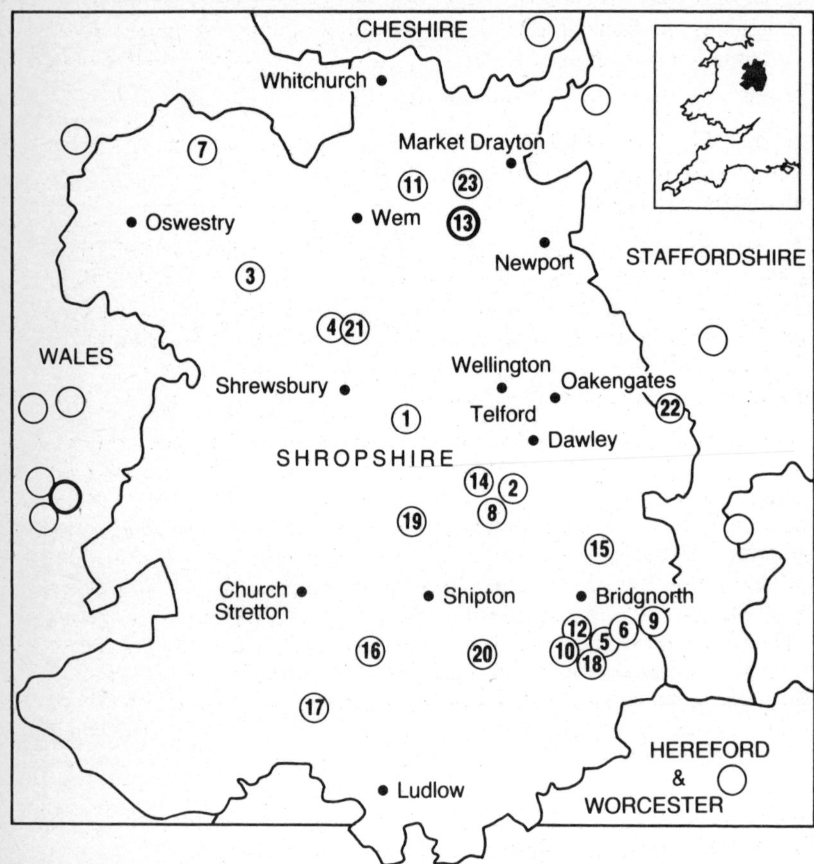

Plain circle numbers can be found by turning to neighbouring counties. Two-starred gardens are ringed in bold.

ATTINGHAM PARK 1

Attingham, Nr Shrewsbury, Shropshire. Tel: (074377) 203
The National Trust

4m SE of Shrewsbury. Turn off A5 at Atcham • Parking • Licensed tearoom, 12.30 - 5 p.m. Picnics allowed along Mile Walk • Toilet facilities • Partly suitable for wheelchairs • Dogs on lead in grounds (not allowed in deer park) • Shop • House open 30th March to Sept, Sat - Wed, 1.30 - 5 p.m. Oct, Sat and Sun, 1.30 - 5 p.m. Last admission 4.30 p.m. • Grounds and park open daily except 25th Dec during daylight hours • Entrance: 80p (house and park £2.70).

The house is really the main attraction, but one can also enjoy a half-mile walk by the River Tern with daffodils in the spring followed by azaleas and rhododendrons. In autumn, colour is provided by dogwoods and American thorns. Foundations of the old mill can be seen below the upper weir. A few perennials near the house but this is a garden mainly of large trees and shrubs.

BENTHALL HALL 2

Broseley, Shropshire. Tel: (0952) 882159
The National Trust

1m SW of Broseley off B4375, 4m NE of Much Wenlock, 8m S of Wellington • Best season: spring and summer • Parking 150 yards down road • Toilet facilities • Partly suitable for wheelchairs • Part of house open same times as garden • Open 31st March to Sept, Wed, Sun and Bank Holiday Mon, 1.30 - 5.30 p.m. Last admission 5 p.m. Parties at other times by arrangement • Entrance: £1 (£2 house and gardens)

A small garden containing some interesting plants and features and some nice topiary. George Maw and Robert Bateman both lived in the house and contributed to the garden design and plant collection. Graham Stuart Thomas was involved in the restoration work. The rose garden has some lovely plants and a small pool and there is a delightful raised scree bed. A good collection of geraniums and ground-cover plants together with a peony bed, clematis and roses through trees and shrubs create a pleasant garden to stroll through. The crocus introduced by George Maw and daffodils in spring provide interest, and the many large trees of Scots pine, beech and oak are stunning features. A monument to botanical history. Visitors should also view the house and other properties in the area.

BROWNHILL HOUSE 3

Ruyton XI Towns, Shropshire. Tel: (0939) 260626
Roger and Yolande Brown

10m NW of Shrewsbury on B4397 in the village • Best season: end May/mid-July • Parking at the Bridge Inn 100 yards away • Teas • Toilet facilities • Plants for sale • Open 25th to 27th May, 20th, 21st July, 2 - 6 p.m. and by appointment May to Aug • Entrance: £1, children free

This garden is a great credit to the owners who have incorporated a wide range of design features in a most difficult sloping site of one and a half acres. There are about 300 steps through the garden which includes a laburnum walk, patio with a pond, riverside beds with polygonum, astilbe and wild flowers, a bog garden with iris and primulas. Herbaceous borders, a rock garden with shrubs, a range of shrubs and conifers and a good vegetable garden and soft fruit as well as 16 different types of fruit and nut trees; also grape vines and a peach tree. The variety of features is remarkable in a garden started from scratch in 1972.

BURFORD HOUSE GARDENS
(see Hereford & Worcs)

DAVID AUSTIN ROSES 4
Bowling Green Lane, Albrighton, Nr Wolverhampton, Shropshire.
Tel: (0902) 373931
Mr and Mrs David Austin

8m NW of Wolverhampton, 4m from Shifnal, between the A41 and A464. Take junction 3 off M54 towards Albrighton. Turn right at sign 'Roses and Shrubs' then take the second right (Bowling Green Lane) • Best season: late June/July • Parking • Refreshments: teas, coffee and biscuits • Toilet facilities • Suitable for wheelchairs • Dogs on leads • Plant centre • Open Feb to Nov, Mon - Fri, 9 a.m. - 5 p.m., Sat and Sun, 10 a.m. - 6 p.m., Dec and Jan, Mon - Fri, 9 a.m. - 5 p.m., Sat and Sun, 10 a.m. - dusk

David Austin is one of the country's leading rose breeders so this is an ideal place for inspecting roses. There are about 700 varieties, including shrub, old roses, climbing and species. At flowering time there is a riot of colour. They are well displayed and elsewhere there are iris, a peony garden and hardy plants. The nursery stocks a good range of plants other than roses. David Austin's private garden is occasionally open to the public and a charge is made for this.

DINGLE BANK 5
Chelmarsh Common, Nr Bridgnorth, Shropshire. Tel: (0746) 861418
Mr and Mrs Trevor Ford

3m S of Bridgnorth on Highley Road • Best season: summer • Parking 300 yards away at The Bull's Head, Chelmarsh • Plants for sale at nursery • Open 16th June and by appointment • Entrance: £1 (covers this garden and The Paddocks next door)

A pleasant garden developed by the owners with a wide range of conifers, perennials, grasses, lilies and shrubs. Roses and clematis climb through trees. There is also a bog garden. The keen gardener can compare the plants growing here with those available at the nursery. One can then walk through the gate to the cottage-style garden next door.

THE DOROTHY CLIVE GARDEN
(see Staffordshire)

DUDMASTON 6

Quatt, Nr Bridgnorth, Shropshire. Tel: (0746) 780866
The National Trust

4m SE of Bridgnorth on A442 • Best season: late May but planted for spring, summer and autumn colour • Parking • Teas • Toilet facilities • Partly suitable for wheelchairs • Dogs on lead in garden and Dingle only • Plants for sale • Shop • House open £2.40 • Garden open 31st March to Sept, Wed and Sun, 2.30 - 6 p.m. Last admission 5.30 p.m. Special opening for pre-booked parties only Thurs p.m. • Entrance: £1.50 (house and garden £2.50)

An eight-acre garden of appeal and interest with its large pool and bog garden and the associated plants along with island beds with shrubs, azaleas, rhododendrons, viburnum and lovely old roses. Some large specimen trees bring an air of peace to the garden, and there are old fruit trees including mulberry and medlars to add to the interest of old shrubs. Alas, there are no plant labels to help identify the specimens.

ERWAY FARM HOUSE 7

Nr Overton on Dee, Shropshire. Tel: (069175) 479
Mr and Mrs Alan Palmer

3m N of Ellesmere, 2m S of Overton on Dee. On B5068 Ellesmere - St Martins road after Dudleston Heath, turn right then second left • Best season: late May • Parking • Toilet facilities • Plants for sale • Open Easter Sun and Mon, and 7th, 8th May, 2 - 6 p.m. • Entrance: £1, children free. Parties by appointment

It is difficult to describe adequately the wonderful range of plants this garden contains. Starting early in the year are masses of galanthus, hellebores, aconites, and Sprengeri tulips, followed by hostas, iris, peonies and roses. There are many shrubs and trees, including rare willows, under which grow lilies, alliums, hardy cyclamen and fritillarias. Other rare specimens include *Ulmus × hollandica* 'Wredei' and *Abutilon vitifolium*. A charming cottage garden is being made to add summer interest; other plants provide autumn colour. A true plantsperson's garden.

FARLEY HOUSE 8

Nr Much Wenlock, Shropshire. Tel: (0952) 727017
Mr and Mrs R.W. Collingwood

In Much Wenlock on the A458, turn left by garage on to A4169 signed Ironbridge, garden is 1m on left • Parking very limited on main road • Toilet facilities • Plants for sale • Open by arrangement April to Oct • Entrance: 80p

This one-acre garden has been created on a hillside since 1980 by the present owners, and it is interesting to see how they have gradually cleared land to create island beds containing a wide variety of plants. The garden is not yet finished. It has a cottage-garden feel and this is reflected in the plants. Paved area with alpines and raised beds and a peat bed. Small vegetable garden. Nice troughs and range of conifers. There is something of interest in this garden over many months.

FOUR WINDS
(see Wales)

GATACRE PARK 9
Six Ashes, Nr Bridgnorth, Shropshire. Tel: (038488) 211
Lady Thompson

6m SE of Bridgnorth on A58 Stourbridge - Bridgnorth road • Parking • Teas • Toilet facilities • Plants for sale • Open 12th, 19th May, 2 - 6 p.m. • Entrance: £1, OAP 50p, children free. Parties by arrangement

This eight-acre, peaceful garden has a wide range of features and plants. Vast rhododendrons and azaleas in the woodland area contrast with the Italianate sunken garden with a rectangular lily pool, and columnar trees and a yew arch. Island beds of shrubs and herbaceous plants provide good colour and foliage contrasts and include a vast yucca. Nearby on the lawn is a wonderful specimen of *Liriodendron tulipifera* and a large mulberry tree. Elsewhere is fascinating topiary, ranging from teapots, teddy bears and a corkscrew to the Gatacre monster. There are roses, acers, herbaceous borders, an excellent walled garden and good climbers around the house.

GLAZELEY OLD RECTORY 10
Glazeley, Nr Bridgnorth, Shropshire. Tel: (074635) 221
Mr and Mrs J.A. Goodall

3½m S of Bridgnorth on B4363 • Best season: spring and July • Parking by church • Teas. Teas and lunch for parties by arrangement • Toilet facilities • Suitable for wheelchairs • Plants for sale • Open for parties by appointment and 7th July, 2 - 6 p.m. • Entrance: £1, children 25p

This two-acre garden was for many years a nursery and is well designed, leading from one interesting area to another, with a wonderful collection of plants. There is a heather border, paved garden, bed of potentillas, a glade garden with hellebores, hostas, alliums and agapanthus, scree bed, a bog area with primulas and rodgersias, a fern collection and several good herbaceous borders. There are imaginative colour and foliage combinations and many unusual plants; in spring masses of bulbs.

HAWKSTONE HALL 11

Weston-under-Redcastle, Nr Shrewsbury, Shropshire. Tel: (063084) 242
Redemptorists

13m NE of Shrewsbury, 6m SW of Market Drayton on A442. Enter from Marchamley • Teas • Toilet facilities • Principal rooms of house open • Garden open 27th May and 5th to 31st Aug, 2 - 5 p.m. Coach parties by arrangement at weekends • Entrance: £1.75, children 75p (house and gardens)

Large old garden surrounding a Georgian mansion which is undergoing restoration. A lily pool with adjacent rockery and some beautiful old trees including a monkey puzzle. Rhododendrons provide spring colour. At the Hall is an attractive winter garden and also a courtyard garden with ideas for those with restricted space.

HAYE HOUSE 12

Eardington, Nr. Bridgnorth, Shropshire. Tel: (0746) 764884
Mrs Eileen Paradise

2½m S of Bridgnorth on the B4555 Highley road. Through village of Eardington, then farmhouse 1m on left • Best season: July • Parking in courtyard • Teas with home-made cakes by prior arrangement • Toilet facilities • Partly suitable for wheelchairs • Plants possibly for sale • Open by arrangement • Entrance: £1

The owner is a National Flower Demonstrator and accepts parties for demonstrations. The garden is planned to provide appropriate material and specimens. Half the vegetable garden contains foliage material. The old tennis court on the outskirts is being planted up with trailing plants. Of particular interest to flower arrangers but also to keen gardeners.

HODNET HALL ★★ 13

Hodnet, Shropshire. Tel: (063084) 202
Mr A.E.H. and The Hon. Mrs Heber-Percy

5½m SW of Market Drayton, 12m NE of Shrewsbury at junction of A53 and A442 • Best season: early summer • Parking for cars and coaches • Refreshments: snacks and teas • Toilet facilities • Partly suitable for wheelchairs • Dogs on lead • Plants for sale • Shop • Open Good Fri to Sept, daily, 2 - 5 p.m., Sun and Bank Holidays, 12 noon - 5.30 p.m. • Entrance: £2, OAP and parties per person £1.60, children £1

This garden has been superbly planted to give interest through the seasons - daffodils and blossom in spring, then primulas, rhododendrons, azaleas, laburnums and lilacs, followed by roses, peonies and astilbes merging in summer with the hydrangeas and shrubs that continue until the autumn foliage and berries round off the year. There are great trees on the estate and a magnolia walk along with many unusual plants. One of the oak trees is mentioned in the Domesday Book. Arranged around a chain of lakes which comprise one of the largest water gardens in England, it is the home of a romantic bevy of black swans. Magnificent at all seasons. The walled kitchen garden is set aside for the sale of shrubs, fruit, flowers and vegetables.

LIMEBURNERS ★ 14

Lincoln Hill, Ironbridge, Shropshire. Tel: (095245) 3715
Mr and Mrs J.E. Derry

Turn off B4380 W of Ironbridge up Lincoln Hill and garden is on left at top • Toilet facilities • Partly suitable for wheelchairs • Open April to Sept by appointment • Entrance: £1, children 25p

Walking round this delightful garden there are always surprises in store and a wealth of interesting plants to see. The wildlife garden has a wide range of trees and shrubs and the use of ground-cover plants must help to reduce maintenance. Nice to see roses climbing through shrubs; the planting combinations throughout the garden are excellent. The owners have even managed to provide colour on a limestone bank. Further developments keep taking place, including a new lilium area.

LOWER HALL ★ 15

Worfield, Nr Bridgnorth, Shropshire. Tel: (07464) 607
Mr and Mrs C.F. Dumbell

A454 Wolverhampton/Bridgnorth road, turn right to Worfield and after passing village stores and pub turn right • Best season: May to July • Parking in driveway or nearby roads • Tea and biscuits for parties • Toilet facilities • Suitable for wheelchairs • Dogs on lead • Plants for sale • Open by pre-arrangement with owners and for charity 23rd, 30th June • Entrance: £1.50, OAP £120, children free

This modern plantsman's garden has been created by the present owners since 1964 with help from the designer Lanning Roper. The walled garden has old brick paths and fruit trees through which climb roses and clematis; over the walls the village cottages and the Tudor house provide a fine backcloth to the garden. Everywhere the use of colour combinations and plant associations is good - a red border, another of white and green, giving a cool effect. The water garden contains two weirs and the woodland garden includes rare magnolias, a collection of birch to provide bark interest, conifers, acers, amelanchiers - everything to provide all-year variety and colour.

MILLICHOPE PARK 16

Munslow, Craven Arms, Shropshire. Tel: (058476) 234
Mr and Mrs L. Bury

8m NE of Craven Arms, 11m from Ludlow on B4368 Craven Arms road • Parking • Refreshments for June opening date. Picnics allowed in woodland • Toilet facilities • Dogs on leads • Plants for sale when available • Open 12th May, 23rd June, 2 - 6 p.m. and by appointment • Entrance: £1.50, children 50p

This 13-acre garden stands on the slopes of Wenlock Edge looking across to the Brown Clee Hill, and the view from the house includes a splendid artificial lake and vast trees, including a cedar of Lebanon, Douglas firs, copper beeches, Californian redwoods and an 140-foot *Abies procera*. Wandering through the woodland in spring, visitors enjoy masses of wild flowers - primroses, violets, bluebells and rhododendrons. The herbaceous borders are in the form of several small gardens surrounded by yew hedges. There is a series of small lakes and a pool surrounded by bog plants. Good pieces of sculpture and a lovely old temple.

OLDFIELD 17

Nr Long Meadow End, Craven Arms, Shropshire. Tel: (0588) 672733
Mr and Mrs P. Housden

From Craven Arms take B4368 towards Clun. After 1½m turn right at telephone box, after 200 yards, turn left over cattle grid then on ¾m • Best season: July to Oct • Parking • Teas on open day and for pre-booked parties • Toilet facilities • Partly suitable for wheelchairs • Open 7th July and parties by arrangement • Entrance: £1, children 50p

The owners have worked hard since 1980 to create this three-acre garden with its pool and bog garden. Roses surround the house and are also used for ground cover. A range of soft fruits and fan and espalier-trained trees, a vegetable garden and old and new woodland areas. Other attractions include bee hives and bonsai trees. A new shrubbery contains some fine specimens including golden birch and there are five different oaks, *Quercus rubra*, alder and acers in the Oak Wood. The walls of an old ruin form a delightful paved area with iris and euphorbias amongst other lovely plants. The garden continues to be developed with the aim of all year round colour.

THE PADDOCKS 18

Chelmarsh Common, Chelmarsh, Nr Bridgnorth, Shropshire.
Tel: (0746) 861271
Mr and Mrs P. Hales

3m S of Bridgnorth on Highley Road • Best season: summer • Parking 300 yards away at The Bulls Head, Chelmarsh • Open 16th June, 2 - 6 p.m. or by prior appointment • Entrance: £1 (covers this garden and Dingle Bank next door)

A contrast to the more formal garden next door, with good use of old materials to make paths, pergolas and a rockery. Typical cottage plants have been used and the garden is divided into 'room' areas. There is a stream garden with a bog area with good ideas for the amateur gardener. With the nursery attached to Dingle Bank next door (see entry) the two gardens contain a vast range of plants. A charming small rose garden has been added.

PREEN MANOR ★ 19

Church Preen, Nr Church Stretton, Shropshire. Tel: (06943) 207
Mr and Mrs P. Trevor-Jones

5m SW of Much Wenlock on B4371, 3m turn right for Church Preen and Hughley and after 1½m turn left for Church Preen, over crossroads and drive ½m on right • Parking • Teas • Plants for sale if available • Open to parties by arrangement in June and July only • Entrance: £1.25, children 25p

An exceptional garden designed by Norman Shaw with many features and set in a park with fine old trees. The present owners have restored and replanned it and round every corner or through a gateway there is always a surprise. The gravel garden has a yellow and white border and elsewhere is a silver border. The chess garden has replaced the swimming pool and there is a pot garden filling a corner. The vegetable garden has a parterre design and each bed has variety. The bog garden is attractive, and the unusual fernery is sited amongst some ruins. One could spend a day here trying to absorb the design features and superb planting and enjoying the setting.

RUTHALL MANOR ★ 20

Ditton Priors, Bridgnorth, Shropshire. Tel: (074634) 608
Mr and Mrs G.T. Clarke

From Morville take B4368 and turn off for Ditton Priors. Weston Road from village church and take 2nd left road • Best season: Easter to Oct • Parking in adjacent field • Tea shop in village from 11 a.m. – 5 p.m. • Toilet facilities • Suitable for wheelchairs • Plants possibly for sale • Open for parties by arrangement • Entrance: £1 for conducted tour

This one-acre garden has been cleverly designed since 1972 for ease of maintenance and planted to give pleasure to keen plant lovers. There are some unusual specimens and a collection of daphnes and birches and a group of sorbus, ilex, robinia and willows. By the pool is a collection of primulas, astilbes and iris. Good foliage and colour contrasts and something of interest all through the year. There is also a small vegetable garden and a collection of ferns.

SWALLOW HAYES 21

Rectory Road, Albrighton, Shropshire. Tel: (0902) 372624
Mrs Michael Edwards

7m NW of Wolverhampton. Turn off A41 into Rectory Road after garden centre • Best season: May/June and autumn • Parking in drive and nearby road • Teas on open days • Toilet facilities • Suitable for wheelchairs • Dogs on lead • Plants for sale when available • Open 25th April, 9th, 19th, 30th May, 2nd June and for parties by arrangement • Entrance: £1, children 10p

A delightful two-acre modern garden with many design features and a beautiful display of plants, shrubs and trees. Although planted for easy maintenance, it contains 2000 different types of plants and provides all-year interest. Alpine border divided into various soil conditions, Mediterranean wall with tender plants. Small pools, herbs, a woodland area, colour and foliage contrasts. The National collection of witch hazels and lupins and an interesting area of small gardens for one to copy at home. Vegetables and fruit trees; further developments in hand.

WESTON PARK ★ 22

Weston-under-Lizard, Nr Shifnal, Shropshire. Tel: (095276) 207
The Earl and Countess of Bradford

On A5 7m W of junction 12 on M6 and 3m N of junction 3 on M54 • Best season: May/June • Parking • Cafeteria in old stables providing home baking and estate produce. Also picnic teas • Toilet facilities • Partly suitable for wheelchairs • Dogs • Shop • House open on certain occasions at additional entrance fee • Gardens open April/May, weekends and Bank Holidays, June/July, daily except Mon and Fri, Aug, daily, Sept weekends only, 11 a.m. – 7 p.m. • Entrance: £2.75, OAP and children £1.75

A distinctive 'Capability' Brown creation covering almost 1,000 acres of delightful woodland planted with rhododendrons and azaleas, together with beautiful pools. Some magnificent trees form a handsome backcloth to many shrubs. A rose walk leads to the deer park and there is a walled garden. The rose garden by the house and the Italian parterre garden have been restored. There are many architectural features – The Temple of Diana, Roman bridge and the orangery all designed by James Paine. For children there is an adventure playground, the Weston Park Railway, a pets corner, pottery, aquarium and museum.

WOLLERTON OLD HALL 23

Wollerton, Hodnet, Shropshire.
Tel: (0630) 84769, or (0630) 84756 during office hours
Mr and Mrs John Jenkins

From Shrewsbury take A53 to Hodnet. Turn right towards Market Drayton, then right just after Wollerton sign. Keep right at red brick animal shelter. The garden is the third on left • Parking • Toilet facilities • Plants for sale • Open June to Sept, Fri, 2 - 6 p.m. • Entrance: £1, children 50p

Mrs Jenkins has returned to her childhood home and has remade the knot garden; small gardens have been created using brick walls, beech and yew hedges with paths made of a variety of materials. Roses and clematis scramble over iron arches, and the white garden is charming. A wide variety of shrubs and perennials have been cleverly planted to give foliage and colour associations, and the old brick walls are clothed with climbers.

GARDENS OPEN RARELY

The following gardens are open to the public on three days or less in the year, although they may also be open by appointment if this is stated in the text. For details see individual entry.
May 12 Gatacre Park; Millichope Park; **May 19** Gatacre Park; **June 16** Dingle Bank; The Paddocks; **June 23** Lower Hall; Millichope Park; **June 30** Lower Hall; **July 7** Glazeley Old Rectory; Oldfield.

SOMERSET

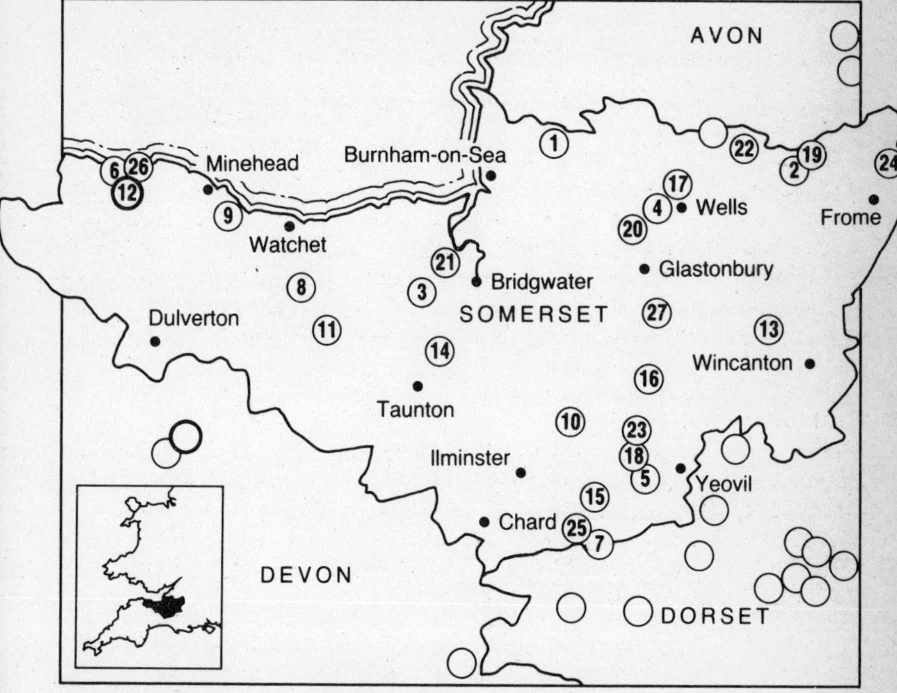

Plain circle numbers can be found by turning to neighbouring counties. Two-starred gardens are ringed in bold.

AMBLESIDE AVIARIES AND GARDENS 1

Lower Weare, Nr Axbridge, Somerset. Tel: (0934) 732362
Mrs R.K. Pickford

1½m SW of Axbridge on A38 • Best season: May • Parking • Coaches by appointment • Refreshments: licensed restaurant, cream teas, ice-creams • Toilet facilities • Suitable for wheelchairs • Souvenir and gift shop • Open March to Oct daily, Nov to Feb Sat and Sun only, 10 a.m. - 5 p.m. Closed 25th Dec to 16th Jan • Entrance: £1.75, OAP 90p, children 2 - 14 75p

The trees around the large pool, which is bisected by a bridge, are really all that remain of the original plan by the owner of some 40 years ago who conceived the idea of a water garden as depicted on the 'Willow Pattern' plate. The cherry blossom reflected in the lily pond, silhouetted by willows of different varieties, give an oriental effect. The aviaries do not intrude on the water garden and the variety of ducks adds to the atmosphere of rural peace in spite of the busy road running alongside a high hedge.

AMMERDOWN HOUSE ★ 2

Kilmersdon, Radstock, Somerset.
Lord Hylton

On the B3139, ½m off A362 Radstock to Frome road • Best season: summer • Parking • Open 1st April, 26th Aug, 11 a.m. - 5 p.m. • Entrance: £1.40

A Bath-stone house perched on the crest of a hill with panoramic views on one side and a Lutyens garden on the other. This garden was a brilliant conception by Lutyens who wanted to link the house with the orangery. When one walks through the Italianate 'rooms' of yew and sculpture and parterre, one is unaware of the tricks of space that are being played. Massive yew planting, now mature and fully 12 foot high, creates enclosed formal areas which lead irresistably one from another - the awkward-shaped spaces between being almost entirely filled with hedging. Upkeep seems to have been pared to a minimum but the originality and grandeur remain as do some particularly nice details such as the clipped Portuguese laurels, honeysuckles trained over nice umbrellas and ancient lemon verbenas in pots in the orangery.

BARFORD PARK ★ 3

Enmore, Nr Bridgwater, Somerset. Tel: (0278) 67269
Mr and Mrs M. Stancombe

5m W of Bridgwater. Turn right to Spaxton off the Enmore Road from Bridgwater • Best season: June/July • Parking • Teas by arrangement • Partly suitable for wheelchairs • Dogs on lead • House open • Garden open May to Sept, Wed, Thurs and Bank Holidays • Entrance: 50p (£2 house and garden), children free

This is a garden in the eighteenth-century style developed over the last 32 years. Set in parkland and protected by a ha-ha on three sides, it has many features. After watching the golden orfe darting around the lily pond, stroll down a sweep of lawn to a stand of tall trees. There, in the woodland glade is a carpet of many shades of primulas. The eighteenth-century walled garden is unusually situated in view of the terrace - a sweep of lawn with deep herbaceous borders on each side make a colourful vista.

THE BISHOPS PALACE ★ 4

Wells, Somerset. Tel: (0749) 78691
The Church Commissioners

In centre of Wells, adjacent to Cathedral • Public parking in city car parks nearby • Light refreshments • Toilet facilities • Bishop's Chapel open • Garden open Easter to Oct, Sun, Thurs and Bank Holidays, 2 - 6 p.m. Also for exhibitions and charity days • Entrance: £1, children 50p, family £3. Season ticket available

The ruins of the banqueting hall have been 'room scaped' with shrubs and herbaceous plants. A shrub rose garden has been planted near the water (from the wells). An unusual garden ornament has been carved from the root of a very old yew tree, depicting Adam and Eve being expelled from the Garden of Eden by an angel with a flaming sword. There are fine mature trees from plantings in the mid-nineteenth century, e.g. black walnut, gingko; and an acre of the walled garden was laid out as an arboretum to commemorate the Queen's Silver Jubilee in 1977. An interesting collection which includes the Chinese foxglove tree and a European hornbeam.

BRYMPTON D'EVERCY ★ 5

Yeovil, Somerset. Tel: (0935) 862528
Mr and Mrs Charles Clive-Ponsonby-Fane

Just W of Yeovil, signposted off A30 and A3088 • Best seasons: spring and June/July • Parking • Home-made teas • Toilet facilities • Partly suitable for wheelchairs • Plants for sale • Shop • House, vineyard and distillery open • Garden open Easter to Sept, Sat - Wed, 2 - 6 p.m. • Entrance: £3.20 (house and gardens). Discounts for OAPs and NT members Mon - Wed

The quiet elegance of the forecourt, a smooth lawn edged with yellow and white herbaceous plants, hardly prepares one for the wealth of colour on which the door of the south terrace opens. Shrub roses, escallonias, hibiscus and cistus flourish in the narrow bed along the many-windowed stone wall up which climb 'Albertine' roses, wisteria, *Robinia hispida* 'Rosea', abutilons, and a creamy, variegated euonymus. On the lower terrace lilies, alstroemerias and erigerons have been planted between roses. Across the sweep of lawn the pond, fringed with iris and gunneras, shimmers with water lilies and is backed by an interesing grouping of oaks, yews, acacias, golden-leaved poplars contrasting with copper beech and *Liriodendron tulipifera*. On the north side of the house the vineyard is planted on the south-facing slope of a small hill protected from the wind by the surrounding arboretum which is now developing.

CHAPEL KNAP ★ 6

Porlock Weir, Somerset. Tel: (0643) 862364
Dr and Mrs H.K.N. Lister

From A39 to Porlock, take the road to Porlock Weir then turn left to Worthy toll road • Best season: May/June • Parking in narrow road, and 4 minutes' walk away at Weir • Refreshments: tea and coffee • Toilet facilities • Open Easter to Sept, Tues, 10 a.m. - 5.30 p.m. • Entrance: £1, children free

An unusual garden overlooking Porlock Bay which, because of its sheltered position, high rainfall and frost-free climate, contains many sub-tropical plants normally associated with conservatory or greenhouse. The backcloth of the sea, large pine trees (*Pinus radiata*) and Chusan palms give the garden a

Mediterranean feel not often found in the West of England. It contains the National collection or argyranthemums and hoherias. Greencombe (see entry) is nearby.

CLAPTON COURT ★ 7

Clapton, Crewkerne, Somerset. Tel: (0460) 73220/72200
Captain S.J. Loder

3m S of Crewkerne on B3165 • Parking • Coaches and private parties by arrangement only • Refreshments: light lunches and teas for parties by arrangement • Toilet facilities • Partly suitable for wheelchairs • Unusual plants for sale Feb to Oct in large centre • Open March to Oct, Mon – Fri, 10.30 a.m. – 5 p.m., Sun, 2 – 5 p.m. and Easter Sat only, 2 – 5 p.m. • Entrance: £3, children under 14 £1, groups of 20 or more £2.40 per person

A very well-kept formal garden, with rare plants and shrubs clearly labelled, rubbing shoulders with some homely indigenous varieties. The woodland garden developed by the present owner on a steep slope set amongst some mature trees has a stream controlled by a series of small brooks that provides the conditions required for rarer wild plants. Many of the plants are 'Loderi' varieties and hybrids of rhododendrons which were introduced by Captain Loder's great uncle who developed the famous Leonardslee garden in Sussex. Captain Loder has completely redesigned and replanted the rose garden in a new formal design.

COMBE SYDENHAM HALL 8

Monksilver, Taunton, Somerset. Tel: (0984) 56284
Mr and Mrs W. Theed

5m S of Watchet on B3188 between Monksilver and Elworthy • Parking inc. coaches • Light refreshments, home-made teas • Toilet facilities • Plants for sale • Shop (inc. trout from estate) • Open Easter to Oct, Mon – Fri, 11 a.m. – 5 p.m. • Entrance: £2.50, OAP/children £1.80 (garden and country park)

Set in a deer park, the small formal Elizabethan parterre-garden is being restored and restocked with old types of roses. The pink lavender is a source of pride to Mrs Theed who also cultivates the old herb garden. Quince trees and a peacock house create the atmosphere of a domestic garden in Tudor times.

DUNSTER CASTLE ★ 9

Dunster, Nr Minehead, Somerset. Tel: (0643) 821314
The National Trust

3m SE of Minehead on A39 • Best season: May/June • Parking • Refreshments in Dunster • Toilet facilities • Dogs in park only • National

Trust shop • Castle open 25th March to Sept, Sa
Oct, Sat - Wed, 12 noon - 4 p.m. Open Bank Holi
March to 3rd Nov, daily, 11 a.m. - 5 p.m. or dusk if
£1.90, children 80p (castle and gardens £4, children £

The family which had lived here since the fourteenth ... National Trust in 1976. A very fine herbaceous border b... surrounds a lawn by the keep and is well worth the steep cli... the formal terraces below thrive a variety of sub-tropical plan... ...lias and azaleas. There are views across to Exmoor, the Quantocks a... the Bristol Channel. The park totals 28 acres in all.

EAST LAMBROOK MANOR ★ 10

Nr South Petherton, Somerset. Tel: (0460) 40328
Mr and Mrs A. Norton

2m NE of South Petherton off A303 • Parking • No coaches • Refreshments: coffee and biscuits only but parties by arrangement • Toilet facilities • Plants for sale (mailing list) • Shop for Margery Fish publications • Open 15th Jan to Oct, Mon - Sat and Bank Holiday Sun and Mon, 10 a.m. - 5 p.m. • Entrance: £1.65, OAP £1.50, school age children 50p

Margery Fish established these gardens for endangered species and the present owners have carried on her tradition. The result is an impression of luxuriant growth. The garden's ring paths are half-hidden by the profusion of plants and its controlled wilderness of colour and scent give the discerning a chance to find rare plants and shrubs.

FORDE ABBEY

(see Dorset)

GAULDEN MANOR ★ 11

Tolland, Nr Lydeard St Lawrence, Somerset. Tel: (09847) 213
Mr J.H.N. Starkie

9m NW of Taunton off A358 • Parking • Teas by arrangement for parties • Toilet facilities • Shop • House open • Garden open Easter Sun and Mon, and 5th May to 1st Sept, Sun, Thurs and Bank Holidays, 2 - 5.30 p.m. • Entrance: £1 (house and gardens £2.50)

Garden seats at vantage points give the visitor a chance to appreciate the many different vistas provided in this country garden which includes a bog garden, herb garden, butterfly garden and herbaceous borders of selected colour. A short walk through a woodland glade leads to a secret garden of white flowering plants. Visitors should not miss the small duck garden near the tea house with carvings on the fence posts.

…MBE ★★ 12

…omerset. Tel: (0643) 862363
…ncombe Garden Trust (Miss Joan Loraine)

½m W of Porlock off B3226 • Parking • Coaches by arrangement • Toilet facility • Partly suitable for wheelchairs • Plants for sale • Open April to July, Sat - Mon, 2 - 6 p.m. or by appointment • Entrance: £1.80, children 50p

Created in 1946 by Horace Stroud, this garden was extended by the present owner over the last 21 years. Overlooking the Severn, set on a hillside where the sun cannot penetrate for nearly two months in the winter, it glows with colour. The formal lawns and beds round the house are immaculate and by contrast the woodland area, terraced on the hillside, provides a nature walk of great interest. A wide variety of rhododendrons and azaleas flower in the shelter of mature trees, where ferns and woodland plants flourish. No sprays or chemicals are used in the cultivation of this completely 'organic' garden which contains the National collection of polystichum.

HADSPEN HOUSE ★ 13

Castle Cary, Somerset. Tel: (0963) 50939
Mr N.A. Hobhouse

2m SE of Castle Cary on A371 • Parking • Coaches by arrangement • Teas on Sun and Bank Holidays • Toilet facilities • Partly suitable for wheelchairs • Plants for sale • Open March to 1st Oct, Thurs - Sun but open Bank Holiday Mon, 9 a.m. - 6 p.m. • Entrance: £2, children 50p

This family garden, developed over the last 200 years, was reclaimed by Penelope Hobhouse after the last war. A large curved wall encloses a garden, sectioned by paved paths, which offers vistas of individual interest including herbaceous plants, old-fashioned roses and even vegetables. A wild-flower meadow set in parkland contrasts well with the ornamental garden near the house.

HESTERCOMBE HOUSE GARDENS 14

Cheddon Fitzpaine, Taunton, Somerset. Tel: (0823) 337222
Somerset County Council

Close to the village of Cheddon Fitzpaine just N of Taunton, follow the 'Daisy' sign to the garden • Best season: midsummer • Parking • Coaches by arrangement only • Picnics on lawn • Toilet facilities in house • Wheelchairs limited to four main areas • Open all year, Mon - Fri, 9 a.m. - 5 p.m., Sat and Sun, 2 - 5 p.m. • Entrance: suggested donation of £1. Garden plan and guide available 50p each

This is a superb product of the collaboration between Edwin Lutyens and Gertrude Jekyll, blending the formal art of architecture with the art of plants. On a limited budget the Somerset County Council has endeavoured to maintain the gardens, respecting the colour groupings of the original designs and keeping the water courses flowing as they would have in Edwardian days. The *Oxford Companion* describes this as Lutyens at his best in the detailed design of steps, pools, walls, paving and seating. The canal, pergola and orangery are fine examples of his work. The Council's programme to restore the gardens to Gertrude Jekyll's original plant design, which they have discovered, is proceeding well. The Eastern Terrace is completed and is a good example.

LOWER SEVERALLS 15

Haselbury Road, Crewkerne, Somerset. Tel: (0460) 73234
Audrey and Mary Pring

1½m NE of Crewkerne off B3165 • Parking on road • Teas on charity open days • Suitable for wheelchairs • Plants for sale • Open March to Oct, weekdays except Thurs, 10 a.m. - 5 p.m., Sun, 2 - 5 p.m. and 9th, 30th June for charity • Entrance: by collecting box, 50p for charity

A typical cottage garden with herbaceous border against stone-walled house. The garden is being enlarged through stone pillars which make a frame for the view of the valley over lawn and varied shrubs, a bank of hostas and a bog garden. Specialists in geraniums and salvias.

LYTES CARY MANOR 16

Nr Somerton, Somerset. Tel: (045822) 3297
The National Trust

2½m NE of Ilchester, signposted from A303 • Best season: late May/early June • Parking (¼m walk) • Suitable for wheelchairs • Plants for sale inc. good selection of perennials • Open 30th March to 30th Oct, Mon, Wed and Sat, 2 - 6 p.m. or dusk if earlier. Last admission 5.30 p.m. • Entrance: £2.50, children £1.30

This garden was revived by its former owner with advice from Graham Stuart Thomas. Pleasing lawns with hedges in Elizabethan style and some topiary. A wide herbaceous border along the length of a stone wall. A large orchard with naturalised bulbs and mown walks adds to the peaceful ambience. Regretfully there is no trace of the original herb garden for which Lytes Cary was famed in the sixteenth century, but a border along the south front is stocked with species of plants cultivated in those days.

MILTON LODGE ★ 17

Wells, Somerset. Tel: (0749) 72168
Mr D.C. Tudway Quilter

½m N of Wells. From A39 to Bristol turn N up Old Bristol Road • Best season: midsummer • Car park on left before reaching drive to house • No coaches • Teas on Sun • Toilet facilities • Open Easter to Oct, daily except Sat, 2 - 6 p.m. • Entrance: £1, children 50p. Private parties by special arrangement (but see above)

The garden, replanted by the present owners in the 1960s, is cultivated down the side of a hill overlooking the Vale of Avalon, affording a magnificent view of Wells Cathedral. A wide variety of plants all suitable for the alkaline soil provide a succession of colours and interest during the summer season, interspersed with ancient oak, cedar and established gingko trees. The 1990 gales badly damaged the adjacent seven-acre arboretum which is usually included in the admission fee. It has had to be closed but may be open again in 1991.

MONTACUTE HOUSE ★ 18

Montacute, Yeovil, Somerset. Tel: (0935) 823289
The National Trust

4m W of Yeovil. NT signs off A3088 and A303 near Ilchester • Best season: June to Sept • Parking • Refreshments: light lunches and teas • Toilet facilities • Suitable for wheelchairs • Dogs on lead. Special walks in park • Plants for sale March to mid-Dec • National Trust shop • House open 30th March to 3rd Nov, daily except Tues, 12.30 - 5.30 p.m. • Gardens open 30th March to March 1992, daily except Tues, 12 noon - 5 p.m. Other times by arrangement with administrator. Park open daily throughout year 12.30 - 5.30 p.m. or dusk if earlier • Entrance: £2 (4th Nov to March £1) (house and garden £4)

This Elizabethan garden of grass lawns surrounded by clipped yews set in terraces is a triumph of formality. Colours are provided by herbaceous borders from mid-summer. The arboretum of rare trees is so far not labelled. The gardens are surrounded by graceful parklands giving vistas and an impression of space. The house provided a backcloth for George Curzon's affair with Elinor Glyn.

R.T. HERBS AND GARDEN 20

Kilmersdon, Radstock, Somerset. Tel: (0761) 35470
Mr and Mrs R. Taylor

6m NE of Shepton Mallet on B3139 • Best season: spring/summer • Public car park adjacent • Refreshments in local pub • Plants for sale • Open daily, 9 a.m. - 6 p.m. or dusk • Entrance: donation box for charity

This is a working garden far removed from the gracious lawns of a stately home but demonstrating the potential of a narrow plot to become a graceful and attractive garden. The wide variety of herbs mingled with herbaceous plants and wild flowers attracts bees, butterflies and insects during the summer and provides feeding grounds for wildlife during the winter months.

SEITHE 20

Godney, Wells, Somerset. Tel: (0934) 712278
John and Renata White

5m W of Wells on B3139. Turn left at Panborough • Parking • Teas • Toilet facility • Suitable for wheelchairs • Organic plants, vegetables and dried flowers for sale • Open 5th May, 11th Aug, 2 - 6 p.m. • Entrance: £1, children free

From house and pond area surrounded by a distinctive range of bamboos, an arch in a towering hedge of clipped × *Cupressocyparis leylandii* leads to a garden of rich organically-grown vegetables surrounded by cologne shrubs and herbaceous plants. This unusual combination has been developed by the owners over many years from an unpromising tip.

SHERBORNE GARDEN

(see Avon)

SOMERSET COLLEGE OF AGRICULTURE AND HORTICULTURE ★ 21

Cannington, Somerset. Tel: (0278) 652226
Somerset County Council

3m NW of Bridgwater on A39 • Parking • Teas for parties by arrangement • Toilet facilities • Suitable for wheelchairs • Plant centre opening early summer 1991 • Open all year, Mon - Fri, 10 a.m. - 6 p.m. or dusk in winter, Sat/Sun, 9 a.m. - 5 p.m. • Entrance: £1, children free

The College was founded in 1922 in the grounds of an old Benedictine priory. Plant specialists may find here the fulfillment of their wildest expectations: the National collection of ceanothus, fremontia, wisteria, osteospermum, abutilon, phormium, cordyline and yucca. Various greenhouses reproduce the conditions - Mediterranean, alpine etc. - for house plants of a different clime. Younger gardeners will be interested in the documented development over the last few years of a butterfly garden. On the other side of the A39 from the College buildings an open area has been landscaped to include a nine-hole golf course and a putting green as well as science plots.

STON EASTON PARK ★ 22

Ston Easton, Somerset. Tel: (076121) 631
Peter and Christine Smedley

11m from Bath, 6m from Wells on A37 • Parking • Teas at hotel • Toilet facilities in hotel • Open by appointment only • Entrance: free

Ston Easton Park is a listed Grade I Palladian house and park. The grounds were laid out and planned by Humphrey Repton in 1792/3. Penelope Hobhouse is working with the Smedleys on the restoration of the park, now the grounds of their hotel. For the opportunity to study the restoration of a great eighteenth-century park in progress it is worth making an appointment to visit. A suitably impressive drive winds past old stables to the plain Palladian magnificence of the house. As always Humphrey Repton made a Red Book with his proposals for improvements. There is a terrace, wide lawns, woods, cedars, beeches, oaks, willows and some new yew hedges. The glory is the view from the great Saloon - or the terrace - over the River Norr which has a bridge and cascades for the correct romantic effect. Vast kitchen garden with glasshouses, a cutting garden and yards of beautifully presented fruit and vegetables. As an example of the dedication of the restoration it took seven years to repair the kitchen garden walls, three and a half years for either side.

TINTINHULL HOUSE GARDEN ★ 23

Tintinhull, Yeovil, Somerset. Tel: (0935) 76233
The National Trust

5m NW of Yeovil, ½m S of A303 • Parking • Teas in courtyard • Suitable for wheelchairs and special parking by arrangement • Open 30th March to Sept, Wed, Thurs, Sat and Bank Holiday Mons, 2 - 6 p.m. • Entrance: £2.50

A relatively small modern garden, barely one acre, which achieves an impression of greater size with a series of vistas created under the influence of Gertrude Jekyll and Hidcote. The wide variety of plants are not labelled in order to retain the charm of a private garden but an inventory is available for interested visitors.

THE TROPICAL BIRD GARDENS 24

Rode, Nr Bath, Somerset. Tel: (0373) 830326
Mr and Mrs D. Risdon

5m NE of Frome, signed off A361 • Parking • Refreshments: licensed cafeteria in summer, light refreshments in winter • Toilet facilities • Suitable for wheelchairs • Clematis for sale in season • Shop • Open all year except 25th Dec, summer 10 a.m. - 6.30 p.m., winter 10 a.m. - dusk. Last admission 1 hour before closing • Entrance: £2.80, OAP £2.30, children £1.40

The gardens have been developed to provide the background and natural habitat, as far as possible, for the birds. The clematis collection was started in

1985 and is now established. Mrs Risdon is the membership secretary of the International Clematis Society (GB and Ireland Branch). The tree trail was badly damaged in the 1990 gales but it is expected to be open again in 1991 when a detailed guide will name the wide variety of trees.

WAYFORD MANOR ★ 25

Clapton, Crewkerne, Somerset. Tel: (0460) 73253
Mr R.L. Goffe

3m SW of Crewkerne off B3165 at Clapton • Parking • Teas for parties • Dogs on lead • Plants for sale • Open 21st April, 12th May, 2nd June, 2 - 6 p.m. Parties by appointment • Entrance: £1, children 30p

A very well-maintained garden of flowering shrubs and trees, rhododendrons and spring bulbs, against the stonework of an Elizabethan house. This is a fine example of the work of Harold Peto who redesigned the garden in 1902.

WOODBOROUGH 26

Porlock Weir, Somerset. Tel: (0643) 862406
Mr and Mrs R.D. Milne

From A39 take B3226 towards Porlock Weir. At Porlock Vale House on right, take left tarmac lane uphill. Garden is the first on right • Best season: May • Limited parking. No coaches • Cream teas • Dogs on lead • Open Easter and Sat, Sun and Bank Holiday Mons in May, 11 a.m. - 5.30 p.m. and at other times by appointment • Entrance: £1 for charities, children free

Sturdy footwear is recommended when visiting this fascinating garden created on a steep (1 in 4) hillside with magnificent views over Porlock Bay. The wide variety of rhododendrons includes some of the lesser-known hybrids, the Ghent azalea has been identified among the many others. A bog garden and two pools add interest over a longer season. Mr and Mrs Milne are hoping to share with visitors their hard-won experience in garden restoration and battle with the dreaded honey fungus.

WOOTTON HOUSE ★ 27

Butleigh Wootton, Nr Glastonbury, Somerset. Tel: (0458) 42348
The Hon. Mrs J. Acland-Hood

3m S of Glastonbury. Minor road to Butleigh from Glastonbury, turn right to Butleigh Wootton. Continue through the village to house • Parking in road • Teas on charity day • Suitable for wheelchairs • Dogs on lead • Open by appointment (except in spring) and 8th Sept, 2 - 5.30 p.m. • Entrance: £1

The present garden design has been developed since 1900. It is a beautiful example of a private country-house garden. A terrace with a view to the Beacon Hill in the Mendips framed by herbaceous beds set in a sweep of lawn. The old-fashioned rose garden against a stone well leads to the woodland area where anemones and fritillaries grow as well as cyclamen. In the park is a monument to Admiral Hood, a family ancestor.

GARDENS OPEN RARELY

The following gardens are open to the public on three days or less in the year, although they may also be open by appointment if this is stated in the text. For details see individual entry.

April 1 Ammerdown House; **April 21** Wayford Manor; **May 5** Seithe; **May 12** Wayford Manor; **June 2** Wayford Manor; **Aug 11** Seithe; **Aug 26** Ammerdown House; **Sept 8** Wootton House.

STAFFORDSHIRE

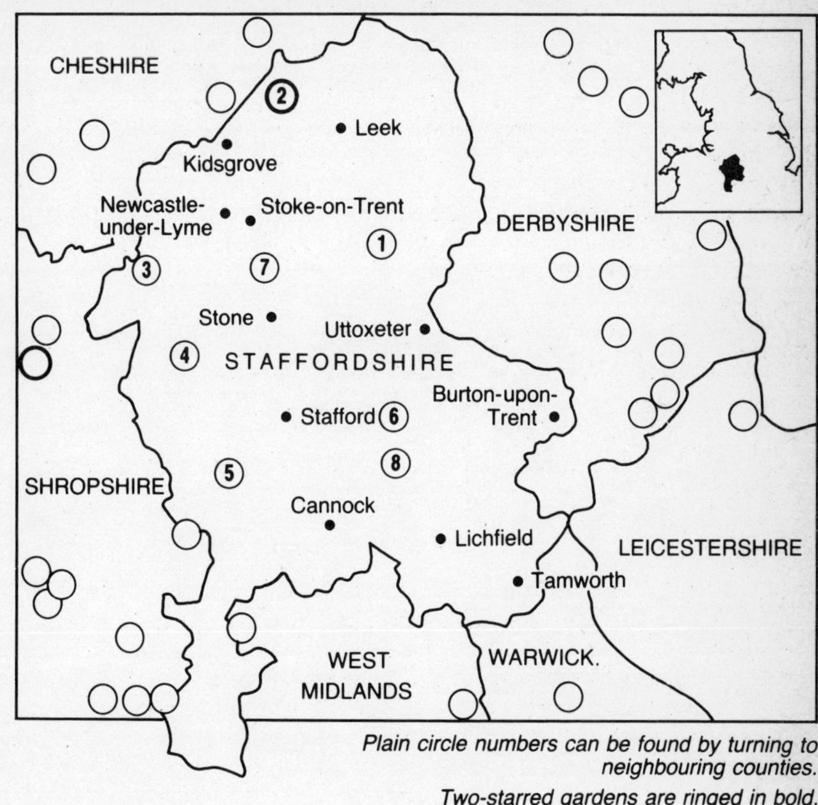

Plain circle numbers can be found by turning to neighbouring counties.

Two-starred gardens are ringed in bold.

ALTON TOWERS ★ 1

Alton, Staffordshire. Tel: (0538) 702200
Alton Towers

From N take M6 junction 16 or M1 junction 28, from S take M6 junction 15 or M1 junction 24. Signposted • Best season: spring/summer • Parking • Refreshments: restaurants, kiosks, picnic areas • Toilet facilities • Suitable for wheelchairs • Dogs on lead • Shop • Ruin open. Pleasure park open at additional cost, Easter to early Nov • Garden open all year • Entrance: end March to early Nov £9.50, OAP £4.50, children 4 – 14 £7.50, children under 4 free (pleasure park and gardens). Early Nov to end March £2, children £1 (pleasure park closed)

This fantastic garden of ornamental architecture was one of the last great follies, created in the early nineteenth century. It contains many beautiful and unusual features including the Chinese Pagoda fountain, a copy of the To Ho pagoda in Canton. The enormous rock garden is planted with a range of conifers, acers and sedums. The fine conservatory houses geraniums and other colour according to the season and the terraces have rose and herbaceous borders. There is a Dutch garden, Her Ladyship's Garden featuring yew and rose beds, the Italian garden, a yew arch walkway and woodland walks. There is water to add further beauty and interest. In addition, there are all the attractions of the pleasure park in season.

BIDDULPH GRANGE GARDEN ★★ 2

Biddulph Grange, Biddulph, Stoke-on-Trent, Staffordshire.
Tel: (074377) 649/343
The National Trust

10m N of Stoke-on-Trent off A527 and 4m from Kidsgrove and Congleton • Best season: May • Parking • Tearoom • Access for disabled difficult so contact head gardener • Shop • Open May to 3rd Nov, Wed - Fri, 2 - 6 p.m., Sat, Sun and Bank Holiday Mon, 11 a.m. - 6 p.m. Last admission 5.30 p.m. or dusk if earlier. 9th Nov to 18th Dec, Sat and Sun, 12 noon - 4 p.m. • Entrance: £3

One of the most remarkable and innovative gardens of the nineteenth century. Designed by James Bateman and Edward Cooke, it contains a series of smaller gardens separated by rocky outcrops, tunnels, walls and tree-lined banks. An Egyptian Garden contains a pyramid of clipped yews and stone sphinx and a stone monster. In the Chinese Garden is a pagoda, joss house and water buffalo and a fine pool. Masses of rhododendrons reflect in the waters of a lily pool, and elsewhere is a rocky glen and sunken dahlia walk. Beautiful trees form a backcloth to this most interesting garden of about 15 acres. Alton Towers (see entry) is nearby.

THE DOROTHY CLIVE GARDEN ★ 3

Willoughbridge, Nr Market Drayton, Shropshire. Tel: (063081 237
Willoughbridge Garden Trust

7m N of Market Drayton, 1m E of Woore on A51 between Nantwich and Stone • Parking inc. car park for disabled • Refreshments in tea room • Toilet facilities • Partly suitable for wheelchairs • Plants for sale in certain seasons • Open April to Oct, daily, 10 a.m. - 5.30 p.m. • Entrance: £1.50, children 50p

Created by the late Colonel Clive in memory of his wife with the help of distinguished gardeners including John Codrington, this garden has wide appeal because of both its design and inspired planting. The coloured guide identifies the highlights season by season. These include the rhododendrons and azaleas in the quarry garden and the pool with the scree garden rising on the hillside above it. In spring there are unusual bulbs and primulas, in summer colourful shrubs, unusual perennials and many conifers; other trees provide autumn colour. The scree garden must give gardeners many good ideas. A garden of great peace and pleasure.

ECCLESHALL CASTLE GARDENS 4

Eccleshall, Staffordshire. Tel: (0785) 850204
Mr and Mrs Mark Carter

½m N of Eccleshall on A519. 6m from M6 junction 14 or 10m from M6 junction 15 • Best season: April/May and July • Parking • Teas • Toilet facilities • Dogs on lead • Open for charity Easter to Sept, daily except Sat, 2 – 5.30 p.m. • Entrance: £1, children 50p

The entrance is along the lime avenue, probably over 200 years old; there are many other old trees in the grounds, and new ones are being planted. The 650-year-old walls of the moat garden and the beautiful arches of the bridge and the renovated fourteenth-century tower are features of this old-world garden. The rose garden, espalier pear trees, rows of indigenous hornbeam, herbaceous borders and masses of rhododendrons create a sense of tranquillity. At present there is some disruption as work goes on to restore the garden to its former glory, but with a visit to the William and Mary mansion included one can enjoy its charm nonetheless.

LITTLE ONN HALL 5

Church Eaton, Near Stafford, Staffordshire. Tel: (0785) 840154
Mr and Mrs I.H. Kidson

6m SW of Stafford, 2m S of Church Eaton, midway between the A5 and A518 • Parking • Teas • Partly suitable for wheelchairs • Open 19th May, 9th June, 2 – 6 p.m. • Entrance: £1.50, children 50p

Entering this six-acre garden the driveway is flanked with long herbaceous borders backed by yew hedges and elsewhere are more herbaceous borders. The large rose garden has standards, shrub and hybrid teas. An unusual-shaped pool known as the 'Dog Bone' has water lilies and elsewhere in the garden are bog plants. Since 1971 the present owners have been planting new trees and are trying to maintain the original design by Thomas H. Mawson of Windermere. There are many rhododendrons, spring bulbs and large beeches and conifers thus ensuring colour for quite a long season. Some areas are somewhat overgrown, but the moat garden gives the garden a sense of mystery and charm.

SHUGBOROUGH ★ 6

Great Haywood, Milford, Staffordshire. Tel: (0889) 881388
The National Trust

6m E of Stafford on A513 • Best season: July • Parking • Refreshments: lunches and snacks in tea room, also picnic areas • Toilet facilities • Suitable for wheelchairs • Dogs on lead in park only • Shop • House, museum and adjacent farm open at same time as gardens • Open 29th March to 27th Oct, daily, 11 a.m. - 5 p.m., 28th Oct to 21st Dec, 11 a.m. - 4 p.m., 2nd Jan to 28th March 1992, 10.30 a.m. - 4 p.m. for pre-booked parties only. Also open for pre-booked parties all year round from 10.30 a.m. • Entrance: £1 per vehicle to parkland. House, museum and farm £6 (OAP £3)

Of interest to garden historians as there are many buildings and monuments in neo-Grecian style ascribed to James 'Athenian' Stuart and built for Admiral Anson from the 1740s onwards. These are some of the earliest examples of English neo-classicism and there is also an early example of chinoiserie based on a sketch made by one of the officers on Admiral Anson's voyage round the world. However, the buildings are 'somewhat randomly scattered rather than sited according to a programme' as at Stourhead, according to the *Oxford Companion*. As for the garden, the Victorian layout was revitalized for the Trust in the mid-1960s by Graham Stuart Thomas who designed a rose garden with various elements in the French style, with roses appropriate to the period. There is also a woodland walk.

TRENTHAM PARK GARDENS 7

Trentham, Stoke-on-Trent, Staffordshire. Tel: (0782) 657341
Country Sports International

On A34 S of Stoke-on-Trent. 2m from M6 junction 15 • Best season: summer • Parking • Refreshments • Toilet facilities • Suitable for wheelchairs • Dogs on lead • Garden centre and conference centre with restaurant facilities adjacent • Open all year 9 a.m. - dusk • Entrance: £2.50, OAP and children £1.50. Half price after 6 p.m.

These 400 acres of parkland were designed by 'Capability' Brown. Nesfield added a large Italian garden and Sir Charles Barry laid out formal gardens for the Duke of Sutherland. The gardens have been greatly simplified but still retain many features such as Brown's large lake on which one can now water sport or go boating. Rose garden and displays of bedding plants, a good selection of shrubs including hebes, potentillas and buddleias. Magnificent trees both alongside the River Trent, which flows through the gardens, and in the woodland area by the lake. The Italian garden has masses of colour from annuals and also some yew trees. A clematis walk has been replanted, but the rock garden needs some attention. A good place for a family day-out as there are picnic areas, a riding school with pony rides, a children's play area, wildfowl pens and a Shire and Craft Centre. There is a Video Gallery along with a newly opened Nature Trail and Heritage Trail.

WOLSELEY GARDEN PARK ★ 8

Wolseley Bridge, Stafford, Staffordshire.
Tel: (0889) 574888; 24 hour information line (0889) 574766
Sir Charles and Lady Wolseley

At junction of A51 with A513 between Rugeley and Stafford • Parking • Refreshments • Toilet facilities • Suitable for wheelchairs • Plants for sale at Cramphorn garden centre in park • Shop • Open daily. Times vary seasonally but 10 a.m. - 6 p.m. in summer • Entrance: charges seasonally variable, advertised.

An outstanding new 50-acre garden development as part of the owners' plan to make the site a major leisure and educational centre. Major features include a two-acre walled rose garden, a water bog garden with broad walk, rockery, a large collection of willows, a large new lake set in a water meadow, a woodland spring garden with flowering shrubs and bulbs. There is a scented garden for the particular enjoyment of the blind and partially sighted and a winter garden aimed at giving colour Nov - March. Similar 'theme' gardens are being developed by the team of designers. Summer visitors will also be intrigued by the sight of the archeaologists excavating the remains of the twelfth-century castle.

GARDENS OPEN RARELY

The following garden is open to the public on only two days in the year. For details see individual entry.
May 19 Little Onn Hall; **June 9** Little Onn Hall.

SUFFOLK

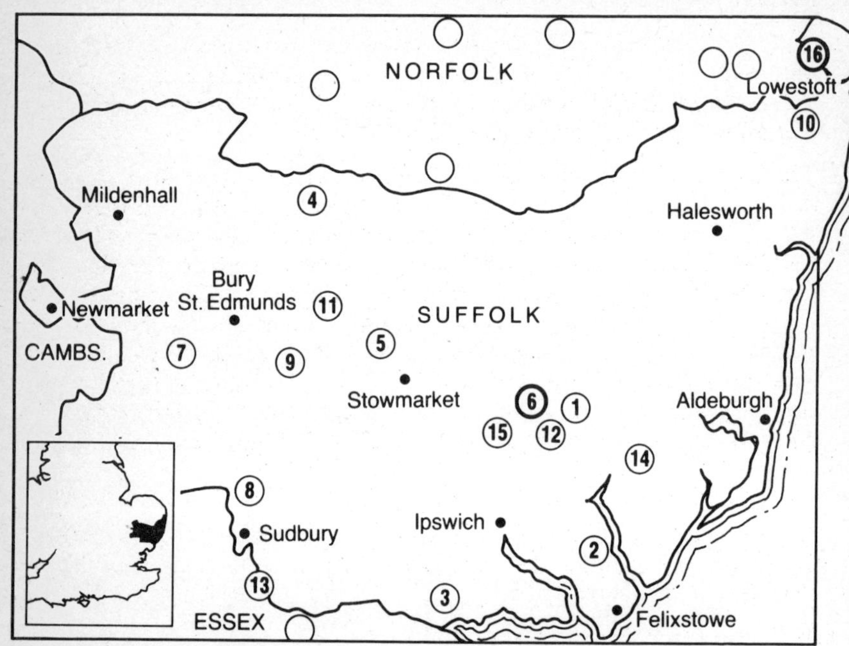

Plain circle numbers can be found by turning to neighbouring counties. Two-starred gardens are ringed in bold.

AKENFIELD 1

1 Park Lane, Charsfield, Woodbridge, Suffolk. Tel: (047337) 402
Mrs Peggy Cole

3m W of Wickham Market on B1078 • *Plants for sale* • *Open end May to Sept, daily, 10.30 a.m. - 7 p.m.* • *Entrance: 75p*

Akenfield, formerly a council house, has a quarter of an acre cottage garden full of charm, and overflowing with flowers and vegetables. To one side the front garden is planted with roses and bedding plants, to the other a small honeysuckle arch leads to a patio with containers of flowers, hanging baskets - and a shed full of home-made wines which is an irresistible attraction to robins who nest among the bottles. Opposite the patio is a tiny water garden complete with waterfall and wishing well. The back garden is divided in two; to one side is a vegetable garden with about thirty different kinds of vegetables and a hen house at the far end. On the other side there are two large greenhouses, overflowing with pot plants, tomatoes and cucumbers. Beyond are small gardens connected by archways, apple trees and a grape vine; hanging baskets and even bottles hold more plants.

BUCKLESHAM HALL ★ 2

Bucklesham, Ipswich, Suffolk. Tel: (047388) 263
Mr and Mrs P.A. Ravenshear

6m E of Ipswich, ½m E of Bucklesham village. Entrance opposte and just N of Bucklesham primary school • Parking. Coaches by appointment • Refreshments by special arrangement • Plants for sale • Shop • Open by appointment • Entrance: £2, OAP and children £1.50

The great interest of Bucklesham is how these five acres of interlocking gardens, terraces and lakes have been created from scratch by the present owners since 1973. Round the house are secret gardens so packed with flowers that no weed could survive; newly planted beds of old-fashioned roses overflow their borders, and a courtyard garden has been created with the use of every kind of container. Descending terraces of lawns, ponds and streams lead to the woodland and beyond; round each corner is a new vista. Skill, wide horticultural knowledge and imagination have enabled Mr and Mrs Ravenshear to achieve their aim of displaying plants, shrubs and trees of interest to the plantsman in tranquil surroundings appealing to the layman, all with minimum maintenance.

EAST BERGHOLT LODGE 3

Via Colchester, Suffolk. Tel: (0206) 298278
Captain C. Wake-Walker RN

Halfway between Colchester and Ipswich on A12. Take B1070, first right and through white gate at crossroads • Parking • Teas and picnic area • Toilet facilities • Partly suitable for wheelchairs • Dogs on lead • Plants for sale • Open by appointment and some Suns in May and June, 2 – 6 p.m. or as arranged • Entrance: £1, OAP 50p, children under 12 free

The gardens at East Bergholt are rather wild and informal but beautiful, with terraced, semi-formal areas developed by the family since 1912, full of old-fashioned roses. Snowdrops, daffodils, bluebells and many wild flowers lead to woodland where damage by the 1987 gales is still being cleared. Walking is quite an adventure but the paths and rides lead the visitor to discover over 350 different varieties of trees and shrubs grown in a natural setting teeming with wildlife.

EUSTON HALL ★ 4

Euston, Thetford, Suffolk. Tel: (0842) 766366
The Duke and Duchess of Grafton

3m S of Thetford on A1088 • Best season: June and July • Parking • Refreshments • Toilet facilities • Suitable for wheelchairs • Plants for sale • Shop • House open • Garden open 6th June to 26th Sept, Thurs, 2.30 – 5 p.m. and 30th June and 1st Sept, 2.30 – 5.30 p.m. • Entrance: £2, OAP £1.50, children 50p, parties of 12 or more £1.50

Fronted by terraces, the Hall stands among extensive lawns and parkland along a winding river, the work of William Kent in the 1740s, (followed by 'Capability' Brown) as is the splendid domed temple isolated on an eminence to the east, and also the pretty garden house in the formal garden by the house, developed by the present Duke. The pleasure grounds, laid out in the seventeenth century by John Evelyn, have grown into a forest of yew but straight rides trace out the original formal layout. Also from this period are the stone gate piers which, together with the remnants of a great avenue, mark the original approach to the house. A small lake reflects the house across the park, and there are many fine specimen trees and a wealth of shrub roses.

HAUGHLEY PARK ★ 5

Nr Stowmarket, Suffolk. Tel: (0359) 40205
Mr A.J. Williams

4m NW of Stowmarket, signposted Haughley Park off A45 • Parking. Coaches by appointment • Picnics in grounds • Toilet facilities inc. disabled • Suitable for wheelchairs • Dogs on lead • House open • Garden open May to Sept, Tues, 3 - 6 p.m. • Entrance: £1.50, children 50p

A hundred acres of rolling parkland edged by 50 more acres of woodland surround the seventeenth-century Jacobean mansion. Unexpected secret gardens edged by clipped hedges or flint and brick walls hide their immaculate flower beds, climbers and flowering shrubs; each garden has its own character. The main lawn is surrounded by herbaceous borders, with, at the end, a splendid lime avenue drawing the eye across many miles of open countryside. Rhododendrons, azaleas and camellias grow on soil which is, unexpectedly for Suffolk, lime-free. The trees include a splendid *Davidia involucrata*, a 40 foot-wide magnolia and a flourishing oak, over 30 foot in girth, reputed to be 1000 years old. Beyond is the walled kitchen garden, the greenhouses and the shrubbery. In spring the broad rides and walks through the ancient woodland reveal not only the newly planted trees, specimen rhododendrons and other ornamental shrubs but 10 acres of bluebells and, more remarkably, two acres of lilies-of-the-valley.

HELMINGHAM HALL ★★ 6

Stowmarket, Suffolk.
Tel: (047339) 217/363 (Contact Mrs McGregor)
Lord Tollemache

9m NE of Ipswich on B1077. 6m E of A45 on B1078 then signposted • Parking • Teas in coach house, picnic facilities • Toilet facilities • Suitable for wheelchairs (garden but not coach house) • Dogs on lead • Plants for sale • Gift shop. Safari rides to see deer, Highland cattle and Soay sheep • Open 28th April to 28th Sept, Sun, 2 - 6 p.m. • Entrance: £2, OAP £1.70, children £1.10, parties of 20 or more £1.60 per person

The double-moated Tudor mansion house of great splendour and charm, built of warm red brick, stands in a 400-acre deer park. A nineteenth-century parterre, edged with a magnificent spring border, leads to the Elizabethan kitchen garden which is surrounded by the Saxon moat with banks covered in daffodils. Within the walls the kitchen garden has been transformed into an enchanting garden most subtly planted; the meticulously maintained herbaceous borders and old-fashioned roses surround beds of vegetables separated by arched tunnels of sweet peas and runner beans. Beyond is a meadow garden with, leading from it, a yew walk with philadelphus and shade-loving plants. On the other side of the Hall is a newly created garden dating from 1982. Designed by Lady Salisbury and planted by the Tollemaches, it is an historical knot garden and herb garden, with a magnificent collection of shrub roses underplanted with campanulas and geraniums, framed by a yew hedge. All the plants are chosen to be contemporary with the house.

ICKWORTH 7

The Rotunda, Horringer, Bury St Edmunds, Suffolk.
Tel: (028488) 270/288
The National Trust

3m SW of Bury St Edmunds, W of A143 • Parking inc. disabled near house • Refreshments: restaurant in house when open • Toilet facilities in house • Suitable for wheelchairs but paths are gravel • Shop • House open • Garden open 30th March to April, Sat, Sun and Bank Holidays, 1.30 - 5.30 p.m. Last admission 5 p.m. May to Sept, daily except Mon and Thurs, 1.30 - 5.30 p.m. Oct, Sat and Sun, 1.30 - 5.30 p.m. Park all year, daily, 7 a.m. - 7 p.m. • Entrance: £1 (house and garden £3.50), parties of 15 or more £3 per person

Until recently the gardens at Ickworth were disappointing but over the last few years there have been some exciting changes. Research has shown that the earliest plantings appear to have been an unusual attempt to re-create a realistic Italian landscape to complement the emphatically Italian building. Much of what the visitor sees today is the recent restoration of this theme. Cypress and other sharp Mediterranean trees punctuate secret gardens surrounded by newly planted hedges and the main path to the south terrace is bordered with the evergreen shrub phillyrea, which will be clipped to window height. The south garden is further enclosed by a fine terrace which has a wonderful view of the garden and surrounding parkland. The north gardens, to the front of the house as you drive up, were largely planted in the 1870s and have now been considerably replanted following general neglect and the 1987 gales. Although many of the great trees still remain, there has been an impressive planting of cedars to restore a unique feature - the cedar woodland as well as a small arboretum. The north gardens are at their best in the spring months with lawns of spring bulbs and wild flowers.

MELFORD HALL ★ 8

Long Melford, Sudbury, Suffolk. Tel: (0787) 880286
The National Trust. Sir Richard Hyde Parker, Bart

E side of A134, 14m S of Bury St Edmunds, 3m N of Sudbury • Parking • Refreshments in Long Melford, picnics in car park • Toilet facilities by main entrance • Mostly suitable for wheelchairs, one wheelchair provided. Disabled driven to Hall • House open with special Beatrix Potter exhibition • Open 30th March to April, weekends only and Bank Holiday Mons. Closed Good Fri. May to Sept, Wed, Thurs, Sat, Sun, Bank Holiday Mon, 2 - 5.30 p.m. Oct, Sat and Sun, 2 - 5.30 p.m. Pre-booked parties Wed and Thurs only. Last admission 5 p.m. • Entrance: £2.40, children £1

This magnificent sixteenth-century Hall of mellow red brick is set in a park and formal gardens. A plan by Samuel Pierse of 1613 shows that the park was separated from the Hall by a walled enclosure outside which was the moat. Part of this is now the sunken garden. The avenue in front of the house is currently being replanted with oak grown from acorns taken from the existing trees. The octagonal brick pavilion, a rare and beautiful example of Tudor architecture, on the north side of the path, overlooks the village green and the herbaceous borders inside the garden which are being restored to their original Victorian and Edwardian design and planting. Outside the pavilion are clipped box hedges and a bowling green terrace which lead past dense shrubbery. The garden has many good specimen trees including the rare Oriental tree *Xanthoceras sorbifolium*. Great domes of box punctuate the lawns and an interesting detail is the arrangement of yew hedges and golden yew to the north of the house. Outside the walls are topiary figures. Round the pond and fountain are beds originally planted with herbs in 1937 and now being gradually improved. Kerdwell, also near Long Melford, is open at specified times in the summer and has a range of 'period' gardens.

NETHERFIELD HERBS 9

37 Nether Street, Rougham, Nr Bury St Edmunds, Suffolk.
Tel: (0359) 70452
Mrs L. Bremness

Extremely difficult to find. 4m SE of Bury St Edmunds between the A45 and the A134. Aim for Rougham Green and ask for directions • Parking. No coaches • Plants for sale • Open daily, 10.30 a.m. - 5.30 p.m. • Entrance: free

Twisting lanes through beautiful unspoilt countryside eventually bring the visitor to a small, early cottage, charmingly restored, buried in a garden full of specialist herbs. Box hedges outline the beds in which culinary, medicinal, cosmetic, aromatic and decorative herbs and perennials grow in exotic confusion. Over 100 varieties of herb plants are for sale - as well as books on how to use and grow them; herb pillows, sachets and pot pourri, essential oils and herbal teas.

NORTH COVE HALL 10

North Cove, Beccles, Suffolk. Tel: (050276) 631
Mr and Mrs B. Blower.

3½m E of Beccles, 50 yards off A146 Lowestoft road • Best season: summer • Parking • Refreshments • Toilet facilities • Suitable for wheelchairs • Dogs on lead • Plants for sale • Open 30th June, 2.30 - 6 p.m. • Entrance: £1, OAP 70p, children free

Climbing roses adorn the eighteenth-century house which is set in lawns with parkland beyond. Belts of trees and shrubs, including shrub roses, hide a large deep pool with steeply-sloping grassy banks. There are many conifers here, ranging from a border of dwarf forms to ancient yews and cedars. Beyond the pool are herbaceous borders and kitchen garden, backed by high brick walls. A woodland walk runs outside the walls - a mature davidia is among the trees to be seen here.

NORTON BIRD GARDENS 11

Norton, Bury St Edmunds, Suffolk. Tel: (0359) 30957
Mr and Mrs D.W.G. Frost

5m E of Bury St Edmunds. Signposted off A45 and A143 and close to A1089 • Refreshments. Picnics allowed • Toilet facilities inc. disabled • Suitable for wheelchairs • Shop • Open daily, 11 a.m. - 6 p.m. or dusk in winter • Entrance: £2.50, OAP £2, children £1, under 5 free. Reduction for parties of 20 or more

Among beds of roses and perennials, ornamental trees and shrubs wander peacocks and other exotic birds. Huge aviaries are planted with more shrubs and even small trees, giving a special charm to the wonderful collection of over 100 species of tropical and European birds. Black swans and many different kinds of ornamental duck swim in the ponds, flamingos adding a very exotic touch. The tropical house has not only sugar birds, tanagers, hummingbirds and many other species, but tropical plants which help create a familiar atmosphere for the birds to breed and raise their young. The charm of the bird garden lies not only in its many exotic birds, lovingly cared for, but in the wonderful collection of more familiar owls, bantams, pheasants - and even guinea pigs, who rush round their own garden plot and in and out of an amazing Wendy house.

OTLEY HALL 12

Otley, Ipswich, Suffolk. Tel: (047339) 264
Mr J.G. Mosesson

8m NE of Ipswich, ½m from centre of Otley • Parking • Refreshments • Toilet facilities • Suitable for wheelchairs • Dogs on lead • House open • Garden open Bank Holiday Suns and Mons, 2 - 6 p.m. and April to Sept by appointment • Entrance: £3, children £1.50

One of the most remarkable small houses in Suffolk, the romantic fifteenth-century Otley Hall, a Grade I listed building, is surrounded by 10 acres of formal and informal gardens. The house is moated; flowers tumble down the banks edged with flowering shrubs and ancient trees; behind is a grassy walk widening here and there into formal and informal gardens, an orchard and two romantic nutteries. Elegant black swans enhance the beauty of two medieval fish ponds, linked by a formal canal, which face the south entrance of the house. On the far side is a large mound with views over woodland and surrounding countryside. The gardens were originally designed by Frederick Inigo Thomas in 1915 and were influenced by the French eighteenth-century style; today the layout and planting, which dates only from the 1960s, provides an authentic and enchanting setting for the ancient manor house.

PARADISE CENTRE 13

Lamarsh Bures, Suffolk. Tel: (0787) 269449
Hedy and Cees Stapel-Jack

Through village of Lamarsh, lane opposite white Georgian house, on right up lane • Parking • Refreshments and picnic area • Toilet facilities • Plants for sale • A paddock with unusual pets will amuse the children • Open Bank Holidays, Sat and Sun or by appointment, 10 a.m. - 5 p.m. • Entrance: free

A nursery specialising in unusual plants and bulbs, especially those which are shade-loving, naturalizing in a sloping five-acre garden, attractively laid out amongst the trees and hills of the lovely Stour Valley. In autumn the garden is carpeted with autumn crocus, including the double variety and sweeps of cyclamen leading down to three ponds full of golden orfe and Koi carp. The banks are edged with bog plants and giant gunnera. Children will particularly enjoy the many ornamental duck, the African pygmy goats and other wildlife.

THE ROOKERY 14

Eyke, Woodbridge, Suffolk. Tel: (0394) 460226
Captain and Mrs R. Sheepshanks

5m E of Woodbridge. Turn N off B1084 Woodbridge - Orford road when sign says Rendlesham 2 • Parking • Refreshments on charity days • Suitable for wheelchairs • Plants for sale on charity days • Open by appointment and 5th, 19th May and one day in June, 2 - 6 p.m. • Entrance: £1.50, OAP and children £1

The gales which devastated so many fine gardens had occasionally the unexpected advantage of opening up large areas which were subsequently, as at the Rookery, planted as an arboretum with many rare specimen trees. Captain and Mrs Sheepshanks have designed a garden which is landscaped on differing levels, providing views and vistas; the visitors' curiosity is constantly aroused as to what is round the next corner. A small pond, a bog garden, shrubbery and evergreen walk, spring bulbs and large collection of cornus add to the general interest. The old vegetable garden is now a flourishing vineyard of one acre.

SHRUBLAND HALL ★★ 15

Coddenham, Suffolk. Tel: (0473) 830404
Lord de Saumarez

4m N of Ipswich. Turn off A45 to B1113 at Claydon • Parking • Refreshments and picnic area in car park • Toilet facilities • Suitable for wheelchairs • Plants for sale • Open 14th July, 2 - 6 p.m. • Entrance: £1.50

The magnificence of Shrubland Hall is reflected in the Victorian gardens, laid out by Sir Charles Barry and later modified by William Robinson. They are amongst the most important of their type remaining in England. From the upper terrace outside the house one descends by a stunning cascade of a hundred steps and descending terraces to a garden of formal beds, fountain and eye-catcher arch. Beyond is the wild garden which merges into the woods and is bordered by the park with its many fine trees, some reputed to be 8000 years old. The gardens are punctuated by a series of enchanting follies ranging from a Swiss cottage to an alpine garden and magnificent conservatory. Lord and Lady de Saumarez have an extensive programme of restoration which includes the box maze and the old dell garden. Many trees blown down in the gales are being cleared and replaced.

SOMERLEYTON HALL ★★ 16

Nr Lowestoft, Suffolk. Tel: (0502) 730224/730308
Lord and Lady Somerleyton

8m from Yarmouth, 6m NW of Lowestoft off B1074 signposted • Parking • Teas and picnics • Toilet facilities inc. disabled • Suitable for wheelchairs • Gift shop • House open. On certain days the miniature railway runs • Open Easter Sun to Sept, Thurs, Sun and Bank Holidays, 2 - 5.30 p.m. • Entrance: £3, OAP £2.40, children £1.55, parties of 15 or more £2.40 per person, children £1.35

An Elizabethan house extensively rebuilt in the mid-nineteenth century as a grand Italianate palace and the gardens splendidly reflect this magnificence with 12 acres of formal gardens, a beautiful walled garden, an aviary and a loggia surrounding a sunken garden displaying statues from the old, now demolished, winter garden. A major programme of replanting and restoration has included replacing many of the great trees in the park which were lost in the gales and cutting back the overgrown yews of the maze, originally laid out by William Nesfield in 1846. Not to be missed are the extraordinary peach cases and ridge-and-furrow greenhouse designed by Sir Joseph Paxton, and now containing peaches, grapes and a rich variety of tender plants. A Victorian kitchen garden and a museum of gardening are being developed.

GARDENS OPEN RARELY

The following gardens are open to the public on three days or less in the year, although they may also be open by appointment if this is stated in the text. For details see individual entry.

May 5 The Rookery; **May 19** The Rookery; **June 30** North Cove Hall; **July 14** Shrubland Hall.

SURREY

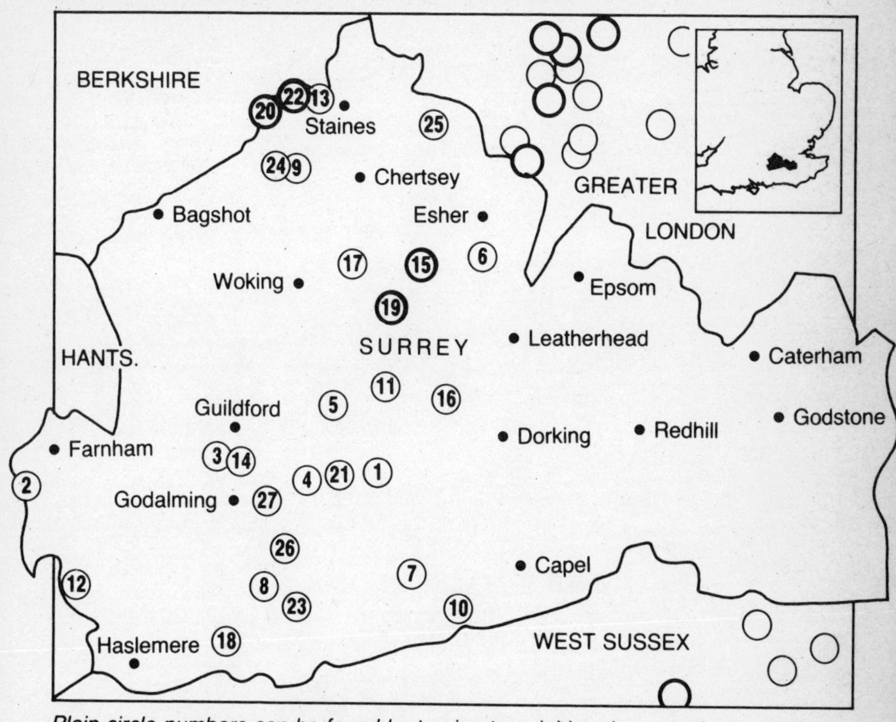

Plain circle numbers can be found by turning to neighbouring counties. Two-starred gardens are ringed in bold.

ALBURY PARK MANSION 1

Albury, Guildford, Surrey. Tel: (048641) 2964 (Administrator)
Country Houses Association Ltd

Turn off A25 onto A248 (signposted Albury). Turn left just before village and entrance is immediately left • Best season: spring, early summer • Parking • Toilet facilities • House open (Pugin) also old Saxon church • Open May to Sept, Wed and Thurs, 2 - 5 p.m. • Entrance: £1.50, children under 16 50p

The gardens remaining around the house are mainly under grass with gravel walks, a ha-ha and stream providing the boundaries. A small formal rose garden, azaleas and rhododendrons are to be seen and an herbaceous border. However, it is the trees that are most impressive – several oaks, a tulip tree and a very old London plane amongst them. There is a tree chart of the estate in the house. Although not open to visitors, the azaleas and rhododendrons on the estate are visible from the garden in spring and are a beautiful sight when in bloom. The pleasure grounds which lie north of the Tillingbourne remain in the ownership of the Trustees of the Albury Estate and are not open to the public. This is unfortunate as the layout owes much to the assistance given by John Evelyn to his neighbour, later 6th Duke of Norfolk, in or before the 1660s. These included the terraces, one in the style of a Roman bath, a tunnel, now walled in at one end, and a canal. In 1882 William Cobbett on one of his rural rides described them as 'without exception the prettiest in England; that is to say, that I ever saw in England.' The gale in January 1990 badly damaged surrounding parkland and some specialist trees were lost.

BIRDWORLD 2

Holt Pound, Nr Farnham, Surrey. Tel: (0420) 22140
The Harvey family

3m S of Farnham on A325 • Best season: Aug • Parking • Refreshments: café for light lunches, coffee and teas • Toilet facilities • Suitable for wheelchairs. Wheelchairs available for hire • Shop • Open daily except 25th Dec, summer 9.30 a.m. - 6 p.m., winter 9.30 a.m. - 3.30 p.m. • Entrance: £2.95, OAP £2.30, children £1.60

First-time visitors to Birdworld will be surprised by the extensive gardens which provide a backdrop to the bird sanctuary. With its wide flat paths and ample seating there is plenty of space to enjoy the variety of planting on show. Although lacking a unifying theme (and the family disagree over which comes first, the birds or the gardens), the variety ensures that the gardens are attractive and colourful on all of the 364 days a year that they are open. Features include summer bedding, hanging baskets, wall baskets, rose garden, heather bed, ornamental grasses border, pergola and climbing roses, pond and white garden.

BRADSTONE BROOK 3

Shalford, Guildford, Surrey. Tel: (0483) 68686
Scott, Brownrigg & Turner

3m S of Guildford on A281 towards Horsham then A248 to Dorking. Sign on left past the Common • Parking • Teas • Open for charity 19th May, 14th July, 2 - 6 p.m. • Entrance: £1.50, children 50p

The layout for this 20-acre garden was Gertrude Jekyll's, particularly the water garden, but the area was derelict for 25 years until discovered by the present owners 10 years ago. Set against the background of the Surrey hills, the Edwardian house is framed by lawns and an ornamental rose garden with lavender and box hedges. Other features include an alpine garden, a lily tank and several woodland walks to a variegated beech and the snowdrop tree, *Halesia carolina*, that flowers in late spring/early summer, and swamp cypresses. Over 150,000 bulbs and some trees under preservation orders including a *Betula nigra* said to be the largest in the country.

CHILWORTH MANOR 4

Chilworth, Surrey. Tel: (0483) 61414
Lady Heald

3½m SE of Guildford off A248. In the centre of Chilworth village on right up Blacksmiths Lane • Best season: spring and June • Parking • Refreshments: teas in house on Sat and Sun. Picnicking from 12.30 p.m. • Toilet facilities • Partly suitable for wheelchairs • Dogs on lead • House open Sat and Sun • Open 6th - 10th April, 11th - 15th May, 15th - 19th June, 20th - 24th July, 3rd - 7th Aug, 2 - 6 p.m. (house and garden open on Sat and Sun, garden only open Mon - Wed) • Entrance: £1.00 (house £1.00), children free

A lovely old garden, particularly in spring and summer, but something to see all the year round. Laid out in the seventeenth century, a walled garden was carved in three tiers out of the side of the hill early in the next century by Sarah, Duchess of Marlborough before she moved to Blenheim. The high walls, backed by wisteria, shelter many fine plants, a herbaceous border, lavender walks and shrubs. There is also a rock garden and a woodland area with magnolias, rhododendrons, azaleas, an oak tree reputed to be 400 years old and a Judas tree. Our visitor, there in spring, was impressed by the candelabra primulas along the stream and golden carp in the monastic stewponds. At weekends, the house is decorated by various Surrey flower clubs in turn.

CLANDON PARK 5

West Clandon, Guildford, Surrey. Tel: (0483) 222482
The National Trust

3m E of Guildford. Take A247 or A3 to Ripley and join A247 via B2215 • Parking. Disabled drivers only near front of house • Refreshments: licensed restaurant when house is open, lunches 12.30 - 2 p.m., teas for visitors to the house only. Picnic area • Toilet facilities inc. disabled • Suitable for wheelchairs • Dogs on lead in picnic area and car park only • Shop • House open • Gardens open 29th March to Oct, daily except Thurs and Fri, 1.30 - 5.30 p.m., Bank Holiday Mon and preceding Sun, 11 a.m. - 5.30 p.m. Last admission 5 p.m. • Entrance £3 (Mon - Wed, £2.50)

Built by a Venetian architect in the early 1730s for the 2nd Lord Onslow, whose family still owns the park, although the house and seven-acre garden are owned by the Trust. It is a pleasant garden to visit and look around. An interesting feature is the Maori meeting house, known as Hinemihi, brought from New Zealand by Lord Onslow, which is said to be one of the oldest in existence. Also note the grotto and parterre. The garden is on a hillside and gives a fine view of the lake which is in the private park. Nearby garden centre (not NT).

CLAREMONT LANDSCAPE GARDEN ★ 6

Portsmouth Road, Esher, Surrey. Tel: (0372) 69421
The National Trust

E of A307, S of Esher just out of the town • Parking • Refreshments in tea room 12th Jan to March, Sat and Sun, 11 a.m. - 4 p.m., April to Oct, daily except Mon, 11 a.m. - 5.30 p.m. Nov to 15th Dec, daily except Mon, 11 a.m. - 4.30 p.m. 11th Jan - March 1992, Sat and Sun, 11 a.m. - 4 p.m. • Toilet facilities • Partly suitable for wheelchairs • Dogs on lead • Shop • House (not NT) not open • Garden open all year, daily, March, 9 a.m. - 5 p.m., April to Oct, 9 a.m. - 7 p.m. (10th to 14th July garden closes 4 p.m.), Nov to March 1992, 9 a.m. - 5 p.m. or sunset if earlier. Last admission ½ hour before closing. Closed 25th Dec and 1st Jan • Entrance: Mon - Sat £1.20, Sun and Bank Holiday Mon £2. Guided tours for 15 or more £1 extra by prior booking.

The *Oxford Companion* describes this as one of the most significant historic landscapes in the country. The 50 acres being restored by the Trust is only part of the original estate which was broken up in 1922 and part became a school. The great landscape designers of the eighteenth century each adapted it in turn for the owner, the immensely wealthy man who eventually became Duke of Newcastle. First he retained Vanburgh, then Bridgeman, then Kent. Later, when Clive of India purchased the estate he brought in 'Capability' Brown who also designed the house, now the school and, in typical form, diverted the London–Portsmouth road to improve the viewpoints, the most striking of which is the grass amphitheatre. In the nineteenth century it was a favourite retreat of Queen Victoria and her younger son. A useful leaflet describes the various contributions to the park, which will appeal to everyone by its sensitive reconstruction of the eighteenth-century English style, even if it has nothing specific to offer the plantsperson, except a few fine trees. The garden is a very popular recreation park for local families, sunbathers and picknickers.

COVERWOOD LAKES AND GARDEN 7

Peaslake Road, Ewhurst, Surrey. Tel: (0306) 731103
Mr and Mrs C.G. Metson

7m SW of Dorking. Off A25 ½m S of Peaslake • Parking • Home-made teas • Toilet facilities • Suitable for wheelchairs • Plants for sale • Open 6th, 12th, 19th May and one day in Oct (gardens only), 26th, 29th May, 2nd, 9th June (gardens and farm), 2 - 6.30 p.m. • Entrance: £1.50, children 75p (£2, children 75p gardens and farm). Reductions for large parties by prior arrangement

The original gardens were designed in 1910 by a rich Edwardian business-man. Now it is a woodland estate surrounding four lakes the water for which arises from the natural springs in the bog garden. Each lake has a different character from the towering rhododendrons reflecting in the calm water of the highest to the largest alongside the arboretum. This was planted early in

1990 and contains 100 different kinds of trees which prospered through the baking summer of 1990. Bordering the paths are a great many varieties of hostas, trilliums and candelabra primulas. Lilies of the valley form a green and white carpet below a wide variety of rhododendrons and azaleas. The farm specialises in pedigree Poll Hereford cattle.

FEATHERCOMBE GARDENS 8

Feathercombe, Hambledon, Nr Godalming, Surrey.
Tel: (0483) 860257
Miss Parker

5m S of Godalming, E of A283 between Hydestile and Hambledon • Parking • Picnic area available • Toilet facilities • Partly suitable for wheelchairs • Dogs on lead • Plants for sale • Open 5th, 6th, 26th, 27th May, 2 - 6 p.m. • Entrance: £1, children 10p

Although mainly worth visiting for the good display of rhododendrons and azaleas, there are fine views across three counties framed by larches and some tree heaths which are now 20 to 30 feet high. Now that the garden is maintained solely by the family, some of the features in the original design of 1910 by Eric and Ruth Parker have had to be changed through lack of labour which is a great pity. Ruth Parker was one of Leonard Messel's daughters and there must have been strong connections between her garden at Feathercombe and his at Nymans (see entry).

GORSE HILL MANOR 9

Gorse Hill Road, Virginia Water, Surrey. Tel: (0344) 842101
Mrs E. Barbour Paton

From A30 turn opposite Wheatsheaf Hotel in Virginia Water into Christchurch Road – continue on this road to roundabout, take second exit (still in Christchurch Road), take third turning immediately left (opposite shops) into Gorse Hill Road. The Manor is at the end, last house on the left • Best seasons: spring and autumn • Parking • Toilet facilities • Open by appointment only. Parties up to 40 and individuals welcome, but no very young children • Entrance: by collecting box

A typical Surrey house and garden of the 1930s, comprising three acres of garden, six of forestry and the rest grazing livestock and residence for donkeys. There are good trees and shrubs, altogether over 450 varieties including acers, magnolias, camellias and viburnums, all identified. There is croquet and putting for children who do not want to study the garden but very young children are not admitted. On a clear day there is a splendid view across to Chobham, a distance of several miles.

HAMPTON COURT

(see London)

HANNAH PESCHAR GALLERY GARDEN 10

Black and White Cottage, Standon Lane, Ockley, Surrey.
Tel: (030679) 269
Hannah Peschar

1m SW of Ockley. Signposted from Cat Hill Lane onwards as Black and White Cottage • Parking • Teas for parties by arrangement • Toilet facilities • Suitable for wheelchairs (but not gallery) • Sculpture gallery open • Garden open 14th April to Oct, Fri and Sat, 11 a.m. - 6 p.m., Sun, 2 - 5 p.m. and by appointment for buyers or group visits (except Mon) • Entrance: £3, children £1.50. Guided tours for parties £5 per person inc. tea or coffee

This delightful Surrey woodland garden is of primary interest to those who enjoy contemporary outdoor sculpture, as Mrs Peschar represents a wide range of artists whose work is displayed in natural settings, including water. The exhibits change, of course, as they are sold, and anyone planning to place objects of art outdoors will find a study of the sculptures here a source of inspiration. Note too the way art contributes to function as in the bridge made by landscape designer Anthony Paul.

HATCHLANDS 11

East Clandon, Guildford, Surrey. Tel: (0483) 222787
The National Trust

E of East Clandon, N of A246 • Best season: spring and summer • Parking. Disabled visitors may be set down at house • Home-made teas • Toilet facilities • Suitable for wheelchairs • House open • Garden open 31st March to 20th Oct, Tues, Wed, Thurs, Sun and Bank Holiday Mon, also Sats in Aug, 2 - 5.30 p.m. Last admission 5 p.m. • Entrance: £2.80 (house and garden)

The main interest is in the Gertrude Jekyll garden which is being returned to its original dimensions and being replanted to her original plans (1914 revision). It will be one to two years before completion as plants are coming from abroad and some have to be propagated. There is a wild meadow featuring cowslips and many wild flowers. It is never cut until July. Mature London plane and cedar trees. Further improvements will include regrading to Humphrey Repton's original design.

HIGH MEADOW 12

Tilford Road, Churt, Surrey. Tel: (0428) 606129
Mr and Mrs John Humphries

3m N of Hindhead. Take A287 from Hindhead then fork left to Tilford. House is nearly 2m on right • Parking at Avalon PYO farm on left past turning to house. Disabled may park in drive to house • Teas • Toilet facilities • Plants for sale • Open 5th May, 2nd, 30th June, 11th Aug, 1st Sept, 2 - 6 p.m. Entrance: £1, children free

As the name suggests this garden is situated high on a meadowside protected by a series of hedges of beech, holly and cupressus. A small terrace is overlooked by a pergola with a variety of climbers. Unusually-shaped beds surround grass of putting-green quality and contain a wealth of colour co-ordinated shrubs, roses and herbaceous plants which are cleverly graded by height. There is a small pool set in a rock garden, a bog plant section, rockery and small peat garden. A plantsman's garden.

LONDON UNIVERSITY BOTANIC GARDENS 13

Egham Hill, Egham, Surrey. Tel: (0784) 433303
University of London.

On A30, 2m SW of M25 junction 13. Opposite Royal Holloway and Bedford New College • Best seasons: spring and autumn • Parking in surrounding streets • Teas on open days • Toilet facilities • Suitable for wheelchairs • Plants for sale when available • Guided tours of Gardens and College on open days • Open by appointment all year, 9 a.m. - 4 p.m. and on 28th April, 1st May, 9th Oct, 27th Nov, 2 - 6 p.m. for charity • Entrance: £2

Founded in 1950 to grow plant material needed for teaching and research work at the University, this botanic garden grew as land became available in surrounding areas and it also assumed a more public role. There are around 500 different species of plants all labelled, 11 plant-houses, two of which are tropical. Here, rarities include an unusual succulent from Hawaii (*Brighamia citrina*) and the New Zealand *Elingamita johnsonii*. Many beds of unusual plants, naturally occuring forms rather than cultivars. Unusual plants are grouped in family beds. Some of these plants may be on sale, but a request to the Curator or Head Gardener on availability of others and their cost may be made. Some are rarely on sale elsewhere. There is a rock garden and an arboretum, which is considered one of the finest post-war plantings, including an extensive collection of Southern beech species and rarities like golden larch and American plane. Unique Memorial walk of dawn redwoods (sequoias). Ferns, mosses, liverworts and carnivorous plants in the gardens. On open days there are guided lecture tours by expert botanists at extra charge. The Government's policy towards universities resulting in what are politely called 'financial restraints' means that the botanic garden area, having grown, is now being reduced, and the surplus areas handed over to Royal Holloway and Bedford New College private grounds. No wonder Britain's advanced education, once second to none, is becoming second to a good many. Visitors can slow, if not reverse, this decline by becoming 'Friends' of LUBG.

LOSELEY PARK 14

Nr Guildford, Surrey. Tel: (0483) 304440
Mr and Mrs J. More-Molyneux

3m SE of Guildford off B3000 • Parking • Refreshments: wholefood restaurant offering organic lunches, snacks and teas. Open 11 a.m. - 5 p.m. in season • Toilet facilities • Shop selling own organic produce. Open 11 a.m. - 5 p.m. in season, Fri, 10 a.m. - 1 p.m. in closed season • House open • Garden open 29th May to 28th Sept, Wed - Sat, 2 - 5 p.m. Also Bank Holidays 27th May and 26th Aug • Entrance: free

The house, garden and farm provide interest and entertainment for all the family by offering such attractions as farm tours and trailer rides. The Elizabethan house is set in a sweep of lawn surrounded by parkland. The secluded garden to the side of the house has yew hedges creating 'rooms', an herbaceous bed with familiar plants and a moat walk. Through the hedge to the vegetable garden catch a glimpse of the organically-grown vegetables, a very good advertisement for the system.

PAINSHILL PARK ★★ 15

Portsmouth Road, Cobham, Surrey. Tel: (0932) 68113
Elmbridge Borough Council on lease to Painshill Park Trust

1m W of Cobham on A245. Entrance on right, 200 yards E of A3/A245 roundabout • Limited parking • Teas and light refreshments • Toilet facilities inc. disabled • Partly suitable for wheelchairs • Shop in Visitor Centre • Open 14th April to 13th Oct, Sun, 2 - 6 p.m. Last admission 5 p.m. Also all year by appointment for parties of 10 or more • Entrance: £2.50, OAP and children over 10, £1.50. Set charge for parties £2.50 per person inc. refreshments

Painshill was developed by Charles Hamilton (1704 - 86), a great English landscape designer who acquired the lease in 1738 and got severely into debt by his ambitious plans. He should be better known and is described by the *Oxford Companion* as 'a brilliant and subtle deisgner (who) could create illusion and vary scene and mood. His work strikes a delicate balance between art and nature, between the artist and the plantsman'. His work was nearly lost to posterity but after 30 years of neglect and delay it was rescued at the eleventh hour when it was bought by Elmbridge Borough Council and an independent Trust was established in 1981. There are now 158 acres of which 14 are taken up by the lake. A great deal of work has already been done, and Charles Hamilton's garden is coming to life again. There are about 100 trees surviving at Painshill that were planted between 1738 - 1773, including the great cedar of Lebanon, the largest in England (120 × 32 feet) and the pencil cedar (*Juniperus virginiana*) approx 60 × 6½ feet – the tallest in England with a mountain ash growing from the trunk seven feet from the ground. Another unusual sight is a beech and London plane with branches apparently fused together. Features include Gothic temple, water wheel, grotto island and ruined abbey.

POLESDEN LACEY ★ 16

Great Bookham, Nr Dorking, Surrey. Tel: (0372) 53401
The National Trust

3m W of Dorking off A246 • Parking 150 yards away • Refreshments: lunches, teas, etc. in licensed restaurant open Jan to March, Sat and Sun, 11 a.m. – 4.30 p.m., 29th March to Oct, Wed – Sun and Bank Holiday Mons, 11 a.m. – 5.30 p.m. (closed 2.30 – 3 p.m.). Picnic site in grounds (not in formal areas) • Toilet facilities • Partly suitable for wheelchairs • Dogs on lead • Shop • House open March and Nov, Sat and Sun, 1.30 – 5.30 p.m. and Bank Holiday Mon and preceeding Sun, 11 a.m. – 5.30 p.m. • Garden open all year, 11 a.m. – dusk • Entrance: 29 March to Oct, £2, Nov to March, £1.20. Reduced rates for parties, weekdays by pre-arrangement. House, Sun and Mon £3 extra, other days £1.80 extra

This 17-acre garden has grown up over several centuries. Richard Brinsley Sheridan, the dramatist who owned the house for over 20 years, lengthened the Long Walk before he died here in 1816. The present house was built a few years later by Cubitt in the Greek classical manner for an owner who made extensive alterations and planted over 20,000 trees. The garden was further developed early this century and given to the Trust in 1944. The walled rose garden is in four square areas divided by paths and covered by wooden pergolas and the area is dominated by a well-head covered by an ancient Chinese wisteria. There are small gardens of peonies, bearded irises, beds of different kinds of lavender. A winter garden overshadowed by four iron trees. A long border of herbaceous plants is a colourful sight in summer. There is also a sunken garden. A fully detailed garden guide is available giving numbered lists of plants, shrubs and flowers.

PYRFORD COURT 17

Pyrford Common Road, Pyrford, Woking, Surrey. Tel: (0483) 765880
Mr C. Laikin

2m W of Woking. M25 Junction 10. B367 junction with Upshott Lane • Parking • Refreshments: tea and biscuits • Toilet facilities • Suitable for wheelchairs • Dogs on lead • Open by appointment and 19th, 26th May, 2 – 6.30 p.m. 20th Oct, 12 noon – 4 p.m. • Entrance: £1.25, children 50p

Transformed at the turn of the century by Lord and Lady Iveagh with advice from Gertrude Jekyll, this varied garden covers about 20 acres, both formal and woodland. The wild garden to the South is a blaze of colour in the autumn, especially the Japanese maples. The north lawn of around four acres is bordered by a high brick wall with a pillared loggia and features several pear-shaped Irish yews. Noticeable on the wall is a loquat, *Eriobotrya japonica*. The wisterias on the pergola walk are from Japanese raised seedlings imported about 70 years ago from Yokohama and are remarkable for their extremely long flower panicles. The ornamental grape, *Vitis coignetiae*, is a fine sight at the end of the pergola walk, brilliant when in autumn colours. By the stream is a rare flowering camellia (*C.* × *Williamsii* 'Hiraethlyn') which flowers in October. There are views to the North Downs and to Guildford cathedral.

RAMSTER 18

Chiddingfold, Surrey. Tel: (0428) 4422
Mr and Mrs P. Gunn

1½m S of Chiddingfold on A283 • Best season: spring • Parking • Refreshments: teas on Sat, Sun and Bank Holiday Mon. Lunches for pre-booked coach parties • Toilet facilities • Suitable for wheelchairs • Dogs on lead • Plants for sale • Open 20th April to 9th June, 2 - 6 p.m. and parties by appointment • Entrance: £1.50, children free

Laid out in 1904 by Gauntlett Nurseries of Chiddingfold and owned by the same family for close to 70 years. Twenty acres of peaceful woodland with views of lakes and hillsides filled with colour and interest. Planting includes Californian redwoods, cedars, firs, camellias, rhododendrons and azaleas plus the rarer *Styrax obassia*, *Tetracentron sinense*, and *Kalopanax pictus*. A camellia garden, magnolia bed and widespread bluebells and daffodils ensure flowers are on view throughout the spring. Especially notable is an avenue of *Acer palmatum* 'Dissectum'. The 'Embroidery for Gardens' exhibition takes place from 18th to 31st May.

ROYAL HORTICULURAL SOCIETY'S GARDEN ★★ 19

Wisley, Woking, Surrey. Tel: (0483) 224234
Royal Horticultural Society

7m from Guildford, 4m from Cobham, 1m from Ripley, W of London on A3 and M25 (junction 10) • Parking • Refreshments: licensed restaurant and self service cafeteria • Toilet facilities inc. disabled • Suitable for wheelchairs • Plants for sale • Shop • To non-members of the RHS open Feb to Oct, Mon - Sat, 10 a.m. - 7 p.m. or dusk if earlier, Nov to Jan, 10 a.m. - 4.30 p.m. (Sun for RHS members only) • Entrance: by membership or £3.50, children 6 - 14 £1.50, under 6 free

George Fox Wilson, a former treasurer of the RHS, established a famous woodland garden here *c.* 1880. After his death it was purchased by Sir Thomas Hanbury (owner of the famous La Mortola garden in Italy) and together with surrounding land became the site of the fourth RHS garden. Despite the lack of any inspired and cohesive overall plan, the mundanity of some of the demonstration gardens and the unimaginative and rather bleak nature of some of the newly planted areas, The Royal Horticultural Society's garden at Wisley fulfils its teaching role so splendidly that it warrants a Grade I classification. Impeccably planted and tended, the garden thrills the thousands of visitors it attracts each year who are understandably impressed by one of the finest alpine rock gardens in Europe, a fine range of plants in the glasshouse range and yards of quintessentially English, deep and richly-appealing herbaceous border. Of great future interest will be the development of the collection of Mediterranean plants established on the southern side of Battleston Hill after the great storms of October 1987. Bonuses available from a Wisley visit are that it is possible to browse among what is arguably the best selection of modern gardening books available anywhere in the world and to buy very well grown plants in the sales area after obtaining informed advice upon their performance.

THE SAVILL GARDEN ★★ 20

Wick Lane, Englefield Green, Surrey. Tel: (0753) 860222
and Windsor Great Park, Berkshire
Administered by the Crown Estate Commissioners

5m from Windsor. From A30, turn into Wick Road and follow signs, or follow signs from Englefield Green • Parking • Refreshments: licensed self-service restaurant open Feb to 22nd Dec (0784) 32326. Picnics allowed in car park area • Toilet facilities inc. disabled • Suitable for wheelchairs • Plants for sale • Gift and bookshop • Open daily, 10 a.m. – 6 p.m. (7 p.m. at weekends) or sunset. Closed 25th to 28th Dec • Entrance: £2.20, OAP £2, accompanied children under 16 free. Parties of 20 or more £2 per person. Guided tours are available – apply to Keeper

The violent storms of recent years have taken such a toll of the tall trees that much of the high canopy has been reduced and the garden has lost some of its former more enclosed woodland feel. Nevertheless covering some 35 acres of woodland, it contains a fine range of rhododendrons, camellias, magnolias, hydrangeas and a great variety of other trees and shrubs producing a wealth of colour throughout the seasons, particularly in spring and summer – meconopsis and primulas in June especially. In the shadier areas a wonderful collection of hostas and ferns flourishes. Daffodils in impressive drifts dominate in the spring while lilies are the highlight of high summer. The tweedy autumn colours in the Savill Garden are almost as satisfying in their mellowness as its jauntier spring hues. A more formal area is devoted to modern roses, herbaceous borders, a range of alpines and a very interesting and attractive dry garden. Windsor Castle gardens nearby (admission free, 10 a.m. – 7.15 p.m., 4.15 p.m. in winter) retain the formal gardens designed by W.J. Aiton for George IV. The Valley Gardens are also nearby (see entry).

VALE END 21

Albury, Surrey. Tel: (048641) 2594
Mr and Mrs J. Foulsham

4½m SE of Guildford. From Albury take A248 W for ½m • Best season: summer/autumn • Limited parking • Refreshments • Toilet facilities • Dogs on lead • Plants for sale when available • Open 30th June, 2 - 6 p.m., 4th Aug, 10 a.m. - 5 p.m. and by appointment • Entrance: £1

A one-acre walled cottage garden surrounding an eighteenth to twentieth-century house. Fine views from terrace across sloping lawns to mill pond and woodlands with a wide variety of herbaceous plants and roses, ornamental pond. This garden is entirely maintained by its owners and as well as being in a beautiful setting will interest plantsmen because on a light, well-watered soil, the owners have interspersed old favourites with 'little gems' such as diascia. There is a fine magnolia with a spread of over 40 feet and a small fruit and vegetable garden.

THE VALLEY GARDENS (Windsor Great Park) ★★ 22

Wick Road, Englefield Green, Surrey. Tel: (0753) 860222
Crown Estate

5m from Windsor. From A30 turn into Wick Road and follow signs for Savill Garden (½m to W) and drive to car park adjoining Valley Gardens, avoiding a 2m round walk • Parking • Refreshments at Savill Garden • Plants for sale at Savill Garden • Open all year, 8 a.m. - 7 p.m. or sunset if earlier. Possible closure if weather inclement • Entrance: £2 car and occupants (10p, 50p and £1 coins only)

One of Britain's most discriminating and experienced garden visitors, Arthur Hellyer suggests that The Valley Gardens are among the best examples of the 'natural' gardening style in England. With hardly any artefacts or attempts to introduce architectural features they are merely a tract of undulating grassland (on the north side of Virginia Water) which is divided by several shallow valleys, that has been enriched by the introduction of a fine collection of trees and shrubs. It was started by the royal gardener Sir Eric Savill when he ran out of room in the Savill Garden to continue making 'natural' landscapes. One of the valleys is filled with deciduous azaleas. In another, 'The Punchbowl', evergreen azaleas rise in tiers below a canopy of maples. Notable too are collections of flowering cherries, a heather garden which amply demonstrates the ability to provide colour during all seasons, and one of the world's most extensive collection of hollies. Lovers of formal gardening might be forgiven for suggesting that the Valley Garden has something of the rather too open, amorphous, scrupulously-kept, American golf-course feel.

VANN 23

Hambledon, Surrey. Tel: (042868) 3413
Mr and Mrs M.B. Caroe

6m S of Godalming, E of A283 at Chiddingfold • Best season: spring • Parking in road • Refreshments: homemade teas in barn on Sun/Bank Holiday Mon. Lunches bookable for parties by arrangement • Limited toilet facilities • Limited access for wheelchairs • Dogs on lead • Plants for sale • Open by appointment on 14th April, 6th May, 23rd June, 2 - 7 p.m., 15th to 20th April, 7th to 12th May, 24th to 29th June, 10 a.m. - 6 p.m. • Entrance: £1.20, children 30p

The six different areas within this garden will provide some interest for most types of gardener. From the student of garden design viewing the water garden still containing plants selected by Gertrude Jekyll, to the admirer of the formal garden complete with clipped yews and regular brick paths, there is something for everyone. Of particular interest is the yew walk now planted with deer-resistant plants providing foliage of all year interest. Colourful annuals are introduced when the spring bulbs are over.

VIRGINIA WATER LAKE ★ 24

London Road, Surrey. Tel: (0753) 853747
Crown Estate, Great Park, Windsor

Off A30, adjacent to junction with A329 • Parking £1 • No refreshments, but picnics permitted • Toilet facilities • Suitable for wheelchairs • Dogs • Open all year • Entrance: free

This was a grand eighteenth-century ornamental addition to Windsor Great Park by the Duke of Cumberland who became its ranger in 1746. It had dams, rockwork, a cascade and grotto. There was a fake 'Mandarin Yacht', a Chinese pavilion and a Gothic belvedere with a mighty single arch bridge spanning the water. Alas, almost all have disappeared but the woodland and the lovely one and a half mile lake, full of fish and wildfowl survive, and there is still a colonnade of pillars.

THE WALLED GARDEN 25

Sunbury Park, Thames Street, Sunbury-on-Thames, Surrey.
Tel: (0784) 451499 (Community Services)
Surrey County Council; maintained by Spelthorne Borough Council

In Sunbury-on-Thames via B375 Thames Street. Entrance through car park • Best seasons: spring and summer • Parking • Toilet facilities • Suitable for wheelchairs • Open all year except 25th Dec, 8 a.m. - dusk • Entrance: free

Although no house remains, this eighteenth-century walled garden has been developed since 1985 into a pleasant open space of about two acres designed to include garden styles from past centuries. Also four large areas of island beds display collections of plants from all parts of the world. The rose garden is composed entirely of species roses and varieties which were either introduced or widely planted during the reign of Queen Victoria. During the summer exhibitions of sculpture, paintings, etc, are on view and a band plays at published times.

THE WATER GARDENS, Kingston upon Thames

(see London)

WINKWORTH ARBORETUM 26

Hascombe, Nr Godalming, Surrey. Tel: (048632) 477
The National Trust

2m SE of Godalming, E of B2130 • Best season: spring/autumn • Parking inc. disabled • Refreshments: teashop open April to Oct, Tues - Sun, 2 - 6 p.m. or dusk if earlier. March, Nov, Dec, Sat and Sun only • Toilet facilities • Dogs • Shop (048632) 265 • Open all year, daily, dawn - dusk • Entrance: £1.50, and there may be a parking charge

The public footpath through Winkworth ensures access 365 days of the year, so it's a great place to take the family for a walk on Christmas Day or any other! The 60 plant families and 150 genera grown here provide variety and interest throughout the year. In the spring there are the azaleas, rhododendrons, cherries and maples and in the autumn sorbus, liquidambar, acers and *Cotinus coggygria*. Its hillside setting and two lakes give pleasing views from almost all of the site. Clearer labelling would help the enthusiast to identify the more unusual species. Contains the National whitebeam collection. Some 262 trees were damaged in the 1990 gales and work is being concentrated on clearing the debris.

WINTERSHALL MANOR 27

Bramley, Surrey.
Mr and Mrs Peter Hutley

2½m S of Bramley on A281 from Guildford towards Horsham. Right turn to Selhurst Common, fork right and the Manor is on the left • Parking • Teas from 3.30 p.m. • Toilet facilities • Suitable for wheelchairs • Open 12th May, 1st Sept, 2 - 6 p.m. • Entrance: £1, OAP 50p, children 20p

This formal garden with roses and colourful herbaceous walk is steeped in history. The old mulberry tree planted by James II was badly damaged by the January 1990 gale but has fruited later. Garden railings were put up to celebrate the Battle of Waterloo. Walks through 100 acres of park and woodland with bluebells, rhododendrons and daffodils. Suitable areas for picnics are provided and there is a small chapel to St Francis for the contemplative who will wish to remember that the spring-fed lakes date from Benedictine times.

WISLEY

(see Royal Horticultural Society)

GARDENS OPEN RARELY

The following gardens are open to the public on three days or less in the year, although they may also be open by appointment if this is stated in the text. For details see individual entry.

May 12 Wintershall Manor; **May 19** Bradstone Brook; Pyrford Court; **May 26** Pyrford Court; **June 30** Vale End; **July 14** Bradstone Brook; **Aug 4** Vale End; **Sept 1** Wintershall Manor; **Oct 20** Pyrford Court.

SUSSEX (East)

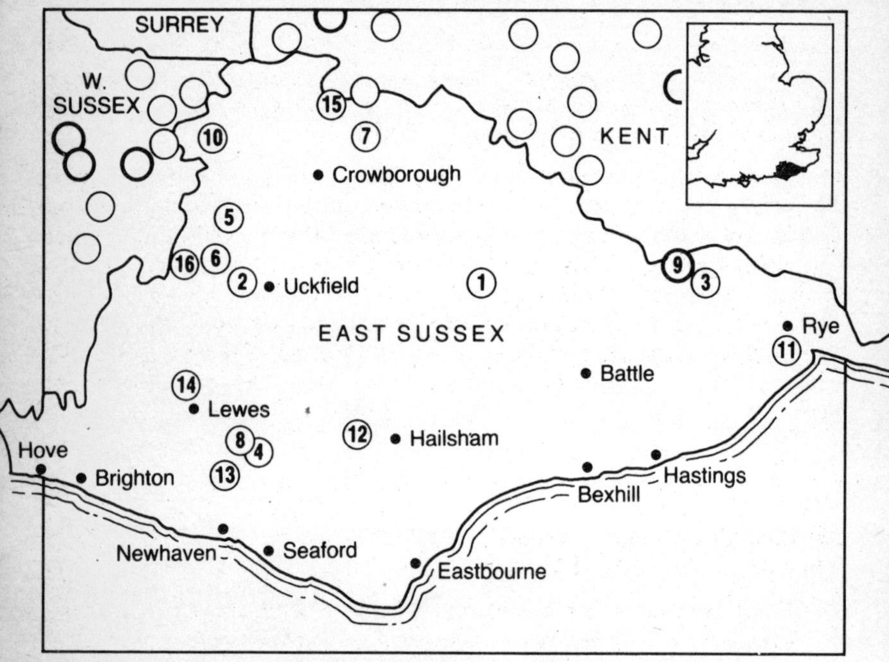

Plain circle numbers can be found by turning to neighbouring counties.
Two-starred gardens are ringed in bold.

BATEMAN'S 1

Burwash, Etchingham, East Sussex. Tel: (0435) 882302
The National Trust

½ S of Burwash on A265 towards Lewes • Parking • Refreshments: light lunches, coffees, teas. Picnics in Quarry Garden and Copse • Toilet facilities • Suitable for wheelchairs • Shop • House open and mill which grinds flour in season • Gardens open 29th March to Oct, daily except Thurs and Fri but open Good Fri, 11 a.m. – 5.30 p.m. Last admission 4.30 p.m. • Entrance: weekdays £3, weekends, Good Fri and Bank Holidays £3.50. Pre-booked parties reduced rates. All prices inc. house and mill

Kipling wrote one of the most-quoted poems about English gardening which is perhaps why Bateman's where he lived from 1902–36 is much visited. Not of great botanical interest, but it is well-kept and pleasant to sit in. Formal, with lawns, yew hedges, rose garden with pond, and wild garden, much of which was his doing, although the garden was laid out before he bought the house (built 1634).

BEECHES FARM 2

Buckham Hill, Nr Uckfield, East Sussex. Tel: (0825) 2391
Mrs V. Thomas

1½m W of Uckfield on Isfield road off A2102 • Parking • Teas on charity open days • Dogs on lead • Vegetables for sale when in season • House open by appointment with seven days notice. £1 extra • Open all year, daily, 10 a.m. - 5 p.m. and for charity • Entrance: 50p, children 25p

One wall of this sixteenth-century tile-hung farmhouse is covered by a *Magnolia grandiflora* and it is surrounded by a dozen or more enormous and very attractive containers, once used for cooling the local smelted iron ore. The circular rose garden has mainly old French, musk and moss roses. There are beds of lilies near the house and various borders of annuals add colour to the lawned areas. There is a newly planted 'glade' and *Eucalyptus niphophila* and *dalrympleana* are settling in well. The garden has been cleverly planted for winter colour and is one of the few in Sussex open between October and February.

BRICKWALL 3

Northiam, East Sussex. Tel: (0797) 223329
The Frewen Educational Trust

On B2088 Rye road • Best season: July • Parking • Suitable for wheelchairs • Dogs on lead • Shop with postcards and booklets • House open • Garden open Easter to Sept, Sat and Bank Holiday Mons, 2 - 5 p.m. • Entrance: £1.50, children under 10 free. Coach parties by arrangement

Brickwall is an interesting example of a Stuart garden, and care has been taken to use the plants chosen by Jane Frewen when she was making and planting it between 1680–1720, such as day lilies, bergamot, *Lychnis chalcedonica*, Cheddar pinks and columbines. There are large lavender beds, a number of ancient mulberries, groups of clipped yew, and a superb pleached beech walk. A striking modern addition is the Chess Garden with green and golden yew chessmen in iron frames, set in squares of white and black limestone chips. This garden is not far from Great Dixter (see entry) and a visit to both would make an excellent day out.

CHARLESTON FARMHOUSE 4

Nr Firle, Lewes, East Sussex. Tel: (032183) 265
The Charleston Trust

6m E of Lewes on A27 • Best season: spring and midsummer • Parking 50p • Refreshments • Toilet facilities • Plants for sale • Shop • House open • Garden open April to Oct, Wed, Thurs, Sat (guided tours of house), Sun, Bank Holiday Mon, 2 - 6 p.m. Last admission 5 p.m. • Entrance: £3.50, children £2.75 (house and garden)

In terms of pure gardening this does not deserve a grading, but it is of national interest because it was created by leaders of the Bloomsbury movement. The walled garden has been meticulously restored through painstaking research and the memories of people who visited when Vanessa Bell and Duncan Grant lived at the farmhouse and of those like Angelica Garnett and Quentin Bell who spent their childhood there. It is a delightful example of a garden created during the 1920s by an idiosyncratic group of highly creative people, and might be called an artist's garden. The crush of visitors may result in limitation on access.

CHELWOOD VACHERY ★ 5

Nutley, Nr Uckfield, East Sussex. Tel: (082571) 3404
BAT Industries

3m S of Forest Row on A22 • Best season: spring • Parking • Refreshments • Toilet facilities • Suitable for wheelchairs • Dogs on lead • Plants for sale • Open 19th May, 2 – 6 p.m. and by appointment for parties and small groups • Entrance: £1.50, children 60p

The house built in 1906 was bought by a Mr Nettlefold in 1925 and bought by BAT as a conference centre in 1955. Nearly 130 acres of woodland and formal garden offer a wide variety of plantings and interest. Even the well-preserved tea room rewards careful inspection of its kingpost and mouldings. Over 280 varieties of heathers are to be found either in their own areas or as underplanting for acer, azalea or dwarf conifer collections. The rock garden is shingeled over polythene for practical purposes, and among the myriad plants are more than 20 varieties of gentians. A Zen garden by the wisteria walk is a simple yet dominant feature, as is the nearby grave of Mr Nettlefold's retriever. Ten varieties of magnolias mingle with rhododendrons. A substantial broad-leaved planting scheme is under way to replace the damage from the 1987 gales, and wildlife conservation is much in mind, with bird and bat boxes and wild flowers. There are three large lakes, two smaller ones, bog gardens, and several small ponds and waterfalls. Amongst the variety of interesting species are *Stransvaesia davidiana* 'Palette', *Viburnum opulus* 'Fructuluteo', *Salix hyptilloides* 'Pink Tassel', *Populus × candicans* 'Aurora', *Magnolia × thompsoniana* (60 feet tall) and *Ceratostigma willmottianum*. The peacocks and guinea fowl roaming around, together with the careful, ample labelling, make this a garden for all.

CLINTON LODGE ★ 6

Fletching, Nr Uckfield, East Sussex. Tel: (0825) 722952
Mr and Mrs Cullum

4m W of Uckfield from A272. Turn N at Piltdown from Fletching, 1½m in main village street surrounded by a yew hedge • Parking on street • Refreshments • Toilet facilities • Suitable for wheelchairs • Dogs on lead • Open 17th June, 2 – 6 p.m. • Entrance: £1.50

This Queen Anne house was built for the first Lord Sheffield's daughter who married Henry Clinton. The garden of about four acres of clay soil is basically divided into areas by period. There is an Elizabethan herb garden with well-tended camomile paths and turf seats, and four knot gardens are being developed. A lawn and ha-ha at the rear of the house with views to distant woods create an eighteenth-century atmosphere, a white, yellow and blue Victorian herbaceous border with its 'hot' colours purposely absent, and a pre-Raphaelite alley of white roses, purple vines and lilies; the twentieth century is represented in the area surrounding the swimming pool. There are also various walks of quince, vines and white cherry underplanted with white bluebells, and a rose garden of musk and English roses complete with fully-occupied dovecote. Pillars of ceanothus and roses cover the walls in early summer, and less formal areas of orchard and wild flowers complete a garden of outstanding imagination and charm. All minor storm damage has been repaired and trees staked.

CROWN HOUSE 7

Eridge Green, Nr Tunbridge Wells, East Sussex. Tel: (0892) 864389
Major and Mrs L. Cave

3m SW of Tunbridge Wells. Take A26 Tunbridge Wells – Crowborough road. In Eridge take the Rotherfield turn S. House is first on the right • Parking on road • Homemade teas • Toilet facilities • Suitable for wheelchairs • Plants for sale • Shop for home-made produce • Open 13th, 14th July, 2 – 6.30 p.m. and by appointment • Entrance: £1, children 25p for charity

This gently sloping one and a half-acre garden contains several different areas of interest. Dominating the side of the house is a colourful umbrella of old-fashioned musk roses, astilbes, golden flame spiraea and catmint. At the front of the house the alpine garden is to be extended and a further pond added. The rose garden is underplanted with cranesbill and is surrounded by a yew hedge and *Clematis montana* 'Rubens'. The heather bed, herb garden and herbaceous borders are all carefully tended, giving a great variety of colour and interest which extend to the aviary, containing budgerigars, cockatiels and green parrots.

FIRLE PLACE 8

Lewes, East Sussex. Tel: (0273) 858335
Viscount Gage

On A27 Lewes – Eastbourne road. Entrance 1m from house • Best season: summer • Parking • Refreshments: cold buffet, licensed 12.30 – 2 p.m., Sussex cream teas 3 p.m. onwards • Toilet facilities • Parkland suitable for wheelchairs • Dogs on leads • Small selection of plants for sale • Shop • House open 5th May to Sept, Wed, Thurs, Sun and unguided Connoisseurs Days first Wed of every month • Garden open 5th May to Sept, Sun, Wed and

Thurs, and Bank Holiday Suns and Mons, 12.30 - 5.30 p.m. • Entrance: £3, children £1 (house and garden). Parties of 25 or more by appointment £2.75 per person. Connoisseurs Day £3.50 per person. No charge for terrace

The accessible part of the garden is nowadays small although attractive. The house, with its honey-coloured Normandy stonework, lies at the foot of the South Downs and has long views over the parkland and a nearby lake. Immediately below the Georgian façade, a terrace (where tea can be taken) overlooks the formal area of Italianate terraces and balustrades, a fountain and a ha-ha. There are several seats from which to enjoy the surroundings.

GREAT DIXTER ★★ 9

Dixter Road, Northiam, East Sussex. Tel: (0797) 253160
The Lloyd family

½m N of Northiam. Turn off A28 at Northiam post office • Parking • Refreshments • Toilet facilities • Plants for sale at nursery. Extensive choice of clematis • Shop • House open • Garden open 29th March to 13th Oct, daily except Mon, 2 - 5 p.m. Open all Bank Holiday Mons and 19th, 20th and 26th, 27th Oct. Open from 11 a.m. on 25th to 27th May, Suns in July and Aug and 26th Aug • Entrance: £2, children 25p (house and garden £3, children 50p. Concessionary rates for OAP and National Trust members on Fridays only when house and garden £2.50)

Probably too well-known to need describing, Great Dixter was bought by Nathaniel Lloyd in 1910. The fifteenth-century house was restored by Lutyens. The sunken garden was designed and constructed by Mr Nathaniel Lloyd. His son Christopher has continued his family's fine gardening tradition, striving to maintain the garden with a dwindling labour force. Composed of a series of gardens, these include fine topiary, a magnificent long mixed border, and enchanting rose garden, gardens where vegetables and flowers mingle, and throughout the complex of gardens are pockets of wild flowers. The spring at Great Dixter is famous for the huge drifts of naturalised bulbs. Truly a plantsman's garden, but a joy for anyone who enjoys gardening in the finest tradition.

KIDBROOK PARK 10

Forest Row, East Sussex. Tel: (0342) 822275
Rudolph Steiner Trust

At Forest Row 1m W of A22. Entrance in Priory Road • Best season: summer • Parking • Toilet facilities (not disabled) • Suitable for wheelchairs • Dogs on lead • Open Aug, daily, 2 - 5.30 p.m. • Entrance: £1, children 50p

A sandstone house built in 1725 now used as Michael Hall School, and its park lies on the northern boundary of the Ashdown Forest. Work is in progress to restore the main elements of Repton's design, though this has been hampered by the loss of 1500 trees during the 1987 gales. 'Swallow' spring, cascades, stepping stones, a pond and a twentieth-century weir add interest, together with wild and bog gardens. The parkland is obviously a shadow of its former glory. Maps can be obtained showing recommended walks through the 125 acres.

LAMB HOUSE 11

West Street, Rye, East Sussex.
The National Trust

In centre of Rye, in West Street, near the church • Parking difficult • House open. Home of Henry James, American novelist, 1898–1916. Later, the brothers Benson, now televised writers, lived there • Open April to Oct, Wed and Sat, 2 – 6 p.m. Last admission 5.30 p.m. • Entrance: £1.40 (house and garden). No reductions for children or parties

Americans are frequent visitors to this house where James wrote some of his best books and studied the English character including its passion for gardening. Although not of considerable botanic interest, this high-walled garden has great charm and it is surprising to find it so big – one acre in the middle of overcrowded Rye. It is well-maintained by the Trust's tenants who have done much in recent years to add style to the charm.

MICHELHAM PRIORY ★ 12

Upper Dicker, Hailsham, East Sussex. Tel: (0323) 844224
The Sussex Archaeological Society

10m N of Eastbourne off the A22 and A27. Signposted • Best season: spring/summer • Parking • Refreshments and picnic area • Toilet facilities inc. disabled • Suitable for wheelchairs • Dogs on lead in car park • Herbs and some herbaceous plants for sale • Shop • House and working watermill open. Blacksmiths and Rope museum • Garden open 25th March to Oct, daily, 11 a.m. – 5.30 p.m., Nov, Feb and March, Sun, 11 a.m. – 4 p.m. • Entrance: £2.50, OAP £2.20, children £1.30

A major feature is the Physic Garden, a reconstruction of a monastic physic garden, based on that at ninth-century St Gall, which was regarded as the ideal. The 11 beds contain medicinal plants for specific complaints. Many of them are the herbs of the hedgerows. A serpentine moatside border has been planted and there are plans to extend it. The monastery stew ponds are also being planted up. A large herbaceous border, backed by a shrubbery, was designed and planted by local horticultural students. Before the Dissolution of the Monasteries, this had been an Augustinian priory, founded in 1229.

MONK'S HOUSE ★ 13

Rodmell, Lewes, East Sussex.
The National Trust

4m SE of Lewes off former A275 now C7. In Rodmell village follow signs to Church. Sign is 400 yards from the house • Parking further down narrow road • Toilet facilities • House open • Garden open 30th March to April, Wed and Sat, 2 - 5 p.m., May to Oct, Wed and Sat, 2 - 6 p.m. Last admission ½ hour before closing • Entrance: £1.50. No reduction for children or parties

The cottage home of Virginia and Leonard Woolf from 1919 until his death in 1969. In autumn 1989 work commenced on redesigning the garden on the basis of the Woolf's notebooks and writings. Leonard Woolf had kept the village self-sufficient in vegetables, as well as showing them, and the original vegetable area is still thriving. There are two ponds, one in dewpond style. An orchard, underplanted with spring and autumn bulbs, contains a comprehensive collection of daffodils. The one and three quarter-acre garden is a mixture of chalk and clay, nurturing a wide variety of species. Flint stone walls and yew hedges frame the more formal herbaceous areas, leading to a typical Sussex flint church at the bottom of the garden. Among the interesting specimen trees are *Salix hastata* 'Wehrhanii', Chinese lantern (20 feet tall), *Magnolia liliflora*, walnut, mulberry, and *Catalpa bignonioides* (Indian bean). Literary folk will want to compare and contrast this garden with the other Bloomsbury lot's house at Charleston Farmhouse (see entry).

OFFHAM HOUSE 14

Offham, Nr Lewes, East Sussex Tel: (0273) 474824
Mr and Mrs H.N.A. Goodman

2m N of Lewes on A275, ½m from Cooksbridge Station • Best season: late spring, high summer • Limited parking on property, more on road • Refreshments • Toilet facilities • Suitable for wheelchairs • Dogs on lead • Plants for sale • Open 5th May, 3rd June, 2 - 6 p.m. • Entrance: £1, children 25p

This garden offers a wide variety of interest and perspectives. Lawns sweep from the extremely attractive house (with its well-blended, lush conservatory) to a colourful shrubbery, which contains shrub roses and a variety of trees, including an evergreen or holm oak, a tulip tree underplanted with bulbs, and a weeping mulberry; beyond is an arboretum with a weeping elm and collections of acers and sorbus. The colourful well-stocked herbaceous borders contain a variety of penstemons, euphorbias and salvias as well as an unusual sundial, contemporary with the house. Other features include a spring path with early purple orchids and fritillaries, a collection of lilacs, a cherry orchard (with several Japanese varieties), and an unusually long bed of peonies and aquilegias. A fine new addition is the herb garden, which is bursting with life: bergamots, alpine strawberries and marjorams, mixed with *Tricyrtis stolonifera*, *Phygelius aequalis* 'Yellow Trumpet', euphorbias and verbenas are framed by box, lavenders and thymes. At the front of the house is a fountain and a splendid example of davidia (pocket handkerchief tree). A particularly large and well-kept greenhouse is the backbone to this fine, well-tended garden.

PENNS IN THE ROCKS 15

Groombridge, East Sussex. Tel: (0892) 864244
Lord and Lady Gibson

7m SW of Tunbridge Wells on Groombridge – Crowborough road just S of Plumeyfeather Corner • Parking • Refreshments • Toilet facilities • Suitable for wheelchairs • Dogs in park only • Open 6th May, one day late June/early July, and 4th Aug • Entrance: £1, first 2 children 50p, further children free

The name comes from the distinguished American Quaker whose family owned the property from 1672 to 1762 and from the Tunbridge Wells rock formations in the garden. It has emerged over the years into a happy combination of formality and informality within a lovely setting. Lady Dorothy Wellesley developed it extensively and built the temple on the slope facing the Georgian house. The present owners have much developed the grounds since purchasing the house in 1956. It is approached by a long drive through parkland full of wild daffodils and other spring flowers. Pleached limes, a walled garden, a stream and pools, a clipped yew hedge, statuary, old roses and extensive borders provide more formal features, and many well-placed seats help visitors enjoy its beauties.

SHEFFIELD PARK GARDEN ★ 16

Nr Uckfield, East Sussex. Tel: (0825) 790655
The National Trust

5m NW of Uckfield, midway between East Grinstead and Lewes on E of A275 • Teas at Oak Hall (not National Trust) • Toilet facilities • Partly suitable for wheelchairs. Wheelchairs available • Shop • House under separate ownership and divided from garden by screen planting • Open 30th March to 20th Nov, Tues – Sat (closed Good Fri and Tues following Bank Holiday Mon), 11 a.m. – 6 p.m. or sunset if earlier. Sun and Bank Holiday Mons, 2 – 6 p.m. or sunset if earlier, Suns in Oct and Nov, 1 p.m. – sunset. Last admission 1 hour before closing • Entrance: April, and June to Sept, £3.80. May, Oct and Nov £3.60

One hundred-acre garden and arboretum with two lakes installed by 'Capability' Brown for the Earl of Sheffield in 1776. Repton also worked here in 1789 and was responsible for the string of lakes up to the mansion. Later still, the lakes were extended and cascades added. Between 1909 and 1934 a collection of trees and shrubs notable for their autumn colour was added, including many specimens of *Nyssa sylvatica*. These and other fine specimen trees, particularly North American varieties, provide good all-year-round interest. Features include good water lilies in the lakes, the Victorian Queen's Walk and, in autumn, two borders of the Chinese *Gentiana sino-ornata* of amazing colour. The Trust is continuing to open up new areas.

GARDENS OPEN RARELY

The following gardens are open to the public on three days or less in the year, although they may also be open by appointment if this is stated in the text. For details see individual entry.

May 5 Offham House; **May 6** Penns in the Rocks; **May 19** Chelwood Vachery; **June 3** Offham House; **June 17** Clinton Lodge; **July 13** Crown House; **July 14** Crown House; **Aug 4** Penns in the Rocks.

SUSSEX (West)

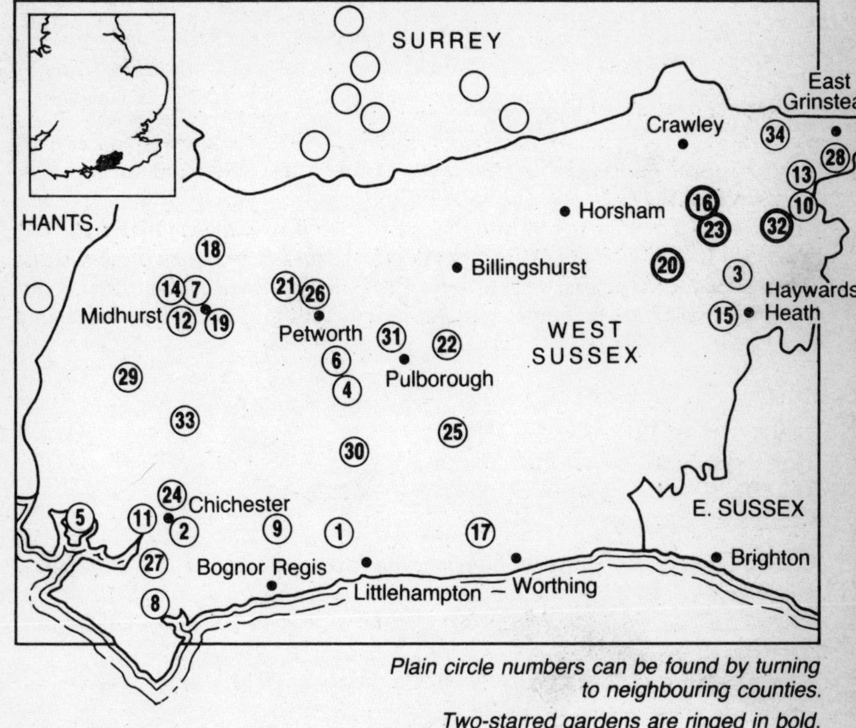

Plain circle numbers can be found by turning to neighbouring counties.

Two-starred gardens are ringed in bold.

BERRI COURT ★ 1

Yapton, Arundel, West Sussex. Tel: (0243) 551663
Mr and Mrs J.C. Turner

5m SW of Arundel, on A2024 Chichester/Littlehampton road in centre of village between Black Dog pub and Post Office • Parking by Baptist Church opposite • Suitable for wheelchairs • Dogs on lead • Open 30th June, 1st July, 2 - 5 p.m., 20th, 21st Oct, 12 noon - 4 p.m. • Entrance: £1, children 30p

A series of sheltered gardens within a three-acre garden of great interest to plant enthusiasts, created over a period of 20 years. There is a mass of daffodils in spring with azaleas and rhododendrons. The borders have an impressive display of shrubs and herbaceous plants and many varieties of shrub and climbing roses. Around the house are magnificent *Magnolia grandiflora*, *Drimys winteri* and *Clematis rehderiana*. Eucalyptus grove.

BISHOP'S PALACE 2

Chichester, West Sussex.
Diocese of Chichester

From South Street, turn into Canon Lane, left through the Palace Gatehouse • Parking in public car parks • Refreshments: refectory in Cathedral cloisters • Toilet facilities in Cathedral cloisters • Suitable for wheelchairs • Cathedral shop • Open daily, 8 a.m. to 9 p.m. or sunset • Entrance: free

After roaming the Cathedral pass down St Richard's Walk from the cloisters, turn right in the close, through the Palace gatehouse and follow the path to the gardens. These lie just within the city walls and have many tall ilex and bay trees. Well kept herbaceous borders and shrubs. A place to linger in the shadow of the Cathedral with a view of the medieval palace. On the way out along Canon Lane the houses and gardens of the close should not be passed in a hurry.

BORDE HILL GARDEN ★ 3

Haywards Heath, West Sussex.
Tel: (0444) 450326 or weekends (0444) 412151
Borde Hill Gardens Ltd

1½m N of Haywards Heath on Balcombe-Haywards Heath road • Best season: March – May • Parking • Refreshments • Toilet facilities • Suitable for wheelchairs • Dogs on lead • Plants for sale • Shop • Open Good Friday to last weekend in Oct, daily, and weekends in March, 10 a.m. – 6 p.m. • Entrance: £2, OAP £1.25, children 75p, parties of 20 or more £1.25 per person, individual season tickets £8, family season tickets £15

The garden was started by Col. Stephenson Clarke when he bought the Borde Hill property in 1893. Many of the trees, shrubs and particularly the rhododendrons were grown from seed collected by great plant hunters like Reginald Farrer, George Forrest, Frank Kingdon-Ward and Joseph Rock. There is a sad lack of labels on the plants, and parts of the garden, especially the bog and bamboo garden, show signs of neglect. However, the garden is important for its collection of exotics.

CHAMPS HILL 4

Coldwaltham, Pulborough, West Sussex. Tel: (0798) 831868
Mr and Mrs D. Bowerman

From A29 at Coldwaltham turn W towards Coates/Fittleworth. Champs Hill is 300 yards up on right • Parking • Teas in May and Aug but not in March • Open 10th March, 5th, 12th, 17th to 19th, 26th May, 16th to 18th Aug, 11 a.m. – 5 p.m., Sun, 1 – 5 p.m. • Entrance: £1, children free

Champs Hill house is approached by a long drive through the 27-acre garden with one of the most interesting collections of heathers in the area. The current owners plan to plant parts of the garden with something different. The sandy soil and high woodland walks make this a pleasant place for a country walk with views over the Arun, while keeping the plantsperson in the family occupied provided he or she likes heathers.

CHIDMERE HOUSE 5

Chidham, Chichester, West Sussex. Tel: (0243) 572287/873096
Mr T. Baxendale

E of Emsworth, W of Chichester, S off A259 Turn right at southern end of Chidham village • Best season: spring • Parking in road • Toilet facilities • Suitable for wheelchairs • Dogs on lead • Open 7th, 8th April, 19th, 20th May, 23rd, 24th June, 25th, 26th Aug, 2 - 7 p.m. • Entrance: 80p, children 30p

Chidmere gardens were laid out in 1930–36 by the present owner's father on the site of a farm and orchard. Modelled on Hidcote they incorporate impressive allées bordered by tall yew and hornbeam hedges together with a sizeable lake. The house (not open) is medieval in origin and, together with the outbuildings, it has been blended into a setting which looks far older than the 1930s. Trees include a davidia, *Gingko biloba*, *Prunus serrula*. There is a good collection of flowering shrubs and interesting French statues from the nineteenth century. In spring the daffodils in the orchard and plantation make a spectacular display.

COATES MANOR ★ 6

Fittleworth, Pulborough, West Sussex. Tel: (0798) 82356
Mrs G.H. Thorp

½m S of Fittleworth off B2138 • Suitable for wheelchairs • Plants for sale • Open 16th, 17th, 18th June, 11 a.m. - 6 p.m. and by appointment • Entrance: £1, children 20p

An unusual garden, which, Mrs Thorpe modestly explains, has been planned for ease of maintenance, using only plants which respond to local conditions. As an experienced flower arranger, she uses trees and shrubs which give long-term pleasure in the form of interesting foliage, berries and autumn colour. The front border running along the road blends a fine copper beech with *Elaeagnus pungens* and a purple-leaved *Cotinus coggygria*. The house is covered with a large-leaved variegated ivy and, particularly on the back lawn, there are some fine specimen trees, including a dramatically-sited *Liquidambar styraciflua* 'Worplesden', giving autumn colour. In addition to the two main gardens there is a delightful small walled garden to the side of the house with ceanothus, clematis and a host of scented honeysuckles and borders containing *Choisya ternata* and *Philadelphus coronarius*. This is a truly inspiring one-acre garden.

COWDRAY PARK 7

Midhurst, West Sussex. Tel: (0730) 812423/812215
Viscount Cowdray

N of Midhurst on A272 Petworth Road • Best season: May/June • Parking • Toilet facilities • Suitable for wheelchairs • Dogs on lead • Garden of new house only open on 19th May • Entrance: £1

Fine hilly deer park enclosing the remains of the Tudor House, burned down in 1793. The gardens surrounding the present-day house include a fine collection of rhododendrons, interesting to compare with nearby Ramster Gardens, fine cedars and azaleas and a sunken garden.

DANESACRE ★ 8

Mill Lane, Sidlesham, Nr Chichester, West Sussex. Tel: (0243) 641322
Captain A.J. Petrie-Hay

From B2145 Selsey road, turn E 300 yards after petrol station at Sidlesham down Rookery Lane. Enter Mill Lane and house is second on right • Parking in road • Teas • Plants for sale • Open 1st June, 2 - 5.30 p.m. • Entrance: £1, OAP 50p, children under 15 20p

A rather special plantsman's garden, taking full advantage of the south coast climate to grow an unusual variety of hardy and semi-hardy plants. There is a sizeable pond and marsh area, playing host to many different species of exotic waterfowl, which make an idyllic backdrop to the colourful display of plants seen at their best in May and June. These include lapageria, schisandra, mitraria, erythrina and feijoa.

DENMANS ★ 9

Denmans Lane, Fontwell, West Sussex. Tel: (0243) 542808
Mrs J.H. Robinson/Mr J. Brookes

5m E of Chichester. Turn S off a27, W of Fontwell racecourse • Best season: late May/early June • Parking • Refreshments: dairy tea shop offering coffee, light lunches and teas from 10 a.m. - 5 p.m. • Toilet facilities • Plants for sale • Shop • The Clock House is home to John Brookes' school of garden design running day courses on a variety of horticultural topics • Open 4th March to 15th Dec, daily, 9 a.m. - 5 p.m. • Entrance: £1.80, OAP £1.60, children £1, groups of 12 or more £1.50 per person

A small walled garden of approximately three and a half acres purchased originally as a vegetable garden by the Robinsons in 1946 and gradually extended and redesigned by Mrs Robinson who retired in 1984 when John Brookes took over. With so much colour and variety, one does not at first realize that there are relatively few flowers. Use is made of groups of trees and shrubs with matching foliage to provide background colour for low-growing and ground cover plants of similar shades that self-seed and naturalize at the front of borders and through gravel paths. For example *Robinia pseudoacacia* 'Frisia', a variegated holly, *Elaeagnus pungens* 'Maculata', marjoram 'Aureum' and *Alchemilla mollis* provide yellow accents in one border, whilst in another *Berberis thunbergii* 'Atropurpurea', *Cotinus coggygria* 'Foliis Purpureis', *Sedum spectabile* and *Anemone* x *hybrida* 'Max Vogel' are all toning shades of pink. The idea of growing in gravel beds came to Mrs Robinson when visiting Greece and has been skilfully extended by John Brookes to include a lake.

DUCKYLS 10

Sharpthorne, Nr East Grinstead, West Sussex. Tel: (0342) 801352
Sir Michael and Lady Taylor

4m SW of East Grinstead, 6m E of Crawley. Take B2028 S at Turners Hill and fork left after 1m to W Hoathly. Left at sign to Gravetye Manor garden on right • Parking • Toilet facilities • Partly suitable for wheelchairs • Dogs on led • Plants for sale if available • Open 28th, 29th, 30th April, 2 - 6 p.m. Parties by appointment • Entrance: £1, children 25p

These 14 acres of terraced and hilly grounds, established with rhododendrons and azaleas, are gradually being developed into many interesting individual areas without any loss of the overall grandeur. The 1987 gales actually helped in thinning out some of the older, less vigorous trees and carpets of bluebells, daffodils, fritillaries, common primroses and violets burgeon. A *Clethra alnifolia* (sweet pepper bush) has reappeared from beneath brambles, and many of the old paths can now be taken, leading through colourful pink pearls, griersonianum and chaetomallum to two ponds and a bog garden. Dogwoods and *Kalmia latifolia* are benefitting from a hard cut-back. The orchard has several wild orchids - early purple, green-winged and common-spotted - and the undisturbed areas nurture a wide variety of butterflies and birds. The more formal areas reflect the present owners' keen interest in auriculas and double primroses, in particular 'Duckyls Red' (which received an R.H.S. Award of Merit). Among other features, the restored rose garden and several newly planted alpine areas, rare poultry and magnificent views across to Wierwood Reservoir make this an ever-inviting garden.

FISHBOURNE ROMAN PALACE GARDEN 11

Salthill Road, Fishbourne, West Sussex. Tel: (0243) 785859
Sussex Archaeological Society

1½m W of Chichester off A259 • Refreshments: cafeteria for light lunches, teas and coffees. Closed Dec to Feb • Toilet facilities inc. disabled • Suitable for wheelchairs • Guide dogs only • Plants and herbs which would have been in use in Roman times for sale • Roman remains open • Open March to Nov, daily. March, April and Oct, 10 a.m. - 5 p.m., May to Sept, 10 a.m. - 6 p.m., Nov, 10 a.m. - 4 p.m., Dec to Feb, Sun, 10 a.m. - 4 p.m. • Entrance: £2.50, OAP and students £1.80, children £1, family tickets (2 adults, 2 children) £6, pre-booked parties of 20 or more adults £1.80 per person

Definitely not a plantsman's garden (in fact there are very few plants in evidence), but one which will appeal to students of history and garden design. Fishbourne is the fascinating recreation of a Roman palace and garden probably built for the local King Tiberius Claudius Cogidubnus about AD 75-100. Visitors would be advised to look at the model of the palace in the museum before viewing the site itself in order to better appreciate the symmetry of the design, as only half of the garden has been excavated. Whilst there is evidence, from the trenches filled with loam that were discovered during excavation, of the layout of paths and surrounding hedges, the planting is an imaginative reconstruction using only types known to have been grown in the Roman period.

FITZHALL 12

Iping, Nr Midhurst, West Sussex. Tel: (073081) 3634
Mr and Mrs Bridger

W of Midhurst off A272. Turn S opposite Iping turnoff • Parking • Teas • Toilet facilities • Partly suitable for wheelchairs • Plants for sale • Shop • Open April to Sept, daily, 2 - 6 p.m. • Entrance: £1.20, children 60p

Three generations of the Bridger family work together to restore and maintain the nine-acre garden on a high South Down site. Surrounded by high rhododendron and yew hedges, the lawns east of the house include fine herbaceous borders, shrubs and heathers, but perhaps the best surprise is the hidden herb garden, enclosed by fine yew hedges. This in turn gives onto a flagstone walk between two gardens full of cyclamen, roses, herbaceous plants. A short woodland walk, carpeted in April with bulbs, leads to a highly productive vegetable garden with produce on sale. Children will be interested in the farm animals.

GRAVETYE MANOR ★ 13

Vowels Lane, Nr East Grinstead, West Sussex. Tel: (0342) 810567
Mr P. Herbert

4m from East Grinstead off M23 and A22, turn towards West Hoathly, but drive carefully as entrance somewhat concealed • Best season: spring • Parking in Vowels Lane car park • Refreshments at hotel and for country club members only • Toilet facilities for hotel guests and country club members only • Dogs on lead • Open all year to hotel guests, perimeter footpath only for public. Small groups by appointment • Entrance: free

This historically important garden has been carefully restored in the style set out by William Robinson. It has a wild meadow leading down to trout lakes from terraced formal gardens. The elliptical kitchen garden enclosed by

Sussex sandstone walls is unique and is cultivated to produce fresh vegetables for the hotel kitchen. It is worth giving yourself a treat, either spending a weekend at Gravetye, or going for lunch but enquire about prices before making plans as this is an expensive as well as enjoyable experience. Either way you will be able to appreciate the garden, lakes and woods.

HAMMERWOOD HOUSE GARDEN 14

Iping, Midhurst, West Sussex. Tel: (0730) 813635
Mrs John Lakin

3m W of Midhurst, 1m N of A272 • Best season: spring • Parking • Refreshments • Toilet facilities • Suitable for wheelchairs • Dogs on lead • Plants for sale • Open 5th, 19th May, 2 - 6.30 p.m. • Entrance: £1.20, children 50p

This is a peaceful country garden formerly part of a Regency vicarage that has been planted with care and a fine eye for good plants. Although the rhododendrons and azaleas give it its most spectacular flowering season, there are some good seedling abutilons and specimen trees. Across a meadow from the main garden is the semi-wild garden set in a small wood.

HEASELANDS ★ 15

Haywards Heath, West Sussex. Tel: (0444) 454181
Mrs Ernest Kleinwort

1m from Haywards Heath on A273 • Parking • Teas • Toilet facilities inc. disabled • Suitable for wheelchairs • Open 8th, 12th, 15th, 19th, 22nd, 26th, 29th May, 2 - 6 p.m. Special arrangements on other days. Coaches/parties by appointment • Entrance: £1.20, children 30p

Beautiful home and gardens created by owners from the original farmhouse, meadow and woodlands. Earliest work consisted of planting shelter belts, then the sunken garden, rock gardens, tennis court, swimming pool - the yew hedges for the enclosed gardens were constructed and planted before the war. Other garden features have been formed over the last 30 years. The guide book photographs of rhododendron and azalea displays promise worthwhile visits, there being 82 rhododendron hybrids. There are large duck ponds and a goose paddock, and the kitchen garden also contains aviaries where birds are bred. A visit in October on a mild, sunny afternoon to view the autumn colour is highly recommended.

HIGH BEECHES GARDENS ★★ 16

Handcross, West Sussex. Tel: (0444) 400589
High Beeches Gardens Conservation Trust

1m E of Handcross, S of B2110 • Best seasons: spring and autumn • Parking • Refreshments on Spring Bank Holidays and for autumn event on 20th Oct • Toilet facilities inc. disabled • Open Easter to mid-June, Sept to Oct, daily except Sun and Wed, 1 - 5 p.m. Also Spring Bank Holiday 10 a.m. - 5 p.m. • Entrance: £2 (accompanied children under 14 free). Guided parties of 10 or more by appointment, £3 per person, any day or time with lunches by arrangement

A garden bearing the mark of the Loder family, which is now being maintained by the Boscawen family as Col. Loder designed it in 1906. The early planting was influenced by John Millais, son of the pre-Raphaelite artist; Arthur Soames of Sheffield Park, Sussex, and William Robinson, whose philosophy of allowing plants to grow naturally has greatly influenced the development of the garden. A series of valleys or ghylls, the garden was badly damaged by the October 1987 gales, but skilful remedial work has removed the most harrowing scars. It has a superb collection of rhododendrons and specimen trees. Willow gentians grow wild, and the front meadow, which has not been ploughed in living memory, is filled with native grasses and wild flowers. The woodland garden is also a haven for wild flowers. Autumn colouring is outstanding.

HIGHDOWN 17

Littlehampton Road, Goring-by-Sea, West Sussex. Tel: (0903) 48067
Worthing Borough Council

3m W of Worthing, N of A259 • Best season: April • Parking • Refreshments at peak times • Toilet facilities inc. disabled • Suitable for wheelchairs (1 available for hire on request) • Open April to Oct, Mon - Fri, 10 a.m. - 4.30 p.m., weekends and Bank Holidays, 10 a.m. - 8 p.m. or dusk • Entrance: by donation

Created by Sir Frederick Stern from a bare chalk pit in 1910, Highdown was donated to Worthing Corporation in 1968. Without a rhododendron or camellia in sight, Highdown makes a refreshing change for those used to gardening on acid soil. From such an unpromising site a garden has been created illustrating the scope and possibilities of a garden of chalk-loving plants. These include buddleia, mahonia, paulownia, althaea and paeonia, as well as rarities such as *Itea ilicifolia* and *Clerodendrum trichotomum fargesii*.

KING EDWARD VII HOSPITAL 18

Midhurst, West Sussex. Tel: (0730) 812341
King Edward VII Hospital Trust

3m NW of Midhurst on A286. Well signed down a 1m drive • Parking • Refreshments • Toilet facilities • Suitable for wheelchairs • Dogs on lead • Shop • Open 18th May, 2 - 5 p.m. • Entrance: by collecting box

Gertrude Jekyll laid out a series of fine herbaceous borders on terraces immediately south of the large hospital opened for officers after World War I. The terraces overlook extensive parkland and playing fields with an elevated view towards the South Downs Way. There are good woodland walks to the north of the hospital which stands in parkland of 152 acres. Also good beds of chrysanthemums etc. grown for the hospital shop.

LANE END 19

Sheep Lane, Midhurst, West Sussex. Tel: (0730) 813151
Mrs C.J. Epril

In centre of Midhurst • Best season: spring • Parking in town car parks • Partly suitable for wheelchairs • Open 25th, 26th, 27th May and 1st, 2nd, 3rd June, 11 a.m. - 6 p.m. • Entrance: £1, children free

This garden is as packed with interest as it is with plants. Created since 1972 on a sharp bulldozed slope, great use is made of raised beds, rock garden feature, and a large heather bank, all leading down to a semi-wild garden of shrubs and fine specimen forest trees. It is hard to believe that the garden is in a busy rural town.

LEONARDSLEE GARDENS ★★ 20

Lower Beeding, Nr Horsham, West Sussex. Tel: (0403) 891212
The Loder family

3m SW of Handcross and M23 on the A279/A281 • Best season: mid-April to mid-June and autumn • Parking • Refreshments: café and licensed restaurant • Toilet facilities • Large selection of plants, esp. rhododendrons, for sale • Shop • Open 13th April to 16th June, daily, 10 a.m. - 6 p.m., 22nd June to 29th Sept, Sat and Sun only, 12 noon - 6 p.m., Oct, Sat and Sun, 10 a.m. - 6 p.m. • Entrance: £2 - £4 (depending on season), children £1 - £2

This famous garden was started by Sir Edmund Loder, a member of the family which has left its mark on a number of great gardens in West Sussex. Sir Edmund raised the famous Rhododendron Loderi hybrids, with their enormous scented flowers. The gardens, with their seven lakes, contain a superb collection of rhododendrons, azaleas, acers, two magnificent dawn redwoods (*Metasequoia glyptostroboides*), as well as a wide variety of shrubs. Far from being depressed by the hurricane damage of 1987, Mr Robin Loder, who runs the gardens, is using the natural clearance to develop and replant and eventually extend the gardens and parklands to over 200 acres. A great deal of money and care has been expended on the excellent facilities for visitors.

THE MANOR OF DEAN 21

Tillingworth, Petworth, West Sussex.
Miss S.M. Mitford

Turn N from A272 ¼m W of Tillington • Best season: spring • Parking nearby • Tea and biscuits 50p • Shop for produce • Open for charity on 24th - 26th March, 21st - 23rd April, 19th - 21st May, 14th - 16th July, 18th - 20th Aug, 8th - 10th Sept, 6th - 8th Oct, 2 - 6 p.m. • Entrance: 50p, children 20p

A charming garden, with old walls and terraces, some dating from the building of the house in 1615, also old sundial and other impressive stone ornaments. Some rare plants still survive from Captain Mitford's subscription to the Kingdon-Ward expeditions, the last of the great plant-hunting journeys. The one-acre walled kitchen garden is still used for growing vegetables and also houses a greenhouse containing a fine yellow rose, grown from a cutting from the wedding bouquet of the present owner's great-grandmother. Throughout the garden there are fine lilies and dense banks of the wild Swiss mauve crocus.

MILL HOUSE 22

Nutbourne, Nr Pulborough, West Sussex. Tel: (0798) 813314
Sir Francis and Lady Avery Jones

At far end of cul de sac immediately to the left of Nutbourne Manor Vineyard (signposted) • Open by appointment and 30th June, 1st July, 2 - 6 p.m. • Entrance: £1.50, combined with other Nutbourne gardens

Mill House garden slopes steeply to a fast-running stream surrounded by bamboo thickets and a water garden. The steep banks are a profusion of wild flowers in June/July and the house itself is surrounded by a cottage garden. There is a fine walled herb garden containing about 140 different species to the side. Other gardens open in Nutbourne include Ebbsworth and Manor Farm and you can also visit the neighbouring Nutbourne Manor Vineyard, of 14 acres, predominantly vines imported from Germany.

NYMANS ★★ 23

Handcross, Nr Haywards Heath, West Sussex. Tel: (0444) 400321
The National Trust

At the southern end of Handcross village, off M23 and A279. Well signposted • Best season: spring and summer • Parking • Teahouse • Toilet facilities

• Suitable for wheelchairs • Plants for sale • Shop • Open 29th March to Oct, daily except Mon and Fri (but open Good Fri and Bank Holiday Mon), 11 a.m. – 7 p.m. or sunset if earlier. Last admission 1 hour before closing • Entrance: £2.80, pre-booked parties £2.30 per person

For 100 years the Messel family have developed Nymans gardens to accommodate a very wide collection of plants, of which rhododendrons, magnolias, camellias and eucryphias are outstanding. The large circular rose garden has been restored and replanted with the old-fashioned roses for which the garden is also famous. Wild and woodland gardening, influenced by William Robinson, dominate Nymans, but there are fine examples of more formal gardening, such as the circular garden sheltered by camellias, and planted with annuals, and the walled garden with its fine double borders of perennial and annual herbaceous plants. Lord and Lady Ross made a fine decision when leaving the relics of a nineteenth-century Gothic portion of the house standing after it was gutted by fire in the 1950s as it provides the garden with a wonderfully romantic backdrop. Leaflets for sale.

PALLANT HOUSE 24

North Pallant, Chichester, West Sussex. Tel: (0243) 774557
Pallant House Gallery Trust

Proceed from the station up South Street. Turn left in West Pallant • Parking on street with vouchers obtainable from most local shops • Toilet facilities • House open • Garden open all year, Tues – Sat, 10 a.m. – 5.30 p.m. Last admission 4.45 p.m. • Entrance: £1.80, OAP, children £1

A small Dutch-style garden close to Pallant House, an interesting local museum, lovingly restored in 1982 by Claud Phillimore, a well-known architect and leading light of the Georgian group. The use of Versailles tubs and eighteenth-century pots enables the tender exotics which were so new and exciting to fashionable men of the eighteenth century to be changed constantly to provide a succession of flowers. The sheltered site allows for some unusual tender plants (e.g. *Syringa × persica*, *Punica granatum* and *Rosa bracteata*) which were all introduced in the eighteenth century, while the small square beds, box edgings, hoggin-covered paths, trellis work and ornaments add to the effect of a strictly period but nevertheless charming town garden.

PARHAM HOUSE AND GARDENS ★ 25

Pulborough, West Sussex. Tel: (0903) 74 2021
Mrs P.A. Tritton

4m SE of Pulborough on A283 • Parking • Refreshments in big kitchen 2.30 – 5.30 p.m. Picnic area • Toilet facilities • Suitable for wheelchairs (garden only) • Dogs on lead • Plants for sale • Shop • House open as garden but 2 – 6 p.m. • Open Easter Sun to 1st Sun in Oct, Wed, Thurs, Sun and Bank

Holidays, 1 - 6 p.m. Last admission 5.30 p.m. • *Entrance: £1.60, children 75p (house and garden £3.20, OAP £2.50, children £1.50)*

The gardens of this Elizabethan house are approached through the Fountain Court. A broad gravelled path leads down a slope through a wrought-iron gate guarded by a pair of Istrian stone lions to the walled garden of about four acres. This retains its original quadrant layout divided by broad walks and includes an orchard. In 1982 it was redesigned retaining its character and atmosphere; the borders were replanted to give interest for many months, with shrubs as well as herbaceous plants. In one corner is the enchanting miniature house, a delight for both children and adults. The pleasure grounds of about seven acres provide lawns and walks under stately trees to the lake, with views over the cricket ground to the South Downs. Veronica's Maze planned for 1991.

PETWORTH HOUSE ★ 26

Petworth, West Sussex. Tel: (0798) 42207
The National Trust

6½m E of Midhurst on A272 in the centre of Petworth • *Parking ½m N of Petworth on A283* • *Refreshments: lunch 12.30 - 2.30 p.m., teas 3 - 5.30 p.m.* • *Toilet facilities* • *Suitable for wheelchairs. Disabled arrangements with administrator* • *Dogs on lead* • *Shop* • *House open 29th March to Oct, daily except Mon and Fri (but open Good Fri and Bank Holiday Mon, though closed following (Tues), 1 - 5.30 p.m. Last admission 5 p.m. Entrance £2.70, children £1.35* • *Deer park open all year, daily, 9 a.m. - sunset. Gardens and car park open 29th March to Oct, daily except Mon and Fri (but open Good Friday and Bank Holiday Mon. Closed Tues following), 12.30 - 5.30 p.m.* • *Entrance: park free. House and gardens £3.30*

The park grew from a small enclosure for fruit and vegetables in the sixteenth century to its present size of 705 acres, and is enclosed by an impressive 14-mile-long stone wall. George London worked here as did 'Capability' Brown. The latter toiled from 1753-63 for the 2nd Lord Egremont modifying the contours of the ground, planting cedars and many other trees and constructing the serpentine lake in front of the house. It was one of Brown's earliest designs, planned while he was still at Stowe. Turner painted fine views of the park (as well as the interior of the house) and it is interesting to see these and have them in one's mind as one strolls around the park as he must have done many times while staying at Petworth. This is not a garden for the botanist, but it is a very splendid experience, all year round, for any lover of man's improvements over nature, and individual trees and shrubs, including Japanese maples and rhododendrons, deserve close study. Trees lost in recent gales, but restoration in progress.

RYMANS 27

Apuldram, Chichester, West Sussex. Tel: (0243) 783147
Lord and Lady Phillimore

1½m SW of Chichester. Turn right off A286 signposted Apuldram and turn right again • Parking • Partly suitable for wheelchairs • House open for art exhibitions sometimes • Open 7th, 28th April, 2 – 5.30 p.m., 23rd June, 8th July, 26th Aug, 2 – 6 p.m. • Entrance: £1, children 30p

Surrounding this fifteenth-century house are three pretty walled gardens laid out by the owners, and containing ponds, rose borders and fine cherry trees; past a huge ilex is the orchard which is a mass of bulbs in spring. The tennis court has flowering shrub borders and the eighteenth-century walled kitchen garden contains herbaceous borders, fruit trees and vegetables. The 200 yard long poplar avenue leads to the church (not to be missed) and gives a good view towards Chichester and the cathedral. Along the avenue is a wood of mixed trees underplanted with late varieties of narcissus. The owners have specialised in unusual plants and shrubs, many from South Africa and New Zealand.

STANDEN ★ 28

East Grinstead, West Sussex. Tel: (0342) 323029
The National Trust

2m S of East Grinstead signposted from A22 at Felbridge, and also B2110 • Best season: May/June • Parking • Refreshments • Toilet facilities • Partly suitable for wheelchairs • Dogs in car park and woodland walks only • Shop • House open as garden, 1 – 5.30 p.m. • Open 29th March to Oct, Wed – Sun and Bank Holiday Mon (closed Tues following), 12 noon – 5.30 p.m. • Entrance: £1.40 (£3.20 house and garden)

The house and estate have close connections with William Morris, and the late Victorian garden reflects much of the romantic era of the latter part of the nineteenth century. It is made up of a succession of small, very English gardens. Perhaps the most outstanding is the little quarry, which has survived as a Victorian fernery. Good views from this hillside-garden across the Medway Valley. The house, designed by Philip Webb, will be of interest to architectural pundits.

TELEGRAPH HOUSE ★ 29

North Marden, Chichester, West Sussex. Tel: (0730 825) 206
Mr and Mrs D. Gault

Turn N on B2141 Chichester/South Harting road opposite North Marden • Parking • Teas on charity open days • Toilet facilities • Suitable for wheelchairs • Open 22nd, 23rd June, 20th, 21st July and by appointment May to Aug, 2 – 5 p.m. • Entrance: £1.50, children 50p

Originally a semaphore station used to convey news from Portsmouth to the Admiralty, Telegraph House is approached up a magnificent one-mile drive of copper beeches, and the gardens sit in a park which includes a yew wood with a 40-minute woodland walk. The views, as far as the Isle of Wight, are preserved while an impressive array of roses, autumn and spring crocuses, and herbaceous plants and shrubs are enclosed by immaculate yew and hornbeam hedges. It is very interesting to see what the owners have managed to develop from a chalky, windswept site, albeit in a magnificent setting, over a period of 20 years.

UPPER HOUSE 30

West Burton, Pulborough, West Sussex. Tel: (0798) 831604
Mr and Mrs C.M. Humber

5m SW of Pulborough. Turn right off A29 at Bury/West Burton crossroads • Teas • Partly suitable for wheelchairs • Plants for sale • Open 1st to 5th June, 2 - 6 p.m. Groups by appointment at other times • Entrance: 75p, children 25p

A large garden that incorporates several different 'rooms' each enclosed within yew hedges. One side of the house gives on to a paved garden with a wide variety of herbs. By the front door is a large *Magnolia grandiflora* and shrubs surrounding a gravelled drive. A large Victorian greenhouse in an immaculate state of preservation, in front of which you can see a rose garden which the owners have now replanted. Beyond this can be found a lawn enclosed by a close-clipped yew hedge. There is a new water garden and bog area at one end. This is a generous country-house garden, with a deceptive air of having happened by chance.

UPPER LODGE 31

Stopham, Pulborough, West Sussex.
Mr J.W. Harrington

From Pulborough take A283 westwards towards Fittleworth. At Stopham, the Lodge is on the left by the telephone box past the entrance to Stopham House • Plants for sale • Open 9th, 13th, 15th, 16th, 29th April, 2 - 5 p.m., 6th, 7th, 13th, 20th, 27th, 28th May, 2 - 6 p.m. • Entrance: 50p

By no means the cottage garden that the name Lodge might suggest. The acid soil has enabled Mr Harrington to concentrate on an impressive range of azaleas and rhododendrons within a comparatively small area, raised from the road and with views over the surrounding park and farmland. There is usually a good range of shrubs for sale and it is a particularly useful garden to visit for those with similar acid soil.

WAKEHURST PLACE GARDEN ★★ 32

Ardingley, Nr Haywards Heath, West Sussex. Tel: (0444) 892701
The National Trust/The Royal Botanic Gardens, Kew

From London take A(M)23, A272, B2028 or A22, B2110 • Parking • Refreshments: self-service teas, Easter to mid-Oct, and at other times in bookshop • Toilet facilities • Partly suitable for wheelchairs • Bookshop • Part of house open • Gardens open all year, except 25th Dec and 1st Jan. Nov to Jan, 10 a.m. - 4 p.m.; Feb and Oct, 10 a.m. - 5 p.m.; March, 10 a.m. - 6 p.m.; April to Sept, 10 a.m. - 7 p.m. Last admission ½ hour before closing • Entrance: Prices and opening times subject to variation

Dating from Norman times, the estate was bought by Gerald W.E. Loder (Lord Wakehurst) in 1903. He spent 33 years developing the woodland and formal gardens, a work carried on by Sir Henry Price. The gardens are leased to the Ministry of Agriculture, Fisheries and Food to be used as an annexe of the Royal Botanic Gardens, Kew. It has a fine collection of rhododendrons, kalmias, camellias, corylopsis and viburnums. Unique is the Himalayan glade planted with species growing at 10,000 feet in the Himalayas. Many tender plants such as callistemon, olearias, crinodendron, leptospermums, mimosa and hoherias flourish. Wakehurst is a place for the botanist, plantsman and garden lover.

WEST DEAN GARDENS ★ 33

West Dean, Nr Chichester, West Sussex.
Tel: (024363) 303
Edward James Foundation

5m N of Chichester on A286 • Best season: spring/early summer • Parking • Toilet facilities • Suitable for wheelchairs • Plants for sale • Open March to Oct, daily, 11 a.m. - 6 p.m. Last admission 5 p.m. • Entrance: £2, OAP £1.75, children £1. Parties by appointment £1.50 per person

This estate was acquired in 1891 by William James who planted fine trees in the 30 acres of informal nineteenth-century gardens which surround an impressive flint house by Wyatt. Range of plants slightly limited by alkaline soil and severe frost pockets. There is a sunken garden, with a deep pond; 300-foot pergola built in 1911 by Harold Peto, leads to a gazebo, surrounded by rare evergreens (*Clematis armandii*, *Cupressus goveniana*, *Cryptomeria japonica*) and fine fern-leafed beeches (*Fagus sylvatica heterophylla*). In addition to the romantic water garden (designed by Gertrude Jekyll) and wild garden, there is a sizeable walled garden with lovingly restored greenhouses containing an amusing collection of antique lawnmowers. The garden borders the Weald and Downland Museum of traditional rural life from 1400 to 1900. The house is now a training college. The arboretum forms part of the gardens and, despite the depredations of the gales, is full of interest for the tree lover.

YEW TREE COTTAGE ★ 34

Crawley Down, Turners Hill, West Sussex. Tel: (0342) 714633
Mrs Hudson

1m S of A264. Down lane opposite Cretan Pottery shop on B2028, take right turn and the cottage is the second of semi-detached on left • Best season: spring/ summer • Parking • Plants for sale • House open for small groups 50p extra • Garden open 29th, 30th June, 2 - 6 p.m. and by appointment for small groups • Entrance: 50p, children 20p. Also joint entrance with Ridge House

A plantsman's delight and an encouragement to all with small gardens, it is not surprising that this third of an acre plot has been a prizewinner. Developments continue and the vegetable garden is now a small Jekyll-style masterpiece. The front garden is divided between a scree with alpines and herbs and a shrubbery with a golden area including *Hypericum aurea*, physocarpus, forsythia and *Philadelphus aurea*. To the rear of the house a mature quince, underplanted with campanulas and rue, stands over a well, while the borders are bursting with colour and unusual plants. Ballerina and Felicia geraniums, *Mertensia asiatica*, pink phlomis, *Babtisia australis*, toad lilies, mutabilis and *Cheiranthus linifolius*, sweet rocket and *Rhododendron impeditum* are but a few of the interesting plants in this exceptional garden.

GARDENS OPEN RARELY

The following gardens are open to the public on three days or less in the year, although they may also be open by appointment if this is stated in the text. For details see individual entry.

April 28 Duckyls; **April 29** Duckyls; **April 30** Duckyls; **May 5** Hammerwood House Garden; **May 18** King Edward VII Hospital; **May 19** Cowdray Park; Hammerwood House Garden; **June 1** Danesacre; **June 16** Coates Manor; **June 17** Coates Manor; **June 30** Mill House; Yew Tree Cottage; **July 1** Mill House.

TYNE AND WEAR

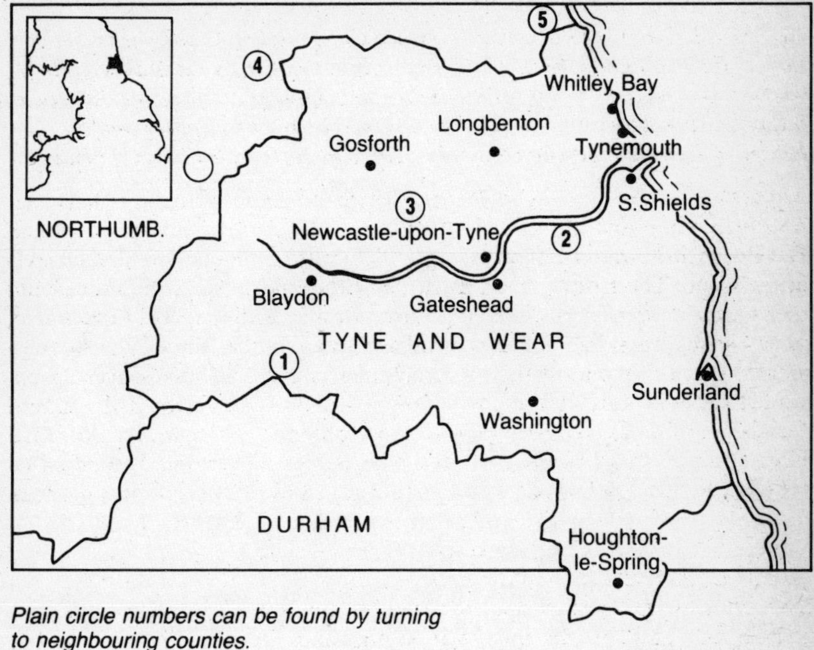

Plain circle numbers can be found by turning to neighbouring counties.

BEDE MONASTERY MUSEUM 1

Church Bank, Jarrow, Tyne and Wear.
Tel: (091) 4892106
Bede Monastery Museum

6m E of Gateshead off A185 • Best season: summer • Parking • Refreshments • Toilet facilities • Suitable for wheelchairs • Dogs on lead • Plants for sale • House open as garden. Entrance: 60p, student 40p, OAP and children 30p • Garden open April to Oct, daily except Mon but open Bank Holiday Mons, 10 a.m. – 5.30 p.m., Nov to Mar, 11 a.m. – 4.30 p.m., Suns, 2.30 – 5.30 p.m. • Entrance: free

A nicely planted small herb garden with a wide range in four sections: culinary, Anglo-Saxon medicinal, aromatic and medicinal. Currently in need of attention but interesting to the herbalist.

GIBSIDE CHAPEL AND GROUNDS 2

Burnopfield, Newcastle-upon-Tyne, Tyne and Wear.
Tel: (0207) 542255
The National Trust

6m SW of Gateshead, 20m NW of Durham from B6314, off A694 Rowlands Gill • Light teas and picnic area in car park • Dogs on lead • Shop • Chapel open and service 1st Sun each month, 3 p.m. Concerts and guided walks • Open 29th March to Oct, daily except Mon (but open Bank Holiday Mon), 11 a.m. - 5 p.m. Last admission 4.30 p.m. • Entrance: £1.50, children 75p, parties £1.20 per person.

The chapel is an outstanding example of English Palladian architecture by James Paine. There is no 'real' garden but the fine avenue of Turkey oaks leading to the derelict Gibside Hall is memorable. The chapel is surrounded by woods managed by the Forestry Commission and has three Wellingtonia firs. There is a Victorian walled kitchen garden which is an open space waiting to be filled.

JESMOND DENE 3

Jesmond, Newcastle-upon-Tyne, Tyne and Wear. Tel: (091) 2328520
Newcastle City Parks Department

1m W of city centre along Jesmond Road • Best season: summer • Parking in Freeman Road • Toilet facilities • Partly suitable for wheelchairs • Dogs on lead • Open all year • Entrance: free

Presented to the city by Lord Armstrong, the famous engineer, in 1883 and only a mile from the city centre, this steep-sided thickly-wooded dene provides extensive walks in an entirely natural setting, complete with a waterfall, a ruined mill and some fine old buildings (and even a well-run pets corner). From Freeman Road the upper park has a play pond and good bedding plants. Quite exceptional condition for a city park.

KIRKLEY HALL COLLEGE ★ 4

Ponteland, Newcastle-upon-Tyne, Northumberland. Tel: (0661) 860808
Northumberland County Council

11m NW of Newcastle off A696, right at Ponteland on C151 for 2½m. RAC signposted • Parking • Refreshments • Toilet facilities • Suitable for wheelchairs • Plants for sale • Open daily, 10 a.m. - dusk • Entrance: £1.20, OAP and children 8 - 16 60p, family ticket £3, parties of 21 or more, 70p per person

The 10-acre grounds with their three-acre walled garden form a showcase for all the gardening arts from propagation onwards. Inside the walls are climbers, borders and bedding plants in profusion, all pleasingly grouped and labelled. The grounds contain a succession of beds, skilfully shaped to follow the rolling contours of the land, each carefully composed for variety of profile and continuity of colour - the heathers being spectacular. Then to the Hall with its outstanding array of beautifully planted containers on terraces down to a most attractive sunken garden and a wildlife pond. National collections include beech, ivy and willow. The whole is a thoroughly professional and delightful achievement by the College.

SEATON DELAVAL HALL 5

Seaton Sluice, Whitley Bay, Tyne and Wear.
Tel: (091) 2373040/2371493
Lord Hastings

10m NE of Newcastle, ½m inland from Seaton Sluice on A190 • Best season: mid-summer • Parking • Toilet facilities • Partly suitable for wheelchairs • Dogs on lead • Souvenir stall • House open • Garden open May to Sept, Wed, Sun and Bank Holidays, 2 - 6 p.m. • Entrance: £1, OAP and children 50p

The original grounds of this architectural masterpiece by Vanburgh no doubt matched its magnificence, but little is known save for an early painting showing a swan lake. A notable weeping ash survives from that time, and there is a venerable rose garden. Since 1950 an excellent parterre has been laid out, now embellished by a large Italianate pond and fountains. An attractive shrubbery (rhododendron, azalea, etc) and herbaceous borders have also been established on the south side towards the fine Normal chapel. Replanting continues and the garden is obviously in good hands.

WARWICKSHIRE

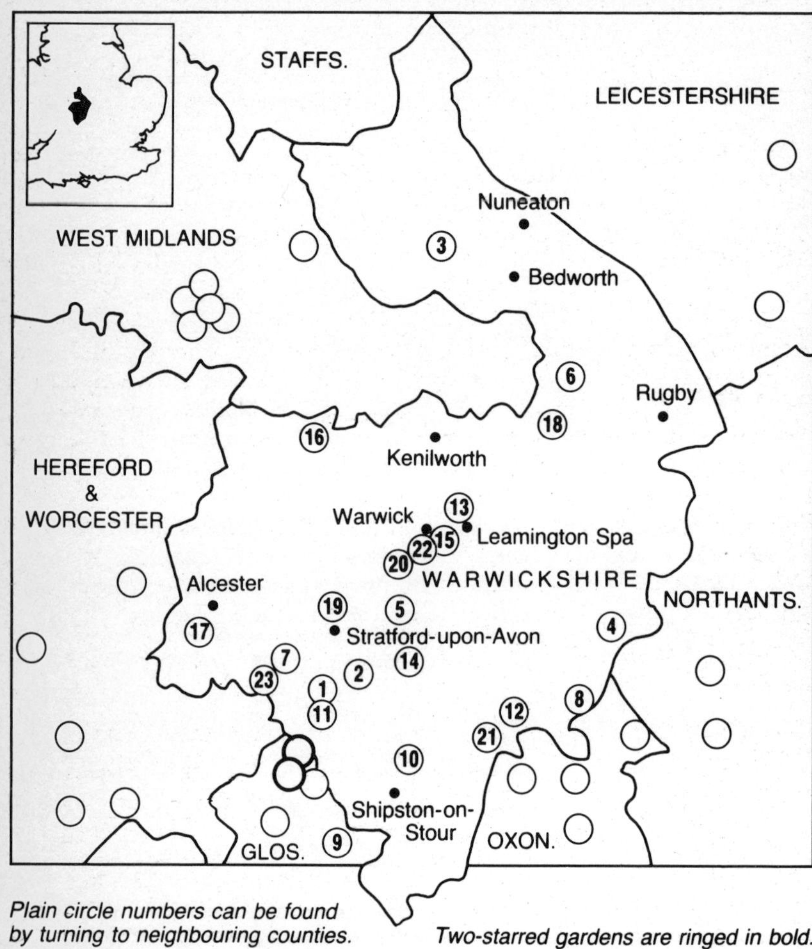

Plain circle numbers can be found by turning to neighbouring counties.

Two-starred gardens are ringed in bold.

ADMINGTON HALL 1

Admington, Nr Quinton, Warwickshire. Tel: (0789) 450279
Mr and Mrs J.P. Wilkerson

6½m S of Stratford-upon-Avon between A34 and A46 • Best season: June to Aug • Parking in road and field opposite • Teas • Toilet facilities • Partly suitable for wheelchairs • Dogs on lead • Plants for sale • Open 1st, 2nd June, 2 – 6 p.m. Parties by appointment • Entrance: £1, children 50p

This recently-made garden contains a 1620 dovecote which is older than the house. There are 12 clipped yews, eleven inside the garden and one outside the gate which may represent the apostles. A pool with fish and ducks is surrounded with a range of water-loving plants, and a stream meanders through the garden. The walled garden contains a wide range of vegetables and fruit, and old trees of chestnut, oak, beech and cedar provide a backcloth to the herbaceous borders. Peaceful walks through the woodland area.

ALSCOT PARK 2

Alscot, Warwickshire. Tel: (0789) 292623
Mrs James West

2½m S of Stratford-upon-Avon on A34 • Parking • Teas • Toilet facilities • Suitable for wheelchairs • Dogs • Plants for sale • Open 16th June, 7th July, 2 - 6 p.m. • Entrance: 80p, children 20p

A typical eighteenth-century park with one of the earliest mock-Gothic houses (not open), this has all the requisite main features - extensive lawns, fine trees, orangery, deer park, river and lakes. There is a small garden round the house but the main interest lies in the new garden developed by Mrs West near the orangery, now the site of a pool area. Around it a large semi-formal garden features old-fashioned roses, a mixed flower and vegetable garden and strong lines of hedging. Note the fine quality of the seats, urns, ornaments, etc.

ARBURY HALL ★ 3

Arbury, Nr Nuneaton, Warwickshire. Tel: (0203) 382804
Viscount and Viscountess Daventry

10m from Coventry, 7m from Meriden at Astley off the B4102 Fillongley/ Nuneaton road • Best season: spring/summer • Parking in adjoining field • Teas • Toilet facilities • Suitable for wheelchairs • Dogs on lead • Shop • House open • Garden open Easter to Sept, Sun and Bank Holidays, 2 - 6 p.m. • Entrance: £1.40, children 70p (park and gardens), £2.70, children £1.40 (hall, park and gardens)

A delightful garden with a sense of peace. Bulbs at the start of the season followed by rhododendrons and azaleas, then roses in June and autumn colour from trees and shrubs. Formal rose garden and climbing roses. Lakes with wildfowl, parkland, the drive and bluebell woods. A canal system was installed years ago as a method of transport. Pleached limes and the old walled garden are some of the features of this pleasant garden, along with the beautiful old trees. There is a museum in the old stables containing a collection of veteran cycles, motor cycles, sewing machines and some old farm implements. Gift and craft shop in the Old Dairy.

THE BUTCHERS ARMS 4

Priors Hardwick, Warwickshire. Tel: (0327) 60504
Mr and Mrs I. Pires

6m SE of Southam. From Southam take A425 towards Daventry and turn right to Priors Hardwick • Parking • Teas on charity open day • Toilet facilities • Plants for sale when available • Open 30th June, but also available at other times to clients dining in the restaurant • Entrance: 70p, children 30p

This attractive four-acre garden stimulates design ideas. There are good colour combinations of plants, shrubs and trees and the island beds provide colour through most of the year. The pool is crossed by a pleasing bridge and surrounded by a collection of bog plants. Roses have been planted to climb through old trees, and there is a rockery. A pleasant garden to stroll round either before or after lunch, tea or dinner.

CHARLECOTE PARK 5

Charlecote, Warwickshire. Tel: (0789) 840277
The National Trust

1m W of Wellesbourne, 5m E of Stratford-upon-Avon on road immediately S of bridge • Parking • Refreshments: morning coffee, light lunches, afternoon teas in orangery. Picnics in deer park • Toilet facilities • Partly suitable for wheelchairs • Large commercial plant nursery opposite main gate • Shop • House open. Last admission 5 p.m. • Park open 30th March to Oct, daily except Mon and Thurs but open Bank Holiday Mon, 11 a.m. - 6 p.m. Evening tours for pre-booked parties 2nd Wed in each month inc. house 7.30 - 9.30 p.m. • Entrance: £3.20 (house and garden)

More of picturesque and historic than garden interest. Home of Lucy family since the thirteenth century. Shakespeare reputedly poached the deer, which still populate the park alongside Jacob sheep. Park laid out by 'Capability' Brown who was directed not to destroy the avenues of elms, later eliminated by Dutch elm disease. Orangery and wild garden. Of special interest is the Shakespeare border with 32 plants which feature in the plays, ranging from herbs to quince and medlar, and old roses and carnations.

COOMBE ABBEY COUNTRY PARK 7

Nr Coventry, Warwickshire. Tel: (0203) 453720 Ranger Service

Just outside Coventry on A427 • Best season: June/July • Parking • Refreshments: bar with snacks. Picnics allowed • Toilet facilities • Suitable for wheelchairs • Dogs on lead • Open daily, 9 a.m. - dusk • Entrance: free but pay and display parking charge all year. Seasonal price fluctuations

The great attraction is the wide range of activities to be enjoyed in the 150 acres. There is a courtyard with a pool, boating for children along with an adventure play area, a countryside centre, guided walks, a heron lake, pleasure cruises, a Victorian garden and a selection of beautiful old trees and shrubs. On the west front of the house is the terrace and parterre, and the grounds contain canals and woodland walks among oaks, chestnuts, conifers and copper beeches. A heather border, rhododendrons and herbaceous plants give further interest.

ELM CLOSE 7

Binton Road, Welford on Avon, Warwickshire. Tel: (0789) 750793
Mr and Mrs E.W. Dyer

5m W of Stratford-upon-Avon on A439. Turn left after 4½m to Welford • Parking in road or pub car park nearby • Teas on special days • Toilet facilities • Suitable for wheelchairs • Plants for sale • Open 17th March, 7th April, 12th May, 9th June, 15th Sept, 2 - 6.30 p.m. Also by appointment • Entrance: £1, children free

It is fascinating to see the wide range of plants in a relatively small garden. Clematis are trained over pergolas and climb through trees and shrubs, and there are dwarf conifers, a rock garden, hellebores, a pool, a fruit and vegetable garden, alpine troughs, raised beds and an excellent variety of bulbs; herbaceous plants and shrubs provide interest and colour throughout the year. All visitors are likely to be stimulated by new ideas.

FARNBOROUGH HALL 8

Farnborough, Warwickshire. Tel: (029589) 202
The National Trust/Mr and Mrs Holbech

5m N of Banbury, ½m W off A423 or E off A41 • Suitable for wheelchairs (grounds only) • Dogs on lead (grounds only) • Open April to Sept, Wed and Sat, also 5th, 6th May, 2 - 6 p.m. Terrace walk only every Thurs and Fri, 2 - 6 p.m. Parties of 15 or more by prior arrangement at other times. Last admissions 5.30 p.m. • Entrance: £1.30 (house, grounds and terrace walk £2)

Grounds improved in the eighteenth century with aid of Sanderson Miller, an architect, landscape gardener and dilettante who lived at nearby Radway. The fine S-shaped terrace walk climbs gently along the ridge looking towards Edgehill. Legend has it that the owner, William Holbech, built the walk in order to see, in the distance, another landowning friend. The *Oxford Companion* describes it as a majestic concept marking the movement towards the great landscaped parks at the end of the eighteenth century. Two temples along the walk and an obelisk at the end. The trees are beeches, sycamores and limes. To the north, part of the site of the former orangery, now a rose garden, is a yew walk ending where formerly a cascade linked the oval pond (now woodland) with the remaining long lake across the road from the house. The atmosphere is affected by the building of the M40 extension nearby.

FOXCOTE 9

Nr Shipston-on-Stour, Warwickshire. Tel: (060882) 240
Mr C.B. and the Hon Mrs Holman

4½m W of Shipston-on-Stour, 4m N of Moreton-in-Marsh. It can also be approached by forking left in Ilmington • Parking • Teas • Toilet facilities • Partly suitable for wheelchairs • Dogs on lead • Plants for sale • Open 26th, 27th May, 2 - 6 p.m. • Entrance: 80p, children free

When the owners came here nearly 30 years ago there were mature yew and beech hedges and from this basic structure they have created a strong design which takes advantage of the wonderful setting. The plantsperson would probably call this minimalist gardening although there are good borders on the terraces with roses, irises, lavender and selected annuals which contrast with the fifteenth-century monastery fish ponds below. The owners have rebuilt these, stocked them with trout and created a woodland walk around. Note also the walled kitchen garden, very orderly and highly productive.

HONINGTON HALL AND VILLAGE GARDENS 10

Honington, Nr Shipston-on-Stour, Warwickshire. Tel: (0608) 61434
Sir John Wiggin Bart.

1½m N of Shipston-on-Stour, ½m to E off A34 • Parking • Teas at Honington Hall • Toilet facilities • Suitable for wheelchairs • Dogs • Honington Hall open June to Aug, Wed and Bank Holiday Mons, 2.30 - 5 p.m. Parties at other times by appointment. Village gardens open for charity 30th June (Hall not open) • Entrance: £2, children 50p

Honington is a well-kept village of up-market houses - some may think so well-kept as to have lost the village character. From the A34, the approach is over a charming eighteenth-century bridge from which the Carolean house can be seen to the left. This is surrounded by extensive lawns and fine trees and, like most of the front gardens in the village, well-manicured flower beds. A popular afternoon out, particularly on the day the village gardens are open.

ILMINGTON MANOR 11

Ilmington, Nr Shipston-on-Stour, Warwickshire. Tel: (060882) 230
Mr D.L. Flower

4m NW of Shipston-on-Stour, 8m S of Stratford-upon-Avon • Parking • Teas on charity open days • Toilet facilities • Suitable for wheelchairs • Plants for sale • Open by appointment and 14th April, 5th, 6th May, 23rd June, 7th July, 2 - 6 p.m. • Entrance: £1.50, OAP £1, children free except 14th April when £2 for combined admission to other village gardens

Created from an orchard in 1909, this is now a mature garden with strong formal design which is full of surprises. There is also much to interest the plantsperson. To the right of the drive is a paved pond, with thyme of many varieties ornamenting the stones. Scented and aromatic climbers surround this area. Next, a walk up the pillar border presents an unusual combination of shrubs and herbaceous plants in colour groups. Then, up stone steps, is the formal rose garden and the long double border planted with old and modern shrub roses. The so-called Dutch garden is really an informal cottage garden with a profuse mixture of colour. There is much more – a trough garden, iris and foliage beds, a rock garden and, in the spring, plenty of daffodils and crocus. New plants and trees are still being added. Although the garden is open by appointment, Mr Flower says that he does not have many such visitors, which is curious as it might easily be coupled with a visit to Hidcote or Kiftsgate nearby.

IVY LODGE 12

Radway, Warwickshire. Tel: (029587) 371
Mrs M.A. Willis

7m NW of Banbury via A41 and B4086. 14m SE of Stratford-upon-Avon via A422 • Parking in village • Teas • Suitable for wheelchairs • Open by arrangement for parties and for charity on 27th April, 22nd June, 2 – 6 p.m. • Entrance: £1, children free

Radway nestles below Edgehill, and the garden of Ivy Lodge runs back across the former battlefield. Above on the skyline can be seen the mock castle, now a pub. In spring there is a profusion of bulbs and blossom; in summer a fine collection of roses. The village contains many cottages with interesting gardens and every other year about a dozen are open to the public. Their attractions range from a good collection of garden gnomes to grander efforts such as pleached limes. In 1988/9 the village achieved the 'Best Kept Village' award but despite this it retains a marked villagey character.

JEPHSON GARDENS 13

Royal Leamington Spa, Warwickshire.
Tel: (0926) 4500 (Nigel Bishop, Parks Manager)
Warwick District Council

In centre of Leamington, main entrance off Pump Room • Parking • Refreshments • Toilet facilities • Suitable for wheelchairs • Dogs • Open 8 a.m. (9 a.m. Sun and Bank Holidays) to ½ hour after dusk • Entrance: free

This Spa town has always made a great effort in the floral decoration of its streets, and this activity can be enjoyed at its peak in the intensive bedding out of the principal formal public garden. The garden at the ruined castle on the outskirts of the nearby town of Kenilworth is also worth a detour, not so much for what it is, but in memory of what it has been.

LOXLEY HALL 14

Loxley, Nr Stratford-upon-Avon, Warwickshire. Tel: (0789) 840212
Col. A. Gregory-Hood

4m SE of Stratford-upon-Avon, N off A422 or W off A429 • Parking in village • Teas on charity open days • Suitable for wheelchairs • Dogs • House closed but church open • Garden open 26th May, 30th June, 2.30 - 7 p.m. The sculpture may be visited by appointment with Mr Roy Chandler (0789) 840 212 • Entrance: £1, children 20p

Though not an immaculate garden, this will interest some. Two reasons for visiting are: first, the owner has designed it as a series of 'rooms' in the Sissinghurst tradition and it is interesting to evaluate his success; second, he has added to them examples of contemporary sculpture from a London gallery. One of our inspectors finds the result rather arid, with not much of interest except large areas of grass; others have enjoyed the sculpture. The church next door is said to be one of the oldest in Britain, founded AD761.

THE MILL GARDEN 15

Mill Street, Warwick, Warwickshire.
A.B. Measures

Mill Street is off the A425 to the west just before reaching the Castle • Open Easter to Sept, Sun and other times when possible • Collecting box for charities

From this excellent informal little place, beside the river, planted with a wide selection of unusual plants, one can see the old bridge across which Shakespeare is said to have ridden to London. There is also a herb garden and raised alpine beds. The garden contains part of the National collection of digitalis. (See also Warwick Castle entry.)

PACKWOOD HOUSE ★ 16

Lapworth, Solihull, Warwickshire. Tel: (05643) 2024
The National Trust

2m E of Hockley Heath on A34, 11m SE of central Birmingham • Parking • Picnic site here but licensed facilities at Baddesley Clinton, another NT property nearby • Toilet facilities • Suitable for wheelchairs • Shop • House open as garden. • Open 30th March to Sept, Wed - Sun and Bank Holiday Mon (closed Good Fri), 2 - 6 p.m., Oct, Wed - Sun, 12.30 - 4 p.m. Last admission ½ hour before closing • Entrance: £1.70 (house and garden £2.50)

Hidden away from a rather suburban part of Warwickshire this garden is notable for its intact layout with courtyards, terraces, brick gazebos and mount of the sixteenth and seventeenth centuries when the house was built. Even more remarkable is the almost surreal yew garden, unique in design. Tradition claims that it represents the Sermon on the Mount but in fact the 'Apostles' were planted in the 1850s as a four-square pattern round an orchard. Never mind, the result is now homogenous. There is a spiral 'mount', yew and box, which is a delightful illusion. Note also the clever use made of brick. G. Baron Ash, who gave the property to the Trust, made a sunken garden in the 1930s and restored earlier design features. He also introduced colourful border planting, but the garden also looks splendid early and late in the year when there is scarcely a flower to be seen.

RAGLEY HALL 17

Alcester, Warwickshire. Tel: (0789) 762090
The Marquess of Hertford

1m from Alcester on A435 • Best season: spring • Parking • Refreshments: tearooms and small café open from 11 a.m. • Toilet facilities inc. disabled • Partly suitable for wheelchairs • Shop • House open • Garden open Easter to Sept, 10 a.m. - 6 p.m.

Not a well-cultivated garden but the climbers on the pillar by the house, the rose garden and some lovely old trees are worthy of a visit. There is also a beautiful lake surrounded by lawns with picnic tables, an adventure area with very good facilities and woodland walks and country trails. The house is very popular with visitors.

RYTON GARDENS 18

(National Centre for Organic Gardening)
Ryton-on-Dunsmore, Coventry, Warwickshire. Tel: (0203) 303517
The Henry Doubleday Research Association

5m SE of Coventry. Turn off A45 onto B4029 • Parking • Refreshments: café serving organic food • Toilet facilities • Suitable for wheelchairs • Guide dogs only • Plants for sale • Shop • Open April to Sept, daily, 9 a.m. - 6 p.m., Oct to Mar, daily except Christmas period, 10 a.m. - 4 p.m. • Entrance: £2, OAPs, children under 18, students, unemployed, £1, family £4.50. Tickets last a year

Six acres including conservation area with pond, native woodland, wild flower meadow, wildlife garden, bee garden, soft fruit garden and trained fruit trees, rose garden, herbaceous and shrub borders, herbs, large vegetable plots including old varieties together with examples of compost-making, raised beds, mulching, green manure crops, plants for drying, use of deep beds and methods of attracting beneficial wildlife into the garden. Also an alpine garden. A children's play area and picnic facilities make it somewhere for the family to visit and learn something for their own garden, even if not intending to use organic methods.

SHAKESPEARE GARDENS 19

Stratford-upon-Avon, Warwickshire. Tel: (0789) 204016
Shakespeare Birthplace Trust & Stratford Council

Located in Stratford-upon-Avon and surrounding area • Many tea shops in town • Toilet facilities in town • Shops in properties • Open at individual times for properties, but others open daily 9 a.m. - dusk. Closed 24th to 26th Dec, and on the mornings of 1st Jan and Good Friday • Entrance: to Trust properties by individual charge or £6, children £2.50 for all of them

If it is true that little is known about Shakespeare, less is known about his gardens. The Trustees have done their best to make them an interesting adjunct to the properties, mostly with tourists in mind. They include *The Birthplace Garden*, a small informal collection of over 100 trees, herbs, plants and flowers mentioned by the Bard. *Mary Arden's House*, the front a mélange of box, roses and flowers, the rear a stretch of lawn with, beyond, a wild garden. Country Museum with tools, etc. Light refreshments and picnic area. *Anne Hathaway's Cottage*; a recreation of a typical English cottage garden of a period later than Shakespeare's and the Tree Garden with examples of those mentioned in the Works. *New Place*; the house Shakespeare bought for his retirement, but alas burnt down, and the foundations planted with a garden around which, it is suggested, his orchard and kitchen garden lay. Reconstructed Elizabethan knot garden with oak pallisade and 'tunnell' or 'pleached bower' of that time. *Hall's Croft*; walled garden with little resemblance to its probable form in the period when it was owned by the Bard's son-in-law. *All the above are Trust properties and fee-charged.* Beyond the knot garden is a large free garden with separate access. Also free are Bancroft Gardens in front of the Theatre and a smaller, more intimate stretch behind, looking down along the Avon towards the church where Shakespeare is buried.

SHERBOURNE PARK ★ 20

Sherbourne, Nr Warwick, Warwickshire. Tel: (0926) 624255
Lady Smith-Ryland

½m N of Barford, 3m S of Warwick off A429, close to the junction of the A46 and the M40 extension • Parking • Teas. For parties, lunches and teas by arrangement • Suitable for wheelchairs • Plants for sale in Barford nursery nearby • Open 5th May with plant sale for charity, 2nd, 16th June, 8th Sept. Also by appointment • Entrance: £1.50, OAP £1, children free

A fine park surrounds the early Georgian house (1730), and adjacent Gilbert Scott church (1863), in which Lady Smith-Ryland has developed a series of imaginative smaller gardens characterized by inspired planting. In particular, the 'square' garden at an angle shows great originality. All the conventional features of the English garden - shrubs, herbaceous borders, roses, lilies and so on - are combined in most pleasing and sometimes surprising congruity. There is a temple and a small lake beyond the church. More of the grounds are being developed, and this will ultimately be one of the most distinguished in an area full of gardens of distinction.

UPTON HOUSE ★ 21

Edgehill, Nr Banbury, Warwickshire. Tel: (029587) 266
The National Trust

7m NW of Banbury on A422 • Parking. Coaches by arrangement with administrator • Light refreshments in tearoom • Toilet facilities • Partly suitable for wheelchairs • Dogs • House open as garden but last admission ½ hour before closing • Open 30th March to April, and Oct, Sat, Sun and Bank Holiday Mon (closed Good Fri), 2 - 6 p.m. May to Sept, Sat - Wed, 2 - 6 p.m. • Entrance: £1.80 (house £3.10)

The house itself, which dates from 1695, contains a fine collection of paintings including two grand Stubbs. More interesting to the garden visitor is that it stands on sandstone, 700 feet above sea level, at the ridge of Edgehill, site of the famous battle. Below a great lawn, the garden descends in a series of long terraces, along one side of which is an impressive flight of stone steps, leading down to the large lake below. The grand scale of the plan is the main interest, but there are many unusual plants, particularly perennials and, along the lake, bog plants. About twice a year the Warwickshire Hunt meets at the house, and by following the hunt to the surrouding hills at the back, gardening enthusiasts who are also hunt supporters may enjoy a unique view of the descending terraces and lake.

WARWICK CASTLE ★ 22

Warwick, Warwickshire. Tel: (0926) 495421
The Tussaud's Group

In the centre of Warwick, which is off the A46 bypass • Parking • Refreshments of all kinds in castle and town. Picnics in grounds • Toilet facilities • Shop • Castle open • Garden open all year round except 25th Dec, March to Oct, 10 a.m. - 5.30 p.m., Nov to Feb, 10 a.m. - 4.30 p.m. • Entrance: £5.50, OAP £4, children £3.50, family ticket (2 adults, 2 children) £16, (2 adults, 3 children) £18. Charges include castle and grounds from March 1991

Despite its commercial nature (the previous owner sold 63 acres to Madame Tussauds and 1000 acres to a farmer) this is a pleasant place to visit. There is, however, no reduction in the entrance price for visiting the grounds alone. Some 30 acres of the medieval castle site were set out by 'Capability' Brown, the first work commissioned after he set up on his own. He removed the old formal garden outside the wall and shaped the grounds to frame a view, using great trees, notably cedars of Lebanon. The courtyard was levelled and made into lawns with Scots pines. It is worth climbing the eleventh-century mound to gain a view of the site and country beyond the River Avon – Brown later worked on Castle Park on the other side. The newly-restored conservatory houses tender plants including the *Grevillea* species from Australia, named after the family. From this conservatory, the visitor looks across the large parterre, peopled by shrieking peacocks. This was laid out in the late nineteenth century when the Pageant Field park beyond was also planted with rhododendrons which this visitor finds obtrusive. On the other side of the castle entrance is a formal Victorian rose garden which has been recreated from Robert Marnock's designs of 1868 and a rock garden and pool of *c.* 1900. The present owner's intention is to restore the whole to its appearance in 1901, the period of the main interior rooms, now peopled with waxworks of former distinguished guests.

One interesting way to see the castle is to go first to The Mill Garden (see entry), in Mill Street, Warwick, south of the town. Later from the castle grounds, the visitor can view this area from the riverside by crossing the bridge near the boat house.

WOODPECKERS 23

The Bank, Marcliff, Nr Bidford-on-Avon, Warwickshire.
Tel: (0789) 773416
Dr and Mrs A.J. Cox

7m SW of Stratford-upon-Avon off B4085 between Bidford and Cleeve Prior • Best season: spring/summer • Parking in road and nearby car park • No refreshments but picnics allowed • Suitable for wheelchairs • Plants for sale • Open March to Sept, last Tues of each month, and 21st April, 9th June, 2 - 5 p.m. and by appointment • Entrance: £1

This two and a half-acre garden contains many good ideas and blends in with the surrounding countryside. Island beds and the patio area with troughs provide all year round interest and colour and there are several borders of individual colours. There is a pool and bog garden, an ornamental garden or potager with standard currants and gooseberries, a knot garden and a round greenhouse containing tender plants.

GARDENS OPEN RARELY

The following gardens are open to the public on three days or less in the year, although they may also be open by appointment if this is stated in the text. For details see individual entry.

April 27 Ivy Lodge; **May 26** Foxcote; Loxley Hall; **May 27** Foxcote; **June 1** Admington Hall; **June 2** Admington Hall; **June 16** Alscot Park; **June 22** Ivy Lodge; **June 30** The Butcher's Arms; Loxley Hall; **July 7** Alscot Park.

WILTSHIRE

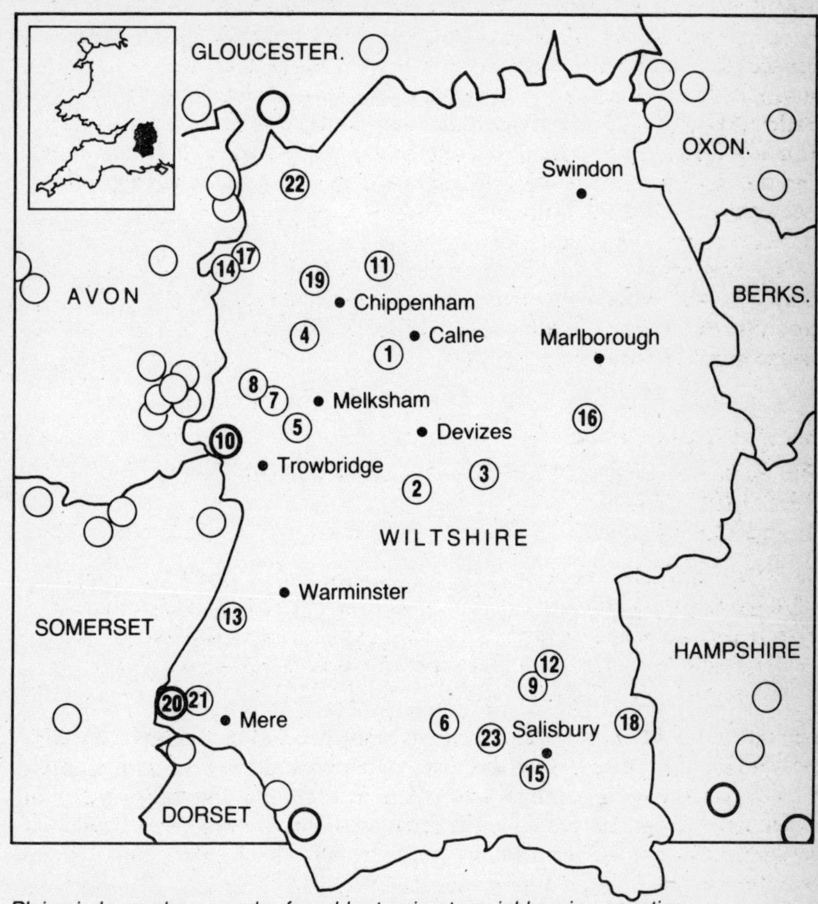

Plain circle numbers can be found by turning to neighbouring counties. Two-starred gardens are ringed in bold.

BOWOOD ★ 1

Bowood House, Derry Hill, Calne, Wiltshire. Tel: (0249) 812102
The Earl and Countess of Shelburne

4½m W of Calne, 5m SE of Chippenham, 8m S of M4. On A342 • Best seasons: spring and autumn • Parking • Licensed restaurant and garden tea-rooms • Toilet facilities • Suitable for wheelchairs • Garden centre specialising in unusual plants • Shop • House open. Also adventure playground for children 12 and under • Gardens open March to Oct, daily, 11 a.m. – 6 p.m. or dusk ir earlier • Entrance: £4, OAP £3.30, children £1.90 (house and garden)

Over 90 acres of 'Capability' Brown landscaped park with a very large lake. At the end of this, a cascade and grotto built by Josiah Lane (1785) and a classical temple. There is an arboretum and pinetum. Thousands of flowering bulbs bloom in spring. The Robert Adam orangery (converted into a gallery) is particularly fine and in front of it are formal Bath-stone terraces with rose beds, standard roses and fastigiate yews. *Fremontodendron californicum* flourishes on the Italianate terrace. The rhododendron walks are situated in a separate 50-acre area, which is only open when the rhododendrons are flowering. Robert Adam's mausoleum ('a little gem' well worth a visit) is in this area.

BROADLEAS 2

Broadleas, Devizes, Wiltshire. Tel: (0380) 722035
Lady Anne Cowdray

1m S of Devizes. Entrance through Devizes (signposted from Long Street) • *Parking* • *Teas on Sun until end of Aug* • *Toilet facilities* • *Own-propagated plants for sale* • *Open Easter to Oct, Sun, Wed, Thurs, 2 - 6 p.m.* • *Entrance: £1.50*

This garden was bought just after World War II and started from nothing by Lady Anne Cowdray in a combe below Devizes. Mature and semi-mature magnolias grow on each side of a steep dell. As good as any Cornish garden, it is stuffed with fine things that one would think too tender for these parts. Large specimens of everything (much of it now forty years old) *Paulownia fargesii*, *Parrotia persica*, all manner of magnolias, azaleas, hydrangeas, hostas, lilies and trilliums of rare and notable species. It is a garden of tireless perfectionism, at its most stunning in spring when sheets of bulbs stretch out beneath the flowering trees. Rarely seen in such quantities for instance are the erythroniums or dog-tooth violets. Many of the more unusual plants, both shrubs and perennials, are grown at Broadleas. There is also a woodland walk, a sunken rose garden and a silver border. This is serious plantsmanship and dendrology.

CHIFFCHAFFS

(see Dorset)

CONOCK MANOR 3

Devizes, Wiltshire. Tel: (0380) 84227
Mr and Mrs Bonar Sykes

5m SE of Devizes off A342 • *Parking* • *Teas* • *Suitable for wheelchairs* • *Open 19th May, 2 - 6 p.m.* • *Entrance: £1, children 20p*

Set between distant views of Marlborough Downs and Salisbury Plain, the Georgian house looks on to the lawns with specimen trees, ha-has and a recently-planted arboretum. From a Reptonesque thatched dairy near the house, a long brick wall and mixed shrub border lead to the stable block, in style early Gothic Revival, with a copper-domed cupola. Beyond, yew and beech hedges and brick walls frame the meticulously-kept kitchen garden and 1930s shrub walk. Box forms attractive bays and clipped balls. Pleached limes, a magnolia garden including malus, sorbus and prunus, and a woodland walk, are other features of this handsome garden.

CORSHAM COURT 4

Corsham, Wiltshire. Tel: (0249) 712214
The Lord Methuen

4m W of Chippenham on A4 • Best season: spring • Parking • Toilet facilities • Suitable for wheelchairs • Dogs on lead • House open • Garden open Jan to Nov, daily except Mon and Fri, 2 – 4.30 p.m. and until 6 p.m. from Good Fri to Sept, except Mon. Open all Bank Holidays • Entrance: £1.50

Approaching from Chippenham, look out for a glimpse of this house on your left, once framed by an avenue of elms now replaced by some lime trees. Surrounded by a landscape of 'Capability' Brown's devising finished off by Humphrey Repton (the lake and boat-house particularly) it is an example of this kind of gardening at its best. Rare and exotic trees look entirely at home: black walnut, Californian redwood, cedars, Wellingtonias, and the most astonishing layered Oriental plane tree, shading beeches, oaks, sycamores and Spanish chestnuts. There are 340 species of trees and 75,000 daffodils in the 40-acre arboretum. The bath-house designed by Brown is a treat and one can get through it into a world of entirely different mood. The Bradford porch leads out into a small enclosed flower garden with catalpa trees. Repton's roses trained over metal arches encircling a round pond is a rare surviving example of the elegance of early nineteenth-century flower gardens. Here the flower borders contain the unusual *Clerodendrum trichotomum* and enormous iron supports for roses and *Clematis* × *jackmanii*. There is a box-edged garden, hornbeam allée, good urns and arbours and seats. In spring the park shines with flowers of countless bulbs under magnolia trees, and in August there are handsome hydrangeas and willow gentians.

THE COURTS 5

Holt, Bradford-on-Avon, Wiltshire. Tel: (0225) 782340
The National Trust

3m SW of Melksham, 3m N of Trowbridge, 2½m E of Bradford-on-Avon on B3107 • Best season: summer • Parking at the village hall • Suitable for wheelchairs • Dogs on lead • Open 29th March to Oct, daily except Sat, 2 – 5 p.m. Out of season by appointment • Entrance: £1.50

Created by Sir George Hastings in 1900–1911, this has been an impressive garden and is still well worth visiting for both the plants and ideas. Extensive bog and water plants. The eighteenth-century house is set in formal areas of garden which give place to wild, bog and orchard gardens beyond. There are many lawns, much topiary, beguiling nooks and lots of good Edwardian features such as stone walls and paths, pergolas, hedges, lily ponds and terraces. A garden in the Hidcote mould.

FITZ HOUSE 6

Teffont Magna, Salisbury, Wiltshire. Tel: (0722) 716257
Major and Mrs Mordaunt-Hare

10m W of Salisbury on B3089 • Open May to Sept, Sat and Sun, 2 - 5.30 p.m. Also 19th May, 16th June for charity • Entrance: £1.75, children 80p

Teffont Magna is an exquisite village threaded along a chalk stream which runs also through the garden of Fitz House. What more could a gardener wish for than the beautiful stone of a sixteenth-century house as a backdrop for a garden and a stream to water it. Good hedges form the 'bones' of this scented garden infilled with massed spring bulbs and handsome shrub planting such as azaleas and roses. The garden is sloping and partly terraced, with large varied flowerbeds and handsome stone retaining walls. It is delightfully peaceful.

GREAT CHALFIELD MANOR 7

Melksham, Wiltshire. Tel: (0225) 464446
The National Trust

3m SW of Melksham on B3107 • Parking • House open • Garden open April to Oct, Tues - Thurs by guided tours only (starting 12.15, 2.15, 3, 3.45 and 4.30 p.m.), 12 noon - 5 p.m. Closed on public holidays. Parties by written appointment on other days • Entrance: £2.80

This house and garden were rescued in the early 1900s by Mr Robert Fuller. The setting is extremely romantic, lost among tree-lined lanes and water meadows. One crosses a stream to enter the courtyard in front of the house with the parish church on the left. Behind the house and the inner court (replanted with pink roses in 1989), the land falls away to an orchard and to the lower moat which is spring-fed. The large lawn or pleasaunce has two topiary houses and a gazebo, all made by Mr Fuller, with a border below. The garden is not for plantsmen but its magic lies in the setting, the mill leat, nine hundred yards long, and in the fact that it is profoundly English and ancient.

HAZELBURY MANOR 8

Nr Box, Corsham, Wiltshire. Tel: (0225) 810715
Mr and Mrs I.D. Pollard

5m SW of Chippenham. From Box take A365 to Melksham, turn left onto B3109, take the next left, and then turn right immediately into private drive • Parking • Teas on charity open days • Toilet facilities • Plants for sale • Open 5th, 6th, 26th, 27th May, 6th, 7th, 13th, 14th July, 2 - 6 p.m. Also pre-booked coach parties any weekday • Entrance: £2.50, children £1.25

Very extensive formal gardens about a sprawling Elizabethan house, immaculately restored and rejuvenated by its present owner. The massive rock garden at the front of the house is impressive although it couldn't be called in keeping with the house and makes as big a twentieth-century statement as the earlier Edwardian garden. This formal garden has a large lawn banked up on either side by high walks between clipped beeches. Every inch is extremely well looked after. In spring the alleys are all carpeted with brilliant polyanthus, cowslips and wallflowers. Mammoth herbaceous borders blaze in summer. There is a beautiful laburnum arched walk, and other notable features are a lime walk and - nearer the house - a terraced alpine garden. A more private and intimate garden nestles in the fortifications on the other side of the house. In this terraced area an old mulberry tree, irises, lavender and standard roses create an atmosphere appropriate to the genuine medieval archery walk. Beyond the fortifications is a new plantation of specimen trees, mostly conifers. There is a great deal to see and nothing is done by half measures. Very impressive.

HEALE HOUSE ★ 9

Middle Woodford, Salisbury, Wiltshire. Tel: (0722) 73504
Major David and Lady Anne Rasch

4m N of Salisbury between A360 and A345 • Parking • Toilet facilities • Suitable for wheelchairs • Dogs on lead • Extensive range of plants for sale, many home-grown • Shop and plant centre open all year (10 a.m. - 5 p.m.) • House not open except to groups of 20 or more booked in advance • Garden open daily except Christmas week, 10 a.m. - 5 p.m. • Entrance: £2

This is an idyllic garden with mature yew hedges. A tributary of the Avon meanders through it providing the perfect boundary and obvious site for the sealing-wax red Japanese bridge and the thatched tea-house which straddles the water. This was made with the help of four Japanese gardeners in 1910 and extends under the shade of *Magnolia × soulangiana* along the boggy banks planted with bog arums, *Rodgersia aesculifolia*, candelabra primulas and irises. There are two terraces immediately beside the house, one rampant with alchemilla, spurges and irises. The other has two stone lily ponds, designed by Harold Peto, and two small borders given height by nine-foot high wood pyramids bearing clematis and honeysuckle. The Long Border contains mostly hybrid musk roses backed by a simple but effective rustic trellis, and also many interesting herbaceous plants. The walled kitchen garden is possibly the most successful part of the garden – it achieves a very satisfying marriage between practicality and pleasure. It is not a regimented vegetable garden but the formal nature of rows of potatoes etc are made a feature and plots are divided by espaliered fruit trees forming an apple and pear tunnel, and by pergolas and hedges. The wonderful flint and brick wall provides protection for many plants including *Cytisus battandieri* and an ancient fig. This is a walled garden where one is encouraged to linger on the seats and in the shaded arbours and enjoy and admire the extraordinary tranquillity of the place. The plant centre is very comprehensive and the shop appeals to the discerning. Unique wrought-iron plant supports can be bought here. Look out for the ancient mulberry and the very old *Cercidiphyllum japonicum*, and *Magnolia grandiflora*. Winner of the Christies – HHA Garden of the Year Award 1984.

IFORD MANOR ★★ 10

Iford, Bradford-on-Avon, Wiltshire. Tel: (02216) 2364
Mr and Mrs J.J.W. Hignett

7m SE of Bath via A36 • Parking • Teas May to Sept, Sun and Bank Holiday Mons • Toilet facilities • Open April and Oct, Sun, 2 – 5 p.m., May to Aug, Tues – Thurs, Sat and Sun and Summer Bank Holidays, 2 – 5 p.m. Other times by appointment • Entrance: £1.50, OAP, students £1

It is always illuminating to see a famous architect and landscape gardener's own garden. Harold Peto found himself a near-ideal house in the steep valley through which the River Frome slides langorously towards Bath. The topography lent itself to the strong architectural framework favoured by Peto and the creation of areas of entirely differing moods. The overriding intention is Italianate with a preponderance of cypresses, juniper, box and yew, punctuated at every turn by sarcophagi, urns, terracotta, marble seats and statues, columns, fountains and loggias. In a different vein is a meadow of naturalised bulbs, most spectacularly martagon lilies. A path leads from here to the cloisters – an Italian-Romanesque building of Harold Peto's confection made with fragments collected from Italy. From here one can admire the whole, and the breath-taking valley and the walled kitchen garden on the other side.

KELLAWAYS 11

Chippenham, Wiltshire. Tel: (0249 74) 203
Mrs D. Hoskins

3m NE of Chippenham on the East Tytherton road • Parking • Teas • Toilet facilities • Partly suitable for wheelchairs • Plants for sale on 16th June • Open March to Nov by appointment and 16th June, 2 – 7 p.m. • Entrance: £1.50, children 20p

June is a very rewarding time to visit because of the old roses which, cleverly underplanted, predominate throughout. Winter is another outstanding time, because of the profusion of winter-flowering shrubs. The Cotswold-stone seventeenth-century house has a stone terrace on the walled garden side bursting with thyme and wild strawberries. The clemency of the walls means that the owner can grow joyous things like sun roses, *Carpenteria californica* and other frailties. A serious cottage garden.

LAKE HOUSE 12

Amesbury, Wiltshire.
Captain O.N. Bailey

Between Amesbury and Salisbury in the Woodford Valley • Best season: spring/summer • Parking • Teas • Toilet facilities • Suitable for wheelchairs • Plants for sale • Open 20th April, 30th June • Entrance: £1, children free

Part of the rich belt of gardens on the network of views round Salisbury which includes Wilton and Heale House. It has that unbeatable basis of the River Avon flowing through water meadows and a backdrop of a flinty-walled Jacobean manor house. A slightly aimless garden, it contains good features, a water garden, yew hedges, pleached limes and mixed herbaceous and shrub borders.

LONGLEAT HOUSE ★ 13

Warminster, Wiltshire. Tel: (09853) 551
The Marquess of Bath

4½m SE of Frome on A362 • Parking • Helicopter landing pad available by prior request • Refreshments: café, licensed restaurant, kiosks • Picnic area by lake • Toilet facilities • Suitable for wheelchairs • Dogs on leads • Shop • House open • Garden open daily except 25th Dec, Easter to Sept, 10 a.m. - 6 p.m., rest of the year, 10 a.m. - 4 p.m. • Entrance: £1, children 50p, coaches free (garden only)

This garden has been rearranged and tinkered with by most of the great names in English landscape history. There is nothing left to show today of the two earliest gardens here, the Elizabethan and that made by London and Wise in the 1680s which must have been one of the most elaborate ever made in England. Sadly it was barely half a century before 'Capability' Brown ironed out the formality and created a chain of lakes set amongst clumps of trees and hanging woods – best admired today from 'Heaven's Gate'. This was slightly altered by Repton in 1804 and added to in the 1870s when it became fashionable to collect exotic trees such as Wellingtonias and monkey puzzles and groves of rhododendrons and azaleas. In this century the fortunes of the garden came under the guiding hand of Russell Page. The park remains both beautiful and rewarding for all who delight in trees. The formal garden focused on the orangery to the south of the house was redeveloped in the nineteenth century. It was simplified and improved upon by Russell Page to great effect. The orangery itself is a dream of wisteria and lemon-scented verbenas. Near the house there is a small, trim rose garden and a quarter of a mile to the south there is a pleasure walk in a developing arboretum, with many spring bulbs and wild flowers. Elsewhere, the safari park and other exhibitions are available to visitors.

MANOR FARM 14

West Kington, Chippenham, Wiltshire. Tel: (0249) 782671
Sir Michael and Lady Farquhar

2m NE of Marshfield • Parking in village • Teas • Toilet facilities • Suitable for wheelchairs • Open 26th May, 8th Sept, 2 - 6 p.m. • Entrance: £1.50 combined with Pound Hill House (see entry)

Created since 1979 from a wilderness of concrete walks, horseradish and gooseberry bushes gone to seed, the garden of Manor Farm now offers suitably romantic views of rose-smothered arbours, pergolas and high walls dripping with old-fashioned climbers - the perfect foil to the square-cut classical villa *c.* 1820. A very personal garden and the labour of love of Lady Farquhar, the garden seems like an extension of the house with a new porch looking down the rose walk, planted with 'Iceberg' and silver plants. The herbaceous border is suitably Jekyllish in blues and pinks. A handsome wrought iron gate and posts topped with eagles offer views of the countryside. There is a ha-ha, a new wild garden and a domestic courtyard where tender plants flourish in tubs.

MOMPESSON HOUSE 15

The Close, Salisbury, Wiltshire. Tel: (0722) 335659
The National Trust

In centre of Salisbury, N side of Chorister's Green in the Cathedral Close • Parking charged for in Close • Teas in Garden Room when house open • Toilet facilities • Suitable for wheelchairs in garden and ground floor of house • House open • Garden open 25th March to 3rd Nov, daily except Thurs and Fri, 12 noon - 5.30 p.m. Last admission 5 p.m. • Entrance: £2.30 (house and garden)

If visiting Salisbury, the Cathedral and the Close are a must, and if you have been fortunate enough to find a parking space, take time also to visit this small walled garden, which is in the old English style. Its reposeful atmosphere is very refreshing. Summer is best, with the old-fashioned roses in bloom, but it is attractive throughout the open season.

OARE HOUSE 16

Oare, Nr Pewsey, Wiltshire. Tel: (0672) 62613
Mr H. Keswick

2m N of Pewsey on A345 • Best season: spring/summer • Parking • Teas on charity open days • Toilet facilities • Partly suitable for wheelchairs • Open 28th April, 28th July, 2 - 6 p.m. • Entrance: 60p, children 20p

The 1740 house was extended by Clough Williams Ellis in the 1920s and the garden created from 1920 to 1960 first by Sir Geoffrey Fry and now by Mr Henry Keswick. It is tantalising to glimpse this house from the road, set back as it is behind towering lime avenues and beech hedges - and when in spring magnolias flower and the grass is awash with narcissi you know the real garden must be something. To the south of the house is an intimate formal 'library garden' of yew hedges reached by a wisteria covered pergola - a gap in the hedge leads the eye down a pleached lime walk to a loggia. Next to this is a narrow secret garden called 'the slip'. On the western side of the house is a long terrace which ends at the flower-bedded swimming pool garden. Far beyond is a wooded slope and a ride leading up into the hilly distance, forming a wonderful vista. The borders are necessarily substantial and planted as they should be with big shrubs and quantities of roses. The kitchen garden contains all the best things arranged in a purposeful manner, with Irish yews, espalier fruit trees, vegetables and an herbaceous border edged with lavender. All this is a model of maintenance on a large scale.

POUND HILL HOUSE 17

West Kington, Wiltshire. Tel: (0249) 782781
Mr and Mrs Philip Stockitt

2m NE of Marshfield • Parking • Teas • Toilet facilities • Suitable for wheelchairs • Plants for sale • Open 26th May, 8th Sept, 2 - 6 p.m. • Entrance: £1.50 combined with Manor Farm (see entry)

An interesting update on the theme of the Cotswold garden, in two acres around a fifteenth-century stone house. It offers the visitor a series of gardening experiences that demonstrate the benefits of a well-trained eye and a professional knowledge of planting. Mrs Stockitt wanted a garden appropriate to the house. 'It's not contrived - gardening should be a refining process. And every year we have a new scheme.' There are lessons to be learned from the easy way the viewer takes in the effect from the yard through to an 'old-fashioned rose' garden (planted and labelled David Austin roses) leading to a Victorian vegetable garden with espaliered fruit trees, then through a clematis tunnel, culminating in a statue. Beyond there is an orchard, a Cotswold garden with topiary, pond, yew-screened tennis court, herbaceous border and drystone walls showing off 'Ballerina' roses, topiary and two trelliswork obelisks, designed by Mrs Stockitt.

ROCHE COURT SCULPTURE GARDEN 18

East Winterslow, Nr Salisbury, Wiltshire. Tel: (0980) 862204
Mr and Mrs Arthur Ponsonby

5m E of Salisbury off A30, S side, following the sign 'Roche Court, Winterslow' • Parking • Partly suitable for wheelchairs • Open April to Sept, Sat and Sun, 11 a.m. - 5 p.m., Oct to March, Sat and Sun, 11 a.m. - 5 p.m. Weekdays by appointment • Entrance: free

This is an exhibition of modern garden or 'public-place' sculpture by such noted practitioners as Armitage, Flanagan, Frink and by dead sculptors in the modern idiom: for example Gill and Hepworth. All works are for sale and information about them can be obtained from the New Art Centre, 41 Sloane Street, London SW1 (071) 235 5844. The garden itself, with pleasant views of Wiltshire downland, is eminently suited to its rôle as open air gallery. There is gorgeous lavender.

SHELDON MANOR 19

Chippenham, Wiltshire. Tel: (0249) 653120
Major M.A. Gibbs

1½m W of Chippenham, S off A420, signposted • Best season: June • Parking • Refreshments: home-made buffet lunches and teas • Toilet facilities • Suitable for wheelchairs • House open (£2.25 house and garden) • Gardens open 31st March, 1st April, 5th May to 6th Oct, Sun, Thurs and Bank Holidays • Entrance: £1.50, OAP £1.35, children over 11 75p, under 11 free

The garden of this ancient house are enclosed by barns and walls. The wonderful courts in front of the house have mostly been put to lawn but a whiff of formality remains in the form of yew hedges and lavender. It is best to visit in mid-June when the good collection of old-fashioned shrub roses, grown in grass, are blazing. The swimming pool is worth seeing as an example of the use of pleached trees and stone work to save it from looking as glaring as most do. Among the rare and interesting shrubs and plants look out for *Rosa gigantea* 'Cooperi', *Grevillea sulphurea*, *Carpenteria californica*, *Cytisus battandieri*, romneya, a white Judas tree and the Chilean fire bush.

STOURHEAD ★★ 20

Stourton, Wiltshire. Tel: (0747) 840348
The National Trust

3m NW of Mere at Stourton off the B3092 • Best season: May for rhododendrons - wonderful in winter when empty • Parking • Refreshments: tearoom, April - 4th Nov or Spread Eagle Inn, lunches, bar snacks • Toilet facilities • Suitable for wheelchairs • Shop • House open 25th March to 3rd Nov, Sat - Wed, 12 noon - 5.30 p.m. or dusk if earlier. Last admission 5 p.m. Other times by written appointment • Gardens open daily all year, 8 a.m. - 7 p.m. (or sunset if earlier, except 24th to 27th July when garden closes at 5 p.m.) • *Entrance: Mar to Oct, £3.50, Nov to Feb, £2.30. House extra £3.50*

Many people go to Stourhead to see the rhododendrons, which are astonishing. However they are not part of the original visionary design by Henry Hoare II in 1741–80, a paragon in its day and almost the greatest surviving garden of its kind. The sequence of arcadian images is revealed gradually if one follows a route anti-clockwise around the lake, having come from the house along the top and seen the lake from above. Each experience is doubly inspiring in that one enjoys the eye-catcher across the lake, almost unattainable and mirage-like, and later when one reaches one's goal – and always some other vision lures one on – the boat-house, the Temple of Flora, the bridge, Temple of Apollo, rock bridge, cascade (these two are tucked away and very surprising), the pantheon, thatched cottage and the grotto. The view from the Temple of Apollo (1765) was described by Horace Walpole as 'one of the most picturesque scenes in the world' by which he meant that it was as fine as a painting. To gain a better idea of how these buildings would have looked had the surrounding planting remained as it was originally, take a walk by Turner's Paddock Lake below the cascade. Between 1791 and 1838 Richard Colt Hoare planted many new species, particularly from America, tulip trees, swamp cypresses, Indian bean trees – the beginning of an arboretum. He also introduced *Rhododendron ponticum*. From 1894 the sixth Baronet replaced these with the latest kinds of hybrid rhododendrons and azaleas, and a large number of copper beeches and conifers, such as the Japanese white pine, Sitka spruce and Californian nutmeg – all are record-sized specimens now. In early summer the scene of azaleas is gorgeous.

STOURTON HOUSE GARDEN ★ 21

Stourton House, Stourton, Nr Warminster, Wiltshire.
Tel: (0747) 840417
Anthony and Elizabeth Bullivant

3m NW of Mere (on A303). Follow signposts to Stourhead, then immediately before Stourhead car park, look out for blue sign boards for Stourton House • *Parking in Stourhead (NT) car park. Free* • *Refreshments: coffees and home-made teas (The Bullivants provide a guide leaflet to more elaborate cateries)* • *Toilet facilities. Disabled 300 yards away in Stourton village* • *Suitable for wheelchairs* • *Unusual and rare plants for sale* • *Shop for dried flowers* • *Open April to Nov, Wed, Thurs, Sun and Bank Holiday Mon, 11 a.m. – 6 p.m. or dusk if earlier. Also for groups of 15 or more on other days by arrangement* • *Entrance: £1.50, children 50p, groups £1.30 per person on open days, £1.50 per person other days. The owners have a series of special days when they concentrate on specific plants: leaflet supplied on request*

This colourful five-acre garden contains treasures in friendly, small spaces: a wild garden, winter garden, secret garden, Apostles walk and seats abound. Rare plants and imaginative designs are everywhere; 200 different varieties of hydrangea, many species of magnolia, unusual daffodils and camellias; euphorbias, chocolate plants and a profusion of flowers for drying. A switchback hedge of Leyland cypress encloses an herbaceous garden of island beds, lavishly planted, and a lily pond with many carnivorous plants and a great urn full of flowers.

THOMPSON'S HILL ★ 22

Sherston, Nr Malmesbury, Wiltshire. Tel: (0666) 840766
Mr and Mrs J.C. Cooper

On B4040. At Sherston turn left opposite church down hill, then bear right up Thompson's Hill until you come to house No 1 • Best season: June • Parking in road • Plants for sale • Open 21st June and by appointment • Entrance: £1

Faultlessly-maintained half-acre garden created over the last ten years on derelict ground. Terraced area behind house, planted in grey colours, enclosed by clipped yew hedges and three Gothic arches with climbing roses and clematis. Beyond, set in lawns, are island beds with mixed herbaceous planting. Old roses and grouped prunus add height and colour. An example of what can be achieved with taste and energy on an unpropitious site.

WILTON HOUSE ★ 23

Wilton, Salisbury, Wiltshire. Tel: (0722) 743115
The Earl of Pembroke

2½m W of Salisbury on A30 in the town centre • Parking • Refreshments: restaurant • Toilet facilities • Suitable for wheelchairs • Plants for sale in garden centre separate from main house and garden area • Shop • Open 29th March to 13th Oct, Tues, Sats and Bank Holiday Mons, 11 a.m. - 6 p.m., Suns 1 - 6 p.m. Last admission 5.15 p.m. • Entrance: grounds only £1.50, children £1.10 (inc. adventure playground). Special rates for parties

The first garden that one sees at Wilton is almost the most recent. The front (north) courtyard of the house has been laid out to a design by David Vicary using formal pleached limes, lavender and a really torrential fountain which baffles the traffic noise on the A30. It has created a cool green place of immense style which manages to answer the architecture of the house. Dotted about this garden are statues, which along with the grotto façade (sadly not viewable), are the last vestiges of one of the earliest gardens here - the complex garden to the south front laid out by Isaac de Caus in 1633. Today it is almost impossible to imagine the elaborations of this garden when one sees only the stretch down to the River Nadder and the Palladian bridge of 1737. Beyond is the vista to Sir William Chambers's Pavilion. Visitors are not allowed into the nineteenth-century terraced garden on the west side, but a walk down the broad gravel near some cedars to the east of the house brings one to the recently established enclosed rose garden, which has a large collection of old-fashioned roses. Adjoining the rose garden, the New Japanese Water Garden is due to open in 1991. Beyond the rose garden is a summerhouse and a statue from the Arundel collection. For children there is a good adventure playground.

GARDENS OPEN RARELY

The following gardens are open to the public on three days or less in the year, although they may also be open by appointment if this is stated in the text. For details see individual entry.

April 20 Lake House; **April 28** Oare House; **May 19** Conock Manor; **May 26** Manor Farm; Pound Hill House; **June 16** Kellaways; **June 21** Thompson's Hill; **June 30** Lake House; **July 28** Oare House; **Sept 8** Manor Farm; Pound Hill House.

YORKSHIRE (North)

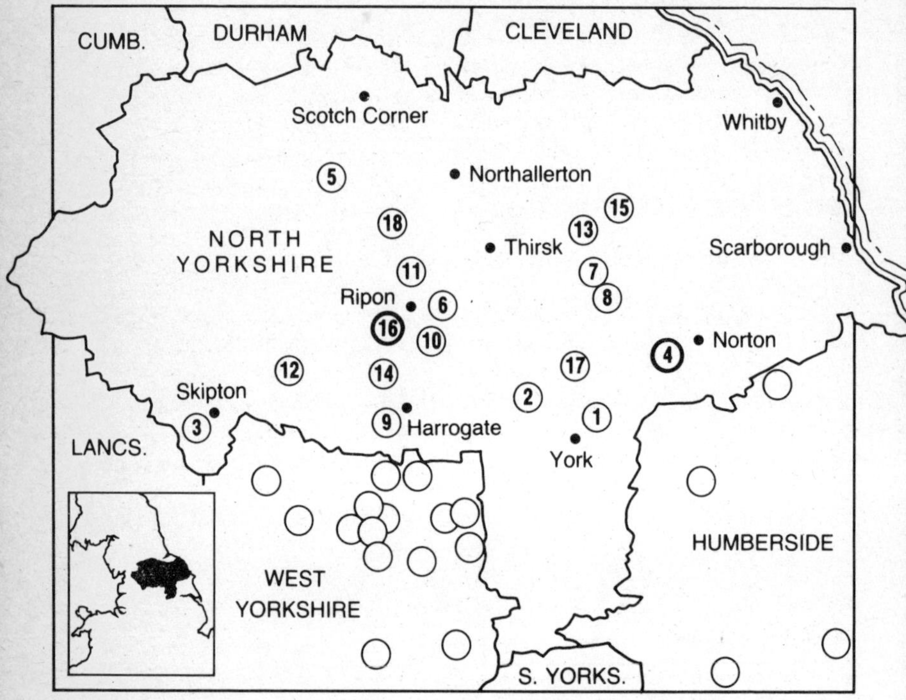

Plain circle numbers can be found by turning to neighbouring counties.
Two-starred gardens are ringed in bold.

ASKHAM BRYAN COLLEGE OF AGRICULTURE AND HORTICULTURE 1

York, North Yorkshire. Tel: (0904) 702121
North Yorkshire County Council

4m W of York on A64 • Parking • Toilet facilities • Suitable for wheelchairs • Plants for sale • Open for special groups by appointment and on 8th June, 1.30 - 5.30 p.m. • Entrance: £1 per car

Although Askham Bryan is one of the prime centres for the teaching of practical amenity-horticulture and has hitherto maintained immaculate grounds and glasshouse collections, they are now showing signs of neglect following financial cutbacks. The outdoor collections have suffered least, the trees, shrubs and roses still being worth travelling to see. Almost all the plants are clearly labelled.

BENINGBROUGH HALL 2

Beningbrough, North Yorkshire. Tel: (0904) 470666
The National Trust

8m NW of York off A19 York – Thirsk road at Shipton • Best seasons: spring and summer • Parking • Refreshments: restaurant 12 noon to 5.30 p.m. Picnics in walled garden • Toilet facilities • Suitable for wheelchairs • House open as garden. Over 100 pictures on loan from National Portrait Gallery • Open 29th March to Oct, Tues, Wed, Thurs, Sat, Sun and Bank Holiday Mon, 12 noon – 6 p.m. or dusk if earlier. Guided garden walk most weekends. Last admission 5.30 p.m. • Entrance: £2.20 (house £3.40)

The main formal garden comprising geometrically-patterned parterres was originally laid out at the time the house was constructed, but was replaced during the late eighteenth century with sweeping lawns and specimen trees, part of an estate of 365 acres. Although generally well-ordered, this is essentially a pleasure garden with an historic framework amongst which considerable recent planting has been integrated. The wilderness and two privy gardens have been restored to eighteenth-century standards, and there is a nineteenth-century American garden and a Victorian conservatory. In conjunction with the imposing Georgian house it is well worthy of a visit.

BROUGHTON HALL 3

Broughton, Nr Skipton, North Yorkshire. Tel: (0756) 799608
Mr H.R. Tempest

4m W of Skipton on the A59, take first left after the Bull Inn • Parking • Toilet facilities • Suitable for wheelchairs • Hall open same times as gardens. Tours on the hour • Open Bank Holiday Mons only at Easter, the two May holidays and Aug, 11 a.m. – 4 p.m. and at other times by arrangement with the owner • Entrance: £3

As well as being a pleasant country house in parklands, this is of interest to the gardening historian as one of the best surviving examples of the Victorian designer Nesfield who spent 30 years laying out the garden. He also sited statues in the park and planted a semi-natural landscape, but it is the parterre on the walled terrace which will most interest Nesfield fans. It has been restored to his design, alas omitting the blue and white gravels he preferred. Nesfield was successful in his time, working for Kew and submitting plans for the forecourt of Buckingham Palace (which might have been rather fun in coloured gravels) but in his later years his passion for parterres fell out of favour.

CASTLE HOWARD ★★ 4

Malton, North Yorkshire. Tel: (065384) 333
Castle Howard Estates Ltd

5m SW of Malton off A64 York – Scarborough Road • Parking • Refreshments: cafeteria • Toilet facilities • Partly suitable for wheelchairs • Plants for sale in large plant centre • Shop • House open • Open 22nd March to 3rd Nov, daily, 10 a.m. – 4.30 p.m. Tours of the woodland garden available for pre-booked groups • Entrance: £5, OAP £4, children £2 (house and garden)

Described as one of the finest examples of 'The Heroic Age of English Landscape Architecture' the grounds were first designed by Sir John Vanburgh assisted by Nicholas Hawksmoor to complement the castle designed by Vanburgh. This layout still generally exists, although in recent times features have been added. Although known principally as a very fine landscape, there is also much for the enthusiastic garden lover. The rose garden developed during the past few years has one of the largest collections of old-fashioned and species roses in Europe. Way Wood and the adjacent area accommodate a very fine collection of rhododendrons, an adjunct to the newly extended arboretum which will soon be one of the largest and most important in the United Kingdom. Most of the plants are well labelled.

CONSTABLE BURTON HALL 5

Leyburn, North Yorkshire. Tel: (0677) 50428
Mr Charles Wyvill

3m E of Leyburn on A684 • Best season: spring/early summer • Parking • Partly suitable for wheelchairs • Open April to mid-Sept, daily, 9 a.m. – 6 p.m. • Entrance: £1

A pleasant garden to visit in beautiful countryside with large specimen trees in a parkland setting probably contemporary with the John Carr house. Essentially a strolling garden rather than one for the plantsperson. Despite obvious signs of labour shortage, it is holding its own.

COPT HEWICK HALL 6

Copt Hewick, Nr Ripon, North Yorkshire. Tel: (0765) 3946
Marquess of Zetland

2m E of Ripon, 1½m W of A1 at Teeside/Thirsk turning • Parking • Teas • Suitable for wheelchairs • Plants for sale • Open 2nd, 30th June, 2 – 5.30 p.m. • Entrance: £1, OAP 75p, children free

Laid out during the Victorian period and with some of those features still remaining, this is an interesting place for the keen plantsperson as it contains a range of choice, unusual and tender plants not often associated with northern gardens. The old walled rose garden is a delight, filled with a collection of old-fashioned, shrub and species roses. Amongst the specimen trees and shrubs growing in this garden are arbutus and halesia.

DUNCOMBE PARK 7

Helmsley, North Yorkshire. Tel: (0439) 70213
Lord Feversham

1m SW of Helmsley on road S of Castle • Parking at Visitor Centre • Refreshments: at tearoom • Toilet facilities • Shop • House open. Extra charge • Garden open Easter Sun to 29th Sept, Sun – Thurs, 11 a.m. – 6 p.m. • Entrance: £2. Discounts for pre-booked groups visiting house and grounds

Home of the Duncombes for 300 years, the mansion has recently been restored to a family home by Lord Feversham. Its 35-acre garden, set in 300 acres of dramatic parkland, dates from *c.*1715 and has been described as 'the supreme masterpiece of the art of the landscape gardener' by Sacheverell Sitwell. Tree-lined terraces, classical temples, statues, vast expanses of lawn and magnificent trees mostly dating from the original eighteenth-century planting. Tallest ash and lime trees according to the *Guinness Book of Records*. One of the earliest ha-has built. Views from terrace of River Rye and the Cascades. Yew walk. Orangery. Woodland and riverside walks.

FOUNTAINS ABBEY

(see Studley Royal)

GILLING CASTLE 8

Gilling East, North Yorkshire. Tel: (04393) 207
The Right Reverend the Abbot of Ampleforth

18m N of York on B1363 York – Helmsley road • Parking • Open July and August, daily, 1 p.m. – dusk • Entrance: 70p, children free

A lovely garden in outstanding scenery. The terraces have been constructed on the south-facing side of the garden, four of them tumbling down the slope from an expansive lawn at the top. Many old-fashioned flowers grow in the borders with a backdrop of majestic trees.

HARLOW CARR GARDENS ★ 9

Crag Lane, Beckwithshaw, Harrogate, North Yorkshire.
Tel: (0423) 565416
Northern Horticultural Society

1½m W of centre of Harrogate on B6162 Otley road • Parking • Refreshments: morning coffee, lunch, teas, picnics, 10 a.m. – 7 p.m. • Toilet facilities • Partly suitable for wheelchairs. Manual and electric wheelchairs available on loan • Guide dogs only • Gift shop • Open all year, daily, 9 a.m. - 7.30 p.m. or dusk • Entrance: £2.50, OAP £2, children free. Groups of 20 or more £2, children under 16 free

A 60-acre site, formerly farmland, established in 1948 by the Northern Horticultural Society as a centre for garden plant trials in the north of England. Now also provides a wide range of horticultural courses for amateur gardeners. It is said that if a plant prospers at Harlow Carr it will grow anywhere in the north. Hosts the National collections of heather and rhubarb cultivars as well as those of hypericum, dryopteris and polypodium. Extensive streamside planting with one of the best collections of moisture-loving plants in the north of England. Large collections of rhododendrons, roses and alpines. Boasts a very fine alpine house and two extensive rock gardens. The arboretum regrettably shows some signs of neglect and some of the shrub borders are rather jaded.

NEWBY HALL AND GARDENS 10

Nr Ripon, North Yorkshire. Tel: (0423) 322583
Mr and Mrs Robin Compton

4m SE of Ripon on B6265 3m W of A1 • Parking • Refreshments: licensed restaurant. Picnic area • Toilet facilities • Suitable for wheelchairs (provided) • Plants for sale • Shop • House open from 12 noon • Gardens open 28th March to 29th Sept, daily except Mon (but open Bank Holiday Mons), 11 a.m. - 5.30 p.m. • Entrance: £2.50, OAP £2.30, children £1.80 (house and gardens £4.50, OAP £3.60, children £2.50). Reduced rate for parties by appointment

The family home of the owners who have set an exceptionally high standard of maintenance while retaining the atmosphere of an established and still lived-in country house. Newby Hall is seventeenth-century with additions and interior by Robert Adam, set in 25 acres of open parkland and some features remain from the eighteenth century, such as east to west walk marked by Venetian statuary, backed by yew and purple plum. The south face has long wide green slopes down to the River Ure, with herbaceous borders on either side backed by clipped hedges and flowering shrubs. Cross walks lead to smaller gardens full of interest. These include species roses, Tropical walled, rock and stepped water gardens as well as a fine woodland area attributed to Ellen Willmott. Facilities for children. Special events are held in June, July and September, such as craft fairs and historic car rallies, with special admission prices.

NORTON CONYERS 11

Ripon, North Yorkshire. Tel: (076584) 333
Sir James Graham, Bart

3½m N of Ripon. Follow Melmerby sign on A61 Ripon – Thirsk road • Parking • Teas Suns and Bank Holidays • Partly suitable for wheelchairs • Dogs on lead • Plants for sale • House open 19th May to 15th Sept, Sun. Also 29th July to 3rd Aug, daily, and Bank Holiday Suns and Mons, 2 – 5 p.m. • Garden open all year, Mon – Fri, 9 a.m. – 5 p.m. and 30th March to 29th Sept, Sat and Sun, 2 – 5.30 p.m. • Entrance: free

The lure of the garden is very much with the past and particularly the association of the house with Charlotte Brontë who made it one of the models for Thornfield Hall in *Jane Eyre*. Norton Conyers has an historic feel that transcends the planting which is pleasant but modest. Most plantings are of the cottage-garden type, although the gardens themselves are quite extensive.

PARCEVALL HALL GARDENS ★ 12

Appletreewick, Skipton, North Yorkshire. Tel: (075672) 311
Walsingham College (Yorkshire Properties) Ltd

1m NE of Appletreewick off B6265 Pateley Bridge – Skipton road • Parking • Picnics in orchard • Plants for sale • Open Easter to Oct, daily, 10 a.m. – 6 p.m. and 28th April, 16th June, 18th Aug • Entrance: £1, children 50p

A garden of great interest to the plantsperson, many of Sir William Milner's treasures having survived years of neglect. The garden is currently being restored and is well worth a visit, if merely to enjoy the spectacular views from the terrace. A fine range of rhododendrons, many originally collected in China, still grow happily here. Fishponds. Rock garden.

RIEVAULX TERRACE AND TEMPLES ★ 13

Rievaulx, Helmsley, North Yorkshire. Tel: (04396) 340
The National Trust

2½m NW of Helmsley on B1257 • Parking. Coach park 200 yards • Picnics • Toilet facilities • Suitable for wheelchairs on terrace. Steps to temples • Dogs on lead • Shop and information centre • Two eighteenth-century temples and exhibition of landscape design in basement of Ionic temple • Open Good Fri to Oct, daily, 10.30 a.m. – 5.30 p.m. Ionic Temple closed 1 – 2 p.m. • Entrance: £1.70, children 80p

This is a unique example of the eighteenth-century passion for the romantic and the picturesque – that is, making landscape look like a picture. The work was done at the behest of Thomas Duncombe around 1754 and consists of a half-mile-long serpentine grass terrace high above Ryedale with fine views. At one end is a Palladian-style Ionic temple with furniture by William Kent and elaborate ceilings. At the other is a Tuscan temple with a raised platform from which are views to the Rye Valley. The concept is wonderfully achieved, but those who expect gardens to have flowers must prepare their minds for higher things.

RIPLEY CASTLE 14

Ripley, Harrogate, North Yorkshire. Tel: (0423) 770152
Sir Thomas Ingilby, Bart

2½m N of Harrogate off A61 Harrogate – Ripon road • Best season: July/Aug • Parking • Refreshments: morning coffee and tea, picnics • Toilet facilities • Suitable for wheelchairs • Gift shop • House open at extra charge • Gardens open Good Friday to Oct, 11 a.m. – 5 p.m. • Entrance: £1, OAP 75p, children 50p. Reduced rates for large parties by appointment

A mid-eighteenth-century 'Capability' Brown landscape with formal gardens developed by Peter Aram for a family that has been here since the thirteenth century. A beautiful landscape, especially during spring at daffodil time. Magnificent specimen trees. The formal areas have seen better days, but the current owner is making considerable strides in their restoration. Lake with attractive Victorian iron bridge. Eighteenth-century orangery and summer houses. Vegetable garden. Woodland walk to a temple with fine views. Extensive new plantings of a rich variety of spring-flowering bulbs are currently being made.

SLEIGHTHOLME DALE LODGE 15

Fadmoor, Nr Kirkbymoorside, North Yorkshire. Tel: (0751) 31942
Dr and Mrs O. James

3m N of Kirkbymoorside, 1m from Fadmoor off A170 • Teas on open days • Open by appointment and 2nd June, 20th July, 2 – 7 p.m. • Entrance: £1

Essentially a hillside garden, but with a walled rose garden and interesting collection of shrubs.

STUDLEY ROYAL AND FOUNTAINS ABBEY ★★ 16

Ripon, North Yorkshire. Tel: (076586) 333
The National Trust

2m SW of Ripon, 9m N of Harrogate. Follow Studley Roger sign off B6265 Ripon – Pateley Bridge road • Light lunches and teas at Studley Royal daily, and Abbey Easter to Oct. Picnic area • Toilet facilities • Suitable for wheelchairs. Powered runabouts available by prior booking • Gift shop • Deer park open all year during daylight hours. Abbey and garden open all year, daily except 24th, 25th Dec and Fri in Nov to Jan as follows: Jan to March and Nov to Dec, 10 a.m. – 5 p.m. or dusk if earlier. April to June, and Sept, 10 a.m. – 7 p.m. July and Aug, 10 a.m. – 8 p.m. Oct, 10 a.m. – 6 p.m. or dusk if earlier.

Guided tours April to Oct, daily at 2.30 p.m. • Entrance: deer park free. Gardens £2 to £2.70 depending on season. Parking £1 at Studley Royal refundable

The gardens were created by John Aislabie, who had been Chancellor of the Exchequer but whose finances were 'ruined' by the South Sea Bubble in 1720 and who retired here to his estate in 1722 and worked until his death in 1742 to make the finest water-garden in the country. The lakes, grotto springs, formal canal and water features plus buildings such as the Temple of Piety turn what is essentially a landscape with large trees and sweeping lawns into one of the most stunning of green gardens. Furthermore, there is the association with the largest and most complete Cistercian foundation in Europe described by the *Oxford Companion* as probably the noblest monastic ruin in Christendom. This can be seen in the distance from the 'surprise view', through a door in a small building.

SUTTON PARK 17

Sutton-in-the-Forest, York, North Yorkshire. Tel: (0347) 810249
Mrs N.M.D. Sheffield

8m N of York on B1363 • Parking. Coaches by appointment • Refreshments: tea room • Toilet facilities • Suitable for wheelchairs • Plants sometimes for sale • Shop • Georgian house open Easter weekend, May to 11th Sept, Bank Holiday Mons and Weds, 1.30 – 5 p.m. and parties of 25 or more by appointment. Also ice-house and nature trail • Gardens open Easter to Oct, daily, 11 a.m. – 5.30 p.m. Parties at other times by appointment at reduced rates • Entrance: £1, children 50p

One of the most distinguished English garden designers of recent times, Percy Cane came to this Georgian house and its terraced site in 1962 with its view over parkland said to have been moulded by 'Capability' Brown. Cane was inspired to take up his profession after a visit to Harold Peto's Easton Lodge (see entry). He started the elegant planting which has been most carefully extended by the present owners. There are several fine features on the terraces – a tall beech hedge curved to take a marble seat, ironwork gazebos and everywhere soft stone. The woodland walk leads to a temple.

THORP PERROW ARBORETUM ★ 18

Bedale, North Yorkshire. Tel: Curator (0677) 25323
Sir John Ropner, Bart

2m S of Bedale, signposted off B6268 Masham road • Best seasons: spring and autumn • Parking • Picnic area • Open all year, dawn – dusk • Entrance: £1.50, OAP and children £1

The arboretum was established some 50 years ago on open farmland by Sir Leonard Ropner and is one of the finest collections of trees in the north of

England, containing over 2000 species. Unfortunately the arboretum suffered some years of neglect, and the present owner is currently undertaking restoration. While many of the trees will never regain their natural habit owing to crowding and lack of pruning, the collection is still undisputedly one of the most comprehensive in the North. In the past year new interpretive signs and a small visitor information facility have greatly improved the pleasure of a visit. A fern walk down to the lake has also been restored.

GARDENS OPEN RARELY

The following gardens are open to the public on three days or less in the year, although they may also be open by appointment if this is stated in the text. For details see individual entry.

June 2 Copt Hewick Hall; Sleightholme Dale Lodge; **June 8** Askham Bryan College; **June 30** Copt Hewick Hall; **July 20** Sleightholme Dale Lodge.

YORKSHIRE (South & West)

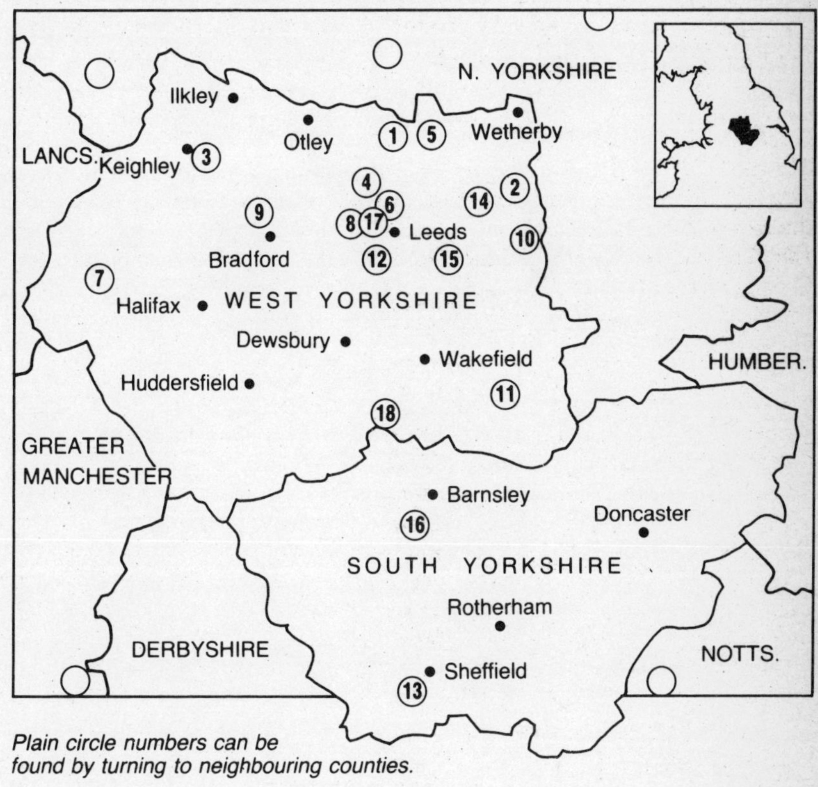

Plain circle numbers can be found by turning to neighbouring counties.

ARTHINGTON HALL 1

Arthington, Otley, West Yorkshire. Tel: (0532) 842115
Mr C.E.W. Sheepshanks

5m E of Otley off A659 • Parking • Teas • Suitable for wheelchairs • Open by appointment only • Entrance: £1, children 20p

A large garden which is improving all the time. Set in beautiful countryside with lovely views it is being enhanced by a developing tree collection, especially maples, and carefully tended woodland walks. There is an area of partly walled garden, greenhouses and both fruit and vegetable gardens.

BRAMHAM PARK ★ 2

Bramham, Nr Wetherby, West Yorkshire. Tel: (0937) 844265
Mr and Mrs G. Lane Fox

5m S of Wetherby just off northbound A1 • Parking • Toilet facilities • Partly suitable for wheelchairs • House open 16th June to 1st Sept, Sun, Tues - Thurs, 1.15 - 5.30 p.m. at extra charge • Gardens open Easter and Spring Bank Holiday weekends and May Day, and 16th June to 1st Sept, Sun, Tues, Wed, Thurs, 1.15 - 5.30 p.m. Last admission 5 p.m. • Entrance: £1.50, OAP £1, children 50p (house and garden £2, OAP £1.50, children £1)

Created by Robert Benson after the style of Le Nôtre some 250 years ago, this is one of the few landscape gardens in the French style to survive in this country. Although great storms have removed many specimen beeches and disrupted the layout of the avenues, the original concept has been maintained and is being perpetuated. Apart from its uniqueness of design, the gardens also have a substantial rose garden which provides summer-long colour and an interesting herbaceous border. However, it is the splendid architectural features and the trees which would have been familiar to the garden's creator, in his day Chancellor of the Exchequer, that are outstanding; as visitors wonder at the beauty of this garden they may well muse how many Chancellors have left such a legacy to the nation.

EAST RIDDLESDEN HALL 3

Bradford Road, Keighley, West Yorkshire. Tel: (0535) 607075
The National Trust

1m NE of Keighley on S side of A650 and 3m NW of Bingley • Parking • Teas • Toilet facilities • Suitable for wheelchairs: not in refreshment room • Dogs on lead • Shop • House open • Gardens open 29th March to 3rd April, and weekends, 12 noon - 5.30 p.m., May to Oct, Sat - Wed, 12 noon - 5.30p.m. Last admission 5 p.m. • Entrance: £2, accompanied children 80p

A traditional seventeenth-century Yorkshire manor house. Neglected through much of nineteenth and twentieth centuries and restored 1983-84 by the National Trust. The great barn is considered one of the finest in the north of England. A well-tended formal walled garden of modest size and a monastic fish pond in grounds running down to the river.

GOLDEN ACRE PARK ★ 4

Otley Road, Leeds, West Yorkshire. Tel: (0523) 463504
Leeds City Council

Off A660 Leeds - Otley road at approach to Bramhope • Parking • Refreshments: morning coffee, teas, lunches • Toilet facilities • Suitable for wheelchairs • Dogs • Gift shop • Open daily during daylight hours • Entrance: free

Until 1945 when it was purchased by Leeds Corporation for £18,500, this was a privately-owned pleasure park. Since then it has been developed as an important public park and minor botanic garden. It is sited on a pleasant undulating site leading down to a lake. Extensively-planted tree collection with most specimens labelled. Rhododendrons are a feature in the spring, alone with alpine plants both in the rock garden and in the alpine house. Golden Acre Park is noted for its very fine collection of houseleeks or sempervivums as well as its heather collection. Demonstration plots are maintained where instruction is provided for home gardeners.

HAREWOOD HOUSE ★ 5

Harewood, Leeds, West Yorkshire. Tel: (0532) 886225
The Earl and Countess of Harewood

7m N of Leeds on A61 • Best seasons: early June and early Oct • Parking • Refreshments: light lunches, teas, etc., restaurant and bar, picnic area • Toilet facilities • Partly suitable for wheelchairs • Dogs on lead • Shop • House open 11 a.m. - 5 p.m. Last admission 4.30 p.m. (£4, children £2, Freedom ticket £5) • Gardens open 24th March to Oct, daily, 10 a.m. - 5 p.m. • Entrance: £2, children £1

Originally laid out in the 1770s by 'Capability' Brown the gardens and park still retain many of his characteristic features, most notably a majestic lake and a well-wooded horizon, although many of his trees have been lost. Nineteenth-century rhododendrons obscure the edge of his lake but afford a fine sight reflected on its surface when flowering in early June. Other features in this woodland setting are a vaguely Japanese bog garden below the lake's cascade. Sir Charles Barry's terrace of the 1840s adds a formal contrast with its parterres and fountains, herbaceous border, bedding schemes and roses. Large quantities of trees and shrubs in these excellently maintained grounds ensure a long season of interest.

THE HOLLIES PARK ★ 6

Weetwood Lane, Leeds, West Yorkshire. Tel: (0523) 782030
Leeds County Council

Entrance off Weetwood Lane, off A660 Leeds - Otley road • Parking • Toilet facilities • Open daily during daylight hours • Entrance: free

The original layout is believed to be Victorian. The gardens were given to Leeds Corporation in 1921 by the Brown famiy in memory of a relative killed during World War I. The fine informal, largely woodland garden features woody plants, especially rhododendrons, many rarely seen growing in this part of the North. Ferns flourish throughout the gardens and a varied collection of hydrangeas provide late summer colour. Many slightly tender subjects, such as eucryphia, embothrium and drimys thrive in the pleasant micro-climate. The home of a number of National collections maintained by

Leeds City Council including probably the most comprehensive philadelphus collection in Europe and also those of hemerocallis and deutzias.

LAND FARM 7

Colden, Nr Hebden Bridge, West Yorkshire. Tel: (0422) 842260
Mr and Mrs J. Williams

Off A646 between Sowerby Bridge and Todmorden. Call at the Visitors' Centre in Hebden Bridge for a map • Best seasons: spring and summer • Plants for sale • Open May to Aug, Sat, Sun and Bank Holiday Mons, 10 a.m. - 5 p.m. • Entrance: £1

A garden created by the owners on a north-facing one-acre site 1000 ft up in the Pennines. Designed as a low-maintenance garden, it nevertheless contains a wide variety of shrubs, herbaceous plants and alpines.

30 LATCHMERE ROAD 8

Leeds, West Yorkshire. Tel: (0225) 60503
Mr and Mrs Joe Brown

NW of Leeds off A6120, along Fillingfir Drive • Plants for sale • Open by appointment to horticultural societies and garden clubs, and every Sun from 23rd June to 4th Aug (except 7th July), 2.30 - 5.30 p.m. • Entrance: 50p, children 25p

A garden of exceptional merit created from scratch over the last 20 years by Mr and Mrs Brown, this is now one of the finest examples of clever design in a small garden. Herbaceous plants, ferns, climbers and shrubs all contribute to a series of mini-features which the visitor passes through in a controlled circuit of the garden. These features include a clematis collection, camomile lawn, sink gardens, pools, patio and limestone garden.

LISTER PARK 9

Keighley Road, Bradford, West Yorkshire. Tel: (0274) 493313
City of Bradford Metropolitan Council

1½m N of Bradford centre (Forster Square) on A650 Bradford - Keighley road • Best seasons: spring and summer • Parking in surrounding streets • Light refreshments: daily except Mon, 10 a.m. - 4 p.m. • Toilet facilities • Suitable for wheelchairs • Dogs on lead • Cartwright Hall, City Art Gallery and Museum open, April to Sept, Tues - Sun, 10 a.m. - 6 p.m., Oct to Mar, Tues - Sun, 10 a.m. - 5 p.m. • Gardens open daily during daylight hours • Entrance: free

This used to be a well-tended park with an excellent garden and botanical garden, including greenhouses with tropical plants. Recently there have been signs of improvement although the botanical garden, which still exists, appears untended, and the main reason for including the park in this guide is that there is a formal floral display in front of Cartwright Hall and an interesting floral clock, a rare example of Victorian ingenuity which is well worth seeing by those living in or passing through the city, perhaps to visit the National Museum of Photography, Film and TV.

LOTHERTON HALL 10

Aberford, West Yorkshire. Tel: (0532) 463510
Leeds City Council

3½m NE of Gosforth on B1217 • Best seasons: spring and summer • Parking. Coaches by appointment • Refreshments and picnics • Toilet facilities • Dogs except in bird garden • Shop • House open. Bird garden closed Mon. Working shire horses • Gardens open all year, daily, 10.30 a.m. - dusk • Entrance: free

A 10-acre garden which grows surprisingly tender shrubs and climbers rare in this raw Northern climate but here protected by walls and tree shelters. The design is thought to owe something to Ellen Willmott and is rather an Edwardian period piece. Formal rose garden, an avenue of yews leading to a white summerhouse, walled garden, sunken garden with lily pond, a well-planted Japanese rockery glen of 1912 and a ha-ha now filled in and planted with primulas, astilbes and meconopsis. Sports lovers will be interested to see the tennis court, one of the earliest of brick construction, but some garden lovers have been disappointed at the lack of seasonal colour between spring and summer. Further restoration and improvement work is taking place and more period plants being introduced.

NOSTELL PRIORY 11

Nr Wakefield, West Yorkshire. Tel: (0924) 863892
The National Trust

6m SE of Wakefield on A638 • Best season: summer for rose garden • Parking • Light refreshments and teas. Picnic site • Toilet facilities inc. disabled • Suitable for wheelchairs • Dogs on lead • Gift shop • House open from 12 noon • Gardens open 30th March to June, Sept to Oct, 12 noon - 5 p.m., Sun, 11 a.m. - 5 p.m. July and Aug, daily except Fri, 12 noon - 5 p.m., Sun, 11 a.m. - 5 p.m. Also open on Bank Holiday Mons, 11 a.m. - 5 p.m., Tues following, 12 noon - 5 p.m. • Entrance: £1.30, children 60p, (house and garden £2.40, children £1.20)

An eighteenth-century mansion set in open parkland with an attractive lake and a variety of well-established trees. A fine, well-tended and well-labelled rose garden is the main gardening feature. There is a children's playground and a picnic area. Special events and fairs are held during the season, some in marquees in front of the house, with a special admission charge (not applied if house and garden only visited).

ROUNDHAY PARK ★ (Tropical World Canal Gardens) 13

Roundhay Road, Leeds, West Yorkshire. Tel: (0523) 661850
Leeds City Council

Off A58 Roundhay Road from Leeds City centre • Parking • Refreshments: light snacks • Toilet facilities • Suitable for wheelchairs • Dogs • Open daily during daylight hours • Entrancee: free

The intensively-cultivated canal gardens area was formerly the kitchen and ornamental gardens of the Nicholson family who sold the site to the Leeds Corporation in 1871. The extensive parkland with its fine trees is an excellent setting for the pure horticultural extravaganza of the canal gardens with their formal bedding and generous collection of Tropical plants in greenhouses. The collections are constantly being added to and are a Mecca for enthusiastic gardeners.

SHEFFIELD BOTANICAL GARDENS 13

Sheffield, South Yorkshire. Tel: (0742) 671115
Sheffield Council

½m from A625 1½SW of Sheffield centre • Parking in surrounding streets • Toilet facilities inc. disabled • Suitable for wheelchairs • Dogs on lead • Plants for sale occasionally, by Friends of Botanical Society • Open daily during daylight hours • Entrance: free

An example of a botanical garden tended by a local authority, with support from and participation by local gardening societies and helpers. Flower displays are changed seasonally. All plants are well-labelled, including those in the special woodland area. A small aviary and an aquarium provide additional features. The gardens, though close to Sheffield centre, are secluded with good seating and grass areas suitable for children and recreation. However, recently the gardens are looking very downtrodden and seem sadly to be going into decline unless action is taken speedily.

SILVER BIRCHES 14

Ling Lane, Scarcroft, Leeds, West Yorkshire. Tel: (0532) 892335
Mr S.C. Thomson

7m NE of Leeds in Ling Lane, Scarcroft off A58 Leeds – Wetherby road • Parking • Tea • Partly suitable for wheelchairs • Plants for sale • Open 19th, 26th May and by appointment June to Oct for parties • Entrance: £1, children 50p

A two and a half-acre garden with tastefully-added shrubs and conifers. Foliage plants are a significant component in the design. There are also good collections of roses, heathers and climbers as well as open water with a range of aquatic plants.

TEMPLE NEWSAM 15

Leeds, West Yorkshire. Tel: (0532) 645535
Leeds City Council

Signposted off junction of A63 and A6120 ring road E of Leeds • Best season: mid-May to early Oct • Parking • Teas and snacks • Toilet facilities • Suitable for wheelchairs • Shop • House open daily except Mon, 10.30 a.m. - 6.15 p.m., 85p, OAP and children 35p • Park open daily, 9 a.m. - dusk • Entrance: free

A pleasant oasis surrounded by urban Leeds. Set in the remnants of a 'Capability' Brown landscape of the 1760s (much reduced by a golf course and open-cast mining) are a wide diversity of gardens. Around the house an Italian paved garden and a Jacobean-style parterre surrounded by pleached lime walks are poorly maintained. A rhododendron and azalea walk leads to small ponds with a bog garden and arboretum, beyond which is a large walled rose garden and greenhouses containing collections of ivies, cacti and some rather dashing climbing pelargoniums. Maintenance could be better.

WENTWORTH CASTLE ★ 16

Stainborough, Barnsley, South Yorkshire. Tel: (0226) 285426
Barnsley Metropolitan Borough Council; leased and managed by the Northern College for Residential Adult Education

Off M1 at Junction 37, 2m down minor road signposted Stainborough • Best season: spring • Parking • Teas • Toilet facilities • House occupied by Northern College • Garden open Spring Bank Holiday. Otherwise parties only for conducted tours booked 3 weeks in advance. This is part of a controlled opening policy during the garden's transition to a public open garden • Entrance: £2, children under 14 £1

One of the most exciting gardens in Yorkshire, laid out mainly under the direction of William Wentworth in 1740, it is currently undergoing a complete review of its activities. Contains one of the finest collections of rhododendrons in the North. These have been established during the past 15 years and form an invaluable educational resource. The owners and tenants at Wentworth are putting together an important development package which will preserve the fabric of the garden and yet enable its already valuable collections to be expanded. It has recently been designated the National collection for the *falconeri* rhododendrons. There are extensive new plantings of magnolias, comprising one of the largest collections in northern England.

YORK GATE ★ 17

Church Lane, Leeds, West Yorkshire. Tel: (0532) 678240
Mrs Sybil B. Spencer

Off A660 Leeds - Otley road, behind Adel Church • Parking, but no coaches • Tea and biscuits • Plants for sale • Open 1st, 2nd June, 2 - 6 p.m. and by appointment • Entrance: £1.50, accompanied children free

Bought by the owner and her late husband in 1951 this was a bleak farmhouse and an unpromising area of land. When her husband died, her son took over the design and in a tragically short life he achieved a garden of impeccable taste and style, using local stone, cobble stones and gravel to create a structure of taste and great interest. As to the design, Arthur Hellyer remarks on its debt to Hidcote, but notes that many of the ideas used there in 10 acres are here confined to barely one. He also comments on the clever use of eye-catching ornaments and topiary. 'This is a garden made for discovery' he says, as 'from no vantage point is it possible to see the whole ... Nor is any route of exploration specially indicated.' This is also a plantsperson's garden maintaining a quality collection arranged in clearly defined model features. These include an extraordinary miniature pinetum as well as fern, peony and iris borders and an exquisite silver and white border. A garden of rare delight.

YORKSHIRE SCULPTURE PARK 18

Bretton Hall, West Bretton, Wakefield, West Yorkshire.
Tel: (0924) 830302
Yorkshire Sculpture Park Charitable Trust

6m SW of Wakefield at West Bretton village. Leave M1 at junction 38 • Parking. Coaches by prior arrangement • Refreshments in Bothy Café • Toilet facilities • Access Sculpture Trail suitable for wheelchairs • Dogs on lead • Shop and Information Centre • Open daily except 25th, 26th Dec and 1st Jan, summer, 10 a.m. - 6 p.m., winter, 10 a.m. - 4 p.m. • Entrance: free

A lecturer at the college initiated this great project for Britain's first permanent sculpture park in 1977, which was the 25th anniversary of the famous Battersea Park exhibitions of sculpture. The Yorkshire Arts Association was set up by a permanent facility the same year. The Palladian-style house and its 260 acres of formal gardens, woods, lakes and parkland provide a fine setting for both temporary exhibitions and the permanent collection that is being built up from them. Work is not bought or given, but available on extended loan from artists, arts councils and, in a few cases, from the Tate Gallery. The layout here makes it possible to view sculpture in 'garden' settings as well as the 'public' settings that demand a more monumental approach by the sculptor. Note also the imaginative use of colour on wooden fencing which leads to the Access Sculpture Trail designed by Don Rankin. The sculptures here are being worked upon *in situ*, evolving and growing with the gardens around them - a splendid example of the subtle relationship between art and nature.

GARDENS OPEN RARELY

The following gardens are open to the public twice in the year, although they may also be open by appointment. For details see individual entry.

May 19 Silver Birches; **May 26** Silver Birches; **June 1** York Gate; **June 2** York Gate.

IRELAND

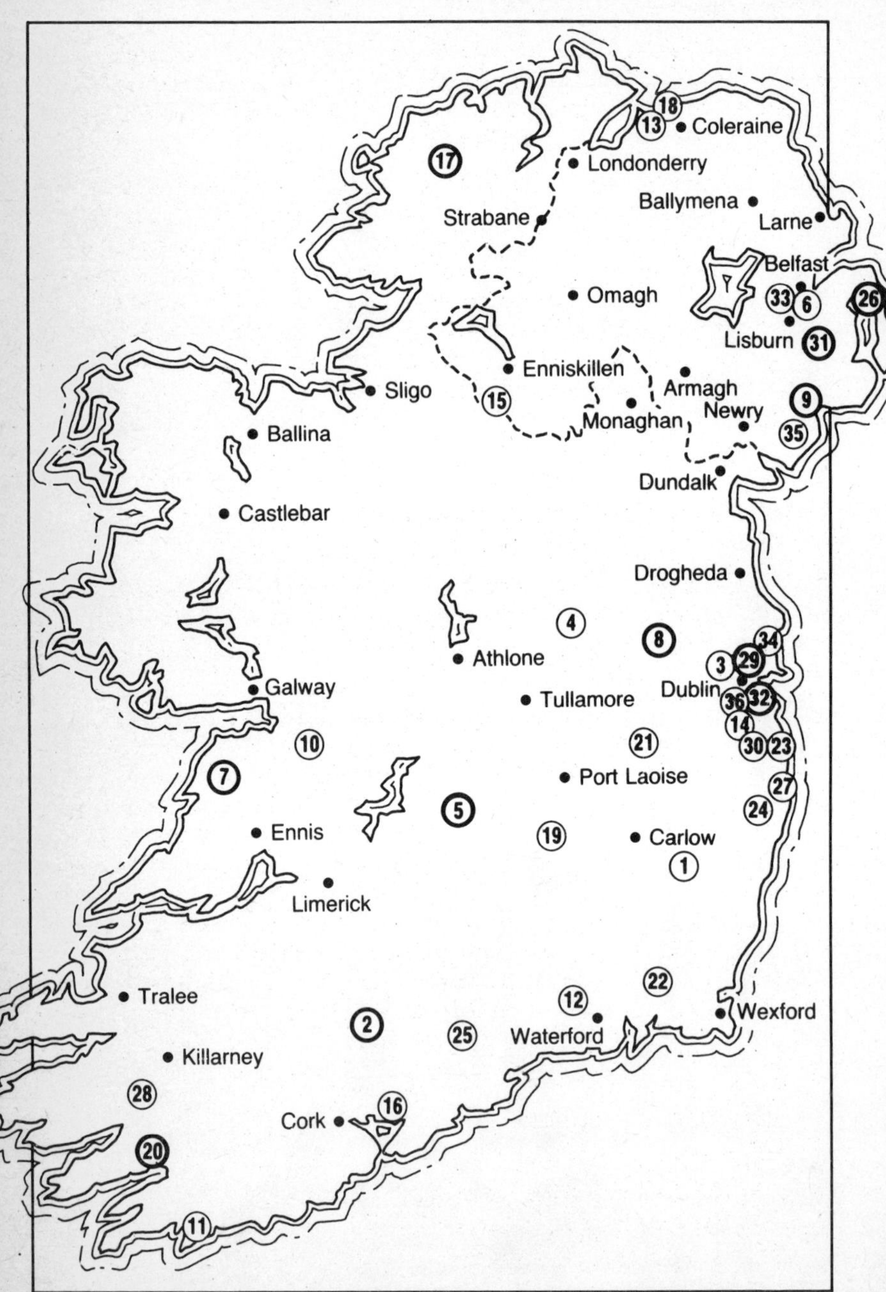

Two-starred gardens are ringed in bold.

ALTAMONT 1

Tullow, Co Carlow, Republic of Ireland. Tel: (0503) 59128
Mr and Mrs North

5m from Tullow, about 1m off main Tullow – Bunclody road • Parking • Home-made teas • Partly suitable for wheelchairs • Dogs on lead • Plants for sale • Open Easter to Oct, Suns, 2 – 6 p.m. Other times by appointment • Entrance: IR£1.50, children under 10 free

The lily-filled lake surrounded by fine, mature trees forms a backdrop for a gently sloping lawn. A central walkway formally planted with Irish yews and roses leads from the house to the lake. There is a beautiful fern-leaved beech, and some much more ancient beeches forming the 'Nun's walk'. A long walk through the demesne leads to the River Slaney with diversions to a bog garden, through a glen of ancient oaks undercarpeted with bluebells in spring. Mrs North's passion for trees is evident in the recent planting, and she has selected old-fashioned roses for her rose beds.

ANNES GROVE ★★ 2

Castletownroche, Co Cork, Republic of Ireland. Tel: (022) 26145
Mr and Mrs F.P. Grove Annesley

2m N of village of Castletownroche, between Fermoy and Malloy • Parking • Picnics • Partly suitable for wheelchairs • Dogs on lead • Open April to Sept, Mon – Fri, 10 a.m. – 5 p.m., Sat and Sun, 1 – 6 p.m. • Entrance: IR£2, OAP and children IR£1

This is an archetypal 'Robinsonian' alias wild garden, but such tags are not helpful. Rhododendron species and cultivers arch over and spill towards the pathways, carpeting them with fallen blossoms. Steep paths descend at various places into the valley of the Awbeg river (which inspired Edmund Spenser). The statuesque conifers planted in the valley make a colourful tapestry behind the river garden, with *Primula florindae* and *P. japonica* cultivars in profusion. Perhaps least successful is the formal garden, maintained with bedding and a short herbaceous border. The glory of Annes Grove is the collection of rhododendron spp. wherein hidden, visitors may see surprises – a superb *Juniperus recurva* 'Castlewellan', a mature handkerchief tree (*Davidia involucrata*) and other exotic, flowering trees. Here is bird-song and the crystal-clear Awbeg, water-buttercups and primroses – peaceful groves.

BEECH PARK ★ 3

Clonsilla, Co Dublin, Republic of Ireland. Tel: (01) 212216
Jonathan and Daphne Shackleton

1m from Clonsilla village on road to Lucan, 10m W of Dublin • Parking • Home-made teas • Toilet facilities • Suitable for wheelchairs • Plants for sale • Open on first Sun of months March to Nov, 2 - 6 p.m. Groups and overseas visitors by arrangement • Entrance: IR£2

In an old walled garden of a Regency house, once bedded with vegetables in season, are raised beds and herbaceous borders brim-full of the choicest perennials and dwarf shrubs. The gems of this highly personal, indeed eclectic, collection begun about 1960 are celmisias (New Zealand mountain daisies), yet the raised beds contain many unusual and uncommon plants, all deliberately selected and superbly cultivated. The herbaceous borders which encircle the walled garden and line its intersecting pathways are planted with as great attention to excellence, and the collection of perennials is outstanding - meconopsis (esp. *M.* × *sheldonii*) phlox, papaver and iris cultivars are striking in season, and a listing of the entire assemblage would occupy a small book. The plants range from old-fashioned, cottage-garden types, some forgotten elsewhere, to the newest and best. David Shackleton, who created this garden, garnering cultivars from Ireland and Britain, died in 1988: his idiosyncratic garden is a wonderfully vivid memorial.

BELVEDERE 4

Mullingar, Co Westmeath, Republic of Ireland. Tel: (044) 40861
Westmeath County Council

4m from Mullingar town, on Tullamore road • Parking • Refreshments in restored stables • Toilet facilities • Suitable for wheelchairs • Dogs on lead • House open • Garden open May to Sept, 12 noon - 6.30 p.m. • Entrance: IR£1, children 50p

The Jealous Wall is one of those typically Gothic–Irish follies, built in 1760 to separate two squabbling brothers. It looks antique and is impressive. Otherwise this garden does not abound in interest, but there are some fine trees and a large walled garden, containing some mundane bedding displays, and it is pleasant to be on the terraces dropping in steps to the shores of Lough Ennel, with views of its waters and islands.

BIRR CASTLE DESMESNE ★★ 5

Birr, Co Offaly, Republic of Ireland. Tel: (0509) 20056
Earl and Countess of Rosse

In town of Birr, 82m W of Dublin • Parking outside castle gates • Refreshments outside castle gate, picnics in walled garden • Toilet facilities • Suitable for wheelchairs • Dogs on lead • Plants for sale • Shop • Exhibitions featuring some aspect of the history of Birr Castle or the Earls of Rosse in gallery open 13th April to 19th May and 25th May to 29th Sept • Castle not open • Garden open daily, 9 a.m. - 1 p.m., 2 - 6 p.m. Closed 25th Dec • Entrance: Jan to mid-April and Oct to Dec: IR£2, children IR£1 Exhibition season (mid-April to Sept) IR£2.80, children IR£1.40. Annual membership scheme

The Victorian Gothic castle dominates vistas which strike through the park and at whose centre is the slumbering 'Leviathan' (a giant telescope which made Birr famous last century). Around, in profusion, are rare trees and shrubs especially many raised from seed received from central China in the mid-1900s. Over one of the rivers is a beautiful suspension bridge, and hidden amongst laurels is a Victorian fernery with recently restored water-works. Evergreen conifers, golden willows, carpets of daffodils, and world-record box hedges, magnolias in the river garden, a new cherry avenue and the original plant of *Paeonia* 'Anne Rosse' are mere selections of the many attractions. It is invigorating to walk around the lake, glimpsing the castle, examining the shrubs and trees (some of which are specially labelled), and revelling in the peace and quiet of central Ireland – three counties can be visited in one brief walk. It is fair to add that the beauties of this garden, which owe so much to Anne, Countess of Rosse, have given her international fame as a gardener.

THE BOTANIC GARDEN PARK 6

Stranmillis, Belfast, Co Antrim, Northern Ireland. Tel: (0232) 324902
Belfast City Council Parks Department

Between Queen's University and the Ulster Museum, Stranmillis • Parking outside • Refreshments: facilities in the Ulster Museum • Toilet facilities • Suitable for wheelchairs • Dogs on lead • Open daily, 7.30 a.m. to dusk. Palm House and Tropical Ravine, summer, weekdays, 10 a.m. – 5 p.m., weekends, 2 – 5 p.m., winter, weekdays, 10 a.m. – 4 p.m., weekends, 2 – 4 p.m. Guided tours and group visits at any time by arrangement • Entrance: free

Established in 1827, this became a public park in 1895. Today it has lots of vulgar bedding for general admiration; it is well done but not to everyone's taste. There are two reasons to visit this otherwise unexceptional park – the curvilinear iron and glass conservatory (1839–1852), one of the finest Victorian glasshouses (Richard Turner built only the wings; the dome is by Young of Edinburgh). It was restored in the 1970s and contains a small collection of tropical plants with massed displays of 'pot mums' and the like in season (again well-grown and finely displayed, but not everyone's favourite). The Tropical Ravine House is the greater delight, and also recently restored. This is 'High Victoriana', with ferns, bananas, lush tropical vines and tree ferns, and goldfish in the Amazon lily pond, and a waterfall worked with a chain-pull! Marvellous, evocative of by-gone crinoline days.

THE BURREN ★★ 7

Co Clare, Republic of Ireland.

North-western Clare, approached from main Galway – Ennis road • No parking problems (except in busy places during Sept) • Burren Display Centre, Kilfenora, 5m from Lisdoonvarna, open Easter to Oct, daily, and in winter by appointment by ringing (065) 88030 • Garden open daily all year. Never closed • Entrance: free

Mankind did assist in creating this enigmatic place which was shaped by nature over 500 million years. From afar it is a desolate, barren rock-scape, perhaps more akin to an outer planet. But the limestone rock weathers to rich soil, its natural fissures providing sheltered crannies for plants, and on it, aided by abundant rain, peat-hummocks form habitats for acid-loving species. Botanists abound (in season) and can be spotted easily as they photograph gentians, bottoms uppermost. The spectacle of spring gentians and mountain avens in May (optimal time around 15th May) is worth seeing once, but far, far too many people think May is the only time to visit The Burren. Mid-winter is as good as any; mid-summer a riot of orchids; early autumn mellow with rowan berries and hazel nuts. As a natural rock garden The Burren has few equals, its flora a rich mixture of arctic and sub-tropical plants - maidenhair ferns and mountain catspaws, Irish orchids and autumn lady's tresses, rock-roses and bloody cranesbills. There are caves and dolmens, castles (with medieval banquets - whatever they may be) and sandy beaches. Comfortable, tough walking shoes are essential; aided by a ramblers' map (several excellent maps are readily available), endless days can be enjoyed walking the 'pavements grey' and the green roads. This was John Betjeman's 'Stony seaboard, far and foreign ...' - but remember to avoid Lisdoonvarna in September unless seeking a companion.

BUTTERSTREAM ★★ 8

Trim, Co Meath, Republic of Ireland.
Jim Reynolds

Best season: summer • Suitable for wheelchairs • Open May to Sept, daily except Mon, 2 - 6 p.m. by written appointment • Entrance: £3

Like all the best gardens, this is a single-handed work of art. A series of compartments contain different arrangements of plants, ranging from a formal box-hedged garden of old roses and lilies, to an informal gold garden carpeted with ferns and hostas. In the main garden a selection of choice herbaceous perennials in an island bed encircled by wide borders processes through the summer from whites and blues to yellows and reds - phlox, kniphofia, lobelia, macleaya, allium are only a few of the genera represented. A formal pool, replete with water lilies and carp, has a distinct Roman feel, and the large tennis lawn has a restrained gallery of clematis, deep purple hedges and rustic summerhouse.

CASTLEWELLAN NATIONAL ARBORETUM ★★ 9

Castlewellan, Co Down, Northern Ireland.
Forest Service, Department of Agriculture (Northern Ireland)

In Castlewellan town, 25m from Belfast, 3m from Newcastle • Parking inc. disabled • Refreshments: summer only • Toilet facilities • Partly suitable for wheelchairs • Dogs on lead • Open all year • Entrance: fee for forest park collected in high season

The walled garden, now called the Annesley Garden, contains an outstanding collection of mature trees and shrubs, many planted before the turn of the century by Lord Annesley. Original specimens of some of Castlewellan's cultivars thrive here, in fine condition. In the spring and summer there are many rhododendrons in bloom, and scarlet Chilean fire-bushes (*Embothrium coccineum*). In early autumn, the snow-carpet is the fallen petals of the unequalled collection of eucryphia. The arboretum has a formal axis, with two fountain pools and steps. An herbaceous border runs along part of this. Beyond the walls is a new garden, planted with heathers, dwarf conifers and limes, and with flowering trees (malus, prunus, etc.). Walks lead into the forest and beside the lough. A caravan and camping ground within the forest park provides a wonderful base for exploring this part of Ireland and for visiting the other County Down gardens. Castlewellan is well known to everyone for the bilious golden Leyland cypress that came from here - don't be dismayed - the arboretum contains many more wonderful plants, some unique, all in their prime. You will not see decrepit trees here - the maintenance is exceptionally good.

COOLE PARK 10

Gort, Co Galway, Republic of Ireland.
Coillte Teoranta (Irish Forestry Board)

2m N of Gort on main Galway road • Parking • Toilet facilities • Suitable for wheelchairs • Dogs • House demolished • Open all year • Entrance: free

This was one of W.B. Yeats' haunts. The house, home of the famous literary figure Lady Gregory, was demolished years ago as an act of thoughtless vandalism and much of the demesne is now planted with conifers. However, beside the remains of the house are two magnificent plane trees, an old mulberry and other exotic trees. In the walled garden is the famous 'Autograph' tree (a copper beech) with the fading initials of the Irish literati including George Bernard Shaw. The walled garden could be greatly improved if the present authorities stopped the horrendous clipping of the shrubs. Walk to the lake and see the swans and linger in the magnificent avenue at the entrance.

CREAGH 11

Skibbereen, Co Cork, Republic of Ireland. Tel: (028) 21267
Mr Peter Harold Barry

4m from Skibbereen on road to Baltimore – entrance on right through white-painted iron gate • Parking at house. Small coaches only • Suitable for wheelchairs • Dogs on lead • Open April to Sept, daily, 10 a.m. – 6 p.m. • Entrance: IR£1, children free

Definitely a garden for those who seek solitude and silence, far from traffic. Paths lead through woodland underplanted with rhododendron species and cultivars, and down to the sea. A serpentine mill-pond is now fringed with gunnera, cordyline and hydrangea, the bold effect inspired by the paintings of 'Le Douanier' Rousseau. There are some fine tender species, including *Telopea truncata*, *Rhododendron* 'Sesterianum', a magnificent *Vitex agnus-castus*, and feathery *Azara microphylla* 'Variegata'. A valiant garden lovingly maintained by the elderly owner, wherein one feels the wilderness is slowly winning, creating a truly wild, Irish pleasaunce.

CURRAGHMORE 12

Portlaw, Co Waterford, Republic of Ireland. Tel: (051) 87102
The Marquis of Waterford

2m from Portlaw, 5m from Carrick-on-Suir and 14m from Waterford • Parking • Suitable for wheelchairs • House open by prior appointment only • Garden open May to Sept, Thurs, 2 – 5 p.m. Also open public holidays • Entrance: IR£1, children IR75p

Some parts of the garden are of early design e.g. the Shell House of 1754 personally decorated by the Countess of Tyrone. However, the main interest is the landscaping, the artificial lake and the views across to the mountains. May and June are the best months to see the azaleas, bluebells and rhododendrons.

DOWNHILL CASTLE 13

Co Derry, Northern Ireland.
The National Trust

5m W of Coleraine on A2 coast road, 1m W of Castlerock • Parking at Bishop's Gate and at Lion Gate • Suitable for wheelchairs • Dogs on lead • Mussenden Temple open Easter to Oct • Grounds always open • Entrance: free

For the architectural historian this is a must – the Mussenden Temple, sited on the clifftop with spectacular views along the coast of Northern Ireland, must be one of the most extraordinary libraries (that was its original purpose) in the world. The walk there is rough, through thistles and sheep droppings. The ruins of Downhill House, the Earl-Bishop's palace, are gaunt, and from the rear towards the Bishop's Gate Miss Jan Eccles has created a garden memorable for the miniature water-meadow full of candelabra primroses (yellow and pink) with startling clumps of dark *Iris kaempferi*. Dressed stones from tumbledown buildings and armless statues are enveloped with happy plantings, bergenia and fuchsia, roses spilling from a rickety pergola, and the sprightly Miss Eccles will be delighted to chat. A gem of a garden to which The National Trust could devote more attention.

FERNHILL ★ 14

Sandyford, Co. Dublin, Republic of Ireland. Tel: (01) 956000
Mrs Sally Walker

On main Dublin - Enniskerry road, 8m from central Dublin • Parking • Toilet facilities • Partly suitable for wheelchairs • Plants for sale • Open March to Nov, Tues - Sat, 11 a.m. - 5 p.m., Sun, 2 - 6 p.m. • Entrance: IR£2, OAP and children IR£1

The plantings of rhododendron species and cultivars provide spectacles of colour from early spring into mid-summer; many of the more tender rhododendrons flourish here. The garden is situated on the eastern slope of the Dublin Mountains and has a laurel lawn, some fine nineteenth-century plantings and an excellent flowering specimen of *Michelia doltsopa*. The walkways through the wooded areas wind steeply past many other shrubs, principally those that thrive on acid soil - pieris and camellia are also outstanding. There is a small rock garden and a water garden near the house, and drifts of daffodils in the spring. A sculpture exhibition has become an annual feature.

FLORENCE COURT 15

Florence Court, Co Fermanagh, Northern Ireland. Tel: (036582) 249
The National Trust

7m SW of Enniskillen, 1m W of village • Parking • Refreshments: teas and lunches in North Pavilion • Toilet facilities • Suitable for wheelchairs in garden only • Dogs on lead • Shop • Eighteenth-century house open 29th March to 7th April, daily, 1 - 6 p.m. Rest of April, May and Sept, Sat, Sun and Bank Holiday Mon only, 1 - 6 p.m. June to Aug, daily except Tues, 1 - 6 p.m. Last admission 5.15 p.m. • Grounds open all year, 10 a.m. - 1 hour before dusk. Parties by arrangement • Entrance: £2

The original, the mother of all Irish yews (*Taxus baccata* 'Fastigiata') still grows in the laurel-infested woodland about a quarter of a mile from the splendid mansion at Florence Court. Well worth the walk; the path allows glimpses of the mountains and the fine 'Brownian' park in front of the house. Some fine weeping beeches and old rhododendrons grow near the house, and work is in progress on revitalizing the walled garden. Strong shoes essential (especially in rainy season!) if you wish to pay respects to the venerable, 250-

year-old tree. Ice-house. The nearby caves (open to public) are worth visiting too, making a rewarding day out, with some fine views.

FOTA ★ 16

Fota Estate, Carrigtwohill, Co Cork, Republic of Ireland.
Tel: (021) 812201
Fota Trust

9m E of Cork City, on road to Cobh • Parking beside arboretum (also serving Fota Wildlife Park). IR£2 per car or IR£1 per adult, children free • Refreshments at Wildlife Park • Toilet facilities at Wildlife Park and in Fota House • Suitable for wheelchairs • Dogs on lead • Shop in Wildlife Park • House open, separate charge • Grounds open April to Sept, daily, 10 a.m. - 6 p.m., Sun, 11 a.m. - 6 p.m., Oct, 2 - 6 p.m. • Entrance: free for arboretum

Many of the superb specimen trees in this garden are undoubtedly among the best examples in Ireland and Britain. By the house is a cedar of Lebanon, undercarpeted with cyclamen; a handkerchief tree (*Davidia involucrata*), exquisite pieris, contorted tree-ferns, *Magnolia campbellii* and much, much more. A banana palm lingers in the border with fuchsia and watsonia cultivars. The Italian garden is, however, a mere shadow, and the orangery derelict, its sentinel *Phoenix dactylifera* patiently waiting the outcome of present uncertainties. At the time of writing the whole island is under a sale-option which may lead to large-scale development altering its unique character. Meanwhile the arboretum slumbers, needful of a clear guiding spirit, but still a delight for those who enjoy trees and shrubs.

GLENVEAGH CASTLE ★★ 17

Glenveagh National Park, Churchill, Letterkenny, Co Donegal, Republic of Ireland.
Tel: (074) 37088/37090
Office of Public Works

15m NW of Letterkenny • Parking at Visitor Centre. Access to garden and castle by official maincoaches only • Refreshments and meals • Toilet facilities • House open, IR£1 • Garden open Easter to last Mon in Oct, daily, 10.30 a.m. - 6.30 p.m. (open to 7.30 p.m. on Sun June to Aug). Other times by arrangement • Entrance: IR£1, OAP 70p, students and children 40p

The centre-piece of the Glenveagh National Park is the garden around Glenveagh Castle. The castle is set beside a mountain lough encircled with high, peat-blanketed mountains, in the middle of windswept moorlands, a most unpromising site. But, as in so many Irish gardens, surprises are countless. The lower lawn garden has fringing shrubberies, and, beyond, steep pathways wind through oak woods in which are planted scented, white-flowered rhododendrons, and numerous other tender shrubs from southern lands. Terraced enclosures with terracotta pots of plants and sculpture are encountered unexpectedly. The jardin potager at the castle has rank on rank of ornamental vegetables and flowering herbs. This is a paradise for plantsmen and gardeners keen on seeing fine specimens of unusual aspect – *Pseudopanax ferox*, *Fascicularia pitcairniifolia*, and many more. Sadly, Glenveagh's great stairway on the mountain is closed to the public, and there have been other changes closing off parts of this wonderland. Linger, and walk the mountain sides. Take the last bus back to the remarkable heather-roofed Visitor Centre with its imaginative landscaping (except the appallingly trained rowans!)

GUY L. WILSON DAFFODIL GARDEN ★ 18

University of Ulster, Coleraine, Co. Londonderry, Northern Ireland.
Tel: (0265) 44141
University of Ulster

On Cromore road, about 1m N of Coleraine town on road to Portstewart • Best season: spring • Parking • Dogs on lead • Open daily • Entrance: free

The daffodils in this garden represent one of the National collections (established under the patronage of the National Council for the Conservation of Plants and Gardens although it was commenced long before the NCCPG scheme). It is principally based on Irish-bred cultivars particularly those of Guy Wilson; however, among the 1000 plus cultivars represented are daffodils from New Zealand and the USA, as well as Britain, and there are both old and modern cultivars. The daffodils are interplanted with shrubs on island beds. The setting is attractive, but the garden now shows signs of diminished care and attention due to cut-backs by the university. Vandalism clearly is a problem – flowers wantonly damaged and picked daffodils strewn on paths were seen on a recent visit. The labels have all been removed (to prevent theft) which makes a nonsense of the collection as an educational facility. The purpose of such a collection is to allow people to look and learn – we must sympathise with the problems faced by the university and hope that some imaginative scheme can be devised to allow visitors to discover the names of the host of daffodils.

HEYWOOD 19

Salesian College, Ballinakill, Co Laois, Republic of Ireland.
Tel: (0502) 3334
Salesian Fathers

Outside Ballinakill village. 3m from Abbeyleix (turn E in town following sign to Ballinakill) • Parking • Partly suitable for wheelchairs • Dogs on lead • Open by appointment • Entrance: free (donations gratefully received)

Edwin Lutyens' walled garden with pergola and lawns is acknowledged as his finest small-scale work in Ireland. It is a gem, now restored close to its original state as far as the walls and ornaments are concerned. The planting is being restored, in the style of Gertrude Jekyll with the advice of Graham Stuart

Thomas. On the driveway leading towards the school buildings is an eighteenth-century folly. There is a long way to go before the garden is again sparkling, but it is still well worth visiting. Please, please do offer financial support when you have visited Heywood - it is a part of our heritage we cannot afford to neglect.

ILNACULLIN ★★ 20

(commonly known as Garinish Island)

Glengarriff, Co Cork, Republic of Ireland. Tel: (027) 63040
National Parks and Monuments Service, Office of Public Works

On an island in Bantry Bay • Toilet facilities • Open March and Oct, daily, 10 a.m. - 4.30 p.m., Sun, 1 - 5 p.m., April to June and Sept, daily, 10 a.m. - 6.30 p.m., Sun, 1 - 6 p.m. July and Aug, daily, 9.30 a.m. - 6.30 p.m., Sun, 11 a.m. - 7 p.m. • Entrance: IR£1.50, students, children and groups of 20 or more IR60p per person. Travel is by boat, charge for which is IR£4 return fare

The boat trip across the sheltered inlets of Bantry Bay, past sun-bathing seals, with views of the Caha Mountains, is doubly rewarding; landing at the slipway you gain entrance to one of Ireland's gardening jewels begun in the early 1900s. Most visitors cluster around the Casita and reflecting pool, designed by Harold Peto, to enjoy (on clear days) spectacular scenery, and some quite indifferent annual bedding. But walk beyond, to the Temple of the Winds, through shrubberies filled with plants usually confined indoors - tree ferns, Southern Hemisphere conifers, rhododendron species and cultivars. A flight of stone steps leads to the Martello tower, and thence the path returns to the walled garden and Italianate garden. Plant enthusiasts can spend many happy hours with such delights as *Lyonothamnus floribundus* var. *aspleniifolius* and a myriad of manuka (*Leptospermum scoparium*, the New Zealand tea-tree); take a picnic and linger; if wet, bring boots or strong shoes and an umbrella. Wonderful.

JAPANESE GARDEN ★ 21

Irish National Stud, Tully, Kildare, Co Kildare, Republic of Ireland. Tel: (045) 21617
Irish National Stud

1m outside Kildare town, 25m SW of Dublin • Parking • Refreshments • Toilet facilities • Plants for sale • Shop • The Irish National Stud and Horse Museum open • Garden open Easter Sunday to Oct, daily 10.30 a.m. - 5 p.m., Sun, 2 - 5.30 p.m. Guided tours on request • Entrance: IR£2, OAP and students IR£1.50, children IR£1

Created between the years 1906–1910. Devised by Colonel William Hall-Walker (later Lord Wavertree), a wealthy Scotsman of a famous brewery family and laid out by the Japanese Eida and his son Minory, the gardens, symbolising the 'Life of Man', are acclaimed as the finest Japanese gardens in

Europe. This is not a plantsman's garden, for few of the plants are Japanese; to be sure there are some excellent old maples, but many of the trees and shrubs are clipped and shaped beyond reason. The overshadowing Scots pines are exquisite. A pathway meanders through artificial caves, into a watery stream, past the tranquil ponds and on to the weeping trees of the grave. Beautiful stone lanterns grace the garden which is in the style of a Japanese 'tea garden'. On a misty day with smoke from a distant fire billowing across, this visitor recalls it as mysterious, beautiful.

JOHN F. KENNEDY ARBORETUM ★ 22

New Ross, Co Wexford, Republic of Ireland. Tel: (051) 88171
Coillte Teoranta (Irish Forestry Board)

8m S of New Ross • Parking • Refreshments: café May to Sept., April weekends only. Picnic area • Toilet facilities • Suitable for wheelchairs • Dogs on lead • Visitor Centre with Kennedy memorial and video • Open daily May to Aug, 10 a.m. - 8 p.m., April and Sept, 10 a.m. - 6.30 p.m., Oct to March, 10 a.m. - 5 p.m. • Entrance: IR£1, family IR£3, season ticket IR £10, coach IR£10, minibus IR£5

A modern spacious arboretum laid out in botanical sequence with rides; from the summit of a nearby hill is a superb panorama of the park and Co Wexford. Best to begin at the viewpoint - turn left just beyond the main entrance and drive to summit car park to see the layout. At the arboretum be prepared for a long walk - fortunately those not keen on gardening tend to linger near the café so that the distant reaches are quiet and empty. Planting began in 1960s and now 4500 different trees and shrubs are growing, ranging from conifers to flowering shrubs. Most species are represented by several specimens, and keen plantsmen can linger long examining the groups. Good labelling. A colourful planting of dwarf conifers is on the western side, a small lake on the east. While primarily a scientific collection, the arboretum is now achieving an established elegance.

KILLRUDDERY 23

Bray, Co Wicklow, Republic of Ireland. Tel: (01) 863405
Earl and Countess of Meath

1m S of Bray on road to Greystones • Parking • Toilet facilities • Partly suitable for wheelchairs • House open with conducted tours at extra charge • Garden open May, June, Sept, daily, 1 - 5 p.m. • Entrance: IR£1, OAP and students IR50p. Children under 12 must be accompanied.

The joy of Killruddery, a seventeenth-century garden with nineteenth-century embellishments, is the formal hedges, known as 'The Angles' set beside the formal canals which lead to a ride into the distant hills. There is a collection of nineteenth-century French cast statuary, a sylvan theatre created in beech, and a fountain pool enclosed in a beech hedge, too. The excellent conservatory (nineteenth-century), alas, has a perspex dome. The landscape features are unique, and Killruddery deserves to be better known, but it is not a garden for keen plantsmen without designer tastes.

KILMACURRAGH ★ 24

Rathdrum, Co Wicklow, Republic of Ireland.
Coillte Teoranta (Irish Forestry Board)

From village of Rathdrum. 25m S of Dublin • Parking at gate only • Dogs on lead • House derelict • Open all year for those on foot, through turnstile • Entrance: free

This garden is rated highly because of its atmosphere and magnificent ancient plants. It has no visitor facilities, but is open without hindrance to those who can find it. Behind the derelict eye-sore of the house there is an incomparable avenue composed of alternating Irish yews and crimson rhododendrons - 'magical' is an overworked word, but the pattern of fallen blossoms on this pathway in May *is* magical. Beyond, paths wind through the arboretum, under rhododendrons taller and older than in most other gardens. The trees at Kilmacurragh include many unequalled specimens - rare conifers abound. If you can, visit it when the crocus blossom is in the meadow, when the rhododendron flowers are tumbling down, at any time for elegant decrepitude. A secret pleasaunce; one hesitates to recommend it - for its secret then is lost.

LISMORE CASTLE 25

Lismore, Co Waterford, Republic of Ireland. Tel: (058) 54424
Duke and Duchess of Devonshire

Entrance in Lismore town • Parking • Open 13th May to 13th Sept, daily except Sat, 1.45 - 4.45 p.m. • Entrance: IR£1.80, children IR90p

Do not come to Ireland just to see Lismore Castle gardens, but the situation of the castle overlooking the River Blackwater is stunning. Entering through the gatehouse, there are two gardens, the upper reached by a stairway in the gatehouse and terraced with patches of vegetables; and the reduced glasshouse by Joseph Paxton (an interesting ridge-furrow house). The view from the main axis to the church spire is fine. In the lower garden are a few meritricious plants, but the principal feature, an ancient yew-walk carpeted softly with the dropped leaves, is wonderful. For that only can this be regarded as a garden of note - the rest is rather mundane. Yet Edmund Spenser is said to have written *The Fairie Queene* here, and it is the Irish home of the Duke of Devonshire who has only Chatsworth (see entry) to console him in England.

MOUNT STEWART HOUSE, GARDEN AND TEMPLE OF THE WINDS ★★ 26

Greyabbey, Newtownards, Co Down, Northern Ireland.
Tel: (024774) 387
The National Trust

On Ards Peninsula, 5m from Newtownards on road (A20) to Portaferry, 15m E of Belfast • Parking 300 yards • Refreshments: light refreshments and teas same time as house • Toilet facilities • Partly suitable for wheelchairs • House open at different times • Garden open 29th March to 7th April, daily, 12 noon - 6 p.m. April to Aug, daily except Tues, 12 noon - 6 p.m. Sept and Oct, Sat and Sun only 12 noon - 6 p.m. • Entrance: £2.50 to garden and Temple of Winds. Parties outside normal opening hours at extra charge

Of all Ireland's gardens this is The One not to miss. Any adjective that evokes beauty can be applied to it, and it's fun too. In the gardens in front of the house is a collection of statuary, satirising British political and public figures - dodos, monkeys and boars. The planting here is formal, with rectangular beds of 'hot' and 'cool' colours. Beyond in the informal gardens are mature trees and shrubs, a botanical collection with few equals, planted with great panache and maintained with outstanding attention to detail. Spires of giant lilies (cardiocrinum), aspiring eucalyptus, banks of rhododendrons, ferns and blue poppies, rivers of candelabra primulas - and much more. Walk along the lakeside path to the hill that affords a view over the lake to the house. Rare tender shrubs such as *Metrosideros umbellata* flourish here outside the walled family cemetery. Leading from it is the Jubilee Avenue and its statue of a white stag. Mount Stewart is a whole day for those keen on plants and it should be seen several times during the year truly to savour its rich tapestry of plants and water, buildings and trees. The Temple of the Winds, James 'Athenian' Stuart's banqueting hall of 1785, is also memorable.

MOUNT USHER ★ 27

Ashford, Co Wicklow, Republic of Ireland. Tel: (0404) 40116/40205
Mrs Madelaine Jay

At Ashford, on main Dublin - Wexford road, 30m S of Dublin • Parking • Refreshments: tea rooms, no picnics • Toilet facilities • Partly suitable for wheelchairs • Shopping courtyard • Open 17th March to Oct, Mon - Sat, 10.30 a.m. - 6 p.m., Sun, 11 a.m. - 6 p.m. • Entrance: IR£2, OAP, students and children IR£1.30

The Vartry river babbles through this exquisite garden over gentle weirs and under bridges which allow visitors to meander through the collections. Mount Usher is a plant-lovers' paradise. *Pinus montezumae* is always first port-of-call, a shimmering tree, magnificent when the bluebells are in flower. The philosophy of Mount Usher eschews chemicals of all kinds, and the lawns are cut in a cycle which allows the bulbs and wildflowers in them to seed naturally. Throughout there are drifts of rhododendrons, fine trees and shrubs including many that are difficult to cultivate outdoors in other parts of Britain and Ireland. The grove of eucalyptus at the lower end of the valley is memorable: a kiwi-fruit vine (*Actinidia chinensis*) cloaks the piers of a bridge, and beside the tennis court is the gigantic original *Eucryphia* x *nymansensis* 'Mount Usher'. In spring, bulbs and magnolias, in summer a procession of rhododendrons, in autumn russet and crimson leaves falling from maples – a garden for all seasons.

MUCKROSS HOUSE AND GARDENS ★ 28

Killarney National Park, Killarney, Co Kerry, Republic of Ireland.
Tel: (064) 31947/31440
National Parks and Monument Service; Office of Public Works

4m from centre of Killarney, on road to Kenmare • Parking • Restaurant • Toilet facilities • Suitable for wheelchairs • Dogs on lead • Craft shop • Open for pedestrians all year, with car access, 8 a.m. – 5 p.m., July and Aug, 8 a.m. – 7 p.m. • Entrance: free

The garden around Muckross House is almost incidental to the spectacle of the lakes and mountains of Killarney. It is principally renowned as a viewing area for the wild grandeur of the mountains. The lawns sweep to clumps of old rhododendrons and Scots pines, and there is a huge natural rock garden which is plagued with noisy children in high season. There is no peace here except on wet winter days. But leave the garden and take the lough-side trails, and enjoy the wildwoods with their unique assemblages of plants – *Sorbus anglica* (English whitebeam), yew and, above all, the almost eternal strawberry tree (*Arbutus unedo*). There is a mystical yew woodland carpeted with mosses. Throughout the National Park the cursed *Rhododendron ponticum* is being slowly and successfully eliminated. Would that the jarveys could go too; don't be tempted to pay for their extravagant transport from the town – the car park is free and beside the house!

NATIONAL BOTANIC GARDENS, GLASNEVIN ★★ 29

Glasnevin, Dublin 9, Republic of Ireland.
Tel: (01) 377596/374388
Department of Agriculture and Food

1m N of central Dublin • Parking very limited in summer and at weekends • Refreshments: arrangements for groups only may be made in advance by writing to the Director • Toilet facilities • Suitable for wheelchairs except for main Palm House • Shop • Open daily except 25th Dec, summer, 9 a.m. – 6 p.m., winter, 9 a.m. – 4.30 p.m. Opening times for glasshouses are posted at entrance • Entrance: free

A fine garden which still retains its Victorian exactitude with close-cut lawns and succulent carpet-bedding (in summer only!), but with an air of decrepitude, and the visitor facilities are parsimonious. The plant collection generally is fine, but in places the shrubs and trees are past their best. In the winter, the glasshouses are worth visiting; by spring there are daffodil-crowded lawns and flowering cherries; the summer highlight is the double, curving herbaceous border, and in autumn the fruit-laden trees and russet foliage can be magical. The Turner conservatory (1843–1869), the finest in Ireland, is being restored. Glasnevin is undoubtedly worth visiting, especially by gardeners with a strong interest in shrubs and perennials; soil conditions preclude large-scale rhododendron planting, and anyone passionate about alpines will be very disappointed. Highlights are hard to enumerate, but a few outstanding plants may be mentioned: *Zelkova carpinifolia* (especially in winter a marvellous 'architectural' tree) the Chain tent (*c.* 1836) with ancient wisteria; *Picea omorika* (at pond); *Fascicularia pitcairniifolia* and *Ochagavia carnea* (at Cactus house); cycads in Palm House; *Parrotia persica* (near entrance, wonderful in February and October); and of course 'The Last Rose of Summer'!

POWERSCOURT ★ 30

Enniskerry, Co Wicklow, Republic of Ireland. Tel: (01) 867676
Dr and Mrs Slazenger

11m S of Dublin, just outside village of Enniskerry • Parking • Refreshments: licensed restaurant • Toilet facilities • Partly suitable for wheelchairs • Dogs on lead • Plants for sale • Shop • House a ruin after a fire in 1974. Craft show and children's play area • Open March to Oct, 9 a.m. – 5.30 p.m. • Entrance: IR£2.50, OAP IR£2, children IR£1. Separate charge for waterfall

Powerscourt is a 'grand garden', a massive statement of the triumph of Art over the Natural Landscape. In its present form, with an amphitheatre of terraces and great central axis (mid-nineteenth century), the garden is largely the design of the inimitable Daniel Robertson. The elaborate High Victorian parterre, garishly bedded-out, has been eliminated and the well-maintained lawns are now peacefully embellished. In some ways Powerscourt is beyond compare – the axis formed by the ceremonious stairway leading down to the Triton Pond and jet, and stretching beyond to the Great Sugarloaf Mountain, is justly famous – it can, however, be glimpsed in a few minutes (and that is what many tourists do). In other ways Powerscourt is over-rated. The herbaceous border is incongruously sited and mediocre. The Japanese garden is merely a miscellany of red-painted bridges and stone lanterns. When you visit Powerscourt give those features a miss and walk along the terrace towards the Pepperpot, through the mature conifers which Lord Powerscourt collected – a big-cone pine (*Pinus coulteri*), the tallest in Ireland and Britain, is here. Wander on, to the edge of the pond, and look up, along the stairway, past the monumental terraces to the façade of the burnt-out house. That's the view of Powerscourt that is breath-taking – a man-made amphitheatre guarded by winged horses. Statuary and the famous perspective gate; an avenue of monkey puzzles and a beech wood along the avenue; these add to Powerscourt's glory.

ROWALLANE ★★ 31

Saintfield, Co Down, Northern Ireland. Tel: (0238) 510131
The National Trust

½m S of Saintfield on A7, Belfast - Downpatrick road • Parking • Refreshments: tea rooms with light refreshments, April to Sept, 2 - 6 p.m. • Toilet facilities • Partly suitable for wheelchairs • Dogs on lead • Trust shop • Open 1st to 28th March, daily, Mon - Fri, 9 a.m. - 5 p.m. 29th March to Oct, weekdays, 10.30 a.m. - 6 p.m., weekends, 2 - 6 p.m. Nov to March 1992, Mon - Fri, 9 a.m. - 5 p.m. Closed 25th, 26th Dec and 1st Jan • Entrance: March to Oct, £2, Nov to Feb, £1. Parties outside normal hours extra charge by appointment only

While famous as a 50-acre rhododendron garden, and certainly excellent in this regard, Rowallane has much more to interest keen gardeners. In summer, the walled garden blossoms in lemon and blue, while hoheria cast white petals in the wind. In secluded places, a handkerchief tree blows; there is a pale-yellow-leaved pieris, a restored Victorian bandstand (music-filled on summer weekends) and orchid meadows. Rock garden with primulas, meconopsis, heathers etc. and several areas of natural wild flowers. Any season will be interesting, and for the real enthusiast there are rhododendron species and cultivars in bloom from October to August. The original plant of *Viburnum plicatum* 'Rowallane' is in the walled garden as is the original *Chaenomeles* x *superba* 'Rowellane'; a feature is made of *Hypericum* 'Rowallane' at the entrance to the walled garden.

45 SANDFORD ROAD ★★ 32

Ranelagh, Dublin 6, Republic of Ireland.
Helen Dillon

Best season: spring - late autumn • Parking in street • Suitable for wheelchairs • Open by written appointment only • Entrance: by arrangement

Within a walled rectangular garden, typical of Dublin's Georgian town houses, Helen Dillon has created one of the best designed and planted gardens in Ireland. As a central foil there is an immaculate lawn which enhances the colourful embroidery of the borders which on exploration turn into a necklace of secret rooms with raised beds for rarities, such as lady's slipper orchids or double-flowered *Trillium grandiflorum*. On the terrace, terracotta pots sprout more rare plants: *Trochocarpa thymifolia* and the blue sweet pea (*Lathyrus nervosus*). Clumps of *Dierama pulcherrimum* arch over the sphinxes, and a small alpine house and conservatory shelter the choicest - *Clematis florida* 'Sieboldii', *Lapageria rosea*, prize-winning ferns, alpines and bulbs. The mixed borders of shrubs and herbaceous perennials are changeful, each season revealing unusual plants and exciting colour combinations. A listing of the plants in Mrs Dillon's garden would not shame a large botanical garden. Each plant has its proper place, all is ordered with no forbidding sense of contrivance. The exuberance overwhelms the formality, and the garden is both a finely-designed pleasaunce and a plantsman's veritable nirvana.

SIR THOMAS AND LADY DIXON PARK 33

Upper Malone Road, Belfast, Northern Ireland.
Belfast Parks Department

S of Belfast city centre, on Upper Malone Road • Best seasons: spring/summer • Parking • Toilet facilities • Suitable for wheelchairs • Dogs • Open all year; walled garden, Mon - Fri, 8 a.m. - 4 p.m., Sat and Sun, 2 - 4 p.m. • Entrance: free

Like regiments of foot soldiers on a battlefield, in lines and squares and circles, roses are paraded. Little else needs to be said, except that in 1991 the World Rose Congress is being held in Northern Ireland, and to provide shelter from the Ulster rain, Turkish tents have been erected in this garden - it looks like a set from a second-rate Hollywood movie. The massed lines of dwarf rhododendron are equally hideous. As for the roses, the new ones being trialled are well-nourished if rather similar. Fine old cultivars are conspicuous by their absence, or, when present, often wrongly labelled. Elsewhere, Dixon Park has excellent trees, a walled garden (containing the International Camellia Trials), and an ice house. It is restful to walk on the signposted trails through the groves.

TALBOT BOTANIC GARDEN ★ 34

Malahide Castle, Malahide, Co Dublin, Republic of Ireland.
Tel: (01) 450940
Dublin County Council

Outside Malahide, 10m N of Dublin • Parking • Refreshments: lunches and teas in castle • Suitable for wheelchairs • Dogs on lead • Shop in castle • House open, additional charge for tours • Garden open May to Sept, daily, 2 - 4.30 p.m. Conducted tour of walled garden Wed, 2 p.m. • Entrance: IR50p, children free if accompanied

Malahide Castle was the home of the Talbot family for many centuries; following the death of Lord Talbot de Malahide it was acquired by Dublin County Council. The garden consists of three parts - the outer demesne (now occupied by playing fields, well-kept lawns and shrubberies, pathways); the main shrubberies (open to the public as above) and the walled garden (open only by special arrangement and on Wednesdays for guided tours). The main shrubberies planted by Lord Talbot contain a varied mixture of trees and shrubs, some of which are outstanding and rare. However, the finest part of the collection is in the walled garden - here Lord Talbot planted such exoticas as *Telopea truncata*, *Bomarea caldasii*, *Garrya* x *issaquahensis*, and numerous others. Olearia was a favourite genus and is well represented here. Australasian genera are also represented (e.g. pittosporum, grevillea, cyathodes, acacia); *Berberis valdiviana* and *Pseudopanax ferox* lurk in an out-of-the-way corner. By the castle is a large cedar of Lebanon with cyclamen below, and a spacious lawn. The garden is worth visiting; the pity is that so many of the shrubs are still clipped into uncomfortable shapes, and that very few of the plants are fully labelled.

TOLLYMORE 35

Newcastle, Co Down, Northern Ireland.
Forest Service, Department of Agriculture (N.I.)

1m from Newcastle, in foothills of Mourne Mountains • *Parking* • *Refreshments* • *Toilet facilities* • *Partly suitable for wheelchairs* • *Dogs* • *Shop* • *Open all year* • *Entrance: car park fee £2*

A fine conifer forest, now a forest park, with walks, treks and rivers on the northern flank of the Mourne Mountains. A small arboretum is adjacent to the main car park and contains some fine trees – *Aesculus indica* and the original *Picea abies* 'Clanbrassilliana'. Of interest perhaps to the more dedicated dendrophiles, but a fine park for the family outing.

TRINITY COLLEGE BOTANIC GARDEN 36

Palmerston Park, Dublin 6, Republic of Ireland. Tel: (01) 972070
School of Botany, Trinity College, Dublin

Adjacent to Palmerston Park, Ranelagh, South Dublin • *Parking in street* • *Suitable for wheelchairs* • *Open Mon – Fri, 9 a.m. – 5 p.m. Appointment preferred* • *Entrance: free*

This is essentially a research garden, but there is a small arboretum, order (family) beds and a collection of Irish native plants, as well as some glasshouses; a fragment of *Todea barbara* from a plant donated in 1892 grows in one glasshouse. Also a collection of *Saxifraga* sp. and the rare Mauritius blue-bell (*Nesocodon mauritianus*). *Melianthus major* flowers well every year, and there are good specimens of *Salix hibernica* and *Sorbus hibernica*. For the botanically curious only.

SCOTLAND

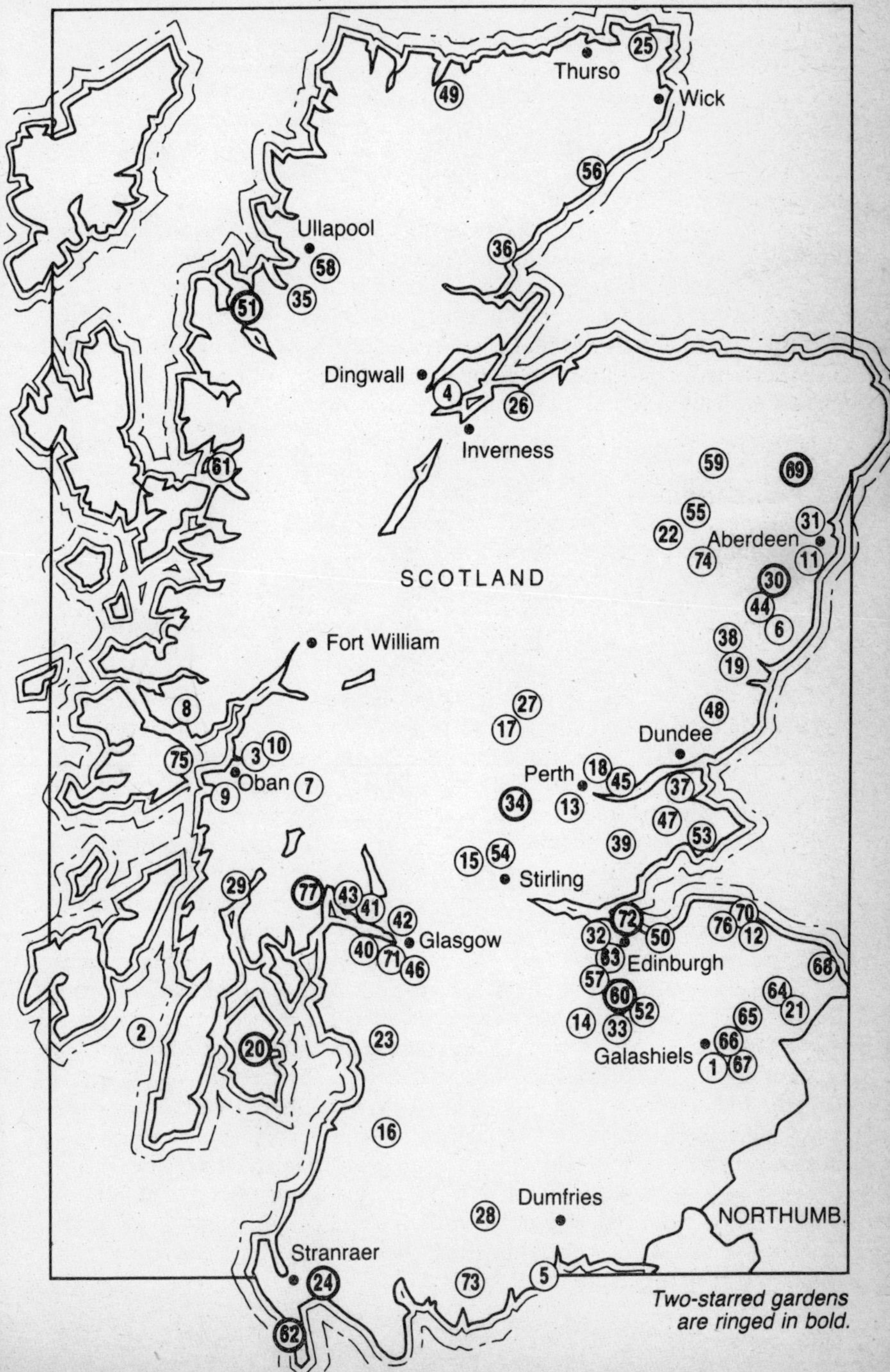

Two-starred gardens are ringed in bold.

ABBOTSFORD 1

Melrose, Roxburghshire, Borders. Tel: (0896) 2043
Mrs P. Maxwell-Scott

3m W of Melrose on A6091, turn SW on to B6360. Just S of A72 • Parking . • Teas and picnics • Toilet facilities • Suitable for wheelchairs. Disabled enter by private entrance • Shop • House open • Garden open mid-March to Oct, Mon - Sat, 10 a.m. - 5 p.m., Sun, 2 - 5 p.m. • Entrance: £2, children £1, rates for parties: £1.60 per person, children 80p

Sir Walter Scott's magnificent house, built between 1817 and 1821 to satisfy his yearning to become a laird, has a garden that is rich in Scottish allusions. A yew hedge to the south of the house has medallions from an old cross inset, and a fountain in the same formal garden came from the same cross. The River Tweed flows past the house and there are fine views across a stretch of garden. Herbaceous beds lead to a gothic-type fern house filled with other plants beside ferns, such as orchids. However, the dedicated Scott scholar will find most interest in the house, amongst historical relics collected by the laird himself.

ACHAMORE GARDENS ★ 2

Isle of Gigha, Argyll, Strathclyde. Tel: (05835) 267
Mr Malcolm Potier

Take A83 to Tayinloan then by ferry to Gigha • Best season: spring • Refreshments at hotel • Toilet facilities • Partly suitable for wheelchairs • Dogs on lead • Plants for sale • Open daily all year round • Entrance: £2, OAP and children £1, collecting box

An amazing idea to create such a superb garden on the Isle of Gigha. The journey there is via most beautiful countryside finishing up with the ferry trip, surrounded by squawking sea birds. In 1944 Sir James Horlick purchased the whole island with the sole purpose to create a garden in which to grow the rare and unusual. This was accomplished with the advice of James Russell. A delightful woodland landscape was planted with a vast collection of rarities from around the world. The garden is especially rich in fine specimens of tender rhododendrons such as *R. lindleyii*, *R. fragrantissimum*, and *R. macabeanum* to name but a few. The overall effect of the garden is tropical. There are many varieties of camellias, cordylines, primulas and Asiatic exotica. A great number of genera are represented by very good specimens, thriving in Gigha's mildness. There is a very fine *Pinus montezumae* in the walled garden: drifts of Asiatic primulas feature around the especially pretty woodland pond. The rhododendrons are unsurpassed in variety, quality and sheer visual magnitude. Gigha is a must, a Mecca for the keen plantsman and avid gardener. Few gardens outside the national botanic collections can claim such diversity and rarity. Although it is true that in recent years the number of gardeners has been reduced and there has been a slight air of neglect, the island now has a new owner who is said to wish to preserve the character of Gigha and keep it open to the public.

ACHNACLOICH 3

Connel, Argyll, Strathclyde. Tel: (063171) 221
Mrs T.E. Nelson

3m E of Connel off A85 • Best season: April to June • Parking • Suitable for wheelchairs • Dogs on lead • Plants for sale • Grounds open 29th March to 22nd June and 3rd Aug to mid-Oct, daily, 10 a.m. - 6 p.m. • Entrance: £1, OAP 50p, children free

A castellated Scottish baronial house beautifully situated above the loch on a rocky cliff. A curved drive sweeps past massed bulbs in spring, and later there are azaleas and fine Japanese maples. Natural woodland with interlinked glades is beautiful in spring with bluebells, primroses and wood anemones. Other gaps are planted with primulas, magnolias and rare rhododenrons. Fine views to Loch Etive and surrounding mountains. Garden walks recently extended.

ALLANGRANGE 4

Munlochy, Black Isle, Ross and Cromarty, Highlands.
Tel: (046381) 249
Major and Mrs A. Cameron

Signposted from A9, 5m N or Inverness • Best season: May to July • Parking: 50p • Teas • Toilet facilties in house • Suitable for wheelchairs • Dogs on lead • Plants for sale • Open 12th May, 9th June, 7th July for charity, 2 - 5.30 p.m. • Entrance: £1, children 20p

A very attractive garden which spills down the hillside in a series of descending terraces merging naturally with the rolling agricultural landscape of the Black Isle. The formal part of the garden incorporates white and mauve gardens, a pair of camomile lawns, many old and shrub roses, tree peonies and a small corner for plants of variegated foliage. In July, climbing Himalayan roses, including *Rosa filipes* 'Kiftsgate' make a spectacular display. There is also a small pool garden, and to the rear of the house a developing woodland garden with unusual rhododendrons, primulas, meconopsis and *Cardiocrinum giganteum*. The hand of an accomplished flower painter, Elizabeth Cameron, shows itself in the garden design, the choice of plants and in the colour combinations in the garden. Well worth the detour from the A9.

ARBIGLAND 5

Kirkbean, Dumfries and Galloway. Tel: (038788) 283
Captain and Mrs J.B. Blackett

From New Abbey, signposted on A710 Solway coast road • Best season: end April to Mid-June, Sept • Parking free • Teas, picnics on beach • Toilet facilities • Dogs on lead • Secluded private sandy beach which can be used by visitors • Open May to Sept, Sun, Tues and Thurs, 2 - 6 p.m. • Entrance: £1, children 50p, under 5 free

The ancient 'broadwalk', lined with fine specimen trees, leads down towards the sea and the woodland garden. One area, called 'Japan' takes its name from the Japanese maples and azaleas which have been arranged around a small burn. Nearby is a large pool, especially attractive in the autumn when it reflects the colours of the trees that surround it; the border around the lawn is full of unusual and interesting plants. The formal sunken garden has been created on the foundations of the original house. The old walled garden, at present disused, dates from the original eighteenth-century house and contains one of the finest *Pieris japonica* in Scotland, over 20 ft high.

ARBUTHNOTT HOUSE 6

Laurencekirk, Grampian.
The Viscount of Arbuthnott

8m from Laurencekirk, 3m from Inverbervie on B967 between A92 and A94 • Parking • Refreshments: tea and biscuits • Toilet facilities • Plants for sale • Garden open for charity on specified days • Entrance: £1, OAP and children 50p (inc. parking)

The policies and the enclosed garden all date from the late seventeenth-century and are contained within the valley of the Bervie Water. The entrance drive is flanked by rhododendrons and the verges full of primroses and celandines in spring. The road crosses a fine bridge topped by imposing urns before reaching the house set high on a promontory with most of the garden sloping very steeply to the river. This garden is unusual in that it has always been treated as an extension of the house, rather than being laid out at some distance. The sloping part has four grassed terraces and this pattern is dissected by diagonal grassed walks radiating out in a manner reminiscent of the Union Jack. This fixed structure creates long garden 'rooms' and vistas as the garden is explored. The garden plan is very old but much of today's mature planting was done by a Lady Arbuthnott in the 1920s and this is continued by the present Lady Arbuthnott. Herbaceous borders, old roses together with shrub roses and ramblers, shrubs underplanted with hostas, meconopsis and lilies, lilacs and viburnums provide colour throughout the summer. A metal stag for target practice stands at the bottom of the slope by the lake.

ARDANAISEIG GARDEN AND HOTEL 7

Kilchrenan, Argyll, Strathclyde. Tel: (08662) 264
Mr and Mrs J.M. Brown and family

4m E from Kilchrenan on route B845 • Best seasons: April, May, July, Oct • Parking • Refreshments at hotel, no children under 8 • Dogs on lead • Plants for sale • Hotel open, formerly Scottish baronial house • Open April to Oct, 10 a.m. - 8 p.m. • Entrance: £1, children free. Collecting box at car park

A picturesque 10-mile drive from Taynauilt down the peninsular makes a fitting introduction to this traditional Argyll garden. Attractive slate paths guide the visitor round 20 acres of well-planted woodland set behind an 1834 baronial house, now a very comfortable hotel, with lovely views across Loch Awe. The species and hybrid rhododendrons are particularly fine. Note the unusual curved walls of the walled garden which has a particularly good herbaceous border for this part of the world.

ARDTORNISH 8

Lochaline, Morvern, Highlands. Tel: (096784) 288 (Estate office)
Mrs John Raven

30m from Corran. From Corran ferry, S of Fort William, cross to Morvern and take route left on A861 towards Lochaline, then left on A884. Gardens 2m before Lochaline on left • Best seasons: April, May and Oct • Parking • Dogs on lead • Plants for sale in kitchen garden • 12 flats in the house available for self-catering accommodation • Open April to Oct, 10 a.m. – 5 p.m. • Entrance: £1, children free. Collecting box

A plantsman's garden with a particularly fine and extensive collection of unusual shrubs, deciduous trees and rhododendrons set against a background of conifers, a loch and outstanding highland scenery. The gardens have developed over the past 100 years or more following the first house on the site, established by a distiller from London in the 1850s. They are on a steeply sloping site and rainfall is heavy. Mrs Raven's late husband wrote a book about their other garden. Docwra's in Hertfordshire (see entry) and it was his ambition to establish a plantsman's paradise here. Apart from the area around the house, there is a pleasing air of informality about the gardens which include a boggy primula garden. Bob's Glen with *Rhododendron thomsonii* and *prattii* and a larger glen with still more species and hybrid rhododendrons. There is an alpine meadow and a flourishing kitchen garden.

ARDUAINE GARDENS ★ 9

by Oban, Argyll, Strathclyde.
Mr H. and Mr M.E. Wright

On the A816, 18m S of Oban, 6m N of Kilmartin. Entrance difficult to find • Parking: Loch Melfort Hotel by arrangement • Refreshments at hotel • Toilet facilities • Dogs on lead • This garden has been open April to Sept, daily except Thurs and Fri, 10 a.m. – 6 p.m., but in recent times it has had to be closed and visitors should check before visiting in 1991 • Entrance: £1, children free

Although not included in many guide books, Arduaine (pronounced Ardoony if you are asking the way) is a very special place. Visitors are gently welcomed and guided round a maze of intertwining pathways which run up and down hills and amongst lawns and a series of interlocking ponds. The romance of the setting overlooking the lovely Asknish Bay is equal to the romance of the gardens' history. Created in the 1900s by J.A. Campbell they were much neglected after 1945 but were tended by a faithful nanny until they were sold in 1971 to the Wright brothers. Here is one of the best collections of rhododendrons in Scotland, as well as many other interesting trees, shrubs and herbaceous plants all planted in harmony with a great understanding of colour and texture.

BARGUILLEAN 10

Taynuilt, Argyll, Strathclyde. Tel: (08662) 375
Mr Sam S. MacDonald

3m from Taynuilt. Minor road to Kilmore off A85 • Best season: April to June • Parking • Dogs on lead • Plants for sale • Open daily, March to Oct, 8 a.m. - 9 p.m. • Entrance: 50p, children free

Nine-acre woodland garden with areas of established rhododendrons, azaleas and confiers and some rare trees and shrubs on a highland hillside overlooking a lochan with views to Ben Cruachan. Much new planting with modern rhododendron hybrids, from the NW of the United States, among native birch and oak woodland makes for interesting comparisons with established rhododendron gardens of the West Coast and is excellent for the evaluation of these cultivars for Scottish gardens. A very peaceful garden, achieving much in a difficult situation. Good nursery adjacent. Abundant wildlife.

BEECHGROVE GARDEN ★ 11

Beechgrove Terrace, Aberdeen, Grampian. Tel: (0224) 625233
BBC Scotland

1½m from city centre • Refreshments: tea and biscuits on charity day • Toilet facilities • Suitable for wheelchairs • Open daily except Fri, 9 a.m. - dusk and for charity 11th Aug, 11 a.m. - 5 p.m. • Entrance: free except on charity day when £1, OAP and children 50p

This garden was begun in 1978 for use in conjunction with BBC Scotland's gardening programme of the same name. During 1990 the garden was cleared except for one area, now referred to as the 'established garden' and new gardens begun. These include two terrace gardens, a housing estate garden suitable for a family, a suburban garden for the more knowledgeable gardener and a 'clay corner' to demonstrate the possibilities for difficult soils. There is a conservatory built for the 1990 series and some small glasshouses. Examples of paving, fencing, vegetables, fruit, a children's play area, a small pool, troughs, etc, complete the garden. It is a very interesting and instructive garden for the aspiring beginner but has less to offer the dedicated plantsman.

BELHAVEN HOUSE ★ 12

Belhaven, Dunbar, East Lothian, Borders. Tel: (0368) 62392
Sir George Taylor

On the outskirts of Dunbar, route A1087 – Belhaven • Parking • Dogs • Open for charity once a year and at other times by appointment • Entrance: 60p

Sir George Taylor's associations with Royal Botanic Garden, Edinburgh, and as Director of Kew Gardens has brought about the development of a small, but fascinating garden, filled with a great many treasured trees, shrubs and herbaceous plants. The peat garden is very good, but it is the trough garden that excels. Some 20 troughs are heavily planted with very choice alpines and rockery plants of great variety. It is a good garden for the keen plantsperson. There is a heavy emphasis on the genus *Primula* on which Sir George is a great authority. Plants from the Past commercial nursery and garden is nearby (see entry). This area of Scotland has great physical beauty and is quite unlike other areas of Britain.

BELL'S CHERRYBANK GARDENS 13

Cherrybank, Perth, Tayside. Tel: (0738) 21111
Arthur Bell & Co Ltd

On A9 into Perth city centre. Gardens located S of main road • Parking • Refreshments: light teas and picnic areas • Toilet facilities • Suitable for wheelchairs • Guide dogs only • Open May to Oct, 11 a.m. – 5.30 p.m. • Entrance: free

This is a modern garden surrounding the commercial offices of Arthur Bell and Sons Ltd, whisky distillers. It is in fact two gardens, the first laid out in the early 1970s, plus the Scottish National heather collection begun in 1983. Their aim is to have the world's largest collection of heathers. Apart from the heathers, the plant collections are not outstanding, but they are well-maintained and beautifully laid out. Interest is sustained throughout the total of 18 acres by water features, modern sculptures, pleasant vistas, a tiny putting green, tubular bells and an aviary. The children's play area includes a roundabout for wheelchair-bound children. A remarkable sundial designed by Ian Hamilton-Finlay, the sculptor, is here (see entry for Little Sparta).

BIGGAR PARK ★ 14

Biggar, Lanarkshire, Strathclyde. Tel: (0899) 20185
Capt and Mrs David Barnes

S end of Biggar on A702, 30m SW of Edinburgh • Parking • Refreshments • Toilet facilities • Suitable for wheelchairs • Dogs on lead • Plants for sale • Open 9th June, 1 – 5.30 p.m., 14th July, 2 – 6 p.m. Visitors welcome by appointment at other times • Entrance: £1

A Japanese garden of tranquillity welcomes one to this well-planned 10-acre plantsman's garden. Sue Barnes' efficient labelling adds greatly to the enjoyment when walking through the woodland, the small arboretum and admiring the well-planted ornamental pond which have all been designed carefully to give year-round interest. This starts with a stunning display of daffodils which are followed by glades of meconopsis, rhododendrons and azaleas in early summer before the huge herbaceous borders burst into colour. The centrepiece, however, must be the outstanding walled garden reached through a fine rockery bank beside the eighteenth-century mansion house. The view through the wrought-iron gate stretches the length of a 50 yard double herbaceous border attractively backed by swags of thick ornamental rope hanging from rose 'pillars', whilst either side is divided into intensively planted sections divided by pleasing grass paths.

BLAIRHOYLE ★ 15

Port of Menteith, by Stirling, Central.
Lt Colonel and Mrs J.D. Pattullo

2m E of Lake of Menteith, 3m W of Thornhill on A8733 • Parking • Toilet facilities • Partly suitable for wheelchairs • Dogs on lead • Plants for sale • Open for charity May to Aug, or by appointment

One of the choicest of the 'private' gardens in Scotland, it and the arboretum were originally laid out by George Crabbie (of ginger wine fame) at the beginning of this century. It is a plantsman's garden of 16 acres with magnificent views across to the Fintry Hills. The renowned arboretum leads down to an ornamental lake and the walled garden bursts with herbaceous plants, roses, fruit and vegetables. Even more attractive are the sweeping lawns which surround and lead into a large, but easily assimilated variety of mature shrubs, trees, rhododendrons, azaleas, primulas, ground-cover plants and heathers.

BLAIRQUHAN 16

Maybole, Ayrshire, Strathclyde. Tel: (06557) 239
James Hunter Blair

7m SE of Maybole on B7045. Signposted • Parking • Refreshments • Toilet facilities • Suitable for wheelchairs • Dogs on lead • Plants for sale • Shop • House open • Garden open mid-July to mid-Aug, except Mon, afternoons only • Entrance: £2.50 (house and garden)

Approached by a three-mile drive along the River Girvan giving good opportunities to admire the 1860 pinetum and the extensive wood and parkland. The three-acre walled garden with original glasshouses is traditionally planted and currently being restocked. Visitors should allow time to see the house which was built in 1820 by William Burn for Sir David Hunter Blair, 3rd Baronet, and contains all the furniture especially made at the time but which has been decorated and arranged with great style by the present owner.

BOLFRACKS 17

Aberfeldy, Perthshire, Tayside. Tel: (0887) 20207
Mr J.D. Hutchison

2m W of Aberfeldy on A827 towards Loch Tay • Limited parking • Plants for sale occasionally • Open mid-April to mid-Oct, daily, 10 a.m. - 6 p.m. • Entrance: £1, concessions 50p. Honesty box at gate

There has been a garden on this site for 200 years, but the present garden was started by the owners' parents in the 1920s and reshaped by the owner over the last 20 years. Three acres of walled plantsman's garden, well laid out and planned to demonstrate the potential of an exposed hillside with a northerly aspect. Astounding views over the Tay Valley are matched by the garden's own interesting features. Gentians do well on this soil. Fine masses of bulbs in spring and good autumn colour. Peat walls and stream garden. A small wild garden is presently being laid out.

BRANKLYN GARDEN 18

Dundee Road, Perth, Tayside. Tel: (0738) 25535
National Trust for Scotland

½m from Queen's Bridge on A85 • Best season: early summer • Parking ¼m from entrance. Disabled parking at gate • Toilet facilities • Paths too narrow for wheelchairs • Plants for sale • NTS sales table • Open March to Oct, daily, 9.30 a.m. to sunset • Entrance: £1.40, OAP and children 70p. Parties £1.20 (60p) per person

John and Dorothy Renton created this garden nearly in sight of the centre of Perth and certainly within sound. Work commenced in 1922 and in 1955 Dorothy was awarded the Veitch Memorial Medal by the Royal Horticultural Society. Branklyn extends to about three acres with the main interest being in alpine and ericaceous plants in its magnificent scree rock garden on the side of the tennis court. There is a splendid collection of dwarf rhododendrons. The National Trust took over the garden in 1968, following the death of Dorothy Renton in 1966 and of her husband the following year, and a substantial restructuring and improvement programme is taking place. Essential work is restoring Branklyn to its rightful position as an outstanding plantsman's garden with its main feature which has been described as 'a true rock-gardener's paradise'. It is impossible to describe all the splendid things to be found here from the fine trees to the comprehensive collection of dwarf and smaller rhododendrons, the meconopsis to the cyprepediums, and the garden will repay many visits.

BRECHIN CASTLE ★ 19

Brechin, Tayside. Tel: (03562) 4566 (Estate office)
The Earl and Countess of Dalhousie

1m from Brechin, route A94 • Best season: late May, early June • Parking • Teas in garden • Open 26th May, 23rd June for charity, 2 - 6 p.m. • Entrance: 50p, children 10p

The main axis of the walled garden is punctuated by a series of individual features. At the first one of these, four Lawson cypresses, a view down steps to the pond garden below is obtained. Subsequent events include a laburnum grove, a birch grove and a cherry grove, all flanked by castellated clipped yew hedges. Arguably one of the best walled gardens in Scotland. The eighteenth-century castle itself is half a mile away, approached by more recent plantings of azaleas and situated on a rocky cliff overlooking the River South Esk.

BRODICK CASTLE ★★ 20

Isle of Arran, Strathclyde. Tel: (0770) 2202
National Trust for Scotland and Cunninghame District Council

On Isle of Arran, 2m from Brodick. Ferry from Ardrossan or Kintyre • Best seasons: late April/early May (woodland garden), May to Aug (formal garden) • Parking free • Restaurant dates as castle • Toilet facilities • Partly suitable for wheelchairs • Dogs on lead • Shop • Castle open 29th March to 7th April, May to Sept, daily, 1 - 5 p.m. From 8th to 30th April and 2nd to 19th Oct open Mon, Wed and Sat, 1 - 5 p.m. (last four 4.40 p.m.) • Park open daily, 9.30 a.m. - dusk • Entrance: £1.80, children 90p (castle and gardens £2.80, children £1.40)

High above the shores of the Firth of Clyde and guarding three approaches to Western Scotland is this red-brick castle, a sign that Arran has been the scene of many territorial disputes over the centuries. Its garden was an overgrown jungle of rhododendrons until the Duchess of Montrose arrived after World War I; she was much helped after 1930 when her daughter married John Boscawen of Tresco Abbey (see entry). Many of the trees and plants here came by boat from Tresco in the Scillies. Others came from subscriptions to the second generation of great plant-hunters like Kingdon-Ward and, in particular, George Forrest, one of the greatest of all collectors. Plants from the Himalayas, Burma and China, normally considered tender, flourish in the Gulf Stream climate. A good display of primulas in bog garden. The walled formal garden to the east of the castle is over 250 years old and has recently been restored as a Victorian garden with herbaceous plants, annuals and roses. It is impossible to list all the treasures of the woodland garden, but perhaps the most surprising is the huge size of the specimens in the lower rhododendron walk where *R. sinogrande* are found, larger than a normal tree with blooms up to two feet long. Memorable views over Brodick Bay.

BUGHTRIG 21

Leitholm, Nr Coldstream, Berwickshire, Borders.
Major General and The Hon. Mrs Charles Ramsey

¼m E of Leitholm on B6461 • Parking • Refreshments • Toilet facilities • Suitable for wheelchairs • Dogs on lead • Plants for sale • Open 30th June, 2.30 - 5.30 p.m. for charity • Entrance: £1, children free

This traditional garden with an 'English' flavour was created by the owner's mother as a more attractive interpretation of the original six-acre walled garden. The immaculately-maintained borders are a lesson to all and the box edgings look as if they have been clipped with nail scissors. There is a pleasing display of herbaceous plants, shrubs, vegetables and young trees. Glasshouses within the walled garden are well-stocked, and there are good specimen trees and quality plantings throughout.

CANDACRAIG 22

Strathdon, Grampian. Tel: (09756) 51226
Mrs E.M. Young

On A97 Huntly - Dinnet road then A944 (formerly B973) Strathdon - Tomintoul road • Best season: July to Aug • Parking • Light refreshments in tearoom • Toilet facilities • Suitable for wheelchairs • Plants for sale • Shop • Open April to Oct, daily (except Tues, April to June and Sept to Oct), 10 a.m. - 5 p.m. • Entrance: April, May, Sept, Oct 80p, children 40p. June to Aug, £1, children 50p

At an altitude of 1000 feet this old walled garden dates from 1820 and covers a three-acre sheltered site in upper Deeside. The garden is now being systematically restored by the present owner and features herbaceous borders, old roses, cottage garden flowers and a wild garden area. There is a Victorian summerhouse in Gothic style.

CARNELL 23

Hurlford. Ayrshire, Strathclyde. Tel: (056384) 236
Mr and Mrs J.R. Findlay and Mrs J.B. Findlay (The Garden House)

4m from Kilmarnock, 6m from Mauchline on A719, 1½m on Ayrshire side of A76 • Parking free • Refreshments on day of opening • Dogs on lead • Plants for sale. Also flowers and home-bakes • Sixteenth-century peel tower • Open 28th July, 2 - 6 p.m. • Entrance: £1, children under 12 free

Exquisite example of 100 yards of linear herbaceous borders facing a rectangular pool with informal planting as a contrast on the opposite bank. Also interesting rock garden, lilies. Walled garden. Burmese and Japanese features. Garden adjacent to house currently being developed. All plants and vegetables grown with organic compost produced *in situ*.

CASTLE KENNEDY AND LOCHINCH GARDENS ★★ 24

Stranraer, Wigtownshire, Dumfries & Galloway. Tel: (0776) 2024
The Earl and Countess of Stair

3m from Stranraer on A75 • Best season: April/May • Parking • Teas • Toilet facilities • Partly suitable for wheelchairs • Dogs on lead • Plants for sale • Shop • Open April to Sept, daily, 10 a.m. – 5 p.m. • Entrance: £1.50, OAP £1, children 50 p. Party rates on application

One of Scotland's most famous gardens set on a peninsular between two lochs and well worth a visit for its sheer 67-acre magnificence and spectacular spring colour. The gardens were originally laid out in 1730 around the ruins of his castle home by Field Marshal the 2nd Earl of Stair who used his unoccupied dragoons to effect a major remoulding of the landscape, combining large formal swathes of mown grassland with massive formal gardens, criss-crossed with avenues and allées of large specimen trees. The garden is internationally famous for its pinetum – currently being replanted, for its good variety of tender trees and for its species rhododendrons including many of Sir Joseph Hooker's original introductions from his Himalayan expeditions. The monkey puzzle avenue, now sadly a little tattered, was once the finest in the noble world and there is also one of two firs and another of hollies underplanted with embothriums and eucryphias. An impressive two-acre circular lily pond puts everyone else's in their proper place and a good walk from this brings you to the ruined castle and its walled garden, well planted with theme borders. The small plant sales area, personally supervised by Lady Stair, is recommended for inexpensive home-grown and unusual plants.

CASTLE OF MEY ★★ 25

Caithness, Highlands.
H.M. Queen Elizabeth the Queen Mother

1½m from Mey • Parking • Teas • Toilet facilities • Suitable for wheelchairs • Dogs on lead • Open for charity 3 days a year • Entrance: 70p, OAP and children under 12, 40p

The castle originates from the late sixteenth century and was renovated by The Queen Mother in 1955. Gardening would not be possible in such an exposed position without the protection of the 'Great Wall of Mey'. Within the walled garden, The Queen Mother has collected her favourite flowers; many were gifts and have special meaning. The personal private feeling pervades the whole garden which is especially well planted and maintained. The colour schemes are very good, blending the garden with the vast natural panorama within which it is situated. The mild sea-temperate climate allows many unusual plants to be grown to so far north.

CAWDOR CASTLE ★ 26

Cawdor, Nairn, Highlands. Tel: (06677) 615
The Earl of Cawdor

Between Inverness and Nairn on the B9090 off the A96 • Best season: summer • Parking • Refreshments: restaurant, teas and picnics • Toilet facilities • Partly suitable for wheelchairs • Plants for sale • Shop • House open • Garden open May to Sept, daily, 10 a.m. - 5.30 p.m. • Entrance: £2.75, OAP and disabled £2, children £1.50. Family ticket £9. Parties of 20 or more on application

Frequently referred to as one of the Highlands' most romantic castles and steeped in history, Cawdor Castle is a fourteenth-century keep with seventeenth- and nineteenth-century additions. The surrounding parkland is handsome and well-kept, though not in the grand tradition of classic landscapes. To the side of the castle is the formal garden where recently-added wrought-iron arches frame extensive herbaceous borders, a peony border, a very old hedge of mixed varieties of *Rosa pimpinellifolia*, the Scots or Burnet rose, a rose tunnel, old apple trees with climbing roses, interesting shrubs and lilies. An abundance of lavender and pinks completes a rather Edwardian atmosphere. The castle wall shelters *Exochorda*, *Abutilon vitifolium*, *Carpenteria californica* and *Rosa banksiae*. Pillar-box red seats create a jarring note in an otherwise splendidly flowery garden. The walled garden below the castle is being developed with a holly maze, a thistle garden and a white garden. There are fine views everywhere of the castle, the park and the surrounding countryside which one can enjoy more actively by walking one of the five nature trails. These vary in length from half to five miles and are an ideal way to admire the magnificent mature woodland.

CLUNY HOUSE 27

Aberfeldy, Perthshire, Tayside. Tel: (0887) 20795
Mr and Mrs J. Mattingley

20m NW of Perth. N of Aberfeldy, over the Wade Bridge, take the Weem to Strathtay Road. Cluny House is signposted about 3m along this road • Best seasons: spring, early summer and late autumn • Limited parking • Plants for sale and plant and seed list available on request • Open March to Oct, 10 a.m. - 6 p.m. • Entrance: £1, children free

Unlike most other gardens this is as truly wild as one can find – friendly weeds grow unchecked for fear of disturbing the NCCPG collection of Asiatic prumulas. Sheltered slopes create a moist micro-climate where all the plants flourish abundantly, including a Wellingtonia with the British near record girth of 35½ft. Superb woodland garden where many of the plants were grown from seed collected by Mrs Mattingley's father during the Ludlow/Sherriff expedition to Bhutan in 1948. Special treats are the carpets of bulbs, trilliums and meconopsis, a fine selection of Japanese acers, *Prunus serrula*, 500 different rhododendrons, *Cardiocrinum giganteum*, 6ft lysichitum and many fine specimen trees. The view over the Tay makes a fitting finale only a few yards from the car park, but best of all was the taste of the fallen walnut picked from beneath the tree!

CORSOCK HOUSE 28

Corsock, Castle Douglas, Dumfries & Galloway.
Mr M.L. Ingall

10m N of Castle Douglas on A712. Also signposted from A75 onto B794 • Best season: May • Parking • Refreshments • Toilet facilities • Dogs on lead • Open 26th May for charity and by arrangement • Entrance: £1, children 50p

A most attractive 20-acre woodland garden with exceptionally fine plantings both of trees (*Fagus sylvatica*, Wellingtonia, oak, Douglas fir, cercidiphyllum, acer) and of rhododendrons (*thomsonii*, *lacteum*, *loderi*, *prattii*, *sutchuenense*). The knowledgeable owner has contributed most imaginatively to the layout of the gardens over the last 20 years, creating glades, planting vistas of azaleas and personally building a temple and *trompe l'oeil* bridge which give the gardens a classical atmosphere. An impressive highlight is the large water garden, again cleverly laid out and with the water-edge plantings set off by a background of mature trees with good autumn colour.

CRARAE GLEN GARDEN ★ 29

Minard, by Inverary, Argyll, Strathclyde. Tel: (0546) 86614
Crarae Gardens Charitable Trust

1m from Minard on A83 • Best season: spring and autumn • Parking • Refreshments: teas and coffee • Toilet facilities • Suitable for wheelchairs • Dogs on short lead • Plants for sale • Shop • Open daily, summer, 9 a.m. – 6 p.m., winter, daylight hours • Entrance: £1.70, children 70p, wheelchairs free

The gardens were originally started by the present owner's grandmother, Grace Campbell, in the early part of this century. Inspired by her great nephew, Reginald Farrer, a famous traveller and plant collector, she and subsequently her son, George Campbell (1894–1967), spent many years creating this superb 'Himalayan ravine' set in a Highland glen. Using surplus seed from the great plant expeditions, numerous gifts from knowledgeable friends and the shared expertise of a network of famous horticulturalists, they planted a variety of rare trees which were Sir George's first love, exotic shrubs and species rhododendrons which now form great canopies above the winding paths. These, together with many other plants from the temperate world make a magnificent spectacle of colour and differing perspectives, the whole enlivened by splendid torrents and waterfalls. The autumn colouring of sorbus, acers, liriodendrons, prunus, cotoneasters and berberis is one of the great features of the garden.

CRATHES CASTLE GARDEN ★★ 30

Crathes Castle, Banchory, Grampian. Tel: (033044) 651
National Trust for Scotland

3m E of Banchory and 15m W of Aberdeen on A93 • Parking 200 yards from gardens, signposted • Refreshments: licensed restaurant • Toilet facilities • Suitable for wheelchairs • No dogs in garden, but nature/dog trail in grounds • Plants for sale • National Trust Shop • House open 29th March to Oct, daily, 11 a.m. - 6 p.m. • Garden open, daily, 9.30 a.m. - dusk • Entrance: £1.20, children 60p (house and garden £3.30, children £1.70)

The first view of Crathes is breath-taking - a romantic castle set in flowing lawns. The building looks much as it did in the mid-sixteenth century but there is no record of how the garden then looked, although the yew topiary of 1702 survives. Sir James Burnett, who came here in 1926, was a keen collector and his wife was an inspired herbaceous planter, and the garden today is their achievement. In all there are eight gardens each reflecting a different theme. Rare shrubs reflect Burnett's interest in the Far East where he served in the army. Splendid wide herbaceous borders with clever plant associations are Lady Burnett's heritage, most famous of which is the white border. There are many specialist areas such as the trough garden and a collection of grasses; the large greenhouses contain a unique collection of carnations. Extensive wild gardens and grounds with picnic areas, with 15 miles of marked trails. Often compared to Hidcote but with evident inspiration from Jekyll, Crathes has wonders for the plantsperson, the designer and the ordinary visitor.

CRUICKSHANK BOTANIC GARDEN 31

St Machar Drive, Old Aberdeen, Grampian. Tel: (0224) 272704
The Cruickshank Trust and University of Aberdeen

1½m N from city centre in Old Aberdeen on A978. Public entry by gate in the Chanonry • Best season: May to Aug • Suitable for wheelchairs • Dogs on lead • Open all year, Mon - Fri, 9 a.m. - 4.30 p.m., May to Sept, Sat and Sun, 2 - 5 p.m. • Entrance: free. Children must be accompanied by an adult

Endowed by Miss Anne H. Cruickshank in 1898 to cater for teaching and research in botany at the University of Aberdeen and for the public good, the original six acres were designed by George Nicholson of Kew. That layout disappeared with World War I tree and shrub plantings. The long wall, herbaceous border and sunken garden date from 1920 but much reverted to vegetable cultivation during World War II. In 1970, the garden was extended and a new rock garden made. A terrace garden was added by the long wall in 1980, a new rose garden in 1986 and the peat walls restored in 1988. The rock garden with a series of connecting pools has interesting alpines, bulbs and dwarf shrubs. A small woodland area is rich in meconopsis, primulas, rhododendrons and hellebores. Proximity to the North Sea does not permit good growth of large conifers with the exception of dawn redwood and *Pinus radiata*. There are fine species lilacs, witch hazels and the long wall shelters more tender exotics. The total area of the present garden is 11 acres, of which 4 acres are planted as an arboretum - this is reached by a path from the summit of the rock gardens.

DALMENY PARK 32

Mons Hill, South Queensferry, Lothian. Tel: (031) 3311784
The Earl of Roseberry

Between South Queensferry and Edinburgh. 7m from the city centre along the Firth of Forth • Parking • Teas • Open May to Sept, Sun - Thurs, 2 - 5 p.m. • Entrance: 60p, children under 14 free. Grounds free

Dalmeny's greatest feature is the Gothic house and its exceptionally fine collections. The gardens are all but gone, though the extensive grounds are heavily planted with good mature trees. Dalmeny is mentioned for one reason - its superb snowdrop wood. Open for charity two Sundays in March, the snowdrop wood must be seen to be believed. Five acres of beech woods atop a hill overlooking the Firth of Forth are drifted with countless wild snowdrops. The views back to Edinburgh are particularly lovely. This is undoubtedly one of Britain's best snowdrop woods; an unforgettable spectacle.

DAWYCK BOTANIC GARDEN 33

Stobo, Peebleshire, Borders. Tel: (07216) 254
Royal Botanic Garden, Edinburgh

8m SW of Peebles, 28m from Edinburgh on B712 • Best season: spring and autumn • Parking • Partly suitable for wheelchairs • Guide dogs only • Open 15th March to 22nd Oct, 10 a.m. - 6 p.m. and at other times by arrangement • Entrance: £1, concessions and children 50p. Special discounts for groups. Season tickets covering Dawyck, Logan and Younger available - telephone Royal Botanic Garden (031) 552 7171

This is a specialist garden of the Royal Botanic Garden, Edinburgh, the home of the famous Dawyck beech; the garden has a large variety of interesting mature trees. These provide an impressive backcloth for many species of flowering shrubs, especially in the spring. There are pleasant woodland walks rich in wildlife interest.

DRUMMOND CASTLE ★★ 34

Muthill, Nr Crieff, Perthshire, Tayside. Tel: (076481) 321
Grimsthorpe and Drummond Castle Trust Ltd

2m S of Crieff on A822 • Best season: June and July • Parking 300 yards past main entrance • Toilet facilities • Partly suitable for wheelchairs • Open April to Oct, Wed and Sun, 2 - 5 p.m. • Entrance: £1.20, concessions 60p

The gardens to this fine castle were first laid out in 1630 by John Drummond, 2nd Earl of Perth. Next to the castle, across a courtyard, is the house and below both is the great parterre garden with, at its centre, the famous sundial made by the master mason to Charles 1. When the garden was revived by Lewis Kennedy, who worked at Drummond from 1818 to 1860, he achieved what the *Oxford Companion* calls 'effectively the re-creation of an idea of the seventeenth-century Scottish garden'. The long St Andrew's cross design has Italian, French and Dutch influences. Beautiful white marble Italian statuary is set in arbours along the southern borders, giving an overall sense of tranquillity and order. The *Oxford Companion* believes that the old arrangement of filling the 'compartments' of the cross with shrubs and herbaceous plants was more effective than today's style in which some may feel the structure is too prominent. The fruit and vegetable gardens and glasshouses should also be visited.

DUNDONNELL 35

By Garve, Ross-shire, Highlands. Tel: (085483) 206
Mr A.S. Roger and Mr N. Roger

24m from Ullapool, 31m from Garve off A832 between Braemore Toll and Gruinard Bay • Parking • Teas • Toilet facilities • Partly suitable for wheelchairs • Plants for sale • Open for charity 5th, 13th June, 11th July, 28th Aug, 2 - 5.30 p.m. • Entrance: £1.50, children 50p

Unlike many of the gardens of Scotland's west coast Dundonnell does not rely on rhododendrons for its effect. It is a very individual garden of grassed walks, box-edged paths, enclosures made by borders of varying sizes all within a garden walled on three sides with the fourth side bounded by the river. Very old yew and holly trees are striking and there are also many exotic trees and shrubs - *Stewartia* species, *Acer palmatum* 'Senkaki', *Quercus pontica*, species hydrangeas, *Decaisnea fargesii* and the bamboo *Chusquea*. The laburnum tunnel is as unexpected as the extensive collection of bonsai, many of considerable size, grown in a slatted house. This is a very tranquil garden to be appreciated at a leisurely pace - even the heavy rainfall will not detract from its charm.

DUNROBIN GARDENS ★ 36

Golspie, Sutherland, Highlands. Tel: (04083) 3177/3266
The Sutherland Trust

1m N of Golspie on A9 • Parking • Toilet facilities • Shop • House open • Garden open May, Mon - Thurs, 10.30 a.m. - 12.30 p.m., June to Sept, Mon - Sat, 10.30 a.m. - 5.30 p.m., Sun, 1 - 5.30 p.m. • Entrance: £2.80, children £1.40, family £6.50, groups £2.50 per person, children £1.25

These Victorian formal gardens were designed in the grand French style to echo the architecture of Dunrobin Castle which rises high above them and looks out over the Moray Firth. They were laid out by the architect Charles Barry, in 1850, when there was a staff of 40 gardeners. There is a staff of only four gardeners now. Descending the stone terraces, one can see the round garden (evocative of the Scottish shield, the head gardener suggests), rose beds, grove, parterre and herbaceous borders laid out beneath. The round ponds, some with fountains, are a particular feature, together with the wrought-iron Westminster gates. The garden is under development - a rhododendron and fern bank has been planted, and other features are planned, within the limitations of a south-east facing site on sandy soil. In the policies (estate lands) there are many woodland walks. An eighteenth-century summerhouse which was converted into a museum in the nineteenth century is now also open to the public.

EARLSHALL CASTLE ★ 37

Leuchars, Fife. Tel: (033483) 205
Major and Mrs D.R. Baxter, Baron and Baroness of Earlshall

Follow signs from centre of Leuchars, A919 • Best season: July and Aug • Parking free • Refreshments • Suitable for wheelchairs in garden • Guide dogs only • Plants for sale occasioanlly • Shop • House open as gardens • Open Good Friday, Easter Sat, Sun and Mon, June to 3rd Sun in Sept, daily except Tues, 2 - 6 p.m. Parties by appointment • Entrance: £2.50, OAP £2, children £1

A walled garden situated beside the restored sixteenth-century castle divided by yew hedges into a series of external 'rooms'. The most significant of these contains topiary 'chessmen' (although some visitors maintain that they are 'abstracts'), and there is also a secret garden, orchard garden, herbaceous border and 'bowling green' with rose terrace, and an attractively laid-out kitchen garden. Interesting garden architecture includes a gardener's cottage, dowry house, summerhouse and arbour, all bearing the stamp of Sir Robert Lorimer's eye for detail. Lorimer, famous for Kellie Castle (see entry) believed in gardens as a place of repose and solitude, formal near the house but becoming 'less trim as it gets further ... and then naturally marries with the demesne that lies beyond'. Altogether, a most delightful retreat from the world outside.

EDZELL CASTLE ★ 38

Edzell, Nr Brechin, Angus, Tayside. Tel: (031) 556840
Department of the Environment

4m N of Brechin. Take A94 and after 2m fork left on B966 • Parking • Toilet facilities • Suitable for wheelchairs • Dogs • Ruins • Open April to Sept, Mon - Sat, 9.30 a.m. - 7 p.m., Sun, 2 - 7 p.m., Oct to March, Mon - Sat, 9.30 a.m. - 4 p.m., Sun, 2 - 4 p.m. • Entrance: £1, OAP and children 50p. Reduced rates for parties

In 1604 Sir David Lindsay made a remarkable small walled garden at his fortress at Edzell; it remains today probably the oldest complete and unaltered garden in the country. By the time they came into the custody of H.M. Office of Works in 1932, the garden and castle had lain in ruins for over 150 years. Although the plantings are new, dating from the 1930s, they are elaborate examples in the manner of the period of the early seventeenth century. Meticulously-kept parterres of box, lawn, and bedding are contained within walls of unique and curious design. There are 43 panels of alternating chequered niches and sculptured symbolic figures. There are large recesses below for bee skeps. The whole is laid out to be viewed from a corner garden-house and the windows of the now-ruined castle. The village of Edzel is quite small and a charming example of an ordered Victorian Scottish highland village. There are shops, a tea room and a small hotel. A must for lovers of the historical and romantic. The pleasaunce is probably unique in its historical context, but the modern plantings make it a disappointing experience in some respects.

FALKLAND PALACE GARDEN 39

Falkland, Fife. Tel: (0337) 57397
National Trust for Scotland

11m N of Kirkcaldy via A912 • Parking 100 yards from palace • Refreshments in village • Toilet facilities • Suitable for wheelchairs • National Trust shop • House and garden open 29th March to Oct, Mon - Sat, 10 a.m. - 6 p.m., Sun, 2 - 6 p.m. (Last tour of palace 5 p.m.) • Entrance: £1.80, children 90p (palace and garden, £2.80, children £1.40)

This was originally the kitchen garden for the sixteenth-century palace where Mary Queen of Scots played as a girl. In World War II it became a forest nursery but was remodelled soon afterwards. The Palace itself lends a gracious and dignified atmosphere to this seven-acre garden as the visitor strolls round the rose garden and admires the herbaceous borders. The shrub island borders are now fully mature and provide a good illustration of how to break up large areas of lawn if that is what you want. In addition, visitors may gain admission from the garden to the royal tennis court (i.e. real tennis) where occasional competitions of this old game are still staged. Features include an outdoor chequers game in the herb garden. Interesting village houses nearby.

FINLAYSTONE 40

Langbank, Renfrewshire, Strathclyde. Tel: (047554) 285
Mr George Gordon Macmillan of Macmillan

On A8 20m from Glasgow, follow large signpost W of Langbank • Best season: spring and autumn • Parking • Refreshments • Toilet facilities • Suitable for wheelchairs • Dogs on lead (off lead in woodland) • Shop open at weekends • House open, April to Aug, Sun, 2.30 - 4.30 p.m. • Garden Open all year, daily, 11 a.m. - 5 p.m. • Entrance: £1, children 60p

Designed, enhanced and tended over the last 50 years by Lady Macmillan, much respected doyenne of Scottish gardens and her family, this spacious garden is imaginatively laid out over 10 acres with a further 70 acres of mature woodland walks. Large, elegant lawns framed by long herbaceous borders, interesting shrubberies and mature copper beech look down over the River Clyde. John Knox's tree, a Celtic paving 'maze' laid out by Lady Macmillan's daughter-in-law Jane, paved fragrant garden with the handicapped in mind and a new bog garden are all added attractions.

GEILSTON HOUSE 41

Nr Cardross, Dunbartonshire, Strathclyde. Tel: (0389) 841467
Miss M.E. Bell

1m W of Cardross on A814 • Best season: May, Oct • Parking • Teas on open day • Suitable for wheelchairs • Plants for sale • Open 25th May for charity, 2 - 5.30 p.m. Other times by appointment • Entrance: 75p, children 25p

A well-maintained walled garden with herbaceous borders and a heather garden which contains about ninety different varieties. Adjoining this garden is a small woodland 'glen garden' where rare and unusual shrubs, trees, rhododendrons and azaleas flourish on the banks of a small burn in picturesque surroundings. The autumn colour is also worth experiencing.

GLASGOW BOTANICAL GARDEN 42

Great Western Road, Glasgow, Strathclyde. Tel: (041) 3342422
Glasgow Corporation

In the centre of Glasgow, corner of Great Western Road and Queen Margaret Drive • Parking outside • Toilet facilities • Suitable for wheelchairs • Dogs on lead • Open daily, 7 a.m. - dusk • Entrance: free

A pleasant afternoon's walk, but disappointing from a horticultural point of view. A few shiny bedding displays do not disguise the fact that apart from a nice herbaceous border the 40 acres of trees, shrubs, herb and teaching gardens are sometimes uninspired, although it has to be said that others have found the gardens inspiring and imaginatively planted. One of the uplifting sights is the rusting old Kibble Palace glasshouse of 1873 where statues peer through temperate-zone plants set in yards of bare, carefully hoed earth. Neighbouring glasshouses offer a comprehensive, if pedestrianly displayed, selection of foliage plants and National collections of orchids and begonias which must be lovely in season.

GLENARN 43

Rhu, Dunbartonshire, Strathclyde. Tel: (0436820) 493
Michael and Sue Thornley

On A814 between Helensburgh and Garelochhead. Go up Pier Road to Glenarn Road • Parking • Refreshments on special open days only • Toilet facilities • Dogs on lead • A few plants for sale • Open 21st March to 21st June, dawn to dusk • Entrance: £1

Established in the 1930s in a Victorian garden by the Gibson family and fed by the famous plant expeditions of that decade, this is a very special woodland garden. Well-kept paths meander round a 10-acre sheltered bowl, sometimes tunnelling under superb giant species rhododendrons (including a *falconeri* grown from Hooker's original seed in 1849), sometimes allowing a glorious vista across the garden to the Clyde estuary, and sometimes stopping the visitor short to gaze with unstinted admiration at 40 foot magnolias, pieris, olearias, eucryphias and hoherias. Michael and Sue Thornley, both professional architects, acquired Glenarn some years ago and with almost no help are successfully replanting and restoring where necessary, whilst still retaining the special atmosphere created by such magnificent growth. An especially pleasing finale is provided by winding down through a nook-and-cranny, granny garden - sadly and inappropriately not suitable for those who find walking very difficult.

GLENBERVIE 44

By Drumlithie, Stonehaven, Kincardineshire, Grampian.
Tel: (05694) 226
Mr and Mrs C.S. MacPhie

8m from Laurencekirk, 6m from Stonehaven off A94 Laurencekirk to Stonehaven road. On a minor road 3m W of Drumlithie village • Parking • Partly suitable for wheelchairs • Open 4th Aug, 2 - 5 p.m. for charity • Entrance: £1

Two very different gardens may be enjoyed at Glenbervie - a traditional Scottish walled garden on a slope and a woodland garden by a stream. Occupying one wall of the enclosed garden is a fine example of a Victorian conservatory with a great diversity of pot plants and climbers on the walls creating a spectacular display. Elsewhere in the walled area is a typical mix of herbaceous plants, fruit, vegetables and summer bedding. There are many shrub and old roses, and on wells and pillars many climbing and rambler roses. In spring there are good displays of bulbs. The woodland garden with its drifts of primulas, ferns and interesting shrubs is beautiful in early summer. There are fine trees near the house.

GLENDOICK GARDENS LTD 45

Glencarse, By Perth, Tayside.
Tel: Nursery (073886) 205; Garden centre (073886) 260
Mr and Mrs Peter Cox

8m from Perth, 11m from Dundee on A85 • Parking in grounds • Toilet facilities • Suitable for wheelchairs • Garden centre open all year at the main road • Open May, Sun, 2 - 5 p.m. and by appointment • Entrance: £1.50

One of the world's most comprehensive collections of rhododendrons is contained within the grounds of this fine Georgian mansion which has an association with Bonnie Prince Charlie who is reputed to have visited the Laird of Glendoick one dark night in 1745. The plant collection was assembled by the late Euan H.M. Cox and has been added to and continued by the present owners.

GREENBANK GARDEN ★ 46

Nr Clarkston Toll, Glasgow, Strathclyde. Tel: (041639) 3281
National Trust for Scotland

Take A726 to Clarkston, turn off opposite railway station, follow signs • Best seasons: spring and summer • Parking • Refreshments • Toilet facilities • Suitable for wheelchairs • Dogs on lead, but not in walled garden • Plants for sale • Shop • Open all year, 9.30 a.m. - sunset except 25th, 26th Dec and 1st, 2nd Jan 1992. Entrance £1.40, children 70p

Large old walled garden of eighteenth-century house divided into many sections, all of which are imaginatively planted. The colour combinations are especially good. All the plants are in very good condition and admirably labelled. An old hard tennis court in the corner has been converted into a spacious and pleasant area for the disabled, with raised beds and a waist-high running water pond. Wheelchair access to the glasshouse and potting shed allows disabled people to attend classes and work here. Woodland walks are filled with spring bulbs and shrubs and there are usually Highland cattle in the paddock.

HILL OF TARVIT 47

Cupar, Fife. Tel: (0334) 53127
National Trust for Scotland

2½m S of Cupar off A916 • Parking • Refreshments and picnic area • Toilet facilities • Partly suitable for wheelchairs • Plants for sale • Shop • House open 29th March to 1st April, 2 - 6 p.m., 6th to 28th April, Sat and Sun, 2 - 6 p.m., May to Oct, daily, 2 - 6 p.m. • Garden open daily, 10 a.m. - sunset • Entrance: £1, children 50p

The garden surrounds the charming Edwardian mansion designed in 1906 for a jute magnate by Sir Robert Lorimer who also laid out the grounds. There is a lovely rose garden and delightful woodland walk to a toposcope. Good size borders are filled with an attractive variety of perennials, annuals and heaths, and the grounds as a whole contain many unusual ornamental trees and shrubs now reaching maturity. The views over Fife are particularly fine. The garden is maintained by the National Trust which regularly upgrades the plantings to include newer and unusual specimens. A good garden for amateurs and keen plantspersons alike.

HOUSE OF PITMUIES 48

Guthrie, by Forfar, Tayside. Tel: (02412) 245
Mrs Farquhar Ogilvie

1½m from Friockheim, route A932 • Best season: June and July • Parking • Refreshments: at Star Inn in nearby village of Friockheim • Toilet facilities • Partly suitable for wheelchairs • Dogs on lead • Plants and soft fruit for sale in season • House open for parties by appointment • Gardens open daily, April to Oct, 2 - 5 p.m. and at other times by appointment • Entrance: £1 by collection box

In the grounds of an attractive eighteenth-century house and courtyard, these beautiful walled gardens lead down towards a small river with an informal riverside walk and two unusual buildings, a turreted dovecote and a Gothic wash-house. There are rhododendron glades with other unusual trees and shrubs, but pride of place must go to the spectacular semi-formal gardens behind the house. Exquisite old-fashioned roses and a series of long borders containing a dramatic palette of massed delphiniums and other herbaceous perennials in July constitute one of the most memorable displays of its type to be found in Scotland.

HOUSE OF TONGUE ★ 49

Tongue, By Lairg, Sutherland, Highlands. Tel: (084755) 209
Countess of Sutherland

1m N of Tongue off A838 • Parking • Open for charity 3rd Aug, 2 - 6 p.m. and by appointment • Entrance: £1, children 50p

Sheltered from wind and salt by tall trees, this walled garden is a haven in an otherwise exposed environment. Adjoining the seventeenth-century house, it is laid-out after the traditional Scottish acre with gravel and grass walks between herbaceous beds and hedged vegetable plots and orchard. A stepped beech-hedged walk leads up to a high terrace which commands a fine view over the Kyle of Tongue. The centrepiece of the garden is Lord Reay's sundial (1714) - a sculpted obelisk of unusual design.

INVERESK LODGE AND VILLAGE 50

Nr Musselburgh, East Lothian, Lothian. Tel: (031) 2265922
Various owners inc. National Trust for Scotland (Lodge)

6m E of Edinburgh, S of Musselburgh via A6124 • Best season: summer • Parking • Lodge open as gardens • Open all year, Mon – Fri, 10 a.m. – 4.30 p.m., Sun, 2 – 5 p.m. • Entrance: 50p, children 25p, honesty box

This large seventeenth-century house in the village of Inveresk, now owned by the National Trust for Scotland, is situated on a steeply sloping site. The high stone retaining walls are well-planted with a wide range of climbers. There are numerous flower beds; a particularly good border is devoted to shrub roses. A peat bed permits a greater diversity of planting. The garden has been completely remade since it came under the ownership of the National Trust for Scotland. No attempt has been made to recreate a period style. The garden is 'modern' in most respects, semi-formal, well planted, very well-maintained and offers a wide selection of plants flowering from spring through autumn. The village itself is a unique, unspoilt example of eighteenth-century villa development with houses dating from the late seventeenth and early eighteenth centuries. All have well laid-out gardens enclosed by high walls and containing a wide range of shrubs and trees as well as some unusual plants. Open one day for charity by admission ticket to cover all gardens. Plant stalls and teas.

INVEREWE GARDEN ★★ 51

Poolewe, Ross and Cromarty, Highlands. Tel: (044586) 356
National Trust for Scotland

6m NE of Gairlock on A832 • Parking • Restaurant 29th Mar to 20th Oct • Toilet facilities • Partly suitable for wheelchairs • Plants for sale • Shop and Visitor Centre • Open all year, daily, 9.30 a.m. – sunset • Entrance: £2.50, children £1.25, adult parties £2, schools £1

This garden is spectacular. Created in 1865 on the shores of the sea loch, Loch Ewe, it covers the entire Am Ploc Ard peninsular. Planned as a wild garden around one dwarf willow on peat and sandstone, it has been developed as a series of walks through herbaceous and rock gardens, wet valley, a rhododendron walk and a curved vegetable garden and orchard. This is a plantsman's garden (labelling is discreet) containing many sub-tropical species from Australia, New Zealand, China and the Americas, sheltered by mature beech, oak and pine trees. New Zealand alpines include the National collection of the genus *Ourisia* (1986). The garden is well-tended and way-marked. The gales of 1989 resulted in the loss of 80 specimen trees. Note: midge repellent is essential and on sale at main desk!

KAILZIE GARDENS 52

Peebles, Peebleshire, Borders. Tel: (0721) 20007
Mrs M.A. Richard

2½m from Peebles on B7062 • Parking • Tea room and restaurant • Toilet facilities • Suitable for wheelchairs • Dogs on lead • Plants for sale when available • Shop • Open April to Oct, 11 a.m. - 5.30 p.m. • Entrance: £1, children 50p

'A Pleasure Garden' is the description in one of the advertisements for Kailzie (pronounced Kailie) and very apt it is too. The gardens of 17 acres are situated in a particularly attractive area of the beautiful Tweed Valley and are surrounded by breath-taking views. The Old Mansion Home was pulled down in 1962 and the vast walled garden, which still houses the magnificent greenhouse, was transformed by Angela Richard, from vegetables to a garden of meandering lawns and island beds. Full of interesting shrubs and plants for drying, there are many surprises including a herb garden, choice flower area, secret gardens, loving seats invitingly placed under garlanded arbours and several pieces of statuary which have been thoughtfully placed. A magnificent fountain at the end of the herbaceous borders leads on to woods and huge stately trees, and from here you may stroll down the Major's walk which is lined with laburnum and underplanted with rhododendrons, azaleas, blue poppies and primulas. From here you can go to the small waterfowl lake.

KELLIE CASTLE 53

Pittenweem, Fife. Tel: (03338) 271
National Trust for Scotland

3m NNW of Pittenweem on B9171 • Best season: summer • Parking, 100 yards, closer parking for disabled • Refreshments in castle • Toilet facilities, not for disabled • Partly suitable for wheelchairs • Shop • House open, 29th March to 1st April, 2 - 6 p.m., 6th to 28th April, Sat and Sun, 2 - 6 p.m., May to Oct, daily, 2 - 6 p.m. (last tour 5.30 p.m.). Garden and grounds, all year, daily 10 a.m. - sunset • Entrance: £1.25, children 50p (castle and garden £2.50, children £1.25)

The garden has no particular relationship to the sixteenth-century house, having been restored by Professor James Lorimer in early Victorian times. Entered by a door in a high wall, the garden is small (one acre) and inspires dreams within every gardener's reach. Simple borders, such as one of catmint only, capture the imagination as hundreds of bees and butterflies work the flowers. Areas of lawn are edged with box hedges, borders, arches and trellises. In one corner, behind a trellis, is a small romantic garden within a garden. A large, white-painted commemorative seat designed by Huw Lorimer provides outstanding focal interest at the end of one of the main walks. The recently-appointed head gardener is establishing a collection of old and unusual vegetable varieties and employing only organic gardening methods, putting heart back into the soil through liberal use of compost. Roses on trellis and on arches abound.

KILBRYDE CASTLE 54

Dunblane, Perthshire, Central. Tel: (0786) 823104
Sir Colin Campbell

Off A820 Dunblane - Doune road • Best season: April to July • Parking • Partly suitable for wheelchairs • Open 31st March, 28th April, 26th May, 30th June, 21st July, 11th Aug, 22nd Sept, 2 - 6 p.m. for charity and also by appointment • Entrance: £1

A good example of a partly-mature 20-acre garden created over the last 10 years by the enthusiastic owner and his highly knowledgeable helper, who are constantly introducing new features and plant content. Imaginatively-placed borders filled with constant colour on wide lawns sloping down to a woodland water garden.

KILDRUMMY CASTLE GARDENS ★ 55

Nr Alford, Aberdeen, Grampian. Tel: (09755) 71264 and 71277
Kildrummy Castle Garden Trust

2m from Mossat, 10m from Alford, 17m from Huntly. Take A944 from Alford, following signs to Kildrummy, left on A97 • Parking: car park free inside hotel main entrance. Coach park up hotel delivery entrance • Toilet facilities • Suitable for wheelchairs • Dogs on lead • Plants for sale • Kildrummy Castle Hotel open, 09755 71288 for reservations • Visitor centre and video room • Woodland walks, children's play area • Open April to Oct, daily, 10 a.m. - 5 p.m. • Entrance: £1, children 9 - 16 50p, 3 - 8 20p

The gardens are set in a deep valley between the ruins of a thirteenth-century castle and a Tudor-style house, now a hotel. The rock garden, by Backhouse of York (1904) occupies the site of the quarry which provided the stone for the castle. The narrowest part of the ravine is traversed by a copy of the fourteenth-century Auld Brig O'Balgownie, Old Aberdeen built by Col. Ogston in 1900. This provides both an excellent viewpoint for the whole garden and also a focus for the water garden commissioned from a firm of Japanese landscape gardeners at the same period. The reflections in the still water of the larger pools increase the impact of the luxurious plantings of *Lysichiton americanum*, primulas, a notable *Schizophragma hydrangeoides*; there are fine maples, rhododendron species and hybrids, oaks and conifers. Although a severe frost pocket, the garden can grow embothriums, dieramas and other choice plants. A garden for all seasons, but especially beautiful in autumn.

LANGWELL 56

Berriedale, Caithness, Highlands. Tel: (059352) 237
Lady Anne Bentinck

2m from Berriedale on the A9 Helmsdale to Wick road • Best season: July to Aug • Parking • Teas on charity open days • Partly suitable for wheelchairs • Plants for sale in adjacent nursery • Open 11th, 18th Aug, 2 - 5.30 p.m. • Entrance: £1

The bare landscape of Caithness does not support too many gardens of interest, but here in the shelter of the Langwell Water is one of the happy exceptions. Reached by a two-mile drive through mature woodland this old walled garden provides the shelter necessary to grow a good range of plants. A map of 1877 already shows a formal plan but the present-day cruciform layout, centred on a sundial, dates from 1916 when it was made by John Murray. An old yew arch dates perhaps from the early 1800s. Murray's hedges of thuya have had to be removed recently but new hedges have been planted. The main area is kept in the old tradition of a mixture of flower borders, fruit and vegetables and there is a small rockery area. At the bottom end is a formal pool surrounded by yew hedging and hidden to one side a small pool filled with water soldiers, *Stratiotes aloides.*

LAWHEAD CROFT 57

Tarbrax, Lanarkshire, Lothian. Tel: (050185) 274
Sue and Hector Riddell

12m from Balerno, 6m from Carnwath on A70 • Best season: summer • Parking • Refreshments on open days • Toilet facilities • Mostly suitable for wheelchairs • Dogs on lead • Open for parties by appointment only • Entrance: £1

Nearly 1000 ft up in the midst of the bleak Lanarkshire moors, Sue and Hector Riddell have planted shelter belts and laboriously carved out a luxuriant garden. Grass walks lead from one interesting border to another, all full of unusual plants. Colour associations and leaf contrasts are carefully thought out. There is an enchanting series of garden rooms all with a different theme. A garden of great ideas including an excellent bonsai collection. Recently most of the vegetable garden has been swept away and replanted in a great sweep of curved, tiered and circular beds of spectacular and original design.

LECHMELM SHRUBBERY AND ARBORETUM 58

Little Leckmelm House, Lochbroom, by Garve, Ross-shire, Highlands. Tel: (0854) 2377
Sir Charles and Lady Troughton

4m E of Ullapool on A835 • Best season: April/May • Open daily, 10 a.m. - 5 p.m. • Entrance: £1, OAP and children 50p

Planted in about 1870, this was derelict for 50 years until reclamation started in 1984 by the present owners. A 10-acre woodland garden with many fine examples of species rhododendron. There are many different pine and cypress trees, now mature, a huge eucalyptus and a magnificent weeping beech. It remains a simple quiet woodland garden, well worth a visit.

LEITH HALL ★ 59

Kennethmont, by Huntly, Aberdeen, Grampian. Tel: (0224) 572215
National Trust for Scotland

1m W of Kennethmont on B9002 and 34m NW of Aberdeen • Parking • Refreshments: picnic area and teas on charity open days • Toilet facilities • Dogs • Stalls on charity open days • House open inc. exhibition: May to Sept, 2 - 6 p.m. (last tour 5.15 p.m.) £2.80, children £1.40, parties £1.60, schools 80p • Garden open all year, daily, 9.30 a.m. - sunset • Entrance: by donation

Since it came into the care of the National Trust for Scotland, the gardens of Leith Hall have been expanded and upgraded. But it is the old garden, remote from the house, that offers the greatest pleasure to the garden enthusiast. This old garden comprises large borders and a large, well-stocked rock garden. The design is simple, romantic and allows a tremendous display of flowers during the whole of summer and early autumn. Especially fine is the magenta *Geranium psilostemon* and a border of solid catmint running from top to bottom of the garden. There are no lawns or open courtyards and no dominating architecture, just massive plantings of perennials and the odd rarity amongst the rocks. The extensive policies offer woodland walks, views and excellent opportunities for birdwatching around the lake.

LITTLE SPARTA ★★ 60

Dunsyre, Nr Lanark, Lanarkshire, Strathclyde.
Mr Ian Hamilton-Finlay

Turn off A721 at Newbigging for Dunsyre. 1m W of Dunsyre is an unmarked very rough farm track up to Little Sparta • Best season: June • Parking • Guide dogs for the blind only • Open by appointment in writing (SAE please) • Entrance: free

A clue as to what is hidden in Ian Hamilton-Finlay's totally unexpected garden is given on arrival at the gate to the property, where a beautifully-carved quotation from Heraclitus greets you. Hamilton-Finlay believes that a garden should appeal to all the senses and particularly should provoke thought, both serious and trivial, and he has therefore revived the art of emblematic gardening which died out in Britain in the seventeenth century. He achieved an international reputation in the process. It is impossible to describe Little Sparta briefly, except to say that he has transformed a sizeable hill farmstead (starting in 1966 with the idea of establishing a testing-ground for his sculptures) into a garden full of images, allusions and symbols. Not all are easily understood or interpreted, which doesn't matter as this is a garden not a crossword puzzle. However, before visiting Little Sparta it may help to read one of the many articles written about it – for example in the King and Rose book *Gardening with Style*.

LOCHALSH WOODLAND GARDEN (Balmacara Estate) ★ 61

Balmacara, Highlands. Tel: (059986) 207
National Trust for Scotland

1m E of Kyle of Lochalsh off A87 • Best season: spring • Parking (½m walk to garden) • Partly suitable for wheelchairs • Open all year, daily, 9 a.m. to sunset • Entrance: £1, children 50p

The garden is approached down the wooded road to the village of Glaick on the lochside and from there, across the water, rise the magnificent mountains of Skye. Woodland planting on this steep-sided, six and a half-acre site was begun in 1887 around Lochalsh House, and the canopy of beeches, larches, oaks and pines is now outstanding. Garden planting was started in 1979 with rhododendrons and shrubs from Tasmania, New Zealand, the Himalayas, China and Japan. Paths created through the woods give a choice of walks, both in terms of gradient and length. Beside these and in glades, fallen branches have been used to build curved, raised beds for the new plantings, which include many primulas and ferns, all of which are labelled. The Coach House Visitor Centre contains interpretive displays on rural industry, geology, and shore, woodland and moorland wildlife. The concept of the woodland garden is in some ways peculiar to the West Highlands because it is one way of creating a micro-climate in which a garden may prosper. Inverewe (see entry) is another excellent example.

LOGAN BOTANIC GARDEN AND LOGAN HOUSE ★★ 62

Port Logan, by Stranraer, Dumfries & Galloway. Tel: (077686) 231
Royal Botanic Gardens, Edinburgh/Sir Ninian Buchan-Hepburn, Bt.

On B7065 ½m S of junction with A716 • Best season: spring • Parking • Teas • Toilet facilities • Suitable for wheelchairs • Open daily, 15th March to Oct, 10 a.m. – 6 p.m. and at other times by arrangement • Entrance: £1.50, concessions £1, children 50p. Special discounts for groups. Season tickets covering Dawyck, Logan and Younger available - telephone Royal Botanic Garden (031) 552 7171

Logan is a fascinating sub-tropical garden situated on the southernmost tip of Scotland - the Rhinns of Galloway. The exceptionally mild climate allowed the creation of a formal garden in the Mediterranean style. The garden was originally started in 1860 by Mrs James McDouall, a great aunt of the present owner, and continued by her two sons, Kenneth and Douglas. It was through their plant collecting abroad and dedication to beauty that this unique garden was created. In 1970 the garden was divided and the walled section was named Logan Botanic Garden, as an annexe to the Royal Botanic Gardens in Edinburgh. The old original and greater part of the garden belongs to Logan House. Now, under the care of The Royal Botanic Gardens Edinburgh, Logan is a fascinating collection of rare and unusual sub-tropical plants. Chusan palms (*Trachycarpus fortunei*), tree ferns (*Cyathea dealbata*), cabbage palms (*Cordyline australis*), and a large number of Australian and New Zealand plants are mixed with hardier temperate plants to give a unique air to this superb garden. Ancient magnolias and meconopsis (Himalayan blue poppies) make a magnificent spring show. Throughout the summer season there are endless banks of flowers appearing along meandering walks that eventually lead to a formal pool filled with various water lilies - surrounded by tree ferns and vast cabbage palms. This garden is a must for the keen plantsman as many of Britain's finest specimens can be found here. The *Gunnera manicata* by the entrance attains a leaf size greater than anywhere else in Britain. Logan is certainly one of Great Britain's finest and most unusual gardens. Logan House garden is open for one day for charity. The fine Queen Anne house has a garden with rare exotic tropical plants and shrubs.

MALLENY HOUSE GARDENS 63

Bolerno, Midlothian, Lothian. Tel: (031449) 2283
National Trust for Scotland

In Balerno village, on A70 Edinburgh - Lanark road • Best seasons: summer and autumn • Parking • Suitable for wheelchairs • Open all year, 10 a.m. - dusk • Entrance: £1, OAP 50p (honesty box)

Aptly described as the National Trust for Scotland's secret garden, Malleny seems an old and valued friend soon after meeting and reflects the thoughtful planning by the head gardener. An impressive Atlantic cedar reigns over this relatively small garden assisted by a square of early seventeenth-century clipped yews and yew hedges. As well as containing the NCCPG collection of nineteenth-century shrub roses and a permanent display from the Scottish Bonsai Association, Malleny's 12ft wide herbaceous borders are superb as is the large glasshouse containing a continual display of flowering plants. Don't forget to admire the attractively laid-out herb and ornamental vegetable garden.

MANDERSTON ★ 64

Duns, Borders. Tel: (0361) 83450
The Lord Palmer

2m E of Duns on A6105 • Best season: early Aug, woodland garden May and June • Parking • Refreshments: tea room in grounds • Toilet facilities • Partly suitable for wheelchairs • Dogs on lead • Plants for sale • Shop • House open as for gardens • Gardens open early May to Sept, Sun and Thurs, end May and Aug Bank Holiday Mons or parties by appointment • Entrance: £3.30 house and garden

One of the last great classic houses to be built in Britain, Manderston was modelled on Robert Adams' Keddleston Hall in Derbyshire (see entry). It was described in 1905 as a 'charming mansion inexhaustible in its attractions' and this might equally well apply to the gardens which remain an impressive example of gardening on the grand scale. Four magnificently formal terraces planted in Edwardian style overlook a narrow serpentine lake and a chinoiserie bridging dam tempts one over to the woodland garden on the far side, thus elegantly effecting the transition from formal to informal. No expense was spared creating the gardens and this air of opulence and good quality is much evident in the formal walled gardens to the north of the house. They are a lasting tribute to the very best of the Edwardian era when 100 gardeners were employed to do what two now do to the same immaculately high standard. Gilded gates open on to a panorama of colourful planting on different levels, with fountains, statuary and a charming rose pergola all complementing each other. Even the greenhouses were given lavish treatment with the walls created from lumps of limestone to resemble an exotic planted grotto.

MELLERSTAIN ★★ 65

Gordon, Etterick, Borders. Tel: (057381) 292
The Earl of Haddington

Halfway between Galashiels and Coldstream. Turn S in Gordon on A6089 and turn W after 2m or turn off B6397 2m N of Smailholm • Parking • Teas • Toilet facilities • Suitable for wheelchairs • Charity gift shop and craft gallery • House open, 12.30 – 5 p.m. (last admission 4.30 p.m.) • Open May to Sept, daily, except Sat, 12.30 – 5 p.m. • Entrance: £1.50, children free (house and garden £3, OAP and parties £2.30 per person, children £1.50)

A bastion of formal garden layout with dignified terraces overlooking an 'arranged' landscape. The house of Mellerstain is a unique example of the work of the Adam family; both William and son, Robert, worked on the building. The garden is formal, comprised of very dignified terraces, ballustraded and 'lightly' planted with climbers and simple topiary. The great glory of the garden is the landscape complete with lake and woodlands in the style of Brown and Repton, but designed early this century by Sir Reginald Blomfield. The view of the Cheviot Hills from the terraces is one of the finest to be found in this lovely area of the Scottish Borders. Mellerstain is a must for lovers of the formal landscape.

MERTOUN 66

St Boswells, Roxburghshire, Borders. Tel: (0835) 23236
The Duke of Sutherland

2m NE of St Boswells on B6404 • Best season: spring and summer • Parking • Toilet facilities • Suitable for wheelchairs • Open April to Sept, Sat and Sun, 2 - 6 p.m. Also open Bank Holiday Mons • Entrance: £1, OAP and children 50p

Overlooking the Tweed and with Mertoun House in the background, this is a lovely garden to wander round and admire the mature specimen trees, azaleas, daffodils and a most attractive ornamental pond flanked by a good herbaceous border. The focal point is the immaculate three-acre walled garden which is everything a proper kitchen garden should be. Walking up from a 1567 dovecote, thought to be the oldest in the county, through a healthy orchard the visitor reaches the traditional box hedges, raised beds and glasshouses of the main area. Neat rows of vegetables, herbs and bright flowers for the house vie for attention with the pruning of the figs and peaches in the well-stocked glasshouses.

MONTEVIOT 67

Nr Jedburgh, Borders. Tel: (08353) 380
Earl and Countess of Ancram

Turn off A68 on B6400 to Nisbet. Entrance second turning on right • Best season: July and August • Parking free • Refreshments in Woodland centre, ½m from house • Toilet facilities • Partly suitable for wheelchairs • Dogs on lead • Plants for sale • Open for charity 23rd June, 2 - 5 p.m. • Entrance: £1, OAP 50p, children under 14 free

The river garden designed by Percy Cane in 1960s which runs down to the River Teviot is currently being restored with herbaceous perennials and shrubs. Beside it, the semi-enclosed terraced rose gardens overlooking the river below have a large collection of hybrid teas, floribundas and shrubs. Beside the house is an attractive formal herb garden. The pinetum is full of unusual trees reaching great heights, and nearby a water garden has recently been created, planted with unusual rhododendrons and azaleas. A circular route around the gardens is also planned. Fine views.

NETHERBYRES 68

Eyemouth, Berwickshire, Borders. Tel: (08907) 50337
Lieutenant-Colonel S.J. Furness

¼m from Eyemouth on A1107 • Best season: July, early Aug • Parking by house • Suitable for wheelchairs • Open occasionally April to Sept for small parties by appointment • Entrance: 70p, children 30p

Having lost its Victorian conservatory and vinery, the garden has perhaps lost a little of its charm, but is worth seeing for the unique elliptical wall and for the traditional mix of flowers, fruit and vegetables grown there.

PITMEDDEN GARDEN ★★ 69

Pitmedden, Gordon, Grampian. Tel: (06513) 2352
National Trust for Scotland

1m W of Pitmedden village on A920 and 1m N of Udny. 14m N of Aberdeen • Parking • Refreshments: picnic area • Toilet facilities inc. disabled • Suitable for wheelchairs and wheelchairs supplied • Dogs • Museum of Farming Life open • Gardens, museum open May to Sept, daily, 10 a.m. - 6 p.m. Grounds open all year, daily, 9.30 - sunset • Entrance: £2.20, children £1.10 from May - Sept. Garden and grounds at other time £1, children 50p (honesty box)

Like Edzell Castle, the great garden of Pitmedden exhibits the taste of seventeenth-century garden makers and their love of patterns made to be viewed from above. The rectangular garden is enclosed by high terraces on three sides and by a wall on the fourth. Very ornamental patterns are cut in box on a grand scale, infilled with rather garish annuals. The overall impact is striking when viewed from either of two period stone gazebos with ogee roofs or when walking along the terraces. Simple topiary and box hedging are abundant. There is a rather curious contemporary fountain made from fragments preserved at Pitmedden and others from the Cross Fountain at Linlithgow. There is a small herb garden near the tea room. Fine borders of herbaceous plants outline the parterre garden the south and west. When the National Trust for Scotland received Pitmedden in 1952 all that survived was the masonry. Since nothing remained of the original plans, contemporary plans for Holyroodhouse Palace gardens were used in recreating what is seen today. A garden well worth visiting at any time of the year.

PLANTS FROM THE PAST 70

The Old House, 1 North Street, Belhaven, Dunbar, East Lothian, Borders.
Tel: (0368) 63223
Dr David Stuart and Mr James Sutherland

1m W of Dunbar. From A1 take A1087 towards Dunbar, through West Barns. Turn left at crossroads after Dunbar town sign, turn first right then first left into North Street • John Muir car park two minutes' walk away and signposted from gates • Partly suitable for wheelchairs • Plants 'from the past' for sale in adjacent nursery • Open March to Sept, daily except Tues, 1 - 5 p.m. • Entrance: by collecting box

Garden historians will delight in this garden which has been renovated during the last five years and planted to an early eighteenth-century design. After the narrow village streets, it is a vivid experience to pass through the gates in the high wall into this gracious parterre. A broad gravel walk directs the eye to the restored eighteenth-century summerhouse, with its terrace and abundantly-filled urns. Viewed from there, the parterre garden appears to consist of a maze-like pattern of flower beds, but take the time to walk the gravel paths between them to appreciate the vibrant colours, subtle textures and evocative, half-remembered scents of the plants. At one side a raised grass walkway leads through to the nursery and sales area in the old kitchen garden where a catalogue of plants is available that includes information on when each species was first grown or introduced into the UK. There is also a cottage garden around the house which has box hedges and old shrub roses but unfortunately this is open only occasionally.

POLLOK HOUSE ★ 71

Glasgow, Strathclyde. Tel: (041) 6320274
City of Glasgow District Council

3½m from city centre, well signposted. A736 in Pollakshaws • Parking • Teas (reservations (041) 6497547) • Toilet facilities • Suitable for wheelchairs • House open and gallery • Gardens open all year, weekdays, 10 a.m. - 5 p.m., Sun, 2 - 5 p.m. Closed 25th Dec and 1st Jan • Entrance: free

Everyone should visit the Burrell Art Collection, Scotland's gem, and Pollok House and gardens are thrown in free. A visit to Pollok House offers a full day's entertainment. The house itself, an Adam design, features a lovely formal terrace of box parterres, beautifully planted and maintained by Glasgow Parks. There are lovely borders near the water and a nineteenth-century woodland garden on the ridge nearby. Stone gazebos with ogee roofs. The grounds are famous for their bluebells in spring. Pollok House holds the famous Stirling Maxwell collection of European decorative arts. In the grounds is the 1985 Museum of the Year, the Burrell Collection, one of the world's finest private collections of the decorative arts. The building was designed to encompass the surrounding woodland. The parkland around is beautifully planted and maintained.

ROYAL BOTANIC GARDEN ★★ 72

Edinburgh, Lothian. Tel: (031) 5527171
Department of Agriculture and Fisheries for Scotland

1½m N of city centre in Leith Walk above Cannongate • Parking • Toilet facilities • Suitable for wheelchairs • Exhibition hall and Inverleigh Visitor Centre open • Garden open daily except 25th Dec and 1st Jan, Mon - Sat, 9 a.m. - dusk, Sun, 11 a.m. - dusk (1 hour before sunset during BST). Plant houses and exhibition hall, Mon - Sat, 10 a.m. - 5 p.m., Sun, 11 a.m. - 5 p.m. (or 15 minutes before garden closes if earlier than 5 p.m.) • Entrance: free

Set on a hillside with magnificent panoramic views of the city, the Royal Botanic Garden of Edinburgh is one of the finest botanic gardens in the world; arguably the finest garden, physically, of its type in Britain. The 75 acres of gardens are filled with hundreds of thousands of plants, trees and shrubs from all over the world with a particular emphasis on Himalayan and Chinese species. The rhododendron collection is vast, the rock garden is among the finest in the world, and the heather collection is renowned. The conservatories hold enormous collections of tropical, sub-tropical and xerophytic plants and were among the earliest to be internally landscaped. The home demonstration gardens are very well done. The perennial border is one of the largest in the UK, approaching 600 feet. The many paths meander through numerous areas of specific interest, all beautifully planted and maintained to the very highest degree. The overall standard of horticulture is superb. The specimen trees are amongst the finest in Britain - the birch collection is unexcelled. This is a garden that takes years to know well. It is forever being improved and replanted.

THREAVE SCHOOL OF GARDENING ★ 73

Stewartry, Castle Douglas, Dumfries and Galloway. Tel: (0556) 2575
National Trust for Scotland

1m W of Castle Douglas off A75 • Parking • Refreshments: restaurant 24th March to Oct, daily, 10 a.m. - 5 p.m. • Toilet facilities • Suitable for wheelchairs • Shop • Visitor centre. Exhibition 29th March to 27th Oct, daily, 9 a.m. - 5.30 p.m. • Garden open all year, daily, 9 a.m. - sunset. • Entrance: £2.50, children £1.25, party rates: £2, OAP and children £1

Nearly 1500 acres of policies (estates), woodland and gardens used as a school since 1960 and catering for young aspiring gardeners. Numerous perennials, annuals, trees and shrubs are used in innovative ways and maintained to a high standard by the resident students of gardening. For the visitor the main interest is a modern design relying heavily on island beds, which can be compared and contrasted with other layouts. Threave is famous for its collection of daffodils and is quite lovely in the spring when these are complemented by the rhododendrons and flowering trees and shrubs. It is an instructive and useful garden to visit rather than a garden of great design or beauty.

TILLYPRONIE 74

Tarland, Grampian. Tel: (03398) 81238
The Hon. Philip Astor

4½m from Tarland via A97 Dinnet - Huntly road • Parking • Teas • Toilet facilities • Partly suitable for wheelchairs • Dogs on lead • Open 25th Aug for charity, 2 - 5 p.m. • Entrance: £1, children 40p

Set on the south-facing slope of a hill at over 1000 feet above sea level this is a cold garden, but shelter belts dating from the mid 1800s ensure that a wide range of plants can be grown. More shelter planting was added in the period 1925-51. The overall layout was completed in the 1920s and was the work of George Dillistone of Tunbridge Wells. The terraces below the house date from the same period and support narrow herbaceous borders. The house walls provide shelter for less hardy climbers and trained *Buddleia davidii* cultivars make a good display in August. Curved stone steps lead between extensive heather gardens onto lawns which sweep down to the ponds which have colourful plantings of astilbes, filipendulas, lysichitons, primulas and ferns. There are fine specimens of *Picea breweriana* and many other conifers and an area devoted to dwarf varieties. Spectacular views over rich farmland and nearby hills end with the Grampians on the horizon. The small pinetum set in pine and birch forest was planted by the late Lord Astor.

TOROSAY CASTLE AND GARDENS 75

Craignure, Isle of Mull, Argyll, Strathclyde. Tel: (06802) 421
Mr Christopher James

1½m from Craignure. Steamer 6 times daily from Oban to Craignure. Motor boat during high season. Miniature steam railway from Craignure ferry. Lochaline to Finnish, then 7m S on A849 • Best season: May • Teas • Toilet facilities • Partly suitable for wheelchairs • Dogs on lead • Shop • Castle open, mid-April to mid-Oct, 10.30 a.m. - 5.30 p.m. Admission extra • Gardens open all year, daily, sunrise - sunset • Entrance: £1, OAP, students, children 50p

House in baronial castle style by Bryce (1858). Main garden formal Italian based on a series of descending terraces with unusual statue walk. This features one of the richest collections of Italian rococo statuary in Britain and alone justifies the crossing from Oban to Mull. Vaguely reminiscent of Powis Castle (see entry), this is a dramatic contrast with the rugged island scenery. The peripheral gardens are also a contrast - an informal water garden and Japanese garden looking out over Duart Bay; also a small rock garden. Rhododendrons and azaleas are a feature but less important than in other west-coast gardens. Collection of Australian and New Zealand trees and shrubs.

TYNINGHAME HOUSE ★ 76

Tyninghame, Nr East Linton, Lothian. Tel: (0620) 860559
Tyninghame Gardens Ltd

25m E of Edinburgh between Haddington and Dunbar. N of A1, 2m E of A198 • Parking • Suitable for wheelchairs • Open 26th May, 21st July for charity • Entrance: £1

Tyninghame is renowned for the gardens created by the Dowager Lady Haddington from 1947 onwards, which have been described as of 'ravishing beauty'. They consist of a formal rose garden, terraces, a secret garden, an Italian garden and an area of woodland. When her husband died in 1986, her son reluctantly sold the house, but those who worried about the garden's future need not to have feared, as the conversion and addition of two houses was handled by Kit Martin with great sensitivity. Tyninghame is close to the sea, with fine views in all directions, and those who are able to visit it on the open days will have a rare opportunity of seeing how the unique character of the garden has been maintained, perhaps enhanced, by the architectural changes around it.

YOUNGER BOTANIC GARDEN ★★ 77

Benmore, Strathclyde. Tel: (0369) 6261
Royal Botanic Gardens Edinburgh

Dunoon, Strathclyde. 1m from junction of A885 and A815 • Best season: May to June • Parking: 10p • Teas at main entrance • Toilet facilities • Suitable for wheelchairs • Open daily, 15th March to Oct, 10 a.m. - 6 p.m. and at other times by arrangement • Entrance: £1.50, concessions £1, children 50p. Special discounts for groups. Season tickets covering Dawyck, Logan and Younger available - telephone Royal Botanic Garden (031) 552 7171

Benmore's 100 acres of woodland gardens have been under development since 1820. The gardens are approached along Britain's finest Wellingtonia (*Sequoiadendron giganteum*) avenue. The tallest is more than 150 feet. Numerous other fine specimen conifers are to be found throughout the gardens. There are exceptionally fine monkey puzzles (*Araucaria araucana*) that retain their lower branches. But Benmore is most famous for its extensive rhododendron and magnolia collections on the hillside beside the River Eachaig in one of Britain's most breath-taking natural settings; the Highlands at their best. A myriad of paths take the visitor along the mountainside through vast plantations of rare shrubs and trees. Marvellous vistas open from time to time. The only obviously man-made feature is a great rectangular lawn enclosed on three sides by walls but open to the mountains on the fourth. This garden is bisected by borders filled with a collection of dwarf conifers. A handsome pavilion overlooks it all. There are other informal beds filled with Australian and New Zealand shrubs and herbaceous plants; a large collection of heathers. Benmore is well worth a visit both for its natural beauty and its vast specimen plant collections. Be prepared for a full day's outing, a great deal of walking, and rain.

GARDENS OPEN RARELY

The following gardens are open to the public on three days or less in the year, although they may also be open by appointment if this is stated in the text. For details see individual entry.

May 12 Allangrange; **May 25** Geilston House; **May 26** Brechin Castle; Corsock House; Tynninghame; **June 9** Allangrange; Biggar Park; **June 23** Brechin Castle; Monteviot; **June 30** Bughtrig; **July 7** Allangrange; **July 28** Arbuthnott House; **July 21** Tynninghame; **July 24** Biggar Park; **July 28** Carnell; **Aug 3** House of Tongue; **Aug 4** Glenbervie; **Aug 11** Beechgrove Garden; Langwell; **Aug 18** Langwell; **Aug 25** Tillypronie.

WALES

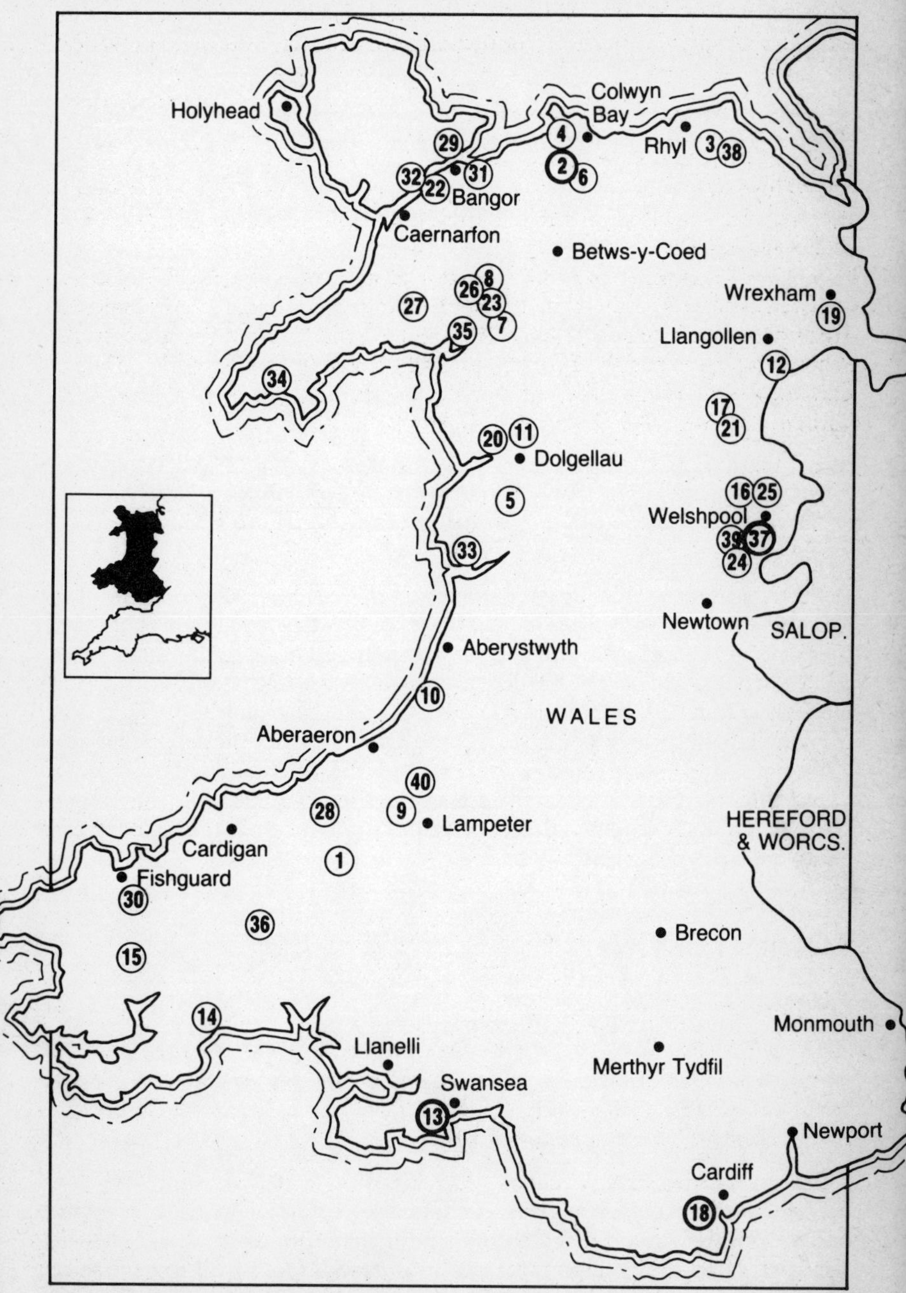

Turn to relevant pages to find gardens in neighbouring counties.
Two-starred gardens are ringed in bold.

BLAENGWRFACH ISAF 1

Bancyffordd, Dyfed. Tel: (055932) 2604
Mrs Gail Farmer

2m W of Llandyssul on Newcastle Emlyn road. First left by Halfmoon pub, 1½m until farm track on right • Best season: spring • Parking very limited • Teas 1m away in village • Plants for sale • Shop, adjacent craft workshops • Open April to June by appointment, 10 a.m. - 5 p.m. • Entrance: 75p, children free

Created over the last 15 years from a green field site, this is essentially a cottage garden, but recent plantings of trees and shrubs to attract wildlife and plants suitable for pressed flowers give great diversity. Good autumn colour.

BODNANT GARDEN ★★ 2

Tal-y-Cafn, Colwyn Bay, Gwynedd. Tel: (0492) 650460
The National Trust

7m S of Llandudno, just off A470 • Best season: May to Aug • Official car park 50 yards from garden nursery • Lunches, teas and light refreshments in Pavilion Restaurant, picnic area in car park • Toilet facilities • Partly suitable for wheelchairs • Plants for sale • Open 16th March to Oct, daily, 10 a.m. - 5 p.m. Last admission 4.30 p.m. • Entrance: £2.50

Bodnant is one of the finest gardens in the country, not only for the magnificent collections of rhododendrons, camellias and magnolias but also for its beautiful setting above the River Conway and the magnificent views of the Snowdonia range. The gardens, which extend to 80 acres, have several interesting features, the most well known being the laburnum arch which is an overwhelming mass of bloom in early June. Others include the dell garden and a lily pool. The whole effect was created by the Aberconway family (who bought Bodnant in 1874) over successive generations, aided by the garden staff, including three generations of Puddles, and by the background of large native trees planted in the 1790s.

BODRHYDDAN 3

Rhuddlan, Clwyd. Tel: (0745) 590414
Lord Langford

Take A5151 Rhuddlan - Dyserth road and turn left. Signposted • Parking • Teas • Suitable for wheelchairs (garden and ground floor of house) • House open • Garden open June to Sept, Tues and Thurs, 2 - 5.30 p.m. • Entrance: £1.50, children 75p (house and garden)

The main feature of the garden is a box-edged parterre designed by William Nesfield. Other points of interest are clipped yew informal walks, three pools, one with rainbow trout, new plantings and ancient specimens of oak. There is also a 1612 pavilion by Inigo Jones which houses St Mary's Well, revered since pagan times and said to have been used for clandestine marriages.

BODYSGALLEN HALL ★ 4

Llandudno, Clwyd. Tel: (0492) 584466
Historic House Hotel

Take A55 from Bangor and at the intersection turn onto A470 towards Llandudno. Hotel and garden are 1m on right • Parking • Refreshments • Open all year • Entrance: free

The owners have restored both house and gardens of this seventeenth-century country house to a high standard. The naturally-occurring limestone outcrops provide an interesting array of rockeries and terraces. One of the major features is a knot garden sympathetically planted with herbs, another is a formal walled rose garden. A number of well-established and interesting trees and shrubs can be seen, including medlar and mulberry. A woodland walk adds a further dimension.

BRYNHYFRYD ★ 5

Corris, Machynlleth, Gwynedd. Tel: (0654) 761278
Mrs David Paish

6m N of Machynlleth off A487 • Parking • Toilet facilities • Open all year by appointment only • Entrance: collecting box

This four-acre mountainside garden has been the subject of TV's *Gardeners' World* and justifiably so. Containing an enormous diversity of plant material, it is extremely steep, which makes for a most interesting visit, especially during the latter half of May when the species rhododendrons and primulas are flowering. Also good specimens of arbutus, halesias, hoherias and magnolias.

BRYN MEIFOD 6

Graig, Glan Conwy, Clwyd. Tel: (0492) 580875
Dr and Mrs K. Lever

Just off A470, 1½m S of Glan Conwy. Follow signs for Aberconwy Nursery • Parking • Toilet facilities • Plants for sale in adjacent nursery. • Open June and Aug, Sun, and May to June, Aug to Sept, Thurs, 2 – 5 p.m. Nursery opening times different • Entrance: by collecting box for charity

The garden, situated next to the Lever's nursery renowned for the quality of plants sold, is being extended and modified. In effect a new garden is being created within the framework of an existing established one, a process of interest in itself. The planting is imaginative and includes some unusual plants in skilfully designed settings which set them off to best effect. There is a lack of artificiality in what is currently a lovely garden with the promise of even more to come, for example a scree area being planted with alpines.

BRYNMELYN 7

Cymerau Isaf, Ffestiniog, Gwynedd. Tel: (076676) 2684
Mr and Mrs A.S. Taylor

2m SW of Ffestiniog on A496 • Best season: spring to autumn • Parking in lay-by opposite junction to Manod (¼m to garden along path at lower gate bearing right after garage) • Open May to Sept, 10 a.m. - 1 p.m., 2 - 5 p.m. Telephone first • Entrance: collecting box

An interesting garden, not only for its range of plant material, but also for its wild mountainside-setting. Divided into smaller gardens each with its own theme and character, it lends itself well to the overall informal style and its nature reserve and woodland setting.

BRYN-Y-BONT 8

Nantmor, Nr Beddgelert, Gwynedd. Tel: (076686) 488
The Misses M. Davies and J. Entwisle

2½m S of Beddgelert, turn left over the Aberglaslyn Bridge onto A4085. After 500 yards turn left up hill marked Nantmoor. Bryn-y-Bont is second house on right • Parking • Teas on certain dates • Plants for sale • Open 5th, 12th May, 23rd June, 11 a.m. - 5 p.m. and April to Oct by appointment. Parties welcome • Entrance: 75p, children free

This is a well-designed garden taking full advantage of the view over the Glaslyn Vale. Mixed borders and rhododendron beds give way to a woodland area where a variety of trees are being introduced. Featured in Radio Wales '*Get gardening*' in 1990.

CAE HIR ★ 9

Cribyn, Lampeter, Dyfed. Tel: (0570) 470839
Mr W. Akkermans

From Lampeter take A482 towards Aberaeron. After 5m at Temple Bar take B4337 signed Llanybydder. Cae Hir is 2m further on left • Best season: summer • Parking • Refreshments • Plants for sale • Shop • Open daily except Mon, 1 - 6 p.m. • Entrance: £1.50, OAP £1.25, children 50p

A six-acre hillside garden, created by the owners since 1985. At its best in early summer when the full effect of the various coloured areas can be seen: a formal blue garden, a circular red garden and an informal yellow garden. Plenty of seating for enjoying the views on the other side of the valley. Be sure to find the bonsai corner tucked behind the hedge. In the lower part of the garden is a small nursery; a water garden is being developed nearby.

CARROG ★ 10

Llanddeiniol, Llanon, Nr Aberystwyth, Dyfed. Tel: (0974) 202369
Mr and Mrs Geoffrey Williams

6m S of Aberystwyth on private road off A487 • Best seasons: spring and summer • Parking • Toilet facilities • Suitable for wheelchairs • Dogs on lead • Open by appointment only • Entrance: £1

From the flowers of varied spring bulbs to the autumn colours of rare maples and birches, this garden is alive with interest for the plant lover. Grass paths wend amongst collections of sorbus, eucalyptus and sweetly scented old-fashioned roses, with rhododendrons flowering well into summer. The walled garden is home for many treasures, such as fremontodendron, rare lilac species and *Abutilon megapotamicum*.

CEFN BERE 11

Cae Deintur, Dolgellau, Gwynedd. Tel: (0341) 422768
Mr and Mrs Maldwyn Thomas

N of Bala – Barmouth road (not by-pass) near Dolgellau, turn at top of the main bridge, turn right within 200 yards, then 2nd right behind school and up hill • Parking at roadside • Refreshments in Dolgellau • Toilet facilities • Open spring and summer months by appointment only • Entrance: collecting box

This relatively small garden has a very diverse plant collection amassed over the last 35 years. Planted informally but within a formal framework, it is a delight to amateur and professional gardeners alike. The alpine house, bulb and peat frames are well worth seeing; so too are the old-fashioned roses.

CHIRK CASTLE ★ 12

Chirk, Clwyd. Tel: (0691) 777701
The National Trust

½m W of Chirk village off A5, up private drive of 1½m • Best season: spring • Parking 200 yards from garden • Refreshments: light lunches and teas, picnic area in car park • Toilet facilities • Partly suitable for wheelchairs • Shop • House open: Good Friday, end March to Sept, daily except Mon and Sat, 12 noon – 5 p.m. Open Bank Holiday Mons • Garden open 28th March to 29th Sept, daily except Mon and Sat, 12 noon – 6 p.m., Oct to 3rd Nov, Sat and Sun only, 12 noon – 6 p.m. Open Bank Holiday Mons. Last admission 4.30 p.m. • Entrance: £3 (castle and garden)

A six-acre garden of trees and flowering shrubs including rhododendrons and azaleas. Interesting formal gardens with some excellent nineteenth-century topiary in yew. Also a rockery garden. Herbaceous borders, ha-ha and folly. The castle dates from 1300 but is set in an eighteenth-century landscaped park.

CLYNE GARDENS ★★ 13

Black Pill, Swansea, West Glamorgan. Tel: (0792) 401737
Swansea City Council

From Swansea take Mumbles road, turn right at Woodman Roast Inn • Best season: spring • Parking • Refreshments at Woodman Roast Inn • Toilet facilities • Suitable for wheelchairs • Dogs on lead • Open all year • Entrance: free

A large (50 acres) well-kept garden to interest everyone from the beginner to the more knowledgeable. There is a stream running through the bog area, fed by a lake via a waterfall and spanned by a Japanese bridge. A tower, built by Admiral Algernon Vivian, the last private owner of the garden, from which to view his rhododendrons, is now dwarfed by them.

COLBY WOODLAND GARDEN 14

Colby Lodge, Amroth, Narberth, Dyfed. Tel: (0558) 822800
The National Trust

Adjoining Amroth beside Carmarthen Bay • Best season: April and May • Parking 50 yards from garden. Disabled may park closer • Refreshments • Toilet facilities • Partly suitable for wheelchairs • Shop • Open 30th March to 2nd Nov, daily, 10 a.m. - 5 p.m. and in winter during daylight hours • Entrance: £1.25

This early nineteenth-century estate garden round a Nash-style house is now mainly woodland with some formal gardens. The walled garden is planted informally for ornamental effect. The woodland garden is planted extensively with rhododendrons and contains some interesting tree species.

THE DINGLE 15

Crundale, Haverfordwest, Dyfed. Tel: (0437) 764370
Mrs A.J. Jones

3m NW of Haverfordwest • Best seasons: spring to autumn • Parking • Teas • Toilet facilities • Suitable for wheelchairs • Plants for sale, small nursery • Shop • Open daily except Tues, March to Oct, 10 a.m. - 6 p.m. • Entrance: £1, children 50p, season ticket £4

A plantsman's secluded garden where foliage and plant structure play an important part in the layout and design. A collection of many rare and unusual plants, including over 150 different old-fashioned and species roses. Formal beds, scree beds, herbaceous borders, water garden and woodland walks all blend within an informal framework.

THE DINGLE ★ 16

Welshpool, Powys. Tel: (0938) 555145
Mr and Mrs Ray Joseph

3m N of Welshpool. Take A490 to Llanfyllin for 1m and then turn left for Groespluan. After 1¾m fork left • Best seasons: early summer and autumn • Parking • Toilet facilities • Plants for sale • Open daily except Tues, 9 a.m. - 6 p.m. • Entrance: £1, children free

Four acres of south-facing, very steep garden, planted with many evergreens for year-round interest. Beds have been created with colour schemes in mind and plants have been carefully chosen to harmonise. A large pool at the bottom gives another dimension to the garden and a breathing space before climbing back to the house.

DOLWEN ★ 17

Cefn Coch, Llanrhaedr-ym-Mochnant, Powys. Tel: (069189) 411
Mrs Frances Denby

On B4580 Oswestry - Llanrhaedr road. Turn sharp right in village at Three Tuns Inn • Parking • Refreshments • Toilet facilities • Plants for sale • Shop • Open May to Sept, Fri and last Sun in May to Aug, 2 - 4.30 p.m. • Entrance: £1

A woodland and water garden situated high in the hills with very good views. The owner has used the land to good advantage. The whole area is very rocky, and large boulders have been used imaginatively to create pools and support bridges across a stream. There is an interesting collection of waterside plants.

DYFFRYN BOTANIC GARDEN ★★ 18

St Nicholas, Cardiff, South Glamorgan. Tel: (0222) 593328

4m W of Cardiff on A4232 turn S on A4050 and then W to Dyffryn • Parking • Refreshments and picnics • Toilet facilities • Suitable for wheelchairs • Dogs on lead • Plants for sale • Shop • House now a conference centre run by Mid Glamorgan and South Glamorgan County Councils. Open air theatre in garden. Butterfly house attached to shop. Extra charge • Gardens open March to Oct, daily, 9 a.m. - dusk • Entrance: £1.50, OAP and children 75p

Dyffryn has been described as The Garden of Wales and one of Wales' best-kept secrets. An Edwardian garden, created out of a Victorian original between 1906 and 1914, it was designed by Thomas Mawson, a leading landscape architect rather overshadowed by his contemporary Lutyens. When the owner died, the garden (and Mawson's services) were retained by his son, Reginald Cory, a distinguished horticulturalist whose special interest was Eastern plants such as those brought here by E.H. Wilson. To the south of the fine house is a large open lawn with ornamental lily pond and, to the west, a series of 'rooms' each enclosed by yew. These are the Roman garden, the paved court, the swimming pool garden and the round garden. Beyond these is the west garden with large beds and borders and fine trees and shrubs. There is also a Japanese garden and a begonia garden. There is a vine walk, particularly splendid in its autumn colours. This is also the time to visit the arboretum which contains some of the finest *Acer griseum* (paperback maple) in the country. Large greenhouse and a cacti collection in the special house in the rose garden. A full description of Dyffryn together with a note on the trees was given in the RHS journal Vol III Pt 4 (April 1986).

ERDDIG ★ 19

Wrexham, Clwyd. Tel: (0978) 355314
The National Trust

2m S of Wrexham off A525 • Best season: spring • Parking 200 yards from garden • Refreshments: licensed restaurant, also light teas and lunches, picnic area in car park • Toilet facilities inc. disabled • Suitable for wheelchairs (wheelchairs provided but house difficult) • Dogs on lead in grounds • Plants for sale • Joiners shop manufacturing quality garden furniture • House open. Last admission 4 p.m. • Gardens open 29th March to 13th Oct, daily except Thurs and Fri (but open Good Friday) 11 a.m. – 6 p.m. Last admission 4 p.m. • Entrance: £2.50 (house and garden £4)

Erddig's gardens, a rare example of early eighteenth-century formal design, were almost lost along with the house. They have been carefully restored. The large walled garden contains varieties of fruit trees known to have been grown there during that period, and there is a canal garden with fish pool. South of the canal walk is a Victorian flower garden. Later Victorian additions include the parterre and walk. National ivy collection here; also a narcissus collection. Parties may have conducted tours with the head gardener by prior arrangement.

FARCHYNYS COTTAGE 20

Bontddu, Gwynedd. Tel: (034149) 245
Mrs G. Townshend

On A496 Dolgellau-Barmouth road, after Bontddu on right. Signposted • Best season: spring • Parking • Teas • Plants for sale when available • Open April to Nov, Mon, Tues, Thurs, Fri and Sun, 11 a.m. – 6 p.m., Wed, 2.30 – 6 p.m. • Entrance: 50p, children 25p by collecting box

This woodland garden overlooking the Mawddach estuary is set in natural oak and conifer woodland which adds to its attraction. There is much new planting, but azaleas, rhododendrons and magnolias are well established and would repay a spring visit when a system of pools and a stream now being completed should be in operation.

FOUR WINDS 21

Llanrhaedr Y.M., Nr Oswestry, Shropshire. Tel: (069189) 423
Mr and Mrs Douglas Job

From Shrewsbury take A5 towards Llangollen, turn left at Knockin and keep on B4396, crossing over A483 • Best season: end June/July • Parking in lane • Refreshments: tea, coffee and cakes • Toilet facilities • Plants for sale • Open June to Sept, Fri 10 a.m. – 6 p.m. and by appointment • Entrance: 50p, children free

This small garden is for lovers of roses (of which there are 150 including shrub), pelargoniums and house plants. Gesneriads are a speciality, and there are African violets including Chinese types, episcias, hoyas, streptocarpus, eccremocarpus, abutilons, plumbagos, clivias and many fuchsias and chrysanthemums.

FOXBRUSH 22

Aber Pwll, Port Dinorwic, Gwynedd. Tel: (0248) 670463
Mr and Mrs B.S. Osborne

3m from Bangor on Caernarvon road, approach to Port Dinorwic on left opposite W Lodge to Vaynol Estate • Parking in layby opposite for cars and coaches • Refreshments on open days only • Toilet facilities • Suitable for wheelchairs • Plants for sale • Craft shop on open days only • Open 31st March, 9th June, 7th July, 18th Aug, 11 a.m. – 5 p.m. and by prior appointment • Entrance: 75p, children 10p

The present owners have created this garden since they bought the site of an old mill in 1968. It is difficult to garden as it is subject to extensive flooding by what was the mill stream through the entire length. An intensively-planted wall is a major feature of the three acres of interesting and varied waterside and cottage garden plants which is being extended each year. Numerous wheelbarrows planted as landscapes are just the right height for wheelchairs and are of particular interest.

FRONHEULOG ★ 23

Llanfrothen, Penrhyndeudraeth, Gwynedd. Tel: (0766) 770558
Mr and Mrs J. Baily Gibson

From Llanfrothen via B4410 Rhyd road after ½m turn left, after 200 yards turn left again; opposite Hen Ysgoldy • Limited parking • Open mid-April to mid-Sept by appointment only • Entrance: by collecting box

A beautifully-kept garden where the natural contours and exposed rocks have been cleverly exploited. A rich variety of heathers and conifers give colour and interest at all times. New and surprising areas continually open up during the visit. A fascinating and imaginative example of cultivating a natural hillside to the best advantage. Dramatic views.

GLAN SEVERN 24

Berriew, Welshpool, Powys. Tel: (0686) 640200
Mr and Mrs N. Thomas

From Welshpool take A483 S. After 5m the entrance is on left by bridge over River Rhiew • Parking • Toilet facilities • Suitable for wheelchairs • Plants for sale • Open by appointment only all year, 2 - 6 p.m. • Entrance: 70p, children 10p

Large mature garden reclaimed by new owners. A three-acre lake with islands where ducks and moorhens breed. The stream which feeds the lake is newly planted along the banks with moisture-loving plants. A large area of lawn contains mature trees, herbaceous borders and a water feature. A grotto which has been carefully restored is now being replanted.

GLEBE HOUSE ★ 25

Guilsfield, Welshpool Powys. Tel: (0938) 553602
Mrs Jenkins and Mrs Habberley

3m N of Welshpool off A490 (Llanfyllin) • Parking • Refreshments on charity open days • Toilet facilities • Suitable for wheelchairs • Plants for sale on charity open days • Open by appointment and 14th April, 28th July for charity, 2 - 6 p.m. • Entrance: 70p, children 10p

This is a real cottage garden. A series of small gardens lead off from each other, with a mixture of shrubs, herbaceous plants, roses, herbs and fruit. Backing everything and climbing up the walls and trees is a large collection of clematis, said to total 130 varieties.

HAFOD GARREGOG 26

Nantmor, Caernarfon, Gwynedd. Tel: (076686) 282
Hugh and Angela Mason

5m N of Penrhyndeudraeth • Parking • Partly suitable for wheelchairs • Dogs on lead • Plants for sale on open days • Open 5th, 12th May, 11 a.m. - 5 p.m. and April to Sept by appointment • Entrance: 75p, children free

A small garden created by the owners since 1971 in a woodland setting with fine mountain views above the River Hafod. The garden is essentially rhododendrons and azaleas, with a lot of other colour, especially foliage colour provided by shrubs. There is a vegetable garden and water garden.

MUR CWYMP 27

Garn Dolbenmaen, Gwynedd. Tel: (076675) 383
Mr and Mrs A.E. Hepher

Garn Dolbenmaen is ¾m from A478. Turn E into village signposted near café. In village turn sharp left by chapel, first right opposite postbox in wall, 3rd gate on right • Parking • Plants for sale when available • Open by appointment only, April to Oct • Entrance: by collecting box

Mur Cwymp is a nine-acre smallholding, two and a half of which are devoted to the garden. The site is 600 ft above sea level and very exposed so shelter belts have been planted. The garden is divided into many small areas, beautifully planted with unusual trees and shrubs. A great surprise and delight to find such a fine garden in an inhospitable position.

PANT-YR-HOLIAD ★ 28

Rhydlewis, Llandysul, Dyfed. Tel: (023975) 493
Mr and Mrs G. Taylor

From Cardigan take coast road to Brynhoffnant. Take B4334 towards Rhydlewis for 1m, turn left and garden 2nd left • Best season: spring • Parking • Teas by appointment • Toilet facilities • Partly suitable for wheelchairs • Plants for sale • Open Easter to Sept, Wed, Fri and Sun, 2 – 5 p.m. • Entrance: £1, children 50p

This five-acre woodland garden was created by the owners in part of a farmstead. It has many unusual trees and shrubs, rhododendrons and azaleas. There is a bog garden and pool with rare-breed ducks. In the more open areas of the garden are terraced beds containing alpines, and a herb garden. A recently constructed summer walk where herbaceous plants predominate should be a very pleasant area when more mature.

PENCARREG ★ 29

Glan Y Menai Drive, Glyn Garth, Nr Menai Bridge, Gwynedd.
Tel: (0248) 713545
Mrs G. Thomas

1½m NE of Menai Bridge towards Beaumaris, Glan Y Menai drive is a turning on the right, Pencarreg is 100 yards down on right • Parking in layby on main road, disabled parking in the main drive • Suitable for wheelchairs • Open all year by appointment only • Entrance: £1 by collecting box

This beautiful garden, with a wealth of species planted for all year interest, has colour which has been achieved by the use of common and unusual shrubs. A small stream creates another delightful and sympathetically-exploited feature. The garden terminates at the cliff edge and this, too has been skilfully planted. The views to the Menai Straits and the Carneddi Mountains in the distance make it obvious why this garden has featured in two television programmes.

PENLAN-UCHAF FARM GARDENS 30

Gwaun Valley, Nr Fishguard, Dyfed. Tel: (0348) 881388
Mr and Mrs Vaughan

From Fishguard take B4313. From Newport take A487 to Cwm Gwaun. Situated next to Sychpant Forest car park • Best seasons: early spring and mid-summer • Parking • Refreshments • Toilet facilities • Partly suitable for wheelchairs • Dogs on lead • Open Easter to Nov, daily, 10a.m. - dusk • Entrance: £1, OAP and children 50p, children under 3 free

A medium-sized garden on a hillside near the top of the Gwaun Valley. The drive is very steep, but the view from the tea room is worth the effort. A very young garden but the owners have realised that its position will make many trees and shrubs an impossibility so they have chosen alpines and summer bedding. Some 12,000 spring bulbs, and fuchsias, geraniums and annuals give plenty of colour later. A raised herb garden, suitable for wheelchairs and the blind, is being developed.

PENRHYN CASTLE ★ 31

Bangor, Gwynedd. Tel: (0248) 353084
The National Trust

3m E of Bangor on A5122 • Best season: spring and summer • Parking • Refreshments: light lunches and teas, picnic in grounds • Toilet facilities inc. disabled • Suitable for wheelchairs, golf buggy available for garden park • Dogs on lead in grounds only • Shop • Castle and museum open as for gardens, 12 noon - 5 p.m. • Gardens open April to June, Sept to Nov, daily except Tues, 12 noon - 5 p.m. July to Aug, daily except Tues, 11 a.m. - 6 p.m. Last admission 4.30 p.m. • Entrance: £1.10, children 60p. Castle and garden: £2.80

Large garden covering 40 acres with some fine specimen trees, shrubs and a Victorian walled garden in terraces with pools, lawns and a wild garden. Although the site of the house dates from the eighteenth century, the gardens are very much early Victorian, dating from the building of the present castle by Thomas Hopper.

PLAS NEWYDD 32

Llanfairpwll, Anglesey, Gwynedd. Tel: (0248) 714795
The National Trust/The Marquess of Anglesey

1m SW of Llanfairpwll • Best season: spring • Parking ¼m from house and garden • Refreshments: light lunches and teas • Toilet facilities inc. disabled • Suitable for wheelchairs • Shop • House open inc. military museum • Gardens open 28th March to 29th Sept, daily except Sat, 12 noon - 5 p.m., 4th Oct to 3rd Nov, Fri and Sun only, 12 noon - 5 p.m. In July and Aug gardens open at 11 a.m. Last admission 4.30 p.m. • Entrance: £3 (house and garden)

An eighteenth-century house by James Wyatt, also an attraction because it contains Rex Whistler's largest wall painting. An informal open-plan garden with shrub plantings in the lawns and parkland. There is a formal Italian-style rose garden to the front of the house. A special rhododendron garden is open in the spring when the gardens are at their best.

PLAS PENHELIG ★ 33

Aberdovey, Gwynedd. Tel: (065472) 676
Mr and Mrs A.C. Richardson

At Aberdovey, between the two railway bridges • Best season: spring • Parking • Teas • Toilet facilities • Plants for sale • Open 31st March to Oct, Wed - Sun, 2.30 - 5.30 p.m. • Entrance: collecting box in hotel reception

A traditional Edwardian estate garden of seven acres reclaimed over the past 10 years. An informal garden with lawns, terraces, pools, fountains, orchard, rock garden and herbaceous borders. Spring bulbs, azaleas, rhododendrons, magnolias, euphorbias, roses and some mature tree heathers of immense size. The jewel is the half-acre walled kitchen garden, including 900 square feet of glass with vines and peaches.

PLAS-YN-RHIW 34

Pwllheli, Gwynedd. Tel: (0758) 88219
The National Trust

12m from Pwllheli on S coast road to Aberdaron • Best season: spring • Parking 80 yards from house and garden. No coaches • Toilet facilities inc. disabled • Shop • House open but to limited numbers • Gardens open 28th March to 29th Sept, daily except Sat, 12 noon - 5 p.m., 6th Oct to 3rd Nov, Sun only, 12 noon - 4 p.m. Last admission ¼ hour before closing • Entrance: £1.50

Essentially a cottage garden around a partly medieval manor house, on west shore of Hell's Mouth Bay. Flowering trees and shrubs, rhododendrons, camellias and magnolias, divided by formal box hedges and grass paths extending to three quarters of an acre. The Trust has recently extended Plas-yn-Rhiw to include 150 acres of woodland, purchased from the Forestry Commission. Snowdrop wood on high ground above garden.

PORTMEIRION ★ 35

Penrhyndeudraeth, Gwynedd.

2m SE of Portmadoc near A487 • Parking in car parks • Refreshments in village • Many areas suitable for wheelchairs • Open throughout the year

Architect Clough Williams-Ellis' wild essay into the picturesque is a triumph of eclecticism with Gothic, Renaissance and Victorian styled buildings arranged as a village around a harbour set in 85 acres of splendidly gardened woodland. It provides one of Britain's most stimulating objects for an excursion and during the period of the June festival in nearby Criccieth there are nine other good gardens open in the district. Write to Criccieth Festival Office, PO Box 3, Criccieth, Gwynedd LL52 0BW for details.

PLAS BRONDANW GARDENS

Llanfrothen, Gwynedd.

5m NE of Porthmadog between Llanfrothen and Croesor • Parking • Refreshments in summer only • Partly suitable for wheelchairs • Gardens open throughout the year • Entrance: £1, children 50p

This garden, in the grounds of the house given to Sir Clough by his father, is quite separate from the village of Portmeirion and was created by the architect over a period of 70 years. His main objective was to provide a series of dramatic and romantic prospects inspired by the great gardens of Italy. It includes architectural features, such as the orangery; visitors should walk up the avenue that leads past a dramatic chasm to the folly, from which there is a fine view of Snowdon.

POST HOUSE GARDENS ★ 36

Cwmbach, Whitland, Dyfed. Tel: (09948) 213
Mrs Jo Kenaghan

From Carmarthen W on A40, take B4298 through Meidrim. Leave by centre lane signposted Llanboidy, turn right at crossroads signposted Blaenwaun then right at next crossroads to Cwmbach • Best seasons: spring and early summer • Parking in official car park • Refreshments • Toilet facilities • Partly suitable for wheelchairs • Plants for sale • Shop • Open all year during daylight hours • Entrance: £1, OAP 75p, children 50p

Four to five acres of woodland valley garden, begun in 1978, wind along the bank of the River Sien. Many rare and unusual trees and shrubs, including 150 species and hybrid rhododendrons, carpeted with snowdrops, anemones, bluebells and wild orchids in the spring. There is a bog garden and a large pool stocked with carp and orfe. Old roses climb into many of the trees in early summer. A glasshouse, built on what was once a water mill, houses the more tender plants, and a conservatory contains plants collected in many parts of the world.

POWIS CASTLE ★★ 37

Welshpool, Powys. Tel: (0938) 4336
The National Trust

¾m from Welshpool on A483, well signposted • Parking • Refreshments: teas and light lunches • Toilet facilities • Partly suitable for wheelchairs (but not castle) • Plants for sale • Shop • Castle open at extra charge • Gardens open 28th March to June, and Sept to 3rd Nov, daily except Mon. In July and Aug, daily except Mon but open Bank Holiday Mon, 11 a.m. – 6 p.m. 'Meet the gardener' tours by special arrangement • Entrance: £3 (castle and garden)

This is a garden originally laid out in 1720 based on even earlier designs. Its most notable features are broad hanging terraces interestingly planted with huge clipped yews. On the second terrace, brick alcoves opposite fine lead urns and figures above the orangery below. Some fruit trees remain on the terraces where in the nineteenth century advantage was taken of the micro-climate to grow fruit and vegetables until a kitchen garden was established. The latter is now a flower garden. Unusual and tender plants and climbers prosper in the shelter of walls and hedges. This garden is not for the faint-hearted because it is very steep, but it's well worth the effort to relish the views which are as fine as any, anywhere. A good collection of old roses. Excellent guide book available with lists of plants.

TREM-AR-FOR 38

125 Cwm Road, Dyserth, Clwyd. Tel: (0745) 570349
Mr and Mrs L. Whittaker

Take A5151 Dyserth – Rhuddlan road. Turn left at crossroads signed Cwm, fork left and at traffic derestriction sign house on left • Best season: spring • Parking • Plants for sale when available • Open by appointment only • Entrance: by collecting box

This small three-quarter-acre garden offers dramatic views of Snowdon and Anglesey and is of great interest to the enthusiastic gardener. Its steep limestone terraces are filled with many rare and interesting plants with special emphasis on alpines.

VAYNOR PARK 39

Berriew, Welshpool, Powys.
Col and Mrs Corbett-Winder

1m from Berriew off B4385 Welshpool – Newtown Road • Best season: May to Oct • Parking • Refreshments and toilet facilities in Berriew • Open May to Oct, daily, 10 a.m. – 6 p.m. • Entrance: donations to charity

Mature parkland garden with fine old trees. Old climbing roses, herbaceous borders, rose garden and fine views of surrounding countryside.

WINLLAN 40

Talsarn, Lampeter, Dyfed. Tel: (0570) 470612
Mr and Mrs Ian Callan

8m NNW of Lampeter on B4342 • Best season: May to mid-July • Parking • Home-made teas on charity open day • Toilet facilities • Partly suitable for wheelchairs • Dogs on lead but not on charity open day • Plants and crafts for sale on charity open day • Small shop • Open 16th June, 2 - 5.30 p.m. and May to early Sept, daily except Fri, 12 noon - 6 p.m. Coaches by appointment • Entrance: £1, children 50p, under 12 free.

The wildlife garden, with its nature trail, has many different features, perhaps the most important being the old hay meadow, the wood, the pond and a long river bank. It is worth mentioning that all of these areas have a very good display of wild flowers - eye-bright burnet, spotted orchid and corncockle to name but a few. The garden abounds with birds, butterflies and dragonflies. The owner or his wife are pleased to discuss the garden with visitors and answer questions.

GARDENS OPEN RARELY

The following gardens are open to the public on three days or less in the year, although they may also be open by appointment. For details see individual entry.

April 14 Glebe House; **May 5** Bryn-Y-Bont; **May 12** Bryn-Y-Bont; **June 23** Bryn-Y-Bont; **July 28** Glebe House.

Glossary of Garden Terms

Bath house A rectangular sunken pool for cold water bathing, with seating approached by steps.

Belvedere A high point on a building, or a summerhouse, which commands a beautiful view.

Bosket A block of very closely planted trees.

Claire-voyée A gap in a wall or hedge which extends the view by allowing a glimpse of the surrounding countryside.

Exedra An area of turf within a semi-circular hedge which is usually used to display ornaments or locate a semi-circular seat; or the seat itself.

Finial An ornament such as an urn or a pointed sculptural form used to cap features like gateposts, the tops of spires, the top corners of buildings, etc.

Folly A decorative building with no serious function except perhaps to lure attention along a vista or to improve the composition of the garden 'picture'.

Gazebo Dog latin for 'I will gaze', used to describe a building usually sited on a high terrace from which the surrounding landscape can be enjoyed.

Ha-ha A deep ditch separating the garden from the landscape beyond. It allows the unscreened view to be enjoyed from the house but is profiled in such a way that livestock cannot enter the garden.

Knot garden Geometric patterns of low growing hedge plants such as box or shrubby germander which are made to appear as though they intertwine like knotted cord. The areas between the hedges are filled with plants or decorative gravels.

Mount An artificial hill usually surmounted by an arbour from which landscapes both inside and beyond the garden can be enjoyed from a different perspective.

Palisade A tall hedge of deciduous trees or shrubs with interlaced branches.

Parterre An intricately patterned formal garden which usually includes other features such as statuary, water basins and fountains, much larger than a knot garden.

Patte d'oie Literally 'goose foot'; a series of usually three formal paths or grand avenues leading fan-wise from a single point through densely planted trees.

Pleaching Training the branches of a line of trees horizontally by pruning and attaching them to canes and wires, so that the remainder can be intertwined as they grow to form a screen of foliage.

Ribbon bed A very narrow band of bedding plants which the Victorians were fond of using to border their lawns.

Rustic work Garden features such as garden houses, fences or seats made from unbarked tree branches – frequently embellished with such decoration as patterns made from sectioned pine cones.

Stilt hedge Clipped trees, such as limes, which have all branches removed for several feet above the ground to reveal a line of bare trunks like stilts.

Tapis vert A long strip of lawn between paths or canals.

Théâtre de verdure Similar to but usually more spacious than an exedra, a turf 'stage' with a back cloth of trimmed hedge and sometimes other hedges disposed like the wings of a theatre.
Treillage Architectural features such as arbours, obelisks or ambitious screens made out of trellis.
Trompe l'oeil A feature designed to deceive the eye, such as a path which narrows as it recedes from a viewpoint to exaggerate the perspective and make the garden seem larger.

Acknowledgements

Our thanks to everyone who has helped with the preparation of the *Guide* - to owners, custodians, professional gardening staff, and many others. In particular, we thank our inspectors and those who advised them. Some of those who have given advice do not wish to be listed, and, although anonymous they have been every bit as valuable. We are also obliged to staff of The National Trust and the National Trust for Scotland for their cooperation. The names which follow include inspectors (but not all of them) and advisors: Rosie Atkins, Mrs David Barnes, Kerry Bate, Kathryn Bradley-Hole, Anne Chamberlain, Anne Collins, Beatrice Cowan, Simon Cramp, Jo and Rosie Currie, Michael Davis, Daphne Dormer, Lady Edmonstone, Michael and Freda Fisher, Lucy Gent, Elizabeth Hamilton, Sarah and Colin Harris, Steve Hipkin, Judith Hitchings, Hilary Hodgson, Jackie Hone, Sophie Hughes, Pam Hummer, Judith Jenkins, Vanessa Johnston, Rosemarie Johnson, Jo Kenaghan, Jean Laughton, Charles Lyte, Janet Macnutt, Michael Mallett, Pat McCrostie, Deirdre McSharry, Lucinda Parry, John and Carol Pease, Stephen Player, Lorna Ramsay, George and Jane Scott, Dr Gordon Smith, Vera Taggart, Andrew Taggart, Sally Tamplin, Bill Tobias, Cynthia Wickham. The editors also express their appreciation of the dedicated assistance of Lizzie Boyd, Angie Hipkin and Wendy Turner.

Your Comments

The next edition of the *Guide* will be improved if readers will write to tell us
(i) if gardens are not included which you think should be
(ii) if you visit a garden in the guide and want to confirm its merits or propose an up-grading
(iii) if you visit a garden and believe its merits are overestimated by our inspector.
Report forms on the following pages can be used for this purpose, or you may just send your comments on a sheet of paper. Handwriting is not always distinct, so if possible please print difficult words and Latin names for plants. Also please print your name clearly. All those who write will help to improve the standards of garden visiting by making good gardens open to the public known to a wider circle. The great thing is to enjoy your garden visiting, just as our inspectors have done. Happy visiting in 1991.

Send your comments to The Good Gardens Guide, Barrie & Jenkins Ltd, 20 Vauxhall Bridge Road, London SW1V 2SA.

Report Form

To the Editors of The Good Gardens Guide, Barrie & Jenkins Ltd,
20 Vauxhall Bridge Road, London SW1V 2SA.

GARDEN

Name:

Address:

Tel:

Name of owner(s):

DETAILS

Location:

Opening times:

Best season:

Entrance charge:

Plants for sale:

House open/times:

DESCRIPTION

Type of garden:

Features/condition:

Please continue overleaf

Brief details of its main characteristics:

Name:

Address:

Date of visit:

Signed:

County Garden of the Year

To the Editors of The Good Gardens Guide, Barrie & Jenkins Ltd,
20 Vauxhall Bridge Road, London SW1V 2SA.

GARDEN

Name:

Address:

County:

Tel:

Name of owner(s):

I recommend this garden for selection as County Garden of the Year for the following reasons:

DESCRIPTION

Type of garden:

Features/condition:

PROPOSER

Name:

Address:

Signature:

Please continue overleaf if necessary

Index

Numbered properties in named roads are to be found in numerical order at the beginning of the index.